N_ inalovei @ yahoo.ca

Ninth Edition

Psychology and Work Today

An Introduction to Industrial and Organizational Psychology

Duane P. Schultz
University of South Florida

Sydney Ellen Schultz

PEARSON
Prentice
Hall

Prentice Hall, Upper Saddle River, New Jersey 07458

Library of Congress Cataloging-in-Publication Data

Schultz, Duane P.
  Psychology and work today : an introduction to industrial and organizational psychology
  / Duane P. Schultz, Sydney Ellen Schultz.-- 9th ed.
    p. cm.
  Includes bibliographical references and index.
  ISBN 0-13-193212-8
    1. Psychology, Industrial. I. Schultz, Sydney Ellen. II. Title.

HF5548.8.S356 2005
158.7--dc22   2005048655

Senior Acquisitions Editor: Jeff Marshall
Editorial Director: Leah Jewell
Editorial Assistant: Patricia Callahan
Assistant Editor: Dawn Stapleton
Director of Marketing: Heather Shelstad
Assistant Managing Editor: Maureen Richardson
Production Liaison: Fran Russello
Permissions Supervisor: Kathleen Karcher
Manufacturing Buyer: Ben Smith
Interior Design: John Ott/TechBooks/GTS
Cover Design: Bruce Kenselaar
Cover Illustration/Photo: Tom and Dee Ann McCarthy/Corbis
Photo Researcher: Beaura Ringrose
Image Permission Coordinator: Nancy Seise
Composition/Full-Service Project Management: Lori Brice/TechBooks/GTS

This book was set in 10/12 Meridien by TechBooks/GTS. It was printed and bound by Courier Companies. The cover printer was Phoenix Color Corp.

Credits and acknowledgments borrowed from other sources and reproduced, with permission, in this textbook appear on appropriate page within text (or on page 499).

Pearson Education LTD. London
Pearson Education Singapore, Pte. Ltd
Pearson Education, Canada, Ltd
Pearson Education–Japan
Pearson Education Australia PTY, Limited

Pearson Education North Asia Ltd
Pearson Educación de Mexico, S.A. de C.V.
Pearson Education Malaysia, Pte. Ltd
Pearson Education, Upper Saddle River, New Jersey

10 9 8 7 6 5 4 3 2 1
ISBN   0-13-193212-8

Brief Contents

iii

Contents

v

Preface

Most of the students taking this introductory course in industrial-organizational (I-O) psychology will work for some kind of organization. Many are already employed while attending college. Our goal in this book is to show them how I-O psychology directly influences their lives as job applicants, trainees, employees, managers, and consumers. In brief, we are teaching students about the nature of work in modern society.

Our focus is on the practical and the applied rather than the scientific ideal. For example, we believe that students must be introduced to topics such as training needs analysis, but they also should know that, in the reality of the workplace, training needs analyses are rarely conducted because companies are reluctant to spend money on them.

It is important that students learn about the major theories, models, research techniques, and findings of the science of I-O psychology, so that they can develop an understanding of the aims and goals of the field. However, students must also be aware that I-O psychology in practice is tempered by the conditions and demands of organizational life. Therefore, we have chosen to discuss theories, methods, and research results within the framework of actual work situations and job-related problems rather than as academic exercises.

Virtually all of the research we cite deals with employees on the job, not college students performing simulated work tasks in the psychology department laboratory. We describe I-O psychology programs in action, showing how they are developed and implemented in a variety of organizational settings, using diverse groups of workers from many countries throughout the world.

Thus, the ninth edition of *Psychology and Work Today* continues to present I-O psychology within the context in which work actually takes place. We recognize the growing ethnic diversity of the workforce, the impact of changing economic conditions, and the effects of modern technology.

We have written this text primarily for students who are not psychology majors and who have little background in the field. These students make up the majority of the enrollment in courses in I-O psychology, business psychology, personnel psychology, and applied psychology in psychology departments and business schools at the community college, college, and university levels.

The changes in this edition mirror the dynamic nature of the field. Chapters have been rewritten and reorganized to incorporate the results of more than 350 new studies reflecting the latest findings and trends within I-O psychology. These articles highlight the globalization of the workforce, as reflected in research studies from more than 30 countries around the world. Some of the topics new to this edition include the selection program for post–September 11 airport screeners, the job stress–related effects of September 11, discrimination based on sexual orientation, effects of applicant characteristics on performance in job interviews, Web-based survey techniques, predictors of workplace violence, organizational citizenship behavior, the role of personality in leadership, engineering psychology applications in everyday life, online shopping and consumer behavior, and collective job satisfaction.

Some topics from the previous edition given expanded coverage are virtual laboratories and Web-based research, online recruiting and testing, career development and training, substance abuse, working hours for managers, personality factors and job performance, and the effect of computers on communication and negotiation at work.

The chapters include outlines, summaries, annotated reading lists, and key terms in boldface type. Definitions for the key terms are presented in the margins and are cumulated in a glossary at the back of the book. Review questions challenge students to analyze material from the chapter; these questions are also suitable for class discussion and written assignments. The popular *Newsbreak* feature has been expanded. These brief sections offer informal discussions of real-world job issues, such as how *not* to interview, temporary employment, being overqualified for a job, and career self-management by learning new skills.

An instructor's manual and test bank to accompany the text has been prepared by Thomas Meriwether from Virginia Military Institute.

We would like to thank the many students and colleagues who wrote to us about the book and who offered valuable suggestions for the new edition. In addition, several reviewers provided perceptive feedback on the manuscript, and we are appreciative of their efforts. They include Anita Blanchard, University of North Carolina–Charlotte; Robert A. Howells, Penn State Erie–The Behrend College; Ann Lynn, Ithaca; and Douglas Peterson, University of South Dakota. Reviewers of past editions include Ken Gray, College of DuPage; Nancy Gussett, Baldwin Wallace College; Diana Punzo, Earlham College; Lori Rosenthal, Emerson College; Keith Syrja, Owens Community College; Jessica M. Sterling, State University of New York–Albany; and Ladd Wheeler, University of Rochester.

Duane P. Schultz
Sydney Ellen Schultz

Part One

The Practice of Industrial-Organizational Psychology

The work of industrial-organizational (I-O) psychologists will affect your behavior and emotional well-being, both on and off the job, whether you are seeking your first job, advancing in your career, or planning for your retirement. In Chapter 1 we describe the scope of I-O psychology. In Chapter 2 we review the research methods I-O psychologists use to collect data, draw conclusions, and make recommendations to management, thus applying their findings to all facets of organizational life.

Chapter 1

Principles, Practices, and Problems

KEY TERMS
REVIEW QUESTIONS
ADDITIONAL READING

IS WORK A FOUR-LETTER WORD?

Not for Tom Gau, it isn't. He's one of the lucky few. This 40-something financial planner from Torrance, California, absolutely, positively enjoys his work. He thrives on it. He talks about it with passion. "I love my job," he told an interviewer.

> I get here at 6 or 7 in the morning. I get out at 9 at night. I manage a lot of money. I'm one of the top producers in the nation. But . . . I'm not here be-cause of that. I'm here to help people. I love helping people. I don't have to work anymore. I'm financially independent. So why am I working these long hours? Because I love helping people (Gladwell, 2000, p. 71).

What about you? Would you work if you didn't need the money? Suppose you won $50 million in the state lottery. Would you still spend most of your adult life working for long hours 5 days a week like Tom Gau? Many people say they would. We're not talking about only movie stars or athletes or superstar musicians. No, we're talking about people in traditional jobs who continue to work hard even though they have more than enough money to live comfortably for the rest of their days.

Think about the CEOs of large corporations, many of whom receive salaries that top $1 million a week. Yet they keep working. Or consider Wall Street traders who rarely take vacations and who put in the same long hours, driven by the same intensity, as they did before they became so successful.

Many surveys have been taken of the rest of us, the people working at less glamorous jobs such as teacher, computer programmer, lab technician, or auto mechanic. The results consistently show that more than three out of four people questioned would continue to work even if they suddenly became financially secure and no longer needed the salary from their job.

People receive much more from their jobs than just a paycheck. Those who are fortunate enough to have found the type of work that suits their abilities experience personal satisfaction, fulfillment, and the pride of accomplishment. These feelings provide their own reward, distinct from income. Thus, work is re-lated not only to economic well-being, but also to emotional security, self-esteem, and contentment. For these people, work is definitely not a four-letter word. And it doesn't have to be for you, either.

Your job can offer a sense of identity and status, defining for you and for oth-ers who and what you are. Your work can give you the chance to learn new skills and master new challenges. It can bring positive social experiences, satisfy-ing your need to belong to a group and providing the security that comes from being an accepted and valued member of a team. A job can furnish the opportu-nity to form friendships and to meet people of diverse backgrounds.

On the other hand, if you are not one of the lucky ones who love what they do, your job can be tedious, monotonous, and even hazardous to your health. Some

Your work helps to define your identity and contributes to your sense of self-esteem.

work environments pose physical dangers; others can produce stress, anxiety, and dissatisfaction. If you are bored with your job, thwarted in your plans for advancement, or angry with your boss, you may bring your discontent home at the end of the workday and foist these negative feelings on your family and friends. Then you may indeed think that work is a four-letter word.

Long-term research has linked work-related stressors with physical and emotional health. The single most reliable predictor of a long life is satisfaction

---

Newsbreak   Getting Engaged

If you were asked to list the aspects of a job that are important to you, the ones that make you excited about and engaged in your work, what would be your answer? Salary? Fringe benefits? Number of vacation days? When 35,000 Americans employed in a variety of jobs were asked that question, few mentioned pay or benefits. In fact, those items didn't even make it in the top ten. The factors that got people most excited about their work were

- challenging tasks.
- participation in decision making.
- some control over the job environment.
- opportunities for career development and advancement.
- competent leadership.
- a sense that their supervisors were concerned with the employees' well-being.

That's a lot to ask for in any job.

Not all the people who responded to the survey said that their own jobs were characterized by these factors. Only some 20 percent reported that they were fully involved with and excited about their jobs. They are the lucky ones. Will you be one of them?

Source: St. Petersburg (FL) Times, September 14, 2003.

---

with one's job. People who are satisfied with their work tend to live longer than people who are dissatisfied with their work.

Selecting the job that is compatible with your interests, skills, and temperament is among the most significant decisions you will ever make. For that reason, this course in industrial-organizational (I-O) psychology may be the most personally relevant of your college career. You will find that I-O psychology will have an impact on your future from the day you apply for your first job until the day you announce your retirement.

The findings and practices of I-O psychologists, second to your own skills and motivation, will determine the positions for which you are hired, the way you are expected to perform your job duties, your rank and compensation, your ultimate level of responsibility, and the personal happiness you derive from your work.

INDUSTRIAL-ORGANIZATIONAL PSYCHOLOGY ON THE JOB

I-O psychologists working in the area of human resources, or employee selection, help initially with the difficult task of choosing a job. Your first formal contacts with I-O psychology outside the classroom are likely to be with recruitment Web sites, application blanks, interviews, psychological tests, and other employee selection measures I-O psychologists have devised to help employers determine whether you are the right person for their job, and whether that job is the most suitable one for you.

After you have satisfied yourself and the organization that the position is appropriate, your advancement will depend on your performance in training programs and on the job, using assessment criteria developed by I-O psychologists.

Because of your college training, it is likely that you will qualify for management positions within the corporate hierarchy. These jobs require that you be aware of and sensitive to the diverse motivational factors and personal concerns that affect the people who work for you. To learn how to lead and motivate your subordinates to put forth their best efforts, you will need to be aware of the findings of I-O psychologists on these factors.

Even if you have no direct subordinates—if, for example, you are an engineer or an accountant or are self-employed—you will still benefit from a knowledge of human relations skills. Knowing how to get along with others can mean the difference between failure and success.

Ideally, you will feel some commitment to your employing organization and will want to see it prosper so that it continues to provide opportunities for your own advancement. The company's output must be produced efficiently and at a high level of quality. The physical plant, equipment, and working conditions should foster a productive working climate. I-O psychologists help design manufacturing and office environments to maximize productivity. In addition, a company's output must be effectively packaged, advertised, and marketed. Psychologists play a role in all these activities.

Thus, at all levels of modern organizational life, psychologists provide essential services to both employees and employers. I-O psychology serves these two masters—you and your company. As it benefits one, it automatically benefits the other.

We offer a note of caution, however. As vital as I-O psychology is, as influential as it will be throughout your working career, it is primarily a tool. And any tool is only as valuable as the skill of the person using it. If the methods and findings of I-O psychology are used improperly by management or are misunderstood by employees, they can do more harm than good. Therefore, it is important for you to know something about I-O psychology, if only for self-defense.

INDUSTRIAL-ORGANIZATIONAL PSYCHOLOGY IN EVERYDAY LIFE

There is more to I-O psychology than its application to the workday world. It also affects your attitudes and your behavior in other areas of life. Consider how you started your day. What governed your choice of toothpaste or bath soap? Why did you choose a particular brand of breakfast cereal this morning? Most likely your decisions were influenced by the psychological image created for the product, by the perceived attractiveness of the package, or by the emotional need a particular brand was intended to satisfy. Did an ad or a slogan tell you that you would be more popular or successful if you wore these jeans or drove that car? I-O psychologists have helped develop advertising and marketing techniques to create, identify, and influence these needs.

Similar psychological techniques are used to promote and sell political candidates. Opinion polls and focus groups are used to inform political leaders about how voters feel about the candidates' public stands on various issues. Polling techniques are also used to determine ratings for television programs.

I-O psychologists assist engineers in the design and layout of displays and controls, such as those on the instrument panel of your car or in various consumer appliances. Psychologists ensure that the controls are comfortable to operate and that the visual displays are easy to interpret. The shape and color of familiar highway signs resulted from I-O psychology research. Psychologists have been involved in the design of aircraft cockpits, cell phones, microwave ovens, and computer monitors and keyboards to make them user-friendly and efficient.

WHAT I-O PSYCHOLOGY MEANS TO YOUR EMPLOYER

Why are the services of I-O psychologists used by so many different types of organizations? Because they work. They promote efficiency, improve morale, and increase corporate profits. Consider the problem of employee absenteeism. Workers who fail to show up cost the company money. Techniques devised and applied by I-O psychologists to reduce absenteeism can result in substantial savings. A bank in Canada with 30,000 employees estimated that it saved $7 million in one year by heeding a consulting psychologist's advice to install a computerized absentee-reporting system. The psychologist's fee and the cost of the system were considerably less than the amount saved.

Another costly problem in organizations is turnover. When employees quit, the company loses the investment made in recruiting, selecting, and training them. Then it must hire and train replacements. At one financial brokerage house in New York, the loss for each employee who quit exceeded $10,000. An I-O psychologist studied the situation and suggested ways to deal with the high incidence of quitting. Implementing these recommendations led to a 10 percent reduction in turnover and a cost saving of $100,000 within the first year. Other research found that regularly scheduled surveys of employee attitudes, formal communication programs between management and workers, and employment tests resulted in more than a 20 percent increase in company profits (Rynes, Brown, & Colbert, 2002).

Enhancing job satisfaction is a major concern in business today. Corporate leaders call on I-O psychologists to improve the attitudes of the workforce toward their jobs and their organizations. Enhanced satisfaction with work can reduce grievances and other labor disputes and decrease absenteeism, turnover, work slowdowns, faulty products, and accidents.

Appropriate employee selection methods, such as psychological tests, designed and monitored by I-O psychologists, help ensure that the most qualified applicants are hired. For example, researchers compared federal government employees who were hired on the basis of their cognitive ability (intelligence) test scores with employees hired on the basis of level of education and work experience. The tests were found to be far superior for selecting better and more productive workers, and the cost savings were substantial.

These examples indicate the importance of the work of I-O psychologists to all types of employing organizations. I-O psychology contributes to organizational efficiency and improves the bottom line on the company's financial report.

THE SCOPE AND HISTORICAL DEVELOPMENT OF I-O PSYCHOLOGY

Psychology is the science of behavior and cognitive processes. **Industrial-organizational psychology** involves the application of the methods, facts, and principles of psychology to people at work. That fact that psychology is a science tells us how it operates. A science deals with observable facts that can be seen, heard, touched, measured, and recorded. Hence, a science is empirical, which means that it relies on verifiable observation, experimentation, and experience, not on opinions, hunches, pet notions, or private prejudices. A science is objective in its approaches and results.

I-O psychology The application of the methods, facts, and principles of the science of psychology to people at work.

It is important to remember that a science is defined by its methods, not by its subject matter. In methods and procedures, I-O psychology attempts to be just as scientific as physics or chemistry. When psychologists observe the behavior of people at work, they do so in the best traditions of science: objectively, dispassionately, and systematically.

The subject matter of I-O psychology is also objective. Psychologists observe and analyze overt human behavior, such as our movements, speech, and writings and other creative works, to analyze and understand the people who are the focus of these observations. These overt behaviors are the only aspects of human existence that can be objectively seen, heard, measured, and recorded. Something more must be involved, however, because psychology is also the science of cognitive processes. Psychologists must study intangible qualities such as motives, emotions, needs, perceptions, thoughts, and feelings. These facets of our inner life cannot be observed directly.

We cannot see motivation, for example. It is an internal driving force inaccessible to observation. Its effects, however, can be seen. An angry person may display that emotion in such behaviors as a flushed face, rapid breathing, and clenched fists. A person driven by a high need to achieve success exhibits that motivation in behaviors that differ from those of a person content merely to get along, whether on the job, at a party, or under observation in a psychology experiment.

We cannot see intelligence directly, but we can observe the overt behavioral manifestations of different levels of intelligence. Psychologists can objectively record that one person performs at a higher level than another person on a test of cognitive abilities and can then infer that the first person is more intelligent. Inference based on the objective observation of behavior enables us to draw conclusions regarding personal factors or conditions, even when we cannot see them directly.

This is how I-O psychologists conduct their work. They observe the behavior of employees on the job under well-controlled and systematic conditions. They record behavioral responses, such as the number of parts produced each hour on an assembly line, the number of keystrokes per minute made by a computer clerk, or the quality of telephone service provided to customers by airline reservations agents. They vary the conditions under which a job is performed and measure any resulting differences in performance. Using these and other techniques, I-O psychologists observe, seeking a better understanding of human behavior. They look, listen, measure, and record objectively and precisely, adhering to the principles of the scientific method.

How did I-O psychology become so necessary to modern organizational life? The field was formed and fashioned of necessity. An urgent practical problem needing a novel solution gave the initial impetus to the field, and the demands of crisis and need have continued to stimulate its growth and influence.

Pioneers in Personnel Selection

Industrial psychology had its formal beginning in the early years of the twentieth century. The honor for sparking the development of the field is usually given to Walter Dill Scott (1869–1955). A college football player at Northwestern University, Scott graduated from a theological seminary, intending to be a missionary in China. By the time he was prepared to undertake this calling, however, he learned that there were no vacancies for missionaries in China. And so he became a psychologist instead.

Scott was the first to apply psychology to advertising, employee selection, and management issues. At the turn of the twentieth century, he spoke out on the potential uses of psychology in advertising. Encouraged by the response of business leaders, Scott wrote several articles and published a book entitled *The Theory and Practice of Advertising* (Scott, 1903), which is generally considered to be the first book about using psychology to help solve problems in the business world. In 1919 Scott formed the first consulting company in industrial psychology, providing services to more than 40 major American corporations, primarily in the area of personnel selection.

In 1913 Hugo Münsterberg (1863–1916), a German psychologist teaching at Harvard University, wrote *The Psychology of Industrial Efficiency*. He was an early advocate of the use of psychological tests to measure a prospective employee's skills and to match that person with the requirements of a particular job. He conducted considerable research in real-world work situations and workplaces, with the goal of improving on-the-job efficiency. His writing, research, and consulting activities helped spread the influence of industrial psychology, and he became a celebrity—America's most famous psychologist. Münsterberg befriended kings, presidents, and movie stars and was one of only two psychologists ever accused of being a spy (the accusation was untrue).

World War I and the Testing Movement

The work of Scott and Münsterberg provided a beginning for the field, but it was a request by the U.S. Army during World War I (1917–1918) that marked the emergence of industrial psychology as an important and useful discipline. Faced with the task of screening and classifying millions of men recruited for military service, the army commissioned psychologists to devise a test to identify people of low intelligence so that they could be eliminated from consideration for training programs. Two tests resulted from their efforts: the Army Alpha, designed for recruits who could read and write, and the Army Beta, which used mazes, pictures, and symbols for recruits who could not read. The Army Beta was also suitable for immigrants who were not fluent in the English language.

Additional tests were prepared for selecting candidates for officer and pilot training and for other military classifications that required special abilities. A personality test, the Personal Data Sheet, which could be administered to large groups of people at one time, was developed to detect neurotic tendencies among the army recruits.

After the war, businesses, manufacturing concerns, school systems, and other organizations that needed to screen and classify large numbers of people demanded more and better testing techniques. The tests devised for the army were adapted for civilian use, and new ones were designed for a variety of situations. Enthusiasm for psychological testing spread throughout the United States. Soon, millions of schoolchildren and job applicants routinely faced batteries of psychological tests. Thus, the initial contributions of industrial psychologists focused on issues in personnel selection—evaluating individuals and placing them in the appropriate grades, jobs, or training programs.

The Hawthorne Studies and Motivational Issues

The scope of the field broadened considerably with one of the most significant examples of psychological research ever undertaken actually on the job. The investigation lasted from 1929 to 1932 and was conducted by psychologist Elton Mayo, head of Harvard University's Department of Industrial Research. Called the **Hawthorne studies** because they were conducted at the Hawthorne, Illinois, plant of the Western Electric Company, this long-term research program took industrial psychology beyond employee selection and placement to the more complex problems of motivation, interpersonal relations, and organizational dynamics (Roethlisberger & Dickson, 1939; see also Hsueh, 2002).

Hawthorne studies A long-term research program at the Hawthorne, Illinois, Western Electric Company plant. It documented the influence of a variety of managerial and organizational factors on employee behavior.

The research began as a straightforward investigation of the effects of the physical work environment on employee efficiency. The researchers asked such questions as: What is the effect on productivity if we increase the lighting in the workroom? Do temperature and humidity levels affect production? What will happen if management provides rest periods for the workers?

The results of the Hawthorne studies surprised both the investigators and the plant managers. They found that social and psychological factors in the work environment were of potentially greater importance than physical factors. For example, changing the level of illumination in a workroom from very bright to dim did not diminish worker efficiency. More subtle factors were operating to induce these workers to maintain their original production level under nearly dark conditions.

With another group of workers, lighting was increased and production levels rose. The researchers made other changes—rest periods, free lunches, a shorter workday—and with the introduction of each change, production increased. However, when all the benefits were suddenly eliminated, production continued to increase. The researchers concluded that physical aspects of the work environment were not as important to employees as management had assumed.

The Hawthorne studies opened up new areas for I-O psychologists to explore, such as the nature of leadership, the formation of informal groups among workers, employee attitudes, communication patterns, and other managerial and organizational variables now recognized as influences on efficiency, motivation, and job satisfaction.

Although the Hawthorne studies have been criticized for a lack of scientific rigor, there is no denying their impact on the way psychologists view the nature of work and on the scope and direction of I-O psychology.

World War II and Engineering Psychology

World War II brought more than 2,000 psychologists directly into the war effort. Their major contribution was the testing, classifying, and training of millions of recruits in various branches of military service. New skills were required to operate sophisticated aircraft, tanks, and ships, and it was necessary to identify persons capable of learning to perform these tasks.

The increasingly complex weapons of war sparked the development of a new field: engineering psychology. Working closely with engineers, psychologists supplied information about human abilities and limitations for operating high-speed aircraft, submarines, and other equipment and thus influenced their design.

I-O psychology achieved greater stature as a result of these contributions to the war effort. Government and industry leaders recognized that psychologists were equipped to solve many practical business problems. The experience also demonstrated to many psychologists, who before the war had worked in the relative isolation of their university laboratories, that there were vital and challenging problems in the real world that they could help solve.

Contemporary Developments in I-O Psychology

The explosive growth of I-O psychology since the end of World War II in 1945 paralleled the growth of American business and technical enterprise. The size and complexity of modern organizations have placed additional demands on the skills of I-O psychologists and provided phenomenal opportunities for the development of the field. New technologies meant that employees needed enhanced and redesigned training programs. The advent of computers, for example, generated the need for programmers and technical support personnel and changed the way many jobs were performed. Psychologists had to determine the abilities required for these jobs, the kinds of people most likely to have these abilities, and the best ways to identify and train them.

The demands on engineering psychologists also increased. Innovations such as supersonic aircraft, missiles, advanced weapons systems, and information technology have required additional training for maximally effective operation. Engineering psychologists became involved in the design of industrial robots, high-tech office equipment, and the redesign of work spaces for today's automated operations.

Organizational issues have assumed greater importance (the *O* side of I-O psychology). Human relations skills are recognized by managers and executives as vital to maintaining the high job performance of their employees. The nature of leadership, the role of motivation and job satisfaction, the impact of the organizational structure and climate, and the processes of decision making are continuously being analyzed. In recognition of the significance of organizational variables, the Division of Industrial Psychology of the American Psychological Association (APA) became the Society for Industrial and Organizational Psychology (SIOP).

CONTEMPORARY CHALLENGES FOR I-O PSYCHOLOGY

The rapidly changing nature of work, together with technological advances and a more diverse population, mean new demands and responsibilities for I-O psychologists in the twenty-first century. One such change relates to the kinds of jobs available, the ways in which they will be performed, and the type of employee who will perform them.

The Virtual Workplace

A prominent organizational psychologist describes the nature of work as follows:

> Consider the new paradigm of work—anytime, anywhere, in real space or in cyberspace. For many employers the virtual workplace, in which employees operate remotely from each other and from managers, is a reality now, and all indications are that it will become even more prevalent in the future (Cascio, 1998, p. 32).

It has become commonplace for organizations to have large numbers of employees who work off-site, telecommuting from a home office, phoning from a car or airplane while traveling on business, or teleconferencing from a hotel room or vacation spot. This dramatic shift in where and how we work is an effect of the information age. Many jobs can be performed anywhere within electronic reach of the home office or the actual workplace, thanks to e-mail, voicemail, pagers, cell phones, laptop computers, and personal data systems.

To function efficiently and productively, these virtual workplaces require at least three types of information access: (1) online material that can be downloaded and printed; (2) databases on customers and products, and automated central files, that can be accessed from remote locations; and (3) a means of tracking employees and their work assignments at any time of day.

The downside of electronically connected virtual workplaces is that employees are often expected to work, or to be available, beyond the normal working hours of the organization. Some companies require their employees to carry phones or beepers at all times, keeping them effectively tethered to the office, with no way to escape the demands of their jobs. As a writer for the *New York Times* noted, "The 24/7 culture of nearly round-the-clock work is endemic to the wired economy." When a sample of 985 I-O psychologists were asked to name the trends most likely to affect the future of the field, 37 percent chose the impact of technology and Internet-related developments as most important (Waclawski, Church, & Berr, 2002).

Virtual Employees

Not only are more people performing their work at locations away from the office, but they are also less likely to be full-time employees who can expect to remain with the same employer for the duration of their career. Whereas previous generations of workers presumed a kind of unwritten psychological contract with their employer—"If I do my job well, my company will keep me on until I'm ready to retire"—today's workers have no such certainty of lifelong job security.

The notion of long-term loyalty and commitment to one organization faded in the closing decades of the twentieth century, during a frenzied period of corporate mergers and acquisitions, downsizing, and plant closures in which millions of workers and managers lost their jobs.

More of today's employees are likely to be contingent workers, freelancers, independent contractors, or part-time seasonal labor. The largest single private employer in the United States is Manpower, Inc., a temporary staffing agency. Millions of Americans work on a freelance basis. At the professional level, the Department of Labor estimates that more than 8 million people can be classified as independent contractors.

Many workers, especially younger ones, report that they prefer contingent work because it provides flexibility, independence, challenges, and the opportunity to continually upgrade their work experience and job skills. Many corporations also prefer this arrangement because they save on administrative expenses and taxes and do not have to provide such benefits as insurance or pension plans.

However, research has shown that the use of temporary workers can have negative effects on the organization's full-time employees. A survey of 415 full-time workers employed by several organizations found that the use of contract workers resulted in a decrease in the full-time workers' loyalty to the organization. The full-time workers also reported that their relations with management had deteriorated (Davis-Blake, Broschak, & George, 2003).

In addition, many organizations expect their full-time employees to train and supervise temporary workers. They also hold their full-time employees accountable for the tasks assigned to the temporary workers. This increases both the workload and the responsibility placed on full-time employees; rarely are they compensated for the extra demands.

A survey of 326 employees (189 of whom were full-time employees) found that they believed their jobs were higher in prestige than those of temporary workers. This is hardly a basis for viewing temporary workers as equals and can lead to unpleasant relationships in the workplace (Chattopadhyay & George, 2001).

Worker Involvement

The ways in which organizations today conduct business are changing drastically, both in existing jobs and in the new jobs that are being created. As a result, employees at blue-collar, supervisory, and upper-management levels are facing revolutionary challenges.

The days when a worker could be taught how to perform a simple task and told to keep doing it that way without question are disappearing. Today's workers want quality management. Their key words are "empowerment," "involvement," and "participation." Workers are expected to master not merely the tasks of a single job, but also to assemble a cluster of personal skills that they can transfer from one job to another. They must continually upgrade these skills and learn to participate in decision-making teams to determine how the work is best carried out. Today's workers are also assuming increasing responsibility for their part in the production or service process, even including the selecting and hiring of new workers.

This involvement of workers affects the ways managers perform their jobs. No longer can they rule by command, telling their employees what to do and when and how to do it. Now they function more as guides and mentors than traditional leaders. These changes require substantial adjustments for workers and managers and are, in part, a response to technological change in the workplace.

Newsbreak   Temporarily Yours

Ten years ago, I took a job stuffing envelopes. It was a necessity: I had just graduated from college and had no idea what I wanted to do with my life, but the lenders who had financed my college education weren't sympathetic to my existential crisis. The job came through a temporary-employment agency, which paid me $7.25 an hour to cram manila envelopes with a company's pap. I lasted one day. Since then, the temp world has changed dramatically. . . .

Temporary employment has grown in part because employers are more cautious about committing themselves. "They want to try people out before hiring them," said James Essey, president of the Tempositions Group of Companies in Manhattan [New York]. Many companies also prefer temps because they may not have to give them full benefits, or any benefits at all.

But it is not only employers who are fickle. Many young people engage in serial workplace monogamy, refusing to enter into serious relationships until they have sowed their corporate oats. "You test each other out, like a trial marriage," said Georgia Ellis, a vice president at Fifth Avenue Temporary Services in Manhattan. "And it doesn't look bad on your résumé, because it doesn't look like you've jumped from place to place. You have an excuse. You're a temp."

Kristin Robinson, 29, has morphed into what is known as a "permanent temp"—one with a long-term assignment. For the last two years, Ms. Robinson, who is also an actress, has had a continuing temporary position as a graphic artist, three days a week, at Andersen Consulting in Manhattan. She freelances the other two days from connections made at other temp jobs. The freedom, she said, is invaluable: "I try to be respectful and give notice, but if I need to leave I leave. And I don't take work home."

Most young corporate nomads, some of whom are actors, musicians, and writers, want to focus on their "real" careers without having to ask, "Do you want fries with that?" They thrive on the flexibility and often use their day jobs as floating office spaces for managing the rest of their lives.

And if they're unhappy in a job, they can simply walk away. Suzanne Lynn, 27, said she left a Greenville, South Carolina, law firm for lunch and, angry about being yelled at, didn't come back. Her agency understood and handed her another assignment. With that kind of freedom and unconditional love, temporary work might be the wave of the future.

Source: Abby Ellin, *New York Times*, April 18, 1999.

Changing Technology and Skills

A radical change in the workplace stems from advances in microelectronics—in word processors, computers, and industrial robots. Work environments large and small have become automated, with sophisticated equipment taking over functions once performed by humans. The majority of office workers today use word-processing or data-processing equipment that eliminates clerical jobs requiring lower-level skills. Workers must be technically proficient in systems and proce-dures unknown to previous generations of employees. Computers, faxes, modems, cell phones, electronic notebooks, e-mail, and the Internet have changed the func-tions of many jobs and created others that never existed before.

Some companies are using electronic equipment as job perks. For example, both Ford and Delta Air Lines provide their employees—whether they work in offices, on the factory floor, or in the maintenance hangar—with computers and printers for home use, plus free Internet access.

With the reduction in the number of manufacturing jobs and the demands of modern technology, there are fewer job opportunities for computer-illiterate or poorly educated men and women. Consider the job of longshoreman, or steve-dore, whose tasks were once described as requiring considerably more brawn than brain. Forty years ago, it took 500 men three months to unload a 900-foot cargo ship. Today, using automated equipment, ten workers can unload a con-tainer ship in 24 hours. In 1969 the International Longshoremen Association had 27,000 members. By 2000 only 2,700 members remained, and their work requires skills not needed 40 years ago, such as the ability to run computerized inventory checks on a ship's cargo.

As many as 25 million Americans over the age of 17 are functionally illiterate, which means they do not have sufficient writing and reading comprehension skills to fill out an application blank for a job. Basic math skills are also lacking. One study showed that when a group of 21- to 25-year-olds were confronted with the task of calculating the change due from a two-item restaurant bill, no more than 34 percent of whites, 20 percent of Hispanics, and 8 percent of blacks could do so correctly.

From an employer's standpoint, it is increasingly difficult to recruit entry-level workers who possess the basic skills needed to learn to perform many jobs. A telecommunications company in the northeastern United States had to interview and test 90,000 job applicants to find 2,000 who could be trained for a job that did not even require a high school diploma. General Motors found that workers who lacked appropriate reading, writing, and math skills had difficulty complet-ing the training programs provided every few years to update skills and acquaint employees with new manufacturing processes.

Globalization of the Workplace

Your job may be going overseas, but you'll still be here—and unemployed. A large number of U.S. companies are outsourcing jobs such as customer relations, tech support, and call centers by having them performed by workers in other countries. IBM, for example, has sent thousands of high-paying information technology jobs to China, where the tasks can be done for a fraction of the pay required by American workers. Microsoft has exported jobs to India, where the annual salary for a computer programmer is $40,000, compared with $80,000 for a programmer in the United States. The concept of globalization means shift-ing jobs to places with lower labor costs and less competition (see, for example, Herbert, 2003). This phenomenon leaves thousands of highly skilled workers in need of retraining to develop job skills compatible with the current needs, and pay scales, of business and industry today.

Newsbreak   What Jobs Will There Be for You?

As some U.S. jobs are being outsourced, others are being eliminated altogether. Still others are being changed so completely by new technology that old skills no longer apply. How can you predict what jobs will be ready for you when you graduate, prepared to begin your working career? Research conducted at Harvard University and at the Massachusetts Institute of Technology about the kinds of jobs likely to be exported found that the most important factor was whether a job could be "routinized," that is, "broken down into repeatable steps that vary little from day to day. Such a job is easier to replace with a clever piece of software or to hand over to a lower-paid worker outside the U.S." (Coy, 2004).

OK, so where does that leave you? According to *Business Week*, the really good jobs in your future will be those that cannot be easily reduced to simple tasks. Such jobs require flexibility, creativity, and the continuing development of your business and social skills. The U.S. Department of Labor lists the most attractive jobs and their average annual salary as the following:

- College educators ($59,000).
- Managers ($84,000).
- Software engineers ($74,000).
- Management consultants ($70,000).
- Artists and designers ($46,000).

Source: Business Week, March 22, 2004.

Diversity Issues

Another change in the workplace is demographic. It involves a shift in the ethnic composition of the workforce. Persons of African, Asian, and Hispanic heritage now constitute at least 35 percent of all new workers. Further, half of all new employees are women. White male workers are becoming a minority. Organizations large and small must be increasingly sensitive to the needs and concerns of a workforce that comprises many cultures and backgrounds.

Up to 800,000 immigrants enter the United States every year. Most of them are eager to work, but many lack English-language training and other literacy skills. They may also be unfamiliar with corporate work habits. This presents an additional challenge to business and industry.

All these changes in the workplace and in the composition of the workforce pose opportunities for I-O psychologists in selecting and training workers, redesigning jobs and equipment, refining management practices, raising morale, and dealing with health and safety issues. These challenges suggest that this is an exciting time to consider a career as an I-O psychologist.

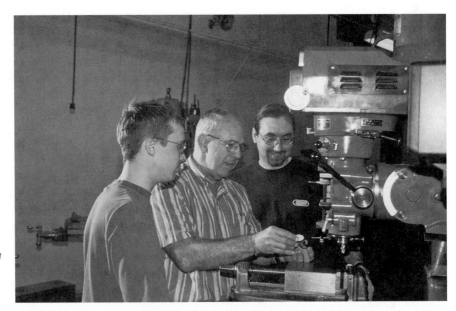

The U.S. workforce today includes a growing number of older workers, who often serve as mentors or trainers for younger workers.

I-O PSYCHOLOGY AS A CAREER: TRAINING AND EMPLOYMENT

Although few people believe that they are qualified to be physicists, chemists, or biologists after taking one or two courses, many people consider themselves expert psychologists even when they have had no formal training. Some think that the practice of psychology requires nothing more than common sense and a lot of time interacting with other people. This will no more make you a psychologist, however, than years of taking medicines will make you a physician.

Modern I-O psychology is a complex and demanding profession that requires university training, practical experience, and continuing study to keep aware of new developments. The minimum requirement for working as an I-O psychologist is a master's degree, which usually requires 42 semester hours and two to three years to complete. Most master's degree students work full time or part time while in school. Of all the graduate degrees granted in I-O psychology each year, two-thirds are at the master's level.

The majority of I-O master's degree graduates find professional jobs in their specialty areas at competitive salaries in industry, government, consulting firms, and research organizations. Their most marketable skills that can be applied to the job are in the areas of psychological test and survey construction and validation, human resources selection and placement, performance appraisal, fair employment practices, and employee training. College course work in motivation, job satisfaction, and organizational development are also useful on the job. Thus, a master's degree program in I-O psychology provides valuable preparation for a productive and rewarding career. However, the higher positions in businesses and universities typically require a doctoral degree, which requires from three to five years of graduate study.

The number of graduate students in I-O psychology continues to grow, with the bulk of the increase being among students at the master's level. These students

---

Newsbreak

But What Can You Do with a B.A. in Psychology?

Fewer than half of all psychology graduates with bachelor's degrees go on to attend graduate school. What happens to them? Where do they find work? What sort of career opportunities can they expect? Relax. If this is your situation, the future looks promising, even if you're not planning on studying for a master's or doctoral degree.

Psychology majors with four-year degrees find employment in all sectors of the economy. Approximately 50 percent work for private corporations, 15 percent are employed by government agencies, 14 percent find jobs in education, 12 percent run their own businesses, and 9 percent work for charitable organizations.

Of those in the corporate sector, most are in managerial positions; the rest work in sales, human resources, training, and other staff functions.

Nearly half of the recent B.A. graduates in psychology report that their job duties are closely related to their course work. They also say that their jobs have high career potential. When employers were asked what skills and abilities they were looking for in job applicants with bachelor's degrees in psychology, they answered that they wanted people with high interpersonal skills and a strong work ethic. Specifically, they sought new college graduates who could get along with others, be a team player, and had the desire to learn new skills.

So, yes, even if you do not plan on graduate school, good jobs are out there for you, but work on your "people skills" and be willing to keep learning.

Sources: J. Kohout, A look at recent baccalaureates in psychology. *Monitor on Psychology,* January 2000, p. 13. Also R. Landrum & R. Harrold, What employees want from psychology graduates, *Teaching of Psychology,* 2003, *30,* 131–133.

---

have a sound practical reason for their choice. They are responding to the projected demand for psychologists. The U.S. Bureau of Labor Statistics expects an increase in job opportunities for psychologists in business and research, in nonprofit organizations, and in computer firms.

The training requirements for a career in I-O psychology are difficult, but the rewards can be great. I-O psychologists have higher salaries than those of any other group of psychologists. In 2000 the median annual income for I-O psychologists with doctoral degrees in the United States was $90,000. The top 10 percent reported annual incomes greater than $180,000. At the master's level, the median salary was $67,000, with the top 10 percent earning more than $185,000 (Katkowski & Medsker, 2001).

In addition, the rewards for I-O psychologists of stimulating work, challenging responsibilities, and intellectual growth are notable. As Ann Howard, a past president of the Society for Industrial and Organizational Psychology, commented, it is a field in which "you can make things happen. You put in a program, and you

TABLE 1–1

Places of Employment and Job Responsibilities of Selected I-O Psychologists

Human Resources Consulting Firm
Test development and validation, interview training, assessment center design, performance appraisal system design, career development programs, attitude surveys.

Market Research, Consulting, and Promotional Services Firm; Marketing Research Project Director
Apply social science research skills to proposal development, analysis, writing, and presentation.

International Airline, Assessment Center Specialist for Overseas Development
Coordinate and supervise assessment center for evaluation of employees being considered for promotion: Develop assessment materials, make recommendations to improve effectiveness, select and train staff to become qualified assessors.

Management Consulting Firm, Senior-Level Manager
Oversee projects involving the systems approach to training, training technologies, and management/career development training.

Human Resource Research and Consulting Associates, I-O Project Manager
Work with interdisciplinary staff (psychologists, sociologists, computer science specialists, and educators) on information systems, test development, survey design, and equal employment issues, including providing expert witness testimony in selected court cases.

Employee Decisions Consulting Firm, Director of Human Resources
Provide services in counseling, coaching executive candidates for job interviews, assessment and test interpretation, and career development.

Pharmaceutical Firm, Manager of Psychological Services
Design psychological strategies for employee testing and job analysis, assess legal considerations in hiring, research and recommend changes in corporate compensation procedures, develop and monitor performance appraisal practices.

Public Utility (Gas and Electric Company), Executive Consultant in Organization Planning and Development
Work with unions, line operations, human resource departments, and senior management groups to redesign human resource systems and implement major organizational changes.

Electronics Corporation, Team Leadership and Communication Trainer
Implement self-directed production work teams: Train workers in manufacturing team concepts, problem-solving techniques, leadership development, communications, and cooperative decision making. Monitor and evaluate programs and document results.

Telecommunications Company, Human Resource Research Intern
Pre-doctoral internship for person admitted to doctoral candidacy at accredited university to conduct research on human resource programs while working with licensed I-O psychologists and human resource professionals.

State College, Assistant Professor of Psychology
Teach courses in organizational behavior, group processes, and tests and measurements; direct undergraduate research projects.

see some results. You might see better people selected, or job satisfaction go up, or turnover go down. But you've made something happen, and that's a very exciting kind of reward."

I-O psychologists work in business, industry, government agencies, service organizations, consulting firms, and universities. Many of the psychologists who teach courses in I-O psychology also undertake research and consulting activities. Employment opportunities, as reflected in examples of job titles, responsibilities, and types of organizations, are shown in Table 1–1.

Smaller organizations that cannot afford a full-time I-O psychologist rely on the services of consulting psychologists who are employed on a contract basis to fill a specific need or solve a particular problem. Consultants may evaluate candidates for employment, design a piece of equipment or an assembly line, establish a training program, conduct a survey on consumer acceptance of a new product, or try to determine why morale or productivity is declining. The value of consulting services lies not only in the technical skills the I-O psychologist offers, but also in the freshness of approach and objectivity that an outsider can bring to the company.

More than half of the I-O psychologists studying for PhDs today are women. There has been a higher rate of increase in the number of women earning doctoral degrees in I-O psychology than in any other specialty. In 2002, 67 percent of the PhD graduates in psychology were women. An intensive recruiting effort for minority graduate students in psychology has had some positive effect. In 2002, 7 percent of new doctorates were Hispanic, 6 percent black, and 4 percent Asian (Bailey, 2004).

I-O psychologists are affiliated primarily with four divisions of the APA: SIOP, the division of Military Psychology, the division of Applied Experimental and Engineering Psychologists, and the Society for Consumer Psychology. Many academic and research-oriented I-O psychologists are also affiliated with the American Psychological Society. Explore the Web sites recommended by psychology graduate students for information on how to survive graduate school and find a job. See www.apa.org/apags (American Psychological Association of Graduate Students), www.users.erols.com/fezworth (PsycHits: the graduate students' psychology reference site), www.socialpsychology.org (the Social Psychology Network), and www.personal.umich.edu/~danhorn/graduate.html (Graduate Student Resources on the Web).

PROBLEMS FOR I-O PSYCHOLOGISTS

No field of study is free of internal and external problems. I-O psychologists face several difficulties, all aggravated by the very factor that has made the field so successful, namely, the demand for its services.

Fraudulent Practitioners

More than any other science, psychology has been victimized by quackery, that is, by the illicit and fraudulent practice of psychology by people who have little or no professional training. This problem is particularly apparent in clinical psychology, where untrained people set themselves up as "counselors" and "therapists" and often do great harm to emotionally disturbed persons who are seeking help.

Quackery also affects I-O psychology. Mary Tenopyr, a past president of SIOP, wrote:

> A major complication in the lives of psychologists in business is the ill-trained or unscrupulous person who offers psychological-type services to companies. . . . Some of the most difficult situations I have had to cope with in my career have resulted from the actions of pseudopsychologists who have captured the ears of high-level managers (Tenopyr, 1992, p. 175).

An uninformed business organization can be just as gullible as an individual. Unethical consulting firms have sold their so-called services to industry and made quick money—and a quicker getaway—before the company realized it had been duped. Not only is such unethical behavior dangerous and unfair to business (consider, for example, all the competent people who were not hired because they performed poorly on the quack's phony test), but it is also harmful to psychology as a science and profession. If a company is damaged by the charlatan's actions, the field as a whole receives the blame. The executives of an organization defrauded in the past will be reluctant to consider legitimate psychological services in the future.

Credentials and Certification

The problem of the phony practitioner is being reduced in clinical psychology because states now license or certify psychologists in the same way they license physicians. It is illegal for people to represent themselves to the public as psychologists or to use any of the tools of psychology unless they have met the licensing or certification requirements. These are usually a graduate degree and satisfactory performance on an exam covering knowledge of all areas of psychology.

These procedures were established specifically to protect the public from charlatans in the areas of clinical and counseling psychology. The question of licensing I-O psychologists is controversial within the profession. Many I-O psychologists practicing in states that offer licensing have chosen to apply for it. Although many SIOP members are licensed, SIOP takes the position that they need not be.

A business must exercise care when seeking the services of a psychologist. It is not enough to flip through the pages of the telephone directory or enter the words "I-O psychology" on a search engine. The educational and professional qualifications of anyone called a psychologist must be examined carefully.

Communication with Management

All sciences develop a specialized technical jargon that its members use to communicate with one another. This vocabulary is sometimes not understood by those outside the discipline. Because I-O psychologists must work closely with people who are not psychologists, that is, with managers and employees, they must make the effort to communicate clearly their ideas, activities, and research results. The recommendations of I-O psychologists will be of no value to an organization if they cannot be comprehended. The reports will be filed in the nearest wastebasket. Psychologists must be able to present their contributions in a way that can be understood by those who are using their services.

Resistance to New Ideas

This problem might be called, "I've always done it this way, and I'm not going to change now!" Psychologists who work in business and industry often meet this attitude—a resistance to change, an unwillingness to try something new or consider novel ideas. When an I-O psychologist recommends altering the usual way of performing a job, workers sometimes view the suggestion as a threat. Employees who are told to modify their work habits to conform to the potentially more efficient system proposed by the psychologist may actively resist because they believe that the company is trying to get them to work harder for the same pay. Insecure workers may also feel that management is criticizing their past job performance. This resistance to change is a serious problem at all levels, from the worker on the assembly line or the phone bank to the CEO at corporate headquarters.

If the findings of I-O psychologists are to have any impact, they must have the support of the managers and employees who will be affected by them. Psychologists need the cooperation of those employees whose jobs will be changed. They must show considerable human relations skills, patience, and persuasiveness in addition to their technical expertise.

Research versus Application?

The question of research versus application continues to concern I-O psychologists in their relations with management. Some managers complain that too little of the research published in I-O psychology journals is oriented toward the practical real-world problems with which they deal every day. This may explain why many human resources managers do not read the published literature in I-O psychology; they may find it too technical, difficult to understand, or impractical and irrelevant to their needs. A survey of 959 members of the Society for Human Resource Management found that fewer than 1 percent reported keeping up with the academic literature. A disturbingly high 75 percent said they *never* read it (Rynes, Brown, & Cogbert, 2002). Psychologists who work for organizations can help alleviate this problem by writing clearly and directly, thus interpreting their research findings in a way that human resources managers would find useful and applicable to their everyday problems on the job.

In addition, there are serious differences between academic I-O psychologists and psychologists who work in applied settings. Although they may receive the same training, once they leave graduate school, their employment experiences and values diverge. Researchers are popularly seen as interested only in theories and methods, not in anything relevant, whereas practitioners are viewed as problem-solvers who ignore theoretical evidence (see Brooks, Grauer, Thornbury, & Highhouse, 2003). Although it is true that much academic research may appear to have no immediate application, psychologists who work directly for organizations know that the two functions, research and application, are interdependent.

Without research, there would be no reliable information to apply to critical problems on the job. This point is often overlooked by managers who demand immediate solutions to specific problems and who cannot understand the hesitation of the psychologist who tells them that the answer can come only from research.

The conflict between research and application arises because organizations often need prompt answers. Production schedules and contract deadlines do not always wait for the design and execution of a research study. Managers facing time constraints may have unrealistic expectations and become impatient when the company psychologist—their so-called "expert" on human behavior—cannot provide a quick fix.

We are not suggesting that whenever I-O psychologists are asked a question, they run to the laboratory to begin a month-long experiment. The history of psychology already provides a wealth of empirical data about human behavior in a variety of situations, and well-trained psychologists know how to apply these findings to specific problems in the workplace. The value of these data, however, depends on the similarity between the situations in which they were obtained and the present situation.

For example, studies about how college sophomores learn complex material are not as relevant to the learning abilities of employees in a chemical company as is research conducted on the learning abilities of employees in a steel company. The steel company research, performed in an actual work setting, will probably provide the more useful results. But a learning study conducted in another chemical company will be even more applicable. And a study conducted on the very workers whose learning habits are in question will be the most useful of all.

Sometimes circumstances do not allow sufficient time or resources for research to be undertaken. SIOP offers the following advice:

> *You can't research every question.* While it is desirable to have a body of research to support your actions, it is not always possible. When you find yourself having to make a decision in the absence of research, you have to take what you know about similar situations and use your own judgment (Baker, 1996, p. 103).

Properly devised research can be of immense value to an organization's productive efficiency, but the needs of the workplace often call for compromise, patience, and understanding by both managers and psychologists. The fundamental issue is not research versus application but research plus application. The two functions are compatible and complementary.

AREAS OF I-O PSYCHOLOGY

We have noted how I-O psychology affects many aspects of the relationship between you and your work. We describe here the specific interests of I-O psychologists that are covered in the following chapters.

The Tools and Techniques of Science (Chapter 2). Psychologists study human behavior through the tools and techniques of science. To understand their work, we must become acquainted with the ways in which they perform research, analyze data, and draw conclusions.

Recruiting and Selecting Employees (Chapters 3 and 4). Despite the opinion of some executives and personnel managers that they can judge job applicants by a handshake, eye contact, or style of dress, selecting and evaluating employees are complex processes that continue long after the initial recruitment and hiring. Throughout your career, questions of promotion and salary increases will arise.

Many of the selection devices, such as interviews and psychological tests, that were used in making your first hiring decision will also be applied to subsequent career decisions. Thus, it is important for you to understand the selection process. It is also to your advantage that your potential employer use the most valid techniques available. Improper matching of the person and the job can lead to inefficiency and dissatisfaction for employer and employee.

Evaluating Employee Performance (Chapter 5).   The periodic evaluation of the quality of your job performance will continue throughout your working career. Promotions, pay increases, transfers, and dismissals will be based on these appraisals. It is vital that these decisions be made as fairly and objectively as possible and not be subject to the personal likes and dislikes of your supervisor. I-O psychologists have devised appraisal methods for many types of jobs. Because your future satisfaction and security depend on these appraisals, it is important that your company have a fair and appropriate system for evaluating your job performance and that you understand how that system works.

Employee Training and Development (Chapter 6).   Virtually every new employee receives some sort of job training. Inexperienced workers must be taught the specific operations they are expected to perform and may also need training in good work habits. Experienced workers who change jobs must be taught the policies and procedures of their new employer. Workers whose jobs are altered by changing technology require retraining. As the machinery of production and the dynamics of organizational life become more complex, the demands made on employees to learn and on employers to teach increase in scope and significance.

Organizational Leadership (Chapter 7).   One of industry's greatest challenges is selecting, training, and developing effective leaders. The problem is of concern to you for two reasons. First, as an employee you will work under a supervisor or manager, and your efficiency and satisfaction will be affected by his or her leadership style. Second, because most business leaders come from the ranks of college-educated persons, you will most likely serve at some level of management in the course of your career. Psychologists are also concerned with the abilities of leaders in various situations and the effects of different leadership styles on subordinates. It is necessary to the continuing growth of any organization that its most competent people be placed in positions of leadership and that they exercise their skills in the most effective manner.

Motivation, Job Satisfaction, and Job Involvement (Chapter 8).   Vital to the efficiency of any organization are the motivations of its employees, the satisfaction they receive from their work, and the extent of their commitment to the company. Many aspects of the work environment affect motivation, satisfaction, and involvement. These include the quality of leadership, advancement opportunities, job security, and characteristics of the physical and psychological work climate. Negative aspects of a job can produce undesirable effects, such as absenteeism, turnover, low productivity, frequent accidents, and labor grievances. I-O psychologists work to identify and modify conditions that can impair the quality of working life before they have serious psychological and economic consequences for employees and employers.

Organizational Psychology (Chapter 9).   Few people work in isolation. Whether our work is in a classroom, a department store, or a software company, it takes place within a particular organizational climate or culture. This culture includes the formal structure and policies of the organization, the nature of its leadership, and the informal groups that arise among workers. Informal groups may dictate norms and behaviors at variance with company policy.

Working Conditions (Chapter 10).   The physical aspects of the work environment were the first to be studied by I-O psychologists. Much research was conducted on lighting, temperature, noise, workspace design, and working hours. Later, attention shifted to more complex social and psychological conditions of work. A job's psychological climate, including such factors as fatigue and boredom, may be more important than the physical climate because psychological effects are subject to greater individual variation.

Employee Safety, Violence, and Health (Chapter 11).   In addition to the tragic physical and personal consequences of industrial accidents, economic losses cost organizations billions of dollars in lost work hours, employee compensation, and the expense of hiring and training new workers. Because the majority of accidents are caused by human error, the work of I-O psychologists is crucial in reducing the accident toll. Psychologists are also involved in efforts to deal with alcohol and drug use on the job, and with violence in the workplace.

Stress in the Workplace (Chapter 12).   Job-induced stress has widespread effects on physical and mental health. It can interfere with job performance and lead to serious illness. Many organizations attempt to deal with the effects of stress through counseling programs and by redesigning jobs to be less stressful.

Engineering Psychology (Chapter 13).   The design of the tools and equipment needed to perform a job is directly related to the physical work environment, to employee motivation and morale, and to job safety. As the machinery of the manufacturing, transportation, and service industries becomes more complex, so do the demands placed on the human operators of this equipment. It is the job of the engineering psychologist to ensure the best working relationship between person and machine by taking account of the strengths and weaknesses of both.

Consumer Psychology (Chapter 14).   The work of consumer psychologists is important to you if you are employed by a company that manufactures and sells consumer products and services, and if you hope to be a smart and informed buyer. Psychologists are involved in defining the markets for consumer goods, determining the effectiveness of advertising campaigns, and analyzing the motivations and needs of the buying public.

Summary

Work provides a sense of personal identity, defines your social status, contributes to your self-esteem, and satisfies your need for belonging to a group. **Industrial-organizational (I-O) psychology** is defined as the application of the methods, facts, and principles of the science of behavior and mental processes to people at work. As a science, psychology relies on observation and experimentation and deals with overt human behavior—behavior that can be observed objectively.

Industrial psychology began in the early twentieth century and grew under the impetus of the two world wars. A major change in industrial psychology came with the recognition of the influence of social and psychological factors on worker behavior, as demonstrated by the **Hawthorne studies** of the 1920s and 1930s. The area of engineering psychology emerged out of the development of the sophisticated weaponry of World War II. Organizational psychology developed in the 1960s in response to a concern with the organizational climate in which work takes place.

Continuing challenges for I-O psychologists relate to virtual workplaces and virtual employees, the demands of new skills, the diversity of the workforce, the changing nature of work itself, and the globalization of work.

To work professionally as an I-O psychologist, you need a master's degree, but you will find a position of greater responsibility with a doctoral degree. I-O psychologists in organizations face several problems brought about, in part, by the demand for their services. These include the fraudulent practice of I-O psychology by persons who are not professionally trained, the difficulty of translating technical jargon so that ideas can be communicated to management, the unwillingness of managers and workers to try new ways of doing things, and the necessity of balancing research and timely solutions to problems.

Areas of I-O psychology discussed in the following chapters are employee selection, psychological testing, performance appraisal, training and development, leadership, motivation and job satisfaction, organizational psychology, working conditions, safety and health, stress, engineering psychology, and consumer psychology.

Key Terms[1]

Hawthorne studies
industrial-organizational (I-O) psychology

Review Questions

1. What's so great about I-O psychology? What has it done for you lately?
2. What aspects of a job would make you want to keep doing it, even if you won a lot of money in a lottery and didn't have to work to earn a living?
3. Give some examples of how I-O psychology can save money for employers.
4. How did each of the following influence the development of industrial psychology: Walter Dill Scott, Hugo Münsterberg, and World War I?
5. What were the Hawthorne studies? How did they change the nature of industrial psychology?
6. How does the hiring of temporary workers affect a company's full-time employees? How do you think you would react if your company suddenly hired temporary workers for your department?
7. How will the trends toward virtual employees, the virtual workplace, and globalization affect your career?

[1]Key terms are defined in the margin of the page on which they are first mentioned. These definitions are cumulated in alphabetical order in the Glossary section at the back of the book.

8. What kinds of jobs can you get with a bachelor's degree, a master's degree, and a doctoral degree in I-O psychology?
9. What unique problems do I-O psychologists face in the workplace?
10. Describe the controversy between research and application in the workplace.

Additional Reading

Anderson, N., Ones, D. S., Sinangil, H. K., & Viswesvaran, C. (Eds.). (2002). *The handbook of industrial, work and organizational psychology. Vol. 1: Personnel psychology; Vol. 2: Organizational psychology.* Thousand Oaks, CA: Sage. A sourcebook of theories, methods, and research findings on all aspects of work design, personnel selection and training, employee behavior, job performance and satisfaction, appraisal and feedback, socialization, communication and decision making, organizational development and change, and person-machine interactions.

Borman, W. C., Ilgen, D. R., & Klimoski, R. J. (Eds.). (2003). *Handbook of psychology. Vol. 12: Industrial and organizational psychology.* New York: Wiley. A sourcebook reviewing various topics in industrial and organizational psychology. Reviewers suggest that this volume has deeper coverage of selected contemporary and future research questions whereas the Anderson volume cited above covers a broader range of issues.

Bowe, J., Bowe, M., & Streeter, S. (Eds.). (2000). *Gig: Americans talk about their jobs at the turn of the millennium.* New York: Crown. Contains 126 oral history interviews from a wide cross section of the U.S. workforce ranging from an air force general to a movie director, a lawn maintenance worker and a waitress. Interesting themes include job satisfaction or dissatisfaction, personal identification with one's work, negative features of glamorous jobs, and appealing features of repetitive jobs.

Donkin, R. (2001). *Blood, sweat and tears: The evolution of work.* New York: Texere. Examines the historical development of work from earliest times to the twenty-first century. Draws together trends from history, political theory, philosophy, religion, psychology, and sociology to examine why people have worked and what they expect to achieve. Discusses major evolutionary changes such as industrialization and the human relations approach to management.

Fraser, J. A. (2001). *White-collar sweatshop: The deterioration of work and its rewards in corporate America.* New York: Norton. A grim portrait of the American workforce as full of stressed-out people caught up in a race they cannot win. Blames the situation on lengthening workdays, fears of layoffs and replacement by temporary workers, dilution of employee benefits, and the pervasive technology that allows the job to follow employees home.

Stockdale, M. S., & Crosby, F. J. (Eds.). (2004). *The psychology and management of workplace diversity.* Victoria, Australia: Blackwell. A clear and well-written guide to managing diversity in the workplace, defining the issues (pro and con) and empirically demonstrating the value of diversity to the organization. Diversity is considered a broader concept than equal employment opportunity or affirmative action in that it is designed to actively further the acceptance of cultural differences. Chapters are devoted to women, African Americans, older workers, disabled workers (including persons considered obese), sexual minorities, and the economic underclass.

Chapter 2

Techniques, Tools, and Tactics

WHY STUDY RESEARCH METHODS?

Why study research methods? OK. Let's put the question more bluntly: What's in it for you? Why do you need to know about how psychologists collect and analyze research data? Although you may not be interested in becoming an industrial-organizational (I-O) psychologist, you will probably have to deal with the findings of I-O psychologists. As a potential manager, you may interact with psychologists to find solutions to management problems, and you will be responsible for making decisions based on the recommendations of the company psychologist or of the consulting psychologist your organization has hired.

Suppose, for example, that you are put in charge of implementing a new manufacturing process to produce color monitors for computers. A modern production facility must be designed and built, and part of your job will be to facilitate the changeover from the old process to the new.

You will have to consider several issues. How will the workers react to an abrupt change in the way they do their jobs? Will they be sufficiently motivated to operate the new equipment and maintain a high standard of production? Will they need retraining? If so, how and where should the training be undertaken? How will the new process affect the company's safety record? These are just a few of the questions you will be expected to answer. If you make a bad decision or a misjudgment, the cost to you and your company will be high.

Using information based on psychological research, I-O psychologists may be able to help you. But if you are to evaluate their advice and recommendations, you must understand how they studied the problems and arrived at their conclusions. You may also be asked to decide whether a research program is worth the time and money. A knowledge of research methods will help you make this decision more wisely.

Our goal in this chapter is not to train you to conduct research but to acquaint you with the requirements, limitations, and methods of the scientific approach. By applying the **scientific method** to problems that are too often dealt with by intuition or guesswork, I-O psychology makes a distinctive contribution to improved management and work practices. If you understand these research tools, you will be able to ensure that they are used properly on the job.

Scientific method A controlled, objective, and systematic approach to research.

Requirements of Psychological Research

Three requirements of scientific research are objective observation, control, and verification.

Objective Observation.   A basic requirement and defining characteristic of scientific research in any discipline is objective observation. Ideally, researchers base their conclusions on objective evidence, which they view without preconceived ideas or biases. For example, when a psychologist chooses a particular test, training method, or workspace design, that choice cannot be determined by private hunches, by the recommendation of some prestigious authority, or even by past research. The decision should be based on an objective evaluation of the facts of the present situation.

Control.   A second requirement of psychological research is that observations must be well controlled and systematic. The conditions under which objective observations are made should be predetermined so that every factor that could possibly influence the outcome is known to the researcher. For example, if we are studying the effects of background music on the efficiency of employees in data-entry jobs, we must control the experimental situation so that no factors other than the music can affect worker productivity.

Duplication and Verification.   The systematic control of objective observation allows for the fulfillment of a third research requirement, that of duplication and verifiability. With careful control of conditions, a scientist working at another time and place can duplicate the conditions under which the earlier experiment was conducted. We can have more confidence in research findings if they have been verified by other investigators. This verification is possible only under carefully controlled conditions. Thus, psychological research in any setting requires (1) systematic planning, (2) control of the experimental situation so that the findings can be duplicated and verified, and (3) objective observation.

Limitations of Psychological Research

Psychologists face many challenges in designing and executing a psychological research program within the confines of a university laboratory. But when a study is undertaken in the real-life setting of a factory or office, the problems are magnified.

Not All Behavior Can Be Studied.   One obvious limitation is that research methods cannot be applied to every problem. For example, social psychologists cannot conduct controlled observations of how people behave in riots. The situation is too complex and dangerous to arrange in advance. Similarly, in industry it is not feasible to conduct systematic research on some mechanical safety devices that might expose workers to possible injury. There is a limit to what people should be asked to risk in the interest of scientific research.

Observing Behavior Can Change It.   A second problem is that the act of observing people in an experiment can interfere with or change the behavior that the psychologist is trying to study. For example, if employees are asked to take a personality test as part of research on job satisfaction, they may deliberately distort their test responses because they do not want to answer personal questions or because they don't like their boss or the company psychologist. For another example, consider research to investigate the effects of jet engine noise on the efficiency of airline mechanics. If the mechanics are aware that they are part of a psychological research study, they may deliberately work faster or slower than they would on a normal workday when they were not being observed.

The Hawthorne Effect.   Sometimes employee behavior changes just because something new has been introduced into the workplace. This phenomenon was first observed during the Hawthorne experiments and so has come to be called the Hawthorne effect. Recall from Chapter 1 that one of the Hawthorne studies involved increasing the level of lighting in a work area. Production rose with each increase in illumination and then remained high even when the lighting level was reduced. It didn't seem to matter whether the light was brighter or dimmer. It was the change, the fact that something new was happening in the workplace, that affected worker productivity. The I-O psychologist conducting the research must determine whether the differences observed in the behavior of the research participants result from the actual working conditions under study or arise from the novelty of the change itself, independent of working conditions.

Artificial Settings.   Some studies must be conducted in artificial settings. Management may not allow the psychologist to disrupt production by experimenting with various work procedures on the assembly line or in the office. As a result, research may have to be conducted in a simulated job environment. In such cases, the research results will be based on performance in a situation that is not identical to the job environment in which the findings are to be applied. This artificiality may reduce the usefulness of the research findings.

College Students as Subjects.   The problem of artificiality is complicated by the fact that much research in I-O psychology is conducted in universities and relies on college students as subjects. A review of five leading journals showed that 87 percent of the studies published used students as subjects. A majority of the studies comparing the characteristics and behaviors of student and non-student samples reveal important differences between the two groups. For example, experienced business managers and college students performing the same task—evaluating applicants for a management position—showed that the students rated the applicants much higher and deserving of higher starting salaries than did the business managers.

Thus, college students may behave differently from employees and managers on the job, and these differences limit the generalizability of the research findings. Although some I-O psychologists argue that research conducted in university laboratories can be generalized to human resources and organizational issues, other psychologists maintain that the differences are so great that only the most cautious generalization is acceptable. To maximize the usefulness of the findings we discuss in this book, we rely primarily on research that studies employees and managers in actual work situations.

METHODS OF PSYCHOLOGICAL RESEARCH

Several methods are available to I-O psychologists who conduct research in the workplace. Selecting the most effective technique is one of the first issues to be resolved in any research program. In most cases, the technique will be determined by the nature of the problem to be investigated. We discuss the following techniques: experiments, naturalistic observations, surveys, and Web-based research.

Experimental method
The scientific way to determine the effect or influence of a variable on the subjects' performance or behavior.

Independent variable In an experiment, this is the stimulus variable that is manipulated to determine its effect on the subjects' behavior.

THE EXPERIMENTAL METHOD

The **experimental method** is simple in its basic concept but can be difficult to implement. The purpose of an experiment is to determine the effect or influence of a variable on the performance or behavior of the people being studied (the research participants, or subjects).

Psychologists distinguish two variables in an experiment. One is the stimulus, or **independent variable,** the effects of which we are interested in determining.

The other is the participants' resulting behavior, called the **dependent variable** because it depends on the independent variable. Both variables can be objectively observed, measured, and recorded.

Designing an Experiment

Consider the following experiment. Management is concerned about the poor productivity of a group of workers who assemble television sets. Company psychologists are asked to study how output could be increased. At first they suggest a number of factors that could be responsible for the low level of production, such as low pay, inadequate training, an unpopular supervisor, and obsolete equipment. After they inspect the workplace, however, the psychologists suspect that the problem is insufficient lighting. They design an experiment to test this hypothesis.

The two variables in the experiment are easy to identify and measure. The independent variable is the level of lighting. This is the stimulus variable, which the psychologists will increase during the experiment to determine the effects. The dependent variable is the workers' response rate—in this case, their measured rate of production with the changed lighting.

The psychologists arrange for the lighting level in the workroom to be increased, and they measure production before the experiment and after two weeks of the brighter lighting. Prior to changing the lighting, each worker assembled an average of three television sets an hour. Two weeks later, individual production averaged eight units an hour, a considerable increase.

Why Did Production Increase?   Can we conclude that the change in the independent variable (the brighter lighting) brought about the change in the dependent variable (the greater productivity)? No. We cannot draw this conclusion on the basis of the experiment as described.

How do we know that some factor other than lighting was not responsible for the higher production? Perhaps the boss was nicer to the workers during the two-week experiment because he knew the company psychologists were hanging around. Maybe the workers purposely produced more because they thought their jobs were being threatened. Maybe sunny weather made the workers happier, or perhaps production increased because of the Hawthorne effect, the fact that some change had been introduced to break the usual monotony of the workday. Many other factors could account for the increase in production, but the psychologists must be certain that nothing operated to influence the subjects' behavior except the stimulus being manipulated.

The Element of Control.   An essential feature of the scientific method was omitted from our experiment: the element of control. Controlling the experimental conditions assures us that any change in the behavior or performance of the research participants is solely attributable to the independent variable.

To produce this necessary control, psychologists use two groups of subjects in an experiment: the **experimental group,** which consists of the subjects exposed to the independent variable, and the **control group.** The experimental and control groups should be as similar as possible in every respect except that the control group is not exposed to the independent variable.

To conduct our experiment properly, then, we must divide the workers into these two groups. Their productivity is measured before and after the experimental period. The production level of the control group serves as a standard against which to compare the resulting performance of the experimental group.

If the groups of workers are similar and if the performance of the experimental group at the end of the experiment is significantly higher than that of the control group, then we can conclude that the improved lighting was responsible for the increased production. Extraneous factors, such as the weather, the supervisor's behavior, or the Hawthorne effect, could not have influenced the subjects' behavior. If any of these factors had been influential, then the performance of both groups would have changed similarly.

Selecting Research Participants

The control group and the experimental group must be as similar as possible. There are two methods experimenters can use to ensure this: the random group design and the matched group design.

Random group design A method for ensuring similarity between experimental and control groups that assigns subjects at random to each condition.

The **random group design** involves assigning the subjects at random to the experimental and control groups. In our experiment, if the company employed 100 television set assemblers, we would arbitrarily assign 50 to the experimental condition and 50 to the control condition. Because the basis for dividing the workers into experimental and control conditions is random, we may assume that the groups are essentially similar. Any possible influencing variables, such as age or length of job experience, should be evenly distributed over the two groups because these factors were not allowed to influence the assignment of the subjects.

Matched group design A method for ensuring similarity between experimental and control groups that matches subjects in both groups on characteristics, such as age, job experience, and intelligence, that could affect the dependent variable.

In the **matched group design,** to ensure similarity between experimental and control groups, subjects in one group are matched with subjects in the other group on the basis of characteristics that could affect their performance (the dependent variable). For our experiment we could find pairs of subjects who are matched on age, job experience, intelligence, and supervisor ratings, and then we could assign one member of each pair to each group. In this way, the experimental and control groups would be as alike as possible.

Although desirable, the matched group technique is costly and difficult to carry out. To find enough pairs of subjects, we would need an even larger pool of potential research participants from whom to choose. Also, it becomes extremely complicated to equate pairs of subjects on more than one factor. Matching people on length of job experience alone presents few problems, but matching them on several factors at the same time is cumbersome.

On the Job: Training Effects on Turnover and Productivity[1]

As a classic example of a typical experiment, let us consider the research conducted in a factory in which sewing machine operators produced women's lingerie. Management had asked a consulting psychologist to find out why 68 percent of the sewing machine operators quit within a year. After taking a survey of employee attitudes and interviewing the supervisors, the psychologist hypothesized that the reason for the high turnover was insufficient job training.

The psychologist devised a study to investigate the effects of several training conditions on the rate of turnover and the rate of productivity. Note that the

[1]*Source:* J. Lefkowitz (1970). Effect of training on the productivity and tenure of sewing machine operators. *Journal of Applied Psychology, 54,* 81–86.

initial problem leading to the research was the high number of people quitting. In the process of designing an experiment to focus on this problem, the psychologist realized that with little extra effort, data could also be secured on a second dependent variable: the level of production.

Subjects and Experimental Design.   The research participants were 208 women employees hired in one year as trainees. The dependent variables were (1) job turnover, defined as the percentage of workers who quit in their first 40 days on the job, and (2) productivity, defined in terms of daily output figures in the first 40 days on the job. The psychologist chose the 40-day period because company records showed that most terminations occurred during that time. The dependent variables were easy to observe, measure, and record with precision.

The independent variable was the level of training. The psychologist specified four training periods. The company's standard practice was to provide one day of training for new employees, conducted in a special training facility. This one-day training was designated as the control condition, against which other training periods would be compared.

Trainees assigned to Group I took the standard one-day training course. Group II received two days of training in the training facility, and Group III received three days of training in the training facility. Group IV had three days of training, but part of it was conducted in the training room and part of it took place in the workroom.

The workers were assigned to each of the four conditions on the basis of the date of their initial employment with the company. Those hired during the first month of the study were placed in Group I, those hired during the second month in Group II, and so on, repeating the cycle throughout the year the study was in progress. Statistical comparisons of each group's initial performance demonstrated their similarity.

Results.   The results of the turnover study revealed that the longer the training received in the training facility (Groups I, II, and III), the lower the rate of turnover (see Figure 2–1). The three-day training period combining on-the-job experience with the training facility (Group IV) did not reduce the turnover rate when it was compared to the three-day training period conducted wholly in the training facility (Group III). As you can see, however, comparing Groups I and III shows that the additional days of training reduced turnover from 53 percent to 33 percent.

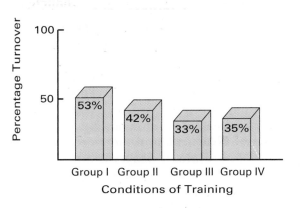

FIGURE 2–1.   Turnover rates of four training conditions.

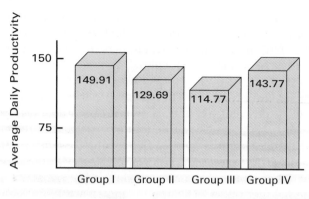

FIGURE 2–2. Production levels of four training conditions.

The second part of the study (the effect of training on productivity) produced unexpected complications. The data showed that the longer the time spent in the training facility, the lower the average daily rate of production (see Figure 2–2). The three days of training in the facility and on the job (Group IV) led to greater productivity than did the three days of training in the facility alone (Group III).

Thus, the independent variable (the different training levels) produced conflicting results on the dependent variables. Greater time in the training room resulted in lower turnover, but it also yielded lower productivity. It is at this point—interpreting the research results—that the training and experience of the I-O psychologist are put to their most severe test. Experiments do not always turn out the way the researcher hopes. Hypotheses are not always confirmed. Results are not always clear and consistent, and considerable interpretive skill is necessary to relate the data to the job or the problem being studied and to explain the options to management.

The psychologist conducting this experiment evaluated the productivity and turnover data and concluded that the three-day integrated training condition (Group IV) would be the most profitable for the company. It yielded a close second-highest level of production and a close second-lowest rate of turnover.

We must keep in mind that I-O research proceeds on two levels: (1) designing the experiment and (2) interpreting and implementing the results. At both levels, psychologists depend on the cooperation of managers and workers who understand the requirements of psychological research.

THE NATURALISTIC OBSERVATION METHOD

Naturalistic observation
The scientific observation of behavior in its natural setting, without any experimental manipulation of the independent variable.

In the study of human behavior at work, it is not always possible to bring the relevant variables under the precise control required by the experimental method. Also, it may be more useful to study behavior as it occurs in real life. We mentioned that one of the limitations of the experimental method is artificiality. To avoid this, psychologists sometimes prefer to observe behavior in its natural setting without introducing any manipulation of the independent variable. This is the essence of the method of **naturalistic observation.** Although this method does not involve the manipulation of the independent variable, the psychologist is still able to maintain some control over the situation.

The advantage of naturalistic observation is that the behaviors being observed and the situations in which they are observed are typical of what occurs in everyday life. The findings of naturalistic observation can be more readily generalized and applied to real life because that is where they were obtained. After all, our ordinary daily activities occur in situations that are not under the stringent control necessary in the experimental method.

This advantage is also a major weakness. Because researchers do not manipulate the independent variable, it is sometimes difficult to conclude with assurance what brought about any resulting change in the subjects' behavior or performance. Another limitation is that the observation cannot be repeated. It is impossible to duplicate the exact conditions that prevailed during the initial observation.

The experimental method also has problems, as we noted. Nevertheless, when it can be used, it is a better choice than naturalistic observation because the experimenter can control and systematically manipulate the independent variable. However, both methods, when applied with precision and interpreted with care, are valuable in the study of human behavior in the workplace.

On the Job: Friendly Behaviors of Store Clerks[2]

A nationwide chain of convenience stores instituted a training program to teach its clerks to be friendly toward customers. The company wanted to determine whether the friendly behaviors would lead to an increase in sales and thus justify the expense of the training. Arranging an experiment would have been difficult and might not have been informative. The company could have compared sales at two stores, one of which had clerks trained to be friendly whereas the other did not, but that might have meant a loss in sales at the control group store and the possible alienation of customers.

The company could have designed a laboratory experiment in which people would pose as courteous clerks and rude clerks. Persons playing the role of customer would be asked if they thought they would buy more from the courteous clerks than from the rude clerks, but that would have been too artificial a situation. Also, the results would not tell the company anything about the impact of friendly behavior on actual sales.

Research Design.   The psychologists decided to conduct a naturalistic observation in which the behavior of 1,319 clerks in 576 convenience stores was secretly watched by trained observers during 11,805 transactions with customers. The clerks had been informed that their level of courtesy would be monitored at some time, but they were not told when and how the observations would take place.

The observers, chosen to fit the profile of a typical customer, pretended to be making purchases. They spent from four to 12 minutes in each store, depending on how many real customers were present. The more crowded the store, the longer the observers could linger without causing the clerks to be suspicious. Observers reported that they thought clerks were suspicious of them in fewer than 3 percent of the observations; these data were excluded from consideration. The clerks' friendly behaviors, as recorded by the observers, included smiling at customers, greeting

[2]*Source:* R. I. Sutton & A. Rafaeli (1988). Untangling the relationship between displayed emotions and organizational sales: The case of convenience stores. *Academy of Management Journal, 31,* 461–487.

customers, thanking customers, and maintaining eye contact with customers. These behaviors, along with the sales figures for each store, were the dependent variables.

Although no independent variables were manipulated, factors that might have influenced behavior and sales were controlled. For example, the proportion of women clerks to men clerks was considered in order to control for variation in courteous behavior by sex; past research had suggested that women tend to be more courteous than men in any setting. The proportion of women to men customers was recorded to control for sex differences in purchasing behavior. Why? Because if some stores were patronized primarily by women, for example, and if women typically made more purchases than men did, then the sales figures for those stores would be higher, independent of the clerks' behavior.

The stores for the observations were selected at random, but all were in heavily populated urban districts. None was from a suburban or rural area where the sales pattern might differ from an urban area. Recognizing that people in various regions of the United States have different buying habits, independent of the company's training program, the data from four sectors—Northeast, South, Midwest, and West—were analyzed separately. Thus, taking the research out of the laboratory and conducting it in the real world still permitted the psychologists to control relevant variables and make objective observations.

Results. To the researchers' surprise, the findings showed that the higher the incidence of courteous behaviors, the lower the sales. Analysis of the data revealed that a store's level of sales influenced the clerks' behaviors, and the courteous behaviors taught in the training program did not lead to increases in sales. The busier the store (the higher the sales), the less time the clerks had to be courteous. In stores with lower sales, clerks had time to be friendlier. The results also confirmed that women clerks were more courteous than men clerks and that clerks in the West were more courteous than those in the Northeast.

The behavior being observed in this example was not as well controlled as it could have been under laboratory conditions, but the greater realism afforded by the use of the real-life situation offset this disadvantage. In many cases, the nature and complexity of the phenomena under investigation determine the most appropriate method of study. In other instances, the psychologist must decide whether to sacrifice some measure of control for greater applicability.

SURVEYS AND OPINION POLLS

Surveys and opinion polls rely on the observation of behavior as it is revealed in the subjects' responses to personal interviews and questionnaires. The focus in the **survey research method** is not on what people do (as in experiments or naturalistic observations) but on what they say they will do.

Survey questionnaires and interviews have many applications in I-O psychology. Psychologists use surveys to ascertain factors that contribute to job satisfaction and morale. Some large organizations maintain a staff of poll-takers to conduct periodic employee surveys on a variety of work-related issues. This polling gives employees the chance to air gripes and complaints (a form of upward communication). It also assesses reactions to changes in work procedures and policies and provides the opportunity for employee participation in policy making.

Survey research method
Interviews, behavioral observations, and questionnaires designed to sample what people say about their feelings or opinions, or how they say they will behave in a given situation.

As a result, surveys have the potential for raising employee morale, reducing turnover, and avoiding costly union grievance procedures. In some plants, maintaining an open channel of communication between employees and employers has prevented unionization. Workers who believe their opinions are heard and valued by management are less likely to feel the need for union representation.

Advertising and motivation research firms use survey techniques to uncover consumer preferences. For example, Campbell Soup Company questioned more than 100,000 consumers to determine their food likes and dislikes. On the basis of the survey results, the company changed the seasonings in its frozen food dinners and introduced a line of low-salt soups.

In addition, public opinion polls are routinely used in political campaigns to assess voter reaction to candidates and to the issues in their platforms.

Problems with Surveys.   Even the best polling organizations have difficulty, however, with the precise measurement of personal opinions and attitudes. One problem is that some people deliberately lie when they are asked questions in a survey. They may say they will do one thing and then do something else. Sometimes they change their minds, for example, telling an interviewer in October that they will vote Republican and then voting Democrat in the November elections.

People may say they prefer a particular brand of clothing or automobile because they believe this choice will make them appear sophisticated. They may claim to drink an expensive imported beer, for example, but if interviewers could look in the refrigerator, they might find cans of an inexpensive local brew instead.

Sometimes people express an opinion in response to a survey question even when they do not have one, because they do not want the interviewer to think they are uninformed. An analysis of 37 surveys found that 64 percent of the respondents claimed to have read the magazine article the poll-takers were questioning them about. In reality, no such article had ever been published. The results also showed that people were more likely to be honest in their responses when they completed a questionnaire in private than when they were asked the same questions in a face-to-face interview.

These difficulties with the survey method can explain some lost elections, failed businesses, and bad management decisions. The fault lies not with the method itself but with the complex, subjective, and sometimes perverse nature of our attitudes, preferences, and behaviors. Keep in mind, however, that properly designed surveys can be highly accurate and that they succeed more often than they fail.

The focus of the survey method is on what people tell interviewers they will do rather than on what they actually do.

Personal Interviews

Four basic ways to collect survey data are personal interviews, paper-and-pencil questionnaires, Web-based questionnaires, and telephone surveys. The personal interview, the most expensive and time-consuming technique, requires a face-to-face meeting with the respondents.

Finding and training capable interviewers is vital because their appearance, manner, and behavior can influence the way people cooperate with them and answer their questions. Research has shown that people respond differently to interview questions, depending on the interviewer's age, race, and sex.

More subtle interviewer variables can also affect survey results. For example, if an interviewer asking questions about drug use shows by smiling or frowning apparent agreement or disagreement with what the respondent is saying, that person may change subsequent answers because of the perception of the interviewer's own opinion about drug use.

Personal, or face-to-face, interviews offer several advantages over other ways of collecting survey data (see, for example, Tourangeau, 2004). In general, personal interviews have higher response rates (some as high as 90 percent) than telephone questionnaires or mailed questionnaires. Personal interviews can reach persons who are unable to read. In addition, interviewers are available to clarify questions the respondents may have about the process.

A disadvantage of these interviews is that some people are uncomfortable disclosing personal information in a face-to-face situation. Also, since many people now choose to live in gated or enclosed housing communities, or in secure apartment or condominium complexes, it is becoming difficult to reach people at these economic levels to participate in surveys.

Paper-and-Pencil Questionnaires

Questionnaires offer a cheaper and more convenient way to obtain information from large numbers of people over a wide geographical area. In I-O psychology today, questionnaires are frequently used to collect information from employees. Because employees can remain anonymous, they are more likely to respond freely and openly. Also, because they can take their time, they can formulate their answers more carefully, and thus, their reported views are often more reliable than those in a personal interview.

The major disadvantage of questionnaire surveys is that the response rate is typically only 40 to 45 percent. Follow-up procedures are sometimes used to try to secure additional returns. A reminder letter or postcard can be mailed to all questionnaire recipients explaining the importance of the survey and requesting cooperation. Letters sent by registered mail and follow-up telephone calls can also be used to encourage compliance. Some companies offer incentives for responding to a survey. A few hold contests with valuable prizes as inducements for returning the questionnaires. Most companies offer only a token payment, such as a dollar bill, which is often sufficient to make respondents feel guilty if they take the money and do not answer the questions.

Web-Based Surveys

Most organizations today use electronic methods to conduct polls of their employees. Questions are posted through e-mail, intranet, or Internet services, and employees respond by using their keyboards to enter their answers. Electronic polls can be completed more quickly than face-to-face polls. Companies such as Allstate, Duke Power, IBM, and Xerox routinely conduct electronic surveys and post the results online, accessible to all their employees.

I-O psychologists have conducted research to compare responses to paper questionnaires with responses to computer-administered questionnaires. Several studies have reported no significant differences (see, for example, Donovan, Drasgow, & Probst, 2000). However, the rates of response vary greatly. A study conducted at

Newsbreak	"Push Polls" Can Win Elections

Public opinion polls not only collect information from voters, but they can also provide information. And some of it may be false or distorted information about a political candidate that can ruin his or her chances of winning. These polls are called "push polls" because they are designed to see if certain negative information can push voters away from one candidate in favor of the candidate who is paying for the poll.

Here's how they work. A polling firm hired by Congressman Green, let us say, calls several thousand registered voters in the congressional district. The callers are asked if they intend to vote for Green or for the opponent, Candidate Brown. Those voters who say they plan to vote for Brown or who have not yet made up their minds are asked a question of this type: "If I told you that Brown was once arrested for fraud—for cheating senior citizens out of their life savings—would that make a difference in your vote?"

Note how the question is phrased. The pollster is not saying that Brown had actually been arrested on such charges—which, in truth, he had not—but merely by raising the issue, the implication is clearly that Brown had been arrested. In this way, thousands of people in the voting district can be fed false information about an opposition candidate in the otherwise innocent guise of taking a poll.

Push polls have been used by candidates of major political parties at all levels of government. And, as you might expect, their use has raised ethical questions. One poll-taker criticized this questionable practice in the trade journal *Campaign Elections*, writing that "The truth is that polls are being used in today's campaigns as much to shape public opinion as to simply report it. Some polling may be used to mislead the public by skewing questions or reporting results out of proper context."

HP (Hewlett-Packard) showed a response rate of less than 26 percent to a paper questionnaire mailed to a sample of employees. When the same survey was sent to employees by e-mail, the response rate exceeded 42 percent. The response rate to a Web-based survey was 60 percent. Also, employees responded faster to the electronic surveys than they did to the mail survey (Frame & Beaty, 2000).

Other studies comparing paper-and-pencil questionnaires with Web-based questionnaires showed that employees in the United States, Japan, and France preferred online survey approaches to the paper-and-pencil format. A significant age difference was found; employees younger than 50 preferred the online approach, while employees older than 50 preferred the paper-and-pencil technique (Church, 2001). Later research supported the finding that the majority of employees preferred the online survey approach. No significant differences in that preference were found by gender, race, or military versus nonmilitary status (Thompson, Surface, Martin, & Sanders, 2003).

Despite the popularity of Web-based surveys, there are several disadvantages to this approach. Since these surveys are faster and less expensive to conduct than other types of surveys, there has been a tendency on the part of management to solicit employee opinions just because it can be done so easily. Sometimes management does not have a clear objective in mind about how it intends to use the survey results. Employees complain about being questioned so frequently when they see that no action is taken in response to their opinions and suggestions. When they believe that their input is not being considered or appreciated, they are likely to disregard future surveys.

There are also concerns about what has been called "ballot stuffing," in which employees make repeated responses to the same survey. This, of course, can bias the results. Some employees are also concerned about privacy. Even if they do not provide their names when responding to a company survey, can they be certain that their anonymity is protected? Such fears prevent some employees from expressing an opinion that they believe may be contrary to company policy. Nevertheless, Web-based surveys have quickly become the most frequently used approach to employee polling.

Telephone Surveys

Telephone surveys offer the advantage of a low cost per interview and the possibility that a single interviewer can contact several hundred people a day. Telephone surveys have been aided by computerized phone systems that speed up the contact process. Telephone surveys cost approximately half as much as personal interviews and obtain comparable data. As you probably know from your own experience, however, it is difficult to reach some people by telephone because modern technology makes it easy for them to avoid unwanted callers. One survey researcher described it as follows: "The majority of American households now have answering machines, caller ID, or both, and substantial numbers of households use them to screen out unwanted calls. Many survey professionals report anecdotally that telephone response rates have plummeted over the last decade" (Tourangeau, 2004, p. 782).

Telephone surveys offer a low cost per interview and the likelihood that an interviewer can contact hundreds of people in the course of a workday.

Newsbreak   Call Me Unresponsive

Blame me, if you wish, for the poor showing of conservatives in opinion polls. I refuse to respond to telephone polls. It's not that I'm unpatriotic, or that I don't want my opinion to count. I vote in every election, and it's partly because my name appears on voter lists that I get so many calls—about one or two a week. I used to respond to pollsters. Why did I swear off them?

- Polls take up my time. The calls interrupt me, whatever I'm doing. What right does Gallup or whoever have to something of mine that he intends to turn around and sell to political parties and publications?
- How do I know it's Gallup or Harris or Fox News or Time/CNN or whoever at the other end of the line? Back when I did answer polls, one pollster asked me what bank I went to and how often I visited it. Thus began my refusals.
- Some questions are too personal, or even dangerous, to answer—like the bank questions. I've also been asked the number of people in my household, whether I have a dog and a gun, and my total household income. These touchy questions get asked late in a poll, since it's harder to stop answering midway than never to begin answering at all.
- Many pollsters are nice, but some are rude. One waited until ten minutes into our conversation before hitting me with the family income stuff. When I declined to answer, she blew up. She said I had to answer or the entire in-depth survey and her time would be wasted. So both of us had wasted our time.
- Some pollsters are salespeople. Under the pretense of polling, a caller might ask, for instance, if you belong to a church, then if you believe in God, and then if you would like to visit his group's new chapel or buy its religion book.
- Many pollsters try to influence opinion. They may ask if you are aware of the horrible things their political opponents have done lately. They don't really want a yes or no; they want to open a discussion in which they mold your views and maybe get a contribution from you for their cause.
- Poll responses often aren't private. They can be recorded and circulated, with respondents' names attached. One evening at a Republican Party caucus, I was treated to a computer printout of a poll taken in my neighborhood. Whom did we intend to vote for, Candidate A, Candidate B, No Opinion, or Refused to Answer? There it was—my entire block, house by house, with my address listed as Refused to Answer. But wasn't it fun gawking at the political leanings of all those people I knew? . . . I do my part by taking opinion poll results with a grain of salt. Others might do likewise.

Source: Genie Dickerson. *New York Times*, July 13, 1999.

Types of Survey Questions

With any survey, regardless of the method used to collect the data, two basic problems must be resolved: (1) what questions will be asked and (2) who will be questioned. In general, surveys use open-end questions or fixed-alternative questions.

Open-end questions
Survey questions to which respondents state their views in their own words. They are similar to essay questions on college exams.

With **open-end questions,** which are similar to the essay questions you have faced on college exams, respondents present their views in their own words without any restrictions. They are encouraged to answer as fully as they desire and to take as much time as they need. If the questionnaire contains many open-end questions, the process will be time-consuming. The usefulness of the replies depends on how skillfully the subjects can verbalize their thoughts and feelings. Open-end questions place considerable pressure on interviewers to be complete and accurate in recording the answers.

Fixed-alternative questions Survey questions to which respondents limit their answers to the choices or alternatives presented. They are similar to multiple-choice questions on college exams.

Fixed-alternative questions, like the multiple-choice exam questions you are familiar with, limit a person's answer to specific alternatives. A typical open-end question might be: How do you feel about raising taxes to provide money for schools? A fixed-alternative question on the same topic might be: With regard to raising taxes to provide more money for schools, are you in favor _____, opposed _____, or undecided_____? Thus, the person is faced with a finite number of choices and a restricted way in which to answer.

Fixed-alternative questions simplify the survey, allowing more questions to be asked in a given period of time. Also, answers to fixed-alternative questions can be recorded more easily and accurately than can answers to open-end questions.

One disadvantage is that the limited number of alternatives may not accurately reflect the respondent's opinion. A person could be in favor of higher school taxes under some circumstances and opposed to them under others. When their answers are restricted to yes, no, or undecided, people cannot make these feelings known to the interviewer. If enough people in the sample have such unexpressed reservations, the results will be misleading.

Usually it is a good idea to pretest the survey questions on a small sample of respondents to make sure that the questions are worded clearly. If subjects misinterpret a question or detect unintended meanings, the results may be biased. For example, a survey by the National Center for Health Statistics questioned Americans about "abdominal pain" until poll-takers discovered that a number of people—enough to skew the survey results—did not understand the phrase, know where the abdomen was located, or even what it was. When respondents were shown a diagram of the body and the abdominal region was pointed out, their answers turned out to be quite different.

The wording of survey questions presents a challenge for I-O psychologists because approximately 25 percent of the American workforce is functionally illiterate. People who cannot read and comprehend questionnaire items and instructions will not be motivated to complete the survey and may not have the ability to do so properly even if they wanted to. For current survey results on a variety of issues, and to participate in surveys, log on to www.ropercenter.uconn.edu, www.gallup.com, or www.pollingreport.com.

Sampling Methods

Suppose a consulting psychologist is asked by the Texas state legislature to ascertain the opinions of automobile owners about a proposed increase in the driver's license fee. To question every car owner in the state would be tedious and difficult, even with sufficient time and money, and it would not be possible to locate and interview everyone. Nor is it necessary. With careful planning, surveying a representative sample of car owners will provide the desired information and predict the responses of the total population.

To select a sample of car owners in Texas, we could stop people at shopping centers, gas stations, or busy intersections. However, this would not guarantee that the people we talked to would be typical of all car owners in the state. The people found at an exclusive shopping mall in the suburbs of Dallas or Houston, for example, would be more likely to represent a higher income bracket than the state's large and diverse population. A better way needs to be found to identify a representative sample of the population for the survey.

Two ways to construct a representative sample of a population are probability sampling and quota sampling. In **probability sampling,** each person in the population has a known probability or chance of being included in the sample. By securing from the state department of motor vehicles a list of all automobile owners, we can select every tenth or 25th name, depending on how large a sample we need. In this way, every person in the population of registered car owners has the same chance (one in ten, or one in 25) of being included in the sample. This method is satisfactory as long as there is a list of everyone in the population. If we wanted to study all eligible voters in the United States, this method would not be useful because only registered voters are listed.

In **quota sampling,** the researcher attempts to construct a duplicate in miniature of the larger population. If it is known from census data that in Texas 20 percent of all car owners are college graduates, 50 percent are men, 40 percent are of Hispanic origin, and so on, then the sample must reflect these proportions. Interviewers are given quotas for people to interview in the various categories and must find appropriate respondents. Because the persons questioned are chosen by the interviewers, however, their personal feelings and prejudices can affect the selection of the sample. One interviewer may prefer to talk only to people who appear well dressed; another might select only women respondents.

Probability sampling
A method for constructing a representative sample of a population for surveys or polls. Each person in the population has a known probability or chance of being included in the sample.

Quota sampling
A method for constructing a representative sample of a population for surveys or polls. Because the sample must reflect the proportions of the larger population, quotas are established for various categories such as age, gender, and ethnic origin.

Noncompliant Employees

Some employees decline to respond to surveys, regardless of how carefully the survey questions are phrased or how attractive the incentives offered for answering them may be. This refusal can bias the results. In some instances employees may have failed to receive a questionnaire or may have misplaced and forgotten about it. But others adamantly refuse to participate in any survey by their employer about their attitudes, opinions, interests, and feelings.

The number of noncompliant employees has been rising, often because managers survey their employees too frequently, asking for information so often that employees become annoyed. When the response rate to organizational questionnaires is thus reduced, the resulting data can provide managers with misleading information.

A study of 194 employees found that people who said they would not fill out a company survey differed in important ways from those who agreed to answer the company's questions (Rogelberg, Luong, Sederburg, & Cristol, 2000). The noncompliant employees were found to have a greater stated intention of quitting their jobs. Compared to the employees who did complete the survey, the noncompliant employees were less committed to the company and less satisfied with their work. Further, these employees placed a low value on the response the company had made to previous surveys. In this instance, then, the replies that management received to its survey came primarily from employees who were highly satisfied with their jobs and supportive of the organization. Therefore, the company did not obtain a representative selection of their employees' views.

VIRTUAL LABORATORIES: WEB-BASED RESEARCH

I-O psychologists now use the Web to conduct research 24/7. In a virtual laboratory, they can run faster and less costly studies and draw upon a larger and more diverse pool of subjects than in a university laboratory or an organizational setting. Web-based research has included questionnaires for job applicants, surveys of employee attitudes, and psychological tests, as well as interactive experiments in which employees respond to stimuli presented on their computer screens.

The linking, or networking, of individual laboratories into a so-called NetLab makes it possible to conduct large-scale studies that collect data from thousands of research participants from different companies and different countries. NetLabs can operate virtual-reality group experiments in which subjects respond to simulations of situations in their actual work environment.

Virtual research offers additional advantages over traditional hands-on research conducted in a workplace or a college laboratory. As one researcher noted, "Surveys and experiments can be delivered quickly to anyone connected to the Web and data can be saved automatically in electronic form, reducing costs in lab space, dedicated equipment, paper, mailing costs, and labor" (Birnbaum, 2004, p. 804).

Recruiting research participants with a broad range of personal characteristics—such as age, gender, level of education, type of work, income, social class, and nationality—can be done far more easily on the Web. We have seen that much psychological research is performed with college students, because they are so readily available on college campuses, where most research is undertaken. In contrast, "Internet chat rooms and bulletin boards provide a rich sample of human behavior that can be mined for studies of communication, prejudice, and organizational behavior, among other topics" (Kraut, et al., 2004, p. 105).

Consider the example of the graduate student who wanted to study elderly people who had expressed an interest in genealogy. Instead of placing notices or advertisements in publications dealing with genealogy, asking people to respond, a process that could have taken several months, the researcher made inquiries to online genealogy groups and enrolled more than 4,000 people for the study in less than a week (Birnbaum, 2004).

Critics of Web-based research note that it is impossible to assess the honesty and accuracy of responses on criteria such as age, gender, and ethnic origin, or to know whether subjects are cheating by being coached on their responses or giving obviously incorrect or frivolous responses just to be contrary. Also, people who are computer literate and comfortable interacting with Internet sources are likely to differ in their educational and socioeconomic characteristics from people who are not so familiar with computers. Thus, the respondents are, in a sense, self-selected and not representative of the population as a whole. However, proponents of Web-based research point out that college students—the typical subjects for psychological research studies—are also not representative of the general population.

Critics also note that the rate of response to online surveys is lower than for those conducted in person or by telephone. The dropout rate is higher for Web-based research than for laboratory studies. It is far easier for an anonymous participant to log off than for a college student to walk out of an experiment being conducted by his or her professor. Nevertheless, a growing number of studies comparing online research with laboratory research and with job-site research shows that the results from all types are similar and consistent (see, for example, Birnbaum, 2004; Gosling, Vazire, Srivastava, & John, 2004; Kraut, et al., 2004). To learn more about Web-based research, including information on how to do it, as well as results from studies in a variety of areas of psychology, go to www.psych.hanover.edu/research/exponnet.html and www.psychexps.olemiss.edu/.

METHODS OF DATA ANALYSIS

In psychological research, as in research in any science, collecting the data is only the first step in the scientific approach to solving problems. Let us assume that we have conducted an experiment to measure the productivity of 200 assembly-line workers, or have administered an aptitude test to 200 applicants for sales jobs. What have we learned? So far, we have simply amassed 200 numbers—the raw scores. Now it is necessary to analyze and interpret these data so that we may draw conclusions about their meaning and apply the results to current situations. To do so, we apply statistical methods to summarize and describe the data.

Descriptive Statistics

You are already familiar with the word *descriptive*. When you describe a person or an event in words, you try to convey a mental picture or image. Similarly, when psychologists use **descriptive statistics,** they are trying to describe or represent their data in a meaningful fashion. Let us examine some research data and see how statistics can describe them.

Descriptive statistics
Ways of describing or representing research data in a concise, meaningful manner.

To evaluate a new test for job applicants that was designed to predict their success in selling satellite TV systems, a psychologist administered the test to 99 applicants. The test scores are shown in Table 2–1. Looking at this swarm of numbers should tell you why it is important to have a way to summarize and describe them. It is not possible to make sense of the data as they are. You cannot formulate a useful prediction or make a meaningful evaluation of the potential job performance of these applicants as a whole by looking at a table of individual numbers.

One way to describe the data is to construct a **frequency distribution** or bar graph by plotting the number of times each score occurs (see Figure 2–3). For convenience in dealing with so many scores, we can group them in equal intervals. Grouping the data is not required, but it does make them easier to work with. The graph offers a clearer idea of the test performance of our group of job applicants than does the table of raw scores alone. Also, the graph provides useful information about group performance by showing that most of the subjects who took the test scored in the middle range.

Frequency distribution
A graphic representation of raw data that shows the number of times each score occurs.

TABLE 2–1					
Raw Scores of 99 Job Applicants for Satellite TV Sales Job					
141	91	92	88	95	113
124	119	108	146	120	123
122	118	98	97	94	89
144	84	110	127	81	120
151	76	89	125	108	90
102	120	112	89	101	118
129	125	142	87	103	147
128	94	94	114	134	114
102	143	134	138	110	128
117	121	141	99	104	127
107	114	67	110	124	122
112	117	144	102	126	121
127	79	105	133	128	118
87	114	110	107	119	133
156	79	112	117	83	114
99	98	156	108	143	99
96		145		120	

Mean, Median, and Mode. Scientific analysis of the data requires that the raw scores also be summarized and described quantitatively. We must be able to represent the data with a single number, a measure of the central tendency of the distribution. To find the typical score in a distribution, we can calculate the mean, median, or mode.

The most common and useful measure of central tendency is the arithmetic average, or **mean,** which is calculated by adding the scores and dividing the resulting sum by the total number of scores. The mean for our group of 99 job applicants is 11,251 divided by 99, yielding 113.6 as the average score. Thus, averaging reduces our raw data to a single number. The mean provides the basis for many higher-level statistical analyses.

The **median** is the score at the midpoint of the distribution. If we arrange the 99 scores in order from lowest to highest, the median is the score obtained by the 50th person. Half the job applicants scored higher than the median, and half scored lower. In our sample, the median is 114, which is close to the mean. The median is a useful measure when dealing with skewed distributions.

The **mode** is the most frequently obtained score in the distribution; a distribution may have more than one mode. With our data, the mode is 114. The mode is seldom applied to describe data but is useful in certain work situations. For example, a store manager concerned with stocking an adequate inventory of stereo sets would want to know which components were being purchased more frequently than others.

Mean The arithmetic average; a way of describing the central tendency of a distribution of data.

Median The score at the midpoint of a statistical distribution; half the scores fall below the median and half above.

Mode The most frequently obtained score in a distribution of data.

Normal Distributions and Skewed Distributions. In Figure 2–3 you can see that most of the job applicants achieved test scores in the middle of the distribution and that only a few scored very high or very low. Many measurements approximate this bell-shaped distribution. In general, this normal curve of distribution occurs when a large number of measurements are taken of a physical or psychological

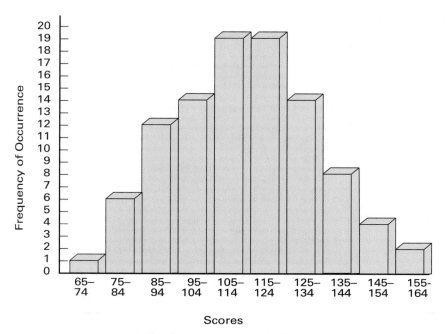

FIGURE 2–3. Distribution of satellite TV sales test scores (grouped data).

characteristic. Whether we measure height, weight, or intelligence, for example, a sample of sufficient size will yield a distribution in which most scores fall near the middle and few fall at the extreme low and high ends.

The **normal distribution** is predicated on the random nature and size of the sample tested. If the sample is not representative of the population but is biased in one direction or another, the distribution will not approximate a normal curve.

Suppose we administered an IQ test to a group of high school dropouts, persons with little formal schooling and little experience in taking standardized tests. Such a group is not typical or representative of the general population, so the distribution of their test scores will not look like the normal curve. When measurements are taken from specially selected groups, the distribution will most likely be an asymmetrical or **skewed distribution** (see Figure 2–4).

Normal distribution
A bell-shaped distribution of data in which most scores fall near the center and few fall at the extreme low and high ends.

Skewed distribution An asymmetrical distribution of data with most scores at either the high or the low end.

FIGURE 2–4. A skewed distribution.

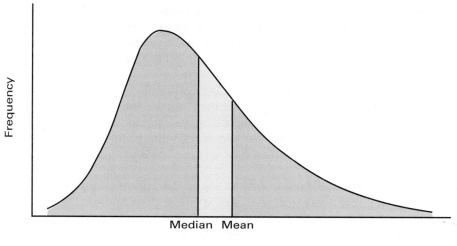

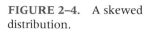

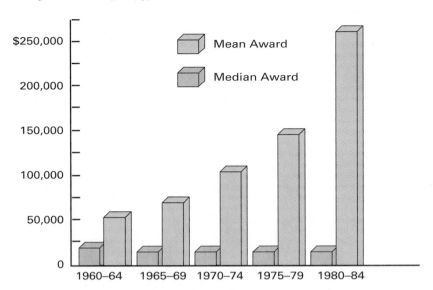

FIGURE 2–5. Median and mean liability awards.

In dealing with skewed distributions, the median is the most useful measure of central tendency. The mean is affected by a few extreme scores in either direction and thus may provide a misleading description of the data. The median is less affected by extreme scores.

You have no doubt heard people say that statistics lie. Although statistics can be used to mislead people, the fault is usually in applying them inappropriately, and not with the statistical techniques themselves. Consider the data in Figure 2–5, for example, which represent median and mean monetary awards in corporate liability cases over a period of 24 years. The mean, or average, awards increased from about $60,000 to $250,000, whereas the median awards decreased slightly during that time period.

The interpretation of these data sparked a controversy. Lawyers, who benefit from larger liability awards to their clients, argued that the liability judgments did not increase over the 24-year period. Insurance companies, who have to pay these liability awards, argued that there had been a fivefold increase.

The lawyers were using *median* liability awards; the insurance companies were citing *mean* liability awards. Both sides were technically correct, although the median is the better measure with a skewed distribution. As an employee, manager, voter, and consumer, you will find that it pays to be skeptical when you hear about "average" figures. Ask which average is being used. Is it the median or the mean?

Variability and the Standard Deviation.   Having calculated and diagrammed the central tendency of a distribution, you may not be happy to learn that more analysis is needed to provide a comprehensive description of a distribution of scores. It is not enough just to know the central tendency. We must also have a numerical indication of the spread of the scores around the center if we are to make good use of the data.

Consider the normal distributions in Figure 2–6. If we take the mean or median as the measure of central tendency of these distributions, we would conclude that the distributions are identical. The means and medians are the same for both curves. You can see, however, that the distributions are not identical. They differ in their spread, or variability.

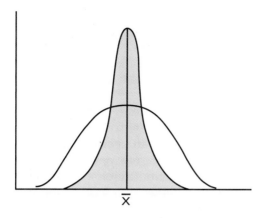

FIGURE 2–6.   Normal curves with the same central tendency but different variability.

The basic measure of variability is the **standard deviation** (SD), a precise distance along the distribution's baseline. Once we determine this distance, we can learn a great deal about the data and describe them more meaningfully.

Let us examine the distribution of IQ scores presented in Figure 2–7. The data form a normal curve with a mean of 100 and a standard deviation of 15. Knowing that the SD is 15 tells us that an IQ score of 115 is 1 SD unit or distance above the mean of 100. An IQ score of 130 is +2 SD units from the mean, and so on. Similarly, an IQ score of 85 is 1 SD distance below the mean (–1 SD).

With the standard deviation, we can determine the percentage of scores in the distribution that fall above or below any particular raw score. Tables based on the mathematical formula for the normal distribution give us the percentage of cases, or frequency of scores, that fall between standard deviation units.

For example, as you can see in Figure 2–7, 99.5 percent of the population has IQ scores below 145, 97.5 percent below 130, and 84 percent below 115. These percentages hold for any measured variable as long as the distribution of the data follows the normal curve. If we know the standard deviation of a distribution, we can determine the meaning of any particular score. We can tell where it falls in terms of the performance of the group as a whole.

Suppose we develop an aptitude test for dental school students that we will use to measure the motor skills needed to manipulate the implements used in dental surgery. Your roommate takes the test and obtains a score of 60. This

Standard deviation
A measure of the variability of a distribution, the standard deviation is a precise distance along the distribution's baseline.

FIGURE 2–7.   Normal distribution of IQ scores showing standard deviation units.

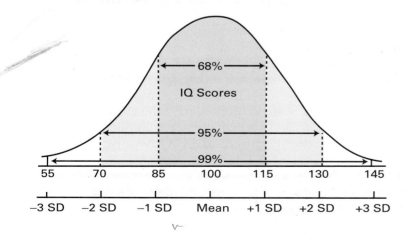

median ⟶ Skewed distribution

number by itself tells us nothing about that student's aptitude relative to that of all the other students. However, if we know that the distribution of test scores follows the normal curve, that the mean is 50, and that the standard deviation is 10, then a score of 60 (+1 SD from the mean) indicates that only 16 percent of the students scored higher and 84 percent scored lower. Your roommate might make a pretty good dentist after all.

There is a method by which raw scores can be converted to standard deviation scores, allowing us to interpret each raw score in the distribution. The standard deviation also permits us to compare the performance of individuals on two or more measures that use different scoring systems. By converting the distributions on all tests to standard deviation units, we can compare performance on one test with performance on another test because the scores will be expressed in the same terms.

Correlation.   We have been discussing the statistical treatment of one variable at a time, such as a set of test scores from a group of job applicants. I-O psychologists more often are concerned with the relationships between two or more variables. Any situation in which a prediction must be made about whether a person is likely to succeed on the job involves matching two or more variables. For example, an employee's performance on a selection test must be compared with a later measure of actual job performance. That is the only way the psychologist can determine whether that selection technique is a valid means of choosing the best people for the job. (We discuss the concept of *validity* in more detail in Chapter 4.) Psychologists use the correlational method to investigate the relationships among variables.

Correlation The relationship between two variables. The strength and direction of the relationship is expressed by the correlation coefficient.

A **correlation** tells the researcher two things: (1) the direction of the relationship between the variables and (2) the strength of that relationship. The direction of the relationship may be positive or negative, depending on whether high scores on one variable are accompanied by high scores or low scores on the other variable.

In a positive relationship, increasing scores on one variable are accompanied by increasing scores on the other variable. For example, a positive correlation between employees' test scores and supervisors' ratings of the employees' job performance tells us that the higher the test score, the higher the supervisory rating. As one variable increases, so does the other. We can predict that job applicants who do well on the aptitude test will likely perform well on the job. In other words, applicants who earn a high test score are apt to get a high rating from their supervisor.

In a negative correlation, increasing scores on one variable are accompanied by decreasing scores on the other variable. In our example, applicants who got high scores on the selection test would be likely to receive low ratings from their supervisors. In other words, those who do well on the test tend to do poorly on the job.

Through the application of the statistical formula for the correlation coefficient, we can calculate the direction and strength of the relationship between the variables. Positive correlations range from zero to +1.00. Negative correlations range from zero to −1.00.

A correlation coefficient of −1.00 indicates just as strong a relationship or correspondence as a coefficient of +1.00. Only the direction is different. In both cases, performance on one variable, such as job ratings, can be predicted from performance on the other variable, such as test scores. The closer the correlation coefficient is to +1.00 or −1.00, the more accurately we can predict performance on one variable from performance on the other. Correlation is a valuable and widely used tool in I-O psychology, and we shall see its use in many examples throughout this book.

Inferential Statistics

In the typical psychology experiment, researchers are interested in comparing the performance levels of two groups—the experimental group and the control group. In an experiment to test the value of a new training method, for example, the job performance of the experimental group, which has had the training, is compared with the control group, which has not been exposed to the new training. An important decision rests on this comparison. Should the new training method be implemented throughout the organization? The decision hinges on the size of the difference between the two groups on their job performance.

Levels of Significance.   How do I-O psychologists know when the difference between the two groups is large enough to justify the cost of establishing the training program throughout the company? They must determine the level of **statistical significance** of the difference between the means of the two groups. Their answer will be expressed in terms of probabilities rather than certainties. The problem is this: Is the difference between the means of the groups large enough that it is unlikely it could have occurred by chance?

Probability.   Applying techniques of **inferential statistics** to the data from the experimental and control groups, we can calculate a **probability** value for the difference between the means. This number represents the probability that the difference could have occurred by chance.

   Psychologists recognize two levels of statistical significance: a probability (p) of .05 and a p of .01. A probability value of .01 means that a difference as large as that obtained in the experiment would occur by chance only one time out of every 100. Thus, a difference at this level of significance could be attributed to the new training method used with the experimental group and not merely to chance. If the probability value was .05, we would have a little less confidence in the results, because this would tell us that there was a probability of 5 in 100 that the difference could have occurred by chance.

Meta-Analysis.   In I-O psychology, **meta-analysis** is a level of analysis higher than significance testing. Meta-analysis involves the large-scale reanalysis of previous studies to determine overall trends. This technique has been adopted by many psychologists as a way of reaching more objective conclusions about issues on which a considerable body of research data exists. Meta-analysis has been used in fields as diverse as I-O psychology, economics, and medical research.

   Regardless of the specific techniques used to analyze research data, statistical tools help the I-O psychologist reach informed decisions and recommendations about crucial problems in business and industry. The use of statistics does not eliminate the need for human decision making, but it does help guide the researcher, manager, or executive in that task. Statistical tools are means to an end, not an end in themselves.

Statistical significance The level of confidence we can have in the results of an experiment. Significance is based on the calculation of probability values.

Inferential statistics Methods for analyzing research data that express relationships in terms of probabilities.

Probability The idea that the differences between the means of experimental and control groups could have occurred by chance.

Meta-analysis The large-scale reanalysis of the results of previous research studies.

Summary

In psychological research, observations must be objective, well controlled and systematic, and capable of being duplicated and verified. Research has several limitations. For example, some problems are too complex to investigate by psychological research methods. The act of observing some behaviors may interfere with them. The novelty of change may alter behavior more than the actual change itself (the Hawthorne effect). Also, some research must be conducted in artificial settings, limiting the generalizability of the findings.

In the **experimental method,** psychologists investigate one influencing variable while holding all others constant. The variable being investigated is the **independent variable;** the behavior that results is the **dependent variable.** Two groups of subjects are used: the **experimental group** and the **control group.** The groups must be as similar as possible, a condition brought about by **random group design** (assigning subjects at random to the two groups) or by **matched group design** (matching the subjects in the groups on a number of personal characteristics).

Naturalistic observation involves observing behavior in its everyday setting. The experimenter can control the independent variables but cannot manipulate them with the precision permitted by the experimental method.

Survey research focuses on attitudes and opinions. Survey techniques include personal interviews conducted face-to-face, paper-and-pencil questionnaires, Web-based questionnaires, and telephone surveys. Research conducted with employees in the United States, Japan, and France has shown that they prefer online surveys to paper-and-pencil surveys. Employees below the age of 50 are more likely to prefer online surveys. Survey questions can be **open-end,** allowing respondents to answer in their own words, or **fixed-alternative,** restricting respondents to a few choices. Representative samples of the people to be questioned in a survey can be selected through **probability sampling,** in which each person in the population has a known chance of being included in the sample, or through **quota sampling,** in which a replica in miniature of the larger population is constructed.

Employees who refuse to answer survey questions may be more dissatisfied with their jobs than are employees who are willing to answer questions. Psychologists also conduct Web-based research in virtual laboratories, where large and diverse subject populations can be studied. Comparisons of Web-based research with laboratory research show that similar results are obtained for the two techniques.

The raw data obtained in a research project can be summarized, described, and analyzed by **descriptive statistics.** Data can be presented in graphs or reduced to a few meaningful numbers. Three ways to measure the central tendency of a distribution of data are the **mean, median,** and **mode.** When sufficient data are collected from a representative sample of the population, they form a bell-shaped or **normal distribution,** in which most of the scores fall in the center or average range. To measure a distribution's variability, psychologists use the **standard deviation,** which is a distance along the distribution's baseline. The standard deviation provides information on the percentage of scores that fall above or below any particular raw score. The **correlation coefficient** denotes the direction and strength of the relationship between two variables and enables psychologists to predict performance on one variable from performance on another variable.

Inferential statistics are used to determine the level of **statistical significance** of the difference between the means of two groups by indicating whether the difference is so large that it is unlikely to have occurred by chance. **Meta-analysis** is a technique for averaging the results of a large number of studies.

control group
correlation
dependent variable
descriptive statistics
experimental group
experimental method
fixed-alternative questions
frequency distribution
independent variable
inferential statistics
matched group design
mean
median
meta-analysis

mode
naturalistic observation
normal distribution
open-end questions
probability
probability sampling
quota sampling
random group design
scientific method
skewed distribution
standard deviation
statistical significance
survey research method

1. Why would knowledge of psychological research methods be of value to you in your working career?

2. What are three basic requirements of psychological research? What are the limitations of psychological research?

3. Distinguish between (a) dependent and independent variables, (b) random group design and matched group design, and (c) experimental groups and control groups.

4. How would you design an experiment to determine why a group of experienced computer operators who had worked for a company for five years suddenly began making data-entry mistakes when their department was moved to a new workplace?

5. Describe advantages and limitations of the naturalistic observation method.

6. What are some of the uses of surveys and public opinion polls? Discuss some of the problems that can limit their usefulness.

7. Describe four methods used to collect survey data.

8. If your job was to conduct a market survey of BMW car owners to find out what changes they wanted to see in new models, what survey research method would you use? Why?

9. What are push polls? How can they influence the outcome of elections?

10. Differentiate between open-end and fixed-alternative survey questions. Discuss the differences between probability sampling and quota sampling.

11. Describe advantages and limitations of conducting psychological research in virtual laboratories.

12. What is the difference between descriptive statistics and inferential statistics?

13. In your opinion, would the world be a better place without statistics? Defend your answer, showing appropriate data.

14. What can the standard deviation reveal about your performance on an IQ test?

15. What does a correlation of $+.85$ tell us about the relationship between your IQ score and your boss's rating of your job performance?

Additional Reading

Birnbaum, M. (2004). Human research and data collection via the Internet. *Annual Review of Psychology,* 55, 803–832. Reviews advantages and disadvantages of laboratory research and research conducted via the World Wide Web. With Web-based studies, researchers can quickly reach large heterogeneous samples or smaller specialized samples, as needed. However, dropout rates are higher.

Boyle, D. (2001). *The sum of our discontent: Why numbers make us irrational.* New York: Texere. Presents compelling, often humorous, examples of the use and misuse of quantification and statistics throughout history.

McConnell, J. H. (2003). *How to design, implement, and interpret an employee survey.* New York: AMACOM. Reviews the development of employee surveys, which are valuable rating tools for managerial performance, in terms of content (the questions asked), process (administering the survey), and feedback once the data have been collected.

Mitchell, M., & Jolley, J. (2001). *Research design explained* (4th ed.). Fort Worth, TX: Harcourt College Publishers. An undergraduate research methods textbook.

Pagano, R. R. (2001). *Understanding statistics in the behavioral sciences* (6th ed.). Belmont, CA: Wadsworth. An introductory statistics textbook.

Smith, F. J. (2003). *Organizational surveys: The diagnosis and betterment of organizations through their members.* Mahwah, NJ: Erlbaum. Reviews the development, implementation, and interpretation of surveys on a variety of employment issues in a diverse set of organizations. Discusses the kind of data surveys can provide and how this information can be applied to improve human resource management and organizational effectiveness.

Tourangeau, R., Rips, J. L., & Rasinski, K. (2000). *The psychology of survey response.* New York: Cambridge University Press. Summarizes and reviews research on the psychological mechanisms of the survey response. Shows how minor variations in the wording of survey questions can affect employee comprehension, judgment, and response.

Part Two

The Development of Human Resources

The I-O psychology specialty referred to as "human resources" includes selecting, training, and evaluating new and current employees. When you apply for a job, you will undergo an extensive selection process. An organization may use techniques ranging from application blanks to sophisticated psychological tests. Once hired, you must be trained to perform the job efficiently. Selection and training techniques will also be used when you are being considered for promotion. The company will want to match your skills with the new job's requirements. When you are promoted to a more responsible job, you must be trained for this new role. Periodically, your supervisor will evaluate your performance. You will want this appraisal to be as fair and objective as possible, and to provide you with feedback about your progress on the job. Employee selection, training, and appraisal methods determine the kind of job for which you will be hired and the way in which you will perform your duties. Chapters 3 and 4 deal with problems of selection. Chapter 3 discusses such selection techniques as application blanks, interviews, letters of recommendation, and assessment centers. Chapter 4 describes intelligence, interest, aptitude, personality, and integrity tests used for selection purposes. Performance appraisal methods are covered in Chapter 5, and training techniques in Chapter 6.

Chapter 3

Employee Selection Principles and Techniques

CHAPTER OUTLINE

Have you ever spent Spring Break in Panama City, Florida? Thousands of students do every year, which is why so many job fairs are held there. Recruiters from a variety of organizations set up booths and try to entice college seniors to go to work for them. A survey of seniors was conducted at the job fair in March 2000. One of the questions was "Do you think you will stay in your first job for more than two years?" The results were unsettling to the recruiters, who rely on hiring new college graduates to help their companies grow. Of the seniors who took part in the survey, two-thirds said they did not expect to remain with their first employer for more than two years (Dunn, 2000).

How long do you think you will want to keep your first job after college? Considerable research suggests that at least half of the graduating seniors in your class will not find enough satisfaction in their work to stay very long with the first organization they join. They may find the job to be different from what they were told by the company recruiter or the interviewer in the human resources department. Or they may find that they did not know themselves so well, that their abilities and interests were not what they thought, or that they were socially or temperamentally unsuited to that particular kind of work.

Whatever the reasons for dissatisfaction with the job, it is an unfortunate situation in which the employee and the employer both stand to lose. This dilemma emphasizes the importance of employee selection principles and practices. Improper matching of the person and the job, of the person's skills and characteristics with the job's demands and requirements, leads to unhappiness and poor performance in the work situation.

Before you enter the personnel office of a potential employer, or before you complete an application blank on a company's Web site, certain preselection factors will already have influenced your choice of job. Some of these are internal, such as your preferences about the kind of work you want to do and your expectations about the organization. Other factors are external, such as the nature of the recruiting effort that brought you in contact with the organization and the amount of realistic information you are given about your possible place in it. Industrial-organizational (I-O) psychologists describe these preselection issues as problems of organizational entry.

ORGANIZATIONAL ENTRY

Your entry into an organization is of immense importance not only for the immediate satisfaction it may bring you, but also for your long-term contentment. Just as the nature of your first love affair will affect your subsequent emotional relationships, so your first job experience will affect your work performance and your expectations about your career.

Research has shown that people who demonstrate success early in their career are more likely to be promoted than those who are less successful early in their career. In other words, employees who start out well, who have positive experiences in the initial stages of their working life, continue to do well.

The amount of challenge your first job provides influences your commitment to your work, your level of achievement, and your motivation to do well for yourself and for your company. The positive impact of a challenging job stimulates a high level of performance and technical competence that can lead to continued success. Research in I-O psychology has documented this relationship between the level of initial job challenge and later success for employees in a variety of occupations in many different organizations.

Finding the right amount of challenge is of major importance in your organizational entry process. It is vital that the challenge offered by your first job be compatible with your expectations and preferences. Indeed, it is crucial to you and your employer that everything about your initial job comes close to satisfying your needs. That is why employers try to learn all they can about the expectations and interests of potential employees.

To find out what people actually do in a variety of jobs, what education and training they need, what their working conditions are like, and what their salaries and job prospects are, see the *Occupational Outlook Handbook* compiled by the U.S. Bureau of Labor Statistics. Check it out online at www.bls.gov.oco/.

EMPLOYEE PREFERENCES

What are you looking for in a job? High salary? Stock options? A comprehensive health insurance plan? A reserved parking space? Although it may be easy to identify the single most important factor for you as an individual, there is no single answer for all employees. I-O psychologists have identified several job characteristics likely to be important to employees. Some of these are listed below. How would you rank them for yourself?

_____ Challenging, interesting, and meaningful work
_____ High salary
_____ Opportunities for advancement
_____ Job security (no danger of being laid off or fired)
_____ Company stock options
_____ Satisfactory working hours
_____ Pleasant working conditions
_____ Compatible co-workers
_____ Signs of respect and appreciation from one's boss
_____ Opportunity to learn new skills

_____ Fair and loyal supervisor
_____ Being asked one's opinion on work issues
_____ Assistance with personal problems

A study of 81 new employees at 14 companies in Germany found that workers who were more committed to personal work goals or preferences before being hired had significantly higher levels of job satisfaction and commitment to their organization after eight months on the job when they believed that their company provided opportunities to attain those goals. Workers who did not believe that their employers provided the proper conditions for attaining personal goals had lower levels of job satisfaction and organizational commitment after eight months on the job (Maier & Brunstein, 2001).

When 113 new college graduates in the United States were surveyed prior to their first job, and four months later, the researchers found that organizational commitment was higher among employees who believed they could achieve their career goals than among employees who believed their company was not likely to provide the opportunity to attain these goals (Saks & Ashforth, 2002). Studies such as these indicate the importance of knowing in advance what your personal goals and career preferences are when you begin the search for your first postcollege job.

Employee preferences can be influenced by external factors such as level of education. College graduates have different expectations from those of high school graduates, who in turn have different preferences from those who did not complete high school. Not all college graduates have the same preferences. Engineering and computer science majors differ from liberal arts majors, and A students differ from C students. Younger workers' preferences differ from those of older workers, white-collar workers' from blue-collar workers', and technical personnel's from managerial personnel's.

Employee preferences change as a function of economic conditions. In an economic downturn when jobs are scarce, new employees in the job market may be more interested in pay and job security and be more willing to remain with an organization even if it does not allow the fulfillment of their goals and preferences. In a robust economic climate when jobs are plentiful, issues such as challenging work or the opportunity to develop new skills rank higher than security or salary.

Many people enter an organization with unrealistic or inflated expectations about the nature of the job and the company, which may explain why so many people leave their first job. The discrepancy between expectations and reality is too great. Expectations begin to clash with reality from the outset, when you have your first contact with a potential employer, typically at your initial meeting with the company recruiter. This marks the first opportunity for each to size up the other, and it is an important step in the preselection process of organizational entry.

THE RECRUITMENT PROCESS

I-O psychologists are concerned with several issues in the recruitment process: the sources employees use to find out about jobs, the characteristics of recruiters, college campus recruiting, and the kinds of information provided to job applicants.

Sources for Recruiting

The traditional recruiting sources available to organizations include online search services, help-wanted ads in newspapers, referrals from current employees, employment agencies and search services, placement services of professional associations, job fairs, and outplacement agencies. Another popular source for recruiting is the college campus. Almost half of all large corporations actively recruit managerial and professional employees through on-campus interviews.

Research involving 133 graduating seniors at three engineering schools showed that, like consumers in the marketplace, they were more attracted to companies that had received favorable publicity through news reports or their own advertising efforts. The more positive publicity an organization had received or generated, the more likely it was to successfully recruit these college seniors (Collins & Stevens, 2002).

Online recruiting is increasingly popular with a majority of medium-sized and larger employers. Electronic bulletin boards post company advertisements for available positions, and job-seekers post their résumés. The use of online sources speeds up the entire recruitment and personnel selection process.

Although online recruiting is effective, it also has problems and limitations. A survey of several hundred job applicants revealed that online recruiting was rated third for level of effectiveness. More effective recruiting sources were (1) networking and personal contacts and (2) professional recruiters and headhunters. Frequently mentioned complaints about online recruiting were (1) slow feedback or follow-up from companies, (2) not enough vacancies listed to make the search worthwhile, and (3) a lack of useful information on the company's Web site (Feldman & Klass, 2002).

A study of 254 college students showed that they were significantly more attracted to a company's Web site if it provided information that was relevant to their values and goals (Dineen, Ash, & Noe, 2002).

Recruiter Characteristics

The behavior and personal characteristics of company recruiters can have a significant impact on how college seniors choose their first job. Psychologists have found that characteristics likely to induce graduating seniors to accept a job offer include behaviors such as smiling, nodding, maintaining eye contact, demonstrating empathy and warmth, and showing thoughtfulness.

Other research on job applicants at on-campus placement centers showed that college seniors preferred recruiters to spend the interview period providing information about the company, soliciting information about the applicant, and answering the applicant's questions. When the college seniors thought that corporate recruiters were spending too much time talking about irrelevant topics, they were significantly less likely to accept a job offer.

Campus Recruiting

College recruiting may not be living up to its potential, and companies may not be realizing full value from their recruitment programs. One explanation for this finding is that fewer than half of corporate recruiters receive training in the proper techniques for interviewing job applicants. Recruiters tend to form a positive or

THEY'LL BE PROUD TO BE HERE.

The Army offers young people great opportunities to learn self-discipline, confidence and teamwork, qualities they need throughout life.

WE'LL BE PROUD TO SEND THEM THERE.

And they can earn up to $40,000 to go to college if they qualify for the Montgomery GI Bill plus the Army College Fund.

CALL 1-800-USA-ARMY   www.goarmy.com

Organizations of all types spend considerable time and money recruiting suitable employees. (Army materials courtesy of the U.S. Government, as represented by the Secretary of the Army.)

On-campus job fairs give college students the opportunity to obtain information on a variety of careers.

negative impression about an applicant's qualifications in the first few minutes of an interview, hardly sufficient time to collect information on which to base a recruiting decision.

Recruiters also tend to spend more time talking with applicants they consider to be qualified and less time with applicants they dismiss on the basis of a superficial judgment. Often recruiters do not agree on the topics to be covered in an interview and sometimes fail to discuss important issues with applicants. All these points reflect a lack of interviewing skills.

In an effort to reduce campus recruiting costs, many organizations have turned to computerized recruitment databases that compile student résumés. Subscribers who are searching for candidates with particular qualifications can prescreen and retrieve these documents.

Whether college recruiting is face-to-face or virtual, one major difficulty faced by corporate recruiters on campus is finding job candidates who have a realistic view of the business world. This is another reason college recruiting often produces less-than-satisfactory results. During the campus recruitment interview, many students obtain a false picture of the job and the organization, sometimes because they have had no experience in corporate life and, therefore, do not know what questions to ask the recruiter. They want to make a good impression and may try to hide attitudes and characteristics they think the recruiter might not like. Another reason for the misleading image is the fault of the recruiters. Their goal is to find people with promise for their company, and to accomplish this, they may paint an idealized picture of their organization and of the new graduate's first job in it.

Newsbreak   **If It Sounds Too Good to Be True . . .**

"Here's what Marc Russell was promised for his first job out of college: a position in a fast-growing consulting company helping Fortune 500 companies solve complex business problems and technological needs, with ample opportunity for rapid career advancement, international travel and stock options. This fairy tale gave way to a scary truth: He spent three months in an empty room in the Seattle suburbs waiting his turn to play Battle Zone on the company's fast computer. That was the good part.

"His longest trip was from Seattle to Portland. He got all of 10 stock options, which he has since lost. His biggest project was working for the King County Jail, where his keenest insight was that the corndogs don't have sticks. He wrote software tracking inmate movement. (How far could they go?) And there was this spooky spooky perk no one warned him about: 'the client threatened to keep us there [in the jail] if he didn't get what he wanted,' Russell says of the prison administrator. 'He was only half joking.'"

And so it so often goes, when the dream job the recruiter promises turns out to be a nightmare. It happens more often than you might think. One executive recruiter advises that you should do everything you can to find out, before you accept the job, whether the promises exceed the realities.

Source: When employers promise the moon, *St. Petersburg (FL) Times*, November 2, 2003; adapted from the *Wall Street Journal*.

Thus, each side may be guilty of misleading the other. The result, when they turn out to be a less-than-perfect match, is likely to be dissatisfaction. The obvious solution is greater honesty, with each party being open about good and bad points. Some corporations deal with this problem by presenting a realistic preview of the job as part of their organizational entry procedures.

Realistic Job Previews

Realistic job previews
A recruitment technique that acquaints prospective employees with positive and negative aspects of a job.

Realistic job previews provide information that is as accurate as possible about all aspects of a job. Such information can be supplied through a brochure or other written description of the job, through a film or videotape, or through an on-the-job sample of the work to see if the applicant can perform the required tasks. The purpose of a realistic job preview is to acquaint prospective employees with both positive and negative aspects of the job. The hope is that this practice will reduce overly optimistic or unrealistic expectations about what the job involves.

Research has supported the finding that realistic job previews correlate positively with job satisfaction, job performance, organizational commitment, and reduced turnover (Ganzach, Pazy, Ohayun, & Brainin, 2002; Kammeyer-Mueller &

Wanberg, 2003). Realistic job previews have also been found to reduce the number of applicants initially accepting jobs because potential employees can learn, even before starting a job, whether certain aspects of the work situation are unappealing or otherwise not appropriate for them.

A REVIEW OF THE SELECTION PROCESS

There is more to proper selection methodology than placing an ad in the newspaper or with an online search service, having people come to the office to fill out an application blank, and questioning them in a brief interview. A successful selection program involves several additional procedures. Let's suppose that the head of the human resources department is told that 200 new employees must be hired to operate the complex machinery that is being installed to produce digital cameras. How will these workers be found?

Job and Worker Analyses

Ideally, the first step is for I-O psychologists to investigate the nature of the job. The organization will not know what abilities potential employees should have unless it can describe in detail what they are expected to do to perform the job effectively. A process called **job analysis** is undertaken to determine the specific skills necessary to the job. From the job analysis, a profile of worker qualifications can be developed.

Job analysis The study of a job to describe in specific terms the nature of the component tasks performed by the workers.

Once these abilities have been specified, the human resources manager must determine the most effective means of identifying these characteristics in potential employees. Does the job require the ability to read complex diagrams? To manipulate small component parts? To demonstrate knowledge of electronics? And how will the company find out whether an applicant has these skills?

A survey of more than 3,000 employees found (perhaps to no one's surprise) that the more complex the skill requirements for a job are, and the more demanding the job is, the greater will be the number, variety, and complexity of the selection methods used for that job (Wilk & Cappelli, 2003).

The necessary background characteristics and aptitudes, as revealed by the job and worker analyses, must be assessed or evaluated in each applicant, for example, by asking specific questions in an interview or by administering appropriate psychological tests. Cutoff test scores or levels for the various abilities will be established. A minimum score on a test or a fixed number of years of education or experience will be proposed, and no one who falls below that level will be hired. It may be necessary for the I-O psychologist to evaluate present workers in the same or similar jobs to determine where the cutoff scores should be set.

Recruitment Decisions

Recruitment decisions are next. Should the company recruit new employees through print or online ads? Through an employment agency? Through referrals from current employees? The number of potential employees attracted by these efforts affects the caliber of those ultimately offered jobs. If ads and referrals bring in only 250 applicants for the 200 jobs, the company must be less selective

Selection ratio The relationship between the number of people to be hired (the number of jobs) and the number available to be hired (the potential labor supply).

in hiring than if there were 400 applicants to choose from. I-O psychologists call this the **selection ratio,** the relationship between the number of people to be hired and the number who are available to be hired. Thus, the potential labor supply directly affects the strictness of the requirements established for the job. If there is a shortage of applicants and the jobs must be filled within a few weeks, some requirements (perhaps the cutoff score on a test of cognitive abilities) will have to be lowered.

A shortage of job applicants may also force the company to expand its recruiting campaign and to offer higher wages, enhanced benefits, or improved working conditions to attract and retain new employees. Thus, the size of the labor supply can greatly influence not only recruitment and selection procedures, but also features of the job itself.

Selection Techniques

Selecting the new employees and classifying them as suitable or unsuitable for the job are accomplished by a variety of techniques, including application blanks, interviews, letters of recommendation, assessment centers, and psychological tests. Hiring decisions typically are based not on a single technique but on a combination of methods. In addition, testing for drug use is now widespread for many types of jobs (see Chapter 12). Some jobs also have physical requirements and may require tests of strength and endurance. Some organizations are testing for HIV, chemical sensitivity, and genetic predisposition to certain diseases.

The next step in the selection process is to test the selection procedures to find out if they have succeeded in identifying the best workers for the jobs. In our example, after the initial 200 workers have been hired, the human resources department must track their progress to see how they perform on the job. This is the major test of the worth of a selection program.

Every new selection program must be investigated to determine its predictive accuracy or validity. This is done by evaluating the performance of the employees selected by the new procedures. For example, after six months on the job, the supervisors of the 200 new workers can be asked to rate their job performance. By comparing these ratings with performance on the selection techniques, we can determine how the two measures correlate. We want to know whether the selection techniques were able to predict which of the applicants turned out to be the better workers.

Suppose we learn that the employees who received high ratings from their supervisors had performed an average of ten points above the cutoff score on a test of manual dexterity and had earned a high school diploma. Employees who received low ratings from their supervisors performed within one or two points of the cutoff score on the manual dexterity test and had not completed high school. These findings tell us that the two factors (manual dexterity and a high school diploma) were able to distinguish between potentially good and potentially poor workers. In the future, then, the human resources department can use these criteria with confidence to select the best people for these jobs.

Keep in mind that to evaluate employee selection procedures we must have some measure of job performance with which to compare performance on the selection techniques. Some ways to appraise and measure work performance are discussed in Chapter 5.

A Sample Selection Program: Airport Screeners

People who want to be airport security screeners must possess a variety of skills and abilities. These were determined by a job analysis performed by several psychologists, who then established a four-step selection program.

1. Applicants complete an online application form to determine whether they possess the minimum qualifications for the job. These include United States citizenship and a high school diploma, GED, or one year of experience as a screener.
2. Applicants take a three-and-a-half-hour computerized test battery designed to measure integrity, work ethic, customer service orientation, English-language proficiency, and technical aptitudes such as visually observing X-ray images. Approximately 48 percent of job applicants pass this series of tests.
3. Applicants undergo a structured interview; a test of physical abilities (such as the ability to lift and search luggage); and a medical evaluation including tests of vision, hearing, cardiovascular function, and a drug urinalysis. Approximately 86 percent of applicants pass this stage.
4. Applicants must pass security and background checks.

When the program began in 2002, the Transportation Security Administration received nearly two million applications. Of those, 340,000 were tested and approximately 50,000 were hired (Kolmstetter, 2003).

FAIR EMPLOYMENT PRACTICES

Successful employee selection programs must conform to the regulations of the Equal Employment Opportunity Commission (EEOC), established in 1972, and the provisions of the 1964 and 1991 Civil Rights Acts. All job applicants, regardless of race, religion, sex, or national origin, are guaranteed equal opportunities in seeking and maintaining employment. Discrimination in hiring is unethical, immoral, and illegal. It has been greatly reduced over the past few decades as a result of this legislation. However, examples of prejudice and discrimination can still be found in the workplace.

One study found that employers were 50 percent more likely to call job applicants for interviews if they had "White-sounding" names such as Brad or Kristen, than if they had "Black-sounding" names such as Tyrone or Tamika (Ferdman, 2003). This finding held true even when the background information on the application form was the same for all applicants, regardless of name.

An analysis of the hiring decisions made for 357 applicants for high-level management positions in the U.S. government civil service found that selection panels composed of people of different races and genders reacted more favorably to female job applicants but more negatively to Black and Hispanic applicants. In addition, African-American males on the selection panels were significantly less likely to hire African-American male job applicants than were female or White members of the selection panels (Powell & Butterfield, 2002).

Adverse Impact on Minority Groups

Adverse impact When a minority group of job applicants or employees is treated markedly worse than the majority group in staffing decisions.

When any minority group of job candidates is treated markedly worse than the majority group, that minority group is said to be the target of **adverse impact** in the selection process. Any selection rate for a minority group that is less than 80 percent of the selection rate for the majority group is evidence of adverse impact.

Let us say that a company had 200 job applicants (100 Blacks and 100 Whites) and hired 100 of them (20 Blacks and 80 Whites). In this instance, 80 percent of the White applicants were hired but only 20 percent of the Black applicants. The selection rate for Blacks was only one-fourth, or 25 percent, of that for Whites, much less than the 80 percent rule for showing adverse impact. This company could be challenged in court for maintaining vastly different rejection rates for minority and majority applicants.

Discriminatory Questions

Interviews and application blanks have also been affected by civil rights legislation. Questions that discriminate against a particular group can lead to lawsuits. For example, it is illegal to ask questions that identify applicants' national origin, race, creed, or color. Applicants cannot be required to name their birthplace or those of their relatives; to identify their religious affiliation, if any; or to give the maiden names of female relatives. It is also unlawful to inquire about the clubs or societies to which applicants belong and to ask them to submit photographs with their employment applications. These questions can be considered discriminatory and have no relation to an applicant's fitness or potential for success on the job.

In addition, employers cannot ask applicants if they have ever been arrested for any crime, because members of some minority groups are much more likely to be arrested on suspicion of wrongdoing. It is lawful, however, to ask applicants if they have ever been convicted of any crime. Conviction could be considered relevant to job performance in certain instances, such as when a person convicted of embezzlement applies for a job as a bank teller.

Reverse Discrimination

Reverse discrimination The phenomenon that may occur when recruiting, hiring, promoting, and other human resources decisions in favor of members of a minority group result in discrimination against members of the majority group.

The impetus to recruit, hire, and promote members of minority groups and to implement EEOC rulings has sometimes resulted in discrimination against members of the majority group. An organization may be so intent, for example, on increasing the number of women in its ranks to meet federal guidelines that it denies equal opportunities to men. In 1992 a White male medical school professor in Florida filed a discrimination lawsuit charging that the university had unfairly denied him a salary increase because the money available for pay raises was distributed only to women and minority faculty. This phenomenon, called **reverse discrimination,** has also occurred in graduate and professional schools, where some White applicants have been denied admission in favor of minority applicants whose grades and test scores were not as high as those of the White applicants.

Reverse discrimination may operate in promotion decisions on the job when women and ethnic minorities are offered greater opportunities for advancement than are similarly qualified White men.

Equal opportunity programs can stigmatize those persons hired or promoted on an affirmative action basis. Majority group member employees may come to believe that preferential hiring practices for women and minorities have led to the hiring of unqualified people. As a result, some White men feel resentful. A backlash against affirmative action programs has been expressed by dissatisfied employees, employers, and political leaders.

A study of 178 college students and 161 employees of a variety of corporations found that both groups of research participants attributed the success of fictitious Black employees to their personal strengths and abilities when the research participants understood the purpose of affirmative action programs. However, those students and employees who believed that companies were simply out to meet minority quotas, even if it meant hiring unqualified people, were significantly less likely to attribute the success of Black employees to their own abilities (Evans, 2003).

A study of 125 White employees of a communications company found that those who held highly prejudiced attitudes and who believed that their employer's affirmative action policies were designed unfairly to benefit Blacks were also dissatisfied with their own promotion opportunities (James, Brief, Dietz, & Cohen, 2001). And a survey of 439 workers who had lost their jobs and were filing for unemployment benefits found that White workers were much more likely to file EEOC claims alleging discrimination as the reason for their firing than were Black workers. The researcher suggested that fewer Blacks filed discrimination complaints because they had less faith in the fairness of "the system" and were more used to experiencing discrimination on the job. Thus, for them, being fired for being Black was nothing new (Goldman, 2001).

A telephone survey of 414 Whites, 392 Blacks, 162 U.S.-born Hispanics, and 177 immigrant Hispanics found that affirmative action programs were most strongly supported by Blacks, and less so by Hispanics. The majority of the Whites polled opposed such programs. In addition, Blacks tended to believe that affirmative action was fair and rarely involved preferential treatment (Kravitz & Klineberg, 2000).

Does Diversity Work?

Affirmative action programs have greatly increased the number of women and ethnic minority employees in the workplace. Has this increased diversity benefited the employees or their employing organizations? One study investigated how 273 Black and White college students were attracted to company Web sites based on how these Web sites depicted the composition of their workforce. Some Web sites showed pictures of only White employees, along with three White managers. The students were told that these managers would be their supervisors if they accepted jobs with the company. A second Web site showed both Black workers and White workers, along with White managers. A third Web site showed the same racial mix of workers and Black as well as White managers. The researcher found that White college students showed no preference for any particular company depicted in the Web sites. Black college students preferred the company site that showed racial diversity among managers (Avery, 2003). This suggests that racial diversity at the managerial level would help in recruiting employees of various minority groups.

Studies have also shown that greater ethnic and gender diversity in an organization allows for different perspectives in problem solving and leads to the generation

Newsbreak   It's No Longer the Back of the Bus

We are unable to get taxis to pick us up in front of office buildings. We are frisked and detained on suburban commuter trains. We are watched in department stores and mistaken for coat-check clerks and restroom attendants while lunching in the best restaurants. We are directed to freight elevators and delivery windows by receptionists who fail to recognize us in our own company offices. We are black professionals in corporate America.

Although I am at my desk each morning facing the same corporate challenges as my white co-workers, a great deal of my job-related stress comes from sources totally unrelated to my job. My father dreamed of the day when his son would work in a towering office with a city view. What he didn't know was that arriving there would not be the end of the struggle for black Americans.

Even though I have been the beneficiary of affirmative action, I can acknowledge some of its flaws—its tendency to create resentment among white men and its potential for generating a sense of "group entitlement" among minorities and women. But my experiences as a corporate lawyer, professor, and black professional in a mostly white environment have shown me that workplace bias in America, even today, is so intractable that it justifies establishing affirmative action as a permanent policy.

For those who believe I am overzealous in suggesting the permanent enforcement of affirmative action, I offer an incident that took place soon after I started a new job as a corporate lawyer in Manhattan.

A receptionist with a security guard in tow came running past my secretary's desk just as I was joining a conference call with a client in my office.

"Excuse me, Larry, but I've got security here," the receptionist said breathlessly, interrupting our call. "Did you see a delivery boy get past reception and come through here with a purple bag?"

I looked to the corner where a Bergdorf Goodman [an upscale department store] bag sat with a hat that I had bought for my wife.

"That's the boy!" shouted the security guard, pointing to me.

When the receptionist saw the shopping bag, recognition and relief washed over her face. "That's so funny," she laughed while closing the door. "We thought you were a delivery boy. Sorry to bother you."

The client looked at me with the slightest hint of skepticism.

Source: Lawrence Otis Graham. The case for affirmative action. *New York Times,* May 21, 1995.

of more and higher-quality ideas. Economic analyses have indicated that companies that are recognized publicly as having a good affirmative action record tend to have higher stock prices and to yield greater returns on investment (Crosby, Iver, Clayton, & Downing, 2003).

Other Forms of Discrimination

Discrimination against Older Workers. The workforce in the United States is aging. Most employers, however, still prefer to hire younger workers, despite consistent evidence from I-O psychology research that older workers are often more productive than younger workers and have lower absenteeism and turnover rates. In general, older employees do not suffer from poorer health, diminished vigor, or declining mental abilities when compared with younger employees.

The stereotypes about older workers persist. Older workers tend to receive more negative performance evaluations than younger workers, appraisals that are likely based more on age than on actual work performance. Older workers are protected by law against age discrimination in hiring and promotion. The Age Discrimination in Employment Act of 1967 legislated against using age to deny employment opportunities to people in the 40-to-65-year-old age bracket. The act was amended in 1978 to raise the age at which employees could be forced to retire from 65 to 70.

Discrimination against Workers with Disabilities. Employees with physical and mental disabilities are protected by federal laws against job discrimination. The Vocational Rehabilitation Act of 1973 made it mandatory for organizations to recruit, hire, and promote qualified disabled persons. The 1990 Americans with Disabilities Act (ADA) prohibits employers, state and local governments, employment agencies, and labor unions from discriminating against qualified individuals with disabilities in job application procedures, hiring, firing, advancement, compensation, job training, and other conditions of employment. The act requires employers to make reasonable accommodations to the physical or mental impairments of a qualified applicant or employee with a disability if it would not impose an undue hardship on normal business operations.

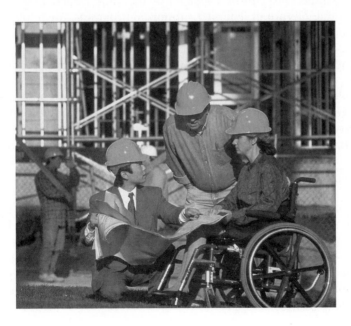

The Americans with Disabilities Act of 1990 prohibits employers from discriminating against qualified persons who have disabilities.

In one "reasonable accommodation" case, a supermarket employee who suffered from fatigue due to lupus (a tubercular disease) was provided with a stool so that she could perform her cashier's job without having to stand throughout her shift. Accommodations for other persons with disabilities include providing oral or Braille instructions to visually impaired job applicants or employees, and constructing ramps and other structural modifications for people who use wheelchairs. Some employers still resist implementing workplace changes on behalf of disabled persons. A survey of 114 managers showed that the greater the adjustment required, the more resistant the managers were to making them (Florey & Harrison, 2000).

An unintended consequence of making accommodations for disabled workers is that such changes may cause resentment among workers who do not have such disabilities (see, for example, Colella, Paetzold, and Belliveau, 2004). Consider again the example of the supermarket cashier with lupus. Other cashiers may feel that they, too, get tired and should not have to stand throughout their shift. Don't they deserve stools? Or what about an employee on antidepressant medication who is allowed to come to work late because the medication makes it difficult to wake up on time? Other employees may also find it hard to wake up in the morning, but since they do not claim a disorder such as depression that is covered by ADA, they are expected to be at work on time. Another issue is that the disabled employee's co-workers may believe that they have to work harder because the disabled employee is working fewer hours.

Prejudice against hiring disabled workers can still be found, even though it is at variance with their actual job performance. Research by I-O psychologists shows that disabled employees perform as well as or better than nondisabled employees. Many large U.S. corporations, such as DuPont, 3M, and McDonnell Douglas, routinely hire disabled workers because they have found that they make good employees. Companies such as McDonald's and Marriott routinely hire people with mild to moderate cognitive impairments and find them to be as productive as their other employees. However, fewer than 20 percent of the people of working age who can be classified as mentally disabled have found jobs, and half of these jobs are in federally subsidized programs. Such jobs include janitor, gardener, grocery store clerk, office receptionist, toll collector, and fast-food restaurant cook.

Passage of the 1990 ADA has led to the filing of thousands of formal job discrimination complaints and lawsuits against employers. Unfortunately, the prospect of legal challenges has made many organizations even more wary of hiring disabled employees. This fear of litigation may explain why the number of disabled persons in the workforce has not increased over the past decade. Russell Redenbaugh, a member of the U.S. Civil Rights Commission who himself is disabled, has concluded that the effect of the Americans with Disabilities Act has been "a complete disappointment."

Discrimination against Women Workers. Women face discrimination in the workplace, particularly when they apply for what are still considered to be traditionally male jobs. The report of the United States Census for the year 2000 found that women remained confined, for the most part, to so-called pink-collar jobs such as nursing, teaching, secretarial and clerical, bookkeeping, waitress and cook, and receptionist. However, women are making great strides in managerial jobs, though they are often restricted to "soft" areas such as human resources or public relations.

Two studies, one of 291 U.S. companies and another of 410 companies, revealed "an overall positive effect of female participation on firm performance." In addition, the companies' "profitability was highest when the workforce was roughly 50 percent female" (Kravitz, 2003, pp. 148, 149). Thus, gender diversity, like ethnic diversity, can contribute to an organization's economic success.

Discrimination Based on Sexual Orientation.   Gay men and lesbian women face discrimination in hiring in public agencies and private companies. To date, no federal civil rights legislation protects homosexuals from workplace discrimination. However, several states now include sexual orientation among the protected categories in their civil rights laws, and a growing number of cities have passed ordinances forbidding job discrimination against gay people.

Many U.S. corporations have implemented antidiscrimination policies with regard to gay persons. Some companies, such as AT&T, Xerox, Lockheed Martin, and Levi Strauss, sponsor support groups and networks for their gay employees. The major American automakers (Ford, General Motors, and DaimlerChrysler), as well as IBM, Citigroup, and some local governments, offer standard fringe benefits to partners of employees in same-sex relationships.

A study of 537 lesbian and gay employees working for 38 different companies found that the presence of formally stated antidiscrimination policies led to higher levels of job satisfaction and organizational commitment among these employees (Button, 2001). Other research showed that gay and lesbian workers who felt discriminated against because of their sexual orientation held negative attitudes toward their work and received fewer promotions than did such employees who did not feel discriminated against (Ragins & Cornwell, 2001).

Research with 379 gay and lesbian employees found that those who believed their work environment was sufficiently supportive to allow them to publicly acknowledge their sexual identity were high in measured job satisfaction and low in anxiety. They also experienced more favorable reactions from co-workers, less job discrimination, and fairer treatment from supervisors than did gay employees who worked in less supportive environments (Griffith & Hebl, 2002).

To learn about a potential employer's diversity policies with regard to sexual orientation, log on to www.gaybusinessworld.com or www.hrc.org; the latter is the Web site of the Human Rights Campaign.

Discrimination Based on Physical Attractiveness.   Some job applicants have a more pleasing appearance than others in terms of currently accepted cultural standards. This type of judgment, called "beautyism" by some, affects hiring and promotion decisions in the business world. Many people believe that physically attractive persons also possess more desirable personal and social traits, an attitude summed up by some I-O psychologists as "what is beautiful is good." Physically attractive persons are perceived as more sociable, dominant, and mentally healthy than less physically attractive persons.

A meta-analysis of studies dealing with the biasing effects of physical attractiveness in the workplace showed that company recruiters and human resources managers were just as susceptible as were college students to being influenced in hiring decisions by the physical attractiveness of the job applicants. This research also showed that the biasing effects were strong for both male and female applicants. However, the results also demonstrated that the biasing effects of attractiveness have decreased over the past few decades (Hosodo, Stone-Romero, & Coats, 2003).

An applicant's height may also serve as an advantage in selection, hiring, and promotion decisions. A meta-analysis of studies involving 8,590 research participants found that height was significantly related to ratings of job performance, leader emergence, and income. Taller people ranked higher on all three measures than did less tall people (Judge & Cable, 2004).

JOB ANALYSIS

The purpose of job analysis is to describe in specific terms the nature of the component tasks performed by workers on a particular job. A job analysis includes information about the tools or equipment used, the operations performed, the education and training required, the wages paid, and any unique aspects of the job such as safety hazards.

Work analysis The study of certain tasks and skills that workers can transfer from one job to another.

It is important to note that many I-O psychology practitioners prefer to use the term **work analysis** instead of job analysis. Work analysis focuses on certain tasks and skills that can be transferred from one job to another. In today's job market, employees must develop and continue to refine a diverse package of skills that they can apply to different jobs. Unlike workers in previous generations, employees in the 21st century cannot expect to spend their working lives performing routine and repetitive tasks.

We mentioned earlier the value of job and work analyses in employee selection. Unless the company knows precisely what a job entails and what is required for successful performance of these tasks, it will have no way of knowing what qualities to seek in applicants for that job.

Job and work analyses have other important uses in organizational life. To establish a training program for a particular job, for example, the nature of the job and the skills it requires must be known. A company cannot expect to train a person to perform a job unless the tasks and operations required for job success can be described.

Job analysis can also aid in efforts to design a job or a workspace for more efficient performance. If a job analysis reveals that a lathe operator has to walk 50 yards from the machine to the storage shelves every time it is necessary to replenish the supply of raw materials, redesigning the work area can eliminate this wasted time and effort. Job analysis can also uncover safety hazards or dangerous operating procedures.

I-O psychologists have devised a number of techniques for conducting job and work analyses. One approach is to refer to previously compiled analyses. The U.S. Department of Labor has developed the Occupational Information Network (O*NET), a database that summarizes such information. It defines, classifies, and describes a variety of occupations. This online database is updated frequently to provide employers with examples and analyses of the knowledge, skills, and abilities employees need to perform these jobs. It is an inexpensive, user-friendly tool for analyzing thousands of jobs and has had a strong impact on both research and application (see Jeanneret & Strong, 2003; Peterson, et al., 2001). In general, the O*NET provides the following information for each job.

- Personal requirements: the skills and knowledge required to perform the work
- Personal characteristics: the abilities, interests, and values needed to perform the work

TABLE 3–1	
O*NET Job Descriptions and Levels of Knowledge	
Category and Operational Definition	**Level of Knowledge**
Administration/Management—Knowledge of principles and processes involved in business and organizational planning, coordination, and execution. Includes strategic planning, resource allocation, manpower modeling, leadership techniques, and production methods.	*High*—Managing a $10 million company. *Low*—Signing a pay voucher.
Clerical—Knowledge of administrative and clerical procedures and systems such as word processing, filing and records management, forms design, and other office procedures and terminology.	*High*—Organizing a storage system for company forms. *Low*—Filing letters alphabetically.
Sales/Marketing—Knowledge of principles and methods involved in showing, promoting, and selling products or services. Includes marketing strategies, product demonstration and sales techniques, and sales control systems.	*High*—Developing a marketing plan for a nationwide phone system. *Low*—Selling cakes at a bake sale.
Computers/Electronics—Knowledge of circuit boards, processors, chips, and computer hardware and software including applications and programming.	*High*—Creating a program to scan for computer viruses. *Low*—Operating a VCR to watch a prerecorded tape.
Engineering/Technology—Knowledge of equipment, tools, and mechanical devices and their applications.	*High*—Designing a clean, efficient power plant. *Low*—Installing a door lock.

- Experience requirements: the training and level of licensing and experience needed for the work
- Job requirements: the work activities and context, including the physical, social, and organizational factors involved in the work
- Labor market: the occupational outlook and pay scales for the work

Table 3–1 shows examples from the O*NET of the knowledge required to perform different types of tasks. Table 3–2 presents descriptions of verbal, quantitative, and cognitive abilities needed for various tasks. To learn more about O*NET and the jobs it describes in such detail, go to http://online.onetcenter.org/.

Other techniques for conducting job and work analyses for specific jobs include interviews, questionnaires, observation, activity logs, and critical incidents.

Interviews.   The use of interviews for job and work analyses involves extensive meetings with the persons directly connected with the job (the so-called subject matter experts). These include the workers performing the job, their supervisors, and the instructors who trained the workers for the job. Job analysts may supplement interviews with questionnaires. The persons being interviewed should be told the purpose of the interview and why it is important to answer the

---

TABLE 3–2

O*NET Examples of Specific Work Abilities

Abilities	Level
VERBAL	
Oral comprehension—The ability to listen to and understand information and ideas presented through spoken words and sentences.	*High*—Understanding a lecture on advanced physics. *Low*—Understanding a television commercial.
Written comprehension—The ability to read and understand information and ideas presented in writing.	*High*—Understanding a book on repairing a missile guidance system. *Low*—Understanding signs on the highway.
Oral expression—The ability to communicate information and ideas in speaking so that other people will understand.	*High*—Explaining advanced principles of genetics to 1st-year college students. *Low*—Cancelling newspaper delivery by phone.
Written expression—The ability to communicate information and ideas in writing so that other people will understand.	*High*—Writing an advanced economics textbook. *Low*—Writing a note to remind your spouse to take something out of the freezer to thaw.
QUANTITATIVE	
Mathematical reasoning—The ability to understand and organize a problem and to select a mathematical method or formula to solve the problem.	*High*—Determining the math required to simulate a spacecraft moon landing. *Low*—Determining the cost of 10 oranges when priced at 2 for 29 cents.
Number facility—The ability to add, subtract, multiply, and divide quickly and correctly.	*High*—Manually calculating the flight path of an aircraft, considering speed, fuel, wind, and altitude. *Low*—Adding 2 and 7.

questions fully and honestly. The questions should be carefully planned and clearly worded to elicit as much information as possible.

Questionnaires.   Two types of questionnaires are used in job analysis: the unstructured questionnaire and the structured questionnaire. In the unstructured, or open-end, approach, the subject matter experts (workers, supervisors, and trainers) describe in their own words the components of the job and the tasks performed.

When the structured questionnaire approach is used, the people being interviewed are provided with descriptions of tasks, operations, and working conditions and are asked to rate the items or to select those items that characterize the job. Research has shown, however, that people can be careless in providing ratings, which can lead to less-than-accurate job and work analyses.

A widely used questionnaire is the Position Analysis Questionnaire (PAQ), which consists of 194 job elements related to specific behaviors and activities. The job elements are organized into six categories of job behavior: information input, mental processes, work output, relationships with other persons, job context, and other job activities and conditions. Employees and supervisors rate each element for its importance to the job in question. Such quantifiable ratings have an obvious advantage over the kind of information yielded by the unstructured questionnaire. As with other types of surveys conducted today, job analysis questionnaires can be administered online as well as in printed versions.

Direct Observation.   A third approach to job and work analyses is the direct observation of workers as they perform their jobs. Because people may behave differently when they know they are being watched, it is necessary for the job analysts to remain as unobtrusive as possible. Also, they should observe a representative sample of workers and make observations at various times throughout the workday to take account of changes caused by factors such as fatigue.

Much of the direct observation conducted today is through electronic performance monitoring. (We discuss in Chapter 5 the use of this technique for employee performance evaluation.) For example, trucking companies use onboard computers to monitor running time, downtime, and speed. Cable television companies monitor maintenance workers electronically to record the time spent per service call.

Systematic Activity Logs.   With systematic activity logs, workers and supervisors maintain detailed written records of their activities during a given time period. If prepared with care, these logs can reveal details about a job that are not otherwise obtainable.

Critical Incidents.   The **critical-incidents technique** is based on the identification of those incidents or behaviors that are necessary to successful job performance. The goal is to have subject matter experts indicate the behaviors that distinguish good from poor workers. The critical-incidents technique focuses on specific actions that lead to desirable or undesirable consequences on the job. A single critical incident is of little value, but hundreds of them can effectively describe the unique behaviors required to perform the job well. (We note in Chapter 6 that critical incidents can also be used to identify areas where employee retraining might be needed.)

Critical-incidents technique A means of identifying specific activities or behaviors that lead to desirable or undesirable consequences on the job.

Job analysis continues to be an important part of the employee selection process. Every employing organization must be able to justify each of its job requirements to show that whatever it asks of a job applicant is related directly to the abilities required to perform the job. The company must not set arbitrary qualifications that can be used to discriminate against groups of workers and to deny them equal opportunity for employment. Detailed job and work analyses provide justification for determining specific job requirements. For example, if a company is charged with sex discrimination because women employees are paid less than men employees for what appears to be the same job, the company would have to show that the men are performing different tasks that justify the greater pay. A job analysis can provide that information. Therefore, organizations take seriously the task of job analysis. Equal employment opportunity and successful selection programs are not possible without it.

Let us consider some specific employee selection techniques currently in use: biographical information forms, interviews, references, and assessment centers. Psychological tests for employee selection are discussed in Chapter 4.

BIOGRAPHICAL INFORMATION

The collection of biographical information, or biodata, on the backgrounds of job applicants is a common method of employee selection. The rationale for this technique is the belief that our past experiences or personal traits can be used to predict our work behavior and potential for success. Because many of our behaviors, values, and attitudes remain consistent throughout life, it is not unreasonable to assume that our behavior in the future will be based on our behavior in the past.

Application Blanks

The initial determination about your suitability for employment is likely to be based on the information you supply on a company's application blank. Today fewer organizations use the standard paper forms, relying instead on applications completed online.

The Home Depot company started using in-store kiosks in 1999 at which prospective employees complete an application form online. The majority of the 40,000 people Home Depot hires every year are processed electronically. Other companies, including Blockbuster and Target, use in-store kiosks to process 80 percent of the hourly employees they hire. Some firms even provide a realistic job preview, using short films to show what life on the job is really like and to highlight what workers are expected to do. Home Depot shows that their jobs include heavy lifting and working some weekends, conditions you would surely like to know about before you file an application form.

Applicants may also answer a series of true-false and multiple-choice questions, devised by I-O psychologists, dealing with personality and ethics issues. Some questions are asked several times, with different wording. In only a few minutes after a form is completed online, the store manager receives a color-coded score for each applicant. A green score is considered so good that the manager will often try to interview the applicant before he or she leaves the store. Yellow scores are considered borderline, and persons who receive red scores, typically 30 percent of all Home Depot applicants, will not be working for the company.

One problem with application blanks, whether completed online or on paper, is the honesty of the applicant's responses. Is the information the applicant supplies complete and correct? Did the person actually graduate from the college indicated on the form? Did he or she really supervise 50 workers in the previous job? Is the reported annual salary correct or exaggerated? A sizable number of job applicants provide misleading or fraudulent information, especially about their previous job title, pay, and degree of responsibility.

In 2001 the newly hired football coach for Notre Dame University was fired after only five days on the job. It turned out that he had not won three football letters as an undergraduate, as he had claimed. In fact, he had never even played football. In addition, he had not received a master's degree, although he had so stated in his application form. Yet he had been a successful football coach for

The standard application blank may include questions about one's life history, work experience, specific skills, interests, community activities, and career goals.

Newsbreak — How Not to Get Hired: Part 1

It pays to proofread your résumé and review your answers on an application blank to correct typographical errors, misspellings, and awkward phrasing, and to consider carefully the image it presents to a prospective employer. The following items are taken from actual résumés, application forms, and cover letters to employers. Do you think any of these people were hired?

"I received a *plague* for Salesperson of the Year."
"I'm a *rabid* typist."
"I have the ability to meet deadlines while maintaining my *composer*."
"I have an excellent eye for *derail*."
"Please excuse any spelling errors on this resume since spelling is not my strong *suite*."
"Objective: To obtain a position that allows me to make use of my *commuter* skills."
"I have formed a partnership with three business *collies*."

And to close a cover letter, one job seeker wrote: "Thank you for your consideration. I hope to hear from you *shorty*."

more than 20 years! Until he went to Notre Dame, however, no one had bothered to check the information he had been providing on applications and résumés.

Similar situations occur in the corporate world. In 2002 the chief executive officer of Bausch & Lomb was found to have lied about having received an MBA degree. Although he was not fired, he did lose a $1.1 million bonus for the year. The chief financial officer of VERITAS Software resigned when it was learned that he had also lied about earning an MBA.

Misrepresentation of one's qualifications is not uncommon, from entry-level workers to company presidents. One organization that does background verifications on new employees for several companies reported that of the 2.6 million background checks it carried out in one year, 44 percent of the applications and résumés were found to contain false statements, usually about degrees obtained (Stanton, 2002).

A survey of human resources managers conducted by the Society for Human Resource Management found that 90 percent of the managers had encountered applicants who had lied about the length of time they had held their previous job. Some 78 percent of the managers later learned that some applicants had lied about having college degrees (Butler, 2000). Many employing organizations do not have the time or resources to confirm the information that applicants supply. Sometimes false information can be reduced by scheduling follow-up interviews and by warning applicants in advance that the company intends to verify the information provided on an application blank.

Many organizations do attempt to confirm the accuracy of biographical information by contacting former employers and the persons named as references.

However, many companies are reluctant to release personal information for fear of lawsuits. A former employee may sue a company for providing unfavorable information, claiming libel or slander. Therefore, many employing organizations hesitate to supply more than limited factual data, such as job title and dates of employment. Few give evaluative information, such as performance ratings, or answer questions about why the employee left or whether the company would rehire the employee. Thus, it is difficult for an organization to verify certain kinds of information provided on an application blank.

Biographical Inventories

Biographical inventory
An employee selection technique covering an applicant's past behavior, attitudes, preferences, and values.

The **biographical inventory,** or biographical information blank, is a more systematized form of application blank. Typically, biographical inventories are longer than application blanks and seek greater detail about a person's background and experiences. The rationale for this extensive probing is that on-the-job behavior is related to attitudes, preferences, and values, as well as to past behavior in a variety of situations.

Whereas a standard application blank might ask for the name of your college, your major field, and the dates you attended, a biographical inventory might ask the following questions about your college experience:

How often did you have problems with other students because of different social groups or cliques?
How often have other students come to you for advice?
How often have you set a goal to do better than anyone else at something?
How often did you feel you needed more self-discipline?

Considerable research is required to determine the background experiences that correlate with job success. The process of validating the items on a biographical inventory is similar to that for any selection technique. Each item must be correlated with a measure of job performance.

Research on biographical inventories confirms their high predictive value. For example, in a study of nearly 400 clerical workers, their biographical data, combined with scores on tests of cognitive ability and personality, were found to be highly accurate predictors of their future job performance (Mount, Witt, & Barrick, 2000).

As with standard application blanks, faking on biographical inventories can be a problem. Some applicants deliberately distort their answers to put a more positive spin on their work and life experiences. Advising applicants that their answers will be checked sometimes reduces this problem. Also, written notice that a scale to detect faking is built into the questionnaire, or that the scoring system will deduct points for dishonest answers, can be effective.

Another approach is to have applicants elaborate on their answers to some of the items on a biographical inventory. An experiment involving 311 applicants for a federal civil service job found that asking them to provide additional information for certain questions such as "How many work groups have you led in the past five years?" resulted in less inflated scores on many of those questions (Schmitt & Kunce, 2002).

As we noted, biographical inventories have been found to be valid predictors of job success. Unfortunately, the technique is not used extensively in business and industry. Some managers claim to be unfamiliar with biographical inventories. Others say they do not have the time, money, or expertise to develop them. And still others are skeptical of research showing the utility of biographical inventories. It appears that the I-O psychologists working for these companies or conducting research on biographical inventories have not been effective in communicating the value of these techniques to the persons who are in a position to apply them.

This situation illustrates the gap that sometimes arises between research and application in I-O psychology. With biographical inventories, researchers have developed a highly successful employee selection tool, but it is seldom used in the workplace. Psychologists need to provide data that persuade human resources managers that this technique for selecting the best employees will save more money in the long run than the initial costs of developing and implementing the inventory.

INTERVIEWS

The personal interview is a widely used employee selection technique. Regardless of any other techniques that are part of an organization's selection program, almost every prospective employer wants the chance to meet an applicant in person before making the offer of a job. It is important to remember that the employment interview, like the college recruiting interview, is a two-way process. Its purpose is to allow a company to evaluate a candidate's suitability for employment. But it also offers the opportunity for candidates, if they ask the right questions, to determine whether the company and the job are right for them. Research has shown that job applicants have more favorable attitudes toward interviews than toward any other selection technique, including biographical inventories and psychological tests (Posthuma, Morgeson, & Campion, 2002).

The personal interview is part of virtually every employee selection program.

Newsbreak   ## How Not to Get Hired: Part 2

Would you show up for a job interview wearing a bathing suit? Would you tilt way back in your chair and prop your feet on the interviewer's desk? Yes, people have actually done those things. Here are descriptions of other not-too-bright interview behaviors taken from the files of corporate interviewers.

- The reason the applicant took so long to answer my question became apparent when he began to snore.
- When I gave the applicant my business card at the beginning of the interview, she immediately crumpled it and tossed it in the waste-basket.
- The interview was going well until the applicant told me that he and his friends always wore the clothing my company manufactured. At that point I told him that we made office products, not clothing.
- She had arranged for a pizza to be delivered to my office during the interview.
- Without asking if I objected, he casually lit a cigar and tossed the match onto the carpet. He did not seem to understand why his behavior annoyed me.
- The applicant was asked to bring a résumé and two references to the interview. She arrived with résumé in hand—and two friends.
- The applicant answered my first few questions then picked up his cell phone and called his parents to tell them the interview was going well.

Interviews, if conducted properly, can supply a great deal of information to employers. An analysis of 338 ratings conducted in 47 interview studies found that personality traits and social skills were the most frequently rated characteristics in employment interviews. The most rated personality traits were conscientiousness, responsibility, dependability, and initiative. The social skills included the ability to work with people and team focus. Mental capacity, job knowledge, and job skills were also considered important. All of these characteristics provide useful information to the persons responsible for making hiring decisions (Huffcutt, Conway, Roth, & Stone, 2001).

Making the Right Impression

The impression you make during an interview will be a decisive factor in whether the organization offers you a job. I-O psychology research has shown that interviewers' assessments of job applicants are often influenced more by their subjective impressions of the applicants than by such specifics as work history, academic qualifications, or extracurricular activities. Personal qualities, such as perceived attractiveness, sociability, and skill at self-promotion, are often key factors in an interviewer's hiring recommendations.

Of course, as you probably know from your own experience, it is possible to act deliberately so as to make the right impression; that is, to present yourself in the most favorable light. I-O psychologists call this skill **impression management,** and have noted two approaches job applicants can take: ingratiation and self-promotion.

Ingratiation refers to ways of behaving that attempt to persuade the interviewer to like you. For example, you may compliment the interviewer's style of dress, or appear to agree with his or her opinions and attitudes. Self-promotion tactics include praising your accomplishments, character traits, and goals. Self-promotion tactics are used more frequently than ingratiation behaviors and result in higher ratings from interviewers (Ellis, West, Ryan, & DeShon, 2002; Posthuma, Morgeson, & Campion, 2002).

Psychologists have identified another construct, called self-monitoring, that influences the image we present to others. This refers to the extent to which people observe, regulate, and control the image of themselves they choose to display in a public setting such as a job interview. Those who are high self-monitors present themselves in whatever way best fits the social climate around them. Low self-monitors remain more true to themselves and behave much the same way in all situations. They do not try to present a different self according to the situation.

As you could guess, high self-monitors have a competitive edge in the workplace. A meta-analysis of 136 samples of more than 3,000 people found that high self-monitors tend to receive more promotions and higher performance ratings than do low self-monitors (Day, Schleicher, Unckless, & Hiller, 2002). Similarly, we could suggest that high self-monitors would tend to receive higher ratings and hiring recommendations in job interviews.

Unstructured Interviews

Three kinds of interviews used in the business world are the standard, or unstructured, interview; the patterned, or structured, interview; and the situational interview.

The **unstructured interview** lacks advance planning. Sometimes it is little more than a general conversation. The format and the questions asked are left to the discretion of the interviewer. It is possible, therefore, that five interviewers conducting separate unstructured interviews with the same applicant will receive five different impressions.

Thus, a basic weakness of the unstructured interview is its lack of consistency in assessing candidates. Interviewers may be interested in different aspects of an applicant's background, experience, or attitudes. The recommendations of the interviewers may then reflect more of the biases and prejudices of the interviewers than the objective qualifications of the applicants.

A now-classic study on this topic, published in 1929, asked 12 interviewers independently to rate 57 applicants on their suitability for a sales job (Hollingworth, 1929). Although the interviewers were experienced sales managers who had conducted many interviews with job applicants, there was a significant lack of agreement among them. Some applicants who were ranked first by one interviewer were ranked last by another. The results of the judgments made about a single applicant are shown in Figure 3–1. You can see that the ratings for this person range from a low of one to a high of 55. This information would be of no help to a manager trying to decide whether to hire this applicant because it offers no firm basis on which to judge the person's suitability.

Impression management
Acting deliberately to make a good impression, to present oneself in the most favorable way.

Unstructured interviews
Interviews in which the format and questions asked are left to the discretion of the interviewer.

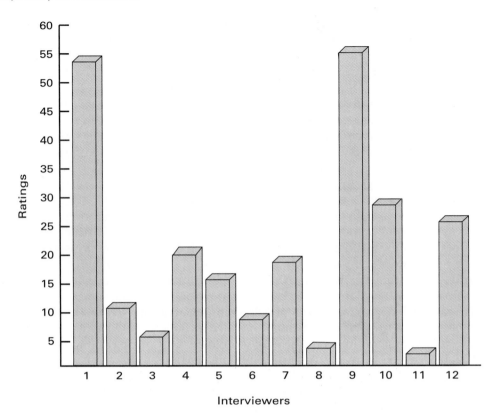

FIGURE 3–1. Data from a classic study showing ratings of one applicant by 12 interviewers.

In addition to a lack of consistency, or reliability, the predictive validity of the unstructured interview is low. This was demonstrated decades ago by Walter Dill Scott, mentioned in Chapter 1 as a founder of the field of industrial psychology. Scott's conclusion has been supported by considerable empirical research.

Training interviewers in the kinds of questions to ask and how to ask them can improve the usefulness of the unstructured interview. Trained interviewers are far less likely to digress into conversation about non-job-related issues than are untrained interviewers. In addition, trained interviewers are able to elicit more pertinent information from the job applicants, information that can be used as the basis for deciding whether to offer the applicants jobs.

Despite the recognized limitations of low reliability and validity, unstructured interviews are still used far too often by employing organizations.

Structured Interviews

Structured interviews
Interviews that use a predetermined list of questions that are asked of every person applying for a particular job.

The **structured interview** uses a predetermined list of questions that are asked of every applicant. Thus, the interview procedure is standardized so that the resulting assessment of the job candidates is less open to interviewer bias.

In conducting a structured interview, the interviewer follows a printed form that contains the questions to be asked. The applicant's responses are recorded on the same form. The interview session has been described as more like an elaborate application blank that the interviewer completes on the basis of what the applicant says.

The following structured interview questions are typical of those used by an organization selecting college graduates for management positions. Because the items deal with work experience, they are intended for graduates who have held at least one job since graduation.

1. What was your first job after completing college?
2. What were your major accomplishments on that job?
3. What were some of the things you did less well, things that point to the need for further training and development?
4. What did you learn about yourself on that job?
5. What aspects of the job did you find most challenging?
6. What sort of work would you like to be doing five years from now?

Because all applicants are asked the questions in the same sequence, there is a more reliable basis for comparison of the candidates than with the random questioning procedures of the unstructured interview.

Structured interviews are a considerable improvement over unstructured interviews and have the potential for higher predictive validity. Research has shown that structured interviews can be as valid predictors of job success as cognitive ability tests. Structured interviews are high in reliability as well. If used properly, structured interviews have the potential for making hiring decisions much easier.

Despite the proven success of structured interviews, however, research with 79 human resources managers from companies in the Netherlands corroborate earlier research with human resources managers in the United States, showing that structured interviews are rarely used in the workplace. They are viewed as too expensive and time-consuming to develop and as impinging too much on the autonomy and independence of the interviewers, who resent having to stick to a prepared script (Van der Zee, Bakker, & Bakker, 2002). Here we have an example of a well-proven technique that is not widely applied, another instance, as we discussed in Chapter 1, of the failure of I-O psychologists to communicate research results to managers.

Situational Interviews

A **situational interview** is developed specifically to meet the requirements of a particular job. The interview questions are not designed to inquire about general work experience or personal characteristics and abilities but rather about the specific behaviors needed for successful performance of the job in question. These behaviors are determined by a job analysis conducted by the critical-incidents technique.

The first step in developing the situational interview is to prepare a list of critical incidents that differentiate between successful and unsuccessful employees currently on the job. These incidents are typically identified by supervisors who have a comprehensive knowledge of the job. The supervisors determine benchmarks for scoring the incidents, assigning a score of five to those behaviors displayed by successful employees, three to behaviors displayed by average employees, and one to behaviors displayed by poor employees. The incidents are rephrased as questions to be asked in the situational interview, and therefore, they represent issues directly related to how an applicant would behave on the job. The numerical benchmarks make it possible to score the interview objectively.

Situational interviews Interviews that focus not on personal characteristics or work experience but on the behaviors needed for successful job performance.

Once constructed, situational interviews are easy to administer and interpret. Because the interview questions are clearly and directly related to job behaviors, this kind of situation can increase the motivation of job applicants to answer accurately and completely.

Situational interviews are used most often to select workers for skilled and semiskilled factory jobs, for sales jobs, and for first-line supervisory positions. Situational interview results correlate positively with measures of later job performance and, in some instances, are more valid than structured interviews.

For higher-level leadership positions, behavior description interviews have proved more useful than situational interviews. In this approach, applicants are asked to relate actual events from their past work experience that might be relevant to the job for which they are applying. A study of 59 candidates for naval officers training and 93 applicants for district manager positions for a major merchandiser demonstrated that behavior descriptions were more predictive of future success than were situational interviews (Huffcutt, Weekley, Wiesner, DeGroot, & Jones, 2001).

Online Interviews

Online interviewing uses computer software to conduct the initial interview. Applicants answer a fixed sequence of multiple-choice questions. All applicants for a specific position are asked the same questions in the same order. Questions on sensitive issues, if appropriate, can be included in an online interview, whereas many interviewers are hesitant to ask about personal matters in the traditional face-to-face interview situation. Corporate users of online interviews report that most applicants are comfortable with this type of screening and are willing to respond with honesty and candor.

As we noted, online screening is now conducted routinely by Target, Macy's, Home Depot, and other large retailing chains. Home Depot's in-store computer kiosks allow selected applicants to complete an interview in less than an hour. The company reported that turnover dropped by more than 11 percent during the first year of the online interview program. Also, managers saved time since they no longer had to interview applicants and score tests. Personal interviews are used only for those applicants who complete and pass the online screening (Richtel, 2000).

Influences on Interviewer Judgments

We discuss several factors that can bias an interviewer's judgment about a job applicant: (1) characteristics of applicants, (2) prior information, (3) the contrast effect, (4) interviewers' prejudices, and (5) the effects of applicant coaching. These influences can be reduced or minimized by training interviewers to recognize their effects.

Characteristics of Applicants. Applicants who display evidence of being extraverted, highly conscientious, and high in the need for achievement are more likely to be hired than are those who do not display these characteristics. In addition, studies conducted in the laboratory, often using college students as research participants, show that physically attractive applicants receive higher ratings from interviewers than do those who are less attractive (Posthuma, Morgeson, & Campion, 2002).

Prior Information. Interviewers generally have some prior information about job candidates, such as recruiter evaluations, application blanks, online screening results, or the results of psychological tests. The nature of that prior information can predispose an interviewer to have a favorable or unfavorable attitude toward an applicant before he or she even shows up for the interview. For example, applicants who performed well on preliminary recruitment screening techniques are generally rated higher by interviewers than are those who did less well in preliminary screening.

The Contrast Effect. Interviewers see many job applicants, often one after another, and how they evaluate a particular applicant may depend on their standards of comparison; that is, the characteristics of the applicants they interviewed previously. For example, after having interviewed three undesirable candidates, an interviewer may rate the next candidate in line as more favorable than the candidate's qualifications merit. That same average candidate may be rated less favorably if the previous candidates have all been highly qualified.

Not only does this contrast tendency highlight the importance of your place in an interviewer's schedule, it also means, as we noted earlier, that interviewers do not always have objective standards for the type of person considered to be a suitable employee. Applicants are not evaluated on an absolute basis, or on their merits alone, but are judged relative to the other applicants interviewed during the same time period. Thus, the standard for the acceptable employee may frequently change.

Interviewers' Prejudices. Another characteristic of interviewers that affects their judgment is their personal likes and dislikes. For example, men sometimes think that women employees are incapable of performing certain jobs. Interviewers of both sexes are more likely to hire women for so-called traditional female jobs, such as schoolteacher or nurse, than for traditional male jobs, such as those in management or engineering. Conversely, some female interviewers are reluctant to consider men for teaching or counseling jobs.

Racial and ethnic prejudice can skew interviewers' evaluations of job candidates, although this bias is not quite as strong today as it was toward previous generations of employees. In a large-scale study in which 708 recruiters interviewed 12,203 applicants, there was no evidence that either difference or similarity in race or gender between interviewers and applicants had any effect on the ratings given (Sacco, Scheu, Ryan, & Schmitt, 2003).

Although prejudice may no longer operate so strongly as an influencing factor, there is no question that interviewers can prejudge applicants who display certain qualities or traits and refuse to consider their other abilities or characteristics. They may also recommend hiring some applicants merely because they display some quality the interviewers like, such as a shared interest in baseball, even though it may bear no relation to job performance.

The phenomenon of generalizing from one trait or characteristic to the entire person in a positive or a negative direction is called the **halo effect.** It influences the decision-making process whenever people have to make personal judgments about others.

Halo effect The tendency to judge all aspects of a person's behavior or character on the basis of a single attribute.

Applicant Coaching.   Being coached or trained apparently can help job applicants perform well in interviews. In one study, 213 candidates for promotion in the police and fire departments of a major city were given up to two hours of training in how the promotion interviews would be conducted. They were also given the opportunity to observe or participate in role-playing sessions in which typical questions were asked and answered. Candidates who received the coaching performed better in the actual job interviews than did those who had not received coaching (Maurer, Solamon, Andrews, & Troxtel, 2001).

As difficult and error-prone as the interview can be, it remains part of virtually every selection program in business, industry, education, and government. The danger lies in placing too much emphasis on its results. If used wisely, however, and in conjunction with other valid selection measures, the interview can be of help to both organization and applicant. Its predictive accuracy can be greatly improved by the use of structured and situational techniques and by appropriate training of interviewers.

REFERENCES AND LETTERS OF RECOMMENDATION

At one time, employee selection programs routinely involved obtaining information about job applicants from persons who knew something about the applicants' background, skills, and work history, such as former teachers, employers, co-workers, and friends. The purpose was to examine other people's impressions of the applicants and to verify the information the applicants reported.

A major limitation of these references was that they often presented a false picture of the applicant. The person providing the reference sometimes deliberately responded in a misleading manner for several reasons. Past employers wanted to be kind and to say only favorable things about former employees. Current employers who hoped to get rid of undesirable employees wrote glowing letters of recommendation. Professors wrote positive letters because they knew that students would be able to read their files in the university placement center.

A more important limitation on the usefulness of references is that many organizations are no longer willing to supply evaluative information of any kind about former employees for fear of lawsuits. If a company makes a false statement about why a former employee was fired, for example, the employee can sue the company for defamation of character. Thousands of such lawsuits have been filed against U.S. corporations. The mere threat of legal action has prevented many companies from cooperating in even the most basic reference-checking effort.

Companies are now advised to refuse to reveal any information about former employees beyond dates of employment, job title, and final salary. If a company chooses to discuss the job performance of a fired employee, it should have for its own protection written evidence from objective performance appraisals citing specific instances documented by date, time, and place. In addition, managers and supervisors should assume that anything they include in a letter of recommendation may one day be scrutinized by a judge and jury.

Even though the amount and kind of information obtained from references is minimal, many employers still make at least a cursory attempt to check references. Because of the legal complications, however, they are used less frequently today as a selection technique than in the past.

Newsbreak   A Deadly Recommendation

Around the Allstate Insurance Company office in Tampa, Florida, where he worked, Paul Calder had frequently seemed to be acting weird. He told people he was an alien. He wrote "blood" and other strange words on his computer screen and refused to let the boss see them. He threatened to kill a masseuse who refused to give him a refund. And then he brought a gun to work.

"I was reasonably sure I had a total lunatic on my hands," his boss said. "A nut case."

The boss was afraid to fire Calder because he believed the employee was capable of killing him and others in the office, but he knew somehow he had to get rid of Calder. So he made up a story about a corporate restructuring that would eliminate Calder's job and offered him severance pay if he would resign. When Calder chose to resign, the boss wrote him a letter of recommendation that was bland and innocuous, as most such letters are nowadays. It did not indicate that there was anything at all wrong with Paul Calder.

The letter said Calder resigned because of organizational restructuring and that his resignation "is in no way a reflection upon Paul's job performance."

To do otherwise—to put an employee's faults and failings on paper—is to open yourself and your organization to a lawsuit for libel or slander. It has become prudent in corporate life today to say nothing about an ex-employee but the bare facts: job title and dates of employment.

Paul Calder found a job with another Tampa insurance company, but his bizarre behavior continued and he was fired. Several months later, he returned to that office to see the people who had fired him. He carried a 9 mm handgun. He killed three men and wounded two women then drove to nearby Clearwater and killed himself.

The families of the murdered employees filed a multimillion-dollar lawsuit against Allstate, Calder's original employer, for failing to disclose the problems with Calder's behavior. Allstate was sued for writing a misleading letter of recommendation, which, ironically, it wrote out of fear of being sued.

Charles Cullen, a 44-year-old male nurse, may have murdered as many as 40 people over 11 years while he held nine different hospital jobs. No hospital would have hired him had they known that he had attempted suicide three times, been committed to mental institutions on four occasions, and was suspected of killing four elderly patients in intensive care units. And he had also been seen running around his neighborhood at night, chasing cats.

Yet no hospital at which he had worked, including those that had fired him, reported to prospective employers anything negative about Cullen's record, for fear of being sued for slander. The only information hospitals were willing to provide was job title and dates of employment. One could say that as a result, he "got away with murder" for a long time.

Sources: L. Dougherty. Shooting victims' families can sue Allstate. *St. Petersburg (FL) Times,* August 8, 1995; Perez-Pena, Kocieniewski, & George, 2004.

ASSESSMENT CENTERS

Assessment center A method of selection and training that involves a simulated job situation in which candidates deal with actual job problems.

The **assessment center** is a widely used method of selection that places candidates who are being considered for hiring or for promotion in a simulated job situation so that their behavior under stress can be observed and evaluated. This approach, initially called **situational testing,** was developed by the German army in the 1920s to select officer candidates of high quality. It was first used extensively in the United States by psychologists during World War II when it was adopted as a selection technique by the Office of Strategic Services (OSS), the forerunner of today's Central Intelligence Agency (CIA).

Situational testing An early term for the assessment-center technique for employee selection and performance appraisal. Employees are placed in a simulated job setting so that their behavior under stress can be observed and evaluated.

Assessment centers usually involve six to 12 candidates at a time who are evaluated as they work through a series of exercises over several days. Candidates are interviewed extensively and may be given intelligence and personality tests, but most of their time is devoted to exercises designed to simulate the actual problems of high-level jobs. The major techniques for eliciting these work samples are the in-basket exercise and the leaderless group discussion.

The In-Basket Technique

In-basket technique An assessment-center exercise that requires job applicants to process memos, letters, and directives found in a typical manager's in-basket.

The **in-basket technique** presents each applicant with the sort of in-basket that is found on virtually every managerial desk, whether in the form of a work tray or the files on a computer. The in-basket used in the assessment-center exercise contains the typical problems, questions, and directives that managers would expect to find when they returned to the office from vacation. The applicants must process this material in a fixed period of time, demonstrating precisely how they would handle the questions and problems on the job. After the exercise, they may be required to justify their decisions during interviews with the assessors.

The program at AT&T relies heavily on the in-basket exercise. Each candidate, playing the role of a manager, must process 25 items (e-mail messages, executive orders, and correspondence) in three hours. Trained assessors observe the candidates to see if they are systematic, establish priorities, delegate authority to subordinates, or become enmeshed in trivialities.

Leaderless Group Discussions

Leaderless group discussion An assessment-center exercise in which job applicants meet to discuss an actual business problem under the pressure of time. Usually, a leader emerges from the group to guide the discussion.

In the **leaderless group discussion,** the applicants meet as a group to discuss an actual business problem. For example, they may be given information about a group of subordinates from among whom they must select one for promotion. As the meeting proceeds, the behavior of the candidates is observed to see how they interact and what leadership and communications skills each person displays.

In the leaderless group discussion exercise at AT&T, a group of six candidates is told that they are managers of a corporation and are directed to increase profits in a fixed period. They are given information about the company and the market, but no one person is appointed leader and no rules are established about how to accomplish their goal. Usually, one candidate assumes the leader's role, and that person's capabilities can be evaluated. The other group members are assessed on their cooperation in performing the tasks assigned to them by the leader.

To induce additional pressure, participants are notified frequently of changes in costs or market conditions, sometimes immediately after the total problem has been solved. The new information must be processed and incorporated into the planning. All the while, the clock ticks, the assessors watch, and the stress mounts. Some participants become angry, disrupting the group's ability to function cohesively. The contrast between those who can operate well under stress and those who cannot becomes obvious.

Assessment centers also use oral presentations and role playing. In the oral presentation exercise, candidates are given a packet of information about some aspect of corporate operations, such as the development of a new product or a new sales campaign. They must organize this material and present it to the group, a task typical of executive responsibilities. In role playing, the candidate acts out the role of manager in a simulated job situation, showing, for example, how he or she would conduct a job interview, fire an incompetent worker, or deal with an irate boss.

Computers and video cameras can be used in assessment centers as a way of reducing costs. Information is provided to the candidates on computer terminals. The assessors videotape the candidates' behavior for later and more extensive evaluation.

Predictive Validity of Assessment Centers

Although researchers are not certain which attributes or dimensions of behavior are being evaluated by the assessment-center situation, they have found the techniques to be useful in predicting subsequent job success not only for managers and executives, but also for entry-level positions. For example, 585 applicants for the police force in Israel participated in a two-day assessment-center exercise. On-the-job evaluations given two to four years later revealed that assessment-center results correlated highly with training and job performance. The level of the applicants' performance in the assessment-center exercise was a valid predictor of their later success on the job (Dayan, Kasten, & Fox, 2002).

A study of 679 university graduates in the Netherlands showed that their job performance as managers seven years later, as reflected in salary growth, showed a high positive correlation with their initial assessment-center performance (Jansen & Stoop, 2001). Similar results were obtained in a study of 66 undergraduate business students in the United States. Follow-up surveys between two and four years later showed a significant positive correlation between their performance in an assessment center while undergraduates and their subsequent level of job satisfaction, promotions, and salary (Waldman & Korbar, 2004).

Other research has focused on the factors or dimensions involved in making assessment-center evaluations. A study of 79 U.S. law enforcement officers concluded that those doing the assessing drew their own initial inferences about the candidates' personality characteristics and that these judgments of the candidates' personality, in turn, influenced the ratings they later gave to the candidates on various dimensions (Haaland & Christiansen, 2002).

A meta-analysis of assessment-center results revealed that four dimensions accounted for most of the predictive validity of the assessment-center technique. Those dimensions were the candidate's ability to solve problems, influence others, organize and plan, and communicate effectively (Arthur, Day, McNelly, & Edens, 2003).

Also, research has indicated that performance on assessment-center tasks tends to demonstrate fewer differences in leadership behaviors and skills between Black applicants and White applicants than is shown on tests of cognitive ability (Goldstein, Yusko, & Nicolopoulos, 2001). I-O psychologists have concluded that assessment-center exercises may be a more equitable way to evaluate the management skills of candidates of different racial and ethnic backgrounds because they focus directly on a person's ability to perform the necessary job-related tasks.

Employee Attitudes toward Assessment Centers

Some job candidates, particularly those who perform poorly, resent assessment-center exercises. Many people believe that a poor evaluation in an assessment center marks the end of their career, no matter how excellent a record they have compiled in their years with the company. Some candidates believe that success in the assessment center depends more on being articulate and personable than on actual competence at managerial tasks. There may be some truth to these charges. Interpersonal skills do count strongly in these assessments, and active and forceful participation is rewarded. However, assessment-center ratings are also based on organizational and decision-making skills, as well as on motivation.

Participation in assessment centers can lead to changes in candidates' perceptions of their interpersonal and administrative skills. Those who perform well tend to believe they have the ability to develop and refine their skills. Those who do poorly tend to have lowered expectations for promotion. In this sense, assessment centers serve as a realistic job preview, demonstrating to applicants what life as a manager or executive would be like.

The assessment-center experience also serves as a training exercise. Candidates can develop and refine their managerial and interpersonal skills by using the feedback they receive from the assessors.

Summary

The proper selection of employees—matching the right person with the right job—is a complex process. Problems of organizational entry involve the applicant's preferences and expectations as well as the company's recruiting efforts. Because our first job experience influences the rest of our working life, it is important that our expectations match the realities of the job. This can be accomplished through a **realistic job preview.**

An employee selection program requires job and work analysis, establishing requirements and cutoff scores, recruiting, administering selection devices, and validating the selection devices by determining how they correlate with measures of subsequent job performance.

Equal employment opportunity legislation mandates fair employment practices in hiring. Selection techniques should be job-related and should minimize **adverse impact** on minority groups. Companies must also try to prevent **reverse discrimination** against qualified members of the majority group. Fair employment practices appear to have had a minimal impact on organizational effectiveness. Targets of discrimination may include minorities, older workers, women, disabled persons, homosexuals, and unattractive people. Greater ethnic diversity in the workplace may reflect in a company's stock price and return on investment and make it easier to hire minority employees.

Job analysis involves a detailed description of the component tasks performed on a job. Job analysts can use already-published work analyses available on O*NET, interview the people directly concerned with the job, observe workers performing the job, have workers keep a systematic activity log, or record critical incidents related to successful job performance. On the basis of the information collected, a job specification can be written that defines the characteristics to be sought in job applicants.

Application blanks on paper or online provide information about job candidates that can be directly related to their probability of success on the job. Weighted application blanks and **biographical inventories** are useful in predicting job success and are similar to psychological tests in objectivity and types of questions. Because many companies are reluctant to release information on former employees for fear of lawsuits, it can be difficult to confirm the accuracy of information provided on applications.

Although the face-to-face or online interview consistently receives unfavorable evaluations in research on employee selection, most companies continue to use it. The weakest type of interview is the **unstructured interview;** the **structured interview** is a more valid predictive device but is seldom used because it appears too expensive and time-consuming. Weaknesses of interviews are failure of interviewers to agree on the merits of a job candidate, failure of interviews to predict job success, subjectivity of interviewers' standards of comparison, and interviewers' personal prejudices. In the **situational interview,** questions relating to actual job behaviors are developed from a critical-incidents job analysis; this may be the most valid type of interview for predicting an applicant's potential for job success. Interviewers' judgments can be biased by applicant characteristics, prior information, the contrast and **halo effects,** personal prejudices, and applicant coaching.

Letters of recommendation are part of most employee selection programs, despite the recognized tendency of writers to be overly kind and the reluctance of employers to reveal more than basic, factual information in order to avoid lawsuits.

In **assessment centers,** used primarily for managerial and executive positions, job candidates perform exercises that realistically simulate problems found on the job. Using the **in-basket technique,** the **leaderless group discussion,** oral presentations, and role playing, applicants are assessed by trained managers on their interpersonal skills and their leadership and decision-making abilities. Assessment centers are valid predictors of success in training programs and job performance.

Key Terms

adverse impact
assessment center
biographical inventory
critical-incidents technique
halo effect
impression management
in-basket technique
job analysis
leaderless group discussion

realistic job previews
reverse discrimination
selection ratio
situational interviews
situational testing
structured interviews
unstructured interviews
work analysis

Review Questions

1. Why do you think most college graduates do not stay long in their first job? What role might company recruiters play in that dissatisfaction?
2. How do a new graduate's work goals and preferences influence the level of satisfaction and commitment he or she finds in a new job?
3. How have online recruiting, applications, testing, and interviewing affected job search behavior? Do you prefer online applications and interviews or the more traditional in-person approach? Why?
4. What are realistic job previews? How do they help both applicants and companies?
5. How does the selection ratio affect recruitment and hiring decisions?
6. Describe how the concept of adverse impact can influence the hiring of minority-group applicants. How might reverse discrimination influence the hiring of majority-group applicants?
7. What is the effect of ethnic diversity in the workplace on the recruiting of minority applicants and on the financial status of the employing organization?
8. What forms of discrimination, other than racial prejudice, are still found in the workplace? How might these effects be reduced?
9. Describe the basic techniques of job analysis.
10. Distinguish between job analysis and work analysis. Describe the role of O*NET in conducting such analyses.
11. What are the advantages and disadvantages of biographical inventories? Why are they rarely used?
12. Distinguish among unstructured, structured, and situational interviews. Which approach is the least valid for predicting job success? Which is the most frequently used?
13. What are two types of impression management? How do they differ from the idea of "self-monitoring"?
14. How are the questions used in situational interviews developed? How do situational interviews differ from behavior description interviews?
15. What factors can influence an interviewer's judgment about a job applicant? Define the contrast effect. Define the halo effect.
16. What is the major problem with obtaining references and letters of recommendation for job applicants? If you were an employer, how would you deal with this issue?
17. When were assessment centers first used in the United States? For what purpose were they devised?
18. Describe two major techniques used in assessment centers.
19. Are assessment centers useful predictors of job performance at all levels? Why do some candidates resent assessment-center evaluations?

Additional Reading

Berry, L. M. (2003). *Employee selection.* Belmont, CA: Thomson/Wadsworth. A textbook that covers the major facets of employee selection and performance appraisal as well as contemporary issues such as test security, the Internet, globalization, international teamwork, and downsizing.

Brannick, M. T., & Levine, E. (2002). *Job analysis: Methods, research, and applications for human resource management in the new millennium.* Thousand Oaks, CA: Sage. A practical, user-friendly guide to everything you've always wanted to know about job analysis. Considers the impact of new technologies, job redesign, and organizational change.

Camp, R., Vielhaber, M. E., & Simonetti, J. L. (2001). *Strategic interviewing: How to hire good people.* San Francisco: Jossey-Bass. A hands-on guide that dispels the myths that interviews are easy to conduct and that gut feelings are a reliable way to assess an applicant's ability to perform a job. Effective interviewing depends on developing realistic goals, defining performance expectations, asking questions related to job performance, determining appropriate answers in advance, maximizing communication in the interview, and using behavioral decision-making criteria rather than personal liking.

Hough, L. M., & Oswald, F. L. (2000). Personnel selection. *Annual Review of Psychology, 51,* 631–664. Reviews research on personnel selection issues including job analysis, interviews, assessment centers, validity generalization, adverse impact, and the use of personality predictors.

Kravitz, D. A., & Klineberg, S. L. (2000). Reactions to two versions of affirmative action among Whites, Blacks, and Hispanics. *Journal of Applied Psychology, 85,* 597–611. Reviews responses of American-born White, Black, and Hispanic job applicants in the Houston, Texas, area to different types of affirmative-action recruitment plans.

Peterson, N. G., Mumford, M. D., Borman, W. C., Jeanneret, P. R., & Fleishman, E. A. (Eds.) (1999). *An occupational information system for the 21st century: The development of O*NET.* Washington, D.C.: American Psychological Association. Describes the development and validation of this global database of job descriptions, the successor to the Dictionary of Occupational Titles (DOT).

Thomas, J. C., & Hersen, M. (Eds.) (2003). *Comprehensive handbook of psychological assessment, Vol. 4: Industrial and organizational assessment.* New York: Wiley. Chapters covering theory, methods, applications, and consequences of testing individuals and groups in the workplace. Deals with test reliability and validity, cross-cultural issues, adverse impact, workers with disabilities, and the effect of technology on test administration and scoring. Considers multiple types of tests including basic skills, cognitive ability, personality, integrity, and interests.

Chapter 4

Psychological Testing

CHAPTER OUTLINE

If you think you'll be finished taking tests when you graduate, think again. You will be taking tests for many more years. How well you perform on them can determine the path of your career, and even your life. Do you plan to continue your education in graduate school to get a master's degree in psychology? Perhaps a law degree or an MBA? Graduate and professional schools all have admissions and certification tests.

Do you expect to find a full-time job right after graduation? Not many organizations will hire you until they see how you score on their tests for job applicants. Once you're hired, you'll be asked to test for training programs and possible promotions. Even NFL football teams administer psychological tests to prospective players. One uses personality tests to detect whether a player might tend to be overly aggressive and likely to cause trouble on or off the field.

Psychological testing is big business in today's workplaces. Industrial-organizational (I-O) psychologists are responsible for designing, standardizing, and scoring the tests that will play an important part in your future. Since there is no escaping psychological tests, it is important for you to know something about them.

PRINCIPLES OF PSYCHOLOGICAL TESTING

Carefully developed and researched psychological tests have several characteristics that set them apart from the tests published in the Sunday newspaper or on a self-help Web site, the ones that ask "Are You a Good Spouse?" or "What Is Your Sex Quotient?" A good test involves more than a list of questions that appear to be relevant to the variable being measured. A proper psychological test is standardized, objective, based on sound norms, reliable, and valid.

Standardization

Standardization refers to the consistency or uniformity of the conditions and procedures for administering a psychological test. If we expect to compare the performance of several job applicants on the same test, then they must all take that test under identical circumstances. This means that every student or job applicant taking the test reads or listens to the same set of instructions, is allowed the same amount of time in which to respond, and is situated in a similar physical environment.

Any change in testing procedure may produce a change in individual test performance. For example, if the air conditioning system in the testing room breaks down during a summer day, the people taking the test may not perform as well as people who took the test under more comfortable conditions. If an inexperienced or careless tester fails to read the complete instructions to a group of job applicants, then those applicants are not taking the test under the same conditions as other applicants.

Appropriate testing procedures can be designed into a test by its developers, but maintaining standardized conditions is the responsibility of the persons administering the test. Therefore, the training of test administrators in proper procedures is vital. An excellent test can be rendered useless by an untrained or inattentive tester.

Standardization The consistency or uniformity of the conditions and procedures for administering a psychological test.

Computer technology is helping to maintain standardized conditions of test administration. Organizations are increasingly using computer-assisted testing to ensure that everyone taking the test receives the same instructions in the same format.

(2) Objectivity

Objectivity refers primarily to the scoring of the test results. For a test to be scored objectively, it is necessary that everyone scoring the test obtain the same results. The scoring process must be free of subjective judgments or biases on the part of the scorer.

In your college career, you have taken both objective and subjective examinations. With **objective tests** (such as those containing multiple-choice and true-false items) scoring is a mechanical process that requires no special training or knowledge. A clerk in a company's human resources department, an undergraduate grader in the psychology department, or a computer program can score an objective test accurately as long as a scoring key with the correct answers has been provided.

Scoring **subjective tests** (such as those containing essay questions) is more difficult, and the results can be influenced by the scorer's personal characteristics, including a like or dislike for the person who took the test. For a fair and equitable assessment of a job applicant, then, an objective test is more desirable.

Objective tests Tests for which the scoring process is free of personal judgment or bias.

Subjective tests Tests that contain items such as essay questions. The scoring process can be influenced by the personal characteristics and attitudes of the scorer.

(3) Test Norms

To interpret the results of a psychological test, a frame of reference or point of comparison must be established so that the performance of one person can be compared with the performance of others. This is accomplished by means of the **test norms,** the distribution of scores of a large group of people similar in nature to the job applicants being tested. The scores of this group, called the **standardization sample,** serve as the point of comparison in determining the relative standing of the applicants on the ability being tested.

Suppose a high school graduate applies for a job that requires mechanical skills and achieves a score of 82 on a test of mechanical ability. This score alone tells us nothing about the level of the applicant's skill, but if we compare that score of 82 with the test norms—the distribution of scores on the test from a large group of high school graduates—then we can ascribe some meaning to the individual score.

If the mean of the test norms is 80 and the standard deviation is 10, we know immediately that an applicant who scores 82 has only an average or moderate amount of mechanical ability. With this comparative information, we are in a better position to evaluate objectively the applicant's chances of succeeding on the job relative to the other applicants tested.

The most widely used psychological tests have sets of norms for men and women, for different age groups, for various racial and ethnic groups, and for levels of education. The adequacy of a test's norms can determine its usefulness in any employee selection program.

Test norms The distribution of test scores of a large group of people similar in nature to the job applicants being tested.

Standardization sample The group of subjects used to establish test norms. The scores of the standardization sample serve as the point of comparison for determining the relative standing of the persons being tested.

Newsbreak	Too Bright for the Job?

Bob Jordan wanted to be a police officer in New London, Connecticut, the town where he lived. He applied for the job, took the Wonderlic Personnel Test, and waited to be called for an interview. No call came. He was sure he had passed the test—the questions seemed so easy—and when he heard that other people who had applied at the same time had been hired, he went to the police station to find out what had happened to his application.

He was advised that he did not "fit the profile" of a successful police officer. Had he performed poorly on the test? Had he scored so low that he was considered unfit for training or too dumb to ever learn how to do the job? No. Bob's problem was that he scored too high.

Too high? He was too smart? Yes. The test norms for the Wonderlic provide an optimum range of scores for a variety of jobs. If your score is too low, the norms suggest that you lack the ability to succeed on the job. And if you score too high, the test makers say that you are too intelligent, that you will be bored by the job and will probably quit before long. According to the test manual, "Simply hiring the highest scoring employee can be self-defeating." Bob Jordan scored six points too high to be considered a good candidate for the job.

An interview with the deputy police chief revealed more information. "Bob Jordan is exactly the type of guy we would want to screen out. Police work is kind of mundane. We don't deal in gunfights every night."

Jordan was so angry that he did what any good American does when he feels he is being treated unfairly. That's right. He sued, claiming he was discriminated against because of his level of intelligence. But a judge ruled that since the police department treated all highly intelligent job applicants the same, it had not discriminated against him. The judge noted that the decision to disqualify Jordan might have been unwise, but he had not been denied equal protection. Jordan now works as a prison guard.

Source: M. Allen. Help wanted: The not-too-high-Q standard. *New York Times,* September 9, 1999.

(4) Reliability

Reliability refers to the consistency or stability of response on a test. If a group takes a cognitive ability test one week and achieves a mean score of 100 and repeats the test a week later and earns a mean score of 72, we would have to conclude that something is wrong. We would describe the test as unreliable because it yields inconsistent measurements. It is common to find a slight variation in test scores when a test is retaken at a later date, but if the fluctuation is great, something is amiss with the test or the scoring method.

Three ways to determine reliability are the test-retest method, the equivalent-forms method, and the split-halves method. The **test-retest method** involves administering a test twice to the same group of people and correlating the two

Reliability The consistency or stability of a response on a psychological test.

Test-retest method A way to determine test reliability that involves administering a new test twice to the same group of subjects and correlating the two sets of scores.

Equivalent-forms method A way to determine test reliability that involves administering similar forms of a new test to the same group of subjects and correlating the two sets of scores.

Split-halves method A way to determine test reliability that involves administering a new test to a group of subjects, dividing in half the total number of items, and correlating the two sets of scores.

Validity The determination of whether a psychological test or other selection device measures what it is intended to measure.

Criterion-related validity A type of validity concerned with the relationship between test scores and subsequent job performance.

Predictive validity An approach to establishing criterion-related validity in which a new test is administered to all job applicants, and all applicants are hired, regardless of test scores. Later, when a measure of job performance can be obtained, test scores are correlated with job performance to see how well the test predicted job success.

Concurrent validity A way to establish criterion-related validity that involves administering a test to employees on the job and correlating their scores with job performance data.

sets of scores. The closer the correlation coefficient (called, in this case, the reliability coefficient) approaches a perfect positive correlation of +1.00, the more reliable the test is considered to be. In choosing a test for employee selection, the reliability coefficient ideally should exceed +.80, although in practice a value of approximately +.70 is considered acceptable. This method has several limitations, however. It is uneconomical to ask employees to take time from their jobs to take the test twice. Also, the effects of learning (remembering the test questions) and the influence of other experiences between the two testing sessions may cause the group to score higher the second time.

The **equivalent-forms method** for determining reliability also uses a test-retest approach, but instead of using the same test a second time, a similar form of the test is administered. The disadvantage of the equivalent-forms method is that it is difficult and costly to develop two separate and equivalent tests.

In the **split-halves method,** the test is taken once, the items are divided in half, and the two sets of scores are correlated. This method is less time-consuming than the other methods because only one administration of the test is required. There is no opportunity for learning or recall to influence the second score.

Validity

Validity is the most important requirement for a psychological test or any other selection device; that is, the test or selection device must be shown to measure what it is intended to measure. I-O psychologists consider several different kinds of validity.

Criterion-Related Validity.   Suppose that an I-O psychologist working for the U.S. Air Force develops a test to measure the proficiency of radar operators. The test will be considered valid if it measures those skills needed for competent performance on the job. One way to determine this is to correlate test scores with some measure, or criterion, of subsequent job performance. If persons who score high on the radar operator proficiency test also perform well on the job, and if those who score low on the test perform poorly on the job, then the validity coefficient between test scores and job performance will be high. We will know that the test truly measures the skills needed to be a good radar operator and is a valid predictor of job success. Validity coefficients of +.30 to +.40 are considered acceptable for employee selection tests.

This approach to defining and establishing validity is called **criterion-related validity.** It is not concerned with the nature or properties of the test itself but rather with the relationship between test scores and later measures of job performance.

Two approaches to establishing criterion-related validity are predictive validity and concurrent validity. **Predictive validity** involves administering the new test to all job applicants for a specified period and hiring them all, regardless of their test scores. At a later date, when some measure of job performance, such as production figures or supervisor ratings, can be obtained on each worker, the test scores and the job performance criteria are correlated to determine how well the test predicted job success. In most organizations, however, top management is unwilling to use this approach because obviously some of the people hired will turn out to be poor workers.

Concurrent validity is more popular with management than is predictive validity. It involves giving the test to employees already on the job and correlating the scores with job performance data. The disadvantage of this method is that by testing only current workers, the validation sample contains mostly the better employees. Poorer workers will probably already have quit or been fired, demoted, or transferred. Therefore, it is difficult to establish by the concurrent validity method whether the test is truly distinguishing between good and poor workers.

Another problem with concurrent validity is that applicants for a job and employees already on the job have different motivations and are likely to perform differently on psychological tests. Applicants may be more highly motivated to perform well on employment tests than current workers, who may feel more secure in their work situation.

The job performance criterion most often used in the establishment of criterion-related validity is ratings assigned by a supervisor to an employee's present level of job performance. Such ratings are made routinely as part of the employee performance appraisal process for all types of jobs. (We discuss performance appraisal in Chapter 5.)

Rational Validity.   I-O psychologists are also interested in **rational validity,** the kind of validity that relates to the nature, properties, and content of a test, independent of its relationship to measures of job performance. In some employment situations it is not feasible to establish criterion-related validity, perhaps because the company is too small to support the expensive and time-consuming validation process or because the job has no precedent. In the initial selection of the original U.S. astronauts, for example, before any space flights had taken place, there were no measures of job performance that could be correlated with test scores.

Two approaches to establishing the rational validity of a test are content validity and construct validity. In **content validity,** the test items are assessed to ensure that they adequately sample the knowledge or skills the test is designed to measure. This assessment can be accomplished by conducting a job analysis and determining if the test items are related to all those abilities needed to perform the job. With a word-processing job, for example, test questions about word-processing computer software are job related, whereas questions about musical abilities may not be. In the classroom, if your professor announces that you will be tested on the first three chapters of this book, then questions about information from other chapters would not be considered content valid.

Construct validity is an attempt to determine the psychological characteristics measured by a test. How do we know that a new test developed to measure intelligence or motivation or emotional stability really does so? One way to measure construct validity statistically is to correlate scores on the new test with scores on established tests that are known to measure these variables. If the correlation is high, then we can have some confidence that the new test is measuring the trait it claims to measure.

Face Validity.   **Face validity** is not a statistical measure but a subjective impression of how well the test items seem to be related to the job in question. Airline pilots would not think it unusual to take tests about mechanics or navigation because these topics are directly related to the job they expect to perform, but they might balk at being asked if they loved their parents or slept with a light on in their room. Such questions might be related to emotional stability, but they do not appear to be related to flying an airplane. If a test lacks face validity, applicants may not take it seriously, and this may lower their test performance.

The best psychological tests include in their manuals the results of validation studies. Without this information, the human resources or personnel manager

Rational validity The type of validity that relates to the nature, properties, and content of a test, independent of its relationship to job performance measures.

Content validity A type of validity that assesses test items to ensure that they adequately sample the skills the test is designed to measure.

Construct validity A type of validity that attempts to determine the psychological characteristics measured by a test.

Face validity A subjective impression of how well test items seem to be related to the requirements of a job.

can have little confidence that the tests in the company's employee selection program are actually measuring the qualities and abilities being sought in new employees. Test validation is expensive, but proper validation procedures will more than pay for themselves.

Validity Generalization

I-O psychologists used to follow a doctrine of situational specificity, which recommended validating a test in every situation—that is, in every job and every organization—for which it was chosen as a selection device. Tests were assumed to be differentially valid, which meant that a test appropriate for selecting laboratory technicians in one company was not automatically considered valid for selecting technicians in another company. Therefore, no test could be used with confidence for employee selection without first determining its validity in the given instance, no matter how valid the test had proven for other, similar jobs.

Validity generalization
The idea that tests valid in one situation may also be valid in another situation.

The idea of situational specificity or differential validity has been replaced by **validity generalization.** On the basis of meta-analyses of previous validation studies, I-O psychologists have concluded that tests valid in one situation may also be valid in another situation. In other words, once established, the validity of a test can be generalized.

The Society for Industrial and Organizational Psychology (SIOP) supports validity generalization. It has also been endorsed by the National Academy of Sciences and is included in the Standards for Educational and Psychological Testing of the American Psychological Association (APA). Validity generalization is widely accepted not only for tests but also for biographical data, assessment centers, interviews, integrity tests, and other selection devices. Many large corporations and government agencies apply the concept of validity generalization in their selection programs.

Validity generalization has important practical implications for psychological testing as an employee selection technique. Organizations have realized that if tests no longer require expensive validation procedures for every job at every level, then they can improve their selection programs by including tests, while saving time and money.

FAIR EMPLOYMENT PRACTICES

One result of fair employment legislation has been an increase in validity research to document whether a test is discriminatory. If studies show that applicants of all races who score below a certain level on a test perform poorly on the job, then the test is not discriminatory by race. I-O psychology research confirms that tests with high validity coefficients have relatively low levels of adverse impact. Criterion-related validation procedures (correlating test scores with job performance measures) are required, when feasible, by the guidelines of the Equal Employment Opportunity Commission (EEOC). Rational validation procedures may also be used to meet EEOC requirements.

A test that is found to be valid for one group is expected to be valid for another. Research has demonstrated that racial differences among average test scores are not the result of test bias but arise from educational, social, and cultural differences. A group of internationally known scientists issued the following statement, published in 1994 in the *Wall Street Journal*:

Intelligence tests are not culturally biased against American blacks or other native-born, English-speaking peoples in the U.S. Rather, IQ scores predict equally accurately for all such Americans, regardless of race and social class.

A report prepared by the APA's Board of Scientific Affairs in 1996 concluded that <u>cognitive</u> ability tests are not biased against African-Americans. In other words, the tests do not discriminate against minority groups. Rather, they reflect in quantitative terms the discrimination that has been created by society over time. Therefore, the consistent finding that Blacks score, on the average, some 15 IQ points, or one standard deviation, below Whites on tests of cognitive ability is a reflection of societal discrimination and not bias or discrimination on the part of the tests themselves (see Roth, Bevier, Bobko, Switzer, & Tyler, 2001).

However, the <u>empirical</u> demonstration of validity does not guarantee that a test will not be declared discriminatory and barred from further use. This occurred with the General Aptitude Test Battery (GATB) used by the U.S. Employment Service. The GATB is a test of cognitive functioning; it also <u>assesses</u> manual and finger dexterity. More than 750 validity studies have confirmed the high validity of the test as a screening instrument for employment. Test validities for Whites and minorities were comparable, although minority job applicants showed lower average scores and, hence, were less likely to be hired.

To avoid the adverse impact that would result from continued use of the GATB, the U.S. Employment Service adopted the controversial practice of **race norming.** Scores for minority applicants were adjusted upward to equalize hiring rates. Thus, political, social, and legal imperatives were given precedence over scientific ones. The 1991 Civil Rights Act prohibits the practice of race norming, specifically banning any form of score adjustment based on race, color, religion, sex, or national origin.

With race norming outlawed, the technique of **banding** was suggested. This was another attempt to equalize hiring rates by race by compensating for the consistently lower scores obtained by minorities on cognitive ability tests. Let us consider a simplified example. A company's human resources director could examine the test scores of job applicants and decide to band or group together all applicant scores between, say, 91 and 100, calling this range of scores "Band 1." Band 2 would encompass all scores between 81 and 90, Band 3 the scores between 71 and 80, and so on. Of course, any bandwidth could be selected; that is, Band 1 might just as easily include all scores between 81 and 100.

To equalize hiring rates by race, then, all applicants included in Band 1 would be considered equal in terms of the ability being tested. No distinction would be drawn between the applicant with a score of 100 and the applicant with a score of 91 if both were in the same band. Further, the order of selection within a band would not necessarily be by test score but rather could be by race. Thus, the person who scored 100 would not always be selected over the person who scored 91; within that band, hiring decisions could be made by racial or ethnic background.

Probably to no one's surprise, studies showed that job applicants who stood to benefit from banding were more likely to believe it was an equitable technique. Many organizations today continue to use banding, but it remains a widely debated and highly emotional issue among the people who develop and use psychological tests for selection purposes (Campion, Outtz, Zedeck, Schmidt, Kehoe, Murphy, & Guion, 2001).

Discrimination against disabled job applicants and employees has been substantially reduced in recent years as a result of EEOC regulations and the Americans

Race norming A controversial practice, now outlawed, of boosting test scores for minority job applicants to equalize hiring rates.

Banding A controversial practice of grouping test scores for minority job applicants to equalize hiring rates.

with Disabilities Act of 1990. Many psychological tests were modified for disabled persons and have been supported by empirical validation studies.

For visually handicapped persons, test questions can be presented orally, in large print, or in Braille, and people can be allowed more time in which to complete the test. Test questions relating to color, shape, and texture cannot be used with persons who were born without sight and have never seen colors and objects. Applicants with hearing disabilities can be given written instead of oral test instructions.

AN OVERVIEW OF A TESTING PROGRAM

The basic steps in establishing a testing program are essentially those necessary for any kind of employee selection program. The first requirement is to investigate the nature of the job for which testing will be used. Once job and worker analyses have been conducted, the appropriate tests to measure the behaviors and abilities related to job success must be chosen or developed.

Where do I-O psychologists find appropriate tests? They can use tests already available or develop new tests specifically for the job and company in question. The best tests include information on reliability, validity, and test norms. Additional evaluative information is provided by the periodically revised *Mental Measurements Yearbook,* which can be accessed at www.unl.edu/buros/. This invaluable resource, begun in 1938, offers current reviews of nearly 4,000 commercially available tests.

There are several issues to consider in deciding whether to use a published test or develop a new one. Cost is always important. It is less expensive to purchase a test than to construct one, especially if only a small number of employees are to be selected. Time is also important. If the organization needs qualified workers as soon as possible, management may be unwilling to wait for a test to be developed.

This situation is an example of the frequent conflict between research and application in I-O psychology, which we discussed in Chapter 1. As one I-O psychologist (who is both a researcher and a practitioner) noted, "Time and money are usually far more salient organizational criteria in decision-making than reliability and validity. Practitioners seemingly are engaged in the continuous art of compromise, navigating what they should be doing through the organizational seas of what they are allowed to do" (Muchinsky, 2004, p. 176).

If an organization decides to develop its own test for a particular job, the I-O psychologist overseeing the project will prepare a list of suitable test items. Then the test must be validated to determine whether it measures what it is supposed to measure. An item analysis will show how effectively each test item discriminates between those who score high on the total test and those who score low. This evaluation involves correlating a person's response on each item with the response on the test as a whole. A perfectly valid test question is one that was answered correctly by everyone who scored high on the complete test and was answered incorrectly by everyone who scored low. Only items with a high correlation coefficient will be retained for the final version of the test.

The level of difficulty of each item must be determined. If the majority of the test questions are too easy, then most people will obtain high scores. The resulting range of scores will be too narrow to distinguish those who are high on the trait or skill being measured from those who are only moderately high. A test on which most items are too difficult presents the opposite problem. It will be difficult

Newsbreak   Testing for Common Sense

If you are planning to go to graduate school to earn an MBA, you will probably be required to take the Graduate Management Admissions Test, the standard test used by business school admissions departments since 1954. This four-hour test assesses verbal, math, and analytical writing skills. It includes 41 verbal questions, two essays, and 37 quantitative questions.

The test is reliable and valid; it is known to predict success in MBA programs. But it is less successful in indicating which of those thousands of MBA students will go on to pursue successful business careers. The test cannot identify the seemingly lazy student who will become, at age 27, CEO of a start-up company worth millions. Nor does the test distinguish the all-A student who will never rise above a paper-pushing job in middle management.

The business school at the University of Michigan is trying to change that situation by adopting a new kind of selection test, one that focuses on "practical intelligence," otherwise known as common sense. The test was developed by Dr. Robert Sternberg, a Yale psychologist, who argues that traditional admissions tests do not pinpoint the ability to advance practical ideas and develop the analytical and creative skills that lead to success in the corporate world.

The practical intelligence test for business school admissions presents applicants with a set of realistic business scenarios, including financial statements, press releases, news articles, and other market information. The applicants are then given a problem to solve by answering a series of questions. The goal of the test is to evaluate an applicant's ability to handle changing situations, learn from misjudgments, and cope with less-than-adequate information—the same everyday challenges that managers confront on the job.

So far, the test has proven to be highly successful in predicting grades in business school; the higher the test scores, the higher the GPAs. The test has also shown to have less gender and racial disparity than the Graduate Management Admissions Test. Women scored significantly higher than men on the test of practical intelligence, and Blacks scored only slightly lower than Whites. On the standard admissions test, Black students scored substantially lower than White students.

The research will follow several successive classes of MBA students as they enter the workplace so that their on-the-job performance can be correlated with test scores to determine the test's validity.

Source: D. Leonhardt. On testing for common sense. *New York Times,* May 24, 2000; see also www.umich.edu/~newsinfo/releases/2001/nov.

to distinguish between those who possess extremely low ability and those who possess moderately low ability.

Much of this validity research requires the determination of some measure of job performance, a criterion with which the test scores can be correlated. Ideally, the test will be administered to a large group of applicants and all will be hired regardless of the test scores. At this point, the value of the test is unknown, so it makes little sense to base hiring decisions on its results. Later, after workers have been on the job long enough to develop some competence, their job performance will be assessed, and these ratings will be compared with the test scores. Economic and time constraints usually preclude this approach to establishing predictive validity. The more common method is to test workers already on the job.

Once the validity and reliability of a new test have been found to be satisfactory, a cutoff score must be set. No one scoring below this level will be hired. The cutoff score depends partly on the available labor supply. The greater the number of applicants, the more selective a company can be. The higher the cutoff score, the higher the quality of the applicants hired. However, by being increasingly selective, the organization must spend more money to recruit and evaluate more applicants to find sufficient numbers who meet or exceed the cutoff score. There is a point of diminishing returns at which the increase in the quality of new hires is less than the cost of recruitment and selection.

Most of the procedures for establishing cutoff scores involve job analyses and criterion-related validity studies to determine the minimum acceptable level of job performance. One frequently used technique asks employees and supervisors to assess the probability that a minimally competent person would answer each test item correctly.

ADMINISTERING PSYCHOLOGICAL TESTS

Psychological tests can be categorized in two ways: (1) how they are constructed and administered and (2) the skills and abilities they are designed to measure.

Individual and Group Tests

Group tests
Psychological tests designed to be administered to a large number of people at the same time.

Some tests are designed so that they can be administered to a large number of people at the same time. These **group tests** can be given to 20, 200, or 2,000 applicants simultaneously. The only limitation is the size of the testing room or the number of computerized testing stations available.

Individual tests
Psychological tests designed to be administered to one person at a time.

Individual tests are administered to one person at a time. Because this makes them more costly than group tests, they are used less frequently by employing organizations. Usually they are reserved for selecting senior management personnel. Individual tests are more popular for vocational guidance and counseling and for diagnostic work with patients.

Computerized Adaptive Tests

Computerized adaptive tests A means of administering psychological tests in which an applicant's response to an item determines the level of difficulty of succeeding items.

Designed for large-scale group testing, **computerized adaptive tests** provide an individual testing situation in which the applicant takes the test at a computer terminal. This approach is sometimes referred to as tailored testing because the test is tailored, or adapted, to the person taking it.

If you were given a standard cognitive ability test in paper-and-pencil format, you would have to answer questions designed to sample the full range of your intelligence. Some questions would be easy because your level of intelligence is higher than the level at which the questions are targeted, whereas other questions would be more difficult because they are at or above your level of intelligence. To complete the test, you must spend time answering all the questions, even the simple ones.

Because individual tests are costly and time-consuming to administer, they are used mostly for vocational counseling and for selecting management personnel.

In computerized adaptive testing, you do not have to waste time answering questions below your level of ability. The computer program begins with a question of average difficulty. If you answer correctly, it proceeds to questions of greater difficulty. Had you answered incorrectly, it would have given you a less difficult question.

Another advantage of computerized adaptive testing is that the testing can be done at any time during the selection process. It is not dependent on finding a qualified test administrator and scheduling a testing session. Because a range of abilities can be measured in a relatively short time, there is less opportunity for the applicant's interest and motivation to diminish. Also, immediate results are available to the human resources department.

Computers also allow for the use of different types of test items. For example, computerized adaptive tests of spatial ability allow the use of three-dimensional objects moving in space instead of two-dimensional stationary images. Questions can be presented with full-motion video and stereo sound. Test-takers can use a standard keyboard response or a joystick, mouse, or trackball to respond to test questions. Other advantages include the worldwide use of a test, instant updating of items without having to reprint paper copies, and instant scoring so that decisions about an applicant's suitability can be made more rapidly (Kersting, 2004; Naglieri, et al., 2004).

Computerized adaptive testing requires a larger initial investment than does a paper-and-pencil test, but it is more economical in the long run. Consultants estimate that the U.S. Department of Defense could save $5 million annually by computerizing the basic enlistment test given to military recruits.

Comparisons of the same tests given in paper-and-pencil format and computerized adaptive versions show little difference in the resulting scores. In one large-scale comparison, 425 employees of a call center took a paper-and-pencil version of a test measuring aspects of personality and judgment. A group of

2,544 job applicants also took the test. A separate group of 2,356 applicants took a Web-based version of the same test that included the same items. The results showed no significant differences in mean scores between the paper-and-pencil and computer versions of the test (Ployhart, Weekley, Holtz, & Kemp, 2003).

One growing problem with computerized tests is that many tests are available on Internet sites and can be accessed from any computer terminal. Since they are not administered in a controlled environment, such as a company's human resources office or testing room, ample opportunity exists for cheating. For example, for an intelligence test, an applicant could consult source books or have someone else present to help with the answers.

Another source of concern is whether Web-based testing might result in adverse impact because of racial differences in computer access and computer literacy. This could result in what some researchers have called a "digital divide," in which people who own and can use computers have an advantage over those who do not (see, for example, Harris, 2003).

Speed and Power Tests

Speed tests Tests that have a fixed time limit, at which point everyone taking the test must stop.

Power tests Tests that have no time limit. Applicants are allowed as much time as they need to complete the test.

The difference between speed tests and power tests is the time allotted for completion of the tests. A **speed test** has a fixed time limit, at which point everyone taking the test must stop. A **power test** has no time limit. Applicants are allowed as much time as they need to complete the test. A power test often contains more difficult items than does a speed test. Large-scale testing programs often include speed tests because all test forms can be collected at the same time.

For some tasks, working speed is an important component of successful job performance. A test for a computer keyboarding job would contain relatively easy questions. Given enough time, most people would be able to respond correctly. The important predictive factor for keyboarding or word processing is the quality of the work that can be performed in a given period: in this case, data entry accuracy and speed. A power test would not be able to evaluate this skill properly.

TYPES OF PSYCHOLOGICAL TESTS

A more familiar distinction among psychological tests for employee selection is in terms of the characteristics or behaviors they are designed to measure. The basic categories are tests of cognitive abilities, interests, aptitudes, motor skills, and personality.

Cognitive Abilities

Cognitive ability tests (intelligence tests) are widely used for employee selection because they are highly effective in predicting success in the workplace. Research studies involving thousands of people in the military services and in a variety of civilian jobs have shown consistently that cognitive ability tests are highly valid for predicting success in job training programs and in actual job performance (Hough & Oswald, 2000; Schmidt & Hunter, 2004).

A meta-analysis of thousands of studies conducted over a period of 85 years compared the predictive validities of 19 selection techniques. The results showed that cognitive ability tests had the highest validity for predicting success in job training and performance (Schmidt & Hunter, 1998). An additional meta-analysis of studies of more than 40,000 people also supported the predictive value of cognitive ability tests for job performance (Bobko, Roth, & Potosky, 1999).

Research on 12 occupational groups in Belgium, France, Germany, Ireland, the Netherlands, Portugal, Spain, Britain, and the Scandinavian countries concluded that tests of cognitive ability were highly valid predictors of success in training programs and job performance for all the countries and occupations included in the meta-analyses (Salgado, Anderson, Moscoso, Bertua, & Fruyt, 2003; Salgado, Anderson, Moscoso, Bertua, Fruyt, & Rolland, 2003).

And if you've been wondering whether it takes a different kind of intelligence, or cognitive ability, to succeed in the workplace than the type needed to succeed in college, I-O psychologists have the answer. A meta-analysis of 163 samples involved 20,352 research participants who took the Miller Analogies cognitive ability test; the test is used for the selection of graduate students and for jobs of moderate to high levels of complexity in business and industry. The research found no significant differences between the abilities needed to succeed in academia and to succeed in the world outside the classroom (Kuncel, Hezlett, & Ones, 2004).

Let us now describe some of the major tests used in the workplace today.

The Otis Self-Administering Tests of Mental Ability has been found useful for screening applicants for jobs such as office clerk, assembly-line worker, and first-line supervisor. The test is group administered and takes little time to complete. It is less useful for professional or high-level managerial positions because it does not discriminate well at the upper range of intelligence.

The Wonderlic Personnel Test, a reliable 50-item measure of general mental ability, is the most popular test for selection, placement, promotion, and reassignment. It is applicable to more than 140 jobs in business and industry, such as flight attendant, bank teller, store manager, and industrial engineer. Because the test has a 12-minute time limit, it is an economical screening device. Test items measure the ability to understand instructions, to solve job-related problems, and to propose ideas that can be applied to new work situations. Test norms are based on more than 450,000 working adults. Computer and hand scoring versions are available.

Wonderlic scores show a high positive correlation with scores on the Wechsler Adult Intelligence Scale, a longer and more complex individual test. A hiring kit to facilitate employer compliance with the Americans with Disabilities Act of 1990 offers large-print, Braille, and audiotape versions of the test. Since its introduction in 1937, the Wonderlic has been administered to more than 130 million job applicants throughout the world. A study of college-age applicants to a computer applications training center found no significant differences between mean scores of persons who took the computerized version and scores of those who took the print version (Dembowski & Callans, 2000).

A nonverbal measure of cognitive ability, the Revised Beta Examination, Third Edition (Beta-III), a 30-minute test, is designed for use with people who read poorly or who cannot read at all. Instructions are provided for English-speaking and Spanish-speaking job applicants. The test has been used extensively for occupational rehabilitation programs in correctional facilities and for unskilled workers in large-scale manufacturing job retraining programs. The six timed subtests include mazes, coding, paper form boards, picture completion, clerical checking,

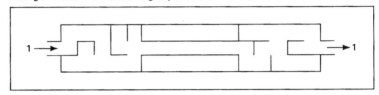

Mazes *ask examinees to mark the shortest distance through a maze without crossing any lines (1.5 minutes)*

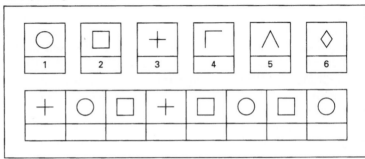

Coding *requires labeling figures with their corresponding numbers (2 minutes)*

FIGURE 4–1. Sample items from Revised Beta Examination, Second Edition (Beta-II). (Reproduced by permission. Copyright 1978 by The Psychological Corporation, San Antonio, TX. All rights reserved.)

and picture absurdities (see Figure 4–1). The Beta-III can be scored for professional, managerial, technical, clerical, sales, crafts, and service occupations.

The Wechsler Adult Intelligence Scale-Revised (WAIS-R) is a lengthy (approximately 75 minutes), individually administered test used primarily for jobs requiring a comprehensive psychological assessment, such as senior management personnel. Its administration, scoring, and interpretation require a well-trained and experienced clinical examiner. The WAIS-R includes 11 subtests, as follows: The verbal subtests are information, digit span, vocabulary, arithmetic, comprehension, and similarities; the performance subtests are picture completion, picture arrangement, block design, object assembly, and digit symbol. Separate verbal and performance measures of cognitive ability can be obtained as well as an overall IQ score. Computer scoring and interpretation are available.

Interests

Interest tests
Psychological tests to assess a person's interests and preferences. These tests are used primarily for career counseling.

Interest tests include items about daily activities from among which applicants select their preferences. The rationale is that if a person exhibits the same pattern of interests and preferences as people who are successful in a given occupation, then the chances are high that the person taking the test will find satisfaction in that occupation.

It is important to remember, however, that just because a person shows a high degree of interest in a particular job, it is no guarantee that he or she has the ability to be successful in that job. What interest test scores show is that the person's interests are compatible with the interests of successful people in that career. If a test shows that a person has no interest in a field, then the chances of succeeding in it are limited.

Two frequently used interest tests are the Strong Interest Inventory and the Kuder Occupational Interest Survey. The Strong is a 317-item, computer-scored

Newsbreak   Can You Pass the Test?

The Wonderlic Personnel Test has been used to evaluate more than 130 million job applicants throughout the world. Chances are good that you may already have taken it. There are 50 questions (a perfect score is 50), but not many people answer all of them correctly. The average score in the United States is 21.6. Minimum scores have been established for many occupations. For example, the minimum score considered appropriate for corporate executive or sales manager is 28; for nursing jobs it is 26; bank teller, 23; cashier, 20; and factory worker, 17. The only way to review the actual questions is to take the test, but Figure 4–2 has 12 examples of the types of questions used. The answers are provided so you can check your score.

1 Assume the first two statements are true. Is the final one true, false or not certain?
  The boy plays baseball.
  All baseball players wear hats.
  The boy wears a hat.

2 Paper sells for 21 cents a pad. What will four pads cost?

3 How many of the five pairs of names listed below are exact duplicates?
  a. *Nieman, K M.*
    Neiman, K. M.
  b. *Thomas, G K.*
    Thomas, C. K.
  c. *Hoff, J. P.*
    Hoff, J. P.
  d. *Pino, L. R.*
    Pina, L. R.
  e. *Warner, T. S.*
    Wanner, T S.

4 "Resent" and "reserve." Do these words:
  a. *Have similar meanings*
  b. *Have contradictory meanings*
  c. *Mean neither the same nor opposite*

5 A tram travels 20 feet in one-fifth of a second. At this same speed, how many feet will it travel in three seconds?

6 When rope is selling at $.10 a foot, how many feet can you buy for 60 cents?

7 The ninth month of the year is:
  a. *October*
  b. *January*
  c. *June*
  d. *September*
  e. *May*

8 Which number in the following group represents the smallest amount?
  a. *7*   d. *33*
  b. *8*   e. *2*
  c. *31*

9 In printing an article of 48,000 words, a printer decides to use two sizes of type. Using the larger type a printed page contains 1,800 words. Using smaller type, a page contains 2,400 words. The article is allotted 21 full pages in a magazine. How many pages must be in smaller type?

10 Three individuals form a partnership and agree to divide the profits equally. X invests $9,000, Y invests $7,000, Z invests $4,000. If the profits are $4,800, how much less does X receive than if the profits were divided in proportion to the amount invested?

11 Assume the first two statements are true. Is the final one true, false or not certain?
  Tom greeted Beth.
  Beth greeted Dawn.
  Tom did not greet Dawn.

12 A boy is 17 years old and his sister is twice as old. When the boy is 23 years old, what will be the age of his sister?

ANSWERS

1	True	7	d
2	84 cents	8	e
3	One	9	17
4	c	10	$560
5	300 feet	11	Not certain
6	6 feet	12	40 years old

FIGURE 4–2. Questions and answers similar to those on the Wonderlic Personnel Test (*New York Times*, November 30, 2003).

group test that covers occupations, school subjects, leisure activities, types of people, and work preferences. Items are rated as "like," "dislike," or "indifferent." Scales for more than 100 vocational, technical, and professional occupations are grouped around six themes on which test-takers are ranked from low interest to high interest. These themes are: artistic, conventional, social, realistic, investigative, and enterprising. In addition, many of the test's occupational scales are gender-differentiated; that is, they have separate male and female norms. Research on the Strong has shown that people's interests tend to remain stable over time.

The Kuder items are arranged in 100 groups of three alternative activities. Within each forced-choice trio, applicants select the most preferred and least preferred activities. The test can be scored for more than 100 occupations. Typical groups of items are as follows:

Visit an art gallery.   Collect autographs.
Browse in a library.   Collect coins.
Visit a museum.   Collect butterflies.

Both of these interest inventories are used primarily for career counseling, where the focus is on trying to select the right kind of occupation for an individual. One problem with using them for personnel selection is the possibility of applicants' faking their responses to make themselves appear more suitable for a particular job. Presumably, when a person is taking an interest test for the purpose of career counseling, he or she will answer more honestly because the results will be used to select a broad area of training and employment rather than a particular job.

Aptitudes

Aptitude tests
Psychological tests to measure specific abilities, such as mechanical or clerical skills.

For many jobs, **aptitude tests** are administered to applicants to measure specific skills. Sometimes these tests must be specially designed for a particular job, but there are also tests available that measure general clerical and mechanical aptitudes.

The Minnesota Clerical Test is a 15-minute individual or group test in two parts: number comparison (matching 200 pairs of numbers) and name comparison (see Figure 4–3). Applicants are instructed to work as fast as possible without making errors. The test measures the perceptual speed and accuracy required to perform various clerical duties. It is useful for any job that requires attention to detail in industries such as utility companies, financial institutions, and manufacturing.

The Revised Minnesota Paper Form Board Test measures those aspects of mechanical ability that require the capacity to visualize and manipulate objects in space, necessary skills for occupations with mechanical or artistic orientation, such as industrial designer or electrician. Applicants are presented with 64 two-dimensional diagrams of geometric shapes cut into two or more pieces and are

FIGURE 4–3. Sample items from Minnesota Clerical Test. (Reproduced by permission. Copyright 1933, renewed 1961, 1979 by The Psychological Corporation, San Antonio, TX. All rights reserved.)

When the two numbers or names in a pair are exactly the same, make a check mark on the line between them.

66273894 _____ 66273984
527384578 _____ 527384578
New York World _____ New York World
Cargill Grain Co. _____ Cargil Grain Co.

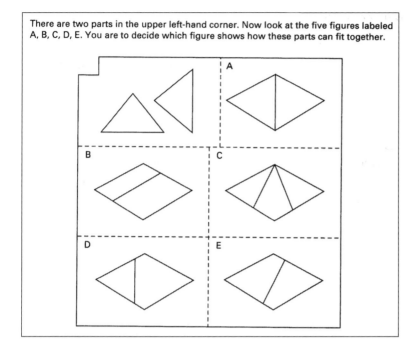

There are two parts in the upper left-hand corner. Now look at the five figures labeled A, B, C, D, E. You are to decide which figure shows how these parts can fit together.

FIGURE 4–4. Sample item from Revised Minnesota Paper Form Board Test. (Reproduced by permission. Copyright 1941, renewed 1969, 1970 by The Psychological Corporation, San Antonio, TX. All rights reserved.)

given 20 minutes to picture how the figures would look as whole geometric shapes (see Figure 4–4). Research shows that the test successfully predicts performance in production jobs, electrical maintenance work, engineering shop work, power sewing machine operation, and various other industrial tasks.

The Bennett Mechanical Comprehension Test uses 68 pictures with questions about the application of physical laws or principles of mechanical operation (see Figure 4–5). Tape-recorded instructions are provided for applicants with limited reading skills. The Bennett is designed for individual or group administration. It takes 30 minutes to complete. The test is used for jobs in aviation, construction, chemical plants, oil refineries, utilities, glass manufacturing, steel, paper and plywood manufacturing, and mining.

FIGURE 4–5. Sample items from Bennett Mechanical Comprehension Test. (Reproduced by permission. Copyright 1950, renewed 1967; 1941, renewed 1969; 1942, renewed 1969; 1967, 1968, 1980 by The Psychological Corporation, San Antonio, TX. All rights reserved.)

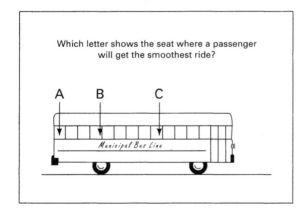

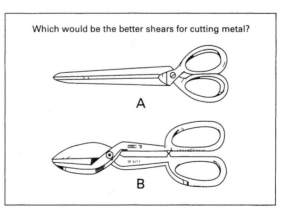

Motor Skills

Many jobs in industry and the military require abilities involving muscle coordination, finger dexterity, and eye-hand coordination.

The Purdue Pegboard is a ten-minute performance test that simulates assembly-line conditions and measures fingertip dexterity and eye-hand coordination necessary for assembly tasks, general factory work, and vocational rehabilitation. The task is to place 50 pegs in a series of holes in a pegboard as rapidly as possible, first with one hand, then the other, then both. Each task is limited to 30 seconds. The test also includes a one-minute task involving the simultaneous use of both hands to assemble pins, collars, and washers. Since it is nonverbal, it can be used with applicants regardless of their language skills.

The O'Connor Finger Dexterity Test and the O'Connor Tweezer Dexterity Test measure how fast an applicant can insert pins into small holes by hand and by the use of tweezers. These tests are standard measures of finger dexterity and have proven to be useful in predicting job success for occupations that require precise manipulative skills.

Personality

Personality tests
Psychological tests that assess personal traits and feelings.

Certain personality characteristics can contribute to job satisfaction and job performance. For example, empathy and nurturance are important traits for counselors to have; autonomy and persistence are vital to investigative reporters; and orderliness and precision are needed by accountants. **Personality test** scores have been found to correlate with job success in virtually all occupations. The predictive validities of personality test scores can be as high as those for assessment centers and biodata questionnaires.

Self-report personality inventories Personality assessment tests that include questions dealing with situations, symptoms, and feelings. Test-takers are asked to indicate how well each item describes themselves or how much they agree with each item.

Two approaches to personality assessment are self-report inventories and projective techniques. **Self-report personality inventories** include items dealing with specific situations, symptoms, or feelings. Applicants are asked to indicate how well each item describes themselves or how much they agree with each item.

Honesty of responses may be the major problem with self-report personality tests. Test questions are often transparent, and people can usually figure out how to respond to make themselves appear to possess whatever qualities they think the organization wants.

Projective techniques A personality assessment technique in which test-takers project their feelings onto an ambiguous stimulus such as an inkblot.

Projective techniques for personality testing present applicants with an ambiguous stimulus such as an inkblot. The task is to tell what is seen in the figure or picture. The rationale is that people will project their thoughts, wishes, and feelings onto the stimulus in an effort to give it meaning. These tests cannot be faked because there are no right and wrong answers.

The best known projective technique is the Rorschach Inkblot Test, in which subjects are shown ten standardized inkblots and asked to describe what they see in the figures. In the Thematic Apperception Test (TAT), subjects are asked to respond to 30 ambiguous pictures of people and situations.

Projective tests are time-consuming and must be administered individually. Examiners must be thoroughly trained and experienced. Because few of the tests have objective scoring keys, there is ample opportunity for subjective bias to affect the scoring and interpretation of the results. Although projective techniques are sometimes used for employee selection at the executive level, research shows that they have low validity.

TABLE 4–1

Simulated Items from the Minnesota Multiphasic Personality Inventory (MMPI)

Answer "true" or "false."
At times I get strong cramps in my intestines.
I am often very tense on the job.
Sometimes there is a feeling like something is pressing in on my head.
I wish I could do over some of the things I have done.
I used to like to do the dances in gym class.
It distresses me that people have the wrong ideas about me.
The things that run through my head sometimes are horrible.
There are those out there who want to get me.
Sometimes I think so fast I can't keep up.
I give up too easily when discussing things with others.

Self-Report Inventories.   The Guilford-Zimmerman Temperament Survey is a widely used paper-and-pencil personality test. The items are statements rather than questions, and the applicant responds by checking "yes," "?," or "no." Three sample items are the following:

You start work on a new project with a great deal of enthusiasm.
You are often in low spirits.
Most people use politeness to cover up what is really cutthroat competition.

The test yields separate scores for ten independent personality traits. As a check against faking or carelessness in responding, there are three falsification scales based on answers to selected items.

The Minnesota Multiphasic Personality Inventory (MMPI-2), first published in 1943 and revised in 1994, is the most frequently used personality test for employee selection and for clinical diagnostic work. The test is widely used in screening for jobs that require a high level of psychological adjustment, such as police officer, firefighter, air traffic controller, and airline flight crew member.

The MMPI-2 consists of 567 statements answered by "true," "false," or "cannot say." The items cover physical and psychological health; political and social attitudes; educational, occupational, family, and marital factors; and neurotic and psychotic behavioral tendencies. A number of items can be scored to determine whether the person taking the test was faking, careless, or misunderstood the instructions. Sample items from the test are shown in Table 4–1.

One problem with any test as popular as the MMPI-2 is that some people will take it more than once, should they apply to different organizations that use it. Among a sample of nearly 2,000 workers in the nuclear power industry, more than 200 were found to have taken the MMPI four times, 102 had taken it five times, 26 had taken it six times, and 3 had responded to all 567 items seven times. The scores of these examinees showed that repeated administrations of the test resulted in less extreme scores. One reason for this finding is that the job applicants became more "test-wise" with each additional exposure to the test. This problem is not unique to the MMPI; it applies to any psychological test used by a large number of employers.

The California Psychological Inventory, developed in 1957 and revised in 1987, consists of 434 items calling for "true" or "false" responses. It provides scores on

TABLE 4–2

The Big Five Personality Factors

Factor	Description
Neuroticism	Worried, insecure, nervous, highly strung
Extraversion	Sociable, talkative, fun-loving, affectionate
Openness	Original, independent, creative, daring
Agreeableness	Good-natured, softhearted, trusting, courteous
Conscientiousness	Careful, reliable, hardworking, organized

20 personality dimensions and has been shown to be useful for predicting success in teaching and in health care occupations (physicians, dentists, and nurses). The test has scales to identify leadership and management potential, creative potential, and social maturity.

The Big Five Personality Factors.   Predictive validities for self-report personality tests are generally in the low to moderate range. However, research using self-report inventories to assess the so-called Big Five personality factors has shown higher validities. These basic personality factors are listed and described in Table 4–2.

Two of these factors, conscientiousness and extraversion, have been found to be particularly effective in predicting job performance. Conscientiousness includes such characteristics as being responsible and dependable, able to plan, organized, and achievement-oriented. Conscientiousness has been found to be a valid predictor for many occupations, including managerial, sales, professional, law enforcement, and skilled and semiskilled jobs.

Extraversion, which includes the characteristics of sociability, talkativeness, ambition, assertiveness, and high activity level, correlates highly with success for salespersons and managers. Extraversion also shows a high positive correlation with success in obtaining a job. College seniors who score high in extraversion and conscientiousness are far more likely to find jobs after graduation than those who score low on these factors. In addition, a survey of 1,886 high-level managers found that those who scored high in agreeableness, openness to experience, and neuroticism were more likely to be seeking to change jobs than were those who scored low on those factors (Boudreau, Boswell, Judge, & Bretz, 2001).

Extraverts do very well in sales jobs. A study of 164 telemarketing sales representatives showed that those who scored high in extraversion had better sales records than those who scored low. Extraverts were also higher in striving for status, that is, in working to perform at a higher level than their peers (Barrick, Stewart, & Piotrowski, 2002).

A meta-analysis of 222 correlations from leadership studies found that extraversion was the most consistent correlate with leadership skill, followed by conscientiousness and openness to experience. The factor of agreeableness was the least relevant of the Big Five factors in predicting leadership success (Judge, Bono, Ilies, & Gerhardt, 2002).

The traits of agreeableness and conscientiousness were found to be highly valid predictors of successful performance when the job involved participation as a member of a work team. A study of 79 four-person human resources work teams showed that high scores on agreeableness and conscientiousness were closely related to task achievement, getting along well with other group members, and dealing effectively with conflicts (Neuman & Wright, 1999).

Much additional research has been conducted on the role of conscientiousness as it relates to work behavior. For example, research has demonstrated that conscientiousness is a consistent predictor of job performance. Employees high in conscientiousness are "predisposed to be organized, exacting, disciplined, diligent, dependable, methodical, and purposeful. Thus, they are more likely than low conscientiousness workers to thoroughly and correctly perform work tasks, to take initiative in solving problems, to remain committed to work performance, to comply with policies, and to stay focused on work tasks" (Witt, Burke, Barrick, & Mount, 2002, p. 164).

A study of 1,673 clerical, sales, and production workers, and truck drivers, found that those who scored high in conscientiousness and in agreeableness received higher ratings of job performance from supervisors than workers who scored high in conscientiousness but low in agreeableness (Witt, Burke, Barrick, & Mount, 2002). A related study of 491 workers in a variety of jobs, including sales, technical support, and software engineering, found that conscientiousness was highly and positively related to high job performance but only among employees who also scored high in social skills. Those who scored high in conscientiousness but low in social skills received lower supervisor ratings (Witt & Ferris, 2003). Again, conscientiousness is the key factor; social skills help, but they are not sufficient to compensate for a lack of diligence.

Other studies have found that conscientiousness is a highly valid predictor of successful performance for U.S. employees working for multinational corporations in other countries, whether they are newly hired or long-term employees (Caligiuri, 2000; Stewart, 1999). In research showing a negative correlation, low scores on conscientiousness were found to be a valid predictor of dysfunctional behaviors such as alcoholism, substance abuse, and reckless driving. People scoring high in conscientiousness were much less likely to exhibit these behaviors than were people scoring low (Sarchione, Cuttler, Muchinsky, & Nelson-Gray, 1998). In view of these and many other similar studies, it is clear that conscientiousness is a desirable characteristic for employees to show and for employers to seek in job applicants.

The factor of openness to experience may also have predictive utility in the workplace, at least for some types of jobs. A study of 166 managers for firms in Europe, who were participating in a cross-cultural training program in Japan, found that those who scored higher in openness to experience received significantly higher ratings from the instructors in the training program than did those who scored lower in openness (Lievens, Harris, Van Keer, & Bisqueret, 2003). Openness was also related to on-the-job creativity. When the supervisors of 149 office workers were asked to rate their employees on creativity—described as suggesting new ideas to improve performance, for example—the employees judged most creative had scored significantly higher on openness to experience than those rated less creative (George & Zhou, 2001).

Openness to experience and emotional stability were found to be vital factors in learning how to fly airplanes. A study of 91 civilian student pilots showed that students with higher levels of openness to experience and emotional stability required significantly less time to learn the necessary skills than did those who scored lower on these factors (Herold, Davis, Fedor, & Parsons, 2002).

Inventories have been developed to measure other specific personality characteristics, such as introversion, self-esteem, sociability, emotional maturity, and

Proactivity
A tendency to take action to try to influence or change one's environment

proactivity. **Proactivity** refers to a tendency to take action to try to influence or change one's environment. The Proactive Personality Scale consists of 17 items to which respondents indicate the extent of their agreement or disagreement. Sample items include the following (Seibert, Kraimer, & Crant, 2001, p. 874):

"No matter what the odds, if I believe in something I will make it happen."
"Nothing is more exciting than seeing my dreams turn into reality."
"I am always looking for better ways of doing things."

People who express a high degree of agreement with such statements are expected to perform well in certain jobs, particularly in sales. Research on nearly 500 people employed in a variety of jobs found that proactivity correlated positively with salary, promotions, and job satisfaction (Seibert, Crant, & Kraimer, 1999). A two-year investigation of 180 full-time employees found that those who scored high on the Proactive Personality Scale at the beginning of the study were rated higher by supervisors two years later on factors such as innovation, career initiative, and learning the political landscape of the workplace. These characteristics were associated with greater career progress and career satisfaction over the course of the study (Seibert, Kraimer, & Crant, 2001).

A final observation on the role of personality in the workplace concerns the predictive value of personality over time. For example, do you think your personality at age 18 will influence the situations you find yourself in when you are older? Researchers in New Zealand measured the traits of positive and negative emotionality in 910 18-year-olds; negative emotionality was described in terms of aggression, alienation, and high stress reactions. The same research participants were surveyed eight years later on the job. Those who scored high on negative emotionality at the age of 18 were generally unsuccessful in their careers. They held low-prestige jobs, were dissatisfied with those jobs, and had difficulty paying bills and getting ahead financially. The researchers noted that "alienated and hostile adolescents appear trapped in a self-fulfilling and vicious cycle. Their personality dispositions lead them to work experiences that undermine their ability to make a successful and rewarding transition into the adult world" (Roberts, Caspi, & Moffitt, 2003, p. 12). Those who scored high on positive emotionality at 18 reported success, happiness, and financial rewards on the job by age 26. They were also engaged in more stimulating work, which at least partially explains their job satisfaction.

Integrity Tests

American companies lose billions of dollars every year to theft, embezzlement, and other forms of employee dishonesty. The polygraph (the so-called lie detector) has been discredited as an effective means of detecting employee theft. A more valid way to predict and detect employee dishonesty is with integrity tests, a paper-and-pencil approach developed as an alternative to the polygraph. I-O psychologists estimate that every year more than 15 million employees and job applicants take integrity tests. Currently, some four dozen such tests are in use.

There are two types of integrity tests: (1) overt integrity tests, which directly assess attitudes toward theft and other dishonest behaviors, and (2) personality-oriented integrity tests, which measure general delinquency, impulse control, and conscientiousness. Both types of test appear to be valid predictors of theft and of such counterproductive behaviors as absenteeism, drug abuse, malingering, and violent behaviors. They have also been found predictive of general job performance as assessed by supervisor ratings (Rynes, Brown, & Colbert, 2002).

Research evidence suggests that most integrity tests are probably measuring the Big Five factor of conscientiousness, which would explain why the tests are such valid predictors of job performance.

Situational Judgment Tests

Situational judgment tests have become increasingly popular. These consist of a series of job-related situations designed to test judgment in the workplace. Applicants choose from among several alternatives to decide which would be the best way and which would be the worst way to respond to the problem. Another approach asks applicants to rate the effectiveness of each of a number of options offered as potential responses to the situation described.

Among the situational judgment tests in current use is the Supervisory Practices Tests, which assesses how well a candidate for a supervisory position would respond to situations that involve making decisions about other people. Test 905 is a situational judgment test used by the U.S. Office of Personnel Management to assess the human relations skills and promotion potential for first-line supervisory jobs in the federal civil service.

A meta-analysis of studies involving more than 10,000 people found that this type of test has high predictive validity for a wide range of jobs. The validity levels are comparable to those for assessment centers, structured interviews, and biographical inventories. Situational judgment tests also correlate highly with cognitive ability tests (McDaniel, Morgeson, Finnegan, Campion, & Braverman, 2001). A study of 823 employees in a government agency, a transportation company, and a manufacturing concern found that a situational judgment test was a valid predictor of job performance in all three kinds of organization (Clevenger, Pereira, Wiechmann, Schmitt, & Harvey, 2001).

LIMITATIONS OF PSYCHOLOGICAL TESTING

Uncritical Use.   A continual danger with psychological tests is their uncritical or inappropriate use by trusting human resources managers who may be taken in by slick brochures and promises of instant success in solving problems of employee selection and equal employment opportunity. A manager may choose a test because it is new, without investigating the test's norms, reliability, or validity. A test may continue to be used despite negative information about its dependability because the employment office is unaware of the research. Often there are no data to support a test because no research has ever been conducted on it. The harm generated by an improper testing program affects not only the organization, but also applicants who may be unfairly disqualified from a job by an ineffective test.

Rejection of Qualified Applicants.   Even the best psychological tests are not perfectly valid. No validity coefficients for tests reach a perfect positive correlation of +1.00. There is always some margin for error in the prediction of job success.

Sometimes unqualified persons will be hired, and sometimes otherwise qualified applicants will be incorrectly identified as unqualified or ineligible on the basis of their test performance. (This type of error also applies to other selection techniques.) These false-positive errors can be reduced when tests with the highest predictive validities are chosen for the selection program.

To minimize these errors, an employee selection program should not be based on a single technique. The use of several techniques allows for the compilation and evaluation of much more information about an applicant.

Faking.   We mentioned earlier that organizations using tests for employee selection must be sensitive to the possibility of faking. However, research evidence on the existence of faking when taking tests is contradictory. In one study, the responses of 1,023 people who took a personality test for the purpose of contributing to research on counseling, where there was no incentive for giving a false personal impression, were compared with the responses of 1,135 job applicants, some of whom may well have had a reason for faking. The test responses of the two groups were found to differ significantly, which the authors said indicated the existence of faking (Stark, Chernyshenko, Chan, Lee, & Drasgow, 2001). Other large-scale studies also compared personality test responses of job applicants with responses of people who were presumed to have no reason to fake their scores. In these cases, no significant differences were found between the two groups (see, for example, Smith & Ellingson, 2002; Smith, Hanges, & Dickson, 2001).

Thus, the matter of faking on selection tests has yet to be fully resolved. However, suppose you are in desperate need of a job and apply for a sales position. You are given a test that includes the following questions:

I enjoy meeting new people.	Yes _____ No _____
I get along well with most people.	Yes _____ No _____
I find it easy to talk to people.	Yes _____ No _____

You can easily anticipate the way the company expects salespersons to answer. Unless these characteristics apply to you, however, your answers will provide the company with a false impression. You may be hired, but you probably will not be successful or satisfied with the job because it requires abilities that you do not possess. In the long run, then, faking test responses works to your disadvantage, but it is hard to convince some avid job seekers of this in advance.

Retaking Selection Tests.   Some job applicants, particularly those applying for government jobs (from the local to the federal level), repeatedly take selection tests in the hope that their scores will improve sufficiently to receive a job offer. As you might expect, with continued practice on selection devices such as cognitive ability tests, scores do improve. It's not that the applicants get smarter, but they do become more familiar with the kinds of questions being asked. Also, with repeated exposure to the test items, they may become less anxious about the testing experience. To investigate the effects of retaking such tests, the scores of 1,515 applicants to a law enforcement agency were examined. The tests in question were for cognitive ability and oral communication skills. More than 40 percent of those who were hired had taken the tests more than once. The scores on both tests increased significantly between the first and second testing experience, and between the second and third testing experience. Also, those who took the tests more than once performed better in the training program, and were less likely to quit, than were those who took the tests only once. The researchers describe these findings as the "persistence" effect, suggesting that applicants who "had to persevere to gain entry into training (repeat testers) were, on average, more motivated to perform than were those who gained entry after a single test" (Hausknecht, Trevor, & Farr, 2002, p. 251).

Ethical Issues.   The APA is concerned about the ethical practices of all psychologists, whether engaged in clinical practice, in academic laboratory research and teaching, or in employee selection. Principles for proper conduct state that psychologists must protect the dignity, worth, and welfare of the persons with whom they deal. Unfortunately, this ideal is sometimes violated in applying psychological tests to employee selection. The APA ethics code describes safeguards for the distribution and use of psychological tests.

1. *Test users.* Persons who administer and interpret psychological tests should be aware of the principles of psychological measurement and validation and the limitations of test interpretation. They must avoid bias and should consider more than one means of assessment. They must adhere to standardized test administration procedures and make every effort to achieve accuracy in recording and scoring test results.
2. *Test security.* Actual test questions should never be reprinted in a public medium such as a newspaper or magazine. It is permissible to publish sample questions (similar to real questions) but not items used in the actual scoring of a test. [The examples in this chapter are sample questions.] Tests should be sold only to professionals who will safeguard their use.
3. *Test interpretation.* Test scores should be given only to those qualified to interpret them. They should not be given to anyone outside the human resources department, such as the applicant's potential supervisor, unless the supervisor has been trained to interpret the scores. The person being tested has the right to know the test score and what it means.
4. *Test publication.* Tests should not be released for use without adequate background research to support the test developers' claims. Informative and current test manuals containing reliability, validity, and normative data should be made available. Advertisements should describe tests accurately, without emotional or persuasive appeals.

Privacy Issues.   One aspect of psychological testing that has come under attack is the use of questions about personal or intimate issues. Critics charge that such personal probing is an unnecessary invasion of privacy. Individual freedom is violated when organizations request or require information that cannot be shown to be related to performance of the job for which the person is applying. Few people question the right of an organization to investigate the background, training, abilities, and personality of job applicants. But personal questions about sex, religion, political beliefs, and health have been successfully challenged in court as unwarranted invasions of privacy. Even if such questions were related to job performance, there remains the issue of how much of ourselves we should be required to reveal to a potential employer.

Newsbreak   Store Sued over Personality Test

When Sibi Soroka applied for a job as a security guard at Target Stores in California, he didn't know he would be asked about his religious beliefs or his sex life. And he didn't like it when he was. As part of the employment screening process, he had to take Psychscreen, a personality test used by Target, which contains items from two well-known psychological tests, the Minnesota Multiphasic Personality Inventory and the California Psychological Inventory.

Soroka felt that his privacy had been invaded when he was asked if he believed there was a devil and a hell in an afterlife. He was also asked whether he was strongly attracted to members of his own sex, or if he dreamed a lot about sex. Questions like these were entirely too personal, he said, and besides, what did his religious beliefs or sexual behavior have to do with being a security guard? Soroka sued Target for violating his right to privacy.

The trial judge denied Soroka's motion for an injunction to prohibit further use of the personality test by Target Stores and ruled that Psychscreen was not an unreasonable device for screening job applicants. Soroka appealed his case to the California Court of Appeals, which ruled in his favor. Psychscreen's questions about religion and sex, wrote the judges in a 39-page decision, violated a job applicant's right to privacy, unless the company could prove that such information was directly related to job performance.

The appeals court ruling did not object to the psychological screening of the store's security guards; it acknowledged that Target had a legitimate and justifiable interest in hiring emotionally stable applicants. Nor did the court find fault with the idea of using personality tests to select guards. What it did criticize was the asking of questions about sex and religion when the company could not provide any empirical demonstration of a compelling interest in that kind of personal information about an applicant.

Although Target Stores appealed to the California Supreme Court, it made an out-of-court settlement with Soroka before a decision could be rendered. Between the legal fees and the undisclosed amount of the settlement, plus the public notoriety, the use of Psychscreen turned out to be an expensive selection technique for this company.

Sources: D. C. Brown (1993). Target Stores settle out of court in *Soroka v. Dayton Hudson. The Industrial-Organizational Psychologist, 31*(2), 88–89. Also D. N. Jackson & J. D. Kovacheff (1993). Personality questionnaires in selection: Privacy issues in the Soroka case. *The Industrial-Organizational Psychologist, 30*(4), 45–50.

Summary

Psychological tests must meet the following criteria: standardization, objectivity, norms, reliability, and validity. **Standardization** refers to the consistency of procedures and conditions under which people take tests. **Objectivity** involves accurate and consistent test scoring that is unbiased by the scorer's personal characteristics and beliefs. **Test norms** are the scores of a group of people who are similar to persons taking the test; norms serve as a point of comparison for individual test scores. **Reliability** refers to the consistency of responses; it can be determined by the test-retest, equivalent-forms, or split-halves methods. **Validity** is concerned with how well a test measures what it is intended to measure. Criterion-related validity is determined by the methods of predictive or concurrent validity. Rational validity is established by content or construct validity. The concept of **face validity** refers to how relevant the test appears to the person taking it. **Validity generalization** indicates that a test valid for one job may be valid for other jobs, and a test valid for one ethnic group may be valid for others.

Fair employment legislation prohibits the use of tests to discriminate against job applicants because of race, color, religion, sex, or national origin. A valid test may be declared discriminatory if adverse impact on minority groups can be demonstrated. **Banding** involves grouping test scores to equalize hiring rates by race to compensate for lower scores obtained by minority applicants on cognitive ability tests.

To establish a testing program, I-O psychologists conduct job and worker analyses, develop suitable tests, conduct an item analysis of each test question, determine the level of difficulty of each question, establish the test's reliability and validity, and set cutoff scores.

Psychological tests differ in terms of how they are constructed and administered and in terms of the type of behavior they measure. Categories include **individual** and **group tests,** and **speed** and **power tests. Computerized adaptive tests,** designed for large groups, involve individual interaction with a computer. Psychological tests can measure cognitive ability, interests, aptitudes, motor skills, and personality. Personality characteristics are assessed by self-report inventories or projective techniques. Cognitive ability tests show high correlations with performance in job training programs as well as actual job performance. The Big Five personality factors, especially extraversion, conscientiousness, agreeableness, and openness to experience, are also valid predictors of job success. Integrity tests are designed to predict and detect employee dishonesty. Two types of integrity tests are overt integrity tests and personality-oriented integrity tests. Situational judgment tests have high predictive validities for a wide range of jobs.

Psychological tests can be of great value in employee selection because of their objectivity and validity. Limitations of tests include uncritical use, unfair rejection of applicants, and faking of responses. Ethical issues include invasion of privacy and confidentiality of test questions and answers.

Key Terms

aptitude tests
banding
computerized adaptive tests
concurrent validity
construct validity
content validity
criterion-related validity
equivalent-forms method
face validity
group tests
individual tests

interest tests
objective tests
personality tests
power tests
predictive validity
proactivity
projective techniques
race norming
rational validity
reliability
self-report personality inventories

speed tests

split-halves method

standardization

standardization sample

subjective tests

test norms

test-retest method

validity

validity generalization

Review Questions

1. Why are standardization and objectivity important in psychological testing?
2. Distinguish three ways of establishing the reliability of a psychological test.
3. Define criterion-related validity, rational validity, and face validity.
4. How would you establish the criterion-related validity of a new psychological test being developed to assess applicants for sales jobs?
5. Describe the technique of banding. What is it used for?
6. Discuss the steps involved in establishing a testing program.
7. In what ways are computerized adaptive testing programs superior to paper-and-pencil testing programs? What are the limitations of computerized testing?
8. How do interest tests differ from aptitude tests? Give an example of each type.
9. How good are tests of cognitive ability in predicting success in training programs and in subsequent job performance? Suggest a type of job for which these tests would be inappropriate or of no value.
10. Give an example of a projective technique. Give an example of a self-report personality inventory. Which is more useful for personnel selection? Why?
11. What are the so-called Big Five personality factors? Which ones do you believe are the most useful for predicting job performance?
12. For what type of job would you hire someone with a high score in extraversion? With a high score in conscientiousness?
13. What is proactivity? How does it relate to job performance?
14. Of what value are integrity tests and situational judgment tests in predicting behavior in the workplace?
15. Discuss the problems and limitations in using psychological tests for selection purposes.
16. What can happen when a job applicant takes the same selection tests several times? In general, how do people who are hired after retaking these tests perform in training programs?

Additional Reading

Barrick, M. R., & Ryan, A. M. (Eds.) (2003). *Personality and work: Reconsidering the role of personality in organizations.* San Francisco: Jossey-Bass. Reviews theories and models of personality with ramifications for the workplace such as personality predictors of job performance, the relationship between job satisfaction and job performance, motivational factors, and personality and counterproductive behaviors (substance abuse, violence, theft, and absenteeism). Also deals with group issues such as the functioning of work teams, self-monitoring and social networking, and person-organization fit.

Hornaday, J. A., & Gibson, L. A. (1998). *The Kuder book of people who like their work.* Atlanta: Motivation Research Corp. A collection of nearly 1,500 job descriptions provided by people who are satisfied with their work. Employees describe their job duties, a typical day, and the abilities and personality characteristics required for job success.

Kaplan, R. M., & Saccuzzo, D. P. (2000). *Psychological testing: Principles, applications, and issues,* 5th ed. Belmont, CA: Wadsworth. A popular textbook reviewing all types of psychological tests.

McCrae, R. R., & Allik, J. (Eds.) (2002). *The five-factor model of personality across cultures.* New York: Kluwer. Reviews the applicability of the five-factor model for individual cultures as well as across some 36 cultures studied. Relates the usefulness of this model for work issues in a global economy and in multinational organizations.

Roberts, B. W., & Hogan, R. (Eds.) (2001). *Personality psychology in the workplace.* Washington, D.C.: American Psychological Association. The results of a conference to improve information exchange between personality psychologists and I-O psychologists. Reviews research relating personality differences to job performance and other aspects of workplace behavior such as organizational citizenship (or prosocial) behavior, cooperation, and initiative. Considers personality-based management issues such as moral integrity in leadership and abuses of power.

Thomas, J. C., & Hersen, M. (Eds.) (2003). *Comprehensive handbook of psychological assessment, Vol. 4: Industrial and organizational assessment.* New York: Wiley. Chapters covering theory, methods, applications, and consequences of testing individuals and groups in the workplace. Deals with test reliability and validity, cross-cultural issues, adverse impact, workers with disabilities, and the effect of technology on test administration and scoring. Considers multiple types of tests including basic skills, cognitive ability, personality, integrity, and interests.

Wainer, H. (2000). *Computerized adaptive testing: A primer,* 2nd ed. Hillsdale, NJ: Erlbaum. An accessible state-of-the-art guide to the elements of computerized adaptive testing including computer technology, test development, statistics, and test theory.

Chapter 5

Performance Appraisal

There's no getting away from it. Someone somewhere will always be monitoring or evaluating your performance at something. Maybe it's your roommate, a classmate or team member, a friend, lover, spouse, or boss. Someone is assessing your behavior and appraising your abilities, whether informally or formally.

Throughout your career, your performance will be monitored and appraised, and your level of salary, rank, and responsibility will depend on how well you satisfy the established criteria for job performance. Of course, the **performance appraisal** of your work is nothing new to you. It has been going on since you started school. Your performance has been appraised continuously through classroom examinations, term papers, standardized tests, and oral presentations—all techniques designed to gauge or assess the quality of your work. In principle, they are similar to the techniques used on the job, and the results of these evaluations obviously have an important bearing on your future.

Although you may not take formal examinations during your years with an organization, performance appraisals at work are just as important as those in college. Your pay raises, promotions, and job duties affect not only your income and standard of living but also your self-esteem, emotional security, and general satisfaction with life. Performance appraisals can also determine whether you keep your job. In a sense, then, you are never finished passing tests; once you have been evaluated and hired by a company, your performance will continue to be assessed.

Keep in mind that performance appraisal can be as beneficial to you as to your company. Just as classroom tests show where you stand and where you need improvement, so the effective performance appraisal program can help you assess your competence and personal development on the job. Performance appraisal will reveal your strengths and weaknesses, enhancing your self-confidence in some areas and motivating you to improve your performance in others.

Performance appraisal
The periodic, formal evaluation of employee performance for the purpose of making career decisions.

FAIR EMPLOYMENT PRACTICES

The Equal Employment Opportunity Commission (EEOC) guidelines apply to any selection procedure that is used for making employment decisions, not only for hiring, but also for promotion, demotion, transfer, layoff, discharge, or early retirement. Therefore, performance appraisal procedures must be validated like tests or any other selection device. Employers who base their personnel decisions on the results of a well-designed performance review program that includes formal appraisal interviews are much more likely to be successful in defending themselves against claims of discrimination.

Racial Bias. Most performance evaluation programs are based on supervisor ratings, which are subjective human judgments that can be influenced by personal factors and prejudices. Race discrimination is known to persist in job assignment, pay, promotion, and other personnel decisions. However, a study of supervisor ratings of 23,316 White employees and Black employees found no evidence of bias against the Black employees (Rotundo & Sackett, 1999).

Age Bias. The evidence with regard to age bias shows that older workers tend to receive significantly lower ratings than do younger workers on measures of self-development, interpersonal skills, and overall job performance. A survey of 185 managers and 290 employees of a large multinational corporation found that older employees who had younger managers received the lowest performance evaluation ratings (Shore, Cleveland, & Goldberg, 2003). We saw in Chapter 3 that job proficiency does not necessarily decline with age. In some cases, then, raters may be basing their assessments on their expectations of an older worker's skills rather than on his or her actual job performance.

Criteria for Compliance.   Performance appraisal systems, which depend on having one person evaluate another, provide opportunities for unfair treatment in terms of pay, promotion, and other job outcomes. For organizations to ensure compliance with fair employment practices, performance appraisals should be based on job analyses to document specific critical incidents and behaviors that are related to successful job performance. The appraisers should focus on these actual job behaviors rather than on personality characteristics. They should review the ratings with the employees who are being evaluated and offer training and counseling to employees who are not performing well.

In addition, appraisers should be trained in their duties, have detailed written instructions about how to conduct the evaluation, and observe the workers on the job. It is vital that all relevant notes, records, and supporting documentation be well organized and maintained to ensure the accuracy and objectivity of the appraisals and to support the company's position in any future legal challenges from workers who claim they were treated unfairly.

PERFORMANCE APPRAISAL: WHY DO IT?

The overall purpose of performance appraisal is to provide an accurate and objective measure of how well a person is performing the job. On the basis of this information, decisions will be made about the employee's future with the organization. In addition, performance evaluations are often used to validate specific selection techniques. Thus, there are two broad purposes for conducting performance appraisals: (1) administrative, for use with personnel decisions such as pay increases and promotions, and (2) research, usually for validating selection instruments. Let us consider the purposes of performance appraisal in more detail.

Validation of Selection Criteria.   We noted in Chapters 3 and 4, on employee selection, that in order to establish the validity of selection devices, they must be correlated with some measure of job performance. Whether we are concerned with psychological tests, interviews, application blanks, or some other technique, we cannot determine their usefulness until we examine the subsequent performance of the workers who were selected and hired on the basis of those techniques. Therefore, a major purpose of performance appraisal is to provide information for validating employee selection techniques.

Training Requirements.   A careful evaluation of employee performance can uncover weaknesses or deficiencies in knowledge, skills, and abilities. Once these are identified, they can be corrected through additional training. Occasionally, an entire work crew or section is found to be deficient on some aspect of the work routine. Information of this sort can lead to the redesign of the training program for new workers and the retraining of current workers to correct the shortcomings. Performance appraisal can also be used to assess the worth of a training program by determining whether job performance improved after the training period.

Employee Improvement.   Performance appraisal programs should provide feedback to employees about their job competence and their progress within the organization. I-O psychologists have found that this kind of information is crucial to maintaining employee morale. Appraisals can also suggest how employees might change certain behaviors or attitudes to improve their work efficiency. This purpose of performance appraisal is similar to that of improving training. In this instance, however, a worker's shortcomings can be altered through self-improvement rather than through formal retraining. Workers have a right to know what is expected of them—what they are doing well, and how they might improve.

Pay, Promotion, and Other Personnel Decisions.   Most people believe they should be rewarded for above average or excellent performance. For example, in your college work, fairness dictates that if your performance on an exam or term paper is superior to that of others taking the course, you should receive a higher grade. If everyone received the same grade regardless of academic performance, there would be little incentive for continued hard work.

In employing organizations, rewards are in the form of salary increases, bonuses, promotions, and transfers to positions providing greater opportunity for advancement. To maintain employee initiative and morale, these changes in status cannot depend on a supervisor's whim or personal bias but must be based on a systematic evaluation of employee worth. Performance appraisals provide the foundation for these career decisions and also help to identify those employees with the potential and talent for contributing to the company's growth.

Opposition to Performance Appraisal

Not everyone is in favor of formal performance appraisal systems. Many employees —especially those affected most directly by such ratings—are less than enthusiastic about them. The list of critics also includes labor unions and managers.

Labor Unions.   Labor unions, which represent approximately 11 percent of the U.S. workforce, require that seniority (length of service) rather than assessment of employee merit be taken as the basis for promotion. However, length of job experience alone is no indication of the ability to perform a higher-level job. For example, a worker with ten years of experience in an auto body plant may know everything about the assembly line. But unless the company has a formal, objective evaluation of that worker's competence in other areas—such as the ability to get along with people or the verbal skills to write reports for management—there is no basis for concluding that the worker will make a good supervisor.

Senior people should be given the first opportunity for promotion, but they must qualify for that promotion because of their abilities, not solely because of length of service. Performance evaluations can provide a reliable basis for these decisions.

Newsbreak | Tough Graders Get Low Scores

Paul Trout is unhappy about his performance appraisals. Not the ones he gives to his students as a professor at Montana State University, but the ones they give him. At the end of every semester, at colleges throughout the United States, students have the opportunity to evaluate how well their teachers are doing their jobs.

Do the instructors show concern for the students? How thoroughly do they know the subject matter? Can they communicate the material clearly and with enthusiasm? Do they grade assignments and tests promptly and fairly? Are they available to discuss students' problems? These are just some of the questions students use to rate their professors. The evaluations are factored into the college's decisions about contract renewals, promotions, salary increases, and tenure.

At Montana State, faculty members need to maintain an average score of 3.6, on a four-point scale, to qualify for a pay raise. "To get scores this high," Professor Trout said, "I have to make a lot of students happy." And to make them happy, he cannot be too demanding. He has to be careful about the amount of work he requires, about his expectations for student performance, and about the standards he sets for grading. A reputation as a tough grader can be costly.

Research on student evaluations shows that students consistently assign low ratings to teachers who set high standards and strict course requirements. Teachers known to offer easy courses receive higher ratings. Have these performance appraisals become nothing more than popularity contests?

According to Trout, "To get high scores, most instructors have to please [their students] or at least not upset them. Even a few students, angry about a demanding workload or a C grade, can have a devastating effect on evaluation scores simply by giving an instructor a zero on every item, as some disgruntled students do."

Is this how you would like your work performance to be evaluated? And what kind of ratings will you give your professor when this semester ends?

Source: P. Trout. Students give top teachers low marks. *St. Petersburg (FL) Times,* March 24, 2000.

Employees. Few of us like being tested or evaluated, particularly if we believe we may receive an unfavorable rating. Not many people are so confident of their skills that they expect consistently to receive praise from their superiors. And few of us welcome criticism, no matter how objective it is or how tactfully it is offered. Because many of us would rather not be assessed and told of our weaknesses or deficiencies, we may react with <u>suspicion</u> or hostility to the idea of performance appraisals.

Managers. Managers who have had unsatisfactory experiences with inadequate or poorly designed appraisal programs may be skeptical about their usefulness.

Some managers dislike playing the role of judge and are unwilling to accept responsibility for making decisions that affect the future of their subordinates. This tendency can lead them to <u>inflate</u> their <u>assessments</u> of the workers' job performance, giving higher ratings than deserved. Also, managers may be uncomfortable providing negative feedback to employees and may lack the skills to conduct the postappraisal interview properly.

Despite these sources of opposition to performance appraisal, it remains a necessary activity in organizational life. Its critics overlook the point that some form of appraisal is inevitable. Some basis must be established for employee selection and training and other personnel decisions. These determinations should not be based on personal likes and dislikes. Job competence must be measured in a way that reflects, as objectively as possible, the qualities and abilities required to do the job.

Techniques of Performance Appraisal

Industrial-organizational (I-O) psychologists have developed a number of techniques to measure job performance. The specific technique used depends on the type of work being evaluated. The abilities needed to work satisfactorily on an assembly line differ from those required on a sales job or a high-level administrative position. The performance measures chosen must reflect the nature and complexity of the job duties. For example, repetitive assembly-line work can be assessed more objectively than the daily activities of a bank executive.

Performance measures may be described as either objective or judgmental. Proficiency on production jobs is more readily appraised by objective performance and output measures. Assessing competence on nonproduction, professional, and managerial jobs, however, requires more judgmental and qualitative measures.

OBJECTIVE PERFORMANCE APPRAISAL METHODS

The measurement of performance on production jobs is relatively easy in principle. It typically involves recording the number of units produced in a given time period. Such measures of quantity are widely used in industry in part because production records are readily available. In practice, performance appraisal of production jobs is not so simple, particularly for nonrepetitive jobs. Quality of output must also be assessed.

Output Measures

Consider the productivity of two employees doing word processing. One enters 70 words a minute, and the other enters 55 words a minute. If we use quantity as the sole measure of job performance, we must give the first worker the higher rating. However, if we examine the quality of their work, we find that the first worker averages 20 errors a minute and the second makes none. We must now adjust the performance evaluations to reflect the quality of output, and the second worker should receive the higher rating.

Even though we have corrected the output data to compensate for the different quality of performance, we must consider the possibility that other factors

Some routine production jobs can be evaluated in terms of the number of units produced in a given period.

can influence or distort the performance measure. Perhaps the employee who made so many keyboard errors works in a vast, open room surrounded by many other employees and a lot of noisy office equipment. The other employee being evaluated may have a private office and few distractions. Or perhaps one is responsible only for short, routine business letters and the other transcribes technical reports from the engineering department. It would be unfair to assign performance ratings without correcting for differences in office environment and level of difficulty of the job tasks.

Another possible contaminating factor is length of job experience. In general, the longer employees are on a job, the greater is their productivity. The performance appraisals of two otherwise identical workers doing the same job may be expected to differ if one has two years of experience and the other 20 years.

Therefore, many factors have to be recognized in evaluating performance on production jobs. The more of these influences that must be taken into account, the less objective is the final appraisal. The impact of these extraneous factors requires raters to make personal judgments. Thus, even with production jobs in which a tangible product can be counted, performance appraisal may not always be completely objective. In repetitive jobs, such as assembly-line work, subjective judgments may have less impact on the final appraisal. In these instances, a straightforward record of quantity and quality of output will suffice as a measure of job performance.

Computerized Performance Monitoring

Work performed at video display terminals can be thought of as a kind of virtual assembly line. Computers are a normal part of the work environment for millions of people the world over, largely in word-processing, data-entry, insurance, and customer-service jobs. Many organizations have programmed their computers to monitor employees' on-the-job activities. Every time a worker produces a unit of work, such as a keystroke, it is automatically counted and stored, providing an objective measure of job performance. Computers can record the number of keystrokes per unit of time, the incidence of errors, the pace of work over the course of a shift, and the number and length of work breaks or rest pauses. Many workers who use computer terminals are subject to this continuous monitoring and evaluating of their job performance by the so-called electronic supervisor, the machine that is always watching. It detects and remembers everything.

Computers are also being used to assess workers in telecommunications jobs, such as airline and hotel reservations agents and telephone operators. An airline based in San Diego, California, monitors its reservations agents throughout the work period, timing their calls and comparing their performance with company standards for the number of seconds spent on each inquiry and the number of minutes allotted for rest breaks. Employees who exceed the standards receive demerits and unfavorable ratings.

Attitudes toward Computerized Monitoring.   Think about it for a minute. How would you like to have every moment of your behavior throughout the workday monitored and recorded? Would it bother you? It may surprise you to learn that a lot of employees, perhaps the majority, are not bothered by electronic performance monitoring. Some of them like it and prefer it to other forms of performance appraisal. Psychologists have found that a person's reaction to electronic monitoring depends on how the data compiled on their job performance are ultimately applied. When the information is used to help employees develop and refine job skills (instead of reprimanding them for taking long rest breaks, for example), most workers report a favorable attitude toward computerized monitoring.

Many employees like this high-tech performance appraisal technique because it ensures that their work will be evaluated objectively, not on the basis of how much their supervisor may like or dislike them. Also, employees believe that such objective measures can provide support for their requests for pay raises or promotions.

Stress and Computerized Monitoring.   Having noted that many employees like computerized performance monitoring, it may seem contradictory to report that they also find it stressful, or so they claim in surveys asking whether the technique causes stress. Keep in mind, as we try to reconcile these disparate findings, that the research results may not be contradictory after all. It is quite conceivable that many employees like computerized monitoring and prefer it over other, more subjective, forms of appraisal, yet still find it stressful. Indeed, it would be surprising if some workers did not claim that all forms of appraisal are stressful to some degree. (If you were asked on a questionnaire whether you find college exams to be stressful, you would probably answer yes.)

The monitoring of an individual's job performance is far more stressful for that employee than when the performance of the work group as a whole is monitored. In the latter case, each worker's performance is combined with that of other group members.

Also, both field studies and laboratory studies show that people who work alone experience greater stress from computerized monitoring than people who work as part of a cohesive group, even when they are monitored individually.

Newsbreak   Big Brother in a Black Box

The reach of computerized performance monitoring is being widened as more and more jobs come online. The see-all, know-all electronic supervisor is now watching assembly-line workers, fast-food workers, machine operators, retail clerks, salespeople, accountants, personnel managers, and health care professionals.

Consider how the typical United Parcel Service (UPS) deliveryman performs his job. Not so long ago, he picked up the packages for his route from the dispatcher in the morning and then was on his own, unobserved and unreachable, until he returned at the end of his shift. Not anymore.

Now he carries a personal computer in a box, all day long. The screen shows his tasks, each one timed to the minute. When he completes a delivery, he enters the details into the computer and the information is instantly transmitted to his supervisor. Thus, the supervisor knows at any time where each delivery person is and whether he is on schedule.

There is no hiding. UPS drivers and millions of other workers are being watched over by what one writer called "the boss that never blinks"—the boss that is always observing, recording, and measuring.

Long-distance truckers are another group being monitored electronically. They used to enjoy considerable freedom. You know the image— alone in their 18-wheel rigs, barreling down the highway, exchanging greetings in their own language on their CB radios, with no one to tell them what to do. Those days are gone. Those trucks now carry computers that are on all the time. Using satellite links and on-board recorders, employers can monitor a driver's speed, rate of braking, and time spent off the road at a stop. Some systems will beep when a driver exceeds the prescribed speed or shifts improperly.

A trucker who hauls mattresses from Indiana to Florida told a reporter that the on-board computer saves time by keeping his daily logbook up-to-date and making it easier for him to get help when his truck has a breakdown, since the company is always aware of his location. Still, there is a downside. "You know they are always watching."

Sources: In a nonstop economy, truckers keep rolling. *New York Times*, November 24, 1999; Truckers face monitoring to make sure they rest. *St. Petersburg (FL) Times*, February 26, 2000; Big brother in a black box. *Civilization*, August/September 1999, pp. 53–55.

The social support provided by the other members of a close-knit work group helps to reduce the stress.

The knowledge of continuous monitoring, of knowing that every action one takes or fails to take is being recorded, can lead workers to focus more on the quantity of their output than the quality. Thus, the stress of computerized monitoring may result in a reduction of work quality, which has a negative effect on overall job performance and satisfaction.

How would you evaluate the job performance of a documentary filmmaker?

As with many innovations in the workplace, computerized performance monitoring has both advantages and disadvantages. As advantages, the technique provides immediate and objective feedback, reduces rater bias in performance evaluations, helps identify training needs, facilitates goal setting, and may contribute to increases in productivity. However, it also invades workers' privacy, may increase stress and reduce job satisfaction, and may lead workers to focus on quantity of output at the expense of quality.

Job-Related Personal Data

Another objective approach to performance appraisal involves the use of personal data, such as absenteeism, earnings history, accidents, and advancement rate. It is usually easier to compile job-related personal information from the files in the human resources office than it is to measure and assess production on the job. I-O psychologists have found that personal data may provide little information about an individual worker's ability on the job, but these data can be used to distinguish good from poor employees. The emphasis here is on a semantic distinction between *workers* and *employees*.

Highly skilled and experienced machine operators who are prone to excessive absenteeism and tardiness may be outstanding workers when they are actually on the job. They may be considered poor employees, however, because the company cannot rely on them to show up regularly and contribute to the efficiency of the organization. Job-related personal data are useful in assessing the relative worth of employees to an organization, but they are not a substitute for measures of job performance.

JUDGMENTAL PERFORMANCE APPRAISAL METHODS

Jobs on which employees do not produce a countable product—or one that makes sense to count—are more difficult to assess. How would you evaluate the performance of firefighters? Should we count the number of fires they put out in a day? How would you appraise brain surgeons? By the number of brains they operate on each week? For business executives, do we tally the number of decisions they make each month?

In each of these instances, I-O psychologists must find some way to assess the merit of the person's work, not by counting or keeping a precise record of output but by observing work behavior over a period of time and rendering a judgment about its quality. To determine how effective or ineffective an employee is, we must ask people who are familiar with the person and the work, usually a supervisor, but sometimes colleagues, subordinates, and even the employee being evaluated.

Written Narratives

Although some organizations use written narratives, which are brief essays describing employee performance, to appraise performance, most also apply numerical rating procedures. Although both narrative and rating approaches are subjective, the narrative technique is more prone to personal bias. An essay written by a supervisor can be ambiguous or misleading when describing an employee's job performance. Sometimes these misstatements are inadvertent, and sometimes they are deliberate, to avoid giving a negative appraisal. An article published in the *Harvard Business Review* listed some common expressions used in written performance appraisals—and suggested what the rater might have meant.

- "exceptionally well qualified" (has committed no major blunders to date)
- "tactful in dealing with superiors" (knows when to keep quiet)
- "quick thinking" (instantly offers plausible-sounding excuses for errors)
- "meticulous attention to detail" (a fussy nitpicker)
- "slightly below average" (stupid)
- "unusually loyal to the company" (no one else wants them!)

In an attempt to reduce ambiguity and personal bias, various merit rating techniques have been developed to provide greater objectivity for judgmental performance appraisals.

Merit Rating Techniques

In many everyday situations we make judgments about the people with whom we come in contact. We assess them in terms of their appearance, intelligence, personality, sense of humor, or athletic skills. On the basis of these informal judgments, we may decide whether to like or dislike them, hire them, become friends with them, or marry them. Our judgments are sometimes faulty; a friend can become an enemy, or a spouse an adversary in divorce court. The reason for errors in judgment lies in the fact that the process is subjective and unstandardized. We do not always judge people on the basis of meaningful or relevant criteria.

Merit rating Objective rating methods designed to provide an objective evaluation of work performance.

The process of judgment in **merit rating** is considerably more formalized and specific because job-related criteria are established to serve as standards for comparison. There is still opportunity for raters to impose personal prejudices on the process, but that is not the fault of the method. Merit rating is designed to yield an objective evaluation of work performance compared with established standards.

Rating scales A performance appraisal technique in which supervisors indicate how or to what degree a worker possesses each relevant job characteristic.

Rating Technique.   Performance **rating scales** are the most frequently used merit rating technique. The supervisor's task is to specify how or to what degree the worker possesses each of the relevant job characteristics. To rate work quality based on observations of the worker's performance, the supervisor expresses a judgment

FIGURE 5–1 Rating Scale.

1	2	3	4	5
Poor		Average		Excellent

on a rating scale such as that shown in Figure 5–1. The worker in this example has been judged to exhibit a slightly above average level of task proficiency.

Some companies rate employees on specific job duties and on broader factors such as cooperation, supervisory skills, time management, communications skills, judgment and initiative, and attendance. In addition, many organizations compare current employee performance with past evaluations, asking supervisors to indicate whether employees have improved, worsened, or shown no change since the last appraisal.

Supervisors may also be asked to note any particular strengths and to explain extenuating circumstances that might have affected a worker's performance. Some companies allow employees to add their own written comments to the evaluation form. A portion of a typical performance rating form is shown in Figure 5–2. Ratings are a popular way of evaluating performance for two reasons: (1) they are relatively easy to construct and (2) they attempt to reduce personal bias.

Ranking Technique. In the **ranking technique,** supervisors list their workers in order from highest to lowest or best to worst on specific characteristics and abilities and on overall job proficiency. You can see that there is a major conceptual difference between rating and ranking. In ranking, each employee is compared with all others in the work group or department. In rating, each employee is compared with his or her past performance or with a company standard. Thus, ranking is not as direct a measure of job performance as is rating.

An advantage of the ranking technique is its simplicity. No elaborate forms or complicated instructions are required. It can be accomplished quickly and is usually accepted by supervisors as a routine task. Supervisors are not being asked to judge workers on factors such as initiative or cooperation, qualities they may not be competent to assess.

However, ranking has its limitations when there are a large number of employees to appraise. Supervisors would have to know all the workers on their shifts quite well in order to make comparative judgments of their efficiency. With a work group of 50 or 100 subordinates, it becomes difficult and tedious to rank them in order of ability or merit.

Another limitation is that because of its simplicity, ranking supplies less evaluative data than does rating. Worker strengths and weaknesses cannot be readily determined by ranking, and there is little feedback or information to provide to workers about how well they are doing or how they might improve their task performance.

The ranking technique for performance appraisal also makes it difficult for supervisors to indicate similarities among workers. For example, in ranking ten workers, a supervisor may believe that three are equally outstanding and two are equally poor, but there is no way to indicate this. The supervisor is forced to rank the workers from highest to lowest. Thus, only one of the

Ranking technique A performance appraisal technique in which supervisors list the workers in their group in order from highest to lowest or best to worst.

Name _____ Position _____ Time in Position _____ Date _____

Department _____ Location _____ Evaluator (Name/Title) _____

Type of Evaluation: Initial 6 Months ☐ Annual ☐ Other _____ Evaluation Period Dates _____

INSTRUCTIONS: Place a check mark (✓) in the box corresponding to the appropriate performance level. Possible elements to consider in evaluation are suggested.

PERFORMANCE RATING LEVELS ——————————————————————————————

Commendable (C) Performance exceeded expectations for the position in most areas and results were fully accomplished in all other areas. Assignments always produce results above "good" performance standards established for this position.

Good (G) Performance met most of the expectations for the position. Overall performance was satisfactory. Assignments and major job duties are accomplished with minimal supervision and direction.

Needs Improvement (NI) Performance is below expectations. Work may lack consistency or require more frequent and closer supervision than normally expected. Attitude or attendance may affect performance.

Unsatisfactory (U) Performance does not meet minimum expectations. This may include below standard performance, lack of ability, lack of application, or disruptions in the workplace. After a final warning and if performance does not improve, the employee will be terminated.

PERFORMANCE RATING FACTORS (Use additional paper if necessary) ——————————————————

Specific Responsibilities and Duties _____	(C)	(G)	(NI)	(U)
1.				
2.				
3.				

PERFORMANCE RATING FACTORS (Continued) — (NA) Does Not Apply (S) Satisfactory (NI) Needs Improvement (U) Unsatisfactory

General Responsibilities and Requirements _____	(NA)	(S)	(NI)	(U)
1. Cooperation. Ability to demonstrate a spirit of willingness and interest when working with superior(s) and co-workers.				
2. Supervision. Ability to direct, control and train subordinates. Also consider degree to which assistants are helped to establish work objectives.				
3. Time Management. Ability to organize time effectively. Also consider ability to set priorities, anticipate problems, estimate time requirements, and meet deadlines.				
4. Communication. Ability to explain, convince and be understood in oral and written communications with employees at all levels. Also consider evidence of an understanding of people's views and of the effect of own actions on others.				
5. Judgment and Initiative. Ability to identify and appropriately solve or refer problems. Willingness to expand responsibilities.				
6. Attendance. Attendance and timeliness meet acceptable standards. Days Absent _____ Days Late _____				

FIGURE 5–2 Performance appraisal form.

three outstanding workers can be at the top of the list even though all three deserve it.

These limitations make the ranking technique a crude measure of performance appraisal. It is usually applied only when a small number of workers are involved and when little information is desired beyond an indication of their relative standing.

COMPLETE THIS SECTION

Principal Strengths _____

Areas for Development _____

Comments: _____

_____

Overall Performance Rating: ☐ Commendable   ☐ Good   ☐ Needs Improvement   ☐ Unsatisfactory

Last Performance Review: ☐ Exceptional   ☐ Commendable   ☐ Good   ☐ Needs Improvement   ☐ Unsatisfactory

Date _____

Evaluated by (Name/Title): _____   _____   _____
                                    Please print   Signature   Date

    Signature of Reviewer: _____   _____
                                                                      Date

    Signature of Employee: _____   _____
                                                                      Date

Note: Employee's comments, if any, should be attached to this form.

FIGURE 5–2   *Continued*

Paired-Comparison Technique. The **paired-comparison technique** requires that each worker be compared with every other worker in the work group or section. It is similar to ranking, and the result is a rank ordering of workers, but the comparative judgments are more systematic and controlled. Comparisons are made between two people at a time, and a judgment is made about which of the pair is superior.

> **Paired-comparison technique** A performance appraisal technique that compares the performance of each worker with that of every other worker in the group.

If specific characteristics are to be rated, the comparisons are repeated for each item. When all possible comparisons have been made, an objective ranked list is obtained that is based on the worker's score in each comparison. If a supervisor evaluates six workers by this technique, comparing each worker with every other worker, 15 paired comparisons must be made because there are 15 possible pairs. The following formula is used (*N* represents the number of persons to be evaluated):

$$\frac{N(N-1)}{2}$$

An advantage of the paired-comparison approach over the ranking technique is that the judgmental process is simpler. The supervisor has to consider only one pair of workers at a time. Another advantage is that it is possible to give the same rank to those of equal ability.

A disadvantage lies in the large number of comparisons required when dealing with many employees. A supervisor with 60 employees would be required to make 1,770 comparisons. If the performance evaluation calls for the appraisal of, say, five separate traits or factors, each of the 1,770 comparisons would have to be made five times. The use of the technique is necessarily restricted to small groups or to a single ranking of overall job effectiveness.

Forced-distribution technique A performance appraisal technique in which supervisors rate employees according to a prescribed distribution of ratings, similar to grading on a curve.

Forced-Distribution Technique.   The **forced-distribution technique** is useful with somewhat larger groups. Supervisors rate their employees in fixed proportions, according to a predetermined distribution of ratings. The standard distribution is as follows:

Superior	10%
Better than average	20%
Average	40%
Below average	20%
Poor	10%

If your college instructors grade on a curve, then you are already familiar with forced distribution. The top 10 percent of the class receives a grade of A, regardless of their specific test scores. The next 20 percent receives Bs, and so on, until all grades are forced into the categories of the distribution resembling the normal curve.

A disadvantage of the forced-distribution technique is that it compels a supervisor to use predetermined rating categories that might not fairly represent that particular group of workers. All workers in a group may be better than average or superior in job performance, and all deserve good ratings. However, the forced-distribution technique dictates that only 30 percent can be rated as above average.

Forced-Choice Technique.   One difficulty with the merit rating techniques we have discussed is that raters are aware of whether they are assigning good or poor ratings to employees. This knowledge may permit their personal biases, animosities, or favoritism to affect the ratings. The **forced-choice technique** prevents raters from knowing how favorable or unfavorable the ratings they are giving their employees are.

Forced-choice technique A performance appraisal technique in which raters are presented with groups of descriptive statements and are asked to select the phrase in each group that is most descriptive or least descriptive of the worker being evaluated.

In the forced-choice technique, raters are presented with groups of descriptive statements and are asked to select the phrase in each group that best describes an employee or is least applicable to that employee. The phrases within each group are designed to appear equally positive or equally negative. For example, raters may be asked to choose one statement in each of the following pairs that best describes a subordinate.

Is reliable
Is agreeable

Is careful
Is diligent

Next, raters may be asked to select one statement in each of these pairs that least describes the subordinate.

Is arrogant
Is not interested in working well

Is uncooperative
Is sloppy in his/her work habits

When given a number of sets of statements, it is difficult for supervisors to distinguish the items that represent desirable or undesirable characteristics. Therefore, they are less likely to deliberately assign favorable or unfavorable ratings.

When I-O psychologists develop statements for forced-choice rating scales, they correlate each item with a measure of job success. Although the statements in each pair may appear to be equally favorable or unfavorable, they have been found to discriminate between more efficient and less efficient workers.

Although the forced-choice technique limits the effect of personal bias and controls for deliberate distortion, it has several disadvantages and is unpopular with raters. Considerable research is necessary to determine the predictive validity for each item. Thus, the technique is more costly to develop than other merit rating methods. The instructions can be difficult to understand, and the task of choosing between similar alternatives in a large number of pairs is tedious. ⟶

Behaviorally Anchored Rating Scales (BARS). **Behaviorally anchored rating scales (BARS)** attempt to evaluate job performance in terms of specific behaviors that are important to success or failure on the job rather than in terms of general attitudes or factors such as communications skills, cooperation, or common sense. The usual way to develop behavioral criteria is through the critical-incidents technique described in Chapter 3 as a method of job analysis.

Supervisors familiar with the job observe the performance of their workers and note those behaviors necessary for effective job performance. A series of critical-incident behaviors are established, some associated with superior performance and others with unsatisfactory performance. These behaviors, based on actual job behaviors, are used as standards for appraising worker effectiveness.

The BARS items can be scored objectively by indicating whether the employee displays that behavior or by selecting on a scale the degree to which the employee displays that behavior. Figure 5–3 shows a BARS for the position of Superman or Wonder Woman, though there are not many applicants for those jobs.

Much of the success of the BARS approach depends on the observational skill of the supervisors in identifying behaviors that are truly critical to successful or unsuccessful performance on the job. If the list of critical incidents is inadequate, any performance appraisal based on these behaviors may be misleading. In some applications of the BARS technique, behaviors are listed in terms of expectations; in this instance, the instrument is called a behavioral expectation scale (BES). One advantage of BARS and BES approaches to performance appraisal is that

Behaviorally anchored rating scales (BARS) A performance appraisal technique in which appraisers rate critical employee behaviors.

Degree of Performance					
Area of Performance	Far Excels Job Requirements	Exceeds Job Requirements	Meets Job Requirements	Needs Improvement	Does Not Meet Minimum Requirements
Quality of work	Leaps tall buildings in a single bound	Leaps tall buildings with running start	Can leap over houses, if prodded	Often stumbles into buildings	Is often knocked down by buildings
Promptness	Is faster than a speeding bullet	Is as fast as a speeding bullet	Would you believe a slow bullet?	Misfires frequently	Wounds self when handling a gun
Initiative	Is stronger than a locomotive	Is as strong as a bull elephant	Almost as strong as a bull	Shoots the bull	Smells like a bull
Adaptability	Walks on water	Strong swimmer	A good water treader	Favorite haunt is the water cooler	Passes water in emergencies
Communication	Talks with God	Talks with the angels	Talks to self	Argues with self	Loses most of these arguments

FIGURE 5–3 A satirical example of a behaviorally anchored rating scale (BARS).

In an MBO program, managers and employees meet to set goals and, later, to review the extent to which those goals were met.

they meet federal fair employment guidelines. The criteria on which workers are assessed are job related because they derive from actual job behaviors.

Behavioral observation scales (BOS) A performance appraisal technique in which appraisers rate the frequency of critical employee behaviors.

Behavioral Observation Scales (BOS).

In the **behavioral observation scale (BOS)** approach to performance appraisal, employees are also evaluated in terms of critical incidents. In that respect, it is similar to BARS. However, the BOS appraisers rate subordinates on the *frequency* of the critical incidents as they are observed to occur over a given period. The ratings are assigned on a five-point scale. The evaluation yields a total score for each employee, obtained by adding the ratings for each critical incident.

The behavioral incidents for the rating scale are developed in the same way as for BARS, through identification by supervisors or other subject matter experts. Similarly, BOS techniques meet equal employment opportunity guidelines because they are related to actual behaviors required for successful job performance.

I-O psychology research comparing BARS and BOS techniques has been inconclusive. Some studies demonstrate the superiority of one technique over the other; other studies fail to confirm these findings.

Management by Objectives (MBO)

Management by objectives (MBO) A performance appraisal technique that involves a mutual agreement between employee and manager on goals to be achieved in a given period.

Management by objectives (MBO) involves a mutual agreement between employees and managers on goals to be achieved in a given time period. Instead of focusing on abilities or traits as in merit rating, or on job behaviors as in BARS and BOS, management by objectives focuses on results—on how well employees accomplish specified goals. The emphasis is on what employees do rather than on what their supervisors think of them or perceive their behaviors to be. Further, MBO actively involves employees in their own evaluations. They are not simply graded or rated by others.

MBO consists of two phases: goal setting and performance review. In goal setting, employees meet individually with supervisors to determine the goals for which they will strive in the time before the next appraisal, usually one year, and to discuss ways of reaching those goals. The goals must be realistic, specific, and as objective as possible. For example, it is not enough for salespersons to say that they will try to sell more products. A fixed number of items or a dollar volume must be established as the goal.

In performance review, employees and supervisors discuss the extent to which the goals were met. Again, this is a mutual process involving both parties. The performance appraisal is based on job results, not on characteristics such as initiative or general skills.

Employees in MBO programs may feel pressured to set higher goals with each appraisal to show evidence of improvement. A supervisor may not accept last year's quota as a sufficient goal for this year's job performance. Thus, the goals may become increasingly unrealistic. Also, MBO is not useful for jobs that cannot be quantified. It would be silly to expect research chemists to agree to make five more scientific breakthroughs this year than last.

The MBO technique satisfies fair employment guidelines and has been found to be effective in increasing employee motivation and productivity.

PERFORMANCE APPRAISAL FOR MANAGERS

The performance appraisal of managerial personnel presents problems not faced in the assessment of other employees. Merit rating techniques are often used to evaluate low- and middle-level managerial personnel, but additional appraisal methods are required. Paradoxically, senior executives are rarely evaluated. They seldom receive feedback or judgments about the quality of their job performance unless the company faces a crisis. Indeed, high-level management failure is sometimes rewarded with generous severance packages. Interviews with top executives have shown that at higher levels of management, performance reviews are less systematic and informative.

Evaluation Techniques

Assessment Centers.   Assessment centers (discussed in Chapter 3 as an employee selection technique) are a popular method of performance appraisal. Managers participate in simulated job tasks such as management games, group problem solving, leaderless group discussions, in-basket tests, and interviews. Recall that assessment centers do not assess actual job behavior but rather a variety of activities that are like those encountered on the job. Assessment-center evaluations appear to have high validity when used for performance appraisal purposes.

Evaluation by Superiors.   The most frequently used technique for the performance appraisal of managers is assessment by their superiors in the organization. Standard rating sheets are rarely used. Typically, the rater writes a brief descriptive essay about the person's job performance. An evaluation by an immediate superior is often supplemented by the judgments of executives at higher levels.

Evaluation by Colleagues: Peer Rating.   **Peer rating** was developed in the 1940s. It is a technique for having managers or executives at the same level assess one another in terms of their general ability to perform the job and their specific traits and behaviors. Although ratings given by peers and colleagues tend to be higher than ratings assigned by superiors, research shows a positive correlation between high peer ratings and subsequent promotion. However, peer ratings show a lower interrater reliability than do ratings by supervisors (Viswesvaran, Schmidt, & Ones, 2003).

Attitudes toward peer rating among managers are generally positive. However, managers are far more favorable toward peer rating when the evaluations

Peer rating A performance appraisal technique in which managers or executives at the same level assess one another's abilities and job behaviors.

are used for career development or improving job skills than when they are used for promotion or other career decisions.

Self-Evaluation.   Another approach to managerial performance appraisal is to ask people to assess their own abilities and job performance. One technique is similar to MBO, discussed earlier in this chapter. Managers and their superiors meet to establish goals for managerial performance—not specific production targets but personal skills to be developed or deficiencies to be corrected. After a time, the managers meet again with their superiors to discuss their progress.

Self-ratings A performance appraisal technique in which managers assess their own abilities and job performance.

Self-ratings tend to be higher than evaluations by superiors and to show greater leniency. Self-ratings also focus more on interpersonal skills, whereas ratings by superiors emphasize initiative and specific job skills. Leniency can be reduced if raters are told that their self-evaluations will be validated against more objective criteria.

A study of 1,888 managers at a large accounting firm compared self-ratings and subordinate ratings collected twice during a one-year period. Those managers who rated themselves much higher than their subordinates did tended to show improvement in their own job performance over time. Those managers who rated themselves lower than their subordinates did tended to show a decline in job performance. These results suggested to the researchers that self-ratings can have a motivating effect for people who tend to overestimate their job performance (Johnson & Ferstl, 1999).

In another study each of 110 supervisors in a state law-enforcement agency was rated on leadership ability by at least two subordinates. The supervisors who received feedback on these ratings later lowered their self-ratings. Supervisors who received no feedback did not change their self-ratings. The researchers concluded that the feedback from subordinates influenced the supervisors' view of their leadership ability (Atwater, Waldman, Atwater, & Cartier, 2000).

Evaluation by Subordinates.   Another approach to the performance appraisal of managers involves evaluation by subordinates, as used in the studies just described. The technique, sometimes described as upward feedback, is similar to having students evaluate their classroom instructors.

Upward feedback is effective in developing and improving leadership abilities. In one global corporation, more than 1,500 employees completed two behavioral observation scales six months apart to rate 238 managers. Managers who received top scores in the first rating did not show improvement at the second rating; they were already seen to be performing well. Managers who received moderate to low ratings initially did show improved leadership effectiveness by the second rating. Thus, the managers who needed to improve did so, most likely in response to the upward feedback from subordinates (Reilly, Smither, & Vasilopoulos, 1996).

Another study showing that subordinates' ratings lead to improved job performance involved 252 bank managers. In research conducted over a five-year period, psychologists found that managers who received poor to moderate ratings from subordinates at the beginning of the period showed far more improvement in subsequent ratings than managers who received higher initial ratings. Managers who met with subordinates to discuss their ratings improved more than managers who did not meet with subordinates (Walker & Smither, 1999).

A study of 454 managers at a telecommunications firm found that ratings by subordinates were significantly more reliable when the results were used for

Rating Your Boss: No Names, Please!

You know the drill. About every six months, your boss calls you in for a chat about how you're doing at your job. It's called a performance appraisal. You sit there, perhaps seething inside, while the boss tells you what you're doing wrong and how you could improve. And you're thinking how you'd like to tell the boss a thing or two about how he or she is doing.

Nowadays some employees can talk back. Growing numbers of companies are asking workers to participate in an upward feedback appraisal process—that is, to appraise the performance of their supervisors and managers. These appraisals or ratings are then used to help determine promotions and pay raises for the boss. Does this sound great? A chance to get back at the supervisor? Maybe get that obnoxious guy fired? But suppose you had to sign your name to the appraisal? Would that affect your comments? Most likely it would, unless, of course, you had already lined up another job.

To test this hypothesis, a management professor at the University of Wisconsin asked 183 employees at an insurance company to rate 38 managers. The employees were all volunteers for the task and were told that the managers would take no reprisals, regardless of what the employees reported. To further reassure the employees, they were given the phone number of a contact in the human resources department whom they could call in the event of any backlash.

Half the employees in the study appraised their bosses anonymously. The other half signed their names to the evaluation form. Did the act of identifying themselves make a difference in the ratings? You bet it did! Employees who signed their names to the appraisal forms gave higher ratings to their managers than did the employees who were doing the ratings anonymously. All employees reported that they would feel much more comfortable rating their bosses if they could remain anonymous.

Upward feedback can be an effective tool for improving manager effectiveness. Just don't sign your name to the form.

Source: D. Antonioni (1994). The effects of feedback accountability on upward appraisal ratings. *Personnel Psychology, 47,* 349–356.

developmental purposes than when they were used for administrative purposes (Greguras, Robie, Schleicher, & Goff, 2003).

360-Degree Feedback

Another approach to performance appraisal involves combining evaluations from several sources into an overall appraisal. Any number of individual ratings sources can be so combined, but the ultimate multisource approach is called 360-degree feedback. It combines the full circle of ratings from all sources—superiors, subordinates, peers, and self, and even evaluations by the organization's customers or clients who have dealings with the person being rated.

Multisource feedback can provide information that would not otherwise be available about the ratees because it provides data from unique perspectives. For example, subordinates and peers have different experiences and relationships with their managers than do the managers' bosses. Multisource feedback may also reduce many forms of bias. If all parties are told that their ratings will be compared with those assigned by others, they are likely to be more objective in their assessments. When combined ratings are consistent, decisions about a manager's future with the organization can be made with greater confidence. Also, if ratings show a high level of agreement, a manager may be more willing to accept criticism because it comes from sources other than the immediate supervisor. When ratings disagree, however, the manager may be reluctant to accept and act on criticism.

In a study conducted in Australia, 63 managers participated in an assessment-center exercise, after which their performance was rated by their supervisors, peers, and subordinates. In addition, each manager rated his or her own performance. Self-ratings were found to be negatively related to assessment-center performance. In other words, managers who rated themselves as having done very well in the assessment-center exercise had actually performed poorly. Peers also tended to overestimate the performance of those who had done poorly. Only supervisor ratings showed a high positive correlation with assessment-center performance. In this example, then, self-ratings, peer ratings, and subordinate ratings did not accurately reflect performance (Atkins & Wood, 2002).

Similar results were obtained from a study of 1,883 managers working for a large U.S. utility company. The managers submitted self-ratings and were also rated by 2,773 subordinates, 12,779 peers, and 3,049 supervisors. The results showed that multisource ratings were not in agreement. Self-ratings were the least discriminating and correlated poorly with the other rating sources (Facteau & Craig, 2001).

A group of 21 bank managers was rated by peers and subordinates before attending a seven-hour feedback workshop on how to influence the behavior of other people. During the workshop the managers were shown the ratings they had received, along with advice about how to interpret that feedback and how to improve their influence tactics. The feedback from peers and subordinates appeared to be effective. Managers who received the feedback significantly increased their use of influence behaviors when compared to managers in a control group who had received no feedback (Seifert, Yukl, & McDonald, 2003).

The use of 360-degree feedback is more costly than appraisals from a single source, but the approach is growing in popularity. Surveys show that 360-degree feedback is already in use in nearly all of the Fortune 500 companies. Despite its popularity, there is, as we noted, little research evidence showing that it is effective. Although studies show that both managers and employees like this type of appraisal, sufficient data to support its use are not yet available.

BIAS IN PERFORMANCE APPRAISAL

Regardless of the sophistication of the techniques used, performance appraisal still involves one person judging, assessing, or estimating the characteristics and performance of another. This inevitably means that human biases and prejudices affect the judgments. Some common sources of error that can distort performance appraisals include the halo effect, constant or systematic bias, most-recent-performance error, inadequate information error, average rating or leniency error, the rater's cognitive processes, the rater's personality, and role conflict.

The Halo Effect

The **halo effect** involves the familiar tendency to judge all aspects of a person's behavior or character on the basis of a single attribute. For example, if we find a person to be physically attractive, we may tend to think of that person also as friendly, likable, and easy to get along with, generalizing from one attribute to personality characteristics and other abilities. A supervisor who scores an employee high on one factor of a merit rating scale may tend to grade that person high on all other factors. This distortion is particularly likely to occur when a high rating is given on one or two traits and the other traits to be rated are difficult to observe, unfamiliar, or not clearly defined.

One way to control for the halo effect is to have more than one person rate a worker, on the assumption that any personal biases will tend to cancel each other out. Another way is to have supervisors rate all subordinates on one trait or characteristic at a time instead of rating each person on all items at once. When workers are judged on a single characteristic, there is a smaller chance for one rating to carry over to other traits.

I-O psychology research suggests that the halo error may be less a problem than previously thought. The halo effect does not appear to diminish the overall quality of ratings; often cannot be detected; and may, in many cases, be illusory. Of course, there are some people who truly are outstanding in all their attributes. In these cases, generalizing from one quality to others is not an error but a simple observation of fact.

Other Sources of Error

Constant or Systematic Bias.   **Constant bias** as a source of performance appraisal error has its basis in the standards or criteria used by raters. Some raters or supervisors expect more than others from their employees. Similarly, in college some professors are known as easy graders and expect less from their students than those known as hard graders. The constant biasing error means that a top rating given by one supervisor may not be equivalent to a top rating given by another supervisor, just as an A from one professor may not mean the same as an A from another professor as an evaluation of merit or ability.

Constant bias can be corrected by requiring supervisors to distribute ratings in accordance with the normal curve. However, as we noted with the forced distribution technique, this means that some workers will receive ratings that are undeserved.

Most-Recent-Performance Error.   Performance appraisals are usually made every six or 12 months. There is an understandable tendency to base ratings on the workers' most recent behavior, without considering their performance throughout the entire rating period since the last appraisal. It is natural for memory to be clearer about events that have occurred more recently, but recent behavior may be atypical or distorted by extraneous factors.

Halo effect The tendency to judge all aspects of a person's behavior or character on the basis of a single attribute.

Constant bias A source of error in performance appraisal based on the different standards used by raters.

For example, if a worker performs poorly in the weeks just before an evaluation because of illness or marital problems, the results may overshadow a previous record of exemplary job performance. If a worker is aware that a performance evaluation is due, he or she may strive to work more efficiently just before the rating. In both cases, performance is not typical of the workers' overall job behavior, and a falsely low or high rating will result.

Most-recent-performance error A source of error in performance appraisal in which a rater tends to evaluate a worker's most recent job behavior rather than behavior throughout the period since the last appraisal.

One way to reduce this **most-recent-performance error** is to require more frequent appraisals. By shortening the time between performance reviews, there is less of a tendency for supervisors to forget a worker's usual behavior. Making supervisors aware of the possibility that this type of error can occur can also be effective in reducing it.

Inadequate Information Error.   Supervisors are required to rate employees at specified intervals whether or not they know enough about the employees to do so fairly and accurately. To admit to superiors that they lack adequate knowledge of their subordinates can be construed as a personal failing. The resulting appraisals will be worth little to the organization or to the employees because they will not be based on a comprehensive knowledge of worker behavior.

Inadequate information error A source of error in performance appraisal in which supervisors rate their subordinates even though they may not know enough about them to do so fairly and accurately.

A way to deal with this **inadequate information error** is to educate raters about the value of performance appraisals and the harm done by ratings based on incomplete information. Supervisors should be given the opportunity to decline to rate employees about whom they have little knowledge and the assurance that they will not be penalized for such refusal.

Average Rating or Leniency Error.   Some raters are reluctant to assign extreme scores in either direction. The tendency is to be lenient and to assign average ratings to all workers. Particularly when dealing with a small number of employees, it is not unusual to find their ratings clustered around the middle of the scale, separated by no more than one or two points. Thus, the range of abilities indicated is restricted, and the ratings are so close that it is difficult to distinguish between good and poor workers. This **average rating error** does not reflect the range of differences that exist among workers, and the ratings provide no useful information to the company or to employees. The challenge for employers is to identify the raters who show this tendency and to take it into consideration when making personnel decisions based on their appraisals of subordinates.

Average rating error A source of error in performance appraisal in which a rater is unwilling to assign very good or very poor ratings. Consequently, most ratings fall in the middle of the rating scale.

Cognitive Processes.   The cognitive or thought processes of raters underlie their judgments of worker effectiveness. We discuss four cognitive variables that can influence evaluations of employee performance: category structures, beliefs, interpersonal affect, and attribution.

1. *Category structures.* The category structures that managers use in evaluating their employees can affect their assessments. When an appraiser thinks about a worker as belonging to a particular category, the information he or she recalls about that worker will be biased toward that category. For example, if an employee is perceived to be a team player, then this becomes a category in the rater's mental picture. The employee's job performance will likely be observed, interpreted, and remembered in terms of how a typical team player is expected to behave rather than in terms of how that employee actually behaves.

2. *Beliefs.* A related cognitive variable that can influence performance appraisals involves raters' beliefs about human nature. These ideas can lead raters to make evaluations in terms of how they view people in general rather than in terms of a specific worker's characteristics and behaviors. For example, supervisors who believe that people are basically good and trustworthy give more generous ratings than those who think that people are spiteful and narrow-minded. Managers who accept the idea of individual differences among people and who are tolerant of those differences may give different ratings from managers who believe most people are alike.

3. *Interpersonal affect.* The cognitive variable of **interpersonal affect** refers to one person's feelings or emotions toward another person. Common sense suggests that, except for those raters who can maintain impartiality and objectivity toward their subordinates, ratings will be influenced by the personal relationship between rater and ratee. In general, raters who have positive emotions or affect toward the persons they are rating give higher marks than do raters who have negative affect. Simply stated, we tend to be more lenient, forgiving, and generous toward people we like.

4. *Attribution.* The concept of **attribution** derives from social psychology research on the way we form impressions of other people. In performance appraisal, one person forms an impression of the abilities and characteristics of another. The rater mentally attributes or assigns reasons to the worker's behavior. These beliefs about why an employee behaves in a particular way can affect the rater's evaluation. For example, a supervisor may observe that two employees frequently seem tired. That supervisor may be lenient and understanding toward the tired employee who has young children but less forgiving of the tired employee who is known to enjoy late-night partying.

Attribution can also be influenced by interpersonal affect. Managers may attribute poor job performance to internal factors, such as lack of motivation or inadequate skills, when they dislike (have negative affect toward) the

Interpersonal affect Our feelings or emotions toward another person. In performance appraisal, the emotional tone of the relationship between manager and employee, whether positive or negative, can influence the assigned ratings.

Attribution A source of error in performance appraisal in which raters attribute or assign positive or negative explanations to an employee's behavior.

person being rated. In other words, the managers appear to believe that the poor performance of the workers they do not like is the fault of the workers themselves. On the other hand, the poor performance of workers they do like may be attributed to external factors such as bad luck, a heavy work-load, or equipment failure.

The attribution error can be reduced by having supervisors spend time performing the job they are evaluating. This experience exposes them to the kinds of external factors that can influence job performance. Raters should also be made aware of how their perceptions of a worker's behavior on the job can differ from the worker's own point of view.

Personality.   It seems obvious that our personality can influence the way we judge or evaluate other people, not only in the workplace, but in all areas of life. For example, a person who is vindictive or hostile toward others will view people differently from someone who is caring and compassionate. Consider the characteristic of self-monitoring. We noted in Chapter 3 that self-monitoring refers to the way people act to control the image of themselves that they choose to display in public. High self-monitors present themselves in whatever way they believe best fits the social situation around them. Low self-monitors stay more true to their own nature and behave generally the same way in all situations.

A study of 210 people employed in government, manufacturing, or service jobs, all of whom had experience in giving performance evaluations, found that high self-monitors gave significantly more lenient and less accurate ratings than did low self-monitors. The researcher suggested that high self-monitors may thus be trying to avoid the disapproval of others. Nevertheless, this provides an example of how one facet of personality can influence the performance evaluation process (Jawahar, 2001).

Other research involved more than 500 rater-ratee pairs employed by an insurance company who were asked to assign peer ratings to one another. The results showed that when both members of the pair had scored high on the personality dimension of conscientiousness, the ratings they gave each other were significantly higher than those of pairs low on conscientiousness. In this case, the degree of personality similarity between rater and ratee influenced the subsequent evaluations (Antonioni & Park, 2001).

Role conflict A situation that arises when there is a disparity between job demands and the employee's personal standards.

Role Conflict.   A final source of error in the performance appraisal process is the amount of role conflict experienced by the supervisor. **Role conflict** refers to the disparity or contradiction between the job's demands and the supervisor's standards of right and wrong. Sometimes the nature of a job requires supervisors to compromise those standards (we shall see in Chapter 12 that role conflict is a source of job stress). Supervisors high in role conflict tend to give higher-than-justified performance evaluations for several reasons: as a way of establishing control over the work situation, as a way of avoiding the confrontation with subordinates that might result from giving them lower ratings, or as a way of obtaining subordinates' gratitude and goodwill.

Whatever the reasons, it is clear from this and similar research that role conflict, and the stress associated with it, may lead supervisors to give higher-than-justified performance ratings. Managers may inflate performance appraisals as a way of satisfying personal needs and dealing with organizational pressures.

HOW TO IMPROVE PERFORMANCE APPRAISALS

The fact that performance appraisals can be so easily biased is no reason to abandon hope of achieving more objective evaluations. We have noted various steps that can be taken to reduce some sources of error. Providing training and feedback to raters, and allowing subordinates to participate, can also decrease errors, increase accuracy, and promote satisfaction with the evaluation process.

Training.   Training the persons who conduct performance appraisals involves (1) creating an awareness that abilities and skills are usually distributed in accordance with the normal curve, so that it is acceptable to find broad differences within a group of workers, and (2) developing the ability to define objective criteria for worker behaviors—the standards or average performance levels against which workers can be compared. I-O psychology research supports the idea that rater training can reduce errors in performance appraisal, particularly leniency and halo. Further, the more actively the raters are involved in the training process, the greater the positive effects. Having raters participate in group discussions and in practice sessions to provide feedback to subordinates generally produces better results than having raters attend lectures about the rating process.

Providing Feedback to Raters.   Providing feedback to raters can also improve performance appraisal. In a now-classic study, marketing managers in a large high-tech company received feedback from trained raters about the evaluations those managers had given their subordinates. The feedback included information about how each manager's ratings differed from the ratings given by other managers. When these marketing managers evaluated their subordinates a year later, they assigned lower ratings than did a control group of marketing managers who had received no feedback about their earlier ratings. More than 90 percent of the managers in the experimental group said that the feedback had influenced their second set of ratings. The researchers concluded that the feedback had reduced the leniency error (Davis & Mount, 1984).

Subordinate Participation.   Allowing employees to participate in the evaluation of their own job performance has been shown to lead to improvements in the appraisal process. In a study of 529 production workers and their supervisors, employees were asked to complete self-appraisal forms and to meet with their supervisors to reconcile discrepancies between self-ratings and supervisor ratings. The researchers found that employee participation led to a significant improvement in employee trust in management and to an enhanced perception of the accuracy of the performance evaluation system (Mayer & Davis, 1999).

Other research has confirmed that allowing employees to have a say in how their job performance is assessed significantly increases satisfaction with and acceptance of the organization's performance appraisal system. Employee participation also leads to a heightened belief in the fairness and usefulness of the appraisal process and to an increase in motivation to improve job performance.

THE POSTAPPRAISAL INTERVIEW

We have noted that two goals of performance appraisal programs are to supply information to management for personnel decisions and to diagnose strengths and weaknesses of employees and provide them with the means for self-improvement. To fulfill the second goal, the job performance ratings and the recommendations of the appraisers must be communicated to the employees.

Offering Feedback.   Offering feedback to employees is usually accomplished during a postappraisal interview between worker and supervisor, a situation that can easily become antagonistic, even hostile, especially when a performance evaluation contains criticism. Negative feedback during a postappraisal interview can make employees angry and lead them to reject any criticism or suggestions. Employees may attempt to shift the blame for alleged deficiencies in job performance by dismissing the usefulness of the appraisal, downgrading the importance of the job, or criticizing the supervisor.

A meta-analysis of 131 studies showed that postappraisal information provided by computer instead of in a personal interview with a supervisor was considered more desirable by the employee and was more effective in improving job performance. Apparently, eliminating the face-to-face interview situation reduced any personal antagonism between worker and supervisor that might otherwise have interfered with the employee's acceptance of criticism (DeNisi & Kluger, 2000).

Not all workers will benefit from feedback, no matter how it is presented. This was demonstrated in a study of 329 tellers in a large international bank in Hong Kong. The difference in how they responded to feedback from their performance evaluations was found to depend on their level of negative affectivity. Employees high in negative affectivity tended to be cynical and distrustful and to dwell on negative rather than positive work experiences. In addition, among the bank

Positive feedback during the postappraisal interview can lead to improvements in job performance.

tellers who received high ratings, job satisfaction and organizational commitment increased for those who had scored low in negative affectivity. Feedback about high ratings did not lead to similar increases in workers who had scored high in negative affectivity (Lam, Yik, & Schaubroeck, 2002).

A one-year study of 176 managers showed that those who received favorable upward feedback from their subordinates tended to improve their job performance more than did those who received unfavorable upward feedback. Those who received negative evaluations from subordinates tended to show a decline in their job performance (Smither & Walker, 2004).

Reaction to Criticism.   The primary purpose of the postappraisal interview is to stimulate employees to improve their job performance. This expectation may be wishful thinking. Some workers, when criticized, will act to exaggerate their faults—coming to work late or showing sloppy work habits—as an imagined means of revenge. If workers are told that they request assistance too frequently, they may stop doing so and, as a result, make more mistakes. In such cases criticism can lead to reduced motivation and job performance.

It may also be unrealistic to expect that a brief meeting every six or 12 months will provide sufficient impetus for employees to change. In addition, it may be unwise to believe that supervisors, unless they are specially trained, possess the insight and skill to diagnose the reasons for a worker's unsatisfactory job performance and to prescribe a program for improvement.

If feedback on employee performance were provided more frequently and competently and not restricted to the formal postappraisal interview, then employee motivation to change job behavior and to persist in that behavior could be enhanced.

Improving Postappraisal Interviews.   Despite the limitations and problems of postappraisal interviews, they can be structured to fulfill the purposes for which they are intended. I-O psychology research has identified several factors related to successful postappraisal interviews. Employees are more likely to be satisfied with postappraisal interviews and to follow their supervisors' suggestions about improving job performance under the following conditions:

1. Employees should be allowed to participate actively in the appraisal process.
2. The postappraisal interviewer should adopt a positive, constructive, and supportive attitude.
3. The interviewer should focus on specific job problems rather than on the employee's personal characteristics.
4. The employee and the supervisor should establish jointly specific goals to be achieved in the period before the next appraisal.
5. The employee should be given the opportunity to question, challenge, and rebut the evaluation without fear of retribution.
6. Discussions of changes in salary and rank should be linked directly to the performance appraisal criteria.

PERFORMANCE APPRAISAL: A POOR RATING?

Performance appraisal may be one of the least popular features of modern organizational life. The general attitude toward performance appraisal is "Oh, gosh, it's appraisal time again. I suppose we had better do it. But what the hell are we doing it for?" A survey of human resources managers found that 90 percent of them were dissatisfied with the performance appraisal system in their organizations. When asked what they would like to change, many said they would eliminate the programs entirely. Some executives express such a high level of dissatisfaction with performance appraisal that they no longer use the term; they call the process "performance management" instead (Toegel & Conger, 2003).

Why do performance appraisal programs get such a poor rating? We have already discussed the opportunities for personal bias and other errors to enter into the evaluations. Here are some additional reasons.

A Poor Rating from Managers.

Consider the person who must make the ratings or conduct the observations and appraisals. Despite a great deal of impressive research supporting the benefits of performance appraisals made by subordinates or peers, the fact remains that on the job, most performance ratings are made by managers or supervisors. Performance appraisal requires their considerable time and effort in addition to their other job duties. They must spend many hours observing subordinates to develop sufficient knowledge on which to base their assessments. They spend additional hours on paperwork, completing the appraisal forms, and yet more time in rater training programs.

In practice, some managers and supervisors resist appraisal programs and fill out the forms only when pressured by their superiors. Thus, the evaluations are often not thorough and systematic but are compiled in haste. Many supervisors loathe the idea of judging employees and taking responsibility for their progress in the organization, and therefore, they are reluctant to give low ratings, even for poor performance.

Further, supervisors may deliberately delay providing feedback, particularly when the evaluation is negative. Or they may inflate the ratings or suppress unfavorable information. By pretending that the employee is performing at a higher level than actual job performance justifies, the supervisor eliminates the potential for confrontation and reduces the negative impact of an unfavorable appraisal.

A Poor Rating from Employees.

Employees do not like performance appraisals, although most recognize that some means of evaluating job performance is necessary. They express concern about the effect of performance assessments on their career, apprehensive that a supervisor will use the appraisal to exaggerate misunderstandings or highlight personality clashes that have nothing to do with job competence. Employees are often not sufficiently informed about the criteria by which they are being judged or even precisely what is expected of them on the job. In addition, employees may be given low ratings for faults that lie within the organization or in the way jobs are structured. These are matters over which employees have no control but for which they may be blamed. In many organizations, the results of performance appraisal programs are never used to help make decisions about promotions or to help employees improve their skills, the major purposes for which such programs were developed. Performance appraisal as conducted in organizations today is largely unsatisfactory, which may help explain why correlations between ratings and results-oriented job performance criteria (such as sales and output data) are relatively low. However, assessments of employee ability at all levels of employment are necessary. The question is not whether to use an employee appraisal system but rather which is the most effective approach to use—and that question has yet to be answered.

Summary

Performance appraisal programs are used to validate selection criteria, determine the need for and success of training programs, improve employee behavior, determine promotions and pay raises, and identify employees with promotion potential. To ensure compliance with EEOC guidelines, performance appraisals must be based on job analyses, must focus on job behaviors rather than personal traits, and must be reviewed with the person being evaluated. Labor unions oppose performance appraisal because of their commitment to seniority as the basis for personnel decisions. Employees dislike performance appraisal because few of us like to be judged or criticized. Managers dislike making appraisals that will affect their subordinates' careers.

Performance appraisals may be objective or judgmental. Objective measures include quantity and quality of output; computer-aided appraisal; and data on accidents, salary, advancement, and absenteeism. Judgmental methods involve having supervisors assess their workers' ability to perform the job. These assessments are made by **merit rating** techniques, including rating, **ranking, paired-comparison, forced-distribution,** and **forced-choice** techniques that involve one person judging the abilities or characteristics of another. The **BARS** and **BOS** approaches to merit rating attempt to evaluate performance in terms of specific behaviors critical to success or failure on the job. BARS and BOS meet EEOC guidelines and can reduce rating errors. **Management by objectives (MBO)** involves mutual agreement between supervisors and subordinates about setting and achieving specific goals.

Evaluating managerial performance may be accomplished through assessment centers or evaluation by supervisors, colleagues (peers), subordinates, or **self-ratings.** Combining ratings into an overall appraisal **(360-degree feedback)** is especially popular.

Sources of rater error include the **halo effect, most-recent-performance error, inadequate information error, average rating error,** the rater's cognitive processes, the rater's personality, and **role conflict.** Three ways to improve performance appraisals are better training for raters, providing feedback to raters, and allowing subordinates to participate in their own ratings.

Performance appraisal results must be communicated to employees to provide them with information about their strengths and weaknesses. Feedback should be given with tact and sensitivity, particularly when criticism is involved, because it can lead to defensiveness and a decline in job performance. Feedback sessions should be informal and frequent and focus on specific goals. Workers should be allowed to participate freely in the discussions.

Key Terms

attribution
average rating (leniency) error
behavioral observation scales (BOS)
behaviorally anchored rating
    scales (BARS)
constant (systematic) bias
forced-choice technique
forced-distribution technique
halo effect
inadequate information error
interpersonal affect

management by objectives (MBO)
merit rating
most-recent-performance error
paired-comparison technique
peer rating
performance appraisal
ranking technique
rating scales
role conflict
self-ratings

1. Why do Equal Employment Opportunity Commission guidelines apply to performance appraisal programs?
2. What has I-O research learned about race and age bias in performance appraisal?
3. Discuss the purposes of performance appraisal. In other words, what are these programs used for?
4. Why do employees and managers both object to performance appraisal programs?
5. In evaluating performance on production jobs, what factors other than worker output should be considered? Why?
6. What are the advantages and disadvantages of computerized performance monitoring? How would you feel about having your work appraised in this way?
7. If you were a manager responsible for periodically evaluating the performance of your 23 subordinates, which merit rating technique would you most like to use? Which would you least like to use?
8. Describe advantages and disadvantages of the ranking technique, the paired-comparison technique, and the forced-choice technique.
9. How would you construct a behaviorally anchored rating scale for evaluating your employees?
10. How do behaviorally anchored rating scales and behavioral observation scales differ? Which provides more accurate information?
11. How does the management by objectives approach to performance appraisal work? Is it likely to increase or decrease employee motivation and job performance?
12. If you were a manager, would you want your job performance to be evaluated by your superior, your peers, your subordinates, or yourself? Explain the reasons for your choice.
13. What are the advantages and disadvantages of performance appraisals conducted by subordinates?
14. Discuss the results of research conducted on 360-degree feedback.
15. What is the halo effect? How might it influence the results of performance appraisals?
16. Distinguish among the following sources of error in performance evaluation: constant bias, most-recent-performance error, leniency error, and role conflict.
17. How can a rater's cognitive processes and personality influence the evaluations he or she makes?
18. In what ways can performance appraisals and the postappraisal interview be improved?
19. In your opinion, what changes to the performance appraisal process might make employees and managers more receptive to the idea of performance evaluation?

Arvey, R. D., & Murphy, K. R. (1998). Performance evaluation in work settings. *Annual Review of Psychology, 49,* 141–168. Reviews recent research on performance appraisal, including rating techniques, sources of bias, and rater training.

Ghorpade, J. (2000). Managing five paradoxes of 360-degree feedback. *Academy of Management Executive, 14*(1), 140–150. Notes the popularity of the 360-degree performance appraisal method in the Fortune 500 companies and discusses several problems relating to privacy, validity, and effectiveness. See also in the same issue, A. S. DeNisi and A. N. Kluger, "Feedback effectiveness: Can 360-degree appraisals be improved?"

Grote, D. (2002). *The performance appraisal question and answer book: A survival guide for managers.* New York: AMACOM. Covers most aspects of performance appraisal including planning, setting goals, execution, evaluation, review, and feedback. Also describes the development of appropriate performance appraisal forms.

London, M. (2003). *Job feedback: Giving, seeking, and using feedback for performance improvement* (2nd ed.). Mahwah, NJ: Erlbaum. Focuses on the benefits of feedback in terms of employee motivation, differences between positive and negative feedback (for example, focusing on specific behaviors rather than assigning blame), accuracy of self-assessments, how employees process feedback, and ways in which appraisers process information about their employees.

Walker, A. G., & Smither, J. W. (1999). A five-year study of upward feedback. *Personnel Psychology, 52,* 393–423. Tracks the improvement of managers and administrators as part of a performance appraisal program that included feedback from subordinates.

Chapter 6

Training and Development

THE SCOPE OF ORGANIZATIONAL TRAINING PROGRAMS

Hamburger University does not have a football team. What it does have is a 130,000-square-foot, state-of-the-art training facility with a faculty of 30 professors. Located in Oak Brook, Illinois, a suburb of Chicago, Hamburger U. was started more than 40 years ago by (who else?) McDonald's. Since then, more than 65,000 managers of the company's restaurants have graduated. In addition, Hamburger U. offers training for employees and franchise holders, who come from all over the world to attend courses. Classes are also given online in more than 20 languages. McDonald's has ten other training centers in countries such as England, Japan, Germany, and Australia. It's expensive, but management believes that the training it offers is one of the main reasons for the organization's success (Margulies, 2004).

Training is big business. "When I look at the money we spend on education and training," said a chemical company executive, "I wonder whether we're running a chemical business or a college." From the high school dropout to the college graduate, from the longtime unemployed to the high-level executive, millions of people today are participating in some form of organizational training in their workplace. Employers spend some $55 billion annually on formal training programs and another $180 billion on informal on-the-job instruction.

Training often begins at an elementary level teaching basic literacy and mathematics skills before offering instruction in specific job skills. When Motorola geared up to meet global competition by converting a plant to cellular technology, the company found that 60 percent of its workforce had difficulty doing simple arithmetic and reading and understanding English. Without remedial training in these skills, the employees could not be taught to perform their new jobs. Polaroid spent $700,000 to offer basic language and math instruction to 1,000 employees. Domino's Pizza teaches reading and math so that employees can follow instructions for making pizza dough.

Training for skilled high-tech jobs is a priority in industry, government, and the military. Aerospace, telecommunications, and Web-based industries rely heavily on reprogrammable robots, multifunctional machinery, and computer-assisted design and manufacturing equipment. The companies need a highly trained workforce to design, operate, and maintain this sophisticated equipment.

As we described in Chapter 1, the nature of work today has changed. We can no longer count on learning one job and keeping it until retirement. We must learn to think not of a single chosen career over a lifetime but of several careers during which we will master a cluster of skills that must be continually upgraded. Our careers require lifelong learning, which means that training has become even more vital today than it was for previous generations.

A Sample Training Program.   Let us describe a classic example of a high-level organizational training program. Western Electric Company established a company college, the Corporate Education Center, to provide instruction in engineering and management. The facility contained state-of-the-art equipment and offered more than 300 courses on a 190-acre campus, complete with dormitories.

Newly hired engineers participated in six-week orientation programs, one during the first six months of employment and a second during the next six months. Engineers were able to choose among various courses in their specialty areas, classes designed to keep them up to date. Supervisors could select courses to upgrade their technical knowledge and managerial skills. The center provided management training at several levels to persons with promotion potential, with courses ranging from planning and interdepartmental relations to urban affairs and industrial-organizational (I-O) psychology.

This ambitious venture is not unusual in American business. Training centers have been established by such organizations as IBM, Xerox, General Electric, and Avis Rent A Car. So, do not be surprised if, during your first month on the job and periodically throughout your career, you find yourself back in the classroom.

Training for Disabled Employees.   Many organizations provide specialized training for disabled employees. At McDonald's more than 9,000 workers with visual, hearing, orthopedic, or learning disabilities, or mental retardation, have been trained for various jobs at the company's fast-food restaurants. In an attempt to dispel stereotypes and to make all employees sensitive to the problems of being disabled, training is provided not only for the disabled employees, but also for the other employees who will be working with them. Over a ten-year period, more than 90 percent of the disabled persons who began training in a "McJobs" program completed it and became productive employees. The company believes that people with disabilities constitute a large pool of underused labor and is determined to train them to do whatever they are capable of doing.

New employees find themselves back in the classroom to learn about company policies and objectives.

Newsbreak

Employees Who Can't Read Directions

Cindy Marano forgot her glasses when she left her office to go to lunch, otherwise she would never have noticed it. Marano, who directs a job training program in Washington, D.C., could not read the menu posted on the wall of her local sandwich shop without her glasses. She asked the middle-aged woman behind the counter to read it to her. At first, the woman pretended not to hear; then she became flustered and rude before finally asking another waitress to read the menu aloud. "Suddenly, the light went on for me," Marano said. The woman was unable to read. And Marano knew, from her work with the job training program, that many of the 40 million Americans who have trouble reading and writing are able to fake it on the job and conceal their handicap, as the waitress had done.

Marano also knew how expensive employee illiteracy is, costing the American economy some $225 billion a year in lost productivity. Someone else very much aware of that cost is Peter Coors, CEO of Colorado's Coors Brewing Company. He calls employee illiteracy a crisis for American industry, and he has taken the lead in promoting corporate awareness and creating industry-based training programs to teach employees how to read.

With today's increasingly high-tech jobs, it is becoming harder to pretend you can read when you can't. Coors found that out when the company instituted a computerized inventory control system. The new system required forklift operators to punch information into a computer, and it soon became obvious that many of them could not do the job. Why? Because they could not recognize the letters on the computer keyboard or read the product codes on the items to be inventoried.

Even low-tech companies lose money to illiteracy. The Outback Steakhouse chain found that some of their cooks were mistakenly preparing more expensive instead of less expensive steaks because they could not read the waiters' orders. Outback started a training program to teach all employees a list of abbreviations, so that even workers for whom English was a new language could do their jobs without making costly mistakes. Other restaurant and fast-food chains use symbols instead of words on their computer screens.

Every company would operate more efficiently if all their employees could read. It would be better for the employees, too. Sharon Thomas, a 34-year-old high school dropout living in Washington was on welfare for 15 years, until she learned to read and was hired for a well-paid job in construction. "I had a lot of hurdles to get over," she said, "but once I was in the workforce, I was so happy. I feel good about myself."

Training and Fair Employment Practices. Organizational training programs may have an adverse impact on minority employees because performance in a training program is often used as a basis for career decisions about promotion, transfer, or dismissal. Any technique that results in personnel decisions has the potential for discriminating against ethnic minority, women, older, or disabled employees.

Therefore, training programs must meet equal employment opportunity guidelines and must be clearly related to job performance before their results can be applied to career decisions.

GOALS OF ORGANIZATIONAL TRAINING PROGRAMS

The first step in establishing a formal training program is the precise formulation of objectives. These objectives must be stated in terms of specific behavioral criteria, the acts or operations employees must perform on the job and the way they should perform them to maximize job efficiency. It is impossible to determine what the training program should include unless the organization knows what the program is supposed to accomplish. In other words, what knowledge, skills, and abilities are critical to learning to perform the job successfully?

Needs assessment An analysis of corporate and individual goals undertaken before designing a training program.

Needs Assessment.   The goals of the training program should be derived from the needs of the organization and the employees. A **needs assessment** should be conducted to determine corporate and individual goals and how a training program would help to achieve them. Such assessments are used to determine specific job components and the skills required to perform them.

Despite the recognized importance of conducting needs assessments, most companies do not do so, probably because the process is so time-consuming and expensive. A meta-analysis of 397 studies of training programs found that only 6 percent of them reported conducting needs assessments prior to establishing the training program (Arthur, Bennett, Edens, & Bell, 2003).

Of course there are situations in which the need for a training program is obvious. For example, a company that automates a manufacturing process, eliminating a number of jobs, may choose to retrain its employees for other work. Rapid expansion that creates new jobs requires a program to train workers to fill the positions. A high accident rate may call for additional safety training. Frequent complaints from dissatisfied customers may lead to employee training in human relations skills. In the absence of a clear indication that training is needed, however, it is management's responsibility to analyze its operations periodically to determine if any aspect could benefit from additional training.

Organizational Analysis.   A general organizational analysis can suggest broad training needs that can then be translated into specific needs of employees or work groups. The next step is a task analysis to identify the specific tasks performed on a job and the knowledge, skills, and abilities needed for those tasks. A person analysis is undertaken to determine which workers need retraining and what kind of training is necessary. These evaluations can be accomplished by job analysis methods, critical incidents, performance appraisal techniques, and self-assessments.

Job analysis is the most frequently used technique for determining training needs and objectives. It yields a detailed list of the characteristics needed to perform a job successfully and the sequence of operations required. From a job analysis, the company can determine how new training procedures can improve job performance.

The critical-incidents technique, which focuses on specific desirable or undesirable job behaviors, provides information on how employees are equipped to cope with significant workday events. For example, how do assembly-line workers deal with jammed machinery? How do supervisors handle disputes among subordinates? How do managers deal with charges of sexual harassment? An analysis of critical incidents can alert the training director to areas in which additional training or instruction is needed.

Performance appraisals are an obvious source of information on training needs. They can document employee weaknesses and lead to recommendations for retraining to correct specific deficiencies. Self-assessment is based on the assumption that the person who is performing a job well is a good source of information about the skills needed to do that job and the areas in which training may be desirable.

STAFFING FOR ORGANIZATIONAL TRAINING PROGRAMS

The quality of an instructor can have a tremendous impact on your performance as a student. Some teachers are able to bring the subject matter to life, to organize and present the material with enthusiasm, and to inspire interest among the class members. Other instructors teaching the same material can make the classroom experience frustrating, tiring, and boring. The most important factor in teaching anything at any level seems not to be competence or expertise in the subject matter. Although competence is necessary, the instructor must also have the ability to teach, to impart information in a clear and compelling manner.

The same principle holds for organizational training. Too often, corporate training is conducted by people who have vast experience on the job but no ability to communicate their skills effectively to others. The solution is to use professional instructors, persons trained in teaching methods and in job skills. Larger organizations maintain full-time training staffs equipped to teach a number of subjects and job skills.

THE PRETRAINING ENVIRONMENT

The pretraining environment established by an organization includes those decisions and cues, communicated directly or indirectly to employees by supervisors and peers, that indicate the value management places on training programs. These factors may include organizational policies, supervisor attitudes toward training, resources available for training, and employee participation in needs assessments. These cues influence the effectiveness of training programs because they tell employees how supportive the company is of training efforts.

The more training opportunities a company offers, the more likely its employees are to believe that training is an important and relevant activity for their careers. Trainees are also more likely to regard training as worthwhile and to be more motivated to achieve in training programs when they know their supervisors support training, know their post-training skills will be assessed, and are given a realistic picture of what the training involves. When these conditions are not met—when the organization's pretraining attitude or climate is perceived as unsupportive—a training program is likely to be rendered ineffective before it even begins.

Pretraining Attributes of Employees

A number of psychological characteristics can influence our desire to learn from a training program as well as the amount and kind of material we are capable of learning. These attributes include individual differences in ability, pretraining expectations, motivation, job involvement, locus of control, and self-efficacy.

Individual Differences in Ability.   Individual differences in training ability can be predicted through cognitive ability tests, biographical data, and performance in an initial training experience, such as a work sample. Trainability tests, such as work samples or minicourses, are also valid predictors of performance in a full course of training. Work samples, when used as measures of trainability, offer a short period of formal job skill instruction followed by a test of job performance in a training facility.

Pretraining Expectations.   Employees' expectations about the outcome of training can influence the program's effectiveness. When a training program fails to live up to the trainees' expectations, they are less likely to complete the program. Trainees whose expectations are not met but who do complete the program are likely to be dissatisfied on the job, to have a low sense of commitment to the organization, and to have a high rate of job turnover. Trainees whose pretraining expectations are met by the training program develop strong organizational commitment, a high sense of self-efficacy, and enhanced motivation to succeed.

Motivation.   The motivation or desire to learn is vital to employees' success in a training program. Learning will not occur unless trainees truly want to learn, regardless of their ability. In every occupation we can find examples of people who have achieved success with less than an optimal level of ability but with a great drive or motivation to succeed.

Research has shown that trainees with higher motivation learn more in training programs than do trainees with lower motivation. Trainees who are highly motivated are more likely to complete the program and to apply their training on the job (Salas & Cannon-Bowers, 2001).

Management can increase trainees' motivation by involving them in decisions about the training program, allowing them to participate in the needs-assessment process, and giving them a choice of training courses. Research has shown that previous negative events or experiences can increase motivation to learn. For example, trainees in an assertiveness training course who had experienced undesirable incidents (when being more assertive might have helped them) were more motivated to learn the training material (Smith-Jentsch, Jentsch, Payne, & Salas, 1996).

Job Involvement.   Trainees who show greater job involvement—whose sense of self-identity is closely linked with their work—show higher motivation to learn than do trainees who are less involved. Long-term career plans are also a factor. Training opportunities may be wasted on employees who display low job involvement and a lack of career interest because their motivation to learn is likely to be low. Further, employees with low job involvement have low potential for showing improvement in their job performance as a result of their training. Thus, pretraining programs to increase job and career involvement may be desirable for some employees.

Locus of Control.   Another variable that affects trainee motivation is locus of control. People identified as having an internal locus of control believe that job performance and such work-related rewards as pay and promotion are under their personal control, dependent on their own behaviors, abilities, and efforts. People with an external locus of control believe that life events in and out of the workplace are beyond their control. They are dependent on such outside forces as luck, chance, or whether their boss likes them.

Employees who have an internal locus of control are likely to be highly motivated to succeed in a training program because they believe that mastering the job skills is under their control and within their capabilities. They are more likely to accept feedback during training and to take action to correct deficiencies. They also show higher levels of job and career involvement than do employees with an external locus of control.

Self-Efficacy.   Another factor that influences employee motivation to succeed in training programs is self-efficacy, the belief in one's capacity to perform a task. It may be described as our sense of adequacy, efficiency, and competence in coping with life's demands. A study of 19,120 people in 25 countries demonstrated that self-efficacy exists in similar ways across these cultures (Scholz, Dona, Sud, & Schwarzer, 2002).

The relationship between self-efficacy and motivation to learn, and between self-efficacy and actual success in training programs, has been amply demonstrated. Several meta-analyses of studies dealing with self-efficacy beliefs concluded that efficacy beliefs contribute significantly to a person's level of motivation and performance in the workplace and in the classroom (Bandura & Locke, 2003).

A meta-analysis of 114 studies involving more than 21,000 employees found that people higher in perceived learning efficacy (their belief in their ability to acquire new skills) were able to learn complex skills more readily than were people low in perceived learning efficacy. This analysis also demonstrated a high positive correlation between self-efficacy and job performance (Stajkovic & Luthans, 1998). Thus, self-efficacy affected performance in the training program and, later, on the job.

In turn, self-efficacy can be influenced by training. Certain types of training, such as behavior modeling, can be used to increase self-efficacy. Even simply telling trainees that the skill they are trying to learn can be mastered through practice can increase self-efficacy.

HOW PEOPLE LEARN: PSYCHOLOGICAL FACTORS

Psychologists have devoted considerable effort to the study of learning. The published literature in the field contains thousands of research reports on human and animal learning under various conditions. In this section we deal with several factors that relate to teaching methods and to the nature of the material to be learned.

Active Practice.   Practice may not always make perfect, as the saying goes, but it does help. For learning to be most effective, trainees must be actively involved in the learning process, not merely passive recipients of information. For example, it is not sufficient to read about the operation of a construction crane or to watch a video of someone operating it. The training program should provide the opportunity for the trainee to sit in the operator's cab and have hands-on practice of the skills required to perform the job.

Imagine learning to drive a car only by listening to a lecture and memorizing traffic regulations. This can make you a better driver, but you will not actually learn how to drive until you sit in the driver's seat and start practicing. The same principle holds for academic material. Actively taking notes during lectures, highlighting and outlining the textbook, and discussing questions with classmates facilitate learning much more than sitting passively in the lecture hall.

Massed and Distributed (Spaced) Practice.   Some tasks are learned more readily when the training program schedules one or a few relatively long practice sessions (massed practice). Other tasks require a large number of relatively short practice sessions (distributed, or spaced, practice). In general, spaced practice results in better learning, particularly for motor skills.

A meta-analysis of 63 studies showed that subjects trained under spaced practice conditions performed significantly better than subjects trained under massed practice conditions. For jobs requiring relatively simple tasks, spaced practice interspersed with short rest periods held the advantage. For more complex tasks, longer rest periods between the spaced practice sessions resulted in more effective learning (Donovan & Radosevich, 1999).

The research evidence is less clear for the learning of verbal skills. Massed practice may be more useful, but much depends on the complexity of the task to be mastered and the type of material to be learned. Short, simple material can be learned well by massed practice because the sessions do not have to be too long for the trainees to absorb the content. More difficult material must be divided into shorter units and learned by distributed practice.

Whole and Part Learning.   The concept of whole or part learning refers to the relative size of the unit of material to be learned. The training course content can be divided into small parts, each of which is studied individually, or the material can be learned as a whole. The decision depends on the nature and complexity of the material and the ability of the trainees. More intelligent trainees are capable of rapidly learning larger units of material than are less intelligent trainees. However, when slower learners are offered the chance to learn the same material in smaller units, they may be able to master it better than when forced to apprehend it as a whole.

Some skills are obviously better suited to the whole learning method. For example, when learning to drive a car, it serves no useful purpose to divide driving behavior into component skills. You do not practice separately and repeatedly movements such as fastening the seat belt, turning on the ignition, releasing the emergency brake, adjusting the rearview mirror, and moving the gearshift lever from park to drive. Driving is an interdependent flow of movements and actions that can be learned more effectively as a whole.

When a task requires the initial learning of several subskills, the part method is more efficient. For example, piano students confronting a new piece of music may choose at first to practice the right-hand and the left-hand parts separately. Trainees can practice these various subskills until a particular level of efficiency has been achieved before integrating them into the total behavior or operation.

Transfer of Training.   Organizational training often takes place in an artificial setting, a training facility that may differ in several ways from the actual job environment. This discrepancy between training and job situations must be bridged. The training program must ensure that there will be a transfer of training—a carryover of the skills mastered during the training program—to the job itself.

The issue is one of relevance: Is the information provided during the training program relevant and meaningful to actual job performance? Is there a correspondence between the behaviors and attitudes taught in the training sessions and the behaviors and attitudes needed to perform the job successfully? Can all the information mastered in the training facility be applied in the production facility or the office? In many instances, the answer to these questions is no.

If there is close correspondence between training requirements and job requirements, positive transfer will develop. The material learned during training will aid or improve job performance. The greater the similarity between the training and work situations, the greater will be the transfer. This question of similarity is increasingly important in view of the growing use of virtual work environments for training purposes.

If there is little similarity between training situations and work situations, negative transfer will result. In that case, the skills learned in the training program will hamper or interfere with job performance. In negative transfer, these skills or behaviors must be unlearned or modified before employees can perform the job.

Several conditions in the post-training environment can facilitate positive transfer. The most important is supervisor support for and reinforcement of the behaviors and skills taught in the training program. In a study to illustrate this point, 80 student pilots working in teams took assertiveness training and were then exposed to situations in a computer-based flight simulator designed to test their level of assertiveness. Positive transfer of training occurred when the team leaders publicly reinforced assertive behavior, thus demonstrating the importance of leader support for using, or transferring, the skills taught in the training program (Smith-Jentsch, Salas, & Brannick, 2001).

Also influential are the opportunity to apply on the job the skills learned in the training program and a follow-up discussion or assessment shortly after completing the training program. Another important factor is the overall organizational climate. The more supportive it is of training, the greater the opportunities for transfer of the training experience to the actual work situation.

A survey of 150 members of a training and development organization dealt with the judgments of training professionals about the effectiveness of on-the-job training programs. The results revealed the expectation that more than 60 percent of employees apply what they learn in training programs directly to their jobs. A year after training, however, that fell to 34 percent. Thus, the effectiveness of transfer appears to decline over time (Saks, 2002).

Feedback.   People learn more readily when they are given a clear idea of how well they are doing. Feedback (sometimes called "knowledge of results") indicates to the trainees their level of progress. Feedback is also important in maintaining motivation. If trainees are not provided with feedback during a training program, they might persist in learning and practicing inappropriate behaviors and incorrect techniques of job performance.

To be maximally effective, feedback must be offered as soon as possible after the inappropriate behavior occurs. If a sequence of operations is being practiced

incorrectly, the desired change is more likely to be brought about if the trainees are told immediately. Overall training progress is greater when the program allows for frequent feedback. The more specific and detailed the correction, the more useful it will be.

Reinforcement.   The greater the reward that follows a behavior, the more easily and rapidly that behavior will be learned. The reward, or reinforcement, can take many forms—a good test grade, a gold star on a chart, a pat on the back from a supervisor, or a promotion for successful completion of a training program. By establishing a program of reinforcement, management can maintain employee motivation and effectively shape behavior by rewarding only those actions that the trainees are supposed to learn and display.

The most frequently used reinforcers in business and industry are money (such as pay raises or bonuses), social recognition (compliments or expressions of approval), and positive feedback about job performance. A meta-analysis of 72 studies conducted on the job found that money improved performance by 23 percent, social recognition improved performance by 17 percent, and feedback improved performance by 10 percent (Stajkovic & Luthans, 2003). Together, the three types of reinforcers are powerful tools for changing on-the-job behavior so that employees may become more productive.

Reinforcement should be provided immediately after the desired behavior has occurred. The longer the delay between behavior and reinforcement, the less effective the reinforcement will be because the trainee may fail to perceive the connection between the correct behavior and the reward for having behaved in that way.

In the early stages of training, reinforcement should be given every time the desired behavior is displayed. Once some learning has taken place, continuous reinforcement is no longer necessary. Then, partial reinforcement will be sufficient, for example, rewarding trainees every third or every tenth time they perform the appropriate behavior.

TRAINING METHODS

Now that we have described the pretraining attributes of trainees and the psychological factors that affect learning, let us consider specific organizational training techniques. Each technique offers advantages and disadvantages, depending on

In an on-the-job training program, new employees practice job skills under the supervision of an experienced worker

the goals of the training program, the abilities of the employees, and the nature of the information to be learned.

On-the-Job Training

One of the oldest and most widely used training methods takes place directly on the job for which the worker is being trained. Under the guidance of an experienced operator, supervisor, or trained instructor, trainees learn while working. They operate the equipment in the production facility or assist customers out on the sales floor and have the opportunity to develop proficiency while they work.

The major advantage of **on-the-job training** is economy; the organization does not have to establish, equip, and maintain a separate training facility. If current workers and supervisors serve as trainers, even the cost of a professional instructor is saved.

A more obvious advantage is positive transfer of training. There is no concern about whether job performance in a training situation will carry over to the actual work situation because training and job situations are the same. In terms of other psychological factors, active practice is provided from the outset. Motivation to learn should be high because the training situation is clearly relevant to the job situation. Feedback is immediate and visible. Good performance will elicit praise, and poor performance will show in a faulty product or dissatisfied customer.

On-the-job training can be expensive in the long run, however. Workers and supervisors must take time from their regular jobs to train new employees. This can lead to an overall reduction in productivity. Additional costs come with the slower work pace of the trainees and any damage they cause to equipment or product because of their inexperience. On certain jobs, permitting untrained workers to operate machinery may be hazardous not only to the trainees, but also to other employees. Accident rates for trainees on the job are typically higher than for experienced workers.

Using current workers or supervisors as trainers does not ensure adequate training for new employees. Just because a person performs a job competently or

On-the-job training
Training that takes place directly on the job for which the person has been hired.

has been on the job for a considerable time does not mean that person has the ability to teach the job to someone else. On-the-job training is often haphazard and inadequate, amounting to no more than the supervisor's saying to the trainees, "Go ahead and start. If you have any questions, come see me."

On-the-job training is also used at the management level. Much managerial and executive training and development occurs through informal and unstructured on-the-job experiences. Indeed, on-the-job experiences can contribute more significantly to the development of managerial ability than any formal classroom instruction.

Vestibule Training

Vestibule training
Training that takes place in a simulated workspace.

Because on-the-job training has the potential for disrupting the production process, many companies prefer **vestibule training.** They establish a simulated workspace in a separate training facility. (A vestibule is a hallway or entrance foyer between the outer door of a building and its main rooms. In the early days of American industry, vestibule schools were organized just inside the doors of industrial plants to introduce new workers to their jobs with a few weeks of specialized training. The word *vestibule* is used in this context to denote that the training program is like an entryway or passageway the employee must cross before getting to the job itself.)

Using the same kind of equipment and operating procedures as the actual work situation, a vestibule training program relies on skilled instructors, rather than experienced workers and supervisors, to teach new workers how to perform their jobs.

Because the sole purpose of vestibule training is training, there is no pressure to maintain a given level of productivity. Trainees do not have to be concerned about making costly or embarrassing errors or about damaging actual production equipment. They can concentrate on learning the skills necessary to be successful on the job.

The greatest disadvantage of vestibule training is the cost. The organization must equip the facility and maintain a teaching staff. This expense is particularly burdensome when there are not enough new workers to make full-time use of the training facility. Further, if the training situation does not correspond closely to the work situation, negative transfer of training will occur, and the trainees may need informal, on-the-job instruction once they start to work. This problem can be aggravated by the common business practice of using obsolete equipment, retired from the production floor, in the training facility. However, if a vestibule training program is properly designed, staffed, and equipped, it can be an effective training technique.

Apprenticeship

Apprenticeship A training method for skilled crafts and trades involving classroom instruction and on-the-job experience.

Perhaps the earliest recorded training method still in use today is the **apprenticeship** program for skilled crafts and trades in private-sector industries such as construction and manufacturing. Programs are available for plumbers, carpenters, electronics technicians, painters, and auto mechanics, among others. Conducted in the classroom and on the job, apprenticeship involves extensive background preparation in the craft as well as actual work experience under the guidance of experts.

Apprenticeships average four to six years. The standard procedure is for the trainees to agree to work for a company for a fixed period in return for a specified program of training and a salary, usually half that earned by skilled and licensed craftspersons. Trainees must complete their apprenticeship before they are allowed to join a union. Membership in a labor union is necessary to securing employment. Thus, apprentice programs constitute a joint effort by industry and organized labor to maintain an adequate supply of skilled workers.

In recent years, apprenticeships in the public sector have grown in popularity. A number of federal, state, and local government agencies have adopted them for skilled blue-collar jobs in civilian and military programs, such as building maintenance worker, highway maintenance worker, prison correctional officer, and firefighter. The Smithsonian Institution in Washington, D.C., operates an apprenticeship program for carpenters, electricians, and plaster masons to build displays for their museums.

Computer-Assisted Instruction

Computer-assisted instruction (CAI), sometimes called computer-based training (CBT), is widely used by private- and public-sector organizations. In CAI the program of instruction, usually on CD-ROM, serves as the teacher. Trainees interact with the material on computer terminals. Their responses are recorded and analyzed automatically, and the difficulty of each item presented is based on the correctness of the response to the previous item.

Computer-assisted instruction (CAI) A computer-based training method in which trainees learn material at their own pace and receive immediate feedback on their progress.

One of the most widespread uses of computer-based training is to teach computer literacy skills. With millions of workers now using computers daily on the job, the development of computer operating skills is critical. Another popular use is in training airline flight crews. The software used by airlines presents displays and touch-panel graphics to simulate the buttons, switches, dials, and signal lights in the cockpit. This type of instruction reduces the number of hours pilots and copilots would otherwise have to spend in a more expensive flight simulator.

With computer-assisted instruction, trainees are actively involved in the learning process and work through the material at their own pace. This means that the trainee, rather than the trainer, decides how long and how often to practice. This freedom to choose can have a downside, particularly for trainees who are not sufficiently motivated to work properly in order to learn the material. Research on 78 technical employees who volunteered for an online course on problem-solving showed that some of them skipped practice sessions or moved too quickly through the course work to adequately understand the material. After the course, the trainees who obtained the lowest test scores were found to have completed less than 70 percent of the practice sessions and to have spent less than six hours working at what was scheduled as a 14-hour course. Those who spend the least time on the training also had low learning self-efficacy levels, meaning that they were not sufficiently confident about their ability to learn the material (Brown, 2001).

Nevertheless, for people with the ability and motivation to succeed, computer-assisted instruction offers many advantages. Trainees receive immediate feedback on their progress and reinforcement for displaying mastery of a skill. The technique offers more individualized instruction than does a traditional lecture-based training course. It is not unlike private tutoring by an excellent teacher who has a comprehensive knowledge of the subject, never becomes impatient or annoyed with the student, and displays no prejudice or error. Because CAI keeps accurate records and maintains a current performance analysis on each trainee, the training staff is free to devote time to any unusual learning problems that arise.

Computer-assisted instruction can be used with even a small number of trainees so that the company does not have to make them wait until there are enough trainees to fill a classroom and schedule a course. It can also be provided to a large number of trainees simultaneously in different locations. Studies have shown that the technique significantly decreases training time and provides positive transfer of training.

Net-Based Training

Net-based training is now being used by companies such as Xerox, Texaco, Unisys, and Crate and Barrel. It involves the Internet and the intranet (the within-company site). The technique is a type of distance learning, and it is transforming traditional training programs by delivering up-to-the-minute programs on demand.

Through net-based training, a company can provide training courses for any number of workers to access from their desks at work or at home, or from laptops and handheld computers while traveling. Instruction is being prepared for nearly every type of training, from certification in information technology to advanced accounting practices and course work for an MBA degree.

Net-based training offers the same advantages as computer-assisted instruction: active involvement of the trainees, the opportunity to proceed at their own pace, immediate feedback and reinforcement, plus flexibility as to the time and place of training.

The cost of net-based training has been estimated to be 20 percent to 35 percent lower than the cost of traditional classroom instruction, where trainers and trainees must assemble on a prescribed schedule. The technique has become a cheaper, better, and faster way of reaching a wider range of employees.

Behavior Modification

The use of positive reinforcement to change behavior has many applications to organizational training. An assessment called a performance audit is conducted first, to determine the problems or behaviors that can be modified for more efficient job performance. A program of positive reinforcement is then introduced to reward employees for displaying the desired behaviors, such as reducing errors or production time per unit. Punishment or reprimands are not used. Although they may temporarily eliminate an undesirable behavior, they may leave in its place anxiety, hostility, and anger. Providing positive reinforcement is much more effective in improving employee productivity and behavior.

Behavior modification
A training program of positive reinforcement to reward employees for displaying desirable job behaviors.

A classic program of **behavior modification** was developed at Emery Air Freight, where the behavioral changes induced were directly connected to job performance. A performance audit revealed two problem areas: (1) despite the employees' belief that they were responding within 90 minutes to 90 percent of customer telephone inquiries, they were actually responding to only 30 percent of the inquiries within that time, and (2) employees were combining packages into containers for shipment only 45 percent of the time, whereas management expected containers to be used 90 percent of the time. The goals of the behavior

---

Newsbreak **She Flew through College**

Morgan Hezlep was 29 years old, working for a San Diego company that designed health care software programs, when she decided that she wanted to go back to college to finish her bachelor's degree. She couldn't quit her job to return to school full time because she needed the salary. And besides, she liked her work. Unfortunately, her company wanted to send her to Boston on a long-term assignment to work with a client establishing a new program.

Then it got more complicated. She didn't want to move to Boston, so her company agreed to fly her back and forth every week. Well, that settled the job problem, but where could she take enough classes to finish her degree? In Boston she would be working all the time, and in San Diego there were no colleges where she could attend weekends only.

Then she learned about an online degree program in computer science offered by Saint Leo University, located near Tampa, Florida. Morgan could do her coursework online during the hours she spent in airports and commuting cross-country by plane. That system gave her about 16 hours a week to study the lectures provided on CD-ROMs and to write the required papers. "I left San Diego every Sunday," she said, "worked Monday through Thursday and flew back home to San Diego on Friday morning. I would get settled in [at the airport], put on my headphones, pop in a CD and begin class."

It took two years to complete the program. In addition to the CD-ROMs, there were weekly online seminars and discussions with professors and other students in a virtual classroom setting. Advisers were always available through a toll-free phone number, fax, or e-mail. Textbooks arrived by mail at the beginning of every course.

Along with her degree, Morgan accumulated more than 300,000 frequent-flyer miles, some of which she applied to the airfare to Tampa for her graduation—the only time she ever saw the campus.

Her new credentials helped her decide to enter a new field. She enrolled in law school, attending actual classes in real buildings every day, and says that her study habits were greatly improved by her online learning experience. "With the online classes," she said, "I was forced to develop good study habits and time management skills. I think the experience made me a more disciplined student."

Source: Commuter school. *St. Petersburg (FL) Times,* July 20, 2003.

---

modification training program were to have employees respond faster to customer inquiries and to use containers for shipment whenever possible.

Managers were taught a number of recognitions and rewards to bestow on employees as reinforcers, ranging from a smile and a nod to specific praise for a job well done. Financial incentives to improve performance were not used. Praise and recognition were found to be sufficient reinforcers for improving job performance and for bringing about positive changes in behavior. Managers were told to reinforce desirable behaviors as soon as they occurred and gradually to shift from constant reinforcement to occasional, or intermittent, reinforcement.

Employees were required to keep a detailed record of their accomplishments so that they could compare their performance with the company standards. This record keeping provided daily feedback on their progress.

The company estimated that the improved productivity and response time saved $3 million in three years, considerably more than the cost of instituting the behavior modification program initially.

Job Rotation

Job rotation A management training technique that assigns trainees to various jobs and departments over a period of a few years.

Job rotation is a popular management training technique. It exposes trainees to different jobs and departments to acquaint them with all facets of their organization. It is frequently used with new college graduates who are just beginning their working careers. Through job rotation, trainees gain perspective on various aspects of organizational life. They have the opportunity to see and be seen by higher management in different departments, and to learn through direct experience where they might best apply their knowledge, abilities, and interests.

The rotation phase of a management career may last several years, taking employees from one department to another or from one plant or office in the United States to others throughout the world. Such changes can promote the development of the management trainees' flexibility, adaptability, and self-efficacy as employees learn to deal successfully with new challenges. Job rotation programs are also used for skilled and semiskilled jobs. They allow workers to increase their skill levels in diverse occupations, and they serve to alleviate the boredom that can result from years of performing the same tasks.

Disadvantages of the job rotation technique include frequent moves, which can disrupt family life and interrupt a spouse's career. If the rotation period is too brief, there may not be sufficient time to become fully acquainted with a particular job. If top management is more interested in using management trainees as temporary office help, instead of as a rising group of managers in need of mentors, the trainees will not have the opportunity to acquire the necessary skills to transfer to upper-management positions. This can defeat the purpose of the program.

Case Studies

Case studies A method of executive training in which trainees analyze a business problem and offer solutions.

The use of **case studies,** a method developed by the Harvard University School of Business, is popular in executive training programs. A complex problem, or case, of the kind faced daily by managers and executives, is presented to the trainees prior to a general meeting. The trainees are expected to familiarize themselves with the information and to find additional relevant material. When they meet as a group, each member must be prepared to interpret the problem and offer a solution. Through the presentation of diverse viewpoints, the trainees come to appreciate different perspectives on a problem and, consequently, different approaches to solving it. Usually the cases have no one correct solution. The group leader does not suggest an answer. The group as a whole must reach consensus and resolve the problem.

A limitation of the case study method is that the solution may not be relevant to the requirements of the job. There may be a discrepancy between the theoretical solution to the case problem and the solution that is practical for

Role playing gives management trainees the chance to try out various supervisory behaviors and to receive feedback from other trainees and instructors.

the organization. Therefore, actions taken on the basis of the case study solution proposed in the training program may not transfer positively to actions that are appropriate on the job.

Business Games

Business games attempt to simulate a complex organizational situation. They are intended to develop problem-solving and decision-making skills and to provide practice in using those skills in a situation in which a management trainee's mistake will not prove costly or embarrassing to the organization.

Trainees compete in teams, each team representing a separate, hypothetical business organization. The team companies are given detailed information about the operation of their organization, including data on finances, sales, advertising, production, personnel, and inventories. Each group must organize itself and assign various tasks and responsibilities to each member. As the teams deal with corporate problems, an instructor evaluates their reasoning processes and decisions. They may be required to consider additional problems based on the outcomes of their initial decisions.

Because the business problems presented to the trainees are so realistic, many trainees form an emotional commitment to their virtual company. They gain experience in making decisions on real-life problems under the pressures of time and the actions taken by rival organizations. For new employees, business games may provide their first exposure to actual job tasks and stresses managers face.

Business games A training method that simulates a complex organizational situation to encourage the development of problem-solving and decision-making skills.

This type of realistic job preview persuades some trainees that they would be happier in another line of work.

In-Basket Training

In-basket technique
An assessment-center exercise that requires job applicants to process memos, letters, and directives found in a typical manager's in-basket.

The **in-basket technique** was discussed in Chapter 3 as a method of employee selection. The same technique is used to train prospective managers. Each trainee is given a stack of letters, memos, customer complaints, employee requests, and other items that present various problems typical of those dealt with by managers on the job. The trainees must take action on each item within a specified period. After completing the tasks, the trainees meet with a trainer to discuss their decisions and receive feedback on the outcomes.

Role Playing

Role playing
A management training technique in which trainees play the role of a supervisor, acting out various behaviors in situations with subordinates.

In **role playing**, management trainees pretend to act out a particular role, displaying whatever behaviors they believe are appropriate in a given situation. For example, they may be asked to imagine themselves to be a supervisor discussing a poor performance appraisal with a subordinate. They act out these situations in front of a group of trainees and instructors, who offer comments on their performance. A trainee may play the role of supervisor at first, then the situation will be reversed and the same trainee will play the employee. Sessions can be videotaped for later analysis. Many people feel foolish or awkward acting out in front of a group, but once they begin, most people develop a sensitivity for the part and project their feelings onto it.

Role playing can be a valuable learning device. It enables trainees to understand the views of subordinates and acquaints them with the roles they will be expected to play as managers. It provides practical experience as well as feedback from other trainees and instructors. Trainees have the opportunity to practice job-related behaviors in a situation in which mistakes or inappropriate behaviors will not jeopardize interpersonal relations on the job.

Behavior Modeling

Behavior modeling
A management training technique in which trainees attempt to imitate the job behaviors of successful supervisors.

The **behavior modeling** approach to management training involves having trainees attempt to imitate or model their behavior on examples of exceptional job performance. It is a popular technique for teaching interpersonal and leadership skills. Behavior modeling is usually conducted with groups of six to 12 supervisors or managers. Sessions may last two to four hours a week for up to four weeks. In the intervals between training sessions, the trainees are on the job, applying what they have learned, which provides them with feedback from their subordinates.

The usual procedure is for a trainer, using a prepared script, to provide a general introduction. Then the trainees watch a videotape of a manager who is acting out appropriate procedures and behaviors for handling a job situation with a subordinate—for example, discussing poor job performance, excessive absenteeism, or low morale.

Next, the trainees engage in behavior rehearsal, practicing the behaviors they saw the model perform. Trainees are not being asked to play a role; instead, they are imitating the actual behaviors they will use on the job, the behaviors the

Newsbreak   Virtual Training

You've seen it in the movies. A jet fighter eases its way upward, below and behind a mammoth flying tanker loaded with aviation fuel. A long thin tube with a funnel extends from the rear of the tanker aircraft. The fighter pilot maneuvers the jet so that its fuel tank port connects with the tiny funnel, while traveling at more than 500 miles an hour. It's called in-flight refueling, a tricky, delicate, and dangerous operation every fighter pilot has to learn.

Lt. Charlie Howard, a newly graduated 26-year-old pilot, is trying to perform the maneuver for the first time. He has listened to the lectures, read the operating manual, and paid close attention to the video showing a pilot's-eye view of the connection, but now he feels his fear mount as he closes in on the monster plane overhead.

He never takes his eyes off the funnel. It's only 20 feet away. He draws closer. Suddenly, his plane is buffeted by high wind gusts and his body is slammed into the seat as the fighter bounces on an updraft. Frantically, Charlie forces the control stick forward, but it is too late. The wind whips faster than he can react, and his tiny plane smashes into the side of the tanker.

"Boom," rings a voice in his ear. "You're dead, Charlie. And so is everybody in the tanker. OK, let's try it again."

Charlie Howard is flying in a virtual aircraft, a flight simulator, wearing a head-mounted virtual reality apparatus that provides lifelike computer-generated images. The only damage he suffered from the "crash" was to his ego, and now he can try the maneuver again and again until he perfects it. Only then will he be permitted to try it in a real airplane.

The U.S. military has invested millions of dollars in virtual training for pilots, air-traffic controllers, and tank commanders, so they can learn their jobs without inflicting harm on themselves and others or damaging expensive equipment.

Virtual reality allows researchers to shape the training to the specific needs of the various branches of the armed forces. U.S. Air Force psychologist Wesley Regian said, "People can practice one part of a more complicated task. Or simulations can start out easy—as with removing the wind in the refueling simulation—and increase in difficulty as a student grasps the basics."

One day Lieutenant Howard will practice refueling in a real plane under genuine wind conditions, but thanks to the I-O psychology research on virtual reality simulation devices, he will be well trained by then. He will have performed the required maneuvers many times already, and survived.

model has displayed. The trainer and the other trainees provide feedback by telling each trainee how closely he or she imitated the model's behavior and where their behavior diverged. This social reinforcement helps trainees gain confidence in their ability to display the appropriate behavior.

The interpersonal and leadership behaviors learned by behavior modeling will transfer directly to the job because the modeled situations between manager and subordinate are actual job situations. Thus, there is a high degree of relevance between behavior modeling as a training technique and the job requirements, a condition that increases trainees' motivation to accept and apply the training.

Reports from organizations using behavior modeling show that the technique is effective in raising employee morale, improving communication with customers, increasing sales, decreasing absenteeism, enhancing supervisory skills, improving production quantity and quality, and reducing employee resistance to change.

Executive Coaching

A new approach to management training involves one-to-one training sessions in which a coach works with a manager to improve a particular aspect of the manager's job performance. Can the manager give a good speech? Can the executive use the Internet? Do performance appraisals show that colleagues and subordinates think the boss has lousy human relations skills? Get a coach!

Executive coaching
A management training technique involving personal sessions with a coach to improve a particular aspect of job performance.

Executive coaching is designed to solve individual problems as they arise. The most frequent use of executive coaching has been as a follow-up to poor ratings on 360-degree feedback appraisals. Recognizing that feedback alone is often not sufficient motivation for a manager to alter his or her behavior, a coach will be brought in to help interpret the feedback and work with the manager to devise strategies for eliciting the desired behavioral changes. Several sessions of coaching may be required to deal with perceived deficiencies.

One year after receiving executive coaching, 1,202 senior managers underwent a 360-degree performance evaluation. Those who had received the coaching were judged to be far more likely to set specific rather than general goals for their subordinates and to solicit ideas for improvement than were those who had received no coaching. The overall performance ratings of those who had received the coaching were also higher than those of the no-coaching control group (Smither, London, Flautt, Vargas, & Kucine, 2003).

Most executives who have received coaching tend to agree with their coaches' recommendations and to rate the process as valuable to their career development.

Diversity Training

We described in Chapter 1 how the nature of the workforce is changing to include more women and ethnic minority workers. To aid their employees in coping with an increasingly diverse workforce, many organizations have instituted **diversity training** programs to teach people to confront personal prejudices that could lead to discriminatory behaviors. Through lectures, videos, role playing, and confrontational exercises, employees are learning, in a way, how it might feel to be a female worker being sexually harassed by a male boss, or a Hispanic worker receiving an unsatisfactory performance appraisal from a Black supervisor. Trainees are forced to deal with their own sexist and racist attitudes, and to learn to be more sensitive to the concerns and viewpoints of others.

Diversity training
Training programs to make employees aware of their personal prejudices and to teach them to be more sensitive to the concerns and views of others.

U.S. companies are spending up to $10 billion annually for diversity training. The success of diversity training depends on several factors: support from management, mandatory attendance, and the size of the organization. Large organizations with strong support from top executives, a staff of diversity specialists, and required attendance for all employees are the most likely to have successful diversity training programs. However, post-training interviews with participants suggest that for some people these programs foster negative reactions as well as charges that the programs are offered only because it appears to be the politically correct thing to do.

CAREER DEVELOPMENT AND PLANNING

We have discussed specific training methods designed to improve employees' knowledge, job skills, and interpersonal relations. Most training programs are mandatory and oriented toward a specific job or specific career stage, such as the entry-level worker, the employee who needs retraining, or the midcareer manager. Some organizations also offer personal development opportunities throughout an employee's career. These career development and planning efforts, which are strictly voluntary, involve a lifelong learning approach.

Organizations as diverse as General Electric, AT&T, Merrill Lynch, TRW, and Xerox operate career development centers. They provide information on company career paths and opportunities and offer counseling and self-analysis programs so that employees can determine how their personal goals coincide with organizational goals. Many companies sponsor workshops to assist employees in career planning and in the development of human relations skills. Employees are encouraged to set career objectives—for example, specifying where they hope to be within the corporate hierarchy in five years' time—and to review these goals periodically. Some companies offer tuition refund plans that enable employees to return to college or graduate school to upgrade job skills or to learn new skills. Employees are also encouraged to participate in in-house training courses.

We have noted that one of the forces of change in the workplace today is the decline of the idea of a lifetime career with a single employer. Increasingly, we may choose to or be forced to change careers several times during the course of our working lives and to continually enhance and upgrade our personal package of skills. This necessity for lifelong learning increases the importance of career development and planning efforts.

A 13-month study followed 800 workers in several different organizations who were involved in career development and learning activities. The researchers reached the following conclusions (Maurer, Weiss, & Barbeite, 2003):

- Prior participation in career development activities was a good predictor of present and future intentions to undertake more such learning activities.
- High self-efficacy led to more favorable attitudes toward career development opportunities, which led, in turn, to higher levels of participation.
- The more supportive of career development activities organizations are, the greater the employee beliefs that their participation will lead to positive personal benefits.
- Older workers receive less organizational support and encouragement for career development activities and feel less capable of undertaking such activities.

In addition, the researchers reported that the major reason for intending to stay with a company, instead of looking for a job with another organization, was the opportunity for career growth, development, and learning provided by the present employer.

Career Development and Life Stages

Psychologists have long recognized individual differences in people's values, goals, and needs at different ages and stages of life. The job or lifestyle that is appropriate in our twenties may be inappropriate for our thirties or fifties. A classic research report noted three distinct career stages (Hall, 1986):

1. *Establishment*. During this stage, approximately ages 20 to 40, people are becoming established in their careers and adjusting to work routines. Toward the middle of this period, they learn whether they are going to be successful or not, through promotions and a sense of personal satisfaction, or through an unwanted transfer or dismissal. If they are successful, they develop feelings of self-efficacy and organizational commitment. If they are unsuccessful, they may need self-analysis, counseling, and a revision of their career plans.
2. *Maintenance*. This stage lasts from approximately ages 40 to 55, the time of the so-called midlife crisis. People become aware that they are aging. They have either approached or achieved their goals or they know they will never reach them. It is a time of self-examination, which may lead to a change in interests, values, and lifestyles. Some people seek challenge and satisfaction in new jobs, hobbies, or relationships. Some organizations offer counseling to their managerial personnel to help them cope with this period.
3. *Decline*. From age 50 or 55 through retirement, employees confront the end of the career to which they devoted their adult life. They must consider the prospect of living on a reduced income and of diminished physical capacity. Retirement brings not only the loss of work and a sense of identity, but also the loss of colleagues with whom to socialize. Additional counseling may be required to assist employees in planning for retirement.

Career development and planning efforts at each stage of working life involve responsibilities shared by employers and employees. Organizations should offer opportunities for personal growth and development. Employees must make effective use of these programs. They should be willing periodically to reanalyze their skills and job performance and to formulate realistic career development plans.

Career Self-Management

As a result of years of corporate mergers, restructuring, downsizing, and outsourcing, many companies today are less able or less willing to provide opportunities for the career development and growth of their employees. They are urging employees to take more responsibility on their own for actively planning and managing their careers. The term **career self-management** refers to the degree to which a person regularly and routinely gathers information and formulates or revises plans for his or her own career, solving problems and making decisions. However, there has been little research on the effectiveness of career self-management training.

Career self-management
A lifelong approach to learning and skill enhancement initiated by the employee rather than by the organization.

Some organizations offer training to help employees assume this responsibility to upgrade their skills and learn new ones. One estimate is that approximately half of all U.S. corporations with a workforce exceeding 100 employees offer career self-management training. A typical program consists of three stages or programs presented on successive days:

Newsbreak   It's Your Career: Make the Most of It

Gary Herman is a 55-year-old systems analyst with the data services division of GTE in Tampa, Florida. He's concerned about his future because he's working in a field where the technology changes so fast and so radically that a person's skills can become obsolete in the space of only a year or two. He spends considerable time reeducating himself to stay marketable.

"People need to be retooled," said James Harris, Herman's boss. "If they don't choose to do that, they could lose their jobs. Either you retrain or you don't move along in your career. It's that simple."

Internet-based technological advancements pose continual challenges for people like Gary Herman. When his employer offered a two-month course on state-of-the-art developments, he added those eight hours per day of study time to his full-time work schedule. His boss had not told him to take the course. Herman knew it was up to him to take advantage of the opportunity to improve his skills. But he also knew that if his next performance appraisal, which included a critical skill reevaluation, did not show that he was making an effort to manage the direction of his career, he would not remain on his chosen career path with GTE and would no longer be marketable elsewhere.

"You have to adopt a pattern of lifelong learning in this field," said John Bonanno, executive director of Boston University's corporate education center. "A lot of what you learn today will, in 2 or 3 years, be obsolete."

But not everyone is capable of being retrained. GTE's training director, Rene Lutthans, found that 25 percent of the employees who participate in such training are unable to master the new skills. "The company tries to find a place for such people, but as projects are phased out, there are no guarantees of employment."

If you can't keep up, you're out. If you don't manage your own career, no one else will.

1. Assessing career attitudes, values, plans, and goals.
2. Analyzing how these goals have or have not been met by the current job.
3. Discussing career strategies to create opportunities to meet one's plans and goals, whether on or off the job. (This stage includes upgrading skills, soliciting feedback from colleagues and supervisors, networking, and being mobile in seeking new job opportunities.)

EVALUATING ORGANIZATIONAL TRAINING PROGRAMS

Regardless of how impressive and sophisticated a training program or facility may appear, or how much employees seem to like it, it is necessary that the outcomes or results be evaluated in systematic and quantitative terms. One way to measure the worth of a training program is to assess the following results: (1) changes in cognitive outcomes, such as the amount of information learned; (2) changes in skill-based outcomes, such as improvements in quantity and quality of production; and (3) changes in affective outcomes, such as positive attitudes and higher motivation. Unless such evaluative research is conducted, the organization will not know how effective its investment of time and money is.

Are employees learning the skills they need for their jobs? Are productivity, safety, and efficiency rising? Have communications and leadership skills improved? Have the attitudes of majority-group employees toward minority-group employees changed? To answer these questions, comparisons must be made of trained and untrained workers performing the same jobs. Or the same workers before and after training can be compared with a control group of workers who were not exposed to the training. Only through such research can the organization determine whether its training program should be modified, extended, or eliminated.

A meta-analysis of 397 studies on training found what the researchers described as a medium to large positive effect of organizational training (Arthur, Bennett, Edens, & Bell, 2003). A survey of 150 members of a training and development organization showed that these training professionals believed that approximately half of all training efforts resulted in an improvement in employee and organizational performance (Katz, 2002).

Even with such a substantial investment at stake, most organizations do not make a systematic effort to evaluate their training programs. Or they may accept subjective or intuitive evidence that the trainees are actually learning something. As a result, many organizations do not have a clear idea whether the millions of dollars they spend on training are worthwhile. One psychologist summed up the attitude this way: "With corporate training, it's often, 'Let's spend the money and hope for the best'" (Ellin, 2000). This failure to examine the effectiveness of training programs is increasingly expensive as more and more training is dependent on computer technology.

In addition to cost, other factors help explain the lack of assessment of the effectiveness of training programs. Many training directors do not have the skills to conduct such research. Also, they may overestimate the usefulness of programs they have initiated and designed. Some companies offer training not because management believes in it or expects it to meet specific corporate goals but merely because their competitors do it.

Some training programs are established because some new technique or management style has produced a flood of anecdotal reports in the popular media attesting to its value. One example is "time management," supposedly a method for learning to use one's time in the most efficient manner. Supporters claimed time management increased employee productivity and satisfaction and reduced stress. With the growing number of magazine articles and television reports about the success of time management, companies hired time-management consultants to train employees in this latest miracle cure for the ills of the workplace. The only problem was time management did not work. No one knows how many companies initiated expensive time-management training programs and maintained them in the absence of data to support their effectiveness.

Assessing the behavioral changes that may occur following training can be difficult. If a worker operates a simple machine or assembles a part, the goal of the training program and the measurement of the outcome are relatively straightforward. The number of items produced per unit time by trained and untrained workers or by workers trained by different techniques can be determined objectively and compared. At this work level, training programs have been shown to be effective. When dealing with human relations, problem solving, or other management behaviors, it is far more difficult to assess the usefulness of the training.

Yet the face validity of management training remains high, despite the lack of supporting data. The programs are popular, everyone says they are necessary, and management looks good for providing them. However, the question remains: Are they truly worthwhile?

Training directors defend their programs by pointing out that management trainees are subsequently promoted to higher levels of responsibility. This is not a valid or sufficient measure of a training program's success because it is usually only the most capable and promising candidates who are chosen to participate in management training initially. These trainees are the ones most likely to be promoted anyway, even without the training programs. Training directors also like to boast that employees like the programs. That's nice, but feelings and other subjective reactions are no substitute for research to investigate whether training results in better job performance. Organizations must be willing to expend the resources necessary to evaluate their elaborate training and development programs. It makes little sense to continue to support such activities without empirical evidence of their worth.

We can see, then, that problems with organizational training provide many challenges for I-O psychologists:

- to identify the abilities required to perform increasingly complex jobs
- to provide job opportunities for unskilled workers
- to assist supervisors in the management of an ethnically diverse workforce
- to retrain workers displaced by changing economic, technological, and political forces
- to help organizations remain competitive in the international marketplace
- to conduct the necessary research to determine the effectiveness of training programs

Summary

Training and development take place at all levels of employment, from unskilled teenagers who need remedial work in basic math and language skills to seasoned corporate vice presidents, from the first day on a job throughout a person's career. Fair employment legislation affects training programs because decisions on placement, promotion, retention, and transfer are often based on performance during training. Therefore, training has the potential to be discriminatory.

The first step in establishing a training program is to specify the training objectives. A **needs assessment** based on organizational, task, and worker analyses is conducted using job analysis, critical incidents, performance appraisal, and self-assessment techniques. The training staff should be knowledgeable about the subject matter, be able to communicate effectively, and have the requisite interpersonal skills.

Pretraining characteristics of the trainees can influence how much they will benefit from a training program. These attributes include individual differences in ability, pretraining expectations, motivation, job involvement, locus of control, and self-efficacy. Psychological factors in learning include active practice of the material, massed or spaced practice, whole or part learning, transfer of training, feedback, and reinforcement.

In **on-the-job training,** trainees learn while actually working at the job. **Vestibule training** takes place in a simulated work area. In **apprenticeship,** trainees undergo classroom instruction and work experience under the guidance of skilled craftspersons. In **computer-assisted instruction,** trainees interact with computer software that presents the material to be learned. Net-based training offers instruction over the Internet or the company's in-house intranet network. This makes training available both on and off the job, whenever and wherever the employees choose to log on. In **behavior modification,** trainees are reinforced, or rewarded, for displaying the desired behaviors.

Job rotation exposes trainees to various jobs at their level of employment. In **case studies,** management trainees analyze, interpret, and discuss a complex business problem. **Business games** require groups of trainees to interact in a simulated business situation. The **in-basket technique,** also a simulation, asks trainees to respond individually to letters, memos, and other office tasks. In **role playing,** trainees act out the problems of workers and managers. **Behavior modeling** has trainees pattern their behavior on that of successful managers. **Executive coaching** offers one-to-one training to improve a particular aspect of a manager's job performance. It is frequently a follow-up to poor ratings on a 360-degree performance appraisal. In **diversity training,** employees learn to confront and deal with racist and sexist attitudes.

Career development is a lifelong learning approach to enhancing job skills and abilities and fostering personal development. Through self-analysis and company counseling and training programs, employees are assisted through various career stages. **Career self-management** refers to lifelong learning and skill enhancement initiated by the employee rather than by the company.

Organizations rarely undertake systematic or quantitative evaluation of their training programs. Many training programs are continued because of subjective beliefs about their effectiveness rather than empirical evidence of actual behavior changes that result from training.

Key Terms

apprenticeship	executive coaching
behavior modeling	in-basket technique
behavior modification	job rotation
business games	needs assessment
career self-management	on-the-job training
case studies	role playing
computer-assisted instruction	vestibule training
diversity training	

Review Questions

1. What is Hamburger U.? What does it tell us about the nature and extent of training in the workplace?
2. What are the purposes of a needs assessment, and how is it conducted?
3. What is the most frequently used technique for determining training needs and objectives? How frequently are training needs empirically determined before instituting a training program?
4. What factors in the pretraining environment influence employee beliefs about the value of the training program?

5. Discuss the influence on training of employees' pretraining expectations and motivation. In what ways can a company increase trainee motivation?

6. How is trainee motivation to perform well in a training program influenced by the factors of locus of control and self-efficacy?

7. Describe the effect on learning of active practice, massed versus distributed practice, and whole versus part learning.

8. How would you establish a training program to teach people to use bulldozers? To use computers?

9. What factors can hinder positive transfer from a training program to on-the-job performance?

10. What reinforcers are used in the workplace? What is their relative importance in improving job performance?

11. Describe the relative merits of vestibule training and on-the-job training.

12. What are the advantages and disadvantages of computer-assisted instruction as compared to more traditional instructor-led training?

13. Distinguish between behavior modification and behavior modeling.

14. How are case studies, business games, and role playing used in management training?

15. How does executive coaching differ from other management training techniques? In the study of senior managers who received executive coaching, how did their behavior change a year later?

16. What factors can influence employee attitudes toward and participation in career development and planning activities?

17. Describe the career stages of working life and the reasons for pursuing career self-management activities.

18. What conclusions can you draw about the necessity, value, extent, and worth of employee training programs?

Additional Reading

Feldman, D. C. (2002). *Work careers: A developmental perspective.* San Francisco: Jossey-Bass. Describes the basics of career development (personality, vocational interests, skills and abilities), issues of career development over the life span (from occupational choices expressed during childhood and adolescence to late career and post retirement), and the influence of changes such as outsourcing, downsizing, and new technologies.

Goldstein, I. L., & Ford, J. K. (2002). *Training in organizations: Needs assessment, development and evaluation* (4th ed.). Belmont, CA: Wadsworth. Offers a systematic approach to training issues including needs assessment, the learning environment, changing work environments, trainer and trainee characteristics, transfer of training, desired outcomes, and training methods. Shows applications for employees, leaders, teams, and organizations.

Kilburg, R. R. (2000). *Executive coaching: Developing managerial wisdom in a world of chaos.* Washington, D.C.: American Psychological Association. Reviews research, theories, and case studies on executive coaching and job performance to help managers learn from mistakes and gain mastery over their organizational roles. Notes the relationship between coaching and counseling for enhancing the growth of high-potential executives.

Kruse, K., & Keil, J. (2000). *Technology-based training: The art and science of design, development and delivery.* San Francisco: Jossey-Bass/Pfeiffer. A practical guide to CD-ROM and Web-based training programs covering basic issues, adult learning principles, interface design, and project management. Describes computer-aided instruction, computer-managed instruction, and computer-supported learning resources. Also includes case studies.

Robinson, P., & Schiff, N. (2001). *If I don't do it now: Career makeovers for the working woman.* New York: Pocket Books. Practical advice for retraining women who want a new career.

Rosinski, P. (2003). *Coaching across cultures: New tools for leveraging national, corporate, and professional differences.* London: Nicholas Brealey. Emphasizes cross-cultural awareness training and executive coaching as critical for managers, executives, and project teams working in multinational corporations or as part of global teams. The goals are to increase the range of effective leadership behaviors, such as communication, and to enhance self-awareness of the impact of such behaviors on employees.

Salas, E., & Cannon-Bowers, J. A. (2001). The science of training: A decade of progress. *Annual Review of Psychology, 52,* 471–499. Reviews training theory, needs analysis, training and post-training conditions, and strategies for motivating trainees. Methods and instructional strategies discussed include distance learning, simulations, games, and team training.

Part Three

Organizational Psychology

Organizational psychology is concerned with the social and psychological climate at work. Few people work alone. Most of us work in groups, such as a crew on an assembly line or the staff of a department in a corporate office. We develop informal cliques that generate and reinforce standards, values, and attitudes that may differ from those of the organization. We are also influenced by the formal structure of the company that employs us. Like informal groups, these formal groups generate a psychological climate or culture of ideals and ideas that affect our feelings about our job. Thus, our attitudes and behaviors in the workplace are influenced by the social climate of the organization and the psychological characteristics of its members. Organizational psychologists study the relationships between these two sets of factors.

Leadership (Chapter 7) is a major influence on work attitudes and behaviors. Organizational psychologists study the impact of various leadership styles and the characteristics and responsibilities of leaders.

Motivation, job satisfaction, and job involvement (Chapter 8) relate to employee needs and the ways organizations can satisfy them. We discuss the nature of employee identification with a job and with organizational goals and how this identification affects job performance and satisfaction.

The chapter on the organization of the organization (Chapter 9) discusses formal and informal groups and their psychological climate. We describe participatory democracy, adaptation to social and technological change, the socialization of new employees, and efforts to improve the quality of our working life.

Organizational psychology affects your working career directly. It influences your motivations, the style of leadership under which you function best, the leadership qualities you may display, and the structure of the organization for which you work. These factors determine the quality of your work experience, which, in turn, influences your general satisfaction with life.

Chapter 7

Leadership

MINORITY EMPLOYEES IN MANAGEMENT
SUMMARY
KEY TERMS
REVIEW QUESTIONS
ADDITIONAL READING

Did you know that half of all new business ventures and start-up companies fail within their first two years? Did you know that only one-third survive as long as five years? In most cases, these costly business failures can be traced to one source: poor leadership. And did you know that worker confidence in senior managers has declined to the point where only about one-third of all employees trust the judgment of their company's executives?

Over all, survey and research results do not present us with a positive or favorable impression of leadership in the workplace today. It is known that more than half of all managers and executives may display, at times, some degree of incompetence. Thus, many employees—perhaps including you—probably work for someone who is an inept leader. Working for such a person can have a negative effect on how you perform your job and how you relate to the people and situations in your life off the job. Poor leadership hurts the company, too, by contributing to work slowdowns, poor customer service, sloppy work habits, and high absenteeism and turnover. The subordinates of a bad boss feel no commitment to their organization, report reduced job and life satisfaction, and experience high levels of stress.

An opinion poll of several hundred workers found that only 11 percent of those who rated their immediate supervisor's performance as excellent said they would be seeking to change jobs in the coming year. In contrast, 40 percent of those who rated their supervisor's performance as poor said they would be looking for another job (Zipkin, 2000).

In addition to incompetence, some leaders can be characterized as abusive. They may ridicule or berate subordinates in front of their co-workers or blame them for something they did not do. They may threaten to fire or demote them. Studies of abusive leaders in civilian and in military organizations found that employees who face verbal abuse on the job develop anger and hatred toward their supervisors. They may resist their supervisors' requests and demands, express low levels of job and life satisfaction, and behave in counterproductive ways within the organization (see, for example, Fitness, 2000; Lewis, 2000; Tepper, Duffy, & Shaw, 2001; Zellars, Tepper, & Duffy, 2002).

Abused workers are not happy workers, nor is their organization functioning at its most productive and effective. On the other hand, consider the results of a meta-analysis of 106 studies involving more than 27,000 employees dealing with their level of trust in the organization's leadership. Employees who reported high levels of trust rated higher in job satisfaction, job performance, and organizational commitment (Dirks & Ferrin, 2002).

Obviously, the quality of leadership is a critical factor in the workplace and in your own working career. It is not surprising that organizations are greatly

Newsbreak   A Bad Boss Can Ruin Your Day

We've all worked for someone like Ellen Brower at some time in our lives, or we've known someone who did. She's arrogant, abrasive, and abusive. She gets angry at the slightest provocation and chews out her employees in front of their colleagues, berating them as incompetent and stupid—and a lot worse. No matter how hard you work, no matter how good a job you do, it's never good enough. She's never satisfied.

You dread going to work, and maybe you have a headache or an upset stomach by the time you reach the office. You have trouble sleeping because of the stress at work, thanks to her. You plan to quit as soon as you can, but until then, you're likely to remain an unhappy employee, getting little from your job but a paycheck. And no amount of money, you tell yourself every day, is worth having to put up with a boss like her.

If you do work for someone like Ellen Brower, you're not alone. Psychologist Robert Hogan of the University of Tulsa says that as many as seven out of every ten managers may be incompetent, exploiting, domineering, irritable, and untrustworthy. They refuse to delegate authority and have poor decision-making skills. In short, they are lousy bosses.

There are thousands of "bad boss" stories, like the one about the manager who would not let his employees phone for an ambulance when an elderly co-worker collapsed at his desk with a heart attack. The boss insisted that they wait until quitting time so that they didn't disrupt the work routine. Besides, as the boss said, "the guy was dead anyway." Or the insensitive department head who refused to believe a female employee who said she had missed work because she had suffered a miscarriage. He insisted that she obtain a written explanation from her physician. When she later requested bereavement leave to deal with her loss, he demanded to see the death certificate.

Some 75 percent of American workers believe that the worst thing about their jobs, and the greatest single cause of stress, is their boss. The most common complaints from workers are that supervisors are unwilling to exercise authority, tyrannize subordinates, and treat employees as if they were stupid.

How did such incompetent people get to be in charge? Hogan says it's because many companies select their best workers and promote them to supervisory positions. The catch is that being the best worker may have nothing to do with having the skills and abilities needed for good leadership. "What these bad guys are good at," Hogan claims, "is sucking up to *their* boss. These people have good social skills. That's how they got their job." Clearly it takes a lot more than social skills to make a good boss.

Sources: A real piece of work: "Worst boss" contest lets employees vent. *Washington Post*, October 16, 1997; R. Hogan, G. J. Curphy, & J. Hogan (1994). What we know about leadership. *American Psychologist, 49,* 493–504.

concerned with selecting, developing, and supporting their managers and executives and in making the best use of their leadership abilities on the job.

In addition to selection and training efforts, I-O psychologists have conducted considerable research on leadership techniques. They have explored the qualities and behaviors of successful and unsuccessful leaders, the effects of different leadership styles on subordinates, and the ways of maximizing leadership abilities.

APPROACHES TO LEADERSHIP

The ways in which leaders behave—the specific actions by which they play out their leadership roles—are based on certain assumptions about human nature. Consciously or unconsciously, leaders operate on the basis of some personal theory of human behavior, a view of what their subordinates are like as people. For example, managers who exercise close supervision on the job—who watch to make sure their employees are doing the work exactly as they have been instructed—hold a different view of human nature from that of managers who give their subordinates the freedom to work independently, in whatever way they think best.

Scientific Management

In the early years of the twentieth century, foremen (the first supervisory level over production workers) were promoted from the ranks of the workers and received little formal training for their leadership role. They had complete control over their subordinates' working lives. Foremen hired and fired, determined production levels, and set pay rates. There were few reins on their authority—no labor union, no industrial relations department, no human resources or personnel manager, no one to whom a worker could complain. Foremen usually gave hiring preference to their relatives and friends, and applied a combination of autocratic behavior, aggression, and physical intimidation to force workers to meet production goals.

Scientific management A management philosophy concerned with increasing productivity that regarded workers as extensions of the machines they operated.

The management philosophy during that period was called **scientific management,** an approach promoted by Frederick W. Taylor, an engineer. Taylor's concern was finding ways to increase productivity by getting the workers and the machines they operated to run faster and more efficiently.

Scientific management regarded workers simply as extensions of the machinery they operated. No consideration was given to the employees as human beings, as people with different needs, abilities, and interests. Workers were considered to be lazy and dishonest and likely to have a low level of intelligence. This view was reinforced by research that psychologists were then conducting on the general level of intelligence in the U.S. population. The psychologist H. H. Goddard argued that people with low intelligence required supervision by people with greater intelligence. "Laborers," Goddard said, "are but little above the child [and] must be told what to do and shown how to do it" (Goddard quoted in Broad & Wade, 1982, p. 198). Therefore, the only way for an organization to increase productivity and efficiency was to compel workers to submit to the dictates of their supervisors and the requirements of the manufacturing process.

The Human Relations Approach

It is difficult to imagine people working under the scientific management approach today. Most modern organizations regard the satisfaction of employee needs as a legitimate corporate responsibility. This changed view, called the human relations approach, arose in the 1920s and 1930s under the impact of the Hawthorne studies (discussed in Chapter 1), which focused attention on workers instead of on the needs of the production equipment.

One change introduced into the work situation in the Hawthorne studies was the style of leadership. At the Hawthorne plant, workers were routinely treated harshly by supervisors who berated them for dropping parts, talking on the job, and taking breaks. As we noted, workers were treated like children who needed to be watched, shouted at, and punished. In the Hawthorne experiments, supervisors were trained to act differently, allowing workers to set their own production pace and to form social groups. They were permitted to talk to one another on the job, and their views about the work were solicited. The new supervisors treated them like human beings, not interchangeable cogs in some giant production machine.

Theory X and Theory Y

The scientific management and human relations approaches to leadership behavior were given formal expression by Douglas McGregor as Theory X and Theory Y (McGregor, 1960; see also Heil, Bennis, & Stephens, 2000). The **Theory X** approach to management assumes that most people are innately lazy and dislike work, avoiding it whenever they can. They must be coerced, watched, and scolded on the job to make them work hard enough to meet the organization's goals. Theory X assumes that most people have no ambition, avoid responsibility, and prefer to be led and directed. Indeed, they would not work at all without a dictatorial leader. Theory X is compatible with scientific management and with the classic organizational style known as **bureaucracy**.

Theory Y proposes that most people seek inner satisfaction and fulfillment from their work. Control and punishment are not necessary to bring about good job performance. According to Theory Y, then, people are industrious and creative and seek challenge and responsibility on the job. They function best under a leader who allows them to participate in setting and working toward personal and organizational goals.

The Theory Y viewpoint is compatible with the human relations movement in management and with the participative, democratic style of organization. An example of the application of Theory Y is the management by objectives (MBO) approach to performance appraisal. We noted that MBO involves a high degree of employee participation in setting goals for job performance and personal growth.

The theoretical distinctions McGregor proposed have long been recognized as useful. How well have they been applied in the workplace? A contemporary scholar wrote that the Theory X view still persists, that is, the "view that workers are ordinarily passive and resistant to the legitimate expectations of management." But, he added, "McGregor's humanistic vision of organizations [his Theory Y concept] is closer to realization today than ever before" (Jacobs, 2004, pp. 293, 295).

Theory X/Theory Y The Theory X approach to management assumes that people are lazy and dislike work and therefore must be led and directed. Theory Y assumes that people find satisfaction in their work and function best under a leader who allows them to participate in working toward both personal and organizational goals.

Bureaucracy A formal, orderly, and rational approach to organizing business enterprises.

THEORIES OF LEADERSHIP

Industrial-organizational (I-O) psychologists recognize that effective leadership depends on the interaction of three factors:

1. the traits and behaviors of the leaders.
2. the characteristics of the followers.
3. the nature of the situation in which leadership occurs.

We describe several theoretical explanations of leadership: contingency theory, path-goal theory, the leader-member exchange, and implicit leadership theory.

Contingency Theory

Contingency theory A leadership theory in which a leader's effectiveness is determined by the interaction between the leader's personal characteristics and the characteristics of the leadership situation.

In **contingency theory,** developed by Fred Fiedler (Fiedler, 1978), leadership effectiveness is determined by the interaction between the leader's personal characteristics and aspects of the situation. Leaders are classified as primarily person-oriented or task-oriented. The type of leader who will be the more effective depends on the leader's degree of control over the situation.

Control is contingent on three factors: the relationship between the leader and followers, the degree of task structure, and the leader's authority or position power. If leaders are popular, are directing a highly structured or routine task, and have the authority or power to enforce discipline, then they have a high degree of control over the situation. We may describe this condition as favorable. For example, army sergeants who get along well with the soldiers in their squad are high-control and effective leaders. On the other hand, an unpopular president of a social club that has no formal goals who has no authority to require attendance or collect dues is a low-control leader in an unfavorable situation. According to contingency theory, the task-oriented leader will be more effective in extremely favorable or extremely unfavorable situations. When the situation is moderately favorable, the person-oriented leader will be more effective.

Contingency theory has stimulated a great deal of research, some of which is supportive and encouraging. However, most of that research was conducted in laboratory settings, not on the job. The validity of contingency theory remains in question, and it has not been determined whether the laboratory findings can be generalized to the workplace.

Path-Goal Theory

Path-goal theory A leadership theory that focuses on the kinds of behaviors leaders should exercise to allow their subordinates to achieve personal and organizational goals.

The **path-goal theory** of leadership focuses on the kinds of behaviors a leader exercises to allow subordinates to achieve their goals. The theory states that leaders can increase their subordinates' motivation, satisfaction, and job performance by administering rewards that depend on the achievement of particular goals. In other words, effective leaders will help employees reach personal and organizational goals by pointing out the paths they should follow and by providing them with the means to do so.

Four styles that leaders can adopt to facilitate employee attainment of goals are as follows (House, 1971; House & Mitchell, 1974):

- Directive leadership—the leader tells subordinates what they should do and how they should do it.

- Supportive leadership—the leader shows concern and support for subordinates.
- Participative leadership—the leader allows subordinates to participate in decisions that affect their work.
- Achievement-oriented leadership—the leader sets challenging goals for subordinates and emphasizes high levels of job performance.

The leadership style that will be most effective depends on characteristics of the situation and the attributes of the subordinates. Leaders must be flexible and should choose whichever style is called for. For example, employees who have a low level of the skills required to perform a task will function better under directive leadership. Employees who have high-level skills need less direction and function better under supportive leadership. Leaders must be able to perceive accurately the nature of the situation and the abilities of their subordinates and respond with the most appropriate approach.

Research findings on the path-goal theory are contradictory, but in general the support is weak. It is a difficult theory to test experimentally because basic concepts, such as "path" and "goal," are hard to define in operational terms.

The Leader-Member Exchange

The **leader-member exchange** model deals with the ways in which the leader-follower relationship (the leader-member exchange, or LMX) affects the leadership process (Graen & Schliemann, 1978). The proponents of this model criticized other leadership theories for focusing on average leadership styles or behaviors and for ignoring individual differences among subordinates. The relationship between each leader-subordinate pair (or dyad) must be considered separately because leaders behave differently with each subordinate.

Subordinates are of two types: the in-group employees, whom the supervisor views as competent, trustworthy, and highly motivated, and the out-group employees, whom the supervisor views as incompetent, untrustworthy, and poorly motivated.

The LMX model also distinguishes two leadership styles: supervision, in which leadership is based on formal authority, and leadership, in which influence is exerted through persuasion. With out-group subordinates, leaders use supervision and assign tasks requiring low levels of ability and responsibility. There is little personal relationship between leaders and out-group members.

With in-group subordinates, leaders practice leadership rather than supervision and assign members important and responsible tasks that require high levels of ability. Leaders and in-group members establish personal relationships in which in-group subordinates provide support and understanding.

On-the-job research has generally supported the leader-member exchange model for various levels of management and has shown that the quality of the leader-subordinate relationship can be improved through training, resulting in the display of more leadership than supervision. Significant improvements in job satisfaction and productivity and decreases in errors have been found among subordinates as a result of training to improve the quality of the LMX.

Two studies of worker-supervisor dyads in a medical center and a distribution company found that employees who believed they had a high LMX with their supervisors also believed they communicated with them more frequently than did those who believed they had a low LMX. In addition, employees in high

Leader-member exchange A leadership theory that focuses on how the leader-follower relationship affects the leadership process.

LMX relationships who communicated frequently with their managers received higher performance ratings than did those in low LMX relationships who communicated frequently with their managers (Kacmar, Witt, Ziunuska, & Gully, 2003; Yrle, Hartman, & Galle, 2002).

A study of 125 salespersons in a large retail organization found that employees who had a strong relationship with their supervisor (a high LMX) were more committed to achieving assigned goals than were employees with a low LMX (Klein & Kim, 1998). Research involving 106 employees and their supervisors in an importing firm found that a high LMX between employee and supervisor was significantly related to delegation of authority. In other words, supervisors in high LMX relationships with their subordinates were far more likely to delegate authority to them. As a result, the employees felt empowered and showed improvements in job performance and job satisfaction (Schriesheim, Neider, & Scandura, 1998). Another study involving 128 manager-employee dyads from 13 organizations also found a high sense of empowerment among employees in high LMX relationships. This sense of empowerment did not appear to exist among employees in low LMX relationships (Gomez & Rosen, 2001).

An analysis of the performance of 317 bank employees confirmed the positive relationship between a high employee-supervisor LMX and high job performance. This study also showed that the relationship was maintained even when the employees and the supervisor were geographically remote from one another, that is, when the employees worked in a different office or a different city from their direct supervisor. The researchers concluded that the mutual trust and respect of a high-quality LMX relationship overcame physical distance so that employees and supervisors worked jointly to accomplish organizational goals (Howell & Hall-Merenda, 1999).

High LMX relationships between superior and subordinate can be characterized as a two-way street. Consider a study of 232 dyads in a large company (Maslyn & Uhl-Bien, 2001). High LMXs were found when both sides put effort into developing the relationship. In low LMXs, one member of the dyad (usually the manager) believed they worked harder at establishing and maintaining the relationships than the other person did. As a result, the managers tended to believe that the low LMX was the other person's fault.

High and low LMXs are also closely related to co-worker exchanges (CWX). A survey of 67 employees at an engineering firm and a health services facility found that when two co-workers had a high LMX with their supervisor, or two co-workers had a low LMX with their supervisor, the co-workers themselves had a high CWX relationship with each other (Sherony & Green, 2002).

Finally, a study of 191 employees of the research and development department of a chemical company found that LMX affected creativity, at least for those employees characterized by a particular cognitive style. The researchers used psychological test results and supervisor ratings to identify employees as cognitive innovators (able to generate ideas that deviated from the norm) or cognitive adapters (able to generate ideas consistent with accepted conventions). Innovators were found to be highly creative on the job, regardless of the nature of their relationship with their supervisor. Adapters were consistently more creative when they had a high LMX relationship with their supervisor than when they had a low LMX relationship (Tierney, Farmer, & Graen, 1999). These on-the-job research findings have given the leader-member exchange model a practical advantage over most other leadership theories.

| Newsbreak | **The Deputy Assistant to the Assistant Deputy . . .** |

Suppose you were offered the following choice: either a $2,000 pay raise or a new job title with the word *manager* in it—not a new job, just a new title. Which would you choose? When the president of On-Line Systems offered his sales force that choice, the $2,000 or the title "sales manager" instead of "salesman," almost everyone opted for the new label.

"The thing that makes people stay," he said, "is not necessarily money. Why do they stay, day after day, coming back to you? It's because they're happy. A showy title makes them feel appreciated."

Employees especially like ego-boosting titles that include "manager" or "director." Managers get their phone calls returned. Clients respond faster to their e-mails and faxes than they do to those from someone with a lower-level title. Being a manager means never being put on hold. All those advantages will make them more productive.

Companies that recruit on college campuses are aware of this phenomenon and have been upgrading the job titles for their starting positions. Instead of seeking a "sales representative," they want a candidate for their "management leadership development program." Same job, but different label. The result? Many more job applicants.

Nowhere is title inflation more blatant than in the government bureaucracy. At the federal level in Washington, D.C., there are, at last count:

484 deputy assistant secretaries
148 associate assistant secretaries
220 assistant assistant secretaries
82 deputy assistant assistant secretaries

Paul Light, a senior fellow at the Brookings Institution who studies what he calls "job title creep," joked about his own job. He says that he needs to have a chief of staff, "but I won't really be somebody until I have a *Deputy* Chief of Staff."

Sources: Please hold for the Deputy Deputy. *New York Times*, March 14, 1999; Title search: What's in a name? *St. Petersburg (FL) Times*, July 26, 1998.

Implicit Leadership Theory

Implicit leadership theory defines leadership from the standpoint of the persons who are being led. According to this view, each of us develops, through our past experiences with different types of leaders, our own implicit theory or image of the ideal leader. If our new manager or boss fits that ideal view or perception, then we will consider him or her to be a good leader. If not, we will consider the new boss to be a poor leader (Lord, Brown, & Freiburg, 1999; Lord & Maher, 1993).

Implicit leadership theory A leadership theory that describes a good leader in terms of one's past experiences with different types of leaders.

This suggests that anyone can be classified as a good leader if that person is perceived by subordinates as fitting their mental image of a good leader's personality. Thus, leadership would be highly subjective. There would be no objective criteria or characteristics that define a person as a good or bad leader. Instead, a person is only a good leader if his or her behavior matches our expectations.

Suppose, for example, that your experiences in the workplace have led you to believe that the ideal manager is kind and considerate and asks for your opinion before making decisions that affect your work environment. This type of leader may make you feel more like a partner than a subordinate. When your new boss turns out to be an authoritarian bureaucrat, you are likely to decide that he or she is not a good leader. A co-worker, however, may have thrived under a different kind of leader; perhaps this employee likes to be told what to do and does not want to participate in decision making. This co-worker may view the new boss as a good leader. According to the implicit leadership theory, then, it appears that great leaders exist only in the eyes of the beholder, that is, in the perceptions of their followers.

It does not follow, however, that a manager could display almost any type of behavior and still be perceived by someone among their subordinates as a good leader. In practical terms, legitimate leadership behavior is limited to attributes that are considered acceptable in the workplace. In a study of 939 workers in a variety of industries in England, a paper-and-pencil test was developed to measure implicit theories of leadership. The results identified four traits associated with good leadership and two traits associated with bad leadership. The positive characteristics were sensitivity, intelligence, dedication, and dynamism. The negative characteristics were tyranny and masculinity. These positive and negative attributes were consistent with employees at all working ages, career stages, and levels of employment (Epitropaki & Martin, 2004).

Implicit personality theory is an unusual approach to leadership. Its usefulness in the workplace has yet to be determined.

STYLES OF LEADERSHIP

Much I-O psychology research focuses on leadership styles and the behaviors by which they are manifested on the job. We discuss the differences between authoritarian and democratic leaders, and between transactional and transformational leaders.

Authoritarian and Democratic Leaders

Authoritarian leadership
A leadership style in which a leader makes all decisions and tells followers what to do.

Democratic leadership
A leadership style in which a leader and followers discuss problems and make decisions jointly.

Leadership in the workplace involves various styles along a continuum. The continuum ranges from a highly **authoritarian leadership** style, in which the leader makes all decisions and tells followers what to do, to a highly **democratic leadership** style, in which leader and followers discuss problems and jointly make all decisions that affect their work. The style that is most effective depends on the nature of the situation and the needs and characteristics of the followers.

In stressful work situations that require unusually rapid and highly efficient job performance, productivity and satisfaction are more likely to be maintained under authoritarian leadership. I-O psychologists suggest that these employees recognize that the nature of their work does not allow time for a participative

For police officers, who hold stressful jobs that require rapid decision-making skills and efficient job performance, authoritarian leadership is desirable. Often, law-enforcement situations do not allow time for a more democratic approach.

approach. For example, firefighters must respond to a fire alarm immediately and follow the directions of their chief. They do not have time to hold a committee meeting to determine the best way to deal with the fire.

Transactional and Transformational Leaders

Transactional leaders conduct their business by identifying the needs of their followers and bestowing rewards to satisfy those needs in exchange for a certain level of performance. Adhering to the path-goal theory, transactional leaders are expected to do the following: "set goals, articulate explicit agreements regarding what the leader expects from organizational members and how they will be rewarded for their efforts and commitment, and provide constructive feedback to keep everybody on task" (Vera & Crossan, 2004, p. 224).

Transactional leaders focus on increasing the efficiency of established routines and procedures and are more concerned with following existing rules than with making changes to the structure of the organization. Thus, they operate most effectively in organizations that have evolved beyond the chaotic, no-rules stage of entrepreneurial development that characterizes so many new companies. Transactional leadership establishes and standardizes practices that will help the organization reach maturity, emphasizing goal-setting, efficiency of operation, and increasing productivity.

Transformational leaders have more latitude in their behavior. They are not limited by their followers' perceptions. Rather than believing that they must act in accordance with what their followers expect of them, transformational leaders work to change or transform their followers' needs and redirect their thinking.

Transformational leaders challenge and inspire subordinates with a sense of purpose and excitement about what can be accomplished. These leaders create a vision of what the corporate culture can be and communicate it to their employees,

Transactional leadership A leadership style that focuses on the social interactions between leaders and followers, based on followers' perceptions of and expectations about the leader's abilities.

Transformational leadership A leadership style in which leaders are not constrained by their followers' perceptions but are free to act to change or transform their followers' views.

stimulating them to develop their abilities while accepting feedback and suggestions. A study of nearly 200 managers (from supervisors to CEOs) in a wide variety of industries found that transformational leaders scored higher on the personality factors of extraversion and agreeableness than did nontransformational leaders (Judge & Bono, 2000). A meta-analysis of 45 leadership studies found that women are far more likely than men to be transformational leaders (Eagly, Johannesen-Schmidt, & Van Engen, 2003).

Three components of transformational leadership have been identified (Bycio, Hackett, & Allen, 1995):

1. Charismatic leadership—the level of confidence and inspiration engendered by the leader
2. Individualized consideration—the amount of attention and support the leader supplies to the followers
3. Intellectual stimulation—the extent to which leaders persuade followers to think differently about how they perform their jobs

Studies of business executives, high-ranking military officers, and high-level administrators in government and universities have found that those described by their subordinates as transformational leaders were more effective on the job. They also had better relations with superiors and made greater contributions to organizational goals than did those described as transactional leaders. Employees reported that they worked harder for transformational leaders than for transactional leaders.

Other research has demonstrated that transformational leaders inspire feelings of worker empowerment and identification with the leader and the work unit. They also motivate subordinates to think and act in ways beyond what they considered possible, bringing out their best qualities. Transformational leadership is capable of producing greater creativity among subordinates as well as a belief in the importance of their tasks (Bass, Avolio, Jung, & Berson, 2003; Bono & Judge, 2003; Kark, Shamir, & Chen, 2003; Shin & Zhou, 2003). The greater effectiveness of transformational leaders has been demonstrated in a wide range of employing organizations and in several countries including the United States, India, Spain, Japan, China, and Austria.

Charismatic leadership
A leadership style characterized by a self-promoting personality, a high energy level, and a willingness to take risks. Charismatic leaders stimulate their followers to think independently.

Often, transformational leaders display **charismatic leadership,** mentioned above as one of three components of this type of leadership. Charismatic leaders have a broad knowledge of their field, a self-promoting personality, a high energy level, and a willingness to take risks and use unconventional strategies. They use their power effectively to serve others and inspire their trust. Charismatic leaders stimulate their followers to think independently and to ask questions. They maintain open communication with subordinates and freely share recognition with them. They tend to generate high job performance and positive work attitudes among their followers.

Charismatic leaders also communicate a vision to their followers. They act to implement that vision, and they display a powerful communications style, such as a captivating tone of voice, animated facial expressions, and a dynamic way of interacting with other people. A study of 25 mid-level managers at a cell phone company in Germany found that the managers could be trained to become more inspirational leaders. The training program, which lasted one-and-a-half days, involved instruction in charismatic leadership behaviors and in preparing and delivering inspirational speeches. Feedback, both positive and negative, was offered on the content and delivery of the speech (Frese, Beimel, & Schoenborn, 2003). Charismatic leaders are the ones who launch new enterprises, direct organizational change, and stimulate impressive gains in employee productivity. But charismatic leaders can also misuse their power over others. They can be insensitive to the needs of their followers and act only for personal gain.

THE ROLE OF POWER IN LEADERSHIP

Among the issues relating to power in leadership behavior are (1) the power that leaders have over their subordinates and (2) the ways in which leaders are motivated by power. Leaders may exert different kinds of power, depending on the situation, the nature of their followers, and their personal characteristics.

Types of Power

Psychologists have proposed five types of leadership power (Yukl & Taber, 1983). These are the first three:

1. *Reward power*. Organizational leaders have the ability to reward subordinates with pay raises and promotions. This power gives leaders a means of control over employees and can affect employee behavior.
2. *Coercive power*. Organizational leaders have an equally strong source of power in their ability to punish subordinates by firing them, by withholding promotions and raises, and by keeping them in undesirable jobs.
3. *Legitimate power*. Legitimate power derives from the organization's formal power structure. The hierarchy of control legitimizes the right of the leader to direct and supervise the activities of followers and the duty of followers to accept that supervision.

These three sources of power are derived from and defined by the formal organization to which leaders and subordinates belong. They are types of power dictated or prescribed by the organization. The next two types of power derive from the leaders themselves and are earned or merited by the leaders' personal characteristics as these are perceived by followers. We might call these attributes *respect* as well as power.

4. *Referent power*. Referent power refers to the degree to which employees identify with their leaders and the leaders' goals, accept those goals as their own, and work with their leaders to achieve the goals.
5. *Expert power*. Expert power refers to the extent to which leaders are believed to have the skills necessary to attain the group's goals. If employees acknowledge their leader's expertise, then they are more likely to become willing and supportive subordinates.

Effects and Uses of Power

As you may know from your own experience, coercive power can be counterproductive. Leaders who rely primarily on coercive power in dealing with subordinates are less likely to be effective than are leaders who exercise the other types of power. People who work for coercive leaders tend to rank low in job satisfaction, productivity, and commitment to the organization. In order, the types of leadership power that research has shown to be most effective are expert power, legitimate power, and referent power.

How does power motivate organizational leaders? High-level executives and middle-level managers often show a great personal need for power. Effective managers tend to demonstrate a higher need for power than do less effective managers. However, the most effective managers do not seek power for personal gain. Their power need is directed toward the organization and is used to achieve organizational goals. As a result, they are usually successful in establishing and maintaining a good work climate, high morale, and high team spirit among their subordinates.

Managers motivated by the need for personal power serve themselves rather than their organization. They are capable of creating loyalty among subordinates, but it is a loyalty toward themselves, not toward the organization. These managers are more effective than those who show no need for power, but they are not as effective as those whose power is oriented toward the organization.

THE ROLE OF EXPECTATIONS: THE PYGMALION EFFECT

Leaders' expectations about their employees' job performance can influence that performance. For example, managers who expect high performance tend to get high performance, and those who expect poor performance tend to get poor performance.

This instance of a self-fulfilling prophecy was first observed in the classroom. In a now-classic demonstration, teachers were told that some of their students had a high level of potential and others had a low level of potential. In reality, there were no such differences between the two groups; the students were equal in their abilities. The differences existed only in the teachers' expectations, as created by the experimental situation. Yet, the group of students with the allegedly high potential later scored significantly higher on IQ tests than did the other group. The teachers had subtly communicated their expectations to their students, thereby affecting the students' academic performance (Rosenthal & Jacobson, 1968).

Pygmalion effect A self-fulfilling prophecy in which managers' expectations about the level of their employees' job performance can influence that performance.

This expectancy effect was labeled the **Pygmalion effect,** named after Pygmalion, a king of Cyprus who fell in love with an ivory statue of a beautiful woman named Galatea. In answer to Pygmalion's prayers, the statue came alive, turning his fantasy into reality.

The self-fulfilling prophecy has been widely demonstrated in the workplace. A meta-analysis of 17 studies involving nearly 3,000 employees in a variety of jobs showed that the phenomenon was particularly strong in the military. It was more prevalent among men than women, and it was also found extensively among disadvantaged employees—those employees considered by management, and by themselves, to have low expectations (McNatt, 2000). Their job performance usually matched their expectations. Other research, involving 30 squads of soldiers in the Israel Defense Force (the Israeli army), confirmed these findings. Women recruits who were held in low esteem by their female superior officers tended to perform poorly (Davidson & Eden, 2000).

It has also been found that expectations of <u>co-workers</u> ca<u>n influence</u> employ<u>ees</u>. A study of 166 engineers, software development specialists, research scientists, physicians, and pharmacists in Taiwan showed that when they believed their co-workers expected them to be creative, their own self-reported identity as a creative person was higher than when co-workers had no such expectations (Farmer, Tierney, & Kung-McIntyre, 2003).

A survey of 584 blue-collar workers and 158 white-collar workers found that employees will come to believe they have creative abilities on the job when their supervisor serves as a model and uses verbal persuasion to enhance employee self-confidence and expectations. In other words, the supervisor can create a self-fulfilling prophecy among the workers that they can be more creative, which has the effect of leading to an actual increase in creativity on the job (Tierney & Farmer, 2002).

Functions of leadership --

THE FUNCTIONS OF LEADERSHIP

A comprehensive research program to identify the functions of leaders on the job began in the late 1940s at Ohio State University. A variety of leadership tasks and behaviors were grouped into two categories of functions called **consideration leadership functions** and **initiating structure leadership functions** (Fleishman & Harris, 1962).

The Consideration Dimension

The functions in the consideration dimension involve awareness of and sensitivity to the feelings of subordinates. These functions are allied <u>with the human relations approach to management</u>. Leaders high in consideration understand and accept subordinates as individuals with unique motivations and needs. Successful leaders must relate to each employee by being considerate of that person's

Consideration leadership functions
Leadership behaviors that involve awareness of and sensitivity to the feelings of subordinates.

Initiating structure leadership functions
Leadership behaviors concerned with organizing, defining, and directing the work activities of subordinates.

Effective managers balance consideration behaviors (sensitivity to subordinates' needs) with initiating structure behaviors (providing a framework within which to meet the company's goals).

Newsbreak   Management Always Wins: The Canoe Race

A Japanese company and an American company decided to have a canoe race on the Missouri River. Both teams practiced long and hard to reach their peak performance before the race. On the day of the race, the Japanese won by a mile.

The American team was crushed. They felt very discouraged and morally depressed. Management prepared a mission statement and made it their goal to uncover the reason for the defeat. A Measurement Team of senior management personnel was formed. They would investigate and recommend appropriate action.

Their finding was that the Japanese team had eight people rowing and one person steering, whereas the American team had one person rowing and eight people steering. So American management hired a consulting firm for an enormous amount of money to advise them. The consulting company concluded that too many people were steering the boat and not enough people were rowing.

To prevent another humiliating loss to the Japanese team the following year, the American rowing team's management was reorganized. The new management structure included four steering managers, three area steering superintendents, and one assistant area steering superintendent liaison. The group then implemented a new performance system intended to give the one person rowing the boat greater incentives to work harder. The system was called the Rowing Team Quality-First Program, designed to give the rower empowerment and job enrichment. It was kicked off with meetings, dinners, and free pens and T-shirts for the rower.

The next year, the Japanese won the boat race by two miles. American management fired the rower for poor performance, halted funds for the development of a new canoe, sold the paddles, and cancelled capital investment for new equipment. They gave awards for high performance to the steering managers and distributed the money saved as bonuses to the senior executives.

Source: An Internet story of unknown source, provided by Marty Salo.

feelings. This necessarily places an additional burden on managers. They must be sympathetic, warm, and understanding of their employees while maintaining production levels and other organizational goals.

The effects of such behaviors on employees can have highly beneficial results for leaders and their organizations. A study of 115 employees of a credit union found that when disagreements occurred between managers and employees, those managers who communicated openly and showed concern for their workers were perceived as more trustworthy and were less likely to be blamed for the disagreement. Employees who worked for managers who were perceived as trustworthy were far more likely to make contributions to their organizations beyond the job requirements, as compared to employees who did not find their managers to be trustworthy (Korsgaard, Brodt, & Whitener, 2002).

You can see the similarity between the consideration leadership function and the leadership styles proposed by some of the theories we discussed earlier. High consideration relates to the person-oriented leader in contingency theory, to participative leadership in path-goal theory, and to the leadership condition in the leader-member exchange model.

The Initiating Structure Dimension

The functions in the initiating structure dimension include tasks traditionally associated with a leadership role—organizing, defining, and directing the work activities of subordinates. Sometimes this aspect of a manager's job conflicts with the demands of the consideration dimension. To accomplish a job (to initiate structure), managers must assign specific tasks to employees, direct the way in which the tasks should be performed, and monitor the work to ensure that it is being done properly.

These work activities may call for some authoritarian behavior and decision making, and there may not be time or opportunity for leaders to consider their subordinates' needs or feelings. A certain amount of work must be accomplished at a specified level of quality in a fixed period of time. The organization's success and the manager's job depend on meeting these standards consistently. Thus, it is not always easy for managers to balance the behaviors of consideration and initiating structure.

The leadership functions in the initiating structure dimension are similar to those of the task-oriented leader in contingency theory, directive leadership in path-goal theory, and supervision in the leader-member exchange model.

Although the consideration and initiation dimensions were developed more than 50 years ago, recent research reveals that they remain valid descriptors of leadership behavior. A meta-analysis of 322 studies found that consideration showed a significant positive correlation with the quality of the leader's performance and the performance of his or her group or organization. Initiating structure was related to leader satisfaction and to group performance. Taken together, both dimensions were linked to leader effectiveness and to the subordinates' level of motivation (Judge, Piccolo, & Ilies, 2004).

CHARACTERISTICS OF SUCCESSFUL LEADERS

The characteristics required for successful leadership vary with a manager's level in the organizational hierarchy. The CEO of an automobile manufacturing company performs different functions and thus needs different abilities from those of a supervisor on the auto painting assembly line. In general, the higher the position on the corporate ladder, the fewer consideration activities and the more initiating structure activities are required. A high-level executive needs fewer human relations skills than a supervisor, because the executive typically controls and interacts directly with fewer subordinates. The corporate vice president may deal only with a half-dozen department heads, whereas the first-line supervisor

A first-line supervisor at an automobile plant meets with subordinates to discuss problems and hear grievances.

may have 100 or more workers to manage. Therefore, leaders at different levels have different functions, characteristics, and problems on the job.

First-Line Supervisors

I-O psychology research on first-line supervisors suggests that supervisors with the most productive work groups have the following qualities:

1. Effective supervisors are person-centered. They rate higher in the consideration function than do unsuccessful supervisors.
2. Effective supervisors are supportive. They are more helpful to employees and more willing to defend them against criticism from higher management.
3. Effective supervisors are democratic. They hold frequent meetings with employees to solicit their views and encourage participation. Less effective supervisors are more autocratic.
4. Effective supervisors are flexible. They allow employees to accomplish their goals in their own way whenever possible, consistent with the goals of the organization. Less effective supervisors dictate how a job is to be performed and permit no deviation.
5. Effective supervisors describe themselves as coaches rather than directors. They emphasize quality, provide clear directions, and give timely feedback to their workers.

Managers and Executives

At higher levels of an organization, managers and executives engage in fewer consideration behaviors and more initiating structure behaviors. In other words, *more work-oriented*

they are less people-oriented and more work-oriented. Successful executives share other characteristics. We discuss the impact of college attendance, personality, the role of power, and the importance of mentoring. We also note the characteristics of unsuccessful executives.

College Experience and Intelligence.

College attendance correlates positively with later job success at the executive level. Employees with a college background rise faster and higher through the management ranks than do those who did not attend college. College grades correlate positively with assessment-center ratings of management potential and later advancement on the job. People who earn higher grades in college show greater potential for promotion, obtain their first promotion early in their career, and rise higher in management than those who earn lower grades. The quality of the college attended is a less useful predictor of later job performance, although assessment-center ratings are higher for managers who attended better-quality colleges.

A more valid predictor of potential and actual promotion is college major. Those who major in humanities and social sciences receive superior ratings in assessment-center exercises and job performance and move faster and farther up the corporate ladder. Those who major in business administration rank second. Mathematics, science, and engineering majors are third. Humanities and social science majors excel in decision making, creativity in solving business problems, intellectual ability, written communications skills, and motivation for advancement. They, and the business majors, rank higher in interpersonal skills, leadership ability, oral communications skills, and flexibility than the math, science, and engineering majors.

For many years it was thought, or assumed, that intelligence was highly related to leadership, that leaders were characteristically more intelligent than their subordinates. Recent research does not support this assumption. Studies have shown a low correlation between intelligence and leadership. In other words, intellectual abilities have not been found to be significantly related to the prediction of performance in leadership positions (see, for example, Fiedler, 2002; Judge, Colbert, & Ilies, 2004).

Personality.

As we saw in Chapter 4, various aspects of personality, especially the Big Five factors, are highly related to job performance. A study of 17 chief executive officers of major corporations also found personality to be an important component of job success at the highest level of management. The factor of conscientiousness was related to a sense of control among the CEOs' top management teams. The factor of emotional stability influenced team cohesion and intellectual flexibility. Agreeableness on the part of CEOs was related to the top management team's feeling of cohesion. Extraversion was related to leader dominance. Openness to experience was related to team risk taking (Peterson, Smith, Martorana, & Owens, 2003).

A study of 571 bank tellers employed by the same firm in both the Hong Kong office and the U.S. office found that managers were far more likely to form relationships of high trust and commitment with subordinates when the subordinates' personalities were similar to their own. Thus, similarity in personality was shown to lead to a high leader-member exchange (Schaubroeck & Lam, 2002).

The Role of Power.   We noted that power was an important motivating force for successful executives. Decades ago, psychologist David McClelland proposed a leadership motive pattern (LMP) that is informally described as "empire building." Executives with a high LMP are believed to be effective managers. They have a high need for power, a lower need for affiliation with other people, and considerable self-control. They have a greater need to influence people than to be liked (McClelland, 1975).

Research on this personality pattern has found it to be highly predictive of success for managers in nontechnical jobs. The managers' need for achievement (the need to perform well) also predicted success in nontechnical positions. In addition, managers high in the LMP prefer jobs that are high in prestige and status.

Mentoring.   People who acquire the support or sponsorship of mentors within the company are often the ones more likely to advance within the corporate hierarchy. A mentor is a coach or counselor who provides support and advice to a younger protégé. Those managers fortunate enough to have had good mentors are far more likely to receive pay increases and promotions, compared to those who do not have mentors. A meta-analysis of 43 studies supported the career-enhancing value of career mentoring, which focuses on aspects of the work, and of psychosocial mentoring, which involves role modeling, counseling, and friendship. Employees who received mentoring had more positive attitudes toward their job and organization and were more successful in terms of promotions and pay raises than were employees who did not receive mentoring (Allen, Eby, Poteet, Lentz, & Lima, 2004).

Unsuccessful Executives.   It is just as important for organizations to know what characteristics lead some managers to fail as it is to understand what makes others succeed. Such failure is usually referred to as "derailment," such as when a train unexpectedly leaves the track.

Executives who once showed management potential but who are later dismissed or retired early typically fail because of personality factors rather than job performance. Derailed executives are judged by their superiors to lack consideration behaviors. Insensitive, arrogant, and aloof, they display an abrasive and domineering leadership style and are overly ambitious to attain personal rather than organizational goals.

One I-O psychologist described unsuccessful executives in terms of flaws or fallacies in their thinking (Sternberg, 2003, pp. 395–396). These are as follows:

1. the unrealistic optimism fallacy, believing they are so smart that they can do whatever they want
2. the egocentrism fallacy, believing they are the only ones who matter, that the people who work for them don't count
3. the omniscience fallacy, believing they know everything and see no limits to their knowledge
4. the omnipotence fallacy, believing they are all-powerful and therefore entitled to do what they want
5. the invulnerability fallacy, believing they can get away with doing what they want because they are too clever to get caught; even if they are caught, believing they will go unpunished because of their importance

PROBLEMS OF LEADERSHIP

First-Line Supervisors

Just as leader characteristics vary with a manager's level in the organizational hierarchy, so do the pressures and problems. In some ways, first-line supervisors have more difficult jobs than executives, yet they receive less formal training in how to manage other people. In fact, supervisors may receive no training at all, and they are not selected as carefully as people who begin their careers at higher-level management positions. Often, the most competent workers are chosen to be supervisors, without any assessment of their leadership potential.

Supervisors promoted from the ranks face conflicting demands and loyalties. Before promotion, they were accepted by those who worked with them and shared their attitudes and values. They may have socialized with co-workers off the job. Their work group gave them a sense of identity and belonging that provided a measure of emotional security.

After they become supervisors, they can no longer enjoy the same relationship with co-workers and friends. Even if they try to remain part of the group, their former co-workers do not respond to them in the same way because of the changed relationship. This costs newly promoted supervisors the emotional security that comes from group affiliation and identification.

Supervisors are the point of contact between management and workers, trying to weigh the conflicting needs of both sides. If supervisors expect to establish and retain the loyalty and cooperation of their workers, they must present management's needs and decisions to the workers and must present the workers' needs to management, serving as a buffer and an open channel of communication. In practice, it is often necessary for supervisors to be more responsive to the demands of their superiors if they hope to keep their jobs.

The trend toward increased worker participation complicates the job of first-line supervisors. They stand to lose what little autonomy they have by being forced to share leadership and decision-making power with subordinates. **Self-managing work groups** are another threat to supervisory power and autonomy. In these programs, instead of sharing power, supervisors must abandon their traditional responsibilities and act as resource persons rather than leaders. If the work groups are less effective than expected, the supervisor will be blamed. If the work groups are effective, top management usually attributes the favorable results to the workers, not to the supervisor.

Computer technology in the workplace has also made supervision more difficult. First-line supervisors are responsible for hardware they often are not trained to understand. Computers can control and monitor quantity and quality of production and provide top management with data on employee performance, output, and other aspects of office or manufacturing processes, thus bypassing any input from the first-line supervisor.

Self-managing work groups Employee groups that allow the members of a work team to manage, control, and monitor all facets of their work, from recruiting, hiring, and training new employees to deciding when to take rest breaks.

Managers and Executives

A department or section head faces stresses that are different from those of the CEO. Middle-level managers, despite comfortable salaries and fringe benefits, typically express considerable discontent. A frequent complaint is the lack of influence in formulating company policy, policy they are expected to implement without question. Middle managers also complain about having insufficient authority and resources to carry out company policy. They must fight for recognition from superiors and compete for support for their ideas and projects. As a result, middle managers often experience considerable frustration as they vie for the few top management slots in the hierarchy.

Another source of dissatisfaction is the feeling of obsolescence that comes to middle-level managers in their late thirties and early forties. Most of them have reached a plateau and will receive no additional promotions. That realization often becomes part of a general midlife crisis, a period of self-examination for middle managers who feel threatened by younger subordinates, by changing cultural values, and by redefined organizational goals. Their productivity, creativity, and motivation may decline, and they may in effect retire on the job, making little contribution to the organization.

Employee participation in decision making is another source of stress for middle managers. Although they have no influence in decisions affecting their own jobs, they see that assembly-line, production, and office workers have gained the right to participate in decision making and job design. Participatory democracy leads to drastic changes in the ways managers can exert control over their employees. Shared leadership results in a loss of managerial authority, status, and power. Democratization may also eliminate traditional management perquisites such as reserved parking spaces, corporate dining rooms, and private offices.

A source of stress more common among high-level managers is the intense commitment of time and energy to the organization. It is not uncommon for executives to work 60- or 80-hour weeks and to bring work home for evenings and weekends. With cell phones, beepers, laptop computers, and fax machines, executives can work at home and while traveling, rarely escaping the demands of the office. This leads to an imbalance in their personal lives, leaving little time for family demands.[1]

The potential rewards of an executive position—power, money, status, challenge, and fulfillment—are great, but so are the demands. Still, there are more positive aspects to life at the top of the organizational hierarchy. Although middle managers are not a particularly happy group, top executives report high job satisfaction. Surveys show that most upper-level executives would remain on the job even if they were financially independent. Their work provides much more than financial satisfaction.

WOMEN IN MANAGEMENT

After decades of being underrepresented in management positions, women employees are finally making progress in the upper ranks of corporate life. In 1995 women held only 8 percent of the top corporate office jobs in Fortune 500 companies. By the year 2000, women held 12.5 percent of these jobs, and two years later the figure was nearly 16 percent. Women still fare poorly in traditionally male industries, such as oil, mining, heavy equipment, and engineering. Many more women corporate officers were reported in apparel and retailing companies (Walsh, 2002).

Women constitute 46 percent of the lower- and middle-level managerial ranks. This is higher than for other industrialized nations: In Sweden and in

---

[1]See Chapter 12 for a more detailed discussion of work-family conflicts.

Britain, 30 percent of these management jobs are held by women, 27 percent in Germany, and 9 percent in Japan (data from French, 2003).

At every level of employment women are paid less than men for doing the same or similar jobs. Evidence suggests that women at all working ages and levels of employment are more reluctant to negotiate or request higher salaries and are more likely to accept whatever pay scale is offered.

A survey of 37 recent master's-degree graduates found that 57 percent of the men negotiated their salary for a management position whereas only 7 percent of the women did so. Those who negotiated received starting salaries that averaged $4,500 higher than those who did not. A study of 38 business school students who were applying for employment showed several differences between male and female applicants. When asked if they believed they were entitled to a higher salary or to a salary equal to what other applicants would receive for the same job, 70 percent of the men said they felt entitled to a higher salary; 70 percent of the women said they were entitled to the same salary as other applicants. In follow-up interviews, 85 percent of the men reported that it was their responsibility to ensure that the organization paid them what they believed they were worth. Only 17 percent of the women agreed with that concept; most of the women believed they were worth whatever the company decided to pay them (Ellin, 2004).

Once hired by an organization, women face other problems on the job. A comparison of 69 women middle- and upper-level managers with 69 men managers at the same levels showed that women reported more barriers to advancement than men did. Women experienced a lack of fit with the corporate culture and felt that they were deliberately excluded from informal networks. They noted difficulty in getting good assignments and were rarely considered for job opportunities that required geographical relocation. These women managers believed that they had to work much harder and meet higher standards than men managers did. In addition, the women found it harder than men to develop mentoring relationships with higher-level executives and to have their achievements recognized by the company's top decision-makers (Lyness & Thompson, 2000).

A common sex stereotype is being applied here: discrimination against women managers by keeping them in jobs that require so-called feminine attributes such as empathy and sensitivity. So-called masculine attributes, such as aggressiveness, ambition, and self-reliance, are seen as more suited to line jobs in manufacturing and sales. It is the line departments that are the stepping-stones to top management. When women do succeed on the job, their superiors (usually men) are likely to attribute that success to luck or other external conditions, not to personal ability. When men succeed, it is usually attributed to personal ability.

Women managers are assessed differently from men managers in terms of their leadership behaviors. When men and women managers display assertiveness, women are typically judged as pushy. These judgments are made by women as well as by men. A woman lawyer wrote:

There's nothing men hate more—especially men in power—than a woman who is [too much] like a man. It's a very negative thing. There was a very well-qualified woman who interviewed at our firm for a position. She had years of experience in the exact practice area that we were recruiting for, but when she showed up, people hated her. Men and women alike said, "She's too mannish." She didn't get the job (Ely, 1995, p. 617).

Men managers expect women managers to be assertive but will tolerate that assertiveness only up to a point. They expect women managers to take risks but always be outstanding, to be tough and ambitious but not "masculine," and to take responsibility but follow the advice of others. In other words, women managers are expected to perform better than men managers, but they should not expect better, or even equal, treatment. The higher the management position in the corporate hierarchy, the more traditionally masculine characteristics managers of both sexes are expected to display.

In an investigation of sex stereotyping on the job, 95 male and 56 female managers were asked to estimate the percentage of men and women managers who were likely to display each of a number of specific leader behaviors. Combined results for both sexes showed that they believed men managers were most likely to be better at delegating, inspiring, providing intellectual stimulation to employees, and problem solving. Women managers were seen as better at mentoring, rewarding, and being supportive of employees (Martell & Desmet, 2001).

Men and women subordinates tend to rate men and women managers as equally effective leaders. Subordinate ratings of men and women managers revealed no gender differences in their task-oriented and people-oriented behaviors, or in their levels of consideration or initiating structure behaviors (the leadership functions we discussed earlier). Research also shows that women managers often display a higher drive to succeed than men managers.

Some evidence suggests that women managers are less effective at maintaining discipline with their subordinates. Interviews with 68 women and 95 men who had been reprimanded by their supervisors revealed that only 40 percent of the employees believed that women bosses had handled the disciplinary procedure appropriately and effectively, whereas 57 percent thought that men bosses had done so (Meece, 2000).

Job satisfaction is higher for women executives than for women in middle- and lower-level management positions. Overall, women managers report greater job satisfaction than do women employees in nonmanagerial positions. Job satisfaction among women managers is not diminished by the fact that most of them believe they have been discriminated against and must work harder than men to achieve the same level of success.

Contrary to expectations, studies of women managers have also found that they experienced the same frequency of mentoring from higher-level managers as did men managers. This equal access to mentors is vital in assisting upward mobility in an organization. Does it make a difference if a woman employee's mentor is male or female? Yes, according to a study of more than 350 women and 250 men in engineering, social work, and journalism jobs. The women who had male mentors earned significantly higher salaries than did the women who had female mentors. Men who had female mentors reported being less satisfied with their mentors than did men who had male mentors. Men with female mentors also felt less accepted by their mentors and believed they were given fewer challenging assignments and less time with their superiors than did men with male mentors (Ragins & Cotton, 1999). It is interesting to speculate on possible explanations for these findings.

Other developmental activities are sometimes less open to women managers. Comparisons of men and women managers consistently show that both formal training programs and on-the-job growth experiences (such as high-profile, challenging assignments that increase one's visibility to senior management) are less available to women. Also, women managers appear to receive considerably less encouragement from superiors than men managers at the same level.

Newsbreak	Tips for Hiring Women: 1943 Version

During World War II (1941–1945), many organizations in the United States found that they needed to hire, for the first time, large numbers of women to perform "men's jobs" because the men had gone off to war. The advice that follows was offered seriously at the time. It was believed to be absolutely necessary to help "the girls" (as they were called then) adjust to working outside the home. Needless to say, the bosses were all men.

- General experience indicates that "husky" girls (those who are just a little on the heavy side) are more even-tempered and efficient than their underweight sisters.
- Give the female employee a definite day-long schedule of duties so that she will keep busy without bothering management for instructions every few minutes. Women make excellent workers when they have their job cut out for them, but they lack initiative in finding work themselves.
- Give every girl an adequate number of rest periods during the day. You have to make allowances for feminine psychology. A girl has more confidence and is more efficient if she can keep her hair tidied, apply fresh lipstick, and wash her hands several times a day.
- Be tactful when issuing instructions or in making criticisms. Women are sensitive. They can't shrug off harsh words the way men do. Never ridicule a girl. It breaks her spirit and cuts off her efficiency.
- Get enough size variety in the workers' uniforms so that each girl can have a proper fit. This point cannot be stressed too much in keeping women happy.

Fortunately, we've come a long way since these tips were published.

Some women managers become discouraged by their lack of progress and opportunity relative to that of men managers and decide to leave the corporate world to start their own companies. A comparison of the reasons given by men and women managers for quitting their corporate jobs found that women were far more likely than men to leave because they believed that their career expectations had not been met. However, even working for themselves, women face discrimination. Women-owned businesses tend to operate in certain occupational categories, notably retail sales, education, and personal services. Nevertheless, women entrepreneurs tend to be as successful as men entrepreneurs.

For more information about the problems and progress of women employees at all levels, visit the Web site for the Women's Bureau of the U.S. Department of Labor: www.dol.gov/wb/. It provides access to publications, statistics, government initiatives, and material about women in so-called nontraditional jobs. There is also an online newsletter. Another useful site is the National Association for Female Executives at www.nafe.com.

MINORITY EMPLOYEES IN MANAGEMENT

Although minority employees have access to management positions in increasing numbers, they continue to face stereotypes, prejudice, and unique problems and challenges. Like women managers, Black and other minority managers meet a glass ceiling that effectively bars them from attaining many top management jobs. That ceiling may be lower for minorities than for women. Most minority employees in management are Black; few are Hispanic or Asian-American. Most of the research on minority personnel in management jobs has studied Black subjects.

Blacks must usually work harder than Whites to prove themselves, and their job performance may be evaluated more stringently. They may find that White employees resent their presence, believing they were hired or promoted with fewer qualifications simply to meet equal employment opportunity requirements. Racist attitudes openly expressed can make everyday interactions with superiors, co-workers, and subordinates unpleasant. Some minority managers quit in frustration. Corning Glass found that Black managers were leaving the company at three times the rate of White managers. Monsanto Chemical reported that the major reasons Black managers gave for quitting were problems with superiors, a sense of not belonging, and a lack of challenge.

Data from the Bureau of Labor Statistics show that minority women have fewer opportunities than White women or minority men in terms of the type of job and salary they are able to obtain. In a survey of 1,735 Black, Asian, and Hispanic women from 30 different companies, more than half of these women employees reported that they had been victims of discrimination. Although the majority of U.S. companies have formulated policies to encourage and promote diversity, the women surveyed said that the policies failed to prevent the subtle racism and sexism they had experienced on the job. They believed that the formal diversity programs were ineffective and that their job opportunities had not improved over the previous five years.

Nearly 35 percent of the women questioned did believe that diversity programs had created a more supportive environment, but only 25 percent felt that the programs had opened a broader career development path for them. When minority women employees were asked to note the greatest hindrance to their career advancement, the most popular answers were the lack of a mentor and the difficulty of networking informally with colleagues.

Conflict may arise when a Black manager is promoted over an equally qualified White manager. Research has shown that the common reaction of those passed over for promotion is that the Black person was given the job on the basis of race. This attitude can create hostility on both sides. Black managers may also have difficulties dealing with other minority employees. Hispanic-Americans and Asian-Americans often believe that Blacks receive preferential treatment. This perception presents problems when Black managers must conduct performance appraisals of subordinates. Minority employees of all races expect Black managers to be more lenient than White managers. Black managers may be pressured by Black subordinates to give them special consideration or overlook poor job performance. Any perceived display of favoritism on the part of a manager can create animosity, which, in turn, can affect the work group's performance.

Research on 2,883 supervisor-subordinate dyads in the U.S. Army found that subordinates were satisfied with their supervisors in the early phases of the relationship. However, that satisfaction later decreased when the supervisors and subordinates were of different races. The lowest level of satisfaction was reported by White subordinates with non-White supervisors (Vecchio & Bullis, 2001).

Workplace diversity training programs can be successful in reducing bias and discrimination on the job and teaching employees of all races to behave with greater sensitivity toward the needs, values, and concerns of all groups.

Summary

Half of all new companies fail within two years because of poor leadership, which also accounts for the finding that half of all corporate decisions are incorrect. Incompetent leadership results in poor employee performance, low job commitment, low job satisfaction, and high stress.

The **scientific management** philosophy, concerned solely with production, was replaced in the 1920s and 1930s by the human relations approach, concerned with satisfying the personal growth needs of employees and maintaining production. McGregor's **Theory X** holds that people dislike work and need strong, directive, and punitive leadership. **Theory Y** holds that people are creative, industrious, responsible, and function best under leaders who allow them to participate in decisions that affect their work.

Contingency theory suggests that leader effectiveness is determined by the interaction between the leader's personal characteristics and aspects of the situation. **Path-goal theory** emphasizes the leadership behaviors that allow subordinates to achieve their goals. **Leader-member exchange** (LMX) is concerned with ways in which leaders behave toward subordinates. **Implicit leadership theory** defines leadership in terms of subordinates' perceptions developed from past experiences working for different kinds of leaders.

Authoritarian and **democratic leaders** differ in the degree of participation they extend to subordinates. **Transactional leaders** focus on establishing routines and procedures and following existing rules to increase the organization's operating efficiency. **Transformational leaders** inspire subordinates and redirect their behavior through personal **charisma,** intellectual stimulation, and consideration. Five types of leadership power are reward power, coercive power, legitimate power, referent power, and expert power.

Through the **Pygmalion effect,** leaders' expectations can affect subordinates' behavior in a self-fulfilling prophecy. Leadership functions are grouped in two categories: **consideration** and **initiating structure.** Consideration behaviors are concerned with subordinates' feelings. Initiating structure behaviors are concerned with achieving organizational productivity goals.

Leadership characteristics vary with the level of leadership; the higher the level, the fewer consideration functions and the more initiating structure functions are required. Successful first-line supervisors are person-centered, supportive, and loyal to the company and to subordinates. They exercise a democratic supervisory style. Effective executives need decision-making and technical skills more than they need human relations skills. People who acquire mentors within a company are more likely to receive pay raises and promotions and have more positive attitudes toward their job. Personality factors, such as the Big Five, correlate highly with managerial success. Executive failure is related more to personality factors than to job performance. Unsuccessful executives may possess fallacies in their thinking such as unrealistic optimism, egocentrism, omniscience, omnipotence, and invulnerability.

Leadership problems vary with organizational level. First-line supervisors may be poorly trained in supervisory skills and face conflicts between organizational demands and demands of subordinates. Participative management, **self-managing work groups,** and computer technology are stressful for supervisors. Middle managers have lost authority because of participative management and may find themselves obsolete at midcareer. Executives face long working hours yet show greater job satisfaction than do persons at lower levels of leadership.

Women managers continue to be paid less than men managers and are reluctant to negotiate for higher salaries. Women managers still face discrimination based on sex stereotypes but are rated by subordinates as equally effective as men managers. Black managers face similar problems of stereotyping and discrimination and may have difficulties dealing with White and other minority subordinates.

Key Terms

authoritarian leadership
bureaucracy
charismatic leadership
consideration leadership functions
contingency theory
democratic leadership
implicit leadership theory
initiating structure leadership
    functions

leader-member exchange
path-goal theory
Pygmalion effect
scientific management
self-managing work groups
Theory X/Theory Y
transactional leadership
transformational leadership

Review Questions

1. In what ways are organizations and their employees affected by incompetent leaders and by abusive leaders?
2. Distinguish between the scientific management and the human relations approaches to leadership.
3. What assumptions about people in general are proposed by Theory X and Theory Y? What kinds of leaders do these propositions call for?
4. In contingency theory, what does a leader's control over a situation depend on?
5. What four leadership styles can facilitate employee attainment of goals, according to path-goal theory?
6. Describe two types of employees and two leadership styles discussed in the leader-member exchange theory.
7. How does the implicit personality theory of leadership differ from other leadership theories?
8. Distinguish between authoritarian and democratic leaders, and between transactional and transformational leaders.

9. What kind of leadership would be most effective for a so-called cutting-edge technology company in its first few years of operation?
10. What are the components of transformational leadership? What are the effects of transformational leaders on employees?
11. Define reward power, coercive power, and legitimate power. How do they differ from referent power and expert power?
12. Which types of leadership power are the most effective? Why do you believe they are the most effective?
13. How would you design an experiment to test for the Pygmalion effect?
14. In what ways do leaders high in the consideration dimension behave differently from leaders high in the initiating structure dimension?
15. What qualities characterize a good first-line supervisor?
16. What problems do first-line supervisors experience on the job, which higher level managers do not face?
17. In what ways do the factors of college experience and personality affect the success of managers and executives?
18. Describe some fallacies in the thinking of unsuccessful executives.
19. What problems do women managers face on the job that are not likely to confront men managers?
20. In what ways have equal employment opportunity regulations benefited minority employees? How have those regulations also caused difficulties for minority employees on the job?

Additional Reading

Avolio, B. J. (1999). *Full leadership development: Building the vital forces in organizations.* Thousand Oaks, CA: Sage Publications. A dynamic presentation of the advantages of the transformational style of leadership.

Book, E. W. (2000). *Why the best man for the job is a woman.* New York: Harper Business. Profiles of women chief executives of Fortune 500 companies. Describes what they have learned from their climb up the organizational ladder and how they balance work and family demands.

Cleveland, J. N., Stockdale, M., & Murphy, K. R. (2000). *Women and men in organizations: Sex and gender issues at work.* Mahwah, NJ: Erlbaum. A clear, comprehensive review of social-psychological research on gender issues that affect behavior in the workplace. Topics include cultural stereotypes, physical attractiveness, communication, discrimination, harassment, power, career management, stress, and health.

Conger, J. A., & Benjamin, B. (1999). *Building leaders: How successful companies develop the next generation.* San Francisco: Jossey-Bass. Describes effective in-house training programs that are tailored to specific organizational needs.

Heil, G., Bennis, W., & Stephens, D. C. (2000). *Douglas McGregor, Revisited: Managing the human side of the enterprise.* New York: Wiley. Reviews McGregor's classic work on the Theory X/Theory Y approaches to management and argues for their continued relevance to organizational issues.

Kanigel, R. (1997). *The one best way: Frederick Winslow Taylor and the enigma of efficiency.* New York: Viking. A biography of Taylor (1856–1915), who promoted the philosophy of scientific management, which depicted workers as extensions of the industrial machinery they were hired to operate.

London, M. (2002). *Leadership development: Paths to self-insight and professional growth.* Mahwah, NJ: Erlbaum. Suggests that effective leaders have achieved an understanding of their own strengths and weaknesses, of the organizational context of their leadership behaviors, and of the needs and relationships of their employees.

O'Neill, M. B. (2000). *Executive coaching with backbone and heart: A systems approach to engaging leaders with their challenges.* San Francisco: Jossey-Bass. A practical, user-friendly guide to the pros and cons of effective executive coaching.

Powell, G. N. (Ed.) (1999). *Handbook of gender and work.* Thousand Oaks, CA: Sage Publications. A reference book on gender issues for the 21st century, including the changing nature of work, so-called corporate masculinity, pay equity, sex segregation in occupations, gender influence on performance evaluation, barriers to leadership, and work-family issues.

Zaccaro, S. J., & Klimoski, R. J. (Eds.) (2001). *The nature of organizational leadership.* San Francisco: Jossey-Bass/Wiley. An examination of effective leadership attributes and performance at management's highest level.

Chapter 8

Motivation, Job Satisfaction, and Job Involvement

CHAPTER OUTLINE

SUMMARY
KEY TERMS
REVIEW QUESTIONS
ADDITIONAL READING

If you ask people why they work, you will probably get some strange looks—and no wonder! Most of us don't have a choice. We have to work in order to survive. In Chapter 1 we did note that for most people, work is not a four-letter word; we can get a lot more from our work than just a paycheck. But that's not the point of this chapter. We're not asking why people work. Instead we're trying to find out what motivates us to work well, to do the best job we are capable of doing. We're concerned here with ways to get people to work more productively, to enhance their feelings of satisfaction and involvement, and to increase their commitment to their organization. This is one of the major problems facing organizations today.

Employers have made tremendous strides in applying the findings of industrial-organizational (I-O) psychology to recruit, select, and train their workers and to provide effective leadership. But none of these functions can improve the quality of the work being performed if employees are not motivated to do the best job possible.

The study of motivation is important to you for two reasons. First, as a consumer you are often the victim of dissatisfied workers who produce faulty products or who process your requests improperly. Second, you will likely spend one-third to one-half of your waking hours at work for 40 to 45 years. That is a long time to feel frustrated, dissatisfied, and unhappy, especially since these feelings will carry over to your family and social life and affect your physical and emotional health.

Psychologists have studied motivation, job satisfaction, job involvement, and organizational commitment. They have proposed various theories to explain employee motivation—why people behave as they do on the job. Some of these theories emphasize the impact of factors in the workplace. Other theories focus on personal characteristics. The theories have stimulated a great deal of research and have spawned a number of techniques to modify work behavior. Thus, they may provide options for making your work life more satisfying and fulfilling.

We discuss here two types of motivation theories: content theories and process theories. Content theories focus on the importance of the work itself and the challenges, growth opportunities, and responsibilities work provides for employees. These theories deal with the content of motivation, that is, with the specific needs that motivate and direct human behavior. Process theories do not focus directly on work but rather deal with the cognitive processes we use in making decisions and choices about our work.

CONTENT THEORIES OF MOTIVATION

We describe four content models: achievement motivation theory, needs hierarchy theory, motivator-hygiene (two-factor) theory, and job-characteristics theory.

People high in the need for achievement are motivated to excel. They derive satisfaction from working hard to accomplish their goals.

Achievement Motivation Theory

We mentioned the need for achievement, or **achievement motivation,** as a characteristic of successful executives. This desire to accomplish something, to do a good job, and to be the best typifies many people, not only business leaders. People who have a high degree of the need for achievement derive great satisfaction from working to accomplish some goal, and they are motivated to excel in whatever task they undertake.

Since the early 1950s, achievement motivation has been studied intensively by David McClelland and his colleagues (Atkinson & Feather, 1966; McClelland, Atkinson, Clark, & Lowell, 1953). Their research, conducted in several countries, shows that successful business managers consistently display a high need to achieve, regardless of the culture. For example, in Poland, which was then a Communist country, the level of concern for achievement was almost as high as in the United States. McClelland concluded that the economic growth of organizations and societies can be related to the level of the achievement need among employees and citizens (McClelland, 1961).

McClelland's research identified three major characteristics of people who have a high need to achieve:

1. They favor a work environment in which they are able to assume responsibility for solving problems.
2. They tend to take calculated risks and to set moderate, attainable goals.
3. They need continuing recognition and feedback about their progress so that they know how well they are doing.

Achievement motivation
The theory of motivation that emphasizes the need to accomplish something, to do a good job, and to be the best.

Studies have shown a high positive correlation between the achievement motivation scores of executives and the financial success of their companies. Research also shows that managers high in the need to achieve display more respect for their subordinates. These managers are more receptive to new ideas and are more accepting of participative management programs than are managers low in the need to achieve. Need achievement is positively related to subsequent promotions among middle- and upper-level managers. Also, both men and women entrepreneurs have been found to score significantly higher in the need to achieve than men and women employees who are not entrepreneurs.

Research suggests two types of goals—mastery and performance—that can satisfy the need for achievement (Barron & Harackiewicz, 2001). Mastery refers to developing competence and self-satisfaction through acquiring knowledge and skills. Performance goals involve developing competence by performing better than other people, such as co-workers, who are in the same situation. Both types of goals can be satisfied by doing one's job to the best of one's abilities.

However, a study of 170 employees of an energy company in the Netherlands showed that employees with a strong mastery orientation were more effective on the job than were those with a strong performance orientation. Also, those with a high mastery orientation established higher-quality leader-member exchanges (LMXs) with their supervisor, which, in turn, were linked to higher job satisfaction and intrinsic motivation. In contrast, employees with a strong performance orientation established lower-quality LMXs and correspondingly were lower in job satisfaction and intrinsic motivation (Janssen & Van Yperen, 2004).

In general, achievement motivation theory provides a plausible explanation for the motivation of some employees and is considered to have widespread application in the workplace.

Needs Hierarchy Theory

Needs hierarchy theory
The theory of motivation that encompasses physiological, safety, belonging, esteem, and self-actualization needs.

Abraham Maslow developed the **needs hierarchy theory** of motivation in which human needs are arranged in a hierarchy of importance (Maslow, 1970). According to Maslow, we always want what we do not yet have. Consequently, the needs that we have already satisfied no longer provide any motivation for our behavior and new needs must rise to prominence. Once we have satisfied our lower-level needs, we can pay attention to higher-level needs. The needs, from lowest to highest, are as follows:

- *Physiological needs:* The basic human needs, including food, air, water, and sleep, and the drives for sex and activity
- *Safety needs:* The needs for physical shelter and for psychological security and stability
- *Belonging and love needs:* The social needs for love, affection, friendship, and affiliation that involve interaction with and acceptance by other people
- *Esteem needs:* The needs for self-esteem and for esteem, admiration, and respect from other people
- *Self-actualization need:* The need for self-fulfillment, for achieving our full potential and realizing our capabilities

These needs should be satisfied in the order presented. People who are hungry or who fear for their physical safety are too busy attempting to satisfy these needs to be concerned about self-esteem or self-fulfillment. In times of economic hardship, when jobs are scarce, most people are so intent on survival that they cannot attend to higher needs such as self-actualization. However, once we reach a sufficient level of physical and economic security, we can move on; that is, we will be motivated to satisfy the next level of needs.

The belonging needs can be important motivating forces on the job. Workers can develop a social support network and a sense of belonging through interactions with co-workers. Esteem needs can be satisfied by buying a bigger house or car, which contributes to the feeling that we are successful, and through on-the-job rewards such as praise from the boss, a promotion, an office with a window, or a reserved parking space. To satisfy the self-actualization need, employees should be provided with opportunities for growth and responsibility so that they can exercise their abilities to the utmost. A routine and boring job will not satisfy the self-actualization need, no matter how high the salary.

Maslow's theory has received little research support and is judged to have low scientific validity and applicability. Its complexity makes it difficult to test empirically. However, the self-actualization concept became popular with managers and executives who accepted this high-level need as a potent motivating force.

Motivator-Hygiene (Two-Factor) Theory

The **motivator-hygiene (two-factor) theory,** which deals with both motivation and job satisfaction, was proposed by Frederick Herzberg. The theory has inspired a great deal of research, although the results have not been consistently supportive. The scientific validity of the theory is low, yet it has led many organizations to redefine the way many jobs are performed in order to increase employee motivation (Herzberg, 1966, 1974).

According to Herzberg, there are two sets of needs: the motivator needs, which produce job satisfaction, and the hygiene needs, which produce job dissatisfaction. The *motivator needs* (the higher needs) motivate employees to high job performance. Motivator needs are internal to the work itself. They include the nature of the individual job tasks and the worker's level of responsibility, achievement, recognition, advancement, and career development and growth. The motivator needs are similar to Maslow's self-actualization need. They can be satisfied by stimulating, challenging, and absorbing work. When these conditions are met, job satisfaction will result. However, when these conditions are not met—when work is not challenging—the result is not necessarily job dissatisfaction.

Job dissatisfaction is produced by the *hygiene needs* (the lower needs). The word *hygiene* relates to the promotion and maintenance of health. Hygiene needs are external to the tasks of a particular job and involve features of the work environment, such as company policy, supervision, interpersonal relations, working conditions, and salary and benefits. When the hygiene needs are not satisfied, the result is job dissatisfaction. However, when the hygiene needs are satisfied, the result is not necessarily job satisfaction, merely an absence of dissatisfaction. The hygiene needs are similar to Maslow's physiological, safety, and belonging needs. Both Maslow and Herzberg insisted that these lower needs be satisfied before a person can be motivated by higher needs.

Herzberg's theory focused attention on the importance of internal job factors as motivating forces for employees. If the motivator needs stimulate employees to perform at their best and to develop a positive attitude toward the job, then

Motivator-hygiene (two-factor) theory
The theory of motivation that explains work motivation and job satisfaction in terms of job tasks and workplace features.

Job enrichment An effort to expand the scope of a job to give employees a greater role in planning, performing, and evaluating their work.

why not redesign the job to maximize opportunities to satisfy motivator needs? This effort, called **job enrichment,** expands jobs to give employees a greater role in planning, performing, and evaluating their work, thus providing the chance to satisfy their motivator needs. Herzberg suggested the following ways of enriching a job:

1. Remove some management controls over employees and increase their accountability and responsibility for their work, thus increasing employee autonomy, authority, and freedom.
2. Create complete or natural work units where possible—for example, allow employees to produce a whole unit instead of one component of that unit. This policy increases the likelihood that employees will regard their work as meaningful within the total organizational process.
3. Provide regular and continuous feedback on productivity and job performance directly to employees instead of through their supervisors.
4. Encourage employees to take on new, challenging tasks and to become experts in a particular task or operation.

All these proposals have the same goals of increasing personal growth, fulfilling the needs for achievement and responsibility, and providing recognition. Proper job enrichment, therefore, involves more than simply giving the workers extra tasks to perform. It means expanding the level of knowledge and skills needed to perform the job.

This was demonstrated in a study involving 1,039 employees of a glass manufacturing plant. The research showed that job enrichment programs significantly increased their sense of self-efficacy—their belief in their ability to do their jobs (Parker, 1998). The program, which offered opportunities for greater accountability, responsibility, and autonomy, enhanced the employees' feelings of adequacy, efficiency, and confidence that they were performing their jobs well.

Job-Characteristics Theory

Job-characteristics theory The theory of motivation that states that specific job characteristics lead to psychological conditions that can increase motivation, performance, and satisfaction in employees who have a high growth need.

The job enrichment movement led two psychologists to ask which specific job characteristics could be enriched. J. Richard Hackman and G. R. Oldham developed the **job-characteristics theory** of motivation based on their research on objective measures of job factors that correlated with employee satisfaction and attendance (Hackman & Oldham, 1976, 1980). Evidence suggested that certain characteristics influence behavior and attitudes at work, but these characteristics do not influence all employees in the same way. For example, the research documented individual differences in the need for growth. People with a high growth need were found to be more affected by changes in job characteristics than were people with a low growth need. Also, changes in these job characteristics did not seem to influence employee attitudes and behavior directly but were filtered by the employees' cognitive processes—that is, their perceptions of the changes.

The presence of certain job characteristics causes employees to experience a positive emotional state when they perform their job well. This condition motivates them to continue to perform well, on the expectation that good performance will lead to good feelings. The strength of an employee's motivation to perform well depends on the strength of the need to grow and develop. The stronger the need, the more one will value the positive emotional feelings that result from good job performance. Thus, the job-characteristics theory states that specific job characteristics lead to psychological conditions that lead, in turn, to higher motivation, performance, and satisfaction—if employees have a high growth need to begin with.

The core job characteristics identified by Hackman and Oldham are as follows:

1. *Skill variety:* the extent to which workers use various skills and abilities on the job. The more challenging a job, the more meaningful it will be.
2. *Task identity:* the unity of a job—that is, whether it involves doing a whole unit of work or completing a product instead of making only part of a product on an assembly line.
3. *Task significance:* the importance of a job to the lives and well-being of co-workers or consumers. For example, the job of aircraft mechanic affects the lives of more people in a more significant way than does the job of postal clerk.
4. *Autonomy:* the amount of independence employees have in scheduling and organizing their work.
5. *Feedback:* the amount of information employees receive about the effectiveness and quality of their job performance.

Jobs can be redesigned to maximize these characteristics in a manner similar to that proposed earlier by Herzberg:

- Combine small, specialized tasks to form larger work units; this enhances skill variety and task identity.
- Arrange tasks in natural, meaningful work units to make the worker responsible for an identifiable unit; this enhances task identity and task significance.
- Give workers responsibility for direct contact with clients or end users; this enhances skill variety, autonomy, and feedback.
- Give workers authority, responsibility, and control over the job tasks; this increases skill variety, task identity, task significance, and autonomy.
- Arrange for workers to learn regularly how well they are performing the job; this increases feedback.

Hackman and Oldham developed the Job Diagnostic Survey (JDS) to measure three aspects of the theory: (1) employees' perceptions of the job characteristics, (2) employees' level of the growth need, and (3) employees' job satisfaction. The JDS is a self-report inventory consisting of short descriptive phrases about the various job characteristics. Respondents rate how accurately each statement describes their job. A revised version, using positively worded items only, has been found to be more valid than the original version.

The job-characteristics theory continues to stimulate research. Studies on job enrichment programs based on this theory have been more supportive and have shown that adding challenge, complexity, and responsibility to some jobs results in greater employee satisfaction, self-efficacy, and motivation (Campion & Berger, 1990).

As you can see, the content theories of motivation we have described share a common core or central concept. They focus on enlarging, enriching, or redefining jobs to provide greater employee responsibility. They note the importance of opportunities for growth, self-actualization, personal achievement, and increased motivation through increasing the amount of accountability, challenge, control, and autonomy at work. Enlarging the scope of a job can provide personal satisfaction and greater motivation to perform well. Boring and routine jobs can be stultifying and decrease satisfaction and motivation. You might keep this in mind when you apply for your next job.

PROCESS THEORIES OF MOTIVATION

We describe three process models: valence-instrumentality-expectancy (VIE) theory, equity theory, and goal-setting theory.

Valence-Instrumentality-Expectancy (VIE) Theory

Valence-instrumentality-expectancy (VIE) theory
The theory of motivation that states that people make choices that are based on their perceived expectations that certain rewards will follow if they behave in a particular way.

The **valence-instrumentality-expectancy (VIE) theory,** originated by Victor Vroom, asserts that people make choices that are based on their perceived expectancy that certain rewards will follow if they behave in a certain way (Vroom, 1964). In the workplace, employees will choose to perform at the level that results in the greatest payoff or benefit. They will be motivated to work hard if they expect this effort to lead to positive outcomes such as a promotion or pay raise and if those outcomes will be instrumental in leading to other desired results.

The psychological value, or valence, of the reward varies with the individual. In other words, our personal perception of the importance of the outcome determines its strength to us as a motivator. A high salary and increased responsibility have a positive valence for many people. Dangerous working conditions have a negative valence for most people. The outcome may not be as satisfying as we expected, but it is the level of expectancy that determines whether we will work hard to obtain that outcome.

The three facets of the VIE theory are related as follows:

1. Employees must decide whether they expect certain job behaviors—such as coming to work on time, following safe procedures, or improving productivity—to have a high probability of leading to a particular outcome (expectancy).
2. Employees must determine whether that outcome will lead to other outcomes—for example, whether a good attendance record leads to a bonus (instrumentality).
3. Employees must decide whether those outcomes have sufficient value to motivate them to behave a certain way (valence).

Think of your own experience in school. If you have decided that getting high grades in the courses you take in your major is important, then that outcome has a high valence for you. If you're not so concerned about your grades in your other courses, then earning high grades in them has a low valence for you. If you want high grades in your major, you have probably developed the expectancy that attending classes, studying hard, and doing more than the minimum requirements will be instrumental in achieving your goal. These calculations are not

Newsbreak   Driven by the Work Ethic

On September 8, 1995, a baseball player made history. He did it by showing up for work. Cal Ripken, Jr., showed up for work 2,131 times, every time his team, the Baltimore Orioles, played a major league baseball game.

The 42,000 fans in Oriole Park at Camden Yards stadium went wild the night Ripken broke the previous record, held by Lou Gehrig, for the longest streak of consecutive games played. The President of the United States witnessed the historic moment and praised Ripken's discipline, determination, and constancy. A television reporter summed up the excitement that gripped the nation when he described Ripken as "a paragon of the work ethic."

The *work ethic* is a term we hear a lot, and it has been a guiding rule and way of life for generations of American workers. It drives, pushes, goads, and motivates people to work hard like Cal Ripken, to do the best job they can, to be on time, and to show up for work every day. If you are curious about the great driving force of the 19th and 20th centuries that led to unimagined heights of industrial, agricultural, and commercial productivity and economic success, then the work ethic is where you should begin. In most progressive economies, work is not a four-letter word.

It wasn't always that way. There was a time when people were not motivated to perform a job well, or even to do it at all. To the ancient Greeks and Romans, there was nothing noble about work. It was a curse of the gods that brutalized the mind and ruined an otherwise good day. The early Hebrews agreed. Work was a punishment from God, although it was also a necessary evil, a way of improving society and atoning for sin.

The early Christians put a more positive spin on work, viewing it as a way to serve God by sharing the proceeds of one's work with people who were less fortunate. Wealth was a means to charity. Work became holy, and idleness sinful.

But it was John Calvin, the 16th-century French Protestant leader, who gave us the ultimate work ethic. Work alone pleases God, he declared, but to achieve that end, work must be methodical and disciplined. "Not leisure and enjoyment but only activity serves to increase the glory of God."

To Calvin, and others who refined what came to be called the Protestant work ethic, work was an emblem of faith. And so was wealth. It was OK to make a lot of money and not feel guilty about it, as long as you did not enjoy it. Old-fashioned, puritanical, nose-to-the-grindstone toil for its own sake became the motivation that drove millions of people to work hard all their lives and to feel virtuous for doing so. And it still drives many of us each and every day to do the best job we can. And to show up for every game.

Sources: R. Todd. All work, no ethic. *Worth Magazine,* January 1996, pp. 78–84; J. Bair & S. J. Sherer. What happened to the work ethic? *College Park Magazine,* Fall 1995, pp. 18–22.

difficult for most of us to make. Indeed, we may not even be aware of them, but they motivate us and guide our behavior nonetheless.

The VIE theory has received a great deal of research support. It appears to agree with personal experience and common sense. The greater our expectation of receiving a reward, assuming it is of sufficient value, the harder we will work for it.

Equity Theory

Equity theory The theory of motivation that states that our motivation on the job is influenced by our perception of how fairly we are treated.

J. Stacy Adams advanced the **equity theory,** the notion that motivation is influenced by our perception of how equitably or fairly we are treated at work (Adams, 1965). He proposed that in any work environment—whether office, shop, factory, or classroom—we assess our inputs (how much effort we put into the work) and our outcomes (how much reward we receive for the work). We calculate, perhaps unconsciously, the ratio of outcome to input and mentally compare it with what we believe are the ratios for our co-workers. If we think we are getting less than other people, the feeling of tension or inequity that results motivates us to act, to do something to bring about a state of equity. If we perceive that we are receiving the same ratio of reward-to-effort that others are receiving, then a state of equity exists.

Other psychologists have extended the equity theory, suggesting three behavioral response patterns to situations of perceived equity or inequity (Huseman, Hatfield, & Miles, 1987; O'Neil & Mone, 1998). These three types are benevolent, equity sensitive, and entitled. The level of reward received by each type affects motivation, job satisfaction, and job performance.

Benevolent persons, described as altruistic, are satisfied when they are underrewarded compared with co-workers and feel guilty when they are equitably rewarded or overrewarded. Equity-sensitive persons (the type described by the equity theory) believe that everyone should be rewarded fairly. They feel distressed when underrewarded and guilty when overrewarded. Entitled persons believe that everything they receive is their due. They are satisfied only when they are overrewarded and are distressed when underrewarded or equitably rewarded.

It seems intuitively correct to state that if we believe we are being treated fairly in comparison to others, in accordance with our expectations, then we will be motivated to maintain our level of job performance. In contrast, if we think we are being treated unfairly, then we will try to reduce that inequity by reducing our level of performance. Consider the example of major league baseball players (infielders and outfielders). If they have their salaries cut or lose at arbitration during their first year as free agents, they are likely to perform at lower levels during the following season. They may reduce their inputs (batting averages and runs batted in) if they believe that their outcomes (salaries) are too low.

Not all research is supportive of the equity theory, but some studies have shown that employee perceptions of inequity are linked to increased levels of resentment, absenteeism and turnover, and burnout (see, for example, Cropanzano & Greenberg, 1997; Van Dierendonck, Schaufeli, & Buunk, 2001).

Goal-Setting Theory

Goal-setting theory The theory of motivation based on the idea that our primary motivation on the job is defined in terms of our desire to achieve a particular goal.

Developed by Edwin Locke, **goal-setting theory** has a commonsense appeal and is clearly relevant to the workplace. Locke argued that our primary motivation in a work situation is defined in terms of our desire to achieve a particular goal (Locke, 1968; Locke & Latham, 1990). The goal represents what we intend to do at a given time in the future. For example, we may set the goal of graduating from college with honors, achieving the highest sales record in the company, or getting a pay raise within a year so we can buy a new house.

Setting specific and challenging performance goals can motivate and guide our behavior, spurring us to perform in more effective ways. Research has shown that having goals leads to better performance than not having goals. Specific goals are more powerful motivating forces than general goals. Goals that are difficult to attain are greater motivators than goals that are easy to attain. However, difficult goals may spur greater motivation toward attaining the goals at the expense of other behaviors, such as helping co-workers. This type of behavior has the potential for reducing overall organizational effectiveness. In addition, goals that are too difficult, perhaps beyond our capabilities, are worse than having no goals in terms of their impact on motivation and job performance.

An important aspect of the goal-setting theory is individual goal commitment, which is defined in terms of the strength of our determination to reach our goal. A meta-analysis of 83 research studies confirmed that goal commitment has a strong positive effect on the level of our task performance (Klein, Wesson, Hollenback, & Alge, 1999). Goal commitment is influenced by three types of factors: external, interactive, and internal. The external factors that affect goal commitment are authority, peer influence, and external rewards. Complying with the dictates of an authority figure such as a boss has been shown to be an inducement to high goal commitment. Goal commitment increases when the authority figure is physically present, supportive, and trusted. Peer group pressure and external rewards such as pay increases also strengthen goal commitment.

The interactive factors that influence our commitment to reaching our goals are competition and the opportunity to participate in setting goals. These factors have been shown to be an inducement to setting higher goals and to working harder to reach them. Internal cognitive factors that facilitate goal commitment are self-administered rewards and our expectation of success. Commitment to the goal is reduced when our expectation of achieving it declines.

Other personal and situational factors have been related to high goal commitment. These include the need for achievement, endurance, aggressiveness, and competitiveness (so-called Type A behavior), success in achieving difficult goals, high self-esteem, and an internal locus of control. In addition, a meta-analysis of 65 studies found that two of the Big Five personality factors are related to performance motivation, as described by the goal-setting theory. People who score high in conscientiousness and low in neuroticism display high levels of goal-setting-induced motivation (Judge & Ilies, 2002).

The goal-setting theory has generated considerable supportive research. Setting goals has been found to produce substantial increases in employee output. In general, the motivating effects of setting goals are strongest for easy tasks and weakest for more complex tasks. These effects generalize across a variety of organizations, jobs, and tasks. I-O psychologists reviewing 35 years of research concluded that "goal-setting theory is among the most valid and practical theories of employee motivation in organizational psychology" (Locke & Latham, 2002, p. 714).

The process theories are concerned with factors and processes internal to the employee. Instead of focusing on characteristics of the work itself, as with content theories, process theories deal with our thoughts and perceptions about our jobs, our calculations about what we stand to gain in return for our efforts, and the decisions we make based on those calculations. We can be motivated to perform at high levels by our expectations of getting the greatest benefit (VIE theory), by how fairly we perceive we are rewarded relative to our co-workers (equity theory), or by setting challenging goals to strive for (goal-setting theory). Or perhaps we can be motivated by some combination of all of them, at different times and in different situations. Process theories share the common theme that how we perceive the work situation will determine how motivated we are to perform at a high level in that situation.

Interest in work motivation theories has shifted since the 1990s, away from developing new theories and more toward extending, empirically testing, and applying proposed ideas in the workplace. The number of purely theoretical articles published in the leading behavioral science journals declined considerably, while the number of empirical studies increased (Steers, Mowday, & Shapiro, 2004). Does it follow that theories of work motivation are no longer a focus of I-O psychology? No. Although the theories described here have some limitations, most are useful in describing some aspect of employee motivation. The diversity of ideas derived from these theories, which are now being tested in and applied to the workplace, shows the progress we are making in understanding the multiple facets of employee motivation (see Locke & Latham, 2004).

JOB SATISFACTION: THE QUALITY OF LIFE AT WORK

Job satisfaction Our positive and negative feelings and attitudes about our jobs.

Job satisfaction refers to the positive and negative feelings and attitudes we hold about our job, and it is the most frequently studied independent variable in I-O psychology (Kinicki, McKee-Ryan, Schriesheim, & Carson, 2002). It depends on many work-related factors, ranging from our assigned parking space to the sense of fulfillment we get from our daily tasks. Personal factors can also influence job satisfaction. These factors include age, health, length of job experience, emotional stability, social status, leisure activities, and family and other social

Assembly-line workers tend to have low job satisfaction. Routine, repetitive work offers little opportunity for personal growth and development.

relationships. Our motivations and aspirations, and how well these are satisfied by our work, also affect our attitudes toward our jobs.

For some employees, job satisfaction is a stable, enduring characteristic, independent of the features of the job. Changes in job status, pay, working conditions, and goals have little effect on the job satisfaction of these people. Their personal tendency toward happiness (satisfaction) or unhappiness (dissatisfaction) varies little over time and circumstances.

I-O psychologists have suggested, based on research conducted with twins, that attitudes toward work and the satisfactions we expect from it may have a hereditary component. In other words, these feelings may be influenced more by our genetic endowment than by features of the work environment. Nevertheless, it is clear that some people are generally more satisfied with life and, thus, with their work. People who have positive attitudes toward their work are likely to have positive feelings about their personal and family life.

So it is generally accepted that job satisfaction and life satisfaction are positively related, but which one causes the other? Or are both influenced by some third factor? To explore this relationship, a sample of 804 employees, selected to be representative of the U.S. workforce, was interviewed and given questionnaires to assess job and life satisfaction. The results showed a positive and reciprocal relationship between job and life satisfaction in the short term; that is, each one influenced the other. Over time, however, the impact of life satisfaction on job satisfaction was significantly stronger, indicating that general life satisfaction may be the more influential of the two factors. This conclusion was supported in a study of 479 police officers. For them, life satisfaction was influenced more by nonwork factors than by satisfaction with their jobs (Hart, 1999). However, it does not follow that attempts to improve job satisfaction are useless. Remember that the two are interrelated. Job satisfaction still has an effect on life satisfaction.

Measuring Job Satisfaction

The approach used most often to measure employee attitudes is the anonymous questionnaire, typically distributed to employees through the company's e-mail network. Because participation is voluntary, not all workers will complete a questionnaire. There is no way of knowing which employees responded and which did not, or how those who failed to respond differ from those who did respond. It might make a difference if more good workers than poor workers completed the questionnaires.

Two popular attitude surveys are the Job Descriptive Index (JDI) and the Minnesota Satisfaction Questionnaire (MSQ). The JDI contains scales to measure five job factors: pay, promotion, supervision, the nature of the work, and the characteristics of one's co-workers. It can be completed in 15 minutes and has been published in several languages. The MSQ is a rating scale for various levels of satisfaction and dissatisfaction, ranging from very satisfied to very dissatisfied. It covers 20 job facets including advancement, independence, recognition, social status, and working conditions. The MSQ takes 30 minutes to complete; a ten-minute form is also available. These questionnaires have high construct validity.

Personal interviews are sometimes used in conjunction with the questionnaires. In these interviews, employees discuss aspects of their jobs with supervisors or interviewers from the organization's human resources department. Another method of measuring job attitudes is the sentence-completion test. Employees

TABLE 8–1	
Level of Satisfaction with Individual Job Facets	
Job Facet	**Percentage of Employees Expressing Satisfaction**
Interest in work	58
Quality of supervisor	55
Commute	55
Vacation policy	51
Job security	50
Sick leave	47
Health plan	40
Wages	37
Flexible work hours plan	37
Promotion policy	22

Source: Survey reported in *St. Petersburg (FL) Times,* August 22, 2002.

are presented with a list of phrases to complete. For example, "My job is _____."
or "My job should be _____." In the critical-incidents technique for evaluating
job satisfaction, employees are asked to describe job incidents that occurred at
times when they felt very good or very bad about their jobs.

Job Facet Satisfaction

Many I-O psychologists suggest that data on overall job satisfaction may not be
an adequate measure of the full range of employees' positive and negative attitudes toward all aspects of the work situation. Employees may be satisfied with
certain conditions and dissatisfied with others. For example, you may like your
work and be comfortable in your office but dislike your boss or your company's
health insurance program. A national survey of 5,000 employees at all levels in a
variety of occupations found that their satisfaction with specific job facets varied
from 22 percent to 58 percent, as shown in Table 8–1.

A single measure of overall job satisfaction fails to make distinctions among
these factors. For this reason, psychologists are focusing on measuring more specific facets or aspects of job satisfaction. Some facets appear to apply to all types of
jobs and organizations, whereas others are present in only certain job categories.

Job Satisfaction Data

Every year the Gallup Poll organization asks a representative sample of U.S.
workers the following question: On the whole, would you say you are satisfied
or dissatisfied with the work you do?

The results show consistently that only 10 to 13 percent of the workers questioned each year say that they are dissatisfied with their jobs. Thus, the majority
of people are assumed to be satisfied with their jobs. However, when more specific questions are asked about job satisfaction, the results are different. For
example, when factory workers are asked if they would like to change jobs, many
say yes, even though they claim to be satisfied with their present jobs. When people
say they are satisfied, they often mean that they are not dissatisfied. Therefore,

when we consider the data on job satisfaction, we must examine the kinds of questions that are asked.

Some job satisfaction studies survey a representative national sample of workers. Others deal with targeted populations, such as the workers in a particular industry, or with specific facets of job satisfaction. Job satisfaction varies with type of occupation. For example, assembly-line workers are significantly less satisfied with their jobs than are office workers. Managers in government agencies are significantly less satisfied than are managers in private industry and business.

Employees of companies on *Fortune* magazine's list of 100 best companies to work for in the United States report high levels of job satisfaction that tend to remain stable over time. Research also shows a high correlation between these employees' positive attitudes toward their companies and the companies' financial performance. The more satisfied workers seem to be, the better is the organization's economic health (Fulmer, Gerhart, & Scott, 2003). To find out more about the top 100 companies and to learn how the ratings were determined, go to the Web site www.greatplacetowork.com.

Impact of Personal Characteristics

Many characteristics of the job and the workplace affect job satisfaction. By redesigning job and work environments, it is possible for management to increase job satisfaction and productivity. Jobs can be redesigned to maximize opportunities to satisfy the needs for achievement, self-actualization, and personal growth. Jobs can be enriched to enhance the motivator needs and the core job characteristics, and to provide higher levels of responsibility.

Personal characteristics linked with job satisfaction include, among others, age, gender, race, cognitive ability, job experience, use of skills, job congruence, organizational justice, personality, job control, and occupational level.

Age. In general, job satisfaction increases with age; the lowest job satisfaction is reported by the youngest workers. This relationship holds for blue-collar and white-collar employees and for men and women employees. Many young people are disappointed with their first jobs because they fail to find sufficient challenge and responsibility. Why does job satisfaction tend to increase with age when the typical reaction to our first job is often disappointment? Three possible explanations have been suggested:

1. The most strongly dissatisfied young workers may drop out of the workforce or change jobs so frequently in their search for satisfaction that they are no longer counted in surveys. This means that the older the sample of employees studied, the fewer dissatisfied people are likely to be included.
2. A sense of resignation develops in some workers as they grow older. They may give up looking for fulfillment and challenge in their work and seek these satisfactions elsewhere. Therefore, they tend to report less dissatisfaction with their jobs.
3. Many older workers have greater opportunities to find fulfillment and self-actualization on the job. Age and experience usually bring increased confidence, competence, esteem, and responsibility. In turn, these feelings lead to a greater sense of accomplishment. In other words, older workers are more likely to have better jobs than are younger workers.

Gender. The research evidence about possible differences in job satisfaction between men and women employees is inconsistent and contradictory. Psychologists have found no clear pattern of differences in job satisfaction. It may not be gender, as such, that relates to job satisfaction as much as the group of factors that vary with gender. For example, women are typically paid less than men for the same work, and their opportunities for promotion are fewer. Most women employees believe that they have to work harder and be more outstanding on the job than men employees before they receive comparable rewards. Obviously, these factors can influence a person's satisfaction.

Race. In general, more White than non-White employees report satisfaction with their jobs. However, before a person can be concerned with job satisfaction, he or she must have a job. Although there is a large, thriving middle class among Black and ethnic minority employees, large numbers of people who want to work are unemployed, are employed irregularly, or are too discouraged to seek employment. Many who have full-time work are confined to low-level jobs that offer marginal pay and little opportunity for advancement or fulfillment. Thus, the primary concern for many workers is not satisfaction but finding a job that pays a decent wage.

Cognitive Ability. Cognitive ability does not appear to be a significant determinant of job satisfaction, but it may be important when related to the type of work a person chooses. For many jobs, there is a range of intelligence associated with high performance and satisfaction. People who are too intelligent for their work may find insufficient challenge, which leads to boredom and dissatisfaction. A survey of 12,686 U.S. workers, a majority of whom were African-American or Hispanic, showed that the more intelligent people held jobs with high interest and challenge. People whose jobs were not sufficiently challenging for their level of intelligence reported great dissatisfaction with their work (Ganzach, 1998). A factor sometimes related to intelligence is level of education. Some studies have shown that education has a slight negative relationship to job satisfaction. The higher the level of formal education, the more likely a person is to be dissatisfied with the job. One explanation is that better-educated persons have higher expectations and believe that their work should provide greater responsibility and fulfillment. Many jobs do not satisfy these expectations. Employees with college degrees are somewhat more satisfied with their jobs than employees who attended college but did not graduate. This finding may be related to the fact that many higher-level positions are open only to college graduates.

Job Experience. During the initial stage of employment, new workers tend to be satisfied with their jobs. This period involves the stimulation and challenge of developing skills and abilities, and the work may seem attractive just because it is new. This early satisfaction wanes unless employees receive feedback on their progress and tangible evidence of their achievements. After a few years on the job, discouragement is common, often being brought on by the feeling that advancement in the company is too slow.

Job satisfaction appears to increase after a number of years of experience and to improve steadily thereafter. The relationship between job satisfaction and length of work experience parallels the relationship with age. They may be the same phenomenon under different labels.

Use of Skills.   A common complaint, particularly among college graduates in engineering and science, is that their jobs do not allow them to exercise their skills or apply the knowledge acquired during their college training. Surveys of engineers show high dissatisfaction with job facets such as pay, working conditions, supervisors, and opportunities for promotion. Other studies show that people are happier at work if they have the chance to use their abilities. Interviews with workers on an automobile assembly line in Sweden revealed that a major factor in their job satisfaction was the opportunity to perform their work at a high level of quality (Eklund, 1995). When working conditions or the actions of co-workers interfered with work quality, job satisfaction declined.

Job Congruence.   **Job congruence** refers to the match between the demands of a job and the abilities of the employee. The higher the congruence—the closer the fit between a person's skills and attributes and the job's requirements—the greater the job satisfaction. Conversely, a poor fit between job demands and personal skills reduces the potential for job satisfaction.

Job congruence The match between our abilities and the requirements of our jobs.

Organizational Justice.   Organizational justice refers to how fairly employees perceive themselves to be treated by their company. When workers believe they are being treated unfairly (a perceived lack of organizational justice), their job performance, job satisfaction, and organizational commitment are likely to decline. Under these circumstances, employees also report higher levels of stress, and they are more likely to file grievances or seek other jobs. Employees who work for large organizations or for companies with an authoritarian culture are likely to have a low opinion of the level of organizational justice in their workplace. Participation in decision making can contribute to an increase in organizational justice (Schminke, Ambrose, & Cropanzano, 2000).

Personality.   Research suggests that employees who are more satisfied in their work are better adjusted and more emotionally stable. Although the relationship seems clear, the cause-and-effect sequence is not. Which comes first, emotional stability or job satisfaction? Emotional instability or job dissatisfaction? Emotional instability can cause discontent in every sphere of life, and prolonged job dissatisfaction can lead to poor emotional adjustment.

Two personality factors related to job satisfaction are alienation and locus of control. Employees who feel less alienated and who have an internal locus of control are more likely to be high in job satisfaction, job involvement, and organizational commitment. A meta-analysis of 135 studies of job satisfaction confirmed the positive relationship between internal locus of control and job satisfaction. The study also found that high self-esteem and self-efficacy, and low neuroticism, are significantly related to high job satisfaction (Judge & Bono, 2001).

Two dimensions of the Type A personality are also related to job satisfaction. *Achievement striving* (the extent to which people work hard and take the work seriously) is positively related to job satisfaction and job performance. *Impatience/irritability* (intolerance, anger, hostility, and a sense of time urgency) is negatively related to job satisfaction. The higher the impatience score, the lower the job satisfaction.

Job satisfaction appears to be highest among employees with a high degree of social and institutional trust, that is, those who believe that people and organizations are basically fair and helpful and can be trusted.

1) age
2) gen

Job satisfaction was also found to be high among employees who scored high on the factors of conscientiousness and positive affectivity (which corresponds to extraversion in the Big Five personality factor model) and low on negative affectivity (neuroticism in the Big Five model) (Brief & Weiss, 2002; Ilies & Judge, 2003; Judge, Heller, & Mount, 2002).

An unusual research program studied the self-evaluations of 384 employed adults, including psychological measures of self-esteem, self-efficacy, locus of control, and neuroticism. This long-term study assessed these factors in childhood and again in adulthood. People who scored high in esteem and efficacy and low in neuroticism, and showed an internal locus of control, showed significantly higher job satisfaction in their middle adult years than did people who scored in the opposite direction. Thus, personality factors measured in childhood showed a direct relationship to job satisfaction measured some 30 years later (Judge, Bono, & Locke, 2000).

Job Control. Based on our earlier description of motivational theories, you might predict that people who can exercise greater control over their job duties will be more highly motivated to perform well and will experience greater satisfaction. This prediction was supported in a study of 412 customer service center workers in England. Those who scored high on a questionnaire called the Job Control Scale were found, one year later, to have better mental health and higher levels of job performance and job satisfaction than did those who reported a low level of job control (Bond & Bunce, 2003).

Occupational Level. The higher the occupational or status level of a job, the higher the job satisfaction. Executives express more positive job attitudes and feelings than do first-line supervisors, who, in turn, are usually more satisfied than their subordinates are. The higher the job level, the greater is the opportunity for satisfying motivator needs. Also, high-level jobs offer greater autonomy, challenge, and responsibility. Satisfaction of Maslow's esteem and self-actualization needs also increases with each level in the organizational hierarchy.

Job satisfaction varies with job category. High job satisfaction is more likely to be reported by entrepreneurs (self-employed persons) and by people in technical, professional, and managerial jobs. The least satisfied employees are in manufacturing and service industries and in wholesale and retail businesses.

Losing Your Job

There can be no job satisfaction without a job. I-O psychology research confirms the obvious. Losing one's job or being laid off is stressful for employees and their families. In Japan, layoffs are considered so traumatic that they are called *kubi kiri,* which means "beheading." Specific consequences of layoffs can include feelings of guilt, resentment, depression, and anxiety about the future, as well as physical complaints, alcohol abuse, drug abuse, divorce, spouse and child abuse, and thoughts of suicide.

Employees with higher-level jobs appear to suffer more greatly from unemployment. Employees with lower-level jobs seem to be more adaptable. Executives, managers, and professionals tend to become defensive and self-critical. Losing a job typically leads to significant changes in lifestyle, expectations, goals, and values. The psychological contract these employees believed they had with their employer has been breached. The unwritten agreement stating that if they worked hard and

Unemployment can lead to anxiety that may persist even after a new job has been found.

showed loyalty to the company, then the company would respond with job security, pay raises, and promotions, can no longer be relied upon. Many people who have lost their jobs feel a sense of betrayal. A study of 756 employees who lost their jobs found that over a two-year period the feeling of loss of personal control was especially harmful. In many cases it led to chronic physical health problems and impaired emotional functioning (Price, Choi, & Vinokur, 2002).

Negative reactions to layoffs can be minimized if management is honest with employees about the reasons for the dismissals. Well-informed employees are more likely to view the layoffs as fair, to continue to speak positively about the company, and to express no intention of suing for wrongful termination. Finding a new position typically reverses the negative effects of losing one's job. However, the nature of the new job relative to the old one can make a difference. A study of 100 workers found that those who were dissatisfied with their new job continued to experience most of the negative effects associated with being dismissed from their previous job (Kinicki, Prussia, & McKee-Ryan, 2000).

A survey of 202 adults who had lost their jobs showed that those who began job-hunting immediately did not improve their chances of finding a new job. Those who waited to begin their job search until they had dealt with such negative emotions as depression and low self-esteem appeared more secure and confident and less nervous during their subsequent job interviews. The people who waited also reported higher job satisfaction with their new jobs than did those who began their job search right away (Gowan, Riordan, & Gatewood, 1999).

When large-scale layoffs occur in an organization, the employees who have kept their jobs are also affected. Often they worry that they will be among the next to be dismissed. A report for the U.S. Department of Labor noted that half of the layoff survivors questioned reported increased job stress, lower morale, and reduced job commitment. Also, 60 percent reported greatly increased workloads because workers remaining on the job still had to meet production goals even though there were fewer workers. Also, the layoff survivors reported a decrease in feelings of commitment to the organization since their friends and co-workers had been dismissed (Shah, 2000).

Newsbreak   Grades Slipping? Maybe It's Not Your Fault

How good are you at assessing your parents' moods? Can you sense when they seem worried or upset about something, like maybe losing a job?

Psychologists have learned that children from ages ten to 17 are keenly aware when their parents experience feelings of insecurity about their work. For example, when children believe that their fathers are uneasy about their work situation, the children's attitudes toward their schoolwork will change and their grades are likely to drop. However, this effect was found only with fathers' jobs. When mothers experienced job insecurity, the children did not seem to be affected.

At Queen's University in Canada, psychologists investigated this situation in college students, even though they were no longer living with their parents at home. Would college students pick up on their parents' job anxiety and insecurity even though they didn't see or talk to them every day? And if so, would their own work, their academic performance, be altered?

The subjects in this experiment were 120 undergraduates under the age of 21. A questionnaire surveyed their perception of their parents' level of job security. A sample question was the following: *My mother/father can be sure of his/her present job as long as he/she does good work.* Two other questionnaires were administered. One measured cognitive functioning, and the other measured the student's level of identification with his or her parents.

Parents were asked to complete a questionnaire about their perceived level of job security. It included such items as this: *I am not really sure how long my present job will last.*

The results showed that college students were sensitive to their parents' feelings about their work, even though they no longer had daily contact with them. Like the younger children studied, the college students' grades fell with a decline in their parents' job security. Again, the effect was greater with fathers than with mothers. However, students who indicated a greater level of identification with their mothers were more likely to show a decline in grades than were students who identified more closely with their fathers.

So if you're a parent, remember that being laid off, or even fearing a layoff, can have consequences for your children. And if you're a college student, maybe you should think twice before calling home and asking Mom or Dad how they're doing at work.

Source: J. Barling, A. Zacharatos, & C. G. Hepburn (1999). Parents' job insecurity affects children's academic performance through cognitive difficulties. *Journal of Applied Psychology, 84*, 437–444.

A survey of 283 employees in a company undergoing a major reorganization showed that their sense of job insecurity, from worry about being laid off, was related to a decrease in their organizational commitment and an increase in their stress levels and health problems. Employees who reported a high sense of job involvement experienced health problems and greater stress than did employees who were less involved with their jobs (Probst, 2000). A study of 1,297 workers in Finland reported that those who were concerned about being downsized experienced decreased levels of work motivation and well-being and a high level of stress. Even rumors about the possibility of company downsizing were sufficient to cause measurable increases in stress (Kalimo, Taris, & Schaufeli, 2003). A meta-analysis of more than 28,000 employees in 50 samples found that feelings of job insecurity correlated highly with health problems, negative attitudes toward their employer, and expressed intention to seek employment elsewhere (Sverke, Hellgren, & Naswall, 2002).

JOB SATISFACTION AND ON-THE-JOB BEHAVIOR

We have described several factors that influence job satisfaction. Now let us consider those aspects of our behavior at work that can be affected by our level of satisfaction.

Productivity.   Ample research has demonstrated a strong and significant relationship between job satisfaction and job performance: The higher the reported satisfaction, the higher the level of performance (see, for example, Judge, Thoresen, Bono, & Patton, 2001). When 4,467 employees, 143 managers, and 9,903 customers of a restaurant chain were surveyed, the results showed that employee satisfaction affected not only customer satisfaction but also the restaurant's level of profitability. When employees reported high job satisfaction, so did customers, who were then likely to spend more money at the restaurant (Koys, 2001).

Most job satisfaction research has focused on individual employees. More recently, I-O psychologists have turned their attention to collective measures of job satisfaction, that is, the satisfaction level of a business unit such as a work team, section, or department. A meta-analysis of 7,939 business units in 36 companies demonstrated that employee satisfaction at the collective level was positively related to customer satisfaction and loyalty, and to employee productivity and safety on the job. High collective job satisfaction was also related to reduced turnover rates (Harter, Schmidt, & Hayes, 2002).

Prosocial and Counterproductive Behavior.   High job satisfaction has been related to **prosocial behavior,** that is, to helpful behavior directed at customers, co-workers, and supervisors to the benefit of employees and their organization. Does it follow that low job satisfaction is related to antisocial actions or to counterproductive behavior that may thwart organizational goals? Negative employee behavior can interfere with production and lead to faulty products, poor service, destructive rumors, theft, and sabotaged equipment. Employees may view these behaviors as a way of striking back at an organization because of real or imagined grievances.

Prosocial behavior
Behaviors directed toward supervisors, co-workers, and clients that are helpful to an organization.

Studies have shown a positive relationship between job dissatisfaction and counterproductive behavior for workers over the age of 30. This does not mean that older workers engage in more negative behaviors than do younger workers; the frequency of negative behaviors is higher for employees under 30. What the research indicates is that only in older workers has counterproductive behavior been related to job dissatisfaction.

Absenteeism.   Absenteeism is widespread and costly for organizations. On any given workday in the United States, up to 20 percent of employees do not show up for work. Absenteeism costs businesses more than $30 billion a year.

Absenteeism has plagued industry since the invention of machines. In textile mills in Wales in the 1840s, the absenteeism rate was approximately 20 percent. During the two-week period following each monthly payday, absenteeism often reached 35 percent. Throughout the 19th century in England, workers typically took off Mondays—"Saint Monday," they called it—to recover from weekend drinking bouts. Factory owners levied stiff fines and dismissed many workers, but that had no impact on attendance.

Much of industry's absenteeism data come from self-reports. Suppose you were filling out a questionnaire dealing with your job performance. One of the questions asked how many days of work you missed over the past year. Would you answer accurately? Or would you underreport the number of times you were absent? Would you be tempted to say that you missed only two days when the actual number was nearer to ten? Studies with diverse groups of workers consistently demonstrate the underreporting of absences by as much as four days a year. Managers also tend to underreport the extent of absenteeism in their work groups. About 90 percent of employees claim to have above-average attendance records. Clearly, many of us are less than honest about admitting the amount of time we lose from work.

If self-report absenteeism data are sometimes inaccurate, then why not use a company's personnel records to get a true indication of the absenteeism situation? That's a good idea in theory, but it does not work well in practice. Many companies do not compile attendance data in any systematic fashion. For managers and professional employees, such as engineers and scientists, such data are rarely collected at all. So when you read a study about absenteeism and learn that the data come from self-reports, you know that the actual number of absences is likely to be higher.

Not surprisingly, the more liberal an organization's sick-leave policy, the higher its absenteeism rate. Absenteeism is also high in companies that do not require proof of illness, such as a physician's note. High-paying manufacturing industries have higher absenteeism rates than do low-paying industries. The more money employees earn, the more likely they are to feel entitled to take time off. Workers in routine jobs often have a higher absence rate than workers in more interesting, challenging jobs.

Societal values may foster absenteeism, as is evident in variations in absentee rates for different countries. In Japan and Switzerland, where job attendance is considered to be a duty, absenteeism rates are low. In Italy, where societal attitudes toward work are more permissive, companies routinely hire 15 percent more workers than needed to make sure that enough people report to work each day to maintain operations.

Management often contributes to an organizational climate that appears to condone absenteeism by failing to enforce company policy. If management is believed to be lenient and unconcerned about absences, some employees will take advantage of the situation. Economic conditions can influence absenteeism rates. In general, when a company is in the process of laying off workers, absenteeism rates decline. Absenteeism increases when the overall employment rate is high, a time when workers feel more secure about their jobs. Also, younger workers are far more likely to take unauthorized time from work than are older workers.

Personal factors can also influence absenteeism. For example, a study of 362 blue-collar workers for an automobile manufacturer in Australia found that those who scored high in positive affectivity (which includes characteristics such as a high activity level, enthusiasm, sociability, and extraversion) had a significantly lower rate of absenteeism on the job than did those who scored low in positive affectivity (Iverson & Deery, 2001). Research on 323 health service workers in England showed that work-related psychological distress and depression correlated significantly with absenteeism rates. Employees who reported greater levels of distress were far more likely to have greater absenteeism than were those who reported less job-related distress (Hardy, Woods, & Wall, 2003).

Research has also suggested that absenteeism can be reduced through a company-sponsored program of rewards and recognition for good attendance records. A garment manufacturer established a program of monthly, quarterly, and annual rewards for low absenteeism rates. For example, employees who did not miss work for a period of a month had their names posted with a gold star. Good attendance for longer periods qualified workers for more expensive gifts such as gold necklaces or penknives. Absenteeism under this program declined significantly from its former level, and employees reported a high degree of satisfaction with the incentive system (Markham, Scott, & McKee, 2002).

Turnover. Turnover is also costly for organizations. Every time someone quits, a replacement must be recruited, selected, trained, and permitted time on the job to gain experience. Evidence relating high turnover to high job dissatisfaction is strong. Studies have shown that both intended and actual turnover can be attributed to dissatisfaction with various aspects of the job such as low pay or poor leadership.

Organizational commitment is strongly related to turnover. The greater a person's commitment to the job and the company, the less likely he or she is to quit. Age, however, does not seem to be a factor that affects turnover. Turnover is higher in times of low unemployment and expanding job opportunities than it is in times of high unemployment and limited opportunities. When people perceive that the economic climate is good and the economy is growing, they find it easier to consider changing jobs in the hope of increasing their job satisfaction.

Jobs that require a high level of creativity tend to be high in challenge, complexity, and autonomy and low on organizational control and supervision. A survey of 2,200 employees showed that people in highly creative and challenging jobs reported higher job satisfaction and lower turnover intentions than did people whose jobs did not offer these characteristics (Shalley, Gilson, & Blum, 2000).

There is a crucial difference between absenteeism and turnover. Whereas absenteeism is almost always harmful to the organization, turnover is not necessarily so. Sometimes it is the unsatisfactory employees who leave the company. I-O psychologists distinguish between *functional turnover*, when poor performers quit, and *dysfunctional turnover*, when good performers quit.

And what about involuntary turnover, such as downsizing or a RIF (reduction in force), when a number of employees are terminated usually as a cost-cutting measure? We noted above that such layoffs have harmful effects not only on the employees who have lost their jobs, but also on the employees who remain with the company. A study of 31 work units of a national financial services company showed that involuntary turnover events had a significant negative effect on the job performance and productivity of the remaining workers. Thus, downsizing was related to the organization's level of productivity (McElroy, Morrow, & Rude, 2001).

MOTIVATION, JOB SATISFACTION, AND PAY

Considerable research has demonstrated a positive relationship between pay and job satisfaction. Pay also affects job and organizational performance. For example, a study of 333 hospitals in California found that high pay among hospital staff members, including physicians and nonphysicians in all job categories, resulted in high positive patient care outcomes and high financial performance for the hospital (Brown, Storman, & Simmering, 2003).

Perceived Pay Equity

The perceived equity or fairness of one's pay can be more important than the actual amount. Survey respondents who believed that people with similar qualifications earned more than they did reported dissatisfaction with their pay. They thought they were being paid less than they deserved. It is not surprising, then, that people who think their salaries are higher than those of their colleagues are likely to be more satisfied with their pay. You may recognize this as a real-world example of the equity theory of motivation, discussed earlier in this chapter.

Most of us develop personal standards of comparison that are based on the minimum salary we consider acceptable, the pay we believe our job deserves, and the amount we think our co-workers are being paid. Thus, satisfaction with pay is determined by the discrepancy between our standards and our actual salary.

Of course, as we have seen, for some groups in American society there is little pay equity, either actual or perceived. In general, women are paid less than men for the same or similar work, and many ethnic minority employees are paid less than Whites. Also, you might think that a family member CEO of a family-controlled company would have a higher salary than a CEO who is not a member of the family of a family-controlled company. A study of 253 family-owned companies over a four-year period revealed, however, that CEOs who were family members actually received lower pay and bonuses than CEOs who were not related to the family (Gomez-Mejia, Larraza-Kintana, & Makri, 2003).

Merit Pay

Merit pay A wage system in which pay is based on level of performance.

Merit pay, or pay for performance, means that the better-performing workers in an organization are paid more than the less productive workers. This wage system is fine in theory but does not translate well to the realities of the workplace. I-O psychologists have studied various influences on the size of the pay raises given under merit pay plans. They have found widespread disagreement among managers about the behaviors that they consider important in making decisions about a worker's pay increase. A worker in one department might receive a sizable raise for job behaviors that bring no recognition in another department. Supervisors who receive substantial pay raises tend to recommend larger raises for their subordinates than do supervisors who receive smaller pay raises.

Pay raises are also related to the degree to which managers rely on their subordinates' expertise and support and whether managers consider such dependence a threat. For example, a manager who is low in self-esteem may want subordinates to provide praise or positive feedback and therefore may be reluctant to give them low pay increases. The manager may fear that if subordinates do

Newsbreak

Unequal Pay for Women, and for Men, Too

Patti Landers was delighted when she got a job as an engineer with the Boeing Company in her home town of Seattle, Washington. Working at Boeing was a family tradition; her father, brother, and husband all had jobs with the aircraft manufacturer. Years before, her grandparents had also worked there. It seemed like a great opportunity, and it was, until Patti compared the amount of her paycheck with what the men in her family were earning—and found a big, big difference. She felt cheated, so she and 37 other women filed a sex discrimination lawsuit against the company.

Boeing denied the allegation that women were paid less than men for doing the same work. But *Business Week* magazine obtained more than 12,000 pages of company documents showing that Boeing had conducted several internal studies that confirmed that men were paid more than women for the same job. Yet Boeing still fought the lawsuit, even though their own documents—which they had taken the trouble to hide in a secure room with an electronic cipher lock—proved that they had known about the pay inequities for ten years.

If the company loses the suit, which has grown to a class-action suit on behalf of 28,000 women employees of Boeing, it could cost the company more than $1 billion, far more money than they saved by paying women workers less than men. A company spokesperson insisted, however, that Boeing was committed to "equal rights."

Company policies such as these are nothing new. The majority of businesses have typically paid women less than men for performing the same or similar jobs. What is new is a study showing that *both women and men* who manage work groups composed mostly of women are paid less than those who manage work groups composed mostly of men.

A study of 2,178 managers in 512 companies demonstrated that in work groups that are 40 to 50 percent female, the managers are paid substantially less than when their work groups have a majority of males. As the percentage of female employees in a work group increases, the pay of their manager decreases. The researchers concluded that pay is unequal for men, too, if the group they manage is composed mostly of women.

Sources: S. Holmes (April 26, 2004). A new black eye for Boeing: Internal documents suggest years of serious compensation gaps for women. *Business Week*, pp. 90–92; C. Ostroff & L. Atwater (2003). Does whom you work with matter? Effects of referent group gender and age composition on managers' compensation. *Journal of Applied Psychology, 88*, 725–740.

not receive a sufficient salary, they will withhold their support or reduce their productivity to make the manager look bad.

There is also evidence that not everyone who receives a merit pay increase reacts to it positively. The effects of merit pay raises were studied over an eight-month period among more than 1,700 hospital employees at all levels from housekeepers to physicians. The effect of the pay increases on employee motivation and job performance was greater among employees who scored low in positive affectivity than among employees who scored high in positive affectivity. In other words, greater pay for better performance was considered to be of greater value by employees who were more introverted and pessimistic and less energetic. Perhaps they needed the recognition and appreciation of the merit pay raise more than did those whose higher positive affectivity (greater energy and optimism) were more independent of the circumstances of their employment (Shaw, Duffy, Mitra, Lockhart, & Bowler, 2003).

Wage-Incentive Pay Systems

Wage-incentive system The primary pay system for production workers, in which the more units produced, the higher the wage.

There are also problems with **wage-incentive systems,** the primary pay scheme for production workers. Through a time-and-motion analysis of a production job, an average or standard number of units produced in a given time can be determined. The wage-incentive system is based on this rate. In theory, the system provides an incentive for high job performance—the more units produced, the higher the wage—but it seldom works in practice. Many work groups establish their own standard for a good shift's production. Regardless of the incentive offered, they will not produce more but will spread out the work to comfortably fill the hours. Surveys show that most workers prefer a straight hourly payment system.

JOB INVOLVEMENT AND ORGANIZATIONAL COMMITMENT

Closely related to motivation and job satisfaction is job involvement; that is, the intensity of a person's psychological identification with the job. Usually, the higher one's identification or involvement with a job is, the greater the job satisfaction. Job involvement is related to several personal and organizational variables.

Personal Factors

Personal characteristics important in job involvement are age, growth needs, and belief in the traditional work ethic. Older workers are usually more involved with their jobs, perhaps because they have more responsibility and challenge and more opportunity to satisfy their growth needs. Older workers are also more likely to believe in the value of hard work. Younger workers, typically in entry-level positions, hold less stimulating and challenging jobs.

Because growth needs are important in job involvement, it follows that the job characteristics most relevant to job involvement are stimulation, autonomy, variety, task identity, feedback, and participation, the characteristics that allow for the satisfaction of the growth needs.

Social factors on the job can also influence job involvement. Employees who work in groups or teams report stronger job involvement than employees who work alone. Participation in decision making is related to job involvement, as is the extent to which employees support organizational goals. Feelings of success and achievement on the job enhance one's level of job involvement.

The relationship between job involvement and job performance is unclear. Employees with high job involvement are more satisfied with, and more successful at, their jobs. Their rates of turnover and absenteeism are lower than those of employees with low job involvement. However, we cannot state with certainty that high job involvement correlates with high performance.

Another variable allied with motivation and job satisfaction is organizational commitment—that is, the degree of psychological identification with or attachment to the company for which we work. Organizational commitment has the following components:

- Acceptance of the organization's values and goals.
- Willingness to exert effort for the organization.
- Having a strong desire to remain affiliated with the organization.

Organizational commitment is related to both personal and organizational factors. Older employees who have been with a company more than two years and who have a high need to achieve are more likely to rate high in organizational commitment. A meta-analysis of 3,630 employees in 27 separate studies showed that the longer a person had been employed by a company, the stronger was the link between organizational commitment and job performance. The researchers suggested that taking measures to increase organizational commitment early in new employees could lead to better job performance (Wright & Bonett, 2002). Scientists and engineers appear to have less organizational commitment than do employees in other occupational groups. In addition, government employees have lower organizational commitment than do employees in the private sector. Government employees are also likely to be lower in job satisfaction.

Organizational Factors

Organizational factors associated with high organizational commitment include job enrichment, autonomy, opportunity to use skills, and positive attitudes toward the work group. Organizational commitment is influenced by employees' perception of how committed the organization is to them. The greater the perceived commitment to employees, the higher the employees' expectations that if they work to meet organizational goals, they will be equitably rewarded.

A study of 746 employees of a university showed that those who scored high in organizational commitment were more dedicated to a company-sponsored program designed to improve work quality than were those who scored low in organizational commitment (Neubert & Cady, 2001). There is also a positive relationship between perceived organizational support and organizational commitment, diligence, innovative management, job performance, and attendance. Organizational commitment is positively related to the amount of support received from supervisors and co-workers and to the degree of satisfaction with supervisors (Bishop & Scott, 2000; Liden, Wayne, & Sparrowe, 2000).

Studies have confirmed a positive relationship between organizational justice and organizational commitment. People who believe their employer treats them fairly are more likely to feel a commitment to the company than are people who believe they are being treated unfairly (Simons & Roberson, 2003).

Gender seems to be related to organizational commitment. The more women employees in a work group, the lower the commitment of the men. With women, however, the reaction is the opposite. The more men there are in a work group, the higher the level of organizational commitment among the women.

Job satisfaction is related to workplace conditions. For some employees, an exercise facility at the workplace fosters a positive attitude toward the job.

Types of Commitment

I-O psychologists have identified three kinds of organizational commitment: affective or attitudinal commitment, behavioral or continuance commitment, and normative commitment (Esnape & Redman, 2003; Meyer & Allen, 1991). In *affective commitment*, the type we have been discussing, the employee identifies with the organization, internalizes its values and attitudes, and complies with its demands. Affective commitment correlates highly with perceived organizational support, as was shown in research with 333 retail employees studied over a two-year period and 226 employees studied over a three-year period (Rhoades, Eisenberger, & Armeli, 2001). The results demonstrated that perceived organizational support was a primary factor in the development of affective commitment.

A review and meta-analysis of more than 70 studies also found a strong positive link between perceived organizational support and affective commitment (Rhoades & Eisenberger, 2002). A study of 211 employee-supervisor dyads showed that supervisor support and recognition was related to perceived organizational support, which, in turn, was related to organizational commitment (Wayne, Shore, Bommer, & Tetrick, 2002). The importance of supervisor support in increasing perceived organizational support was also demonstrated in a study of 493 retail sales employees. That study also found that high perceived organizational support was strongly related to reduced turnover (Eisenberger, Stingchamber, Vandenberghe, Socharski, & Rhoades, 2002).

Other research involving 413 postal workers found a reciprocal relationship between perceived organizational support and affective commitment, which suggests that each factor strengthens the other. The more employees believe their company cares for them and supports their needs, the more strongly they identify with the company and internalize its values and attitudes, and vice versa (Eisenberger, Armeli, Rexwinkel, Lynch, & Rhoades, 2001).

In *behavioral commitment*, the employee is bound to the organization only by peripheral factors such as pension plans and seniority, which would not continue if the employee quit. There is no personal identification with organizational goals and values. Research suggests that affective commitment is positively related to job performance, but behavioral commitment is negatively related to job performance.

Normative commitment involves a sense of obligation to remain with the employer, a feeling that develops when the employees receive benefits such as tuition reimbursement or specific skills training.

Organizational Citizenship Behavior

Organizational citizenship behavior involves putting forth extra effort, doing more for your employer than the minimum requirements of your job. It includes such behaviors as "taking on additional assignments, voluntarily assisting other people at work, keeping up with the developments in one's field or profession, following company rules even when no one is looking, promoting and protecting the organization, and keeping a positive attitude and tolerating inconveniences at work" (Bolino & Turnley, 2003, p. 60).

Good organizational citizens are model employees whose behavior can help ensure the success of an organization. Studies in a variety of businesses—including insurance agencies, paper mills, and fast-food restaurant chains—have demonstrated that employees who are high in organizational citizenship behaviors are more productive and offer better service, which is related to higher customer satisfaction and greater company profits (see, for example, Bolino & Turnley, 2003; Koys, 2001; Walz & Niehoff, 2000).

Some research has shown that people who display organizational citizenship behaviors score high on the factors of conscientiousness, extraversion, optimism, and altruism. They are also team-oriented. A study of 149 nurses in Canada found a strong cognitive component to organizational citizenship behavior. Good organizational citizens based their behaviors on deliberate rational calculations as to how they would benefit from displaying such behaviors on the job (Lee & Allen, 2002). Essentially, they seemed to be saying, "What's in it for me if I behave this way on the job?" But consider this: How much of our motivation, job satisfaction, and job involvement are influenced by pragmatic (some would say, self-serving) calculations?

types of

Summary.....

Summary

Content theories of motivation deal with internal needs that influence behavior. Process theories focus on cognitive processes involved in making decisions. **Achievement motivation** theory posits the need to accomplish something and to be the best in whatever one undertakes. **Needs hierarchy theory** proposes five needs (physiological, safety, belonging, esteem, and self-actualization), each of which must be satisfied before the next becomes prominent. **Motivator-hygiene theory** proposes motivator needs (the nature of the work and its level of achievement and responsibility) and hygiene needs (aspects of the work environment such as pay and supervision). An outgrowth of motivator-hygiene theory is **job enrichment,** the redesign of jobs to maximize motivator factors.

Job-characteristics theory proposes individual differences in growth needs and suggests that employee perceptions of job characteristics influence motivation.

The **valence-instrumentality-expectancy (VIE) theory** describes a person's perceived expectation of the rewards that will follow certain behaviors. **Equity theory** deals with the ratio of outcome to input and how equitably that ratio compares with those of co-workers. **Goal-setting theory** suggests that motivation is defined by one's intention to achieve a particular goal.

Job satisfaction can be measured through questionnaires and interviews. It may be partly an inherited characteristic reciprocally related to overall life satisfaction. Job facet satisfaction refers to individual aspects of the job that can influence employee attitudes. Job satisfaction increases with age, length of job experience, and occupational level. Sex differences in reported job satisfaction are inconsistent. Job satisfaction appears unaffected by cognitive ability, assuming one's job is sufficiently challenging. Other factors affecting job satisfaction include **job congruence,** organizational justice, use of skills, personality, and control. Losing one's job can be damaging to self-esteem and health. Large-scale layoffs also affect those workers remaining on the job.

Research shows a significant relationship between job satisfaction and job performance. The higher the job satisfaction, the higher the performance, a relationship that holds for individuals and for business units such as work teams. Job satisfaction can result in **prosocial behavior;** job dissatisfaction can lead to counterproductive behavior that interferes with organizational goals. Absenteeism is higher among younger workers and in companies with liberal sick-leave policies. Absenteeism is high in low-status jobs and in high-paying jobs and can be caused by low positive affectivity and high levels of stress and depression. Turnover is allied with low job involvement, low organizational commitment, poor promotion opportunities, and dissatisfaction with pay and supervision. In functional turnover, low performers quit; in dysfunctional turnover, high performers quit.

There appears to be a positive relationship between pay and job satisfaction. An important factor in pay satisfaction is its perceived equity and relationship to job performance. Blue-collar workers on **wage-incentive systems** and managers on **merit pay** systems report pay dissatisfaction. Merit pay can lower work motivation because of perceived unfairness; one's true abilities may not be sufficiently rewarded.

Job involvement (intensity of psychological identification with work) is related to job satisfaction. Involvement is affected by personal characteristics such as age, growth needs, and belief in the work ethic, and by job characteristics such as level of challenge and opportunity for employee participation.

Organizational commitment is related to motivation and satisfaction and is greater among older employees and those high in achievement motivation. Also contributing to organizational commitment are job enrichment, autonomy, perceived organizational support, organizational justice, and a positive attitude toward the work group. Three types of commitment are affective commitment, behavioral commitment, and normative commitment.

Organizational citizenship behavior involves doing more for your employer than the job requires. It can lead to higher job performance and can be influenced by personality and by self-serving decisions.

achievement motivation
equity theory
goal-setting theory
job-characteristics theory
job congruence
job enrichment
job satisfaction

merit pay
motivator-hygiene (two-factor) theory
needs hierarchy theory
prosocial behavior
valence-instrumentality-expectancy
  theory
wage-incentive systems

1. Explain the differences between content theories and process theories of motivation. Give an example of each. What do these types of theories have in common?
2. What two types of goals can satisfy the need for achievement?
3. Describe the characteristics of people who are high in the need for achievement.
4. What are the needs in Maslow's needs hierarchy theory? Which needs can be satisfied on the job?
5. Distinguish between motivator needs and hygiene needs. Describe how each type affects job satisfaction.
6. How would you enrich the job of an automobile assembly-line worker?
7. In what ways does the motivator-hygiene theory differ from the job-characteristics theory? In what ways are they similar?
8. Give an example of how the VIE theory can be applied to your job as a student.
9. According to equity theory, what are three ways of responding to perceived equity or inequity? Which way best describes you?
10. Can goal-setting theory be applied to the workplace? If so, give an example of how it would work.
11. How can I-O psychologists measure job satisfaction? What personal characteristics can influence our level of job satisfaction?
12. Describe some effects of losing one's job. How does job loss affect the company employees who were not laid off?
13. What is prosocial behavior? How does it relate to job satisfaction?
14. Discuss the relationship between job satisfaction and job performance for individual employees and for work groups.
15. Why is it difficult to conduct research on absenteeism? What organizational policies may contribute to a high absenteeism rate?
16. Distinguish between functional turnover and dysfunctional turnover.
17. How does a merit pay system differ from a wage-incentive pay system? What are the problems with each of these approaches?
18. What is the difference between job involvement and organizational commitment?
19. Discuss personal and organizational factors that can influence organizational commitment.
20. Describe three types of organizational commitment.
21. What is organizational citizenship behavior? Give two examples of organizational citizenship behavior and tell what you think motivates it.

Additional Reading

Brown, M., & Heywood, J. S. (Eds.) (2003). *Paying for performance: An international comparison.* Armonk, NY: M. E. Sharpe. Discusses the use of pay-for-performance systems to encourage employee productivity in eight Western industrialized countries. Notes cultural differences as well as potential dysfunctional consequences of implementing such systems. Also considers the use of bonuses, promotions, tax breaks, seniority, and profit-sharing as part of an incentive package.

Dessler, G. (1999). How to earn your employees' commitment. *Academy of Management Executive, 13*(2), 58–67. Describes how modern organizations must clearly communicate the organization's mission, guarantee organizational justice, and support employee development.

Ellingson, J. E., Gruys, M. L., & Sackett, P. R. (1998). Factors related to the satisfaction and performance of temporary employees. *Journal of Applied Psychology, 83,* 913–921. Discusses job satisfaction among temp employees (a large but rarely studied subject group) and relates it to whether the decision to undertake temporary work is voluntary or involuntary.

Fraser, J. A. (2001). *White collar sweatshop: The deterioration of work and its rewards in corporate America.* New York: W. W. Norton. Assesses trends in the U.S. corporate workplace based on interviews with employees from entry level through upper management representing all major industries. Suggests from this anecdotal evidence that American workers are overworked, undervalued, struggling to balance work and family demands, vulnerable to job loss, and facing fewer opportunities for promotion.

Ganzach, Y. (1998). Intelligence and job satisfaction. *Academy of Management Journal, 41*(5), 526–539. Reviews research on the relationship between cognitive variables, level of education, and job satisfaction as affected by the complexity of the job.

Greenberg, J., & Cropanzano, R. (Eds.) (2001). *Advances in organizational justice.* Stanford, CA: Stanford University Press. Reviews research, theories, and practical implications of organizational justice, defined as the study of people's perceptions of fairness in their organization. Recognizes differences in perceptions among various ethnic groups and supervisory levels.

Hart, P. M. (1999). Predicting employee life satisfaction. *Journal of Applied Psychology, 84,* 564–584. Reports on personality correlates (such as neuroticism, extraversion, and job satisfaction) that relate to overall life satisfaction in a group of police officers.

Lawler, E. E., III. (2000). *Rewarding excellence: Pay strategies for the new economy.* San Francisco: Jossey-Bass. A model for pay systems recognizing the interdependence of several factors: global competition, changing technology, employee skills and knowledge, organizational structure, business strategies, and rewards for individual and team performance. Notes the importance of an appropriate reward system for attracting, developing, and retaining outstanding employees.

Wright, T. A., & Cropanzano, R. (2000). Psychological well-being and job satisfaction as predictors of job performance. *Journal of Occupational Health Psychology, 5*(1), 84–94. Analyzes the idea that the so-called happy worker is a more productive worker. Relates happiness (psychological well-being) and job satisfaction to job performance.

Chapter 9

The Organization of the Organization

All of us live and work within the framework of some kind of organization, a context that provides written and unwritten, formal and informal rules about how its members conduct themselves. You grew up in an organization called a family. Your parents established a culture that defined the guidelines by which the family functioned—the acceptable attitudes, values, and behaviors that made your family a unique organization, different from the families of your friends and acquaintances.

Perhaps a family in the house across the street had a culture based on orthodox religious beliefs and unusually strict standards of behavior, whereas a family next door was more moderate in its beliefs or reared its children more permissively. These families operated within different organizational styles. They established a structure based on a specific set of expectations, needs, and values that were expected to hold for all family members.

Various organizational styles are also evident in your college classes. One professor may be stern, even dictatorial, allowing no student discussion. Another may operate in a more democratic fashion, asking students to participate in decision making about course content and requirements.

Differences in organizational style in the workplace range from the rigid, hierarchical bureaucracy of the military and the civil service to the open, participatory approach that fosters high employee involvement. Bureaucracies regulate and prescribe what workers do and how they do it; little deviation is tolerated.

The modern organizational style attempts to humanize the workplace and has led to a modification of many traditional bureaucratic practices. Increasing numbers of organizations are treating their employees as integral members of the company and requesting their input in long-range planning and decision making. This shift in organizational style has brought about radical changes in the way work is organized and performed and has led to an improvement in the quality of work life for many employees.

Organizational psychologists study these changing trends in organizational life to determine their impact on employee satisfaction and behavior. We have described how the nature of leadership and the motivation of workers can affect job satisfaction, job performance, and organizational efficiency. In this chapter we describe the impact of organizational factors.

THE CLASSIC ORGANIZATIONAL STYLE: BUREAUCRACY

Bureaucracy A formal, orderly, and rational approach to organizing business enterprises.

The bureaucratic approach and the participatory approach represent two extremes in organizational style. We tend to think of **bureaucracies** in negative terms, as bloated, inefficient structures, top-heavy with layers of management and wrapped in miles of red tape that frustrate creativity.

As we know from our everyday experiences trying to deal with organizations of this type, there is much truth to this view. Yet the bureaucratic organizational style was once as revolutionary as the modern participative style, and it was considered just as humanistic in its intentions. Bureaucracies were devised to improve the quality of work life, and for a while they did.

As a movement of social protest, bureaucracy was designed to correct the inequities, favoritism, and cruelty that characterized organizations at the beginning of the Industrial Revolution. Companies were owned and managed by their founders,

The few executives at the top of the organization chart have little contact with lower-level employees and may have little awareness of their working conditions and personal concerns.

who had absolute control over the terms and conditions of employment. Employees were at the mercy of the owners' whims, prejudices, and decrees.

To correct these abuses, Max Weber, a German sociologist, proposed a new organizational style that would eliminate social and personal injustice (Weber, 1947). Bureaucracy was to be a rational, formal structure organized along impersonal and objective lines—an orderly, predictable system that would function like an efficient machine, unaffected by the prejudices of the factory owners. Workers would have the opportunity to rise from one organizational level to the next on the basis of their ability, not because of their social class or whether the boss liked them. Bureaucracy was a socially responsible improvement over the earlier system and served in its day to humanize the workplace.

The first practical application of the bureaucratic organizational style appeared in the United States even before Weber published his ideas on bureaucracy. The organization chart, which may be the most famous symbol of the bureaucratic approach, came into being in the 1850s. A general superintendent for the New York & Erie Railroad, Daniel McCallum, prepared a chart for his company and insisted that all workers abide by it (Chandler, 1988). McCallum's idea—formalizing the position and status of all employees in a hierarchical structure—quickly became popular and was soon adopted by most American companies. Thus, when Weber formally promoted the rules by which bureaucracies should operate, he was describing an organizational style already widely accepted in the United States.

Weber's ideas about bureaucracy, as depicted on the organization chart, involved breaking down or decentralizing the organization into component parts and operations. Each operation would be linked to others in a fixed rank order of control. The concept of division of labor, fostered by the scientific management approach, simplified jobs and made them more specialized. Responsibility or authority for each operation was delegated downward through the hierarchy, and communication flowed upward through the same channels. This arrangement effectively cut employees off from contact with other levels and sectors of the organization.

Although organization charts look nice and give managers the feeling that employees are in their proper places and that the organization is running smoothly, these neat lines and boxes on paper do not always reflect daily operations on the job. There is, as we shall see, an organization within the organization—an uncharted complex of informal social groupings of workers—that can interfere with the most rigid rules of the most dictatorial structure. And it is often through these informal groups and networks that the work of an organization is (or is not) accomplished.

There are problems with bureaucracies, however. A bureaucratic management tends to ignore human needs and values. They treat employees as inanimate, impersonal boxes on the chart, as interchangeable as the machines they operate. Bureaucracies do not recognize human motivations, such as the needs for personal growth and responsibility, self-actualization, and participation in decision making.

Employees within a bureaucracy have no individual identity and no control over their work or over the organizational policies that influence the quality of their working life. The ideal employees for a bureaucracy are docile, passive, dependent, and childlike. Decisions are made for them, for their own good, because they are considered incapable of deciding for themselves.

By being forced to channel all communication through their immediate supervisor, workers are isolated from higher management and prevented from making suggestions about company practices that affect their jobs and their well-being. Workers in these situations score low on measures of job satisfaction, job performance, and organizational commitment.

Bureaucracies can be criticized not only for their smothering effects on workers, but also for their harmful effects on themselves. Just as they prevent personal growth for employees, bureaucracies minimize opportunities for organizational growth, in part because of the barriers to upward communication. Bureaucracies foster rigidity and permanence and do not adapt quickly or well to the kinds of changing social conditions and technological innovations characteristic of today's workplace. The orderly bureaucratic structure was designed to preserve existing conditions. New developments are viewed as threats. For all its initial revolutionary fervor and humanistic intentions, then, the bureaucracy has not been successful in meeting human needs and changing times.

THE MODERN PARTICIPATIVE ORGANIZATIONAL STYLE

We noted that a major criticism of bureaucracy is its tendency to treat workers as docile, passive, and dependent. The modern participative organizational style takes a different view of human nature, summarized by the Theory Y position of McGregor's Theory X/Theory Y formulation we described in Chapter 7.

Theory X describes a view of human nature compatible with the rigid require-ments of a bureaucracy, which stifles individual motivation and the potential for growth. Workers need strict supervision because they are incapable of acting on their own initiative. This traditional, low-involvement organizational approach has the employees doing the work, middle managers controlling them, and only top management involved in strategy, planning, and long-range leadership.

In contrast, Theory Y assumes that employees are motivated to seek and accept responsibility for their work. In this view, people have a high level of creativity, commitment, and need for personal growth. Theory Y and other motivational conceptions supporting a participative approach suggest that organizations must decrease workers' dependency and subordination in order to take better advan-tage of their potential. Jobs and organizations must become less rigid in design and structure, allowing employees to help determine how best to perform their tasks. Jobs can be enriched to increase challenge and responsibility. Leaders should become less autocratic and more responsive to employee input. Decision making should involve participation at all levels. And organizations must be-come more flexible, capable of changing in response to employee needs and to social, technological, and economic conditions.

This high-involvement management style rests on three assumptions about people, participation, and performance (Lawler, 1986):

1. *Human relations.* People should be treated fairly and with respect. People want to participate, and when they are allowed to do so, they will accept change and become more satisfied with and committed to the organization.
2. *Human resources.* People are a valuable resource because they have knowl-edge and ideas. When they participate in decision making, the result is bet-ter solutions to organizational problems. Organizations must promote the personal development of their employees because it makes them more valuable to the company.
3. *High involvement.* People can be trusted to develop the knowledge and skills to make important decisions about the management of their work. When people are allowed to make such decisions, the result is an improvement in organizational performance.

The kind of work behavior stimulated by high-involvement management has been labeled, simply, "taking charge." Taking charge in this context involves em-ployees in making decisions about how their work should be performed and then implementing those decisions by actively restructuring the way they do their job. In research on this idea, a study of 275 white-collar workers found that they were far more likely to exhibit take-charge behaviors when they perceived that top management was open to their suggestions. Employees who were more likely to take charge were found to be high in self-efficacy and in responsibility for bringing about change. Both of these factors can be enhanced by a supportive management climate (Morrison & Phelps, 1999).

A nationwide survey of thousands of workers in England found that high-involvement management was positively related to higher pay (Forth & Millward, 2004). Research conducted in a large U.S. retail organization on 2,755 employees in 215 work groups reported that a sense of "psychological ownership" was fos-tered by a climate that emphasized self-determination, participative manage-ment, and recognition. This feeling of psychological ownership correlated with

Newsbreak   The Workers Are Taking Over!

It's happening everywhere you look. Employees are taking on more responsibility and making decisions only their bosses used to make. Jobs have been enlarged, expanded, and enriched, and workers have been empowered, given the freedom to take charge and do their work in their own way.

Take the case of a major department store. A salesperson overheard a customer tell a companion that the suit she had bought three weeks ago was now on sale. She wished she had waited for the sale so she could have bought it for less. The alert salesperson asked for the customer's name and credited her account with the difference between the sale price and the original price. The salesperson acted on his own initiative, without asking his supervisor for an OK—without even telling his supervisor! He was empowered to make these decisions for himself.

Nordstrom, the department store that prides itself on both customer and employee satisfaction, posts the following rules for its new employees:

Rule #1: Use your good judgment in all situations.
There will be no additional rules.

The rule says to use your good judgment. This means that decisions and the responsibility for them are in the hands of the employees, not the supervisors. This is nothing short of a revolution in the way we work.

A commercial printing company in Wisconsin encourages its printing press operators to make their own decisions. A corporate spokesperson explained: "Just as each lawyer is a partner and runs his own part of the business, I said each pressman is going to run his own press. I'd rather have 50 people out there thinking independently than for me to sit up here from the top and say, 'This is the way we're going to do it.'"

At Compaq Computer Corporation, three-person teams assemble and test new computers. Each worker is capable of performing different tasks and coping with challenges. Previously, the computers were built on an assembly line, with each worker performing one small task repeatedly. Under the new system, the number of completed units per worker increased 50 percent. Profits improved, and the employees reported greater satisfaction with their jobs. They feel important—and they are. The workers are taking over!

positive employee attitudes toward the organization and with the organization's improved profitability (Wagner, Parker, & Christiansen, 2003).

High-involvement management calls for active employee participation in decision and policy making at all levels and can lead to greater opportunities for personal growth and fulfillment and increased organizational effectiveness. These changes in organizational style have been expressed in various quality-of-work-life (QWL) programs.

TOTAL QUALITY MANAGEMENT

Total quality management (TQM) refers, in general, to the kinds of participative management programs we have been describing. They are characterized by increased employee involvement, responsibility, and participation in jobs that have been expanded, enriched, and enlarged. They adhere to the Theory Y approach to leadership (see Chapter 7) in which employee ideas and decisions play a vital role in the effective functioning of the organization. The overall goal of TQM is to improve the quality of the work being performed within the organization by improving the quality of the employees' working life. For that reason, TQM programs are sometimes called **quality-of-work-life (QWL) programs.** These programs have been implemented—in most cases with great success—to change the nature of leadership from Theory X to Theory Y and to improve employee motivation, job satisfaction, job involvement, and organizational commitment, the issues we discussed in Chapter 8.

An ambitious quality-of-work-life program was undertaken by General Motors with the support of top management and the United Auto Workers union. The program began when company and union officials agreed to form a labor-management committee to assess QWL projects. All projects had to consider extrinsic factors (physical working conditions) as well as intrinsic factors (employee involvement and satisfaction). Teams of industrial-organizational (I-O) psychologists, managers, and employees were empowered to enlarge jobs, redesign production facilities, and revise the old low-involvement bureaucratic organizational structure.

Total quality management (TQM)
Participative management programs characterized by increased employee involvement and responsibility.

Quality-of-work-life (QWL) programs
Organizational programs based on active employee participation in decision and policy making.

Under a quality-of-work-life program, small teams of workers meet periodically to discuss problems of productivity and employee involvement.

They began at a GM assembly plant in Fremont, California, which had been closed because of the poor quality of the cars assembled there. Absenteeism stood at 20 percent, on-the-job use of alcohol and illicit drugs was widespread, and more than 800 grievances had been filed against the company. The plant reopened three years later as New United Motor Manufacturing, Inc. (NUMMI), a joint venture of GM and Toyota that was committed to participative management.

NUMMI employees work in teams of four to six members and perform a variety of tasks throughout the workweek. Cars are built on the traditional assembly line, but employees rotate from one job to another, mastering new skills in the process. They solve production problems and devise ways to increase productivity on their own, without being told what to do by their supervisors.

Artificial status barriers have been eliminated. Workers and managers eat in the same cafeteria, and all begin the workday with a group exercise period. The majority of the employees who worked in the old GM plant like the high-involvement participative organizational style, and the quality of the cars produced has improved markedly.

Encouraged by NUMMI's success, General Motors adopted the participatory approach for its Saturn Motors plant in Spring Hill, Tennessee. Workers are organized into teams of about a dozen members, and they make all major decisions about their work, including the hiring of new employees. Management perks, such as reserved parking places, were eliminated, and communication is encouraged across all levels without employees having to obtain permission from supervisors or union shop stewards. Absenteeism is reported to be less than 1 percent, a rate similar to that of Japanese auto plants, and less than a tenth of other U.S. auto plants.

Productivity increased markedly in all GM plants that instituted QWL programs. Ford and DaimlerChrysler (then Chrysler) started similar programs and reported increases in worker productivity. One result was that the entire U.S. auto industry finally began to catch up with the success of Japanese automakers. In 1999 a Ford plant in Atlanta, Georgia, building the Taurus became the first American plant to surpass Japanese-owned factories in worker productivity.

The major factor driving these advances in the auto industry and other sectors of the economy is increased worker involvement and participation. Management has seen that taking an interest in what workers have to say really does pay off.

Why Some Programs Fail

There are many reports of successful QWL programs, but it should be noted that some have failed. Consider Volvo, which has been building cars by the team approach for decades. Although productivity is lower than at standard assembly plants, the participative approach has resulted in substantial improvements in quality and reductions in turnover and absenteeism. Volvo expanded the concept of worker participation at a new car assembly factory in Sweden in 1988. Instead of having employee teams build a portion of each car, which then moves on to the next team, the teams at the new plant were expected to build an entire car. The results were dismal. It took 50 hours to assemble a car at the new plant, compared to 37 hours using the team approach. At a Volvo plant in Belgium that uses a traditional assembly line, it takes 25 hours to assemble a car. Absenteeism at the plant in Sweden is high because many employees did not realize the

Susan Pacheco-Baker,
Ford Mechanical Engineer.

"Some of our best customer input comes from employees."

Because our employees are customers too, they want the same thing in a car or truck as you do. So at Ford Motor Company we encourage everyone, in every area of the company, to share their ideas. And it's this kind of thinking that has resulted in vehicles like our Ford Explorer having one of the highest customer satisfaction ratings in the industry. People know a good idea when they see it.

Ford • Lincoln • Mercury • Ford Trucks

QUALITY IS JOB 1. IT'S WORKING.

Buckle up–Together we can save lives.   Always insist on genuine Ford Motor Company collision repair parts.

Modern organizations invite employee participation in decision making. (Courtesy of Ford Motor Company.)

demands the redesigned job would entail. In addition, the training period to provide workers with the skills required to assemble an entire car turned out to be longer than anticipated.

Other QWL programs have failed because some employees have no desire to participate in decision making or to assume responsibility for determining the best way to perform their jobs. Some workers prefer, or need, more rather than less direct supervision. Also, QWL efforts can be doomed when managers continue to try to control their subordinates instead of working with them to share power and authority. QWL programs have a high probability of failure when they do not have the forceful advocacy and commitment of senior executives and when supervisors and union shop stewards view such programs as a threat to their power. Managers and supervisors must give up some of the power and authority by which they once directed and controlled their subordinates. They must also learn to share power and to function willingly as coaches, guides, mentors, and resource persons. Many managers find this a difficult adjustment to make.

Two characteristics of today's workplace may tend to dampen the positive effects of QWL programs. These are diversity and the growing number of contingent workers. While the workforce as a whole is becoming increasingly diverse, there are still organizations dominated by a majority of White males. Women and ethnic-minority employees are often left out of the informal social network through which majority employees share job-related information and social support. Thus, minority employees have fewer opportunities to participate in decision making and in efforts to restructure and redesign their jobs. In addition, an organization's permanent, full-time staff may actively exclude contingent employees (such as temporary or contract employees, or virtual workers) from participative programs.

Self-Managing Work Groups

Self-managing work groups Employee groups that allow the members of a work team to manage, control, and monitor all facets of their work, from recruiting, hiring, and training new employees to deciding when to take rest breaks.

Self-managing work groups allow the members of a work team to manage, control, and monitor all facets of their work, from recruiting, hiring, and training new employees to deciding when to take rest breaks. These autonomous work groups have become highly popular in business and industry today.

An early analysis of the first self-managing work groups yielded the following behavioral characteristics (Hackman, 1986):

1. Employees assume personal responsibility and accountability for the outcomes of their work.
2. Employees monitor their own performance and seek feedback on how well they are accomplishing their tasks and meeting organizational goals.
3. Employees manage their performance and take corrective action when necessary to improve their performance and the performance of other group members.
4. Employees seek guidance, assistance, and resources from the organization when they do not have what they need to do the job.
5. Employees help members of their work group and employees in other groups to improve job performance and raise productivity for the organization as a whole.

Self-managing work groups require a level of employee maturity and responsibility not called for in supervisor-managed groups. Self-managing work groups also need clear direction from the organization about production goals, a support staff to provide technical expertise, and adequate material resources. In some cases, engineers and accountants are added to the self-management teams so that they can deal with a full range of problems, operating, in effect, like minibusinesses within the larger organization.

Self-managing work groups also depend on the maturity and responsibility of managers, who must be willing to surrender authority to their subordinates. Indeed, management support is the most critical variable in determining the effectiveness of self-managing work groups. The extent of managerial support is also highly predictive of employee satisfaction.

The term *self-managing* work groups is not quite accurate because all such groups or teams require an external team leader (an employee of the organization who is outside the work group) to serve as a mediator, liaison, and buffer between the work group and the organization. In-depth critical-incident interviews with 19 external team leaders and 38 team members of a Fortune 500 company revealed that successful external team leaders displayed two kinds of behaviors: one focused on the organization and the other on the team (Druskat & Wheeler, 2003).

Organization-focused behaviors involve a high degree of social and political awareness of the needs, values, and concerns of management. Leaders must make sure that team members are aware of those concerns and responsive to them. Team-focused behaviors involve building trust among work group members and showing respect, concern, and care for them. Thus, some type of leadership is necessary for self-managing work groups to function efficiently; a hands-off approach was not found to be effective.

Many studies of self-managing work groups show their positive effects on productivity, quality of work, turnover, and job satisfaction. But self-managing work groups also have their problems. Converting from traditional bureaucratic management to self-management is difficult, expensive, and time-consuming, and many organizations underestimate the extent of the investment required. In particular, they underestimate the amount of training and meeting time involved and have unrealistic expectations about how soon self-managing groups can become productive. The need to monitor and review the progress of self-managing work groups can also dampen the initial enthusiasm for this approach.

Virtual Self-Managing Work Groups

A new type of self-managing work group is the virtual team. Members may work in geographically separate offices (or home offices) for different units of the same company or even in different companies that are linked by the same project. They meet by electronic means to perform a specific task, though they may rarely assemble in person. Their efforts are wired through such information systems as the Desktop Videoconferencing System (DVCS).

Using e-mail and other means of telecommunication, DVCS re-creates the face-to-face interactions and dynamics of actual group meetings. Cameras mounted on computer monitors bring team members into visual contact, allowing their verbal contributions to be supplemented and enlivened by facial expressions and gestures that can be viewed by all team members. An important element of context is thus added to the team members' words and opinions.

Newsbreak   Everybody Wanted to Go Home Early

Did you know that Harman Automotive, Inc., is the most famous automobile rearview mirror factory in the history of I-O psychology? The plant, located in Bolivar, Tennessee, was the first real-life experiment in employee empowerment—giving workers control over their own jobs. When this bold venture began, a quarter of a century ago, it was so phenomenally successful that the Big Three automakers used it as a model when they planned and implemented similar changes in their workplaces.

So many corporate presidents, foundation executives, and university scholars descended on the plant to see the miracle firsthand that the workers soon felt overwhelmed. They were so busy conducting tours that they had little time left for making rearview mirrors. They decided to limit the visitors to one group a week.

And then it all went wrong. Workers decided that they wanted to go home as soon as they met their daily production quota. Managers agreed. They called it "earned idle time." Well, this was fine for the assemblers and polishers, who, by working in teams, could finish their mirrors in half a day. But it caused friction with the workers who ran the huge metal-casting machines. They had to remain on the job for the full shift, to tend to their equipment.

So before long, everybody was demanding a shortened workday. Some managers bent the rules to allow their workers to leave early. Other managers refused. Many employees began to cut corners on quality so they could finish work in the morning and take most of the day off. Some workers devised shipping cartons with raised false bottoms so they would appear to be completely filled with mirrors when they were not. The temptation of paid time off was too great.

One worker said, "It turned us into thieves." A Harvard professor who had helped design the system lamented, "We were too idealistic."

Morale plummeted. Quality and quantity of product dropped. Absenteeism and turnover soared. Applicants for the jobs were easily attracted, however. Everybody had heard about the plant where you could get a full day's pay for a half day's work. The first question new hires asked was, "When can I go home?"

And one day in 1996, everybody went home early. Harman Automotive was forced to close.

Virtual work groups appear to have the potential to increase productivity, job satisfaction, job involvement, and organizational or team commitment. Group members must manage their own projects and evaluate their own performance. Managers must master the means of communication and keep team members "in the loop." Attendance must be mandatory so that all team members have an opportunity to participate.

ORGANIZATIONAL CHANGE

The employee participation programs we have discussed call for radical changes in organizational style. We have noted, however, that bureaucratic organizations by definition are resistant to change. When a structural change is to be introduced into an organization, it often meets with hostility, production slowdowns, strikes, or increased absenteeism and turnover. Whether the change involves new equipment, work schedules, procedures, office layout, or reassignment of personnel, it will usually be resisted at first.

Some organizations are able to change with the cooperation and support of employees and managers. The factor most responsible for determining whether change will be received positively or negatively is the way in which change is proposed and implemented. If change is imposed on employees in an autocratic manner and they are given no explanation or opportunity to participate, then they are likely to react negatively. However, when managers make an effort to explain the nature of the forthcoming change, the reasons for implementing it, and the benefits workers and management can expect from it, then workers are likely to respond positively and accept the change.

A study of 130 public housing employees showed that their openness to change was positively affected by the amount of information they received from management and by the degree of their participation in the planning process. Employees who were the least receptive to change also showed lower job satisfaction, were more likely to quit, and displayed greater irritation with aspects of their jobs (Wanberg & Banas, 2000).

Similar findings resulted from a study of two utility companies that were introducing major changes designed to reduce costs and to offer faster customer service. The changes would alter the ways in which many jobs were performed. Employees participated in the change process through their representation on a steering committee that worked closely with management. Before and during the time the changes were formulated and introduced, more than 100 employees were surveyed. The most significant finding was that employee trust in management increased over the period of the surveys. The researchers suggested that this greater trust was related to employees' beliefs that they had been given ample opportunity to participate in planning for the change and that management had explained and justified the plan sufficiently (Korsgaard, Sapienza, & Schweiger, 2002).

In another example of organizational change, a merger of companies resulted in job losses due to layoffs. Survey data showed that social support from co-workers was the most important coping resource for employees who were not laid off. Another finding was that employees' perceived control over their own job tenure was lowest during the initial stage of the organizational change, a time when layoffs were being rumored but not yet implemented. Once the layoffs had occurred, employees' perceived control increased (Fugate, Kinicki, & Scheck, 2002).

Not all workers' acceptance of change depends solely on external factors such as management explanations. Receptivity to change is also influenced by personality. Some of us are more predisposed than others to try new ways of performing our jobs. This was demonstrated in a cross-cultural study of 514 employees in six companies in the United States, Europe, Asia, and Australia. Workers were tested for positive self-concept, which includes the factors of locus of control, positive affectivity (defined as well-being, confidence, and energy), self-esteem, and self-efficacy. Test scores were also obtained for risk tolerance, which includes openness to experience, low aversion to taking risks, and tolerance for ambiguity. Workers who scored high in positive self-concept and risk tolerance coped with change significantly better than did those who scored low in these characteristics. In addition, high scorers rated high in job satisfaction, organizational commitment, and job performance (Judge, Thoresen, Pucik, & Welbourne, 1999).

A study of 265 nurses also illustrated the importance of organizational commitment in accepting change. This survey showed that affective commitment and normative commitment were more important in employee support for organizational change than was behavioral commitment (Herscovitch & Meyer, 2002).

Are the positive effects of worker participation in planning and implementing change permanent, or do they disappear once the researchers leave the office or factory? To study this question, two I-O psychologists visited a plant more than four years after it had undergone a radical change from a centralized bureaucracy to a flexible, innovative, participatory democracy. The change had been guided by the company president (a psychologist), with full worker participation, and was considered successful in terms of increased corporate profits, productive efficiency, and employee satisfaction.

The consulting psychologists in this now-classic study found that the benefits were evident four years later and that some of the effects were even greater than during the period immediately following the change. The increase in job satisfaction was accompanied by a higher concern with maintaining production levels (Seashore & Bowers, 1970). When properly introduced, then, a change in work procedures or in the entire organizational climate can have long-lasting positive effects.

Organizational Development (OD)

I-O psychologists have focused considerable attention on the problems of total organizational change and on systematic ways to bring about planned change. This effort, called **organizational development (OD),** involves techniques such as sensitivity training, role playing, group discussion, and job enrichment as well as survey feedback and team building.

Organizational development (OD) The study and implementation of planned organizational changes.

In the survey feedback technique, surveys are conducted periodically to assess employee feelings and attitudes. The results are communicated to employees, managers, and work teams throughout the organization. Their task is to provide feedback to higher management by suggesting explanations for the questionnaire findings and by recommending ways to correct the problems identified by employees in the surveys.

The team-building technique is based on the fact that many organizational tasks are performed by small work groups or teams. To enhance a team's morale and problem-solving abilities, OD consultants (called **change agents**) work with the groups to develop self-confidence, group cohesiveness, and working effectiveness.

Change agents Organization development facilitators who work with business groups to implement change and develop group confidence and effectiveness.

Outside consultants or change agents are usually able to view an organization's structure, functions, and culture with greater objectivity than in-house managers. Change agents' first task is diagnosis, using questionnaires and interviews to determine the organization's problems and needs. They evaluate strengths and weaknesses and develop strategies for solving problems and for coping with future changes. However, they must be cautious about introducing change without allowing employees to participate in the process.

The implementation of the recommended strategies, a process called intervention, begins with top management. Unless organizational change has management support, the chance of success is small. The specific intervention techniques depend on the nature of the problem and on the organizational climate. The OD process is flexible and can be adapted to the needs of the situation. In general, regardless of the specific techniques applied, the OD process helps to free the typical bureaucratic organization from its rigidity and formality, allowing more responsiveness and open participation.

OD techniques have been applied by many public and private organizations. Although research results are mixed, some significant increases in productivity have been documented. Job satisfaction seems to be negatively related to OD, however, perhaps because the emphasis is on improvements in productivity rather than on employee considerations.

SOCIALIZATION OF NEW EMPLOYEES

Organizations are constantly undergoing change through the addition of new employees at all levels of the workforce. New workers come with different levels of ability, motivation, and desire to perform their job well. They bring various needs and values that affect the organizations for which they work. At the same time, the culture of the organization makes its impact on the new employees. They have much to learn beyond the necessary job skills. They must learn their role in the hierarchy, the company's values, and the behaviors considered acceptable by their work group.

This learning and adjustment process is called **socialization,** and it is not unlike a rite of passage in which members of a society enter a new stage of life. Those who cope successfully with this adjustment process are generally happier and more productive employees.

Socialization The adjustment process by which new employees learn their role in the organizational hierarchy, their company's values, and the behaviors considered acceptable by their work group.

Positive interactions between current and new employees should be part of a company's socialization program.

Poor socialization to an organization—that is, a negligent or haphazard introduction to company policies and practices—can undermine the accomplishments of the most sophisticated employee selection system. An organization can recruit and hire qualified people and then lose them in the early stages of employment because of an inadequate reception. Improper socialization can foster frustration, anxiety, and dissatisfaction for new employees, which can lead to low job involvement and organizational commitment, low motivation and productivity, and to dismissal or quitting.

Socialization involves several organizational strategies. Ideally, the company should provide new employees with challenging jobs that offer opportunities for growth and development, the mastery of skills, self-confidence, success experiences, positive interactions with superiors, feedback, and co-workers who have high morale and a positive attitude toward the organization.

A study of 154 newly hired accountants found that early socialization links with supervisors (instead of forming links only with co-workers at the same level) fostered the learning of job and social roles and the establishment of organizational commitment (Morrison, 2002). A long-term study of 101 new employees involved surveying them when they were graduating college seniors, with follow-up surveys six months after graduation and two years after graduation. The results showed that they tended to internalize the values of their employer when they received positive social support from more experienced co-workers who served as role models (Cable & Parsons, 2001).

Although institutionalized socialization strategies are effective in teaching new hires about the organization, most new employees are not passive learners in this rite-of-passage process. Many are highly proactive, taking an enthusiastic role in seeking the information they believe they need to adapt to their work environment. A study of 118 newly hired workers during their first three months on the job found that those high in extraversion and openness to new experiences demonstrated significantly higher proactive socialization behaviors than did those lower in these personality attributes. The extraverted employees were more likely to take steps to build relationships and to obtain feedback from co-workers and managers (Wanberg & Kammeyer-Mueller, 2000).

Research involving 70 newly hired employees for high-tech project teams found that newcomers who rated high in self-efficacy held higher expectations about how well they would perform their new job. The study also showed that newcomers' performance expectations were enhanced when they were provided with early success experiences, challenging goals, and positive role models on which to base their own job behaviors (Chen & Klimoski, 2003).

Role ambiguity A situation that arises when job responsibilities are unstructured or poorly defined.

Role conflict A situation that arises when there is a disparity between job demands and the employee's personal standards.

Socialization will occur more quickly when there is greater interaction between new and established employees. Interactions can include asking questions, having informal conversations, and taking coffee breaks together as well as formal activities such as mentoring and performance appraisals. However, some evidence indicates that socialization programs should not rely on the employees who are being replaced by the newcomers. There is the possibility that departing employees will teach their successors established and perhaps inefficient job performance techniques and thus discourage innovation.

I-O psychologists have identified two factors that relate to socialization: **role ambiguity** (when the employee's work role is poorly structured or defined) and **role conflict** (when there is a disparity between job demands and the employee's personal standards). High levels of role ambiguity and role conflict are associated with low levels of job satisfaction, satisfaction with supervisor, and organizational commitment, and with a high rate of turnover. To resolve role ambiguity and role conflict, many new employees act on their own to obtain information about the job and organization from their co-workers and supervisors.

Resocialization

Most of the research we have cited here has dealt with new college graduates entering their first full-time job. But nowadays, most people can expect to change jobs several times during their working life. This means that, throughout your career, you are likely to experience new rites of passage, new socialization experiences (or resocialization) every time you join a different organization. Common sense suggests that having had one or more prior jobs should make socialization to the next job easier. Also, we might expect that performance, job satisfaction, and organizational commitment will be higher among workers who have had previous jobs because of their experience in adjusting to different organizations. However, research has not always supported that position. This shows the importance of careful I-O research. Sometimes our commonsense expectations and intuitive beliefs are not supported by scientific study.

What about employees who stay with the same company but are transferred from one location to another? Do they also need resocialization? Yes, because each unit of the organization will have different values, expectations, and acceptable behaviors. Although there is usually not a formal socialization process for transferees, there is an informal one in which they seek feedback from peers and supervisors to test the adequacy of their job behaviors in their new situation.

A study of 69 transferees in 15 organizations assessed feedback-seeking behaviors. It was found that seeking feedback from peers declined significantly over the first year in the new location, whereas seeking feedback from supervisors remained stable. These results indicate that feedback from supervisors is seen as more important in the resocialization process (Callister, Kramer, & Turban, 1999).

ORGANIZATIONAL CULTURE

A major organizational factor to which new employees must be socialized is the culture of the group they are joining. Just as nations have cultural characteristics—beliefs, customs, and behaviors that distinguish them from other nations—so do organizations. **Organizational culture** may be defined as a general pattern of beliefs, expectations, and values, some conscious and some unconscious, that are expected to guide the behavior of all members of an organization.

An organization's culture is influenced by the type of industry of which it is part; different companies within the same industry can be expected to have a common organizational culture. For example, steel manufacturers share cultural characteristics that are distinct from those of publishers, insurance companies, hospitals, Internet companies, or movie studios because of different market conditions, competitive environments, and customer expectations. Also, society expects different services from, say, an electric power company and a furniture manufacturer. There is a greater societal need for continuous and uninterrupted

Organizational culture
The organization's pattern of beliefs, expectations, and values as manifested in company and industry practices.

Newsbreak   Gimme an Order of Fries—Sir!

When Tom White was hired by Foodmaker, the parent company of the Jack in the Box fast-food chain, he did no work at his level for two months. Although his job title was vice president, he spent this introductory period learning about the company's culture, starting from the bottom up. This meant cooking fries, flipping burgers, and mastering the socialization program called "on boarding."

In addition, he was assigned a mentor and coach who showed him the Foodmaker way of doing things and who closely monitored his progress to make sure he would fit in. Finally, after eight weeks of experiencing in person more of the company's operations than most executives see in eight years, Tom was permitted to start his new job.

"It was probably the first time," he said, "that I've taken a new position and from Day One knew my duties and how to get things done in the organization. Without the on-boarding program, I would probably be six months to a year behind where I am now."

Corporate consultants report that few companies give their executives this type of opportunity to acquaint themselves with the organizational culture before undertaking their new job duties. The result is a high washout rate. Up to half of all new high-level executives quit or are dismissed within three years.

A survey of 46 executives who recently changed jobs revealed that one-third said they would need as long as a year to adjust to their new company. They agreed that the toughest part was adapting to the corporate culture. One human resources director described organizational culture as the "framework in which you get your job done—or not!"

Source: P. Sweeney. Teaching new hires to feel at home, *New York Times,* February 14, 1999.

---

service from the former than from the latter. Different departments within a company, such as research, engineering, and marketing, can develop their own subcultures that may differ from the dominant organizational culture.

Some I-O psychologists use the terms *organizational culture* and *organizational climate* interchangeably, arguing that the concepts share a fundamental similarity. Others note that climate is the surface manifestation of culture. Organizational climate is what we perceive when we observe the way a company functions, whereas organizational culture relates to deeper issues, the causes of an organization's operating style.

From our descriptions of participatory management programs, you have seen that organizational culture can influence a company's effectiveness. For example, companies with a culture of high involvement and high participation consistently outperform companies that do not favor employee participation and involvement.

Person-Organization Fit

The concept of **person-organization fit** can be defined as the degree of congruence between an employee's values and the organization's values. That agreement can be maximized through recruitment, selection, and socialization procedures.

Person-organization fit may be enhanced when the values of newcomers closely agree with those of their supervisors. This was demonstrated in a study of 154 new employees and 101 supervisors from 68 European companies based in the Netherlands. High congruence correlated with low turnover intentions. At the same time, a high level of incongruence or disparity between employee and supervisor values was associated with a low level of organizational commitment from that employee (Van Vianen, 2000).

A related variable is personality. A person-organization fit should encompass not only similar values, but also similar personalities. Most organizations are relatively homogeneous in terms of instilling a modal personality among its managers. A self-selection factor is involved here: Job applicants tend to be attracted to companies whose structure, mission, and attitudes they seem comfortable with. Think about a high-tech company staffed by people in their 20s who dress casually, put in long hours hunched over their computers, and bring their dogs to work. Now imagine a major investment banking firm with people in dark suits who arrive in limousines and conduct their business in hushed voices. The differences in personality are obvious!

Some organizational psychologists advocate revising the typical approach to employee selection, suggesting that companies should evaluate not only whether the applicants' knowledge, skills, and abilities are suitable for a particular job, but also whether those applicants' personalities are compatible with the organization's culture and personality.

Person-organization fit
The congruence between an employee's values and the organization's values.

LABOR UNIONS

One aspect of organizational life that helps define a company's culture is the presence or absence of labor unions, in which workers act collectively to protect and promote their interests. Union members form a subculture within the larger organizational culture. Membership in a union can contribute to job satisfaction and productivity and have a powerful influence on employees' attitudes toward their jobs and their employers.

The socialization of new union members is similar to the process of becoming acclimated to any new organization. Unions offer formal institutionalized socialization as well as informal individual socialization. The formal procedures include orientation lectures and training programs. Informal procedures involve attending union meetings with co-workers, being introduced to the shop steward, or having a work problem solved by the union. A study of 322 union members in Singapore found that loyalty to the union, developed through socialization procedures, was a powerful motivating force, leading union members to behave in ways that promoted the interests of the union and other union members (Tan & Aryee, 2002).

A review of pay scales in the United States shows that unionized employees are paid wages up to 33 percent greater than nonunion employees. In addition to higher pay, membership in a labor union can result in better and safer working conditions, job security, and fringe benefits, thus contributing to satisfaction of what Maslow called the lower-order needs. Union membership can also satisfy higher-order needs for status, belonging, and esteem and can provide a sense of power through the knowledge that unionized employees have an important bargaining tool: the threat of a strike. Some union members report a greater loyalty to their union than to their company.

Unions initially resisted quality-of-work-life programs because they feared such efforts would erode union loyalty. This resistance has been declining as more union members participate in and support QWL programs and other forms of worker participation.

Organized labor currently faces a crisis of declining membership. At the end of World War II, in 1945, more than 35 percent of the U.S. workforce belonged to unions. By 2003 that figure had fallen to 12.9 percent, which nevertheless accounts for approximately 15.8 million union members in the United States. Men are more likely than women to join unions; Black workers are more likely than White, Asian, or Hispanic workers to join unions. Almost 40 percent of government employees belong to unions as compared to less than 10 percent of private sector employees. For information on current workplace issues from the standpoint of labor unions, see the Web site of the AFL-CIO at www.aflcio.org.

Union Grievances

One aspect of union activity that affects employee attitudes and behaviors is the grievance process. Specified in union contracts, the grievance process establishes a formal mechanism for airing and resolving worker complaints. The number and focus of worker grievances serves as an indication of job dissatisfaction and can pinpoint the causes of problems in the workplace. Grievance procedures provide employees with a means of upward communication to management and an approved way of venting frustrations that might otherwise be expressed in work slowdowns, stoppages, or sabotage. Thus, the grievance process can be useful for both workers and managers.

The number of grievances varies with the nature of the job. Monotonous and repetitive assembly-line jobs performed under uncomfortable conditions by unskilled workers are associated with a high grievance rate. Social factors are also important. Highly cohesive work groups tend to file more grievances than do groups that lack a sense of unity. First-line supervisors who are low in consideration behaviors are the targets of more grievances than are supervisors who are high in consideration. In general, when a complaint is resolved in favor of the worker, job satisfaction rises along with the perception that the grievance system is fair and unbiased. When a grievance is settled in favor of management, labor-management relations often deteriorate.

INFORMAL GROUPS: THE ORGANIZATION WITHIN THE ORGANIZATION

Informal work groups develop within every organization. These groups have tremendous power to shape employee attitudes, behavior, and productivity. Workers come together informally to establish and promote a set of norms and values, a subculture within the larger organizational culture. These informal groups do not appear on the organization chart and are beyond the control of management. Often, management is not aware of their existence.

Informal groups determine for new employees how they will come to perceive management and other aspects of organizational culture. These groups can work for or against the organization by encouraging cooperation with company policies and procedures or by thwarting productivity and management goals.

The Hawthorne Studies

The classic Hawthorne studies provided empirical evidence of informal work groups. A team of 14 workers in the telephone bank wiring room of the Western Electric plant was observed for six months. The observer noticed that the group had developed its own standards of behavior and productivity. The workers shared many interests, engaged in rough but friendly teasing, and stood ready to help one another on the job. They valued one another's friendship and acceptance and displayed many of the characteristics of a family. They avoided doing anything that might bring disapproval from the group.

In terms of productivity, the group determined what it considered to be a fair and safe day's output. Management had set one standard, with an incentive to be paid for meeting or exceeding the daily level (an employee could make more money by working faster). But the group had set its own standard, which was below the company's level. The workers believed that if they met or exceeded management's demands, the company would then raise the standard and force them to work harder. Therefore, the informal work group set a leisurely, easily attainable production goal, willing to forgo the opportunity to earn extra money. The workers admitted to the observer that they were capable of producing more but to do so would have defied the group's norms. The group had assumed such prominence in the workers' lives that they considered group acceptance more important than extra pay.

Members of informal work groups usually have similar backgrounds and interests and may determine for themselves an acceptable standard of productivity, which may differ from the one set by management.

Social Loafing

Social loafing The idea that people do not work as hard in a group as they do when working alone.

Another effect of informal work groups is the phenomenon known as **social loafing,** the idea that people do not work as hard in a group as they do when working alone. One explanation for social loafing is that people believe they can get lost in the crowd and that their slower work pace will not be noticed. Also, people tend to expect, on the basis of past experience, that others in the group will goof off, so they might as well do so, too.

Social loafing is less likely to occur when workers believe that their supervisors are aware of how hard they work as individuals. Social loafing is more likely to occur when workers believe that their personal efforts are not recognized by their supervisors. Men are more likely to engage in social loafing than are women. Further, workers in Eastern cultures (which are more collectivist or group-oriented) are less likely to practice social loafing than are employees from Western, more individualistic, cultures.

Workers are likely to engage in social loafing under the following conditions:

1. When their individual outputs cannot be evaluated.
2. When working on tasks that are not meaningful or personally involving.
3. When working with strangers.
4. When they expect their co-workers to perform well on the task.
5. When their work groups are less cohesive.

Group Cohesiveness

Group cohesiveness The focus, closeness, and commonality of interests of a small work group.

Informal groups exist in virtually every type of organization. They are characterized by personal interactions that occur over an extended period because frequent interactions are necessary to the development of closeness **(group cohesiveness)** and a commonality of interests. Groups must also have a focus, such as workers in the same department who share a physical workspace. The groups cannot be too large, or the sense of personal and direct contact will be lost.

Most of us have a need for affiliation and companionship, and this need can be satisfied by an informal work group. The group also serves as a source of information about work procedures and about what constitutes an acceptable day's output. Group closeness was also found to influence employee perceptions of organizational issues. For example, employees who form personal relationships in a work group tend to interpret organizational events in a similar way. Employees in less cohesive informal groups tend to interpret the same events in a different way.

Group norms and standards are pervasive throughout organizational and personal life. The group can influence political and racial attitudes, style of dress, even where to eat or go on vacation. Because group membership satisfies so many needs, employees strive to be accepted by group members. Deviant behavior is rarely encountered, except from new workers who need time to absorb the group's ways.

Informal groups tend to attract and retain people with similar personality characteristics and to take on a consistent affective or emotional tone. As a result, group members tend to have similar moods and feelings about their work. A group's affective tone influences the group's work performance. A negative affective tone is related to a low level of helping behaviors, manifested in rude and uncooperative behavior. Positive affective tone is related to a low level of absenteeism.

Positive affective tone is also positively related to organizational spontaneity, which includes such behaviors as helping co-workers, protecting the organization, making constructive suggestions, developing one's personal skills, and spreading goodwill. Positive affect in a group is likely to be stronger when the group is small and the members work in physical proximity. In that situation, the mood of the individual employee is influenced by the collective mood of the group over time (see, for example, Brief & Weiss, 2002).

We noted that the degree of closeness within a group is called group cohesiveness. The greater the cohesiveness, the greater the group's power over its members and the greater the pressure on group members to conform. Several factors influence cohesiveness. As the group gets larger and there is less opportunity for frequent contact among group members, cohesiveness declines. Larger groups generally splinter into subgroups or competing groups. Diversity of background, interests, and lifestyles reduces group cohesiveness.

Working conditions are also important. Workers under a wage-incentive system that rewards on an individual rather than a team basis find that the resulting personal competition reduces feelings of closeness. Team rewards enhance group cohesiveness by encouraging cooperation; everyone works for a common goal.

Outside pressures and threats affect group cohesiveness. Just as citizens of a nation under attack usually cooperate to submerge personal or regional differences, so will a work group faced with an unfair supervisor or an unpopular policy. A meta-analysis of 64 studies identified three components of group cohesiveness: interpersonal attraction, task commitment, and group pride. The study also found a strong positive relationship between high group cohesiveness and high job performance (Beal, Cohen, Burke, & McLendon, 2003).

TECHNOLOGICAL CHANGE AND ORGANIZATIONAL STRUCTURE

The widespread use of computer-aided manufacturing and office equipment has changed the ways in which daily work is performed and has also affected the formal and informal structure of organizations. Computer technology creates the need for greater coordination and integration of an organization's basic units, which requires the development of new reporting hierarchies. For example, at one plant in which operations were computerized, the engineering staff had to be reorganized so that it reported to the marketing department, a unit with which it previously had had no direct contact. The change was necessary to coordinate customers' needs (marketing) and the development of new products (engineering).

Computer technology requires greater formalization of work procedures. Rules for entering data into computer files must be precise. They permit no employee discretion or deviation. These formal procedures reduce opportunities for individuality in structuring and organizing work. Computers also change the source of decision-making authority, although the direction of the change is not always clear. In practice, automating an office or manufacturing plant sometimes results in greater centralization of decision making, restricting it to fewer levels on the organization chart. In other cases it results in decentralization, giving greater decision-making authority to the worker at the video display terminal. For some jobs, computer operators may be more knowledgeable than their supervisors about the equipment's capabilities. This shift in power from supervisors to employees can disrupt traditional working relationships and leave managers with a reduced understanding of the work they are supposed to be managing.

Computers are also changing the procedures for the meetings that result in corporate decisions. Instead of asking a group of employees to sit around a table and discuss a problem, some organizations hold virtual meetings in which the interaction takes place through computers. Participants express their ideas simultaneously and anonymously and comment on one another's work. Anecdotal evidence from organizations as diverse as hotels, banks, plastics companies, and aircraft manufacturers indicates that virtual meetings are shorter and less stressful. Leaders are able to stick to an agenda because employees do not digress or waste time at the computer to the extent they do in person.

This type of electronic brainstorming typically involves groups of up to 12 participants who are instructed to submit as many ideas as they can, to avoid criticizing others' ideas, and to try to combine and improve the ideas generated by other group members. Thus, the process eliminates two problems inherent in face-to-face group brainstorming: (1) *production blocking*, which is the inability of more than one member to generate ideas at the same time, and (2) *evaluation apprehension*, which is the reluctance of some members to offer their own ideas for fear of being publicly criticized or embarrassed. Software packages for electronic brainstorming allow the members of the virtual group to enter their ideas at any time without interruption and to do so anonymously. Such groups tend to generate more ideas than traditional face-to-face groups, and the ideas are often of higher quality, apparently as a result of being exposed to the ideas of the other group members (Kerr & Tindale, 2004).

Computers can force changes in the organization's informal structure by disrupting traditional lines of communication and power. For example, in companies where workers have side-by-side work stations, they communicate freely and easily about both work-related and personal matters. Where such jobs are automated, workers are often separated by partitions that inhibit talking and socializing.

Reducing the chances for personal interaction reduces the group's cohesiveness. Even though workers have found ways to use their computers for informal communication, this approach lacks the closeness and the privacy afforded by face-to-face contact. It also eliminates the nonverbal cues, such as tone of voice, facial expressions, hand gestures, and other forms of body language that can be as informative as the words themselves. In addition, many companies routinely monitor the messages on their internal e-mail system, an action that discourages its use for promoting the personal and social interactions necessary to maintain group cohesiveness.

Along with the loss of group cohesiveness, computer use on the job has led to employees' growing sense of isolation, both on and off the job. Instead of being able to walk into the neighboring office or down the hall to consult with a colleague in person, you can ask your questions without leaving your cubicle, and thus without any meaningful personal contact. Instead of gossiping around the water cooler, employees are chatting online. Even lunch breaks are at risk as growing numbers of employees rush back to their computer terminals rather than visit with co-workers or run errands. A survey of 1,000 employees found that 14 percent ate by themselves at their desks so they could log on during their free time (Fickenscher, 2000).

The ideas once shared during informal gatherings of employees or generated and exchanged during spontaneous meetings are being lost, along with the opportunities to network and build social support. This situation is especially true for the millions of employees who work at home. Many of these telecommuters spend their entire workday connecting with other people only by electronic means.

Surveys of employees who do business with others online rather than in person reveal that they trust the people with whom they deal in person more than they trust the people they interact with only by electronic means. Those who deal with others face-to-face spend more time getting to know one another through conversation about conventional topics such as family and other personal (nonwork) matters, which can lay a foundation for trust and friendship. Dealing with people only through fax, e-mail, or video conferencing is not the same as being there in person. Such relationships are seen as less personal and less humanized (Olson & Olson, 2003).

The depersonalized nature of communicating through electronic means can affect business negotiations. The greater distrust of the other party, who is known only online, can impede and distort the negotiating process. Surveys of international bankers found that they believed communicating by telephone when engaged in important negotiations was a more real and beneficial way to establish a good personal and working relationship than communicating only online (Bargh & McKenna, 2004).

An additional problem brought on by electronic communication involves the amount of time spent online. Psychologists have suggested that excessive Internet use can lead to a form of addiction. The Center for Internet Studies surveyed 18,000 users and found that nearly 6 percent met the criteria for compulsive Internet use, characteristics similar to those that define compulsive gambling (DeAngelis, 2000). These people were especially hooked on chat rooms, pornography sites, online shopping, and e-mail. One-third of them said they logged on regularly as a form of escape or to alter their mood. For more information log on to the Center for Internet Studies at www.virtual-addiction.com or the Center for Online Addiction at www.netaddiction.com.

Employer monitoring of computer use has a disruptive effect on the employee-employer relationship and, as a result, on the organization as a whole. Workers may come to view their bosses as watchdogs, always spying on their behavior. To examine the pervasiveness of electronic snooping in the workplace, the American Management Association surveyed more than 1,000 major U.S. companies. They found that electronic surveillance of employees has grown rapidly during the past several years. Almost 78 percent of the companies questioned reported that they routinely monitored their employees' behavior on the job, including checking telephone calls, e-mail, voice mail, Internet connections, and computer files. More than half of the firms used blocking software to prevent connections to unauthorized telephone numbers and about a third blocked Internet access to Web sites they deemed inappropriate. Some 43 percent of the companies tracked the amount of time employees spent on the phone and checked the phone numbers to find out if the calls were work related.

A survey of 224 mid-sized companies conducted by the Center for Internet Studies found that 60 percent had disciplined employees for online abuse and

Newsbreak

Are You a Compulsive Multitasker?

Charles Lax is always "on," no matter where he is or what he's doing. When the 44-year-old venture capitalist from Boston flew to Los Angeles for a conference on telecommunications, he wasn't really all there. Only part of him was listening to the presentation he paid $2,000 to attend. He was also surfing the Internet on his laptop while checking his mobile device (part phone, part pager, part Internet tool) for his e-mail. Even as the presentation continued he could not disconnect himself from his electronic devices long enough to concentrate on it. If he did so, he risked facing the one situation he dreaded most: boredom!

"It's hard to concentrate on one thing," he said. "I think I have a condition."

He does. Experts who study such persistent multitasking—the need to be constantly "on," to be always wired or connected—have given it a label, to make it official. They call it *online compulsive disorder*, or OCD. You've seen OCD people in your classes or your workplace. They may be sitting in a meeting room or a lecture hall and exchanging messages with someone across the room on a handheld device, or at their desk talking on two phones simultaneously, or watching their kid's soccer game and reading the news on some information Web site.

Psychologists who have studied OCD find that such people have a short attention span, become frustrated when given long-term projects or assignments, thrive on the constant fixes of information, and have a physical craving for the stimulation they receive from checking voice mail, e-mail, or answering the phone—or, even better, doing all three at once. Does this mean they are more productive than people who prefer to do one thing at a time? Not according to Dr. David Meyer, a psychology professor at the University of Michigan. His research shows that multitaskers hinder their own productivity when they try to do more than two things at the same time. He found that people who switch back and forth between two tasks spend 50 percent longer to complete them than if they worked on one task at a time. But that behavior would not supply the rush, or fulfill the need for excitement and exhilaration that OCD people constantly crave. "It's instant gratification," Charles Lax told a telephone interviewer. "I use it when I'm in a waiting situation—if I'm standing in line. Being able to send an e-mail in real time is just so. . . ." He stopped. "Can you hold for a second? My other line is ringing."

Source: M. Richtel. The lure of data. *New York Times*, July 6, 2003.

30 percent had fired workers for such behavior. The two most frequently reported abuses were using the Internet for personal e-mail on company time and for connecting to pornography sites (DeAngelis, 2000). Another survey questioned 1,000 Internet users and reported that 10 percent believed that their work had suffered as a result of the excessive amount of time they spent surfing Web sites.

Newsbreak   Beware of Big Brother

It pays to be careful when you log on at work these days. What you say could get you fired. That was the painful lesson learned by Michael Smyth, who used to be a sales manager at The Pillsbury Company until he messaged his boss one day and referred to the boss's superior as a "back-stabbing bastard."

Smyth thought his e-mail was private and personal, just like sending a letter through the regular mail. But it wasn't. A co-worker found a printout of the message and brought it to the attention of the "back-stabbing bastard." Smyth was fired right away. He sued for wrongful discharge, arguing that his communication was private, but a judge turned down his claim.

The judge ruled that Smyth forfeited any and all reasonable expectations of privacy when he used the company network, even though his message was clearly intended for only one person. A lawyer for the company pointed out that a warning appears on the screen every time employees log on, reminding them that their mail might be intercepted and read by anyone else on the network.

So be careful what you say online. You don't know who might be monitoring your mail. And be careful where you surf. That can get you in trouble, too.

Andrew Quinn, systems manager in charge of monitoring for a Canadian company, checks every e-mail employees send and receive as well as every Web site with which they connect. "Look at this guy," he told a visiting reporter. "He's sending out jokes on e-mail. That's all he's been doing for the last hour!" What does that tell you about his job productivity?

The *New York Times* fired 23 workers at their Virginia office for sending and receiving obscene messages. Xerox fired 40 workers when records showed that they had spent up to eight hours a day on porn sites. Other workers misuse their work time conducting personal business, day-trading, planning trips, shopping, and playing computer games. This so-called cyberslacking has caused meltdowns of company networks, costing many hours of downtime and hundreds or thousands of dollars for repair. Sometimes the situation gets so bad that business has to be conducted over that low-tech device known as the telephone.

Sources: L. Gvernsey. The Web: New ticket to a pink slip. *New York Times,* December 16, 1999; You've got inappropriate mail. *New York Times,* April 5, 2000; J. L. Seglin. You've got mail; you're being watched. *New York Times,* July 18, 1999.

Another 13 percent blamed easy access to the Internet as being responsible for their inability to stay focused on their jobs (Fickenscher, 2000).

Despite such findings, other survey research has found that employees who know their computer use is being monitored are not less likely to continue to use their computers for nonwork activities than those who do not know their computer activities are being monitored (Everton, Mastrangelo, & Jolton, 2003). Perhaps the first group of people consists of Internet addicts who will continue their addictive behavior despite the consequences, not unlike gamblers or alcoholics.

Employees who are monitored for Internet use also report higher levels of depression, tension, and anxiety, and lower levels of productivity than do employees who are not monitored by their employers (Rosen, 2000).

Some employees, particularly those in food service and health care industries, cannot even find privacy in the bathroom. Sensing devices on soap dispensers and faucets determine whether employees are adhering to basic sanitary requirements and practices by washing their hands. One employer said, "If an employee fails to wash up, his badge may start flashing as a black mark goes directly into his file on the main computer." In addition, up to 35 percent of large companies have installed video cameras as a security measure to prevent employee or customer theft, or to monitor job performance.

A study of 370 high school and college students holding summer jobs asked how they felt about video cameras watching them as they worked. Those who had been told about the electronic monitoring in advance felt it was fair and also said they felt more valued by their employers. Those who were not told in advance believed the procedure was unfair and they felt devalued by their employers (Hovorka-Mead, Ross, Whipple, & Renchin, 2002).

Employees who are being watched and monitored in any fashion by any means often complain that their privacy and dignity are being violated. Employers argue that they need to ensure that their employees are not goofing off. Which side do you agree with?

Summary

Organizational psychologists study organizational climates and styles and the ways they affect employees. The classic organizational style is **bureaucracy,** intended to be a rational structure in which rules of conduct and lines of authority were fixed and in which subjectivity and personal bias had no place. Bureaucracies ignored human needs and could not adapt easily to social and technological change.

The modern organizational style, a high-involvement participatory approach, is more concerned with employees' intellectual, emotional, and motivational characteristics. Workers participate in decision making at all levels. **Total quality management (TQM)** programs restructure job and management requirements to enhance worker participation, involvement, and responsibility. In **self-managing work groups,** a work team controls all aspects of the job through an external team leader who serves as a buffer between the group and the organization. Virtual self-managing work groups are linked electronically. Its members may never meet face-to-face.

Employees and managers may resist changes in work methods, equipment, or policies. If workers are allowed to participate in decisions about the change, they are more likely to support it. **Organizational development (OD)** involves techniques for introducing large-scale changes. The process is carried out by **change agents** who diagnose problems, devise appropriate strategies, and implement the interventions.

New employees undergo an adjustment period called **socialization.** A socialization program should involve a challenging job, appropriate training and feedback, a considerate supervisor, co-workers with high morale and organizational commitment, and a suitable orientation program. Resocialization occurs any time an employee joins a different organization.

Organizational culture is the pattern of beliefs, values, and expectations that guide the behavior of the organization's members. **Person-organization fit**

refers to the congruence between an employee's personality and values and the organization's culture and values.

Membership in a labor union can affect job satisfaction and productivity and can satisfy lower-level needs through pay, job security, and fringe benefits. Membership can also satisfy belonging, esteem, status, and power needs.

Informal work groups, which influence employee attitudes and behavior, exist beyond management control. They operate by their own standards with regard to productivity and worker-management relations. **Social loafing** is the idea that people do not work as hard in a group as they do when working alone. **Group cohesiveness** refers to the degree of closeness of a group. The higher the group cohesiveness, the higher the job performance.

Computer usage has produced changes in organizational structure by causing a power shift from supervisors to employees. Meetings can now be held online (virtual meetings), reducing group cohesiveness and increasing social isolation. Electronic surveillance can reduce employees' trust in their organization.

bureaucracy	role ambiguity
change agents	role conflict
group cohesiveness	self-managing work groups
organizational culture	social loafing
organizational development (OD)	socialization
person-organization fit	total quality management (TQM)
quality-of-work-life (QWL) program	

Key Terms

Review Questions

1. Why was the development of the bureaucratic organizational style considered to be such a revolutionary and humanistic change to the workplace?
2. Describe the problems and weaknesses of bureaucracies for both the individual employee and the organization.
3. According to McGregor's Theory Y, what are workers like? How does this differ from the Theory X view of workers?
4. If your company employed two managers and 50 workers to produce mountain bikes, how would you convert the operation to a high-involvement management system?
5. What are the requirements and advantages of TQM programs? Why do some of them fail?
6. If self-managing work groups are designed to function autonomously, why are external team leaders necessary, and what do they do?
7. How can self-managing work groups function when group members work in different locations instead of together in one facility?
8. What factors influence the ways in which employees accept major organizational change?
9. Describe the procedures involved in OD. What is the role of change agents?
10. In what ways can an organization facilitate the socialization of its new employees? What are the results of the poor socialization of a new employee?
11. Define role ambiguity and role conflict. How do they relate to socialization?

12. What is organizational culture? Give an example of how organizational culture can affect job satisfaction and performance.
13. In what ways can the labor union grievance process benefit workers and employers?
14. What organizational conditions are likely to lead to social loafing? Does social loafing occur when people work alone rather than in groups?
15. Describe three components of group cohesiveness. Is there likely to be greater group cohesiveness in larger groups or in smaller groups? Offer an explanation for your answer.
16. How has computer technology affected work procedures, the conduct of meetings, and the brainstorming process?
17. How extensive is electronic monitoring in the workplace? Give some examples of how it is carried out.
18. What would be your reaction if you learned that your employer was monitoring your computer use? Would it change your behavior? If so, how?

Additional Reading

Ashkanasy, N. M., Wilderom, C. P. M., & Peterson, M. F. (Eds.) (2000). *Handbook of organizational culture and climate*. Thousand Oaks, CA: Sage Publications. Reviews international research, theory, and practice. Includes basic concepts, measurement, assessment, and applications of organizational culture/climate theory to everyday management and human resources problems such as organizational commitment and socialization.

Bar-Haim, A. (2002). *Participation programs in work organizations*. Westport, CT: Quorum. Reviews some 50 years of worker and work team participation programs and notes cultural, historical, and political differences among programs in the United States and European countries.

Boyett, J. H., & Boyett, J. T. (2000). *The Guru guide to entrepreneurship*. New York: Wiley. Profiles 70 highly successful entrepreneurs including the founders of Microsoft, Amazon.com, McDonald's, and Wal-Mart. Describes their organizational styles, including sharing information and perks with employees, and offers self-tests to assess your potential to start and run a business.

Burke, W. W. (2002). *Organization change: Theory and practice*. Thousand Oaks, CA: Sage. A historical review of organizational change and an overview of contemporary models. (The author's view may be summed up as follows: Change happens! Let's do it right!)

Carter, L., Giber, D., & Goldsmith, M. (Eds.) (2001). *Best practices in organizational development and change*. San Francisco: Jossey-Bass/Pfeiffer. Provides case studies to support the idea that organizational development (OD) is to organizations as clinical psychology is to individuals. Describes OD as the application of psychological principles to promote healing, growth, and constructive change in organizations.

Cole, R. E., & Scott, W. R. (Eds.) (2000). *The quality movement and organizational theory*. Thousand Oaks, CA: Sage. Papers from National Science Foundation workshops that review theories and applications of total quality management from the 1980s onward. Notes the importance of the interaction between management's quality initiatives and employees' learning and decision-making processes.

de Caluwe, L., & Vermaak, H. (2003). *Learning to change: A guide for organization change agents.* Thousand Oaks, CA: Sage. Deals with the complexities of planning for organizational change, employee resistance, politically competing management interests, and the role of in-house leaders and outside consultants in implementing change.

Lane, F. S., III. (2003). *The naked employee: How technology is compromising workplace privacy.* New York: AMACOM. Explores techniques used by employers to monitor employee performance as well as the safeguards employees can take to protect their privacy and other rights.

Pencavel, J. (2001). *Worker participation: Lessons from the worker co-ops of the Pacific Northwest.* New York: Russell Sage. An assessment of worker ownership and management of companies in the forest products (lumber) industry. Suggests that employee involvement contributes to a stable workforce, high job satisfaction, high productivity and efficiency, but also a high rate of accidents.

Schein, E. H. (1999). *The corporate culture survival guide.* San Francisco: Jossey-Bass. A readable, practical guide to the creation and evolution of organizational cultures, showing how to guide the inevitable changes. Emphasizes the importance of appropriate leadership in understanding values and shared assumptions in new, midlife, and mature companies.

Schneider, B., & Smith, D. B. (Eds.) (2004). *Personality and organizations.* Mahwah, NJ: Erlbaum. A comprehensive study of the role of personality in organizational life. Reviews effects of personality variables on group performance, communication, organizational climate and culture, person-organization fit, and other aspects of organizational behavior.

Turner, M. E. (Ed.) (2001). *Groups at work: Theory and research.* Mahwah, NJ: Erlbaum. Summarizes research from social and I-O psychology on the influences of power and politics on group decision-making, problem-solving, and leadership. Also describes the processes of organizational socialization and commitment, and the relationship of group functioning to work performance.

Wallace, P. (2004). *The Internet in the workplace: How new technology is transforming work.* New York: Cambridge University Press. Describes how the Internet has made a 24/7 connection to the workplace a reality for many employees and has also led to new styles of teamwork, communication, leadership challenges, and workplace surveillance.

Part Four

Characteristics of the Workplace

We have discussed some of the effects of the social and psychological climate in which work takes place. The structure of the organization, its style of leadership, and the motivations of employees all influence productivity and job satisfaction. We turn now to more tangible aspects of the workplace—physical features, working hours, safety issues, and concerns about physical and emotional health.

Chapter 10 deals with physical conditions of work, including lighting, noise, temperature, color, and music. Work hours and work schedules are discussed, along with factors such as fatigue, monotony, and sexual harassment. Accidents, violence, alcoholism, and drug abuse are covered in Chapter 11. Psychologists help to determine the causes of workplace accidents and violence, and ways to prevent them. Dependence on alcohol or illicit drugs is both a personal tragedy and a personnel problem. Psychologists design employee assistance programs for troubled workers at all occupational levels. Chapter 12 considers the stresses that result from various physical and psychological conditions of work. Psychologists have developed ways of preventing stress and of treating it on and off the job.

Chapter 10

Working Conditions

CHAPTER OUTLINE

PHYSICAL WORKING CONDITIONS

Look around. Are you in the dorm? The library? An office? What is it like? Comfortable and quiet? Noisy and distracting? Bright and attractive? Cold and drab? These are just some of the physical characteristics of a work environment that can determine how well we are able to do our jobs. Whatever our task—whether we are trying to study, repair an engine, or sell a computer—our surroundings can affect our skill, motivation, and satisfaction.

An organization can recruit and select the best employees, train them thoroughly, provide outstanding leaders and an optimal organizational climate to maximize job performance, but if the physical working conditions are uncomfortable, productivity will suffer. Uncongenial work settings can lead to decreased productivity, lower job satisfaction, more mistakes and accidents, and increased absenteeism and turnover.

When a workplace is made more comfortable or working hours more flexible, productivity usually increases, at least temporarily. But the industrial-organizational (I-O) psychologist must be careful in interpreting such changes in performance. What, precisely, has caused the greater productivity? Was it physical changes such as a new climate-control system, brighter lighting, or better soundproofing? Or was it more subtle psychological factors such as employees' more positive attitude toward management for instituting the changes?

Although the results may be beneficial for the company, whatever the cause, management needs to be able to explain the reasons for any improvement in productivity or satisfaction. Suppose they stem from the fact that employees are pleased that their company is treating them as human beings rather than as cogs in a machine. If so, the company will want to know whether there are other human-relations ways to improve satisfaction and productivity that do not involve expensive alterations to the physical workplace.

In many industries, people work at peak efficiency under what appear to be intolerable conditions. And there are many other instances of poor performance and low morale in well-equipped, lavishly decorated surroundings. The effects of changes in physical working conditions may be influenced or modified by how employees perceive, accept, and adapt to these changes. Therefore, the physical features of the workplace must be considered in light of complex psychological factors.

Work Sites

The physical work environment includes many factors, from the size of the parking lot and location of the building to the amount of natural light and noise in the work area. Inadequate parking spaces or a parking lot too far from the building can so irritate employees that their attitude toward the organization is negative before they even reach their work station.

The location of the work site, whether in the downtown of a large city or a more remote suburban area, can also affect employees' satisfaction with their jobs. For example, suburban office parks are often isolated from the shops, restaurants, and other services found in cities. Surveys show that young, single employees typically prefer living and working in cities, whereas married people tend to prefer the quieter suburbs as better places to work and rear children.

Many organizations offer various amenities to attract and retain dedicated employees. Some companies have turned themselves into vacation resorts with

> ## Newsbreak   Employee Gripes
>
> What do you think is the number one complaint made by people who work in offices? What is it about their workplace that bothers them more than anything else? Take a guess. According to the International Facility Management Association, the number one office complaint relates to temperature—the workplace is too cold. And the number two complaint? The office is too hot!
>
> The rest of the top ten complaints reported by office workers are
>
> - Poor janitorial service.
> - Not enough conference space.
> - Not enough storage or filing space at the work station.
> - Poor indoor air quality.
> - Lack of privacy at the work station.
> - Inadequate parking.
> - Computer problems.
> - Workplace is too noisy.
>
> Do any of these apply to your work or study area?

on-site spas, gyms, nurseries, shops, banks, and medical clinics. Why would organizations spend money on what used to be considered frills? At the luxury-laden Citicorp office complex in Tampa, Florida, an employee said, "You spend so much of your life at work; it's nice that you can have things like a fitness center or child-care facility. For me, it builds loyalty." And loyal employees are less likely to quit, take time off, or be sloppy about their work.

Office and Workplace Design

Once inside our place of employment, we may find other physical features that create dissatisfaction or frustration. One source of complaints is the ventilating, heating, and air-conditioning systems in glass-wall, fixed-window buildings. Temperatures are often uncomfortably hot on the sunny side of the building and too cool on the shady side. Other irritants are slow elevators in high-rise buildings, the quality of the food in the company cafeteria, and inconvenient or poorly maintained restrooms.

Office size and design can be related to employee satisfaction and productivity. The layout of a set of offices will affect the behavior of managers who rely on spontaneous encounters as a way of obtaining and exchanging information. The closer their offices, the more likely they are to meet throughout the workday. Physical separation, such as placing suites of management offices on different floors of a building, decreases the amount of contact.

The size of an office building can influence working relationships. The smaller the building, the closer the relationships among employees tend to be. In very large buildings, where employees have fewer interactions, relationships tend to be more formal and impersonal. All these factors, none of which involves actual job tasks, can impair productive efficiency. An unpopular

Landscaped offices have no floor-to-ceiling dividers. These cubicles may enhance communication and work flow, but they can be noisy and distracting.

location, poor design, or inconvenient layout can reduce morale and foster negative attitudes.

Workplace design and location are especially critical for disabled employees who may be barred from certain jobs not because of lack of ability, but because they do not have access to the work area. Steep flights of stairs, narrow doorways, and inadequate restrooms may prevent them from being employed. The 1973 Rehabilitation Act and the 1990 Americans with Disabilities Act require the removal of architectural barriers. All parts of a building must be accessible to persons in wheelchairs. Compliance with the laws has meant modifications to the physical plant, such as automatic doors, ramps and elevators, handholds, wider doorways and corridors, and lower wall telephones and speakerphones. Surveys show that 60 percent of these required changes cost less than $100 and 90 percent cost less than $1,000. Many disabled employees do not need any physical modifications of an office workspace. IBM, which has hired disabled workers for more than 40 years, took the lead in redesigning work stations to provide job opportunities for these employees.

Environmental Psychology and Landscaped Offices

Environmental psychology The study of the effect of workplace design on behavior and attitudes.

The field of **environmental psychology** is concerned with the relationships between people and their physical environment. Combining architecture and psychology, environmental psychologists are concerned with natural and built environments and their impact on behavior. For example, research on office design and layout has focused on communications between and within departments, flow of job tasks among groups, relationships between managers and subordinates, and work group cohesiveness.

One early result of environmental psychology research was the landscaped office. In contrast to private, separated offices, the landscaped office consists of a huge open space with no floor-to-ceiling walls to divide the area into separate

Newsbreak

Can You Get Any Work Done at Work?

Can you get any work done at work? Maybe not if you work in a cubicle as the comic strip *Dilbert* reminds us daily. Cubicle designers and managers may insist that the open office plan, with its low walls surrounding individual work stations, allows the free flow of ideas, but tell that to the employees who spend many hours each workday in that setting. They'll likely tell you that they find it hard to concentrate on their job because of all the nonwork activities and conversation going on around them. Cubicle dwellers will complain to anyone who will listen about being forced to hear of other workers' family problems, medical problems, financial problems, or the cute thing their dog did yesterday. Some say it's easier to work at home, while the office is more suitable for socializing.

Sue Weidermann, a management consultant in Buffalo, New York, found that in one large law firm the employees who worked in cubicles were interrupted by noise, visual distractions, or co-workers who just wanted to have a conversation an average of 16 times a day. And none of these interruptions was related to work. Interruptions that did relate to the job occurred an average of five times a day. Weidermann observed that following an interruption, it took an employee 2.9 minutes to settle down and return to work, which means that approximately an hour out of every workday was spent trying to refocus on the job tasks.

Kathi Heering used to work for a bank but found that she couldn't concentrate in her cubicle. She pleaded with her boss to construct the cubicle walls a few inches higher, so that co-workers couldn't lean over them so easily to chat, but the boss refused. He claimed that the low walls "fortified communication." Unfortunately, the communication was not about work. Now Kathi does her job from home where she enjoys a luxury that she did not have at the office. It's called a door. Whenever her family or her dogs intrude on her work, she simply closes the door.

Source: Laboring to work at work. *Wall Street Journal,* May 8, 2004.

---

rooms. All employees, from clerks to corporate officers, are grouped into cubicles, functional work units that are set off from others only by planters, screens or partitions, or cabinets and bookcases.

Inexpensive to construct and maintain, landscaped offices are believed to facilitate communication and work flow. The openness is supposed to enhance group cohesiveness and cooperation and reduce psychological barriers between employees and managers. Research on employee reactions has revealed both advantages and disadvantages. Employees report that landscaped offices are pleasant and conducive to socializing. Managers report improved communication. Complaints relate to lack of privacy, noise, and difficulty in concentrating. Because cubicles are typically separated only by low dividers, work areas tend to lack the personal touches—such as photos, plants, posters, or souvenirs—that contribute to feelings of individuality and comfort.

Despite these problems with landscaped offices, many organizations have invested considerable money in them and are reluctant to bear the additional expense of reconverting to more private offices. For companies with large numbers of employees at computerized work stations, the landscaped office has become standard.

As real estate costs escalate, organizations are trying to squeeze more employees into smaller facilities. The size of the typical office cubicle or individual work station is steadily shrinking. Some employees who travel frequently no longer have a permanently assigned work area but only a temporary space. For example, consultants who spend much of their time on-site at a client's workplace will phone ahead to reserve a cubicle for their next visit to the home office. Because the practice is not unlike booking a hotel room, it has come to be known as *hoteling*.

Illumination

In addition to studying general issues of workspace design, I-O psychologists have conducted extensive research on specific environmental factors such as lighting, noise, and temperature. These aspects of the work environment are analogous to the hygiene needs proposed by Herzberg. All of these environmental factors have been found to affect job satisfaction.

Continued exposure to inadequate illumination while reading or performing detailed operations can be harmful to one's eyesight. Research confirms that inadequate lighting is a source of distress. High glare, dim bulbs, and a lack of natural light have negative effects on job performance.

Intensity.   Intensity, or level of brightness, is the most common factor associated with illumination. The optimal level of intensity varies with the nature of the task and the age of the worker. Older workers generally need brighter light than do younger workers for satisfactory performance of the same task. A job involving the precise manipulation of small component parts, as in electronics assembly, requires brighter light than an assembly line in a bottling plant. Lighting engineers have recommended minimum intensity levels for a variety of work areas including office buildings (see Table 10–1).

Distribution of Light.   Another important factor in illumination is the distribution of light over the work area. Ideally, lighting will be distributed uniformly throughout the visual field. Illuminating a work station at a much higher intensity than its surroundings leads to eyestrain because of the natural tendency of the eyes to move. When a person looks from a brightly lit area to a dimly lit area, the pupils of the eyes dilate. Returning the gaze to the brighter area causes the pupils to contract. This constant reaction of the pupils leads to eyestrain. When you are sitting at your desk, you should have overhead lighting as well as a desk lamp focused on your work. This arrangement will give a uniform distribution of light throughout the room. Similarly, it is less fatiguing to the eyes to have additional lighting in the room where you are watching television or staring at your computer screen.

Uniform illumination throughout a work area can be provided by indirect lighting in which all light is reflected. Thus, no light will strike the eyes directly. In

TABLE 10–1

Recommended Lighting Levels for Office Workplaces

Description	Range of Footcandles*
General Offices and Private Offices	56–70
Accounting, Bookkeeping, Drafting	120–150
Conference Rooms	10–70
Corridors, Elevators, Escalators, Stairways	16–20
Lobbies, Reception Areas	10–30
Bathrooms	24–30

*A footcandle of light (a standard candle at a distance of one foot) is approximately the brightness produced by a 100-watt bulb held 10 feet above your head on a dark night.

Source: Commonwealth of Pennsylvania Lighting Recommendations. www.pacode.com/secure/data/034/chapter27/chap27toc.html

contrast, direct lighting, with bulbs located at various points in the ceiling, tends to focus or concentrate the light on specific areas, causing bright spots and glare.

Glare. Glare reduces visual efficiency and contributes to eyestrain. Glare is caused by light of a brighter intensity than that to which the eye is accustomed. This brightness may come from the light source or from reflective surfaces. Glare can lead to an increase in errors in detailed work in as short a time as 20 minutes. It can obscure vision, something you may have experienced when driving at night and confronting an oncoming car that has its high-beam headlights on. Glare is also a problem with the video display terminals for computers.

There are several ways to reduce or eliminate glare. Extremely bright light sources can be shielded or kept out of the visual field. Workers can be supplied with visors or eyeshades. Reflective or glossy surfaces can be painted with a dull, matte finish.

Natural Light. There is a definite psychological component with regard to natural (full-spectrum) light versus artificial light. Research has shown that people who work in windowless offices and receive no natural light express a strong desire for windows, regardless of the adequacy of the artificial illumination in their work area. Most workers like to be able to see outside, and they also believe that natural light is better for the eyes than is artificial light. People may have a physiological need for a certain amount of full-spectrum or natural light. Several European countries have laws requiring employers to ensure that all employees can see natural light from their work areas.

Noise

Noise is a common complaint in modern life. Noise makes us irritable and nervous, interferes with sleep, and produces physiological effects such as hearing loss. Noise is a documented occupational hazard for industrial employees such as

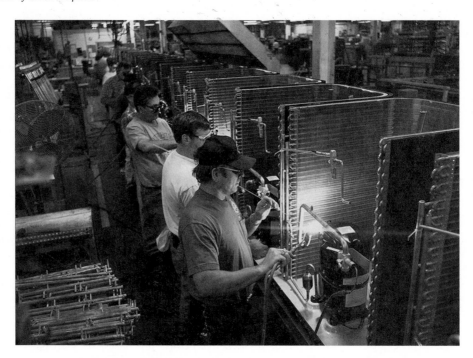

The excessive noise levels in some industrial plants can cause hearing loss.

riveters, boilermakers, aircraft mechanics, and foundry and textile workers. Businesses have been faced with employee claims of hearing damage that total millions of dollars each year.

The National Institute of Occupational Safety and Health (NIOSH) reports that 30 million Americans are routinely exposed to noise levels that eventually will affect their hearing. NIOSH also estimates that at least 20 percent of U.S. employees work in environments that can endanger their hearing. For example, more than 90 percent of coal miners suffer hearing loss by age 50. At least 75 percent of farmers suffer hearing impairment from continued exposure to noisy farm machinery. The president of the National Hearing Conservation Association asserts that "Hearing loss is one of the most common workplace conditions" (Kluger, 2004, p. 56).

The basic unit for measuring noise is the *decibel* (db), which is a measure of the subjective or perceived intensity of a sound. Zero db is the threshold of hearing, the faintest sound most of us can hear. Table 10–2 shows decibel levels in familiar situations. Some loudness levels are threats to hearing. A worker exposed regularly over a long period to decibel levels above 85 can expect to suffer some hearing loss. Exposure to levels over 120 db can cause temporary deafness. Brief exposure to levels in excess of 130 db can cause permanent deafness. The U.S. government has established maximum permissible sound levels for industrial workers: exposure to 90 db for an eight-hour day, 100 db for a two-hour period, and 110 db for a 30-minute period.

When people are exposed to sounds in the 95 to 110 db range, blood vessels constrict, heart rate changes, and the pupils of the eyes dilate. The constriction of the blood vessels continues for some time after the noise ceases, a condition that alters the blood supply throughout the body. Continuous exposure to loud noise is associated with high blood pressure and muscle tension. High noise levels also impair emotional well-being and induce stress. In a study of 40 women clerical workers, three hours' exposure to the noise of a typical open-office arrangement

TABLE 10–2

Decibel Levels for Familiar Sounds

Source of Noise	Decibel Level
Breathing	10
Whisper from 5 feet away	30
Quiet office	40
Conversation 3 feet away	70
City traffic	80
Kitchen appliances	95
Average factory	100
Power lawnmowers	110
Crying babies	110
Noisy restaurant	110
Pneumatic hammers 3 feet away	120
Electronically amplified rock band	140
Jet aircraft at takeoff	150

produced measurable physiological signs of stress. The noise also reduced the employees' motivation to work (Evans & Johnson, 2000). A study of the physiological effects of high noise levels tracked blood pressure changes in workers in Israel over a four-year period. It was found that workers with more complex jobs showed greater increases in blood pressure than those with less complex jobs (Melamed, Fried, & Froom, 2001).

Noise interferes with communication. If the background noise in an office is low (between 50 and 60 db), then two people can conduct a conversation without raising their voices at a distance of up to five feet. As the background noise level rises, workers must talk louder or must leave their work stations and come closer together to be heard. The decibel level of the average factory forces workers and supervisors to shout. It is likely that important information is lost in transmission.

Color

Exaggerated claims have been made about the benefits of color for homes, offices, and factories. It has been suggested that certain colors increase productivity, reduce accidents, and raise employee morale. These claims are not supported by empirical evidence, and there is no validity to any purported relationship between a specific color and productivity, fatigue, or job satisfaction.

However, there is a role for color in the workplace. Color can provide a more pleasant working environment and can be an aid in safety practices. Color is used in many manufacturing plants as a coding device. Fire equipment is red, danger areas yellow, and first-aid stations green. Color-coding allows these areas to be identified quickly. Color can prevent eyestrain because colors differ in their reflective

Newsbreak   Does Beige Make You Sick?

If you start to feel a little drowsy or a little queasy after dinner, maybe it's not what you ate or drank. Maybe it's the color of your dining room. That's the suggestion of one painting contractor, who wrote in the magazine *Paint Dealer* that beige walls create gas and stagnation in the human digestive tract. Should you paint your dining room walls blue? No, that's not a good idea either. Decorators consider blue to be an appetite suppressant. You'll lose weight if you have your meals in a blue room. What about red? Yes! According to the same decorators, red increases your appetite, heart rate, passion, and energy.

And so it goes—various and sometimes competing claims that the right color will change your life, or ruin it. Here's an ad from one manufacturer: "Cool colors, like blue and green, cool and soothe your mind, body, and spirit. It's no wonder we flock to the ocean and mountains to rejuvenate our senses. These blue-based tones are best used in rooms where you want peace and serenity to prevail. Warm colors, like red, orange, and yellow, convey an energy and passion unmatched by their cooler counterparts. Use these high-power hues in rooms where you anticipate activity and motivation, such as a kitchen, child's playroom, or exercise space. You may find your life becomes more than just living. It becomes a sensory experience full of color and feeling!"

Do you believe that? Or do you think they're in the business of selling paint?

---

properties. A white wall reflects more light than a dark one. Thus, the appropriate use of color can make a workroom or office seem brighter or darker. Colors also create different illusions of size. A room painted a darker color seems smaller than it actually is. Light-colored walls give the feeling of space and openness.

On U.S. Navy submarines, the 24 Trident missile tubes, which run through all four decks, are painted reddish orange. The color is darker for tubes at one end of the ship than the other to create the illusion of depth. This makes the cramped quarters appear more spacious than they are. The captain of the USS *Tennessee* told an interviewer, "That's the psychologists looking out for us."

Interior decorators claim that blues and greens are cool colors and that reds and oranges are warm colors. Anecdotal evidence suggests that these colors influence our perception of temperature. In one example, an office was repainted from a drab brown to a bright blue. When winter approached, the employees complained that they were cold even though the indoor office temperature was the same as it had been during previous winters. The temperature was raised five degrees, but the complaints persisted. The office was repainted in warm colors, and the employees said they were too hot. The temperature was lowered five degrees to where it had been before, and complaints ceased.

If a work area is dingy, then repainting it may improve employee morale. A fresh coat of paint in any color can make workers feel better about their environment. But there is little I-O psychologists can conclude with assurance about the effects of color on employee behavior.

Music

The use of music at work is as old as work itself. Workers traditionally sang on the job, even in noisy factories at the time of the Industrial Revolution. During the late 1800s and early 1900s, quieter industries, such as cigar-making, encouraged singing on the job. Some companies hired musicians to play for the workers, and by the 1930s many organizations supported their own bands and singing groups.

Many claims have been made about the effects of music on productivity and morale. Employees are supposed to be happier and more efficient when they listen to music at work. Studies conducted by firms that supply recorded music support these claims, but such research often lacks scientific rigor and control. Early research on music showed that most employees liked the idea of having music during working hours and believed it would make them more productive. This finding depended partly on the kind of work involved. Music has been found to increase production slightly for assembly-line jobs that are reasonably simple and repetitive. Workers regard this type of job as monotonous and not sufficiently demanding to fully engage their attention. Thus, music can provide a focus for these workers, something to occupy the mind and to help the workday pass more quickly and enjoyably. For more demanding work, there is no evidence that music increases productivity because the complexity of the work requires more concentrated attention.

Most of the music piped into factories, offices, corridors, elevators, and waiting rooms is supplied by Muzak, which has been in business since 1934. The company estimates that its background music is played to 100 million people in more than 250,000 companies in a dozen countries. It has more than a million tunes in its database and provides customized pop-rock programs to companies such as Gap, Old Navy, and Harry Winston. Another music provider, PlayNetwork, supplies the music you hear in Starbucks and TGI Friday's. Muzak-style sound is intended to humanize the work environment by giving people an emotional lift. A different program is created for each type of business and each workday. The tempo corresponds to changes in mood and energy levels and is designed to be more stimulating at mid-morning and mid-afternoon. Critics consider such music to be bland or even a form of noise pollution.

Temperature and Humidity

We have all experienced the effects of temperature and humidity on our morale, efficiency, and physical well-being. Some of us are happier and have more vitality in cold weather, whereas others prefer hot weather. Some people are depressed by rainy days, and others barely notice them. Most of us work in facilities where temperature and humidity are controlled. But workers in construction, shipbuilding, and other industries are frequently exposed to temperature extremes.

We noted in a *Newsbreak* that the primary complaint of office workers was that the workplace was too cold; second, that it was too hot. But if employees tried to raise or lower the temperature of their office area, they would probably find out that the thermostats are fakes. They don't really work but are there only to provide the illusion of control. Employees may believe that by changing the thermostat they have initiated some action to correct the sensation of being too hot or too cold, and often that action satisfies them, even though the actual temperature remains the same. Research shows that for people who work outdoors or in facilities that are not air-conditioned (such as warehouses or automobile repair shops), unusually high temperatures seem to have no significant effect on mental work but do lead to lower performance on strenuous physical tasks. Even if productivity did hold steady, workers must expend more energy under difficult climate conditions in order to maintain the same output. Usually, they will need more frequent rest breaks. Motivation is also a factor. Highly motivated workers are better able to maintain production under temperature extremes than are poorly motivated workers.

Automated office equipment has been found to interfere with climate-control systems. A single computer terminal does not generate much heat, but when dozens of terminals, printers, and fax machines are operated in the same area, heat and static electricity levels increase. The drier air also leads to complaints about eye irritation from employees who wear contact lenses.

WORK SCHEDULES

A vital part of the overall work environment is the amount of time we spend on the job. There is no standard universal work schedule. The 40-hour workweek common in the United States is not the norm in every country. Americans spend more hours on the job than do workers in other industrialized nations. Employees in the United States work almost two weeks longer each year than employees in Japan, and 14 weeks longer each year than workers in Norway. Not only do Americans work more hours, they also take fewer annual vacation days. A survey of 1,000 employees conducted by Expedia found that 12 percent of them did not plan to take any vacation days. On average, U.S. workers receive 16 vacation days per year but take only 14 of them. Contrast that with the vacation policies of other nations: Italy, 42 days; France, 37 days; Germany, 35 days; England, 28 days; and Japan, 25 days.

In general, managers work longer hours than employees at other levels but seem to be well rewarded for their efforts. A survey of 47 men managers showed that they averaged a 56.4-hour workweek, and 28.6 percent of them worked more than 61 hours per week. Those who put in the greatest number of hours were paid significantly more than those who worked less, receiving, on average, a $204,993 annual salary compared with $162,285. Those who worked longer hours also reported significantly higher job satisfaction and job involvement. The negative side was a feeling of alienation from one's family and a high level of work-family conflict (Brett & Stroh, 2003).

Although Americans continue to work long hours, they do so in ways that are different from previous generations of workers. The traditional five-day, 40-hour week in which all employees of an organization arrived and left at the same time is being replaced by alternative work schedules. We will discuss the standard workweek, shift work, and alternative schedules such as permanent part-time employment, the four-day workweek, and flexible hours (flextime).

Working Hours

At one time in the United States, people routinely worked 10 hours a day, six days a week. The five-day, 40-hour week became the norm in 1938 with the passage of the Fair Labor Standards Act. The United States became the first country to formally establish a five-day, 40-hour workweek, but this is not necessarily the most efficient work schedule. Workers have accepted it as normal, but in the past they accepted 60 hours and then 48 hours as normal.

Some jobs require workers to punch a time clock at the beginning and end of each work shift.

There is a difference between **nominal working hours** (the prescribed number of hours employees are supposed to spend on the job) and actual working hours (the amount of time employees devote to job duties). The two rarely coincide. Some research shows that employees spend no more than half the workweek actually performing required job tasks. Some of the lost time is scheduled by the company as rest pauses, but most of it is unauthorized and beyond the control of the organization. When employees arrive at the workplace, it may take them a long time to begin work. They may shuffle papers, sharpen pencils, read the news headlines online, or oil machines (whether needed or not). Throughout the workday employees may visit with co-workers, surf the Web, exceed the length of the lunch break, or linger at the coffee machine. Managers lose time waiting for meetings to begin or for telephone calls to be completed, or they may spend time using their e-mail for personal messages.

An interesting relationship has been documented between nominal and actual working hours. When nominal (prescribed) working hours are increased, actual working hours decrease. In other words, the longer the workday or workweek, the lower the worker productivity. This finding holds even for highly motivated workers. In the early days of World War II in England, patriotic fervor reached a peak. Dangerously low in supplies and equipment, the nation was fighting for survival. The government extended the workweek in defense plants from 56 to 69½ hours. At first, productivity increased 10 percent, but it soon fell 12 percent below the previous level. Other consequences of increasing nominal working hours included greater absenteeism and more frequent accidents. In the 69½-hour workweek, actual working hours were only 51. With the shorter 56-hour workweek, actual working hours had been 53. A study conducted by the U.S. Bureau of Labor Statistics during World War II showed that the seven-day workweek that was adopted by many American companies during the war resulted in no greater production than the six-day week. One day of the seven days was lost time.

Nominal working hours
The prescribed number of hours employees are supposed to spend on the job; not all of these hours are actually spent performing job tasks.

This relationship between nominal and actual working hours also applies to overtime when employees are asked to work beyond the normal workday for a markedly higher rate of pay. Much of the extra time is unproductive because people tend to adjust to the longer workday by performing at a slower pace. If productivity drops when the number of required working hours is increased, will productivity rise if the workday is shortened? Some research indicates that it will, but other studies show that a decrease in nominal working hours has no effect on actual working hours. In a case of historical interest, during the Great Depression of the 1930s a manufacturing plant reduced nominal working hours by more than nine hours a week, yet actual working hours fell only five hours a week. Another plant reduced the workweek by 10½ hours, and hourly production rose 21 percent!

Permanent Part-Time Employment

Part-time or half-time employment is the most widespread form of alternative work schedule. More than 25 percent of the U.S. workforce holds part-time jobs. Part-time employment has grown faster than full-time employment, particularly in service and retail trades. By shifting to part-time employment, organizations reduce the costs of keeping full-time staffs (which require higher salary and benefit packages) and increase their scheduling flexibility.

We noted that full-time employment does not mean that the organization is actually getting a full day's work from each employee. Further, management has recognized that much work, such as writing and independent research, can be performed satisfactorily part time. A lower-level assembly line or clerical job can be performed by two persons, each working half time.

The U.S. Department of Health and Human Services found that supervisors of part-time employees were strongly in favor of part-time employment. A study of welfare caseworkers in Massachusetts who worked 20 hours a week showed that they had a lower turnover rate and a higher caseload contact than did full-time employees. State government agencies in Wisconsin found that actual working hours among permanent part-time social workers, attorneys, and research analysts equaled or exceeded the actual working hours of full-time employees.

Part-time employment is attractive to people with pressing family responsibilities and to disabled persons who have mobility problems. Most part-time employees are women, and they tend to be concentrated in lower-level jobs and receive lower rates of pay than do full-time employees. However, increasing numbers of professionals and managers are opting for part-time employment because it gives them the chance to return to school or to explore other career opportunities.

A large-scale study including 794 employees of a grocery store chain, 200 hospital workers, and 243 retail employees found that those who had chosen part-time employment were far more satisfied with their jobs, performed their work better, and were more committed to their organization than were those who were assigned to part-time work against their will (Holton, Lee, & Tidd, 2002).

The Four-Day Workweek

Another way to alter the workweek significantly is to reduce it to four days. This usually involves four days at ten hours a day (a 40-hour week) or four days at nine hours a day (a 36-hour week with no reduction in pay). Union leaders, management consultants, and many companies that have tried the four-day workweek are enthusiastic about it. Typically, the initiative to shorten the workweek came not from employees but from management for several reasons. These include the possibility of increasing worker productivity and efficiency, the idea of using the shorter workweek as an incentive to recruit workers, and the hope of reducing absenteeism, which in many organizations is unusually high on Mondays and Fridays.

Comments from managers and employees on the four-day workweek have been positive. They cite improved job satisfaction and productivity, reduced absenteeism, and easier work scheduling. A nationwide Gallup Poll supported the appeal of the four-day week. Some 45 percent of the men surveyed indicated that they would like a four-day schedule. Women who did not work outside the home opposed the four-day workweek by a ratio of two to one. Women who did work outside the home were far more favorable to the idea of a four-day workweek.

Flexible Work Schedules

Another type of alternative work schedule permits employees to decide for themselves when to begin and end the workday. In the 1960s several companies in Germany tried a flexible working hours **(flextime)** schedule to deal with traffic congestion at rush hours. Under this plan, the workday is divided into four segments, two of which are mandatory and two optional (see Figure 10–1).

In this example, employees can report to work any time between 7:30 a.m. and 9:00 a.m. and leave any time between 4:00 p.m. and 5:30 p.m. The mandatory work periods are the morning hours from 9:00 a.m. until the lunch break and the afternoon hours from lunch to 4:00 p.m. Thus, employees work a minimum 6½-hour workday. The optional daily maximum is 9½ hours. How long each employee will work is established individually as a function of the company's needs.

Flextime offers several advantages. Rush-hour traffic congestion around plants and offices is reduced. Because employees spend less time and energy commuting, they are often more relaxed at work, more satisfied with their jobs, and more likely to begin work promptly. Many workers make only minor changes in their work habits under a flextime schedule. The inflexible demands of car pools, commuter timetables, and family life hold them to schedules much like those they had before flextime. However, employees believe that having the choice of when to arrive and leave work enhances their personal freedom. Studies have found that flextime schedules decreased absenteeism and improved workers' productivity and their satisfaction with the job and the work schedule.

Flexible working hours appear to be most appropriate for jobs such as research and development, clerical and data entry, and light and heavy manufacturing.

Flextime A system of flexible working hours combining core mandatory work periods with elective work periods at the beginning and end of the workday.

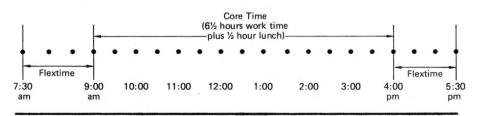

FIGURE 10–1. A typical flexible work schedule.

For some assembly-line and shift-work operations, flextime is difficult to implement because of the interdependence of the work teams. Overall, flextime is a fair, sensible, and low-cost alternative work schedule that is popular with employers and employees.

Surveys conducted by the Families and Work Institute have consistently shown that employees with flexible work option plans were significantly less likely to leave their companies and were more productive than employees who had no flexible options. The surveys also reported that 72 percent of low-wage workers without flexible working hours call in sick when they need time off to deal with child-care or family crises. Under a flexible working hours plan, they might not have to use illness as an excuse to tend to personal needs (see www.familiesandwork.org).

Rest Breaks

Ever since the Hawthorne studies, management has recognized the importance of authorized rest breaks. Their beneficial effects have been amply demonstrated, but there is a more insistent reason for granting them. Why? Because employees will take breaks whether or not the company sanctions them. If the time is going to be taken anyway, the organization might as well appear benevolent and offer the rest pauses as a fringe benefit.

When authorized rest pauses are introduced, unauthorized breaks decline, though they do not disappear. Other benefits of rest periods include increased morale and productivity and reduced fatigue and boredom. This is another instance of how a decrease in nominal working hours can result in an increase in efficiency.

Workers who engage in heavy physical labor need rest pauses because muscles in continuous use will tire and become less effective. Rest pauses also reduce repetitive motion injuries to hands and wrists. For sedentary and intellectual work, a rest break provides a change of stimulation. It allows boredom to dissipate and

Many jobs are repetitive and physically demanding. These workers should be given formal rest periods to reduce boredom and fatigue.

provides the opportunity to think about something else or to socialize with co-workers. Rest pauses may also result in more positive attitudes toward management. When a rest program is implemented, workers tend to believe that it is an expression of management's concern for them as individuals.

Research on data entry clerks and computer operators showed that those who reported higher levels of fatigue and boredom on the job tended to take longer rest breaks than did those who felt less fatigued and bored. Also, psychologists have found that computer workers who do stretching exercises during rest breaks, particularly for arms and shoulders, perform better after the breaks than do workers who engage in no physical movement during their breaks (Jett & George, 2003).

A study of keyboard entry workers in Canada found that microbreaks lasting only 30 seconds, when taken regularly every 20 minutes, reduced physical discomfort in back, shoulder, and forearm muscles to a greater extent than taking microbreaks whenever the workers felt like it or having no breaks at all. With regularly scheduled rest breaks, there was no decline in productivity levels (McLean, Tingley, Scott, & Rickards, 2001).

A much longer rest break—the off hours between the workdays—was the subject of another research study. A survey of 147 workers in Germany showed that those who believed they had sufficiently recovered from the previous day's work were more involved in their work the next day. Those who felt greater stress on the job needed more time to recover from the workday than did those who experienced less stress (Sonnentag, 2003).

Shift Work

Many industries operate around the clock. Workers in electric and natural gas utilities, transportation, steel, automotive assembly, hospital services, and telecommunications typically work one of three shifts, usually 7:00 a.m. to 3:00 p.m., 3:00 p.m. to 11:00 p.m., or 11:00 p.m. to 7:00 a.m. Some companies assign workers to one shift permanently, whereas others rotate assignments, switching workers each week or month to a different shift. Employees working evening or all-night shifts usually receive extra pay to compensate for the inconvenience of the working hours. Some 25 percent of the blue-collar and white-collar workforces perform shift work.

How does shift work affect job performance? Research shows that workers are less productive on the all-night shift than on the day shift. They are also more prone to make errors and to have more serious accidents. Nuclear power plant accidents in the United States and in Russia occurred during the night shift. A nuclear power plant in Pennsylvania was closed by the Nuclear Regulatory Commission when night-shift control room personnel were found to be asleep on the job.

A study of 1,867 oil industry employees in Britain found that shift workers reported greater levels of stress, increased exposure to adverse and risky working conditions, lower feelings of job control, less social support from supervisors, and higher levels of conflict at work than those who worked regular hours during the standard workday (Parkes, 2003).

The disruption of the normal sleep-wake cycle has physiological and psychological consequences. Humans develop a diurnal rhythm, a regular daily cycle of bodily activities that is consistent from one 24-hour period to the next. When this rhythm is disrupted, the body undergoes dramatic changes and sleep becomes

Newsbreak

Asleep on the Job? Good for You!

There was a time when you could be fired for falling asleep on the job. But now a growing number of companies are urging their employees to do just that. They're even providing nap lounges and encouraging workers to "power nap" when they feel sleepy. What's going on here? Why are companies encouraging employees to go to sleep during working hours? The answer is that they will be more alert and efficient when they wake up.

Sleep researchers have demonstrated that no matter how soundly we sleep at night, most of us become drowsy in the early afternoon, whether we've eaten heavily at lunchtime or not. A sleepy worker is not efficient or productive and is likely to make mistakes or cause accidents.

Worse, many of us don't get enough sleep at night, so we begin the workday feeling sluggish. A study by the National Sleep Foundation reported that 64 percent of U.S. workers fail to sleep the recommended eight hours a night. Some 32 percent of the people report sleeping fewer than six hours per night. As you might expect, this widespread lack of sleep affects how well we perform our jobs.

The same study found that 61 percent of the population said that a bad night's sleep impairs their decision-making ability, and 37 percent felt that it prevented them from doing their best work. The obvious antidote is to make up the sleep at work, to take brief power naps during the day to restore alertness and efficiency.

The work of the National Sleep Foundation is changing many corporate cultures. It has a slogan: *Be productive. Take a nap!* Why not do your part today!

Sources: New respect for the nap, a pause that refreshes. *New York Times,* January 4, 2000; Naps, all in a day's work. *St. Petersburg (FL) Times,* March 25, 1999.

difficult. The effect on sleep is the major complaint of employees on night-shift work; that is, they are unable to sleep during the day because of daylight and household routines. Family life suffers, and everyday activities such as shopping become difficult to schedule. Night-shift workers and those on a rotating-shift schedule report a high incidence of stomach disorders, sleep disorders, cardiovascular complaints, marital problems, and irritability.

Fewer problems are encountered with the fixed-shift system than with the rotating-shift system, even when the fixed shift occurs at night. Workers permanently assigned to one shift are more likely to adjust to a new diurnal rhythm. With the rotating-shift system, workers must readjust every week or so, whenever the shift schedule is changed, and this system does not give the body time to adjust to one schedule before being forced to begin another.

There are other ways to alleviate some of the problems associated with shift work. When the rotating-shift system must be used, the changes from one shift to another should be made as seldom as possible—for example, every month instead of every week. Another way to ease the change from one shift to another is to lengthen the time off between shift changes. A longer interim period makes the change less abrupt and allows employees to rest before starting a new schedule. Because the night shift is the most difficult for employees and the least productive for employers, it could be shortened to make it less stressful.

A potentially harmful form of shift work that affects many of us is the erratic work schedule of commercial airline pilots, who often change from night flights to day flights and back, sleeping at irregular intervals and disrupting their bodily rhythms. Studies of civilian and military pilots and flight crews working unusually long and erratic hours (such as ten to 24 hours continuously) confirm the harmful effects of severe disturbances of diurnal rhythms. The airline personnel reported considerable fatigue, slept poorly following their work periods, and took unauthorized naps in the cockpit for up to two hours. Examinations of aircraft flight recorders (so-called black boxes) revealed that deviations in pilot performance correlated positively with subjective feelings of fatigue.

Research conducted by psychologists for NASA's Fatigue Countermeasures Program found that allowing pilots 40-minute rest periods during low workload portions of long flights resulted in significantly increased alertness. Flight crews that were not supposed to nap during the study period did so anyway, although most of the personnel who took unauthorized naps were not aware of having done so.

For information, in English and Spanish, on sleep and alertness problems (including jet lag, insomnia, shift work, and the effects of caffeine) see the Web site for the National Sleep Foundation at www.sleepfoundation.org. You can also participate in a Sleep in America public opinion poll.

PSYCHOLOGICAL AND SOCIAL ISSUES

Other important factors in the work environment relate to the nature of the job and its impact on employees. Does your job provide you with a sense of satisfaction and achievement, or does it make you tired, bored, and ill? We have noted that the design of your job can affect your motivation and satisfaction. Some quality-of-work-life programs have been successful in improving morale and motivation, but jobs designed to be so simple that they make no demands on our intelligence, need for achievement, or attention will lead to boredom, fatigue, and inefficiency.

Job Simplification

Simplified, fragmented, and repetitive work affects mental and physical health. For example, assembly-line workers complain more about their physical health and visit company medical facilities more often than workers who do less repetitive work. Psychologists suggest that people who hold such jobs on a rigid work schedule are more anxious, depressed, and irritable than workers doing the same kinds of jobs on a more flexible schedule. Simplified and repetitive work can lead to the deterioration in cognitive functioning usually associated with old age. These workers are prone to absentmindedness and disorientation.

The history of **job simplification** dates from the beginnings of mass production systems in the early 20th century. If relatively expensive consumer

Job simplification
The reduction of manufacturing jobs to the simplest components that can be mastered by unskilled or semiskilled workers.

goods such as automobiles were to be produced cost-effectively in sufficient quantities to meet consumer demand, then old-style production methods, such as building each unit by hand, would have to change. Mass production called for product consistency and standardization so that parts would be interchangeable. It also required fractionation of job tasks. It was no longer economically or technically feasible for one person to make an entire product. The work had to be meticulously divided so that each worker produced only a small part of the finished product. The ideal was to reduce every manufacturing process to the simplest elements that could be mastered by an unskilled or semiskilled employee.

Job simplification offered tremendous economic advantages to industry and to consumers, permitting the lowest possible cost per unit produced. When Henry Ford established his automobile assembly line, he was able to sell cars at a price within reach of people who previously could not afford them. The same was true for other consumer goods. The factory-produced chair in which you are sitting costs considerably less than a chair handmade by a skilled furniture craftsperson. This was an additional advantage of job simplification: Industry no longer had to rely on the skilled trades, the workers who required years of apprenticeship, expected high wages, and were apt to be independent of mind. The typical assembly line could be staffed by workers who had little skill and could be quickly trained to perform the job. The process made workers more docile and easier to manage. Because they had few marketable skills, they knew they could easily be replaced. Workers were as interchangeable as the parts they produced.

There is no denying that job simplification had a stimulating impact on the American economy. More jobs became available, and people had more money to buy the plentiful consumer goods. The more people bought, the more factories had to be built, which, in turn, meant even more jobs. New products required additional businesses to advertise, sell, and service them. Such economic growth could not have occurred if production methods had remained limited to the handcrafted approach.

Assembly-line workers have paid a price for their role in this industrial development. The farther removed workers are from the finished product, the less meaning and value they attach to their jobs. The carpenter who shaped a table from a piece of lumber knew the pride and fulfillment of achievement and the challenge of using skill and imagination. There is little challenge and satisfaction in operating a machine that attaches bumpers to automobiles day after day, year after year. The worker is an adjunct to the machine, pressing a button or pushing a lever or watching in case something goes wrong. The work has little meaning and quickly becomes frustrating and monotonous. Workers soon grow apathetic, morale declines, and the quantity and quality of production deteriorate.

Job simplification also affects white-collar and managerial jobs because computers have turned many offices into electronic assembly lines. In white-collar jobs, work is increasingly fragmented and simplified. As a result, office workers are becoming cheaper to train and easier to replace.

We noted in Chapter 9 how jobs can be enlarged, enriched, and expanded to provide employees with greater responsibility and challenge. The quality-of-work-life programs we discussed are real-world examples of making jobs more complex rather than simpler. Expanding the job has clear benefits for both employees and employers.

Boredom and Monotony

Two inevitable consequences of job fractionation and simplification—boredom and monotony—are important components of the psychological work environment. Boredom results from the continuous performance of a repetitive and uninteresting activity and can lead to restlessness, discontent, and a draining of interest and energy. However, what is boring for one person may be exciting for another. Although most people find assembly-line work to be monotonous, for example, others do not. And some workers in jobs that appear to be challenging also report feelings of boredom. The relevant factor is motivation. The data entry clerk who is highly motivated to process entries without making errors will be less bored than the worker who lacks this motivation.

One obvious way to alleviate boredom is to enlarge the scope of the job, to make it more complex, stimulating, and challenging. Management can also alter work schedules and the physical and social conditions of the workplace to reduce boredom. Attention to noise reduction, lighting, and pleasant surroundings can help combat the negative effects of repetitive and monotonous work. A congenial informal work group helps, as do rest pauses to provide a change of activity. The greater the change in activity during rest pauses or lunch breaks, the less disruptive will be the effects of boredom.

Fatigue

Psychologists describe two types of fatigue: psychological fatigue, which is similar to boredom, and physiological fatigue, which is caused by excessive use of the muscles. Both types of fatigue can cause poor job performance and lead to errors, accidents, and absenteeism. Prolonged or heavy physical labor produces measurable physiological changes. People whose jobs require heavy lifting and hauling consistently show cardiovascular, metabolic, and muscle fatigue as well as a decline in the ability to maintain their initial productivity level.

Psychological or subjective fatigue is more difficult to assess but is no less disturbing to employees. We are all aware of experiencing strain, irritability, and weakness when we are excessively tired, and we may find it difficult to concentrate, think coherently, and work effectively.

On-the-job research has shown that productivity parallels reported feelings of fatigue. High reported fatigue is a reliable indicator that production will shortly decline. With most physically demanding work, employees say that they are most tired at the beginning of the work period, just before the lunch break, and again at the end of the workday. Thus, fatigue does not build up over the course of the work period but appears and disappears throughout the working hours. This suggests that factors other than physical labor (motivation, for example) can influence feelings of fatigue. It often happens that a person leaves the job at the end of the shift feeling exhausted but finds that the fatigue disappears on arriving home and anticipating some pleasurable activity.

Research conducted in the Netherlands on 322 university employees and 555 nurses showed that as the demands of a job increase, greater feelings of job control will reduce fatigue. Also, as the demands of a job increase, reported feelings of fatigue can lead to a decrease in job satisfaction (Van Yperen & Hagedoorn, 2003; Van Yperen & Janssen, 2002).

An employee experiencing psychological fatigue finds it difficult to concentrate, think coherently, and work effectively.

Research on physiological fatigue shows that workers can undertake greater amounts of physical labor when the work pace is more gradual. Too rapid a rate of heavy work dissipates the body's energy too quickly so that the worker must then function at a slower pace for the remainder of the work period. An analogy can be made with long-distance runners who pace themselves so that they do not consume all their energy before covering the desired distance.

Rest periods are necessary for jobs that involve heavy physical labor and should be taken before fatigue is complete. The greater the amount of fatigue at the time of the rest break, the longer the recovery period must be. For some jobs, more frequent rest breaks are needed. Rest periods must provide total relaxation, not merely a stoppage of work. It is the manual laborer, more than the office worker, who will benefit from pleasant cafeterias and comfortable lounges in which to relax.

Ethnic Harassment

Another social-psychological condition of the workplace that affects productivity, job satisfaction, and emotional and physical health is on-the-job harassment, whether based on race, ethnicity, gender, or other personal characteristics. Harassment may come from co-workers or supervisors, or it may be part of the corporate culture.

The population of a typical workplace, like the population of many a nation, has become increasingly diverse. As organizations employ more people of various racial and ethnic groups, harassment is on the rise. Ethnic harassment is an obvious source of stress. It may be manifested at work as slurs or derogatory comments about a person's racial or ethnic group and may result in the exclusion of the person from work groups or social activities.

A study of 575 Hispanic men and women provided evidence of harassment on the job. Verbal slurs, derogatory comments, and offensive ethnic jokes were found to be more common than behaviors intended to exclude a person on ethnic grounds. People who were targets of verbal harassment reported a lowering of their sense of psychological well-being (Schneider, Hitlan, & Radhakrishnan, 2000).

Gender Harassment

Women employees at all levels in an organization face harassment on the job ranging from suggestive remarks and obscene jokes to threats of job loss and physical assaults. A distinction can be made between sexual harassment and gender harassment. *Sexual harassment* involves unwanted sexual attention and coercion. *Gender harassment* refers to behavior that reflects an insulting, hostile, and degrading attitude toward women. Thus, gender harassment does not necessarily involve sexual harassment. Gender harassment is directed toward all women, whereas sexual harassment is targeted toward a specific woman. To report incidents of sexual harassment and to receive advice on dealing with it, call the toll-free Job Survival Hotline at Nine to Five, a working women's advocacy group (1-800-522-0925). Their Web site, www.9to5.org, focuses on issues of economic fairness, harassment, and work-family policies.

Gender and sexual harassment have been found in many workplaces and have resulted in costly and embarrassing lawsuits for a number of prominent organizations. Chevron paid $2.2 million to four women employees who were further harassed following their initial filing of sexual harassment charges.

Mitsubishi was ordered to pay $34 million to several hundred women employees who charged that the company's Illinois plant failed to respond to their sexual harassment complaints.

A review of harassment claims filed with the Equal Employment Opportunity Commission (EEOC) showed that several types of companies were likely to be the target of lawsuits because they ignored reports of harassment. These include family-owned businesses, firms too small to maintain human resources or personnel departments, factories located in rural areas, and so-called male-dominated industries such as construction. Younger women in low-level jobs, single or divorced women, and women in predominantly male environments report more harassment than do middle-aged or older married women whose jobs are not in male-dominated organizations.

The reported incidence of sexual harassment can be affected by the wording of the survey questions. A meta-analysis of 55 samples (consisting of 86,578 respondents) found two distinct approaches to measuring the incidence of sexual harassment. The *direct query survey* allows the respondent to define what behaviors constitute sexual harassment and to describe freely what happened to them. The *behavioral experiences survey* provides the respondent with a list of incidents defined by the researcher as constituting sexual harassment; respondents then select the experiences or behaviors that correspond to their personal situation.

These approaches reveal striking differences in the reported incidence of harassment. Surveys of women respondents using the direct query approach show a reported incidence of harassment of approximately 35 percent, whereas with the behavioral experiences approach, the reported incidence of harassment is approximately 62 percent (Ilies, Hauserman, Schwochau, & Stibal, 2003). This provides another example of the importance of knowing how a survey was conducted and how the questions were phrased before evaluating and applying the results.

The same meta-analysis compared the incidence of sexual harassment in four work environments: academic, the private sector, government, and the military. The reported incidence of sexual harassment was highest in the military setting; the results were the same for both types of survey questions. More women in the military reported being harassed than in any other work environment. The lowest reported incidence was in academia.

Survey data from 22,372 women in all branches of the military services in the United States revealed that 4 percent of them reported actual or attempted rape by other military personnel. Those most likely to report such physical assaults were lower in rank, hence in status and power (Harned, Ormerod, Palmieri, Collinsworth, & Reed, 2002).

A meta-analysis of gender differences in defining harassment involved 62 research studies. Women perceived a wider range of behaviors as potentially harassing than did men. For example, 89 percent of women perceived sexual touching as harassment; only 59 percent of men shared that view. Men were significantly more likely to believe that physical sexual contact initiated by a woman was a compliment; women were more likely to believe that physical sexual contact initiated by a man was a threat and an instance of harassment (Rotundo, Nguyen, & Sackett, 2001). Thus, there is disagreement about the behaviors that are considered harassing. Another point to keep in mind is that not all incidents of harassment on the job are reported, as we shall see later.

A study of 315 male and 262 female police officers in New Zealand found that gender harassment was a significantly greater source of psychological distress for women than for men. The researchers suggested that harassment is more harmful for women who work in traditionally male occupations such as police departments because in those situations such behaviors can make women feel that "they need to over-perform to be accepted and recognized within the organization. High performance demands are in turn associated with psychological distress" (Parker & Griffin, 2002, p. 13).

Like ethnic harassment, gender harassment can lead to physical ailments (gastrointestinal disorders, headaches, and weight loss) as well as psychological problems (fear, depression, anxiety, and loss of self-esteem). It also has a negative effect on job satisfaction and productivity. Many studies link harassment to low job satisfaction and high stress. A survey of office workers found that 70 percent reported harassment on the job, but it showed no differences in the frequency or consequences of that harassment for White women and non-White women (Munson, Hulin, & Drasgow, 2000).

Research shows that most incidents of sexual harassment on the job are not reported out of fear of retaliation, a fear that may be justified. A study of 6,417 men and women in the U.S. armed forces showed that those who reported sexual harassment to their superiors faced retaliatory measures that led to greater psychological distress and lower job satisfaction. The higher the rank of the perpetrator of the offense, the less likely that the organization took punitive measures or corrective action against the harasser (Bergman, Langhout, Palmieri, Cortina, & Fitzgerald, 2002).

Gender and sexual harassment remain serious problems in the workplace, despite the ongoing publicity given to these issues. Lawsuits have resulted in costly payouts for companies. Training programs designed to make employees more aware of and sensitive to the feelings of others have also had limited effects. A strong organizational culture in which the consequences of sexual harassment on the job are swift and severe can reduce but not eliminate the problem. A committed organizational leadership is also important. A study of 2,749 men and women in the military showed that women who viewed their leaders as making honest and sincere efforts to stop harassment were significantly more willing to report harassment than those whose leaders were more tolerant of harassment. In addition, women who viewed their leaders as sincere about the issue were more satisfied with the procedure for filing complaints about harassment and felt more committed to the organization (Offermann & Malamut, 2002).

A study of 2,038 men and women university employees found that those who experienced sexual harassment at work were more likely to seek mental health services than were those who had not been sexually harassed. This finding held for both men and women. Men were more likely than women to turn to alcohol as solace following sexual harassment incidents on the job (Rospenda, 2002).

For current news about sexual harassment and links to related sites, see the Web site for the National Organization for Women (NOW) at www.now.org/issues/harass. It describes current cases as well as actions being taken to combat on-the-job harassment. For the federal government's policy on sexual harassment and links to the proper way to file a charge of employment discrimination, see www.eeoc.gov/facts/fs-sex.html.

Telecommuting: The Virtual Workplace at Home

We have noted the growing flexibility in work scheduling in recent years. Now a similar flexibility has come to characterize the workplace itself. Many employees work at home, thanks to advances in personal computers, telecommunications, and fax machines. This move toward telecommuting—the decentralizing of work—has affected hundreds of U.S. companies in life insurance, data processing, financial services, airline and hotel reservations, and mail-order merchandising. The U.S. Office of Personnel Management estimates that 23.6 million workers in the United States telecommute at least part time. Men in their early 40s make up 65 percent of this workforce. Telecommuting is particularly attractive to employees with day-care or dependent-care problems and to disabled workers.

Companies that provide for telecommuting cite gains in productivity; reduced costs for office overhead; and, obviously, a decline in absenteeism. People working at home may have fewer interruptions than people working in offices and may be able to concentrate better. They can perform their job in bad weather or when feeling poor, whereas office-based employees in those situations might hesitate to come to work. Research at IBM comparing virtual-office telecommuters with in-house office employees found that telecommuting was associated with high productivity. Women employees in virtual offices were more productive than men employees in virtual offices, but both groups were pleased that they didn't have to spend time commuting. They enjoyed being able to schedule their work outside traditional office hours, and they reported fewer distractions and a more comfortable working environment. A study of 26 highly educated white-collar workers in Sweden found that the blood pressure levels of both men and women were significantly higher when they worked at the office than when they worked at home. This finding suggested to the researchers that working at home was less stressful for these workers (Lundberg & Lindfors, 2002).

Los Angeles County administrators estimated that their telecommuting program involving 2,600 workers saved $11 million a year in increased productivity, reduced absenteeism, decreased overtime pay, and reduced office space. They also claimed that the program cut commuting time by 1.4 million hours, thus eliminating 7,500 tons of carbon monoxide from car exhausts. An AT&T poll of 1,005 home-based workers found that 80 percent believed they were more productive than when working in the company offices. In addition, 61 percent said they got sick less often, and 79 percent appreciated the chance to wear casual clothes while working. Surveys at other companies found increases up to 30 percent in productivity as well as a significant reduction in the nonproductive work time spent socializing. Telecommuting does not appear to be related to any decrease in an employee's opportunity for promotion.

A large-scale study involving 549 employees of an entertainment and broadcasting company found that working in a "virtual" office at home led to higher motivation and greater acceptance of telecommuting than working in a standard desktop office at home. In the latter arrangement, all communication with the company office was conducted electronically. The virtual-reality office re-created at home provided the physical look and the feel of the employees' company workspace and even included the presence of co-workers. Researchers described it as follows: The virtual-reality office included "the office corridors, individual offices, and work areas of the participants. Thus, 'going to work' acquired the meaning of traversing the virtual hallways to reach one's office; 'attending meetings' meant transporting to another virtual office or conference room. The perception created via these rooms is very consistent with the feel created by many popular PC games and Nintendo/PlayStation games that present a 3-D representation of space with the player traveling through the virtual world of the game" (Venkatesh & Johnson, 2002, p. 674).

A growing number of employees work from a home office, an option that is particularly attractive to people with day-care concerns.

Working in the virtual office in the study cited above was very close to actually being in the company office. The researchers concluded that the virtual office situation provided the sense of social inclusion that was missing from the standard desktop approach to telecommuting. After a year of trying both systems, significantly more of the telecommuting employees chose the virtual-reality workplace over the desktop workplace, which they described as "empty" and "barren." Thus, not everyone likes the idea of working at home, at least not with the typical desktop arrangement. Not only do some people miss the social interaction, but they may not be sufficiently disciplined to work steadily without supervision. Some spouses object to having a partner work at home. Children may provide an additional distraction. Some managers believe they will lose their authority over subordinates if the subordinates are not physically present. And labor unions are concerned about the declining loyalty of members who do not work together on the job.

Some telecommuters feel pressured to work harder than they did in their traditional offices. Others say that by working at home, they are never free of the job. When the phone or fax or e-mail summons them after working hours, they feel compelled to respond. Nearly 20 percent of telecommuting programs fail for these reasons. Another reason for unsuccessful programs is that some teleworkers do not get the technical support they need from the employers. Despite these difficulties, many employees prefer working at home. Human resources managers already view telecommuting as one of the most important workplace trends of the century.

Physical working conditions include factors such as the location of the factory or office building, parking facilities, heating and air-conditioning systems, elevators, child-care facilities, cafeterias, and restrooms. **Environmental psychology** is concerned with the impact of these workplace features on employee behaviors and attitudes. In the landscaped office employees are grouped in functional units with no floor-to-ceiling barriers.

Light distribution and glare must be considered in designing illumination for workspaces. Noise in the work area can lead to deafness and to physiological effects such as increased muscle tension and blood pressure. Color is a useful coding device and can create differing illusions of size and temperature and improve the aesthetic appearance of the workplace. Some employees like music on the job, but research shows that it does not influence productivity. Optimal temperature and humidity ranges have been established for different kinds of workplaces. The comfort level of a workspace also depends on humidity level and air circulation.

Temporal working conditions include the number of hours worked and how those hours are arranged. Much scheduled work time is lost to unauthorized breaks. When **nominal working hours** are reduced, production tends to increase. Part-time employment offers opportunities to combine career, family, educational, leisure, and other pursuits, and may result in greater productivity. The four-day workweek seems to result in lower absenteeism and higher morale but has little effect on productivity. **Flextime** is popular with employees but has little effect on productivity or job satisfaction. Rest pauses will be taken whether or not they are officially sanctioned. They are necessary in manual labor to rest the muscles. For sedentary workers, rest pauses provide a change of pace and help alleviate boredom. Shift work disrupts the body's diurnal rhythm and can lead to social and psychological difficulties. In general, productivity is lower on the night shift; serious accidents and errors are higher.

Social-psychological working conditions relate to the design of the job and its effects on employees. **Job simplification** has made many jobs so unchallenging that they are boring and lead to psychological and physiological fatigue that reduce productivity. Repetitive, boring work is also tiring. Boredom can be relieved by enlarging the job scope, improving working conditions, and scheduling rest pauses. Ethnic and gender harassment occur frequently in the workplace and have harmful physical and emotional effects on their victims as well as reducing job satisfaction and productivity.

Computers and telecommunications advances make working at home possible for many types of employees. Telecommuting is associated with higher productivity, lower absenteeism, and corporate savings on office space.

Summary

environmental psychology
flextime

job simplification
nominal working hours

Key Terms

1. Why is it difficult to interpret the effects of a change in the physical work environment that has led to an increase in productivity?
2. According to survey data, what are the major complaints made by office workers about their work environment?

Review Questions

3. Explain how the size and design of offices and the size of an office build-ing can affect productivity and the nature of the working relationships among co-workers.
4. Describe advantages and disadvantages of landscaped offices.
5. What is a foot-candle of light? Why is it a bad idea to illuminate a work station at a much higher level of intensity than its surroundings?
6. How many decibels does it take to cause permanent deafness? What other physiological changes occur as a result of exposure to high noise levels?
7. In what ways can the use of different colors be helpful in the workplace?
8. What are the effects of exposure to very high temperatures on the job? Why do some organizations put fake thermostats in their offices?
9. What is the difference between nominal working hours and actual working hours?
10. What was the effect on actual working hours when nominal working hours were increased in some companies during the years of World War II?
11. What are the advantages to employees and employers of permanent part-time employment, of a four-day workweek, and of a flexible work-ing hours arrangement?
12. If you had a job that required shift work, which shift schedule would you choose? Explain the reason for your choice.
13. When did job simplification begin? What did it involve? How did it ben-efit the U.S. economy?
14. Is there a relationship between job simplification and boredom or mo-notony on the job? If so, explain it.
15. Distinguish among ethnic harassment, sexual harassment, and gender harassment.
16. What are the effects of sexual harassment on female employees? On male employees?
17. In what type of work environment has sexual harassment been found to occur most frequently?
18. Why are most incidents of sexual harassment not reported? What fac-tors can reduce sexual harassment at work?
19. What are some of the reasons employees do not like telecommuting? What are its advantages to employees and employers?

Additional Reading

Avery, C., & Zabel, D. (2000). *The flexible workplace.* Westport, CT: Quorum. A re-source for implementing flexible work arrangements and managing human resources in such situations. Includes pros and cons of telecommuting, flex-time, compressed workweeks, job sharing, permanent part-time employment, and voluntary (or involuntary) reduced work hours. Provides a historical overview as well as current examples. Notes relevant factors such as dual-career families, eldercare responsibilities, globalization and the need for 24/7 staffing, information technology, and environmentalism.

Bell, P., Green, T., Fisher, J., & Baum, A. (2001). *Environmental psychology,* 5th ed. Ft. Worth, TX: Harcourt College Publishers. A standard textbook on environ-mental psychology; covers the influence of physical workplace features on employee behaviors and attitudes.

Fenson, B., & Hill, S. (2003). *Implementing and managing telework: A guide for those who make it happen.* Westport, CT: Praeger. Describes the implementation, operation, and corporate benefits of telecommuting. Cites research showing that successful teleworkers have low affiliation needs and good time management skills. Also discusses security procedures for home computers and system back-ups for company data.

Gibson, C. B., & Cohen, S. G. (Eds.) (2003). *Virtual teams that work.* San Francisco: Jossey-Bass. Describes design, leadership, and employee participation in virtual work teams. Covers team interaction; challenges of electronic communication; culture and language differences; and pitfalls of working across time, distance, and organizational boundaries. Gives examples of the relative effectiveness of virtual versus face-to-face work teams for different tasks.

Hill, E. J., Miller, B. C., Weiner, S. P., & Colihan, S. P. (1998). Influence of the virtual office on aspects of work and work/life balance. *Personnel Psychology, 51,* 667–683. Studies issues of working hours, productivity, and morale among IBM employees in virtual office settings.

Hochschild, A. R. (1997). *The time bind: When work becomes home and home becomes work.* New York: Metropolitan/Holt. Describes an organization in which employees routinely put in 10-hour workdays and identify more with colleagues and subordinates than with family members, deriving greater social support from office relationships than from relationships outside the workplace.

Paludi, M., & Paludi, C. A., Jr. (Eds.) (2003). *Academic and workplace sexual harassment: A handbook of cultural, social science, management, and legal perspectives.* Westport, CT: Praeger. A multidisciplinary, multicultural treatment of sexual harassment issues in public and private sector organizations.

Rothausen, T. J., Gonzalez, J. A., Clarke, N. E., & O'Dell, L. L. (1998). Family-friendly backlash. *Personnel Psychology, 51,* 685–706. Discusses the positive and negative effects on employees of employer-provided on-site child-care facilities.

Chapter 11

Safety, Violence, and Health in the Workplace

Some jobs can kill you, or make you sick, and some jobs lead to a high rate of accidents. The shops, offices, and factories in which we work can be dangerous places. Every year more than 5,000 accidental deaths occur on the job. The number of disabling injuries, although not fully documented, is thought to be in excess of four million each year. Research by the Bureau of Labor Statistics indicates that for every disabling work injury reported, at least ten are not reported by companies attempting to hide a poor safety record. The monetary cost of these injuries is staggering, not only to employees and their organizations, but also to the nation as a whole. Billions of dollars are forfeited through lost time and wages and paid out in medical benefits and workers' compensation claims.

The health of workers in some types of jobs can be undermined by their exposure to toxic chemicals in the workplace. Disabling illnesses caused or aggravated by these on-the-job conditions generally do not kill or maim as suddenly or dramatically as accidents, but they impose emotional and economic costs, shortening the lives of thousands of workers.

Although accidents are the primary cause of death on the job, murder is the second; for women employees it is the leading factor, accounting for 42 percent of women's on-the-job fatalities. Injuries from deliberate acts of violence are becoming more widespread.

In this chapter we examine these and other aspects of workplace health and safety, discussing what industrial-organizational (I-O) psychologists have learned about accidents and violence on the job and what organizations can do about the problem. We deal with alcohol and drug abuse, both of which have adverse effects on employee health, safety, and job performance. We also discuss other health issues in the workplace such as those related to the use of computers and to the presence of employees with HIV.

WORK-RELATED HEALTH PROBLEMS

The toll from work-related diseases is as shocking as the accident rate. These illnesses are more insidious than a sudden, traumatic accident because they develop slowly over years before the worker experiences physical symptoms. For example, coal miners develop a unique respiratory condition called black lung disease, a progressively crippling disorder caused by prolonged inhalation of coal dust. Chemical industries pose health perils to their workers, dangers that are not fully known. Up to ten million workers are exposed daily to chemicals for which safe thresholds have not been established. The Environmental Protection Agency (EPA) has designated as toxic more than 16,000 chemical substances regularly used in the workplace. Some 150 of these are neurotoxins; that is, they cause damage to the human brain and nervous system.

Miners, mill workers, and shipyard workers are exposed to asbestos on the job, facing the danger of lung cancer at seven times the national rate. Textile workers are at risk for brown lung disease, caused by inhaling cotton dust. Medical technicians face dangers from radiation exposure. Office workers face the potentially harmful effects of indoor pollutants.

Astronauts working in the International Space Station report a variety of symptoms, including nausea and headaches, which have been traced to chemical fumes and an accumulation of deadly carbon dioxide. Chemists employed by the

BP Amoco research center near Chicago, Illinois, were developing a rare form of brain cancer at eight times the national average. It was traced to two chemical agents used routinely in their work. The American Academy of Asthma estimates that approximately 15 percent of the asthma sufferers in the United States acquired their disease from chemicals on the job such as latex, nickel, chrome, and mercury. Occupational asthma has now become the single most common work-related respiratory disorder.

An alarming increase in the incidence of job-related cancers among women has been documented among textile workers and workers at dry-cleaning plants. Breast cancer is on the increase among nurses and medical technicians who deal with X-rays and chemotherapy agents. A higher than normal rate of spontaneous abortion (miscarriage) has been found among oncology nurses and among women working in the chemical industry. Table 11–1 lists some frequently used substances, their health effects, and the types of workers who are regularly endangered.

TABLE 11–1

Hazardous Substances and On-the-Job Diseases

Potential Dangers	Potential Diseases	Workers Exposed
Arsenic	Lung cancer, lymphoma	Smelter, chemical, oil-refinery workers; insecticide makers and sprayers
Asbestos	White-lung disease (asbestosis); cancer of lungs and lining of lungs; cancer of other organs	Miners; millers; textile, insulation, and shipyard workers
Benzene	Leukemia; aplastic anemia	Petrochemical and oil-refinery workers; dye users; distillers; painters; shoemakers
Bischloromethylether (BCME)	Lung cancer	Industrial chemical workers
Coal dust	Black-lung disease	Coal miners
Cotton dust	Brown-lung disease (byssinosis); chronic bronchitis; emphysema	Textile workers
Lead	Kidney disease; anemia; central-nervous-system damage; sterility; birth defects	Metal grinders; lead-smelter workers; lead storage-battery workers
Radiation	Cancer of thyroid, lungs, and bone; leukemia; reproductive effects (spontaneous abortion, genetic damage)	Medical technicians; uranium miners; nuclear-power and atomic workers
Vinyl chloride	Cancer of liver, brain	Plastic-industry workers

Newsbreak   The Sick Building Syndrome

Many of us spend our working days sealed off from fresh air, trapped in closed environments. We can't open the windows—in many buildings they're not designed to open—and we breathe only filtered cooled or heated air. The cooling and heating systems in modern office buildings may be cost-efficient to operate, but the results can be dangerous. What we inhale can make us sick.

According to the World Health Organization, the physical complaints brought on by these artificial environments include eye, ear, and throat irritations, dry nasal membranes, skin inflammations, fatigue, headaches, nausea, and dizziness. Consider a few examples. In a sealed office building in San Francisco, California, most of the 250 employees complained of headaches, sinus problems, allergic skin reactions, and general discomfort shortly after the building opened. The symptoms disappeared when the air-filtration system was modified to allow more fresh air to circulate. In another new building, workers became dazed and stuporous most afternoons, especially on hot days. The problem was traced to the roof, where melting tar released fumes that were drawn into the air-conditioning system and dispersed throughout the building. Bacterial infections have also been transmitted through ventilation and air-conditioning systems.

When hundreds of employees in a new $37-million, ten-story county office complex in Florida developed symptoms of asthma, the building had to be abandoned. Experts concluded that construction flaws, a faulty air-conditioning system, a leaky roof, and vinyl wallpaper had combined to make the building a breeding ground for mildew and other contaminants.

Sealed buildings contain an alarming number of chemicals that are not dissipated or diluted by fresh air. Solvents, adhesives, cleaning fluids, fire-retardant materials, paint additives, formaldehyde in insulation, and chemicals in carpeting, wall coverings, and draperies can all be toxic. Copy machines produce ozone, which has been linked to headaches and upper respiratory tract infections. Solvents in carbonless paper are dangerous. Long-term exposure to electronic equipment has been related to headaches, eye problems, and neurological disorders. Harmful levels of microwaves and other sources of radiation have been linked to eye damage, memory loss, thyroid dysfunction, and leukemia. Perhaps some buildings should be labeled: Caution: *Working here may be hazardous to your health!* For more information on the sick building syndrome, visit the Web site www.epa.gov/iaq/pubs/sbs.html.

We noted earlier that more than 5,000 workers are killed by accidents on the job every year and that more than one million suffer injuries. These figures do not include those killed or injured commuting to and from the workplace. More than 90 percent of the employees killed on the job are men, though they constitute little more than half of the workforce. There is an obvious reason for this occurrence: More men than women work in construction and heavy industry, where an accident can have the most severe consequences. More men than women work as long-distance truck drivers, an occupation that contributes to 20 percent of all on-the-job fatalities every year. Obviously, some jobs are more dangerous than others, which means that some workers are subject to greater risk of injury or death at work.

In 1970 the U.S. Congress passed the Occupational Safety and Health Act, establishing the Occupational Safety and Health Administration (OSHA) in the Department of Labor. OSHA's purpose is to assure safe working conditions by developing and enforcing federal safety standards and by sponsoring research on the causes and prevention of accidents and diseases in the workplace. Although progress has been made, OSHA has been so poorly funded that it has not been able to carry out its mandate to make our workplaces safer. More than 35 years after OSHA was established, it still has so few safety inspectors that on average a company can expect to be visited only once every 84 years.

ACCIDENT STATISTICS

We noted in Chapter 2 that statistics do not lie but that sometimes the people who use statistics distort ideas in their own interests, backing up the distortions with data. This is the situation with accident statistics. The problem is defining when an accident is really an accident, which is not as ridiculous as it sounds.

How severe must an accident be for it to be included in an organization's accident statistics? Suppose a bakery worker drops a 100-pound sack of sugar. Is this an accident? Technically, yes. However, whether the company lists it as an accident depends on the consequences, not on the act itself. If the sack does not split and spill sugar all over the equipment and if no one is hurt, the episode will not be recorded as an accident. But what if the sack falls on the worker's foot and breaks a few bones? Is this considered an accident? Not necessarily. Many companies would not list this as an accident, even though the worker is injured and requires medical treatment. The worker may not be able to walk for a while, but if the company provides a desk job until the injury heals, then the employee will not have lost time from work. So here we have an accident that results in an injury, yet it will not be included in the accident statistics, and the company's safety record will remain intact. The definition of an accident in this case depends on whether the injured worker must miss time from work.

A few years ago, a large U.S. meat-packing firm was fined nearly $3 million for failing to report more than 1,000 job-related injuries among its workers. Statistics on railroad accidents investigated by a Washington-based journalist contradicted official government reports. Where Amtrak cited 494 injuries in 25 train wrecks, the independent journalist found 1,338 injuries. It is this failure to record all job-related injuries, not just those that keep workers off the job, that led the Bureau of Labor Statistics to conclude that accidents are significantly underreported.

Incomplete reporting makes research on the causes and prevention of accidents more difficult. The statistics provided by business and industry show the results of only a small proportion of accidents and provide little information on their causes. By concentrating only on lost-time accidents, the data provide an inaccurate picture of overall safety patterns.

An organization likes to boast about having a good safety record. It shows that the company is a caring employer, doing all it can to promote a safe working environment for its employees. To preserve a good safety record and a favorable public image, a company may resort to extreme measures such as closed-door investigations, incomplete reporting, and outright distortion of facts. However, sometimes it is the employees who distort the facts. Some fail to report minor accidents for fear of acquiring a reputation as careless or accident-prone. Others fear disciplinary action if the accident was their fault because they failed to follow prescribed operating procedures or to activate safety devices.

The underreporting and cover-up of accidents has been documented in many countries. In Japan, workers tend to conceal evidence of job-related injuries because of personal shame. To avoid losing face, Japanese workers attempt to hide even major injuries such as broken bones or to insist that they occurred at home. Managers conspire to conceal workplace injuries because they may represent negligence on their part as well.

CAUSES OF ACCIDENTS

Human error is the factor responsible for most accidents, whether they occur in the workplace, on the highway, or in the home. However, conditions of the work environment and the nature of the job tasks can also contribute to accidents.

Workplace Factors

Workplace conditions that affect employee safety include type of industry, hours of work, lighting, temperature, equipment design, safety devices, and social pressure.

Type of Industry.   The frequency and severity of accidents vary as a function of type of industry. A steel mill provides more opportunities for accidents than does a bank. The greater the physical demands made on the worker, the higher the accident rate. Also, stressful and tiring work seems to result in more accidents. Industries such as construction, highway transportation, farming, and mining are high in frequency and severity of accidents. Industries such as warehousing, aircraft and automobile manufacturing, and communications have a low frequency and severity of accidents. Cement and steel companies report a low frequency of accidents, but when accidents do occur, they are usually severe. Electric utilities also record few accidents, but these tend to be severe because of the high voltages involved. Wholesale and retail businesses have high accident rates, but lost-time injuries are rare. Data for some high-risk industries are shown in Table 11–2.

Hours of Work.   We might assume that the higher the number of hours worked, the higher the accident rate, but research does not provide clear support for this idea. However, shift work seems to be related to accident rates. In general, fewer accidents occur during the night shift than during the day shift, although night shift accidents, when they do occur, are usually more serious. This situation may be related to level of illumination. The artificial lighting provided at night can be better for work than the natural lighting conditions during the day.

TABLE 11–2

Risk Levels for Business and Industry

Industry	Injury Rate per 100,000 Full-Time Workers
Mining	23.5
Agriculture	22.7
Construction	12.2
Transportation	11.3
Wholesale trade	4.0
Manufacturing	3.1
Government	2.7
Retail trade	2.1
Services	1.7
Finance	1.0

Source: Bureau of Labor Statistics, 2004. http://www.stats.bls.gov/IIF/home.htm

Lighting.   Good lighting can lead to a reduction in accidents. The insurance industry estimates that poor lighting is a causal factor in one-fourth of all industrial accidents. Accidents are higher in plants that continue production through dusk before the nighttime lighting is turned on. Dusk is also a time of frequent automobile accidents. The relationship between level of illumination and accident rates in industry has been firmly established. An alert management can easily correct the problem of a poorly lit work area.

Temperature.   Studies of factory workers show that accident rates are lowest when the workplace temperature is maintained at 68 to 70 degrees Fahrenheit. Accidents increase when the temperature varies significantly, either warmer or cooler. Studies of coal miners show that minor accidents are three times more frequent under high temperatures (approaching 85° F) than under low temperatures (approaching 62° F). Workers seem to become more careless under the discomfort of higher temperatures. Older workers are more affected than younger workers by climatic extremes and are more likely to have accidents at higher temperatures.

Equipment Design.   Another physical factor related to accidents is the design of the tools, equipment, and machines used on the job. For example, if an engineer locates a stop button where it is difficult to reach, this can have deadly consequences for the worker who needs to shut down the machine immediately. Poor placement of switches and controls, inadequate warning lights for system malfunctions, and dials that are difficult to read have all been blamed for accidents.

Engineering psychologists strive to match equipment requirements with the capabilities of the human operators (see Chapter 13). Their work on safe workplaces and equipment has been highly effective, particularly with regard to cumulative trauma disorders and repetitive motion injuries such as carpal tunnel syndrome. These injuries are caused by continuous and repeated motions of hands and wrists and can affect shoulders and back as well. Repetitive motion injuries are prevalent among office workers using computer terminals and among certain types of factory workers. Redesigning keyboards, providing posture chairs and armrests, and allowing rest pauses are all effective in reducing repetitive motion injuries.

Cumulative trauma disorders are also seen in grocery store checkout clerks who are required to make frequent repetitive wrist movements using electronic scanners. Every product must be moved over or in front of the scanner so that the price of the item will be registered. The optimum workstation design for checkout clerks is one in which the cashier stands and is able to use both hands interchangeably to distribute the workload between both wrists. This reduces the type of injury likely to occur if only one hand is used. The next time you are in a checkout line, notice whether the cashier uses one hand or two when passing items by the scanner.

Safety Devices.   Also important in the design of safe machinery is the development of built-in safety devices and other aids to prevent accidents. Safety devices must function to keep a worker's hand away from sharp moving parts or to automatically disconnect the power supply in an emergency, but they must not interfere with the operation of the machine.

A hazardous work environment such as a natural gas drilling plant must be designed so that emergency controls are within easy reach.

Personal protective equipment—such as respirators, safety glasses with shatterproof lenses, steel-tipped shoes, ear protectors, and padded gloves—can be provided to protect workers in dangerous jobs, but too often they are not used. Sometimes the reasons are practical; for example, workers object to using a safety device that interferes with job performance. A respirator can hinder communication among workers. Thick gloves make it hard to press buttons on a control panel.

Another reason safety equipment is often not used is that it can be uncomfortable. Workers using respirators for jobs performed under high-temperature conditions may find that the device when clamped to their face causes skin irritation. A survey of employees in an automobile glass factory showed that only 30 percent considered them comfortable enough to wear. This attitude obviously influences workers' decisions about whether to use equipment that may protect them from harm but that causes considerable discomfort.

Social Pressure.   Accidents can be caused by the pressure to maintain a production schedule or adhere to a timetable. Workers often perceive the threat of disciplinary action or dismissal if they fail to keep to a schedule. Shutting down a production line or power plant because they think conditions are unsafe costs the company huge sums of money. The employee or manager who assumes the responsibility for such an action may be punished.

Airline pilots who refuse to fly in bad weather or because ice is forming on the aircraft's wings cause passengers to miss connecting flights. Also, they are held responsible for reducing the company's on-time performance record. When pilots see their colleagues reprimanded for similar behavior, they feel considerable pressure to take off on time despite the weather.

Personal Factors

Proper attention to equipment design and to the physical and social conditions of the work environment can help reduce the frequency and severity of accidents. Overall, however, the human element is the more important cause. Some of the personal factors studied by I-O psychologists are alcohol and drug use, cognitive ability, health, fatigue, work experience, job insecurity, age, and personality characteristics.

Alcohol and Drug Use.   Large numbers of employees use alcohol or illegal drugs on the job. An employee with a drinking or drug problem is much more likely to be involved in an accident than is an employee without such a problem. Even drinking off the job can lead to accidents at work. A study of more than 380,000 general aviation pilots showed that pilots with DWI (driving while intoxicated) convictions were 3.5 times more likely to have alcohol-related problems while flying than those who had no DWI convictions (McFadden, 2002).

Cognitive Ability.   It seems reasonable to assume that workers with a lower measured level of intelligence would have more accidents than workers with a higher measured level of intelligence. However, research does not fully support this idea. Some studies have found that cognitive ability is related to accident-free behavior only in certain jobs, such as those requiring judgment and decision making as opposed to those involving repetitive manual labor.

| **Newsbreak** | **How about a Drink *after* You Drive?** |

We all know that driving after we've had a few drinks is not a smart thing to do, but surely there can be no harm in having a few drinks after we've driven. Right? Wrong! At least it would be wrong if you drive a bus, a semi, or a cable car for the San Francisco, California, Municipal Railway System.

A five-year study of 1,836 drivers for the Muni system found that the more they drank in their off-the-job hours, the more likely they were to have an accident or serious injury at work. Drivers who reported having more than ten drinks a week after work were far more likely to file claims against the company for work-related injuries. Also, the amount of drinking after work was directly related to job stress. The more on-the-job stress the workers reported, they more they drank off the job as a way of relieving the stress.

This situation was expensive for the company. Workers compensation claims linked to after-hours drinking was costing the company more than $250,000 a year. That's a high price to pay for drinking off the job and a good reason for companies to identify and monitor employees who appear to suffer greatly from job stress. These employees can be offered counseling and shown ways of coping with stress other than drinking.

Source: Drinking after work could affect job. *St. Petersburg (FL) Times*, September 22, 2002.

Health.   I-O psychologists have documented a relationship between health and accidents. Employees who are in poor health or who are frequently ill tend to be highly susceptible to accidents. Workers with physical disabilities, assuming that their overall health is good and that they have jobs commensurate with their abilities, do not have a disproportionate share of accidents. Those disabled employees are usually highly motivated to work well and safely. One physical characteristic related to accidents is vision. In general, people who have good eyesight have fewer accidents than do people who have poor eyesight.

Fatigue.   Fatigue causes a decrease in productivity and an increase in accidents. During a typical eight-hour workday, periods of increased productivity are accompanied by decreased accidents. In the ten-hour workday in many heavy industries, a sharp rise in the accident rate during the last two hours of the shift has been reported, presumably because of fatigue.

Fatigue is a factor in highway accidents, a subject of study by I-O psychologists because highways are the workplace for bus and truck drivers. Fatigued bus and truck drivers who fall asleep at the wheel are involved in at least 10 percent of the collisions involving other vehicles. Fatigue contributes to one-fourth of all single-car accidents.

Work Experience.   A shorter time on the job tends to mean a higher accident rate. After some months on the job, the accident rate usually drops and continues to decline as work experience increases. This was shown in a 12-year study of 171 firefighters. Those firefighters with more experience on the job suffered less severe injuries from accidents than did those with less experience on the job (Liao, Arvey, Butler, & Nutting, 2001). However, the relationship between accidents and time on the job is not always clear. Although most studies have reported fewer accidents among employees with greater experience, these findings may be biased by self-selection. Workers who have had numerous job-related accidents are likely to have been fired or transferred or have quit to look for safer employment. Therefore, we cannot conclude with certainty that longer work experience, by itself, leads to a reduction in the accident rate. In some cases, the decrease in accidents among experienced workers can be explained by the fact that those who had more accidents have dropped out.

Job Involvement, Empowerment, and Autonomy.   A study of 14,466 workers from more than 2,000 companies found that those employees who scored higher in job involvement, which means they had greater autonomy and responsibility for their work, also scored higher in job satisfaction (an issue we discussed in Chapter 8). This study also reported a positive relationship between high job satisfaction and safety awareness. Thus, the researchers concluded that high job involvement leads to a lower accident rate (Barling, Kelloway, & Iverson, 2003).

Research with 531 workers in 24 work groups within a chemical company found that groups whose workers felt more empowered (who had greater power and authority over their work) had significantly better safety records than groups whose workers did not feel so empowered. The empowered groups performed safety checks and other safety-related behaviors more frequently than did the nonempowered groups (Hechanova-Alampay & Beehr, 2001).

Similarly, a study of 161 factory workers in Australia demonstrated that those workers who were high in feelings of job autonomy had significantly higher safety records over an 18-month period than did those who had a low degree of job autonomy (Parker, Axtell, & Turner, 2001).

Job Insecurity.   Research was conducted on 237 food-processing-plant employees in an organization that had already laid off some of its workers. The results showed that the workers who reported feeling insecure about their jobs and their future with the company had less motivation to adhere to safe working practices and to comply with safety policies. This lack of diligence, in turn, contributed to an increase in workplace accidents and injuries among these insecure employees (Probst & Brubaker, 2001).

Age.   The link between age and accidents is similar to the relationship between experience and accidents because there is an obvious relationship between age and length of work experience. Other factors that interact with age are physical health and attitudes toward the job. Overall health, as well as specific abilities such as vision and hearing, deteriorates with age. However, older workers have greater job knowledge and more highly developed skills. Reaction time and eye-hand coordination may no longer be as good, but older workers usually have a more complete grasp of the job's demands. Their attitudes toward safety tend to be more serious. However, when older workers do have accidents, they are likely to be more costly in terms of physical consequences and time lost from work.

Personality Characteristics.   A popular belief is that people who have a great many accidents have some unique set of personality traits that distinguishes them from people who rarely have accidents. Research does not support this contention, although some studies have found that people who have a high number of accidents manifest such characteristics as neuroticism, hostility, anxiety, social maladjustment, and a sense of fatalism. One study of 219 civilian production workers and 263 U.S. Army mechanics found that those who scored low in conscientiousness were more likely to make a cognitively based mistake or error that led to an accident while performing a routine task than were those who scored high in conscientiousness (Wallace & Vodanovich, 2003). However, any relationship between personality variables and accident frequency is not strong. There is no basis for concluding that people who have frequent accidents have a personality pattern that is clearly different from that of accident-free individuals.

Temporary emotional states can contribute to accidents, however. The person who is angry with a spouse or boss or is preoccupied with money problems is likely to be less attentive on the job and, hence, more susceptible to accidents. This was demonstrated in research involving 127 U.S. Army soldiers who had been involved in automobile accidents during the previous five years and 273 other soldiers who had not been involved in accidents. The difference between the two groups was clear. Those who had experienced accidents reported heightened emotions just prior to the accident. These emotionally stressful states covered a wide range, from divorce and illness to being disturbed by a passenger in the car (Legree, Heffner, Psotka, Medsker, & Martin, 2003).

Accident Proneness.   The theory of **accident proneness** holds that certain people are more likely than others to have accidents and that most accidents are caused by or involve the same few people. The theory also assumes that accident-prone persons are likely to have accidents regardless of the type of situation. An effective way to test this theory is to compare accident records for the same people for two different periods to determine if the people who had accidents in one period also had accidents in the other. Correlations from studies of this type are low, indicating that a person's past accident record is not a valid predictor of future accidents.

In a classic study, one psychologist reexamined accident statistics that had originally been interpreted as supporting the accident-proneness theory (DeReamer, 1980). In analyzing driving records of 30,000 people, it was found that fewer than 4 percent of them accounted for 36 percent of the accidents over a six-year period. These data suggested that a small group of drivers were involved in a large number of accidents. If they could be prevented from driving, then the accident rate could be cut by more than one-third. The data were reanalyzed by comparing accident records for the first three years of the period with accident records for the second three years of the period. It was found that the accidents during the two different periods did not involve the same drivers. Those identified as safe drivers during the first period accounted for more than 96 percent of the accidents in the second period, a finding that is highly damaging to the accident-proneness theory. More recent attempts to measure and validate the concept of accident proneness also have been unsuccessful (see As, 2001; Haight, 2001).

The theory no longer enjoys the credibility it once had, although evidence suggests that some workers may be predisposed to have more accidents in a particular

Accident proneness The idea that some people have personality traits that predispose them to have accidents, and that most accidents are caused by or involve these same few people. This theory is not supported by research.

Newsbreak	Look Out! The Driver Behind You May Be Asleep

That's a chilling thought to remember the next time you travel on an interstate highway. Take a look at those 40-ton 18-wheelers barreling along all around you and then think of this statistic: 78 percent of all truck drivers have a sleep disorder. It's called obstructive sleep apnea, and it causes a sleeping person to stop breathing momentarily and to awaken briefly. Someone with this disorder can wake up literally hundreds of times each night and not know it. The next day, however, the person will be sleepy.

"If someone wakes up every two or three minutes throughout the night," said psychologist William Dement, director of the Sleep Research Center at Stanford University, "it's as though they had very little sleep or no sleep at all." And then that person climbs into the cab of a tractor-trailer and drives at speeds up to 80 miles an hour, trying to keep awake for the duration of a ten- or 12-hour workday. No wonder fatigue is a major factor in truck accidents, when three out of four drivers have such disturbed sleep.

Drivers who fall asleep at the wheel of their rig account for up to 1,500 highway deaths a year. This figure means that while trucks represent only 3 percent of the traffic on the nation's highways, they are involved in 13 percent of all fatalities.

In case you're wondering whether you might be suffering from obstructive sleep apnea, don't worry. The disorder is three times higher among truck drivers than in the general population. One cause may be irregular work and sleep patterns. Long-distance drivers may work half the night, sleep for two hours, and then continue driving. Other factors are lack of regular exercise and a tendency to be overweight.

There are cures for sleep apnea, but first you have to know you have it. Most truckers don't know. They may wonder why they feel so tired during the day, but there is a natural tendency to shrug it off, gulp another cup of coffee, and keep on trucking. That's their job.

Sources: T. Hilchey, Sleeping disorder may affect many truckers. *New York Times*, May 14, 1995; B. Gavzer, Is the long haul too long? *Parade Magazine*, May 16, 1999.

---

type of work. Accident proneness may be specific to the work situation and not a general tendency over all situations, which limits the theory's predictive value.

ACCIDENT PREVENTION

An organization can take several steps to safeguard its employees and reduce accidents in the workplace. These include proper reporting of accidents, attention to workplace design, safety training, management support, and safety publicity campaigns.

Newsbreak	Accidents and Adolescents

Do you hold a job while you are attending school? The chances are good that you do, and you probably had an outside job during your high school years, too. Some 75 percent of high school seniors in the United States are employed, and nearly half of them work more than 20 hours a week. Research shows that 16- to 19-year-olds are the group at the highest risk for on-the-job accidents.

Michael Frone, a psychologist at the Research Institute on Addiction, in Buffalo, New York, wanted to know why. What characteristics of high-school and college-aged men and women could be related to these accidents and injuries? He started his research by investigating substance abuse (no surprise, given his own place of employment). He surveyed 319 adolescents and found that the use of marijuana and alcoholic beverages on the job showed a positive correlation with accidents and injuries.

But he also found other causes. One was simply being a guy. That's right. Male teenagers suffered more work-related injuries than female teenagers did. A high accident rate was also associated with heavy workloads, boring jobs, poor physical health, and a negative emotional outlook. It's hard enough being 18 or 19, but it also appears to be extra hazardous on the job.

Source: M. Frone (1998). Predictors of work injuries among employed adolescents. *Journal of Applied Psychology, 83,* 565–576.

Accident Reports

An accident prevention program is no better than the quality of its accident reports. All accidents, regardless of the consequences, should be investigated and described in detail. A comprehensive accident report should include the following:

- precise time and location of the accident.
- type of job and number of employees performing it.
- personal characteristics of the accident victim.
- nature of the accident and known or suspected causes.
- results of the accident—such as personal injuries and damage to plant, equipment, and supplies.

Workplace Design

Although most accidents are caused by human error, conditions in the physical work environment are potential sources of accidents. Lighting in the workplace must be adequate for the job tasks, and temperature must be maintained at a comfortable level. Work areas should be clean and orderly. Many accidents have been traced to poor housekeeping. Oil or grease spots on the floor, electrical cables underfoot, and equipment stored in hallways or stairwells can cause serious accidents that can easily be prevented. First-aid kits, fire extinguishers, and other safety equipment should be located conveniently throughout a work area and painted in vivid and easily identified colors.

Controls that are hard to reach or that require excessive force to operate and displays that are excessively complicated and so easily misread are design mistakes that are ready sources of accidents. Emergency controls must be made accessible and easy to operate.

Engineering psychologists suggest two general principles for the design of safety devices: (1) The machine should not function unless the safety device is engaged (for example, a power saw that will not operate unless the hand guard is in place) and (2) the safety device must not interfere with production or cause the employee to work harder to maintain the same output.

Safety Training

Most organizational training programs devote time to accident prevention. Workplace dangers and hazards are pointed out, and information is presented on the causes and results of past accidents. Rules for safe operating procedures are taught, along with the location of emergency and first-aid equipment. Periodic drills may be held to maintain awareness of safe working habits. When a company has an increase in accidents, it may mean that retraining of the workforce is necessary. Experienced workers can become careless and need refresher courses to update their work habits. In general, companies that systematically continue safety training efforts are rewarded with substantial reductions in accidents and in hours lost from work. The money saved easily pays the cost of the training programs.

For more information on work-related health and safety issues, see the Web sites for the Occupational Safety and Health Administration (www.osha.gov) and the National Institute for Occupational Safety and Health (www.cdc.gov/niosh/homepage.html).

Management Support

Supervisors play a key role in any successful program for safety training and awareness. Because of their close association with workers, they must be alert to unsafe working conditions and practices. Supervisors are in the best position to remind employees of safe working habits, to arrange proper maintenance of equipment and the work environment, and to foster a climate of safety within the organization. They are also able to recommend when retraining is advisable. If supervisors do not insist on adherence to safe working procedures, then any safety training program will be less than maximally effective. By example as well as instruction, supervisors can maintain employee motivation to work safely and to prevent accidents.

A study of 381 workers and 36 supervisors in a maintenance and repair center in Israel showed that leaders could be trained to improve safety practices on the job. Supervisors were provided with feedback about safety-related episodes over a period of eight weeks. This led to a significant increase in the supervisors' safety awareness, which, in turn, led to a significant decrease in the accident rate among their workers. It also led to an increase in the workers' use of safety-related equipment (Zohar, 2002).

Other research confirms the vital role of the supervisor in establishing an appropriate climate for safety on the job. A study of 127 transportation teams in the

Safety devices such as face shields should be easy to use and should not interfere with production.

U.S. Army showed that high-quality leader-member exchange relationships (LMXs) led to a positive safety climate characterized by a greater emphasis on safe job behaviors. Low-quality LMXs did not lead to greater safety awareness (Hofmann, Morgeson, & Gerras, 2003).

Studies conducted in Canada on 174 restaurant workers and 164 young employees (under age 25) in a variety of jobs also demonstrated the importance of a supervisory emphasis on safe practices on the job. The results showed that transformational leadership led to an enhanced safety climate at work and a consequent reduction in injuries on the job (Barling, Loughlin, & Kelloway, 2002).

However, it is important to remember that supervisors cannot be expected to practice safety awareness unless their superiors reinforce that concern. If higher management tolerates sloppy accident reporting or expresses even a neutral attitude toward safety, this does not encourage attention to safe practices. Active high-level management support of safety is a key dimension of an appropriate organizational climate. All levels of supervision must demonstrate to subordinates that safety is everyone's responsibility.

In a study of 1,590 employees in ten manufacturing and mining companies in Australia, the attitude toward safety promoted by management was shown to be significantly related to safe job performance (Griffin & Neal, 2000). And research on 534 production workers in 53 work groups in Israel found that the group safety climate created by the immediate supervisor significantly affected the rate of on-the-job injuries. The higher the group perceived its safety climate, the lower its accident rate (Zohar, 2000).

A study of 136 production workers showed that a strong company-wide safety climate can significantly reduce the anticipated adverse effects of job insecurity on compliance with safe job practices. The author suggested that organizations that focus on production, perhaps at the expense of safety, send a message to their employees that high productivity is the best way to keep their jobs. On the other hand, organizations that support a safe working environment send a message to their employees that compliance with safety practices is necessary to retain their jobs (Probst, 2004). This, the pertinent I-O research today, demonstrates that all levels of management must establish and reinforce a climate of safety to keep accidents and injuries at a minimum.

Safety Publicity Campaigns

To motivate employees to follow the safe work habits they have been taught, many organizations conduct publicity and promotional campaigns with posters and booklets, charts showing the number of accident-free days, and contests with appealing prizes.

Posters and Booklets.   Posters are a frequently used device, but their effectiveness depends on the kind of message depicted. Negative themes coupled with gruesome pictures of mangled bodies ("Don't do this—or this is what will happen!") are particularly ineffective. These fear-oriented appeals create resentment and anger toward the company and the message. The most effective safety posters stress positive themes (for example, "Wear hard hat in this area" or "Hold on to railing").

Warning signs and posters should be as conspicuous as possible, placed where they will be seen by the appropriate employees. Research has shown that for greatest effectiveness signs should be in large bold print with the lettering in high contrast against the background. The use of color, prominent borders, easily recognized pictorial symbols, and flashing lights are also desirable (Wogalter, Conzola, & Smith-Jackson, 2002). I-O psychologists recommend the following criteria for posters and warning signs:

- *Signal word.* Warnings should have signal or key words that are appropriate to the level of danger, for example, DANGER, WARNING, or CAUTION.
- *Hazard statement.* Warnings should tell clearly what the dangers are.
- *Consequences.* Warnings should tell clearly the results of failing to comply.
- *Instructions.* Warnings should tell workers what to do or what not to do to avoid the danger. The example in Figure 11–1 meets these criteria.

Booklets of safety instructions and rules are relatively ineffective in encouraging safe working practices no matter how widely they are distributed. It is easy to ensure that all workers receive a booklet, but it is far more difficult to make them read it.

Safety Contests.   Safety contests can be effective in maintaining interest in accident prevention. Some contests reward workers on an individual basis for accident-free work over a given period. Other contests operate on a group basis, rewarding a work crew or department. Contests can be competitive, pitting one work unit

FIGURE 11–1.   An effective warning poster.

WARNING	(Signal word)
UNDERGROUND GAS LINE	(Hazard statement)
EXPLOSION AND FIRE POSSIBLE	(Consequences)
NO DIGGING	(Instructions)

against another to see which has fewer accidents. Such contests may make workers more conscious of safe operating procedures and thus reduce accident rates, but the effects may not last much longer than the life of the contest. One solution is to hold continuous contests, changing the awards frequently enough to maintain employee interest. An obvious disadvantage of safety contests is that they encourage workers, supervisors, and managers to suppress the accurate reporting of accidents.

Safety in Home Offices.   With an increasing number of employees now telecommuting, the problem of safety in home offices has become a national concern. Home-based workers report computer-related discomfort and injury to necks, backs, shoulders, and arms from poorly designed chairs and awkwardly positioned keyboards and monitors. Other dangers include overloaded power outlets, poor lighting, and hazards from children's toys underfoot or outstretched power cords.

Safety experts suggest that many accidents in these offices go unreported because employees do not want to risk losing the opportunity to work at home. OSHA has raised the issue of safety for home work environments. Should employers be held liable when employees are injured while working at home, or is safety at a home office the responsibility of the employee who chooses to work at home?

VIOLENCE IN THE WORKPLACE

Murder is the second leading cause of death on the job and the primary cause of death for women in the workplace. In addition, every year more than two million employees are physically assaulted at work or threatened with assault. The office, shop, and factory have become very dangerous places.

You have seen the stories on the TV news. A disgruntled ex-employee who has been fired returns to the office or store or factory with a gun and starts shooting, usually killing or wounding former co-workers and the supervisor who fired the employee. Because of the publicity given such incidents that have occurred in post offices, the phrase "going postal" has become a generic shorthand description of the phenomenon. In fact, postal workers are less likely to be harmed on the job than many other types of workers.

It is important to put such events in perspective. You need not fear that the person at the next desk is looking at you suspiciously. Although disturbed workers have, indeed, gone on murderous rampages, three-fourths of workplace fatalities involve deliberate robberies rather than random, vengeful acts.

Victims of violence are typically taxicab drivers, convenience store clerks, pizza delivery drivers, and owners of small inner-city grocery and liquor stores. Ex-employees or co-workers commit approximately one-third of workplace homicides. Women are especially vulnerable to workplace violence. Many are murdered by boyfriends or husbands who choose the women's workplaces as the sites of their actions. Some companies provide security for women employees who are being stalked by abusive partners. For a detailed examination of the risk factors and prevention strategies associated with workplace violence, see www.osha.gov/SLTC/workplaceviolence/.

I-O psychologists have described different levels of violence in the workplace, beginning with incivility, which involves the display of disrespect and condescension toward, or the degradation of, one person or group by another person or group.

This does not involve physical violence but can make the workplace an unpleasant and stressful environment. A study of 1,180 public-sector workers found that 71 percent of them reported at least one instance of incivility over a five-year period. As many as one-third of these acts were instigated by people in positions of power within the organization. Women were more often the targets of incivility than were men, but the effects for all employees were lower job satisfaction, greater psychological distress, and psychological withdrawal from the job (Cortina, Magley, Williams, & Langhout, 2003).

Another level of violence in the workplace is unruliness, which includes the following aggressive and violent behaviors:

- Threatening or bullying other employees.
- Punching, kicking, throwing, or damaging something in anger.
- The loud and harsh use of profanity.
- Exhibiting emotional and irrational behavior when thwarted.
- Defacing or destroying company property.

As you can see, none of these behaviors involves homicide or physical assault, yet the tendency toward unruliness may contribute to an atmosphere of violence and may even be found to become a significant precursor to violence.

Additional research describes a profile of characteristics of persons believed to be most likely to commit destructive acts. These are shown in Table 11–3. A telephone survey of 300 employed adults found that alcohol abuse correlated positively with committing acts of violence. Interestingly, heavy drinking also correlated positively with becoming a victim of violence (McFarlin, Fals-Stewart, Major, & Justice, 2000).

A number of other factors have been related to violence at work including the geographic location of the workplace. A survey of 250 plants in a variety of locations found that the highest level of aggressive behavior occurred in plants located in communities with high crime rates. The lower the community's crime rate was, the lower the level of aggression within the workplace located in that community (Dietz, Robinson, Folger, Baron, & Schulz, 2003).

Another factor involves imitation. A study of 149 employees of group health care facilities found that those who saw co-workers engage in aggressive behavior, or

---

TABLE 11–3

Characteristics of Violent Employees

- Male between the ages of 30 and 50
- Alcohol or drug abuser
- Past history of violent behavior, serious psychiatric disorder, and impulsive behavior
- History of trauma, abuse, and neglect
- A loner with few social outlets
- Identifies strongly with the job
- Expresses feelings of shame or humiliation

who themselves were targets of aggressive behavior, were more likely to engage in aggressive behavior on the job (Glomb & Liao, 2003).

Research on 489 employed men in their 30s who worked for a variety of organizations revealed that those employees who perceived themselves as victims were highly likely to demonstrate aggression on the job. This effect of perceived victimization was stronger among those who had a history of alcohol abuse or antisocial behavior in other settings (Jockin, Arvey, & McGue, 2001). In a related study involving 141 government employees, those who felt victimized were less likely to seek revenge if the offender held a higher status position within the organization. Those who felt victimized by people in lower status positions were more likely to seek revenge against the perpetrator of the aggressive act (Aquino, Tripp, & Bies, 2001).

Other research on predictors of workplace aggression has explored the impact of individual differences. One study of 115 workers in two companies found that the measured trait of anger, defined as a stable personality trait that predisposes a person to experience anger in almost any situation, was directly linked to aggression on the job. The higher the level of the trait anger, the higher the incidence of workplace aggression (Douglas & Martinko, 2001). Another study involving 213 workers in several organizations confirmed the importance of the trait of anger in workplace aggression. This study also reported that employees who scored low on a measure of self-control tended to be more aggressive on the job.

Research on 254 workers in 71 different jobs in Canada also dealt with the effects of aggression and violence. Employees who were victims of aggressive acts by co-workers scored lower on measures of physical and emotional well-being and affective commitment to the organization. The researchers suggested that this was likely to reduce their subsequent job satisfaction and job performance (LeBlank & Kelloway, 2002).

Protecting Employees from Violence

Ideally, companies would not hire anyone who is prone to violence, but employee selection techniques are not yet sufficiently accurate to accomplish that goal. In an effort to address this problem, two psychologists developed a seven-item scale to measure what they call "interpersonal deviance," that is, behaviors that are harmful to other people in the organization (Bennett & Robinson, 2000). The scale is useful for research purposes, but its value as an employee selection device is not yet established. Further, it seems doubtful that seriously antisocial job applicants would answer the questions honestly. Consider the following items. Would you hire someone who answered "yes" to any of them?

1. Have you made fun of someone at work?
2. Have you said something hurtful to someone at work?
3. Have you made ethnic, religious, or racial remarks at work?
4. Have you cursed at someone at work?
5. Have you played a mean prank on someone at work?
6. Have you acted rudely toward someone at work?
7. Have you publicly embarrassed someone at work?

Even if human resources directors or personnel managers had the selection techniques to identify applicants with violence-prone personality profiles, not all such people would commit acts of violence on the job. Indeed, unless they were faced with sudden adverse situations, such as receiving a poor performance evaluation or a harsh reprimand, or being fired, they might never exhibit even minor unpleasant behaviors.

I-O psychologists recommend several positive steps to deal with workplace violence. Managers can be trained to recognize potentially violent workers. Difficult employees can be offered counseling. Supervisors can be taught tactful ways of communicating bad news such as disciplinary actions or terminations. OSHA has developed more tangible suggestions for reducing workplace violence, including installing metal detectors, alarm systems, extra lighting, video surveillance cameras, and bulletproof barriers. The agency also recommends hiring more security guards.

As usual, support from the organization will be beneficial. A study of 225 health care workers in Canada investigated two types of organizational support: *instrumental support*, which involved directly helping employees in need, and *informational support*, which involved providing employees with information they could use to help themselves deal with these problems. The results showed that both types of organization support led to a reduction in negative psychological health consequences of experiencing aggression in the workplace. Instrumental support was found to be more powerful than informational support because it also led to a reduction in physical health problems and negative affect that resulted from aggression on the job (Schat & Kelloway, 2003).

ALCOHOLISM IN THE WORKPLACE

More than 14 million people in the United States are known to be alcoholics, although the actual figure may be higher. The U.S. Public Health Service considers alcoholism to be a major health threat, along with heart disease and cancer. Alcoholism is defined as an illness characterized by an inability to control the consumption of alcohol to the extent that intoxication is inevitable, once drinking has begun. Medically, alcoholism is an addiction, a pathological drug dependence that is harmful to health and that interferes with normal functioning.

Up to 10 percent of the American workforce is estimated to be alcoholic at a cost to employers in excess of $100 billion a year. This cost is attributable to absenteeism; tardiness; errors and accidents; low productivity; inefficiency; and, often, the dismissal of valuable employees in whom money and training time was invested. Although there is no dispute that alcoholism is a serious problem for American business, not everyone agrees on the extent of alcoholism in the workforce. It is possible that the problem is overstated by therapists, consultants, and directors of rehabilitation programs, the people whose livelihood depends on the idea that alcoholism is rampant and that their programs can cure it.

Alcoholic employees can be found at all levels of organizational life. According to the National Institute on Alcohol Abuse and Alcoholism (NIAAA), more than 70 percent of known alcoholics are professional, semiprofessional, or managerial employees. More than half of all alcoholics have attended college. The greatest incidence of alcoholism is in the 35-to-55 age group.

The Drug Free Workplace Act of 1988 makes employers who hold $25,000 or more in federal government contracts responsible for the prevention of substance abuse on the job. The law requires these employers to notify employees that the possession, sale, or use of alcohol or illegal drugs on the job is prohibited. If employees are convicted of alcohol or drug offenses, employers are required to impose disciplinary action such as mandatory treatment programs, suspension without pay, or discharge.

Effects on Job Performance

Alcoholics tend to believe that drinking will not affect their behavior at work and that no one will detect a difference in the way they perform their jobs. This is untrue. The debilitating effects of excessive drinking are evident almost immediately. However, in the beginning stages only a trained observer will notice them.

Although behavioral changes occur gradually, after a few years of steady drinking an employee's job performance and efficiency will have deteriorated so greatly that the changes will be obvious to supervisors and co-workers. The downward path of an alcoholic's behavior is depicted in Figure 11–2. The signs of altered job performance include excessive absenteeism, long lunch breaks, lies, errors, and low productivity. In the middle phase, gross changes are apparent that can no longer be overlooked. By this time, the alcoholic has usually received a warning from supervisors and is no longer being considered for promotion.

As the performance curve shows, everything goes downhill—career, family life, reputation, and financial stability. Ironically, each crisis precipitated by excessive drinking provides yet another reason to continue drinking. Unless the person recognizes the problem and accepts help, this cycle can lead to career failure, imprisonment, hospitalization, or an early death. When a worker's superiors continue to ignore excessive drinking, mistakenly believing that they are being kind or helpful, they are only prolonging the problem. Intervention at an early stage is vital to an alcoholic's recovery.

The Alcoholic Executive

The plight of any alcoholic employee is tragic, but when the alcoholic is an executive, the cost to the company is greater. When an organization loses an executive because of a drinking problem, it is deprived of someone in whom it has invested considerable training, a high salary and fringe benefits, and significant responsibilities, a person whose judgment and decision-making abilities have been considered important to the organization's success.

Alcoholic executives, more than lower-level employees, are adept at concealing their problem for a longer period. They may be aided by their subordinates, who are often willing to cover up for their bosses' indispositions. Thus, alcoholic executives can escape detection longer than people in the accounting office, the warehouse, or on the assembly line.

There is another comfort for alcoholic executives. They are not as apt to be fired as are lower-level employees. The executive is more likely to be retained and given a make-work job until retirement. Although management recognizes the problem of alcoholism on the factory floor, it is more reluctant to admit that it exists in the office next door.

Laboratory studies of the process of negotiation, a skill widely practiced by high-level managers and executives, showed that people who negotiate deals while under the influence of alcohol make costly mistakes for their organization.

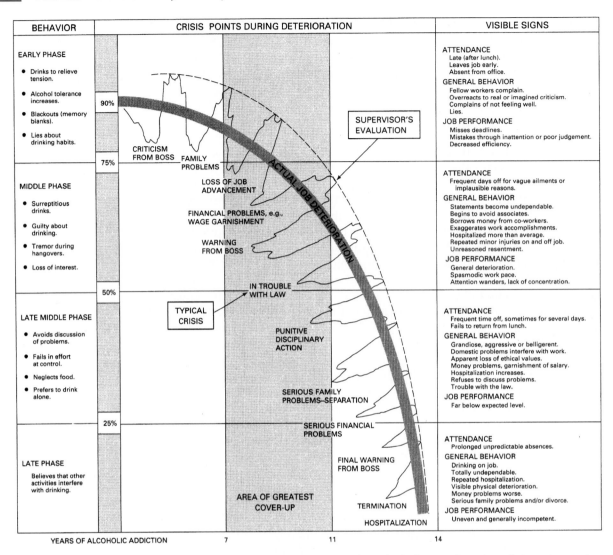

FIGURE 11–2. Deterioration in behavior and job performance of an alcoholic as a function of time. (From A. Carding, "Booze and business," *Administrative Management*, 1967, *30*, 21. Copyright Doyle Lindley, Bechtel Corporation. Reproduced by permission.)

Subjects who conducted negotiations while intoxicated (having a blood alcohol level of 0.05) were significantly more aggressive in their dealings with others than were negotiators who were sober. Those who had been drinking were far more likely to insult, mislead, and threaten the people with whom they were bargaining. In addition, they were found to be cognitively impaired, which led them to make errors of judgment, focus on irrelevant information, and misinterpret or ignore key points of the problem under consideration (Schweitzer & Kerr, 2000).

Employee assistance programs (EAPs) Counseling and rehabilitative services for various employee problems, notably alcohol and drug abuse.

Rehabilitation Programs

Many federal government agencies and more than half of the largest U.S. corporations sponsor formal alcoholic rehabilitation programs. These efforts, called **employee assistance programs (EAPs),** return as much as 20 dollars for every dollar

Newsbreak	**Brian's a Hard Charger!**

Brian's a hard charger. That's what Brian Early's friends and colleagues used to say about the mid-twenties accounts manager. They also used to say that sometimes he drank more than he could handle. They didn't realize that Brian was drinking most of the time. "I was getting up the next morning and smoking dope just to get rid of the headache" from his hangover, he admitted.

But Brian was able to hide his problem from his co-workers and bosses because he had layers of protection, like most managers. He arranged his own workday and travel schedule, was often out of the office on legitimate business, where he could drink without being seen by colleagues, and he had a support staff to cover for him who did much of the work that he was supposed to be doing. Also, even if his subordinates suspected that he was drinking heavily, they feared retaliation if they went over his head to complain about his behavior.

Like many alcoholics, Brian denied he had a problem. A psychologist who counsels alcoholic executives wrote, "Their work becomes the foundation of their denial." The person says, in effect, "I can't be an alcoholic because I'm handling all these things at work." In the end, it was not Brian's boss who told him he had to get help. It was his wife, before she left him. That got his attention. He checked himself into a treatment center, endured the symptoms of withdrawal, and has not had a drink for 22 years. He carved out a successful new career, and yes, his wife returned to him. But Brian never forgot the way he had once behaved. He regularly attends support group meetings and is always on guard against the kinds of stresses that led him so easily to drink. And he likes to say he holds one comforting thought: "My worst day today is still better than my last day drunk."

Source: P. Olsen, Detoured but not stopped by alcohol. *New York Times*, May 25, 2003.

invested in them in terms of reduced absenteeism, reduced health care costs, and higher productivity. Most EAPs offer counseling services for various employee problems, but their major concerns are alcohol and drug abuse.

Employers can offer a strong motivation for alcoholic employees to seek treatment because they hold out the hope of retaining a job. Psychologists and physicians who work with alcoholics agree that fear of losing one's job can carry more weight than threats from spouses or the possibility of an early death. To alcoholics, keeping their jobs may be their last defense against admitting that they have a drinking problem. When that defense is jeopardized, the desire to seek and accept help is usually great.

Most programs to combat alcohol abuse follow a three-step process suggested by the National Council on Alcoholism:

1. *Education of managers and supervisors.* The purpose is to persuade management that alcoholism is not a moral or ethical issue but a medical problem, a treatable illness.

2. *Early detection of alcoholic employees.* Managers should be trained to detect the symptoms of alcoholism and the resulting behavioral and performance changes. Early detection improves the alcoholic worker's chances for recovery.

3. *Referral of alcoholic employees for help.* Some companies rely on in-house physicians and psychologists to supervise rehabilitation programs for alcoholic employees. Other companies refer employees to outside clinics. Most organizations provide for treatment on company time and continue the workers' salaries while they are in treatment programs.

An especially effective treatment approach involves co-workers who are members of Alcoholics Anonymous. That organization has a high success rate in dealing with alcoholism because its members know the effects firsthand. There is some evidence, albeit weak, to suggest that recovering alcoholics become better workers. Their performance no longer suffers from their drinking, and they may expend extra effort, realizing that this is their last chance. However, even if the job performance of recovering alcoholics does not improve, at least the company has reclaimed experienced workers who would otherwise have been lost.

For information on all aspects of alcoholism on the job, see the Web site maintained by the U.S. Office of Personnel Management at www.opm.gov/ehs/alcohol. asp. In addition, databases, research programs, and other resources are available from the National Institute on Alcohol Abuse and Alcoholism of the National Institutes of Health at www.niaaa.nih.gov. Another informative source is www. alcoholismhelp.com.

DRUG USE IN THE WORKPLACE

The use of illegal drugs on the job is a serious problem. Marijuana is the principal substance used; amphetamines, opiates, cocaine, PCP, and ecstasy have also been found in the workplace. In addition, prescription drugs such as tranquilizers, painkillers, and stimulants can be overused. Data show that one out of every ten current and prospective employees has used or will use drugs. The National Institute of Drug Abuse reports that the use of illegal drugs is more widespread among younger employees, ages 18 to 25.

Consider some recent findings on the extent of drug use among the workforce and the general population (Frone, 2003).

- 14.8 million Americans use illicit drugs.
- 11 percent of people between ages 12 and 17 use illicit drugs.
- The highest rate of drug use is among the 18–25 age group, peaking at 17.4 percent at age 21.
- Drug use is higher among men (8.7 percent) than women (4.9 percent).
- 77 percent of drug users hold jobs.
- The availability of illicit drugs in the workplace (notably marijuana) obviously affects the rate of drug use; the greater the availability, the higher the use.

Although drug abuse has been detected at all corporate levels, it is highest among skilled and semiskilled laborers and lowest among managerial and professional personnel. The overuse of prescription drugs is highest among middle-aged and older workers. Drug users are found in all types of jobs. One nuclear power plant caught security guards using drugs. The U.S. Navy discovered that the majority of one aircraft carrier's crew regularly smoked marijuana. And an oil company learned that offshore drilling rig crews in the Gulf of Mexico were often under the influence of illegal drugs.

The drug-dependent worker may present a more serious problem than the alcoholic worker in terms of the disruptive effects on production and efficiency. Drug users are potentially more dangerous because they may attempt to sell drugs to other workers to finance their own habit.

Effects on Job Performance

Behavioral effects of drug use on the job will vary with the type of drug taken. In general, however, the new user shows marked changes in behavior. There is a negligence about appearance, personal hygiene, and dress. Some take to wearing dark glasses. Emotional outbursts are common, along with a tendency to borrow money. There is also likely to be impairment in judgment and reflexes; sluggishness of movement; dilation or contraction of the pupils of the eyes; bloodshot eyes; and, in extreme cases, needle marks on the arms or elsewhere on the body. These behavioral changes affect job performance.

In addition, drug abusers have been found to have up to four times the number of accidents, three times the number of absences, three times the number of health benefit claims, and five times the number of workers' compensation claims. They are far more likely to be late for work and they rate low in job satisfaction.

Questionnaire surveys of 470 adults taken when they were in their mid-twenties, and again in their early thirties, found that early use of drugs was highly predictive of later drug abuse. In other words, those who reported drug problems in their twenties continued to abuse drugs into their early thirties. Their continuing drug abuse led to job instability, lowered job satisfaction, and a reduced tendency to conform to generally accepted societal norms. However, those who received early social support for confronting their drug problem were less likely to be using drugs by the time of the second survey. Also, they were more likely to rate themselves higher in job satisfaction than were those who did not receive early social support (Galaif, Newcomb, & Carmona, 2001).

Depending on what there is to steal from an organization, drug use can lead to an increase in employee theft. Thus, drug users are likely to become marginal employees who are a burden to management and a threat to the morale and safety of co-workers. In hazardous occupations, such as construction and transportation, drug users, like alcoholics, can be a menace to the public. Proponents of on-the-job drug screening argue that public safety is the best reason for mandatory drug testing. The public has a right to expect that operators of buses, trains, and airplanes will not have their judgment or reaction time impaired by drugs.

The U.S. Department of Labor reports that small businesses (with 24 or fewer workers) are more strongly affected by employee drug abuse than are large companies (500 or more workers). Only 13 percent of known drug users work for large organizations; 44 percent work for smaller companies. The practical explanation for this finding is that smaller companies are less likely to have programs designed to detect or combat drug use on the job. Therefore, drug users at a smaller company are less likely to get caught. In addition, a mistake made by a drug-impaired employee at a small company (say, one worker out of 25) can be more economically devastating and potentially dangerous than an error made by one employee out of 1,000 (Report: *Alcohol and drug abuse in America today*, 2004).

Drug Testing Programs

The chances are high that you will be tested for drug use when you next apply for a job. Most companies that test for drug use refuse to hire applicants who test positive. Drug testing is now part of the employee selection process, and the results of your drug test can override your performance on other selection measures.

Psychologists have suggested the following guidelines to make drug testing programs as equitable as possible:

- The organization should issue a statement to employees describing its policy on drug abuse and testing.
- If employees belong to a union, the company's drug policies and testing procedures should be submitted to collective bargaining before being put into effect. Employers who refuse to bargain with the union are subject to charges of unfair labor practices.
- Drug testing procedures should apply to all employees. No specific group should be singled out for testing.
- Current employees should be tested only in documented cases of job impairment or because of other valid indications of probable cause.
- Employees should be informed in advance of drug testing procedures, including the drugs being screened for, the types of tests, and the consequences of refusing to be tested.
- Positive test results should be confirmed by a second test.
- Results of drug tests should be kept confidential.

A telephone survey of 1,484 people employed full time or part time found that those who had used marijuana during the previous month were significantly more likely to believe that drug testing by employers was unfair than were workers who had not used marijuana during the previous month. A second finding of this survey was that those who held safety-sensitive jobs, where impaired performance could cause injury to the public, to co-workers, or to the employee, were significantly more likely to believe that drug testing by their company was fair, as compared to those whose jobs were not safety sensitive (Paronto, Truxillo, Bauer, & Leo, 2002).

Drug testing is controversial. It can be argued that testing infringes on employees' rights to privacy, confidentiality, and security from unreasonable search and seizure. Primarily for these reasons, some organizations have been reluctant to institute widespread drug testing programs for employees and instead require organizations to reassign workers in dangerous jobs to alternative tasks if they are known to be drug users.

The validity of drug testing is also an issue. The Centers for Disease Control and Prevention reports that mass drug screening, particularly with inexpensive and unsophisticated tests, can incorrectly indicate the presence of drugs in up to two-thirds of the cases. This high rate of false positives means that a disturbingly large number of job applicants and employees are mistakenly labeled as drug users.

The lack of accuracy of the tests can be attributed to false readings, laboratory errors, and cheating by employees. Other substances in urine or blood samples can mimic the presence of drugs. Poppy seeds can falsely indicate the use of opiates. Marijuana can be inaccurately indicated by over-the-counter cough and cold products such as Contac or by painkillers such as Advil and Nuprin. An herbal tea that is a normal part of the diet in certain South American countries can lead to a positive test for cocaine. Laboratory technicians can inadvertently mix up samples. Some years ago, the U.S. Army found that half the urine samples of a group of 60,000 soldiers had been so carelessly handled in the laboratory that none of the test results could be considered reliable.

People being tested for drug use may try to cheat the system by substituting someone else's drug-free urine or by adding an adulterant such as laundry bleach to mask traces of drugs. For this reason, most employers insist that employees urinate in the presence of an observer, a practice most people find offensive.

Drug users are highly likely to have accidents on the job. (Reproduced by permission of Partnership for a Drug-Free America.)

The first step taken by many organizations to deal with drug use on the job is a clear and direct statement to employees and job applicants about the policy concerning drug use, drug testing, and the consequences of violating that policy.

The second step is screening all job applicants, not only with drug testing, but also by paying attention to gaps in employment history, criminal conviction records, dishonorable military discharges, and physical signs of addiction.

The third and most difficult step is to detect employees who are using or selling drugs on the job. One company hired an ex-addict to work at various jobs throughout the plant and identify drug users. Another company hired private detectives to pose as employees. Some employers have used drug-sniffing dogs to detect the presence of drugs in the workplace and in employees' cars in the company parking lot.

Most organizations differentiate between occasional users of soft drugs and addicts or pushers of hard drugs. If occasional users have a good performance record and agree to accept help, companies will usually arrange for a treatment program. If users refuse help, they will likely be fired. Drug pushers are subject to arrest.

Workers who are treated successfully for drug problems and return to their jobs show reduced absenteeism, accidents, sick leave, and claims for health benefits. In general, EAPs report success rates of up to 80 percent, with success defined as remaining drug-free and maintaining satisfactory job performance for one year after treatment. Once drug users have lost their jobs, the recovery rate drops to about 5 percent, a clear indication of the importance of detecting and treating a worker's substance abuse problem while he or she is still employed.

Research involving 260 city government employees showed the usefulness of group training for building acceptance of and trust in EAPs. Group training specifically oriented toward drug abuse problems significantly increased the tendency for employees to seek help for up to six months after the end of the training program (Bennett & Lehman, 2000).

For information about drug abuse issues in the workplace, see the Web site of the National Institute on Drug Abuse at www.nida.nih.gov and the site for the U.S. Department of Labor at www.dol.gov/workingpartners/-57k.

COMPUTERS AND PHYSICAL HEALTH ISSUES

Some employees who work with computers report a high incidence of back pain, physical fatigue, and visual disturbances. These problems can often be eased by altering the design of the work area and correcting poor lighting conditions. The city government of San Francisco, California, passed legislation to regulate the use of video display terminals in the workplace in order to reduce eyestrain, muscle fatigue, and repetitive motion injuries. The law follows guidelines recommended by engineering psychologists and requires that workers be provided with adjustable chairs and adequate lighting and that computer terminals be equipped with detachable keyboards and adjustable screens. In addition, employees whose jobs do not include regular rest breaks must be given 15 minutes of alternative work every two hours.

Carpal tunnel syndrome
A repetitive motion disorder that may involve numbness; tingling; or pain in fingers, hands, and forearms.

Carpal tunnel syndrome, a repetitive motion disorder of the wrist, has plagued workers in many occupations for decades. Any job that requires repeated identical or similar motions can lead to this painful, crippling nerve injury. Once reported mainly by blue-collar workers such as meat cutters, carpenters, jack-hammer operators, and assembly-line workers, it received little recognition or publicity.

With the advent of computers, white-collar workers, such as newspaper re-porters and editors, started feeling those characteristic shooting pains in hands and forearms accompanied by tingling and numbness in the fingers. That was when carpal tunnel syndrome became famous. And when media people started hurting, they wrote articles about this newfound condition. Psychologists and medical researchers began to study it, and OSHA became alarmed. For more information about carpal tunnel syndrome, see the Web site for the National Institute of Neurological Disorders and Strokes at www.ninds.nih.gov/health_and_medical/disorders/carpal_doc.htm_19k.

Repetitive motion injuries are said to afflict more than two million people in the American workforce, many suffering damage to the point of needing surgery to relieve the pressure on the affected nerve. The condition can often be pre-vented by proper attention to engineering psychology guidelines of the kind leg-islated by the city of San Francisco.

There are additional health concerns for people who manufacture computer chips. This work is potentially dangerous because it exposes employees to ar-senic, cyanide, acids, and noxious solvents. Some workers claim that the job causes headaches and loss of concentration, and they are concerned about long-term health effects. Research to date neither confirms nor refutes these charges. Nevertheless, companies such as AT&T have taken the precaution of transferring pregnant women from computer chip manufacturing areas to other worksta-tions. Other companies inform employees of the hazards and offer the opportu-nity for a transfer.

Studies have shown a higher rate of miscarriages among pregnant women who work with computers more than 20 hours a week, compared to pregnant women who do other kinds of office work. Research on animals has related the low-frequency, pulsed, electromagnetic radiation emitted by video display termi-nals to miscarriages and birth defects. However, the evidence with human sub-jects is less certain.

Psychologists suggest that the source of the problem is the stressful assembly-line atmosphere in which many computer operators function rather than the ra-diation emitted by the display screens. In an investigation of pregnant women in several occupations, clerical employees had a higher miscarriage rate than did managerial and professional employees who spent a comparable amount of time at a computer terminal. The jobs of the managerial and professional women em-ployees may have been less stressful and more satisfying. Research on pregnant women workers in several countries found no significant evidence of increased risk of miscarriages or birth defects from working with computers.

The issue raises a problem of discrimination. Some companies practice what is called **protective exclusion,** barring women of childbearing age from certain jobs, such as computer chip production, out of fear of eventual lawsuits should it be shown that computer work is related to miscarriages, birth defects, or other health problems. In some companies, women job applicants have been asked to supply urine samples that were tested, without the applicants' knowledge or consent, for evidence of pregnancy. In instances where women were not hired on the basis of such a policy, it constitutes sex discrimination.

Protective exclusion The practice of barring certain groups of employees, such as women of childbearing age, from potentially hazardous jobs because of fear of lawsuits.

In 1991 the U.S. Supreme Court struck down this practice of protective exclusion as a form of sex discrimination and ruled that employers could not exclude women from jobs in which exposure to toxic substances might harm a developing fetus. The case before the court involved the Johnson Controls battery plant, which had excluded women of childbearing age (except those who could prove they were sterile) from high-paying assembly-line jobs that exposed them to potentially harmful lead fumes. Some women had undergone surgery to be rendered sterile rather than transfer to lower-paying jobs. It is interesting that the company's fetal-protection policy had never been applied to men even though the men's sperm was at risk of becoming malformed, a condition that could lead to birth defects.

Computers emit other forms of radiation, including X-rays and infrared, magnetic, and electrostatic fields. The long-term effects of these emissions have not been determined.

HIV IN THE WORKPLACE

An HIV-positive person in a work group can have a profound effect on job performance and morale, engendering the fear of becoming infected among ill-informed co-workers. At a New England telecommunications company, 30 employees walked off the job when they learned that a co-worker had been diagnosed as HIV positive. Some people erroneously believe that all those who test positive for HIV must be homosexuals or drug abusers. A study of 160 human resources managers in Singapore confirmed the results of previous research conducted in Western nations that the more information a person has about HIV, the lower the fear of exposure to the condition in the workplace is. Inadequate knowledge or incorrect information leads people to exaggerate the risk of contagion by casual contact on the job. Thus, these people become fearful about working with someone diagnosed as HIV positive (Lim, 2003).

Another problem confronting organizations is the increasing cost of health insurance, especially for employees with high medical bills. The AIDS epidemic was the first large-scale health crisis to occur since employer-paid health insurance became a standard employee fringe benefit in the United States. Insurers are prohibited by law from excluding HIV coverage in their policies. A survey of 1991 HIV/AIDS patients found that the fear of losing health benefits, and the concern over job discrimination, were major barriers to returning to work after they had taken time off for treatment. Other reentry issues were whether employers would make accommodations such as allowing time off for continuing doctor's visits or providing less strenuous job duties (Martin, Brooks, Ortiz, & Veniegas, 2003).

Employers cannot discriminate against persons with AIDS in hiring or other career decisions, nor can they fire AIDS patients because of fear of contagion. The Centers for Disease Control has concluded that the disease cannot be spread through casual contact and work. Only about one-fourth of U.S. companies have policies and programs to deal with HIV-positive employees. Some companies educate employees about the disease by presenting factual information in newsletters, booklets, and videotapes. Informal question-and-answer sessions with medical experts are also helpful. Such company-sponsored educational programs can have the additional benefit of inducing employees to modify their own behavior in ways that will reduce their risk of contracting or spreading the virus.

Summary

OSHA's goal is to enforce federal industrial safety standards to protect workers from accidents and health problems on the job. One problem with research on accidents is that many organizations distort accident data through incomplete reporting in an effort to maintain good safety records. Workplace factors that affect accidents are type of industry, work schedules, lighting, temperature, and equipment design. Personal factors contributing to accidents include alcohol and drug use, health, fatigue, work experience, job insecurity, age, job involvement, and personality variables such as conscientiousness. The theory of **accident proneness** has little research support.

To prevent accidents, organizations should practice complete reporting and analysis of accidents, consider the design of the job and work environments, provide managerial support for safe work practices, provide safety training and a strong safety climate, and sponsor safety publicity campaigns.

Workplace violence is increasing. Behaviors expressing incivility, anger, and hostility threaten workers at all levels. Factors related to workplace violence include the level of violence in the community, being a target or victim of workplace violence, and the psychological trait of anger. Those most likely to commit acts of violence are men between ages 30 and 50 with a history of substance abuse and psychiatric disorders.

Alcoholism on the job has been linked to tardiness, absenteeism, low productivity, and emotional problems. Organizations try to assist alcoholic employees through **employee assistance programs (EAPs)** and by training managers to detect signs of alcoholism in their workers. Drug use on the job has been found at all occupational levels. In general, organizations treat drug users more severely than they do alcoholics. The use of drug testing in employee selection is widespread, though the tests may not be accurate and may violate privacy rights. Effects on employee health of prolonged computer use, such as **carpal tunnel syndrome,** are being investigated.

The presence of HIV-positive employees can affect the morale and productivity of others in the workplace. However, the more information employees have about the condition, the lower their erroneous fear of becoming infected through casual contact is.

Key Terms

accident proneness
carpal tunnel syndrome

employee assistance programs (EAPs)
protective exclusion

Review Questions

1. In what ways can work affect your health? Give specific examples.
2. Describe some of the symptoms and causes of sick building syndrome.
3. Why is it difficult to define an on-the-job accident?
4. What physical conditions of the workplace can contribute to accidents?
5. In what ways can the design of equipment and safety devices reduce workplace accidents?
6. How does each of the following contribute to accidents in the workplace: alcohol and drug use; health; age and work experience; job insecurity?
7. What roles do personality characteristics and job involvement play in workplace accidents?

8. Discuss the effects of safety training and management support in reducing accidents on the job.
9. Describe how you would design a warning poster to caution employees about the dangers of getting too close to a high-voltage cable.
10. Describe different levels of violence in the workplace. Note the relative incidence of each type and some of the overall effects of workplace violence.
11. What factors have been linked to violence on the job?
12. Define the personality trait *anger* and describe how it relates to workplace violence.
13. Why is it easier for an alcoholic executive to escape detection than for a lower-level employee?
14. Describe the three-step process of the National Council on Alcoholism to combat alcohol abuse on the job.
15. What factors influence drug abuse in the workplace? What are the effects of drug use among employees?
16. Discuss arguments for and against drug testing in the workplace. Do you think it is fair for an employer to require you to take a drug test as a condition for employment?
17. How, and why, do employers treat alcoholics differently from drug users?
18. How is prolonged computer use related to physical health problems? How can such potential problems be reduced on the job?
19. If you were a manager who learned that an employee had tested positive for HIV, what problems would you anticipate from the rest of your employees? How would you deal with the situation?

Additional Reading

Barling, J., & Frone, M. R. (Eds.) (2004). *The psychology of workplace safety.* Washington, D.C.: American Psychological Association. Reviews causes and prevention of workplace injuries and deaths in industrialized and in developing nations. Relates occupational accidents to poor worker-management communication, deficient safety culture, inadequate training, and lack of incentive-based pay systems.

Bennett, J. B., & Lehman, W. E. K. (Eds.) (2003). *Preventing workplace substance abuse: Beyond drug testing to wellness.* Washington, D.C.: American Psychological Association. Reports on long-term research programs that emphasize wellness rather than punishment or disciplinary actions for alcohol and drug abusers in the workplace. Attempts to deal with causes of substance abuse such as job stressors, work-family conflicts, lack of social support, inadequate health promotion information, and deficient coping skills.

Fox, S., & Spector, P. E. (Eds.) (2005). *Counterproductive work behavior.* Washington, D.C.: American Psychological Association. A comprehensive survey of workplace behaviors that are dangerous to individuals and to organizations, such as bullying, emotional abuse, revenge, and aggression. Considers environmental factors of the workplace as well as personal characteristics of perpetrators and victims.

Lewis, G. W., & Zare, N. C. (1999). *Workplace hostility: Myth and reality.* Philadelphia: Taylor & Francis. Offers a profile of the at-risk employee, including behavioral warning signs for the potential for violence (such as attendance records, job performance problems, and verbal and nonverbal cues). Suggests courses of action for the organization including referral for psychological evaluation, legal action, and the development and implementation of corporate anti-violence policies.

Schwenk, C. R., & Rhodes, S. L. (Eds.) (1999). *Marijuana and the workplace*. Westport, CT: Quorum. Reviews research on the effects of marijuana use on job performance and behavior in the workplace. Covers issues such as motivation, attention, learning and memory, and psychomotor skills as well as violent behavior, socially deviant behavior, and criminal conduct.

Chapter 12

Stress in the Workplace

TREATING STRESS IN THE WORKPLACE

We have seen several ways in which work can be harmful to your health. Accidents and violence on the job and exposure to noxious chemicals in factories and sealed office buildings account for substantial numbers of injuries and deaths every year. Another danger—**stress**—affects millions of employees, but it operates in more silent and subtle ways. Whereas poorly designed chairs or toxic fumes are physical agents that affect health, productivity, and morale, stress is a psychological agent that influences physical and emotional well-being and our ability to perform our jobs.

Stress Physiological and psychological responses to excessive and usually unpleasant stimulation and to threatening events in the environment.

Stress-related diseases are widespread among employees throughout the world. A national survey conducted by a life insurance company found that nearly half of all employed adults considered their jobs to be extremely stressful. One of every three Americans has seriously considered quitting his or her job because of stress.

As many as half of all visits to physicians are precipitated by stress. Further, a major share of physical complaints may be psychosomatic—that is, actual physical

With portable electronic equipment, employees are always connected to their office. The constant job-induced stress may reduce efficiency and lead to physical complaints.

Newsbreak   War Reporters

It has long been known that military forces in combat experience high levels of stress, both during wartime and for a long time after. But what about the war reporters we see on television, the men and women in flak jackets and helmets who brave combat conditions to bring the war home to the rest of us? According to Dr. Anthony Feinstein, a psychiatrist at the University of Toronto, war correspondents also experience high levels of stress. Feinstein studied 140 reporters from six major news organizations who had covered combat in several wars. When he compared them with 107 other journalists from the same organizations who had never covered war situations, he found striking differences between the two groups.

War reporters had been severely traumatized by the events they had witnessed, often to a degree that impaired their normal functioning. They showed substantially higher rates of serious depression and post-traumatic stress disorder (PTSD) than those who had not reported from war zones. The PTSD often persisted for years. The war reporters also exhibited a wide range of social and emotional problems with symptoms including flashbacks, recurring nightmares, irritability, and difficulty concentrating. Also, they were frequently unable to adjust to civilian society back home. They were reluctant to spend time with old friends, unless they had shared similar experiences, and had difficulty maintaining personal relationships. Some sought solace in alcohol.

Nevertheless, the war reporters in this study claimed to know little about PTSD and did not recognize their symptoms as typical of stress. They were aware that something was wrong and that they were deeply troubled but remained, as the researcher described it, "surprisingly unaware of what afflicted them."

Sources: A. Feinstein (2002). A hazardous profession: War, journalists, and psychopathology. *American Journal of Psychiatry, 159*(9), 1570–1579; A. Goode, War horrors take a toll on reporters at the front. *New York Times*, September 17, 2002.

disorders caused by or related to emotional factors such as stress on the job. Physical problems associated with stress include high blood pressure (hypertension), ulcers, colitis, heart disease, arthritis, skin diseases, allergies, headaches, neck and lower back pain, and cancer. Stress has been linked to an increase in infectious diseases and may be implicated in disorders that involve suppression of the immune system.

Stress in the workplace is also costly to employers, as reflected in lower productivity, reduced motivation, and increased errors and accidents. High stress is related to increases in turnover intentions and counterproductive behavior, such as theft and drug and alcohol abuse. Job stress contributes to spiraling health care costs. The estimated expenditures for only two stress-related conditions—heart disease and ulcers—is approximately $45 billion a year, which makes stress more costly for organizations than accidents. For every worker killed in a job-related accident, at least 50 suffer some form of heart disease. Research on more than 960,000 workers in the United States and in Sweden reported that employees in high-stress jobs had a rate of heart disease four times greater than did employees in low-stress jobs.

A survey of more than one million workers in Britain found that more than half of them reported physical health problems that resulted from the stress of unusually long working hours. British psychologists report that job stress accounts for 60 percent of all workplace accidents in that country (Cartwright, 2000).

Other research shows that employees who report the greatest amount of job stress cost their employers significantly more in health care benefits than employees who report experiencing little stress on the job. A survey of 14 university employees who completed daily Internet diary accounts of stressful events over the course of one semester showed that the job stress increased over the period of the study. Individual sources of job stress remained relatively minor over time, but as these stressful events accumulated, the overall effect became more severe. And as stress levels increased, job satisfaction and morale decreased (Fuller, et al., 2003).

Stress affects employees at all levels and types of jobs. It is unlikely that you can avoid the consequences of stress during your career, any more than you can avoid them in college. Some level of stress will probably affect the quality of your working life and, in turn, other aspects of your daily living.

OCCUPATIONAL HEALTH PSYCHOLOGY

Continuing problems of workplace stress led to a field of study called **occupational health psychology.** This concern for occupational health and employee well-being can be traced to the early years of industrial psychology practice. The German psychologist, Hugo Münsterberg, who taught at Harvard University, helped found the field of industrial psychology. Among the issues he considered were accidents and worker safety. During World War I (1914–1918), the British government established the Industrial Fatigue Research Board to study problems of inefficiency and fatigue in manual laborers. Since then, a great deal of research has been conducted on all aspects of employee health.

In 1990 psychologist Jonathan Raymond proposed the term *occupational health psychology* for this field. The Academy of Management formed the Health and Well-Being Focus Group in its Organizational Behavior division. Similarly, the American Psychological Association and the National Institute for Occupational Safety and Health (NIOSH) launched programs to support the formal development of the field of occupational health psychology. International conferences were convened, graduate school programs established at major universities, and publication of the *Journal of Occupational Health Psychology* was begun.

The goal of occupational health psychology, is to understand and combat the harmful effects of stress on employee health and safety. Much of the research discussed in this chapter is an outgrowth of this effort. For more information on occupational health psychology, visit the NIOSH Web site at www.cdc.gov/niosh/ohp.html-27k. For general information on stress, see www.stress.org (the American Institute of Stress) and www.workhealth.org (the Job Stress Network home page of the Center for Social Epidemiology).

Occupational health psychology The field of study dealing with the health effects of job stress and other aspects of employee well-being.

PHYSIOLOGICAL EFFECTS OF STRESS

Some of us feel stress every time we take an exam. People undergo stress when a car runs a stop sign and almost hits them or when a shadowy figure chases them down a dark street. When something like that happens, we become anxious, tense, and fearful. Stress involves physiological and psychological responses to excessive and usually unpleasant stimulation and to threatening events in the environment.

Dramatic physiological changes occur during stress. Adrenaline, released from the adrenal glands, speeds up all bodily functions. Blood pressure rises, heart rate increases, and extra sugar is released into the bloodstream. The increased blood circulation brings additional energy to the brain and muscles, making the person stronger and more alert to cope with the threat. A stressful situation mobilizes and directs one's energy, boosting it beyond its normal level. With the excess energy of this so-called fight-or-flight response, an organism (human or other animal) will either fight the source of the stress (perhaps an attacker or a predator) or flee from it.

Most of the research conducted on the fight-or-flight phenomenon has been conducted on male subjects. Only recently have enough data been compiled on female subjects to note that they respond differently to stress. Researchers characterize women's response to stress as "tend-and-befriend." *Tending* involves nurturing activities designed to protect themselves and their offspring from the stress; *befriending* refers to the development of social groups or networks that also help defend against stress (Taylor, et al., 2000). And although behavioral responses to stress may vary by gender, the physiological changes induced by stress (noted in the previous paragraph) are experienced by both men and women.

Most of us will not encounter extreme emergency situations, and few jobs expose people to threatening events such as those faced by police, firefighters, or soldiers in combat. For the majority of us, the stresses we face on the job are psychological or emotional in nature, such as an argument with the boss, the belief that we have been treated unfairly, or concern about a promotion. These constitute what we commonly refer to as hassles or insults of everyday life. Individually, they are low-level sources of stress, but they are hard on the body because they accumulate. Each stress adds to the previous one and can tax the body's energy reserves because of the physiological changes it produces. If stressors are frequently found in the workplace, the body remains in a state of high physiological arousal and alertness for long periods, a condition that can lead to physiological damage as well as psychosomatic illnesses.

Psychosomatic disorders are not imaginary; they involve specific tissue and organ damage. Although their origin lies in psychological and emotional factors, they have a definite physical impact on the body. Further, the illnesses brought about by stress can serve as new sources of stress. When physical health has declined, resistance has been lowered, and bodily energy has been reduced. As a result, motivation and job performance are bound to suffer. A large-scale meta-analysis of more than 300 research articles dealing with stress found that chronic stressors such as worry over losing one's job, or the fear of unemployment, can suppress the body's immune system. This leaves the individual more vulnerable to disease with fewer physiological resources with which to combat it (Segerstrom & Miller, 2004).

It is important to note that not all employees are affected by stress in the same way. Consider air traffic controllers, who have one of industry's most stressful jobs. Hour after hour they must exercise constant vigilance, tracking aircraft at various speeds and altitudes converging on or departing from the same point. Their work is hectic, difficult, and demanding, with the additional burden of being responsible for thousands of lives throughout each workday. Research on the physiological functioning of air traffic controllers shows that their bodies reflect the pressures of the job. As the number of aircraft in their sector increases, coronary arteries become more constricted and blood pressure rises. The incidence of hypertension among air traffic controllers is three times higher than normal for their age group.

This would appear to be a classic example of the deadly effects of stress. We would guess that the rate of heart attacks, strokes, and other stress-related disabilities is many times higher among air traffic controllers than among the rest of the population. But research indicates that this is not so. On some measures, air traffic controllers are healthier than the general population. Although some air traffic controllers show a pattern of disease and early death, others are apparently unaffected.

Job Satisfaction and Feelings of Control

What makes the difference? Why don't the job pressures affect them all in the same way? The difference seems to lie in the level of job satisfaction controllers get from their work. Those who report being very satisfied with their jobs suffer fewer harmful effects of stress. Those who are very dissatisfied with their jobs show many more stress-related effects.

A study of 1,886 business managers in the United States identified two kinds of daily work stress (Cavanaugh, Boswell, Roehling, & Boudreau, 2000):

1. *Challenge-related stress,* which includes time pressure and a high level of responsibility that lead to feelings of fulfillment and achievement.
2. *Hindrance-related stress,* which includes excessive job demands and constraints (such as red tape, poor support from higher management, and job insecurity) that interfere with achieving goals.

Thus, not all stress is considered harmful. Challenge-related stress is motivating and positively related to job satisfaction. Hindrance-related stress is associated with frustration and low job satisfaction.

High job satisfaction contributes to health and longevity. Although both types of stress noted above cause similar physiological changes, only hindrance-related stress was shown to lead to detrimental health effects. This accounts for the fact that some people in high-stress jobs, such as air traffic controllers, maintain generally good health.

Consider another high-stress occupation—that of corporate executive. It is widely assumed that executives experience enormous job stress and consequently have a higher rate of heart attacks than does the general population. Research does not support this position. High-level executives have 40 percent fewer heart attacks than do middle-level managers, who are popularly assumed to work under less stressful conditions.

The primary reason top executives are relatively less affected by job stress is that they have more autonomy and control over their work than do middle-level managers. Research has shown that being able to control workplace events can significantly reduce perceived job stress. People with low levels of job control are far more likely to develop heart disease than are those with greater control over the demands and responsibilities of their job.

Research on 97 government employees in Britain found that reorganizing their jobs to give them more choice and control over their work tasks resulted in significant improvements in their self-reported mental health, job performance, and absence rates for illness over a one-year period (Bond & Bunce, 2001). A study of 118 policemen in Singapore revealed that measures of heart rate and blood pressure, taken every 30 minutes on the job, rose significantly in situations in which they had low control (Bishop, et al., 2003).

INDIVIDUAL DIFFERENCES IN STRESS RESPONSES

If we are to examine thoroughly the causes of stress on the job, then we must take account of personal factors that can render employees vulnerable to stress. Not all stressors at work affect people the same way. A source of stress that can ruin the health of one worker may have no noticeable effect on that of a colleague.

We have mentioned two factors that may reduce a person's susceptibility to stress: high job satisfaction and control over the conditions of one's work. Several other variables have been related to our vulnerability to the effects of stress. One factor involved in coping with stress is social support, our network of family and social ties. The person who lives alone or is emotionally alienated from others is more likely to be sensitive to stress than is someone who has strong ties to family, friends, and colleagues. Family support can help compensate for negative feelings about one's job and can enhance self-esteem, acceptance, and worth. Social support on the job, such as a cohesive work group or a good relationship with one's boss, can also reduce the effects of stress. This was demonstrated in a study of 61 nurses and 32 accountants in Britain. Low social support from colleagues and supervisors at work was linked to elevated heart rate not only during the workday, but also during the evening hours after the work period had ended (Evans & Steptoe, 2003).

Thus, a lack of social support can increase the risk of heart disease. In general, the lower the level of available social support, the greater the health risks. Variations in social support over the course of the workday have been found to affect blood pressure. Studies of men and women in various occupations showed that blood pressure rose when social support was low and dropped when social support was high.

General physical health is related to susceptibility to stress. People in better physical condition suffer fewer harmful effects from a stressful work environment than do people in poorer physical condition. Physical exercise is a good way to improve general well-being. Many companies provide exercise facilities to help employees alleviate stress.

Our level of ability to perform our jobs can make us more or less resistant to stress. Employees with high skill levels usually find their work less stressful than do employees with lower skill levels. You may have noticed this effect in your college classmates. Students who are barely able to keep up with the course work are usually more anxious about exams than are students who have less difficulty mastering the required material.

Newsbreak   Perils of the Road Warrior

Have you been in an airport lately? Then you know how stressful air travel has become—long lines at the security checkpoints, flight delays, cancelled departures, cramped aisles and seats. And if you think it's stressful taking a flight every now and then for vacation or to go home for the holidays, what must it be like for employees whose jobs require that they travel frequently? Some employees make more than 100 business trips a year, often covering several cities in a week's time: a meeting in New York on Monday, a Denver conference on Tuesday, a presentation in Germany on Wednesday. Sound glamorous? Maybe if you have your own corporate jet, but for most business travelers who don't have that perk, travel is a drudge.

A survey of frequent business travelers conducted by Hyatt hotels found that one of every three employees said they would like to stop traveling, but they were sure it would hurt their careers. More than half said that in the future they would turn down a job that required so much travel. Those with families were particularly inconvenienced. They carried the additional burden of guilt for being away from home and missing so many of their children's activities.

Other surveys show that flight delays are a source of stress for up to 50 percent of all business travelers. Long waits for baggage are an annoyance for 30 percent. Questionnaires completed by Hilton hotels customers indicated that more than half did not sleep well, despite the luxurious and well-equipped accommodations.

An additional problem for business travelers is becoming ill while away from home. A study of international business travelers conducted by Coca-Cola reported that diarrhea is the most common health complaint, followed by colds and other respiratory ailments linked by the poor air quality on airplanes. Half of all business travelers admitted to overeating while on the road, and one-fourth said they drank more than usual. The World Bank noted that their employees who travel frequently account for 80 percent more of the organization's medical claims than their employees who do not travel. Frequent travelers are also three times as likely to seek psychological help for anxiety and acute stress reactions as are employees who rarely travel. Even spouses of frequent business travelers develop problems. Their rate of insurance claims for psychological disorders is twice as high as for spouses of nontravelers.

Clearly, it's not easy being a road warrior. The excitement may not be all you imagined.

Sources: R. S. DeFrank, R. Knonpaske, & J. M. Ivancevich (2000). Executive travel stress: Perils of the road warrior. *Academy of Management Executive, 14*(2), 58–71; J. Sharkey, Business travel. *New York Times*, January 12, 2000; A. Tugend. All stressed out and everywhere to go. *New York Times*, May 25, 2004.

being able to control their workplac

The Type A Personality

Type A/Type B personalities Personality patterns related to one's ability to tolerate stress; Type A persons have been associated with heart disease, anger, hostility, time urgency, and depression; Type B persons may work as hard as Type As but show fewer stress effects.

Personality factors have been related to our tolerance of stress. This relationship is particularly apparent with **Type A** and **Type B personalities** and their differential susceptibility to heart disease, which, as we noted, is a major consequence of stress (Friedman & Rosenman, 1974). Although specific physical factors such as smoking, obesity, and lack of exercise are implicated in heart disease, they may account for no more than 25 percent of the cases. The rest may be linked to aspects of the Type A personality pattern. In contrast, Type Bs rarely have heart attacks before the age of 70, regardless of the nature of their jobs or their personal habits.

Two primary characteristics of the Type A personality are a high competitive drive and a constant sense of time urgency. Type As are described as intensely ambitious and aggressive, always striving to achieve, racing against the clock, rushing from one self-imposed deadline to another. They are attracted to high-stress, fast-paced, competitive, and demanding jobs. A study of 175 hospital workers and 110 employees of a telecommunications company in Canada confirmed the relationship between Type A behavior and high job stress as well as physical health problems (Jamal & Baba, 2003).

Type As are thought to be in a continual state of tension, perpetually under stress. Even when their work environment is relatively free of stressors, they carry their own stress as a fundamental part of their personality. Type As also tend to be extraverted and high in self-esteem. They show a high level of job involvement and score high in the needs for achievement and power. Table 12–1 shows some typical Type A behaviors.

Type B personalities may be just as ambitious as Type As, but they have few of the other characteristics. Type Bs experience less stress at work and at leisure. They may work as hard and in equally stressful environments, but they suffer fewer harmful effects. These two personality types respond differently to prolonged stress over which they have little control. For example, Type As will struggle to master a difficult situation, but if they are not successful, they will become frustrated and give up. Type Bs in a similar situation will try to function as effectively as possible and will not give up.

The early research on the Type A and Type B personality dimensions, conducted in the 1960s and 1970s, described a clear link between Type A behavior and coronary heart disease. More recent research has not found that relationship to be so consistent, although few psychologists are willing to state that there is no relationship at all. For example, a meta-analysis of 87 studies reported a modest relationship between Type A behavior and heart disease but a stronger relationship between heart disease and the emotions of anger, hostility, and depression. These researchers concluded that the coronary-prone personality may be someone who also has negative emotions such as anger and anxiety in addition to the personality characteristics noted above (Booth-Kewley & Friedman, 1987).

The Hardiness Factor

Hardiness A personality variable that may explain individual differences in vulnerability to stress. So-called hardy persons believe they can control the events in their lives and thus may be more resistant to stress.

Another personality variable that may account for individual differences in vulnerability to stress is **hardiness.** People characterized as being high in hardiness have attitudes that may make them more resistant to stress. Hardy people believe they can control or influence the events in their lives. They are deeply

TABLE 12–1

Are You a Type A Person?

Do you

_____   always do everything very rapidly? *Type A people eat, move, walk, and talk at a brisk pace. They speak with emphasis on certain words, and the ends of their sentences are spoken much faster than the beginnings.*

_____   become extremely impatient with the speed at which things are accomplished? *Type A people continually say "yes, yes" or "uh-huh" to whomever is talking to them, and even finish other persons' sentences for them. They become outraged by a slow car ahead of them or a slow-moving line in a restaurant or theater. When they read, they skim the material quickly and prefer summaries or condensations of books.*

_____   always think about or try to do two or more things at the same time? *For example, Type A people may think about one thing while talking to someone about something else, or they may try to eat and drive at the same time, in an effort to get more accomplished in a given period of time.*

_____   feel guilty when you are on vacation or trying to relax for a few hours?

_____   fail to be aware of interesting or beautiful things? *Type A people do not notice a lovely sunset or the new flowers of spring. If asked, they cannot recall the furnishings or details of an office or home they just visited.*

_____   always try to schedule more events and activities than you can properly attend to? *This is another manifestation of the sense of time urgency Type A people feel.*

_____   have nervous gestures or tics such as clenching your fists or banging on a desk to emphasize a point you are making? *These gestures point to the continuing tension at the root of the Type A personality.*

_____   consistently evaluate your worth in quantitative terms? *For Type A persons, numbers alone define their sense of accomplishment and importance. Type A executives boast about their salary or their company's profits. Type A surgeons tell how many operations they have performed, and Type A students report how many A's they have received in school. These people focus on the quantitative rather than the qualitative aspects of life.*

committed to their work and to other activities of interest, and they view change as exciting and challenging rather than threatening.

Hardiness can be assessed by a 20-item scale designed to measure three components: control, commitment, and challenge (Kobasa, 1979, 1982). Research has shown that hardy persons develop fewer physical complaints under highly stressful conditions than do persons who are not hardy. For example, among a group of 88 adults who lost their jobs, considered to be a highly stressful life event, those who scored higher in hardiness used a variety of coping techniques,

People high on the personality variable of hardiness may be more resistant to stress. They are committed to their work, believe they can control events in their lives, and view change as exciting and challenging.

such as problem solving and positive reappraisals of their employment options, to a greater extent than did those who scored low in hardiness (Crowley, Hayslip, & Hobdy, 2003).

Thus, hardiness may moderate the effects of stress through the way people evaluate and interpret the experiences and events in their lives.

Self-Efficacy

Self-efficacy refers to the belief in one's ability to accomplish a task. It is the sense of how adequate, efficient, and competent we feel about coping with life's demands. People who are high in self-efficacy are less bothered by stress than are people who are low in self-efficacy. For example, a study of 2,293 U.S. Army soldiers subjected them to both psychological and physical stress associated with overly long workdays and unusual physical demands. Soldiers who scored high in self-efficacy reacted more positively to work stressors than did soldiers who scored low (Jex, Bliese, Buzzell, & Primeau, 2001).

A study of 226 U.S. bank tellers showed that employees high in self-efficacy who believed that they had a high level of control over their jobs were more resistant to psychological stress than were employees with low self-efficacy (Schaubroeck, Lam, & Xie, 2000). Even when tellers who scored low in self-efficacy had high perceived control over their jobs, they still experienced the effects of stress. Thus, the researchers concluded that the determining factor in stress tolerance was self-efficacy, a finding confirmed in a follow-up study of 217 employees of a survey research company (Schaubroeck, Jones, & Xie, 2001). For more information on self-efficacy research, see www.emory.edu/education/mfp/effpage.html-101k.

Locus of control One's belief about the source of one's rewards. People with an internal locus of control believe that job performance, pay, and promotion are under their control and dependent on their own behavior. People with an external locus of control believe such events depend on outside forces such as luck.

Locus of Control

The personality variable of internal versus external **locus of control** influences a person's reaction to stress. People who rate high on internal control believe that

Newsbreak

At Wendy's, Every Second Counts

"Hi! May I take your order, please?" Try again. "HimayItakeyourorder-please." Talk about stress! Say it fast, as fast as you can, over and over, several hundred times a day. Your boss is holding a stopwatch to make sure you're not speaking too slowly. That's what's happening at Wendy's, the fast-food chain striving to become the fastest in the world.

"Every second is business lost," explained a Wendy's manager, eyeing the clock. He was pleased. His store had knocked eight seconds off the average takeout delivery time. A survey of 25 fast-food restaurants found that customers' cars idled an average of 203.6 seconds from the instant they arrived at the menu board until they left the pickup window with their food. At Wendy's they cut that average down to 150.3 seconds, which put them 16.7 seconds ahead of McDonald's and 21 seconds ahead of Burger King.

But that's still not fast enough. For every six seconds saved at the drive-through, sales rise by 1 percent. A store that can increase its drive-through efficiency by 10 percent stands to grow its sales more than $50,000 a year.

If the timer beeps before you've finished your task, you know you're falling behind. If you can't take an order, make change, and deliver the food in less than a minute, you're too damn slow. If you can't cook 300 burgers in less than seven seconds each, you should get out of the kitchen. Every second counts, and the boss is counting.

Source: Faster food. *St. Petersburg (FL) Times,* May 19, 2000.

they can influence the forces and events that shape their lives. People who rate high on external control believe that life is determined by other people and by outside events and forces such as luck or chance. A study of 361 nurses in Germany found that those who scored high in external locus of control reported experiencing higher levels of stress and burnout on the job than those who scored high in internal locus of control (Schmitz, Neumann, & Oppermann, 2000).

Self-Esteem

Self-esteem, which is similar to self-efficacy, refers to how we feel about ourselves. In the workplace this concept is referred to as **organization-based self-esteem** (OBSE). People high in OBSE have a high sense of personal adequacy and see themselves as important, effective, and worthwhile members of their organizations. Research shows that people low in OBSE are more affected by job stress than people high in OBSE. Workers low in OBSE are likely to be more susceptible to the effects of role conflict (a major workplace stressor) and to poor support from their supervisors. Low OBSE workers also tend to be more passive in coping with stress.

Negative Affectivity

Another personality characteristic that may influence our vulnerability to stress is **negative affectivity,** which is closely related to neuroticism, one of the

Organization-based self-esteem A personality dimension relating to our assessment of our adequacy and worth with regard to our place in the employing organization.

Negative affectivity A personality dimension characterized by a generalized life and job dissatisfaction and by a focus on negative aspects of life events.

Construction work can be stressful not only because of physical hazards but also because of external factors such as completion deadlines.

so-called Big Five personality dimensions. People who measure high in negative affectivity are likely to experience distress and dissatisfaction in all areas of life, not just on the job. They focus on the negative aspects of their experiences and dwell on their failures, weaknesses, and shortcomings. Although some research has found that people high in negative affectivity are likely to show high levels of stress, as measured by self-report inventories, other studies have failed to confirm any such effect (Spector, Chen, & O'Connell, 2000). Clearly, more research is needed.

Type of Occupation

Stress levels differ as a function of occupation. NIOSH ranked 130 jobs in terms of the level of stress they engender. The jobs with the highest stress levels include laborer, secretary, clinical laboratory technician, nurse, first-line supervisor, restaurant server, machine operator, farm worker, and miner. Other stressful occupations are police officer, firefighter, computer programmer, dental technician, electrician, plumber, social worker, telephone operator, and city bus driver. One of the least stressful jobs is college professor. In general, clerical and blue-collar workers suffer more stress than do managerial and professional employees, largely because they have less opportunity to make decisions about their work and less control over working conditions.

Sex Differences

Women consistently report higher levels of job stress than men do. Research has shown that women employees report headaches, anxiety, depression, sleep disturbances, and eating disorders more frequently than men employees do. Women also report more smoking and alcohol and drug use in response to workplace stress. Women in highly stressful jobs are more likely to experience spontaneous abortion and shorter menstrual cycles than are women in less stressful jobs. On the positive side, women are far more likely than men are to take advantage of social support networks to help them cope with stress (Nelson & Burke, 2000). Women homemakers also experience high levels of stress. The demands of family and the roles of wife and mother can lead to overwork, to dissatisfaction and a sense of loss of control, and to conflict with the need to seek employment outside the home. Many women homemakers report feeling depressed, believing that more demands are placed on them than on women with paying jobs.

WORK-FAMILY CONFLICTS

Both men and women report conflicts between the demands of family and the demands of the job, but the difficulties are usually greater for women. Work-family conflict has been documented among workers in many countries (see, for example, Yang, Chen, Choi, & Zou, 2000). However, the intensity of that conflict may vary from one culture to another. This was demonstrated in a large-scale study of 2,487 managers from 15 countries. Western, or Anglo, cultures included the United States, Canada, Australia, England, and New Zealand. Eastern cultures included Hong Kong, Taiwan, and China. Latin cultures included Argentina, Brazil, Colombia, Ecuador, Mexico, Peru, and Uruguay.

The results showed that in the Western, more individualistic, cultures, there was a greater relationship between the number of hours worked and the strength of the work-family conflict than among managers in more collectivist Eastern and Latin cultures. The researchers suggested that "Anglos view working extra hours as taking away from their families, which may provoke feelings of guilt and greater levels of work-family pressure." Employees

Both men and women employees report conflicts between the demands of family life and the demands of the job, but the difficulties are usually greater for women.

Newsbreak   It Gets Worse after Work

Susan R. is a manager at AT&T in Basking Ridge, New Jersey, and she is a daily victim of stress caused by work overload, both on and off the job. When she leaves her office at five o'clock, the workday is far from over. For many women like Susan, the most difficult part of the day is just beginning.

She must leave precisely at five, not a minute later, even if she's in the middle of a meeting. "It's a frantic rush to get out of the office," she said. "It's so stressful." What's her hurry? She has to pick up her four-year-old son from his day-care center then drive across town at the height of rush-hour traffic to collect her seven-year-old daughter from her after-school program. If she's not on time, she'll be met by a fretting child and a harried teacher (who's probably late picking up her own kids), and then she will be docked for a late fee.

A quick stop at the grocery store to buy food for dinner and she dashes home to let the dog out, prepare the meal, referee fights between the children, pay attention to her husband (who doesn't do much to help), supervise the children's homework, do the laundry, and so it goes. . . .

By the time she's gotten the kids to bed, Susan has put in more than a 12-hour workday. No wonder she's exhausted and stressed out. And she's not alone. Even for wives whose husbands share more of the child-care and household duties, the primary responsibility still falls on the woman. And if she's a single working mom, it can be worse.

How do they do it all? Where do they find the time and energy? "They steal it from themselves," said a sociologist who studied the lives of 300 mothers who had jobs outside the home. In order to spend time with their children, these women cut down on sleep and on their own free time. Today, working mothers sleep nearly six hours less per week and have 12 fewer hours for their own activities than do mothers who do not have outside jobs. "There's no time for hobbies or socializing," one woman said. "I can't tell you the last time I went out."

Having it all—a family and a job—can lead to a lot of stress along the way.

Sources: A. L. Kelly. For employed moms, the pinnacle of stress comes after work ends. *New York Times*, June 13, 1999; Working moms don't shirk time with kids. *St. Petersburg (FL) Times*, March 28, 2000.

in the other cultures were more accepting of the necessity of working longer hours because, in general, earning a living was more difficult (Spector, et al., 2004, p. 135).

The stressors associated with work-family conflict are apparently independent of type of job and working conditions, and they affect managerial as well as non-managerial employees. Today, in the United States, more than 60 percent of all women with children six years of age or younger are employed outside the home.

These working women are essentially holding two full-time jobs: one in the office, shop, or factory and the other at home. Spouses may help out, but the primary responsibility for family life remains with women. It is typically the woman worker who is called when a child becomes ill or who must adjust her work schedule when an elderly parent needs care.

A survey of 513 workers at a Fortune 500 company in the United States also found that the greater the number of hours worked, the higher the reported feeling that work was interfering with family life, and the higher the levels of reported stress. Employees who worked longer hours identified strongly with their careers. They believed that they had insufficient time each day to accomplish all of their work and that their bosses expected them to put in extra hours (Major, Klein, & Ehrart, 2002).

As you might expect, women are reported to be more affected than men by work-family conflicts, primarily because so many women come home from work to their second job—caring for their children and spouse and managing their household. A study of 623 men and women employed outside the home found that women devoted an average of seven more hours each week to their families than men did. In addition, the men averaged two hours a week more personal free time than the women did (Rothbard & Edwards, 2003).

However, despite this gender gap in work-family relationships, in general, women with paying jobs outside the home enjoy better health than full-time homemakers. Employed women score higher on measures of psychological well-being and have a lower risk of cardiovascular illness. The psychological and physical health advantages for employed women are greatest for women in high-status careers (Nelson & Burke, 2000).

Organizational Solutions for Work-Family Conflicts

As research continues on work-family conflicts, and as the data showing potentially harmful effects accumulate, organizations have instituted measures to deal with these effects. For example, providing day-care facilities at the workplace can relieve some of the concerns of employees with young children. Other approaches include flexible work scheduling, supportive supervision, telecommuting, and opportunities for part-time work.

Research has shown that flexible work scheduling and supportive supervision are highly effective ways in which organizations can help reduce work-family conflicts among employees. Both supportive bosses and flexible working hours lead to increases in employee perceptions of having some personal control over their work and family demands. These feelings of greater control lead, in turn, to lower levels of conflict and stress, and higher job satisfaction.

Another source of organizational support involves maternity or paternity leave. The 1993 U.S. Family and Medical Leave Act provides up to 12 weeks of parental leave. There is some evidence, however, that women in high-paying, high-status professional and managerial jobs are penalized for taking too much parental leave. Extended time off has been associated with fewer subsequent promotions, smaller pay increases, and lower performance evaluations.

Organizations that try to assist their employees in reducing work-family conflicts may benefit financially from these initiatives. A study of 231 Fortune 500 companies found that those that offered programs to reduce work-family conflict had higher stock prices and thus a higher shareholder return compared to companies that did not offer such benefits (Arthur, 2003). However, the higher share price may have resulted from the publicity given those organizations that offered such benefits, or it may have been related to other factors. As we noted in Chapter 2, correlation does not necessarily imply causation.

CAUSES OF STRESS IN THE WORKPLACE

Many aspects of the work environment can induce stress. Some of these are work overload, work underload, organizational change, role conflict, and role ambiguity.

Work Overload and Work Underload

Work overload Too much work to perform in the time available or work that is too difficult for the employee to perform.

Psychologists use the term **work overload** to describe the common condition of overwork. They have identified two types: quantitative overload and qualitative overload.

Quantitative overload is the condition of having too much work to do in the time available. It is an obvious source of stress and has been linked to stress-related ailments such as coronary heart disease. The key factor seems to be the degree of control workers have over the rate at which they work rather than the amount of work itself. In general, the less control employees have over their work pace, the greater the stress. *Qualitative* overload involves work that is too difficult. Having insufficient ability to perform a job is stressful. Even employees with considerable ability can find themselves in situations in which they cannot cope with the job's demands.

A study of 94 employees of an accounting firm in Britain showed that work overload was directly linked to self-reported psychological stress, burnout, and the belief that work was interfering with family life (Harvey, Kelloway, & Duncan-Leiper, 2003). Questionnaire surveys of 241 workers in Canada showed that those who felt they had job demands that were significantly higher than those of other workers performed less physical exercise than those who felt they had lower job demands (Payne, Jones, & Harris, 2002). The combination of high job demands and little exercise is consistent with the relationship mentioned above between work-related stress and coronary heart disease.

Work underload Work that is too simple or insufficiently challenging for one's abilities.

The opposite condition, **work underload**—having work that is too simple or is insufficient to fill one's time or challenge one's abilities—is also stressful. A study of 63 musicians in a symphony orchestra found that they sometimes faced both overload and underload—overload when the job tasks were too difficult and underload when the tasks did not make full use of the musicians' skills (Parasuraman & Purohit, 2000). Other research relates work underload to increased boredom and monotony (also a factor in stress) and to reduced job satisfaction.

Thus, an absence of challenge in the workplace is not necessarily beneficial. A certain level of job stress can be stimulating, invigorating, and desirable. Our goal should be to find the optimum level under which we can function and remain in good health and to avoid the extremes of work overload and work underload.

Organizational Change

Another stressor is change. Employees who see change as exciting and challenging are less vulnerable to stress than are those who view change as a threat. It is the way we perceive or respond to change, rather than the change itself, that is the source of the stress. Many people resist change, preferring the familiar so that they will know what to expect.

Consider the relationship between employees and supervisors. Once that relationship has been established, assuming it is positive, all parties feel comfortable with it because each knows what to expect from the other. The situation is predictable, safe, and secure. When the supervisor leaves and employees face a new boss, they no longer know what behaviors will be tolerated, how much work will be expected, or how their job performance will be evaluated. Such changes in the work environment can be stressful. Other stressful changes include revised work procedures, required training courses, and new workplace facilities. Company mergers can lead to concerns about job security, new managers, and different organizational policies.

A stressful change for many older employees is the presence of younger workers and workers of diverse ethnic backgrounds who bring to the workplace unfamiliar attitudes, habits, and cultural values. Employee participation in decision making and other changes in the organizational culture can be stressful for higher-level managers.

Role Ambiguity and Role Conflict

An employee's role in the organization can be a source of stress. **Role ambiguity** arises when the scope and responsibilities of the job are unstructured or poorly defined. The employee is not sure what is expected or even what to do. This is particularly crucial for new employees, whose job guidelines may be unclear. Adequate orientation and socialization programs for new employees can reduce role ambiguity.

Industrial-organizational (I-O) psychologists have proposed three components of role ambiguity:

- Performance criteria ambiguity—uncertainty about the standards used to evaluate a worker's job performance.
- Work method ambiguity—uncertainty about the methods or procedures appropriate to the successful performance of the job.
- Scheduling ambiguity—uncertainty about the timing or sequencing of work.

You can readily see how for most jobs it would not be too difficult for supervisors to alleviate role ambiguity by establishing and promoting consistent standards and procedures.

Role conflict arises when a disparity exists in job requirements or between the job's demands and the employee's values and expectations. For example, when a supervisor is told to allow subordinates to participate in decision making and at the same time is pressured to increase production, the supervisor faces an obvious conflict. To meet production goals immediately may require authoritarian behavior, yet meeting participation goals requires democratic behavior.

Role ambiguity A situation that arises when job responsibilities are unstructured or poorly defined.

Role conflict A situation that arises when there is a disparity between job demands and the employee's personal standards.

When the job requires behaviors that contradict an employee's moral code, such as when a salesperson is asked to sell a product known to be inferior or dangerous, role conflict can develop. The salesperson can quit, but the threat of unemployment may be a greater stressor than the role conflict.

Other Stressors

Supervisors and managers can be major sources of stress to their subordinates. Research confirms that poor leadership behaviors—such as when supervisors fail to be supportive of their employees or refuse to allow participation in decision making—can lead to stress.

Problems of career development—such as when an employee fails to receive an anticipated promotion—may also lead to stress. If career aspirations are not satisfied, frustration can be intense. Overpromotion can be stressful when employees are advanced beyond their level of competence to positions with which they cannot cope, leading to qualitative overload. The fear of failure on the job can induce considerable stress. Performance appraisal is a source of stress. Few people like being evaluated relative to others. Also, a poor evaluation can have a significant impact on one's career.

Taking responsibility for subordinates can be a stressor for supervisors and managers. Evaluating employees for salary, promotion, or termination decisions; providing incentives and rewards; and managing their output on a daily basis can lead to stress. Managers are much more likely to report stress-related physical complaints than are employees such as accountants whose daily responsibilities do not include supervising others.

The use of computers can also be a source of stress. A study in Sweden of 25 employees between the ages of 18 and 24 showed that they had misgivings about using computers despite recognizing their advantages. They reported that computer access generally improved the quality of life but that computers also had negative stress effects related to work and information overload, and a lack of personal connection to other people. They also believed that computers demanded that they always be available to respond quickly to e-mail and to information on the Internet (Gustafsson, Dellve, Edlund, & Hagberg, 2003).

A study of computer use in Austria involved 26 people using the Internet. The researchers found that interruptions and delays in system response time during online searches produced signs of physiological stress including increased heart rate and increased emotional activity as measured by skin conductance (Trimmel, Meixner-Pendleton, & Haring, 2003).

A person otherwise free of stress on the job can be adversely affected by a boss or co-worker who is experiencing stress (a so-called stress carrier). The anxiety exhibited by one stressed employee can easily affect other people. A study of 109 women working in a variety of jobs showed that interpersonal conflicts at work were a source of stress and related to affective well-being. Interpersonal conflicts outside the workplace were perceived as not nearly so stressful (Potter, Smith, Strobel, & Zautra, 2002).

A survey of 458 workers in Britain showed that temporary employees reported lower levels of job stress than did permanent employees. The researchers suggested that the temporary contract employees were less likely to experience stressful conditions such as having to participate in decision making, and role overload or role conflict (Parker, Griffin, Sprigg, & Wall, 2002).

[handwritten: Computer-Control performer] *[handwritten checkmark]*

Assembly-line work is associated with stress because it is repetitive, monotonous, noisy, and lacks challenge and control. Other physical working conditions that are common sources of job stress are temperature extremes, poor lighting, shift work, and indoor pollution.

Computer-controlled performance monitoring can be stressful. Machine pacing of mail sorting and other repetitive keyboard tasks increases stress and is related to absenteeism, poor performance, and muscle fatigue. Automated monitoring of keystrokes and keyboard time is stressful, like having an ever-vigilant supervisor constantly looking over one's shoulder.

The September 11th Attacks

[handwritten: performance appraisal is a source of stress.]

A nationwide survey of workers in the United States conducted a few days after the terrorist attacks in New York and Washington, D.C., on September 11, 2001, found that 90 percent of those polled reported having one or more symptoms of stress. Additional research conducted in the United States and in other countries after the event showed that the stress reactions to the attacks did not necessarily persist. One online questionnaire survey of 5,860 employees taken three months later found that the most prominent reactions were fear, denial, and anger. The anger was not directed toward the terrorists but toward what the employees believed was their company's lack of attention to employees' emotional needs and personal safety. Employees reported a low post-9/11 level of trust in their organizations and in their immediate supervisors. In addition, women, people with children, and people who lived within 150 miles of the World Trade Center in New York City experienced higher reported stress reactions immediately following the tragedy than did others (Mainiero & Gibson, 2003).

A large multinational corporation was in the midst of conducting its annual employee survey at the time of the attacks, thus affording a unique opportunity to assess attitudes immediately before and after the event. More than 70,000 employees were included at locations in the United States, Western Europe, Asia, Latin America, Australia, and South America. The results showed no evidence of significant changes in employee attitudes or feelings about their jobs or organizations, or in personal stress reactions, from the period before to after the attacks. We note, however, that none of the employees in question was located in New York or Washington, D.C., where the attacks occurred (Ryan, West, & Carr, 2003).

EFFECTS OF STRESS IN THE WORKPLACE

We have noted some of the long-term health consequences of stress, those psychosomatic disorders that arise from prolonged exposure to stressful conditions. In addition, there are long-term psychological consequences, such as tension, depression, irritability, anxiety, low self-esteem, resentment, psychological fatigue, and neuroticism. Research has also linked high work-related stress to spouse abuse; child abuse; and aggressive behavior on the job, such as overt hostility and sabotage. Other effects of work stress include mass psychogenic illness, burnout, and some types of workaholism.

Mass Psychogenic Illness

Mass psychogenic illness A stress-related disorder manifested in a variety of physical symptoms that spread rapidly among a group of workers; popularly called assembly-line hysteria.

A stress-related disorder among assembly-line workers is **mass psychogenic illness,** popularly known as assembly-line hysteria. This stress-induced malady typically affects greater numbers of women than men. It strikes suddenly, spreading so quickly throughout a production facility that the line may have to be shut down.

Consider the case of an electronics plant in Ohio. One morning, an assembly-line worker complained of dizziness, nausea, muscular weakness, and difficulty breathing. Within minutes, nearly 40 employees went to the company health clinic with the same symptoms. The illness spread, and the plant had to be closed. Managers speculated that something was wrong with the air—perhaps some chemical, gas, virus, or other infectious agent. Physicians, toxicologists, and industrial hygienists were called in to investigate. They found nothing in the factory to explain the problem. The cause was determined to be mass psychogenic illness, a stress-related disorder that has no physical origin and that spreads by contagion.

On another assembly line, employees were packing frozen fish in boxes for shipping. One employee remarked about a strange odor. Suddenly, workers began to choke, experiencing dizziness, nausea, and trouble breathing. The plant was closed, and investigators were summoned to search the building. They found nothing, no toxic agent in the air, in the drinking water, or in the fish that the workers were processing. There was no apparent physical cause for the illness, yet there was no denying that the workers were physically sick.

Although there is no physical cause, such as a virus in the air-conditioning system or a contaminant in the drinking water, physical stressors in the workplace have been found to trigger the onset of mass psychogenic illness. For example, the noise, speed, poor lighting, variable temperatures, unpleasant odors, and work overload conditions common to assembly lines can lead to mass psychogenic illness. Often, pressure to increase production on the line may contribute to the phenomenon. This situation may involve considerable overtime work, which most employees are not in a position to refuse. Poor relations with supervisors can also be a factor. If management has not established formal grievance procedures or if communication and feedback between employees and management are poor, then the resulting friction will be a source of stress.

Another stressor related to mass psychogenic illness is social isolation. Employees who are unable to communicate with one another because of the noise and the rapid work pace can experience feelings of isolation and a lack of social support from co-workers. Work-family conflict, especially for women, can be a source of stress, which may help explain why more women than men fall victim to assembly-line hysteria.

Burnout

Burnout A condition of job stress that results from overwork.

The effects of job stress that result from overwork can be seen in the condition called **burnout.** Employees suffering from burnout become less energetic and less interested in their jobs. They are emotionally exhausted, apathetic, depressed, irritable, and bored. They tend to find fault with all aspects of their work environment, including co-workers, and react negatively to the suggestions of others. The quality of their work deteriorates but not necessarily the quantity.

Employees suffering from burnout tend to become rigid about their work, following rules and procedures compulsively because they are too exhausted to be flexible or to consider alternative approaches. In time, the burned-out employee will have an impact on the emotional health and efficiency of co-workers and subordinates. Advanced burnout is characterized by even lower energy, self-esteem, self-efficacy, and job involvement, as well as an increase in physical stress symptoms, turnover, and social withdrawal at the very time social support is most needed. Deterioration in job performance becomes noticeable, and poor performance appraisals are usually the result (Cropanzano, Rupp, & Byrne, 2003; deCroon, Sluiter, Blonk, Broersen, & Frings-Dresen, 2004; VanderPloeg, Dorresteijn, & Kleber, 2003).

Three components of the burnout syndrome have been proposed (Maslach, Schaufeli, & Leiter, 2001):

1. Emotional exhaustion—the feeling of being drained and empty that is caused by excessive psychological and emotional demands, often brought about by work overload or unrealistically high expectations.
2. Depersonalization—a feeling of callousness and cynicism and a reduced sensitivity toward others.
3. Reduced sense of personal accomplishment (inefficacy)—the feeling that one's actions and efforts are wasted and worthless.

The Maslach Burnout Inventory was developed to measure this condition (Maslach & Jackson, 1986). It consists of four subscales to assess the components of emotional exhaustion, depersonalization, personal accomplishment, and a related factor called personal involvement. Studies show the test to have high reliability and validity. High scores on the burnout scale have been related to exhaustion and to work overload in various occupations.

Sample items from the Burnout Inventory include the following. Do they apply to anyone you know?

- I feel emotionally drained by my work.
- I feel used up at the end of the workday.
- I feel like I'm at the end of my rope.
- I worry that this job is hardening me emotionally.

Age is a significant predictor of burnout. Thus, burnout is an early-career phenomenon, more likely to occur among younger workers than among those over age 40. Women are no more likely than men to experience burnout, but marital status is related to the condition. Single and divorced persons have been found to be more likely than married persons to experience emotional exhaustion. Emotional exhaustion has also been related to lack of opportunity for promotion. Burnout typically strikes employees who are highly dedicated and committed to their work—those who put in overtime, take work home, or come to the office on weekends.

Other factors have been related to burnout, including feelings of time pressure, high levels of role conflict and role ambiguity, and a lack of social support from supervisors. A study of 374 workers in Germany, in industrial jobs, human service jobs (teachers and nurses), and transportation jobs (air traffic controllers), showed that excessive job demands and lack of job resources were significantly related to exhaustion and disengagement from work (Demerouti, Bakker, Nachreiner, & Schaufeli, 2001).

Another study conducted in Germany involved 591 flight attendants, travel agents, and shoe sales clerks. The results showed that dealing with customers contributed to job stress and burnout. Four customer-related social stressors were described: disproportionate customer expectations; verbally aggressive customers; hostile, humorless, or unpleasant customers; and unclear customer demands, which lead to employee role ambiguity (Dormann & Zapf, 2004).

A study of 40 managers of large companies, and 125 other employees in a variety of clerical, managerial, and professional jobs, found that burnout was negatively associated with decision-making opportunities involving one's work. Burnout (particularly the depersonalization component) was more likely to occur when employees were given little choice about participating in making decisions relating to their jobs. Thus, the less influence they believed they had over their jobs, the greater the effects of burnout (Posig & Kickul, 2003).

Several personality characteristics have been related to burnout. A study of 296 nurses in acute care hospitals demonstrated that those who scored high on the Big Five personality factor of neuroticism were far more likely to experience burnout than were those who scored low on this factor. Those high in extraversion and agreeableness were less likely to develop burnout, primarily because these qualities allowed them to engage in more interpersonal and social activities, such as talking with co-workers about their job stresses. That type of interpersonal relationship provided social support, which was not experienced by those who scored low in extraversion and agreeableness (Zellars & Perrewe, 2001). The likelihood of experiencing burnout on the job is also higher among Type A personalities and among people who score low in hardiness, high in external locus of control, or low in self-esteem.

Burnout may also vary among cultures, although the evidence to date is not definitive. Some studies suggest that average burnout levels are significantly lower in European countries than in the United States, and that employees in Japan and Taiwan may experience the highest levels of burnout. Other studies have shown that English-speaking nations have higher average burnout scores (Maslach, Schaufeli, & Leiter, 2001; Savicki, 2002).

Burnout affects people in different ways. Burnout victims may feel insecure and have unfulfilling personal lives. Because they lack self-esteem and recognition off the job, they try to find it on the job. By working hard and making significant contributions to the company, they earn esteem and tangible rewards and also prove to themselves that they are worthwhile. The price for prolonged overwork is an accumulation of stress and the depletion of the body's energy. This condition, in turn, leads to physical and psychological problems.

Workaholism or Job Engagement?

Workaholism So-called addiction to work because of anxiety and insecurity or because of a genuine liking for the job.

Employees experiencing burnout are sometimes described as **workaholics,** people who are addicted to their work. However, not all of those labeled as workaholics strive to perform well because they are driven by anxiety and insecurity. Some genuinely like their work and derive satisfaction from it. To them, work is not an unhealthy compulsion that gradually wears them down. Rather, work provides a healthy, enriching, and stimulating focus for their lives. These workaholics are happy, well-adjusted people who enjoy their jobs. They seldom take vacations because they feel no need to escape from their work. However, because of their intense sense of commitment, they can be a source of stress to others.

Psychologists estimate that 5 percent of all employees are workaholics and that the majority of these are content. These healthy workaholics are likely to have supportive families; autonomy and variety on the job; and tasks that match their levels of knowledge, skills, and abilities. Workaholics who lack these qualities tend to be discontent and dissatisfied. They are more susceptible to burnout and to the negative effects of stress. We have a distinction, then, between healthy and unhealthy workaholics. Healthy workaholics, or work enthusiasts, are highly committed to and involved with their work and derive such intense enjoyment from it that it seems inappropriate to consider them as suffering from a type of addictive behavior. I-O psychologists have proposed a new label for employees who truly love their work; they are described as being high in **job engagement** (Maslach, Schaufeli, & Leiter, 2001).

Job engagement The true enjoyment of work, characterizing people who score high in energy, involvement, and efficacy.

Job engagement is still defined in terms of the three components of burnout— emotional exhaustion, depersonalization, and inefficacy—but those people who score high in job engagement are described as high in energy, involvement, and efficacy. In addition, they are vigorous, resilient, willing to commit fully to their work, seldom fatigued, and persistent in the face of difficulties. They are enthusiastic about their work and take pride in it. Work is the center and focus of their lives, and they are both unwilling and unable to detach themselves from it. Work is the source of their satisfaction, challenge, and fulfillment.

To take an online test to determine whether you are a healthy or unhealthy workaholic, go to Workaholics Anonymous at www.workaholics-anonymous.org/. For a workaholics support group, visit www.io.com/~workanon/.

TREATING STRESS IN THE WORKPLACE

Organizational stress-management interventions include altering the organizational climate and providing treatment under employee assistance programs (EAPs). Individual techniques for dealing with stress include relaxation training, biofeedback, and behavior modification.

Organizational Techniques

Controlling the Organizational Climate. Because one of the stressors of modern organizational life is planned change, the organization should provide sufficient support to enable employees to adapt to change. Stress can be prevented or reduced by allowing employees to participate in decisions about changes in work practices and in the organizational structure. Participation helps employees accept change and allows them to express their opinions and air their complaints.

Providing Control. The belief that we can exercise some control over our work greatly reduces the effects of stress. This was demonstrated in a nationwide survey of 2,048 U.S. workers. The results showed that those who perceived fewer constraints on their job, and greater decision-making ability, reported lower levels of job stress (Ettner & Grzywacz, 2001). Organizations can improve employees' sense of control by enriching, enlarging, and expanding jobs to provide greater responsibility and decision-making authority.

Defining Employee Roles. To reduce the stress caused by role ambiguity, managers should tell subordinates clearly what is expected of them and what their job responsibilities are.

Eliminating Work Overload and Work Underload. Appropriate employee selection and training programs, equitable promotion decisions, fair distribution of work, and proper matching of job requirements with employee abilities can help eliminate the stress of work overload and work underload.

Providing Social Support. Social support networks can reduce personal vulnerability to stress effects. A study of 211 traffic police officers found that burnout was lowest among those who reported receiving the greatest support from their supervisors and their families (Baruch-Feldman, Brondolo, Ben-Dayan, & Schwartz, 2002). Organizations can enhance social support by promoting cohesive work groups and by training supervisors to show empathy and concern for subordinates.

Bringing Your Pet to Work. A growing number of companies allow their employees to bring their pets (usually dogs) to work with them. A study of 193 people who worked for employers with pet-tolerant policies found that those who brought pets to work reported lower levels of stress than those who did not bring their pets or who had no pets (Wells & Perrine, 2001).

Providing Stress-Management Programs. EAPs can include in-house counseling programs on managing stress. Evaluative research has been conducted on EAPs that teach individual stress control and inoculation techniques such as relaxation, biofeedback, and cognitive restructuring. Studies show that these programs can reduce the level of physiological arousal associated with high stress. Participants who master behavioral and cognitive stress-relief techniques report less tension, fewer sleep disturbances, and an improved ability to cope with workplace stressors.

A study of 130 employees in the Netherlands who participated in a corporate stress-management training program found significant reductions in anxiety and psychological distress, and improvements in assertiveness. These effects lasted up to six months. Social workers and other employees who received two days of training in managing stress were found to be just as effective in helping other employees reduce stress as were highly trained clinical psychologists (deJong & Emmelkamp, 2000). Obviously, using trained employees rather than clinical psychologists as instructors would greatly reduce the cost of a stress-management program.

Providing Fitness Programs. The number of organizations offering wellness or physical fitness programs to promote occupational health is now well more than 80 percent. By enhancing physical and emotional well-being, employees may become less vulnerable to the effects of stress. The focus is on counseling employees to change or modify unhealthy behaviors and to maintain a healthy lifestyle. Although such programs are sponsored by the organization, the responsibility for healthful behaviors—such as exercise, proper diet, and stopping smoking—rests with the employee.

Some corporate stress-management programs are directed toward Type A executives in the hope of reducing the incidence of coronary heart disease. Xerox estimates that the cost to the company of the loss of an executive is $600,000. Stress reduction and behavioral change techniques are considerably less expensive. Exercises to alter Type A behaviors include speaking more slowly and learning not to interrupt others when they are talking. Executives can be trained in such management practices as delegating responsibility, establishing daily goals, setting priorities, and avoiding stress-producing situations.

Individual Techniques

Some individual techniques for dealing with stress can be taught in company-sponsored EAPs or stress-reduction programs. Others can be adopted personally, such as a program of physical exercise. Exercise can increase stamina and endurance, reduce risk factors for coronary heart disease, and dissipate excess energy and tension. Many companies sponsor physical fitness programs and provide exercise facilities and running tracks at the workplace. Other individual techniques for reducing stress are relaxation training, biofeedback, and behavior modification.

Relaxation Training.   As early as the 1930s, **relaxation training** was promoted as a way to reduce stress. Patients were taught to concentrate on one part of the body after another, systematically tensing and relaxing the muscles. By focusing on the sensations produced by the relaxed state, they could achieve progressively deeper relaxation. Psychologists have proposed several refinements of this basic technique. In autogenic training, subjects learn to relax by imagining that their limbs are growing warm and heavy. In meditation, subjects concentrate on deep, regular breathing and the repetition of a phrase or sound. The relaxation-response approach combines these two techniques. The quieting reflex technique teaches subjects to achieve the relaxed state more quickly. Feedback on muscle tension can be combined with these approaches, along with self-measurement of blood pressure before and after relaxation exercises.

Relaxation training A stress-reduction technique that concentrates on relaxing one part of the body after another.

Biofeedback.   **Biofeedback** is a popular technique for dealing with stress effects. It involves the electronic measurement of physiological processes such as heart rate, blood pressure, and muscle tension. These measurements are converted into signals, such as flashing lights or beeps, which provide feedback on how a bodily process is operating.

Using the feedback, people then learn to control their internal states. For example, suppose that a light is activated on a monitor whenever your heart is beating at a relaxed rate. With practice, you can learn to keep the light on by maintaining that relaxed heart rate. Precisely how you learn to do this has not been established, but with enough practice, you can control your heart rate and soon will no longer need feedback from the light to do so.

Biofeedback can be used to control muscle tension, blood pressure, body temperature, brain waves, and stomach acid. By reducing the physiological changes that accompany stress, people can reduce the incidence of stress-related disorders.

Biofeedback A stress-reduction technique that involves electronic monitoring of physiological processes, such that people can learn to control muscle tension, blood pressure, and brain waves.

Newsbreak — Take a Vacation—But Will It Work?

Workers in the United States don't take enough time off as a way of slowing down and recharging to help avoid stress, work overload, and burnout. Europeans take much more annual vacation time than Americans do. American workers get fewer paid vacation days than French or German workers, and many American workers do not even use the days to which they are entitled. A survey conducted by Expedia, the online travel service, of 2,019 adults found that at least 30 percent gave up earned vacation time every year. On average, every full-time U.S. worker misses out on three vacation days a year. Worse, each year we tend to take less time off than we did the year before.

The Expedia survey also showed that 32 percent of the people who take vacations manage to take their work with them, checking e-mail or office voice mail regularly. They are carrying the stress of their job with them. Consequently, companies such as Radio Shack, expressing concern about employee burnout, are trying to induce employees to change their behavior by introducing what they call a "guilt-free" vacation program. Radio Shack has one simple rule: Don't call the office while you're on vacation! Other companies concerned about the problem insist that employees at all levels actually take their vacations instead of accumulating the time for extra pay.

Does it work? Is a forced vacation the best way to relieve stress and prevent burnout? Dr. Dov Eden, a management professor at Tel Aviv University in Israel, studied 76 clerical workers before and after their vacations. The results were not encouraging. The benefits from the break dissipated after only three weeks. Employees quickly returned to their prevacation levels of stress. It was as if they had never been away. Dr. James Quick, a professor of organizational behavior at the University of Texas at Arlington, discovered that the incidence of heart attacks rises on Monday mornings, when people return to work from their weekend break. He suggested that a longer vacation may bring an even greater risk. So what's the choice? Your work may be stressful, but now it appears that your vacation can also be harmful to your health!

Sources: D. Galant. Now for the hard part: It's over. *New York Times,* July 12, 2000; Bosses beg workers to get away. *St. Petersburg (FL) Times,* July 7, 2000. Yahoo Financial News, June 6, 2004 (www.biz.yahoo.com).

Behavior Modification. Behavior modification techniques are effective in rendering Type A persons less vulnerable to stress. Characteristics that can be altered by behavior modification include intense drive, self-imposed deadlines, and a high rate of activity. Behavior modification involves the conditioning of positive emotional responses to stressful events.

Summary

Occupational health psychology is concerned with the effects of stress in the workplace. Stress lowers productivity, increases absenteeism and turnover, and causes physiological changes. Prolonged stress can be a factor in the psychosomatic origins of illnesses, including heart disease, gastrointestinal distress, arthritis, skin diseases, allergies, headaches, and cancer. Factors that can reduce stress include high job satisfaction, control, high autonomy and power, social support, good health, job skills, and certain personality characteristics.

People identified as **Type A** may be more prone to heart attacks. They have a high competitive drive; a sense of time urgency; and high levels of hostility, aggression, anger, and impatience. **Type B** persons lack these characteristics and may be less vulnerable to stress effects. People high in **hardiness** (a belief that they can control life events, a commitment to work, and a view that change is stimulating) are less vulnerable to stress effects. Similarly, people high in self-efficacy, internal **locus of control**, and self-esteem, and low in negative affectivity, are less vulnerable to stress.

Causes of stress include work-family conflicts, **work overload, work underload,** organizational change, **role ambiguity, role conflict,** career development problems, supervision, contact with stress carriers, machine-paced jobs, and physical conditions of the workplace. Consequences of stress include long-term effects of psychosomatic disorders and short-term effects on health, behavior, and job performance.

Mass psychogenic illness affects more women than men and is spread quickly among co-workers. It is related to physical and psychological stressors. **Burnout** is related to prolonged overwork, feelings of time pressure, high role conflict and role ambiguity, and lack of social support. It results in lower productivity, exhaustion, irritability, rigidity, and social withdrawal. Those high in the Big Five factor of neuroticism who are Type A personalities are more likely to experience burnout. Burnout victims are sometimes considered to be **workaholics** who are compulsively driven to work hard out of insecurity and lack of fulfillment in their personal lives. Healthy workaholics, who score high in **job engagement,** derive satisfaction from work and are free of the stress effects of burnout.

Organizational techniques for coping with stress include emotional climate control, social support, redefinition of employee roles, and elimination of work overload and underload. Individual techniques include physical exercise, **relaxation training, biofeedback,** behavior modification, vacations, and quitting a highly stressful job.

Key Terms

biofeedback
burnout
hardiness
job engagement
locus of control
mass psychogenic illness
negative affectivity
occupational health psychology
organization-based self-esteem

relaxation training
role ambiguity
role conflict
stress
Type A/Type B personalities
work overload
work underload
workaholism

<table>
<tr><td>

</td><td>

1. How can you tell when you are experiencing stress? Describe some of the mental and physical characteristics.
2. Describe the history and purpose of occupational health psychology.
3. What physiological changes occur in the body in reaction to stress?
4. Explain how the cumulative effect of minor hassles and insults of everyday life can affect our health.
5. What are the major job-related factors that can prevent the harmful effects of job stress?
6. Explain why air traffic controllers and senior executives may be less affected by stress than middle-level managers?
7. Describe characteristics of the Type A and Type B personalities. Why is one type more susceptible to stress effects than the other?
8. How do the following personality characteristics account for individual differences in reactions to stress: hardiness, self-efficacy, locus of control, and negative affectivity?
9. Define the concept of organization-based self-esteem. How can it influence a person's reaction to job stress?
10. Why are work-family conflicts generally greater for women than for men?
11. In what ways do work-family conflicts differ among Western, Eastern, and Latin cultures? In your opinion, what accounts for these differences?
12. How can organizations reduce problems associated with work-family conflicts?
13. Explain the differences between qualitative work overload and quantitative work overload.
14. How can work underload be as stressful as work overload?
15. Describe how each of the following can be a source of stress: organizational change, role ambiguity, role conflict.
16. What do surveys of U.S. workers reveal about the stress effects of the terrorist attacks of September 11th?
17. Describe physical and psychological factors associated with mass psychogenic illness. In what kinds of jobs is this phenomenon most likely to occur?
18. What are the major causes and components of burnout? What personality characteristics are related to burnout?
19. Define job engagement. How does it differ from workaholism? Describe the characteristics of a person who scores high in job engagement.
20. What approaches can organizations take to treat job stress? How do you deal with the stresses in your own life?

</td></tr>
</table>

<table>
<tr><td>

</td><td>

Allen, D. (2001). *Getting things done: The art of stress-free productivity.* New York: Viking. Offers advice on decision making to minimize stress and maximize productivity. Suggests dividing tasks into categories: do it yourself, delegate it, defer action on it, or drop it.

Cooper, C. L., Dewe, P. J., & O'Driscoll, M. P. (2002). *Organizational stress: A review and critique of theory, research, and applications.* Thousand Oaks, CA: Sage. Organizes the results of hundreds of research studies to present a coherent picture of occupational stress and burnout.

</td></tr>
</table>

Maslach, C., Schaufeli, W. B., & Leiter, M. P. (2001). Job burnout. *Annual Review of Psychology, 52,* 397–422. Burnout, the prolonged response to chronic emotional and interpersonal job stressors, is described in terms of exhaustion, cynicism, and inefficacy. Describes recent research on "engagement," the antithesis of burnout, which suggests possible interventions to alleviate the burnout syndrome.

Nelson, D. L., & Burke, R. J. (2000). Women executives: Health, stress, and success. *Academy of Management Executive, 14*(2), 107–121. Explores the unique health issues of women with high-level paying jobs outside the home. Describes stressors, ways of coping, and effects on organizational effectiveness.

Nelson, D. L., & Burke, R. J. (Eds.) (2002). *Gender, work stress, and health.* Washington, D.C.: American Psychological Association. Summarizes the findings of literature reviews and empirical studies describing gender differences in coping responses to stress. Describes prevention and intervention strategies and suggests areas for additional research.

Quick, J. C., & Tetrick, L. E. (Eds.) (2003). *Handbook of occupational health psychology.* Washington, D.C.: American Psychological Association. International coverage of occupational health issues, relating stress to various psychogenic illnesses and to fatigue, burnout, family dysfunction, and job dissatisfaction.

Wright, T. A., & Cropanzano, R. (2000). The role of organizational behavior in occupational health psychology. *Journal of Occupational Health Psychology, 5,* 5–10. Introduces a special section of nine articles highlighting the effects on organizations of employee health and psychological well-being.

Part Five

Engineering Psychology

Engineering psychologists are involved in the design of comfortable, safe, and efficient workplaces. From the adjustability of office chairs and the brightness level of the data displayed on your computer monitor to the controls in your car, psychologists study many aspects of working life to make jobs less stressful and employees more productive. Chapter 13 describes the contributions of engineering psychologists to the design of tools, equipment, and work areas to ensure that these are compatible with the needs and abilities of employees.

Chapter 13

Engineering Psychology

CHAPTER OUTLINE

HISTORY AND SCOPE OF ENGINEERING PSYCHOLOGY

We have discussed various ways in which industrial-organizational (I-O) psychologists contribute to the organizational goals of increasing employee efficiency, productivity, and job satisfaction. We have seen how employees with the best abilities can be recruited and selected, trained for their jobs, and supervised and motivated effectively. We have also described techniques that can be applied to optimize the quality of work life and the conditions of the work environment. But we have mentioned only briefly a factor as influential as any of those discussed—the design of the machinery and equipment employees use to do their jobs and the workspaces in which those tasks are performed.

Tools, equipment, and work stations must be compatible with the workers who use them. We may think of this as a team operation, a person and a machine functioning together to perform a task that could not be accomplished by either working alone. If the person and the machine are to work smoothly in this person-machine system, they must be compatible so that each makes use of the strengths of the other and, where necessary, compensates for the weaknesses of the other.

Engineering psychology
The design of machines and equipment for human use, and the determination of the appropriate human behaviors for the efficient operation of the machines. The field is also called human factors, human engineering, and ergonomics.

This pairing of operator and machine is the province of **engineering psychology,** also called human factors, or human engineering. British psychologists use the term *ergonomics,* which is derived from the Greek word *ergon*, meaning "work," and *nomos*, meaning "natural laws." In conjunction with engineers, engineering psychologists apply their knowledge of psychology to the formulation of natural laws of work. Thus, engineering psychology is the science of designing or engineering machines and equipment for human use and of engineering human behavior for the efficient operation of the machines.

Until the 1940s, the design of machinery, equipment, and industrial plants was solely the responsibility of engineers. They made design decisions on the basis of mechanical, electrical, space, and size considerations. They paid little attention to the workers who would have to operate the machines. The machine was considered to be a constant factor, incapable of being changed to meet human needs. It was the employee who would have to adapt. No matter how uncomfortable, tiring, or unsafe the equipment was, the human operators—the only flexible part of the person-machine system—had to adjust, to make the best of the situation and fit themselves to the machine's requirements.

Adapting the worker to the machine was accomplished through time-and-motion study, a forerunner of engineering psychology, in which jobs were analyzed to determine how they could be simplified. Of course, this approach to designing machines while ignoring the needs of the people who operated them could not be maintained. Machines were becoming too complex, requiring levels of speed, skill, and attention that threatened to exceed human capacities to monitor and control them.

The weapons developed for use in World War II placed greater demands on human abilities, not only muscle strength but also sensing, perceiving, judging, and making split-second decisions. For example, pilots of sophisticated fighter aircraft were allowed little time to react to a dangerous situation, to determine a course of action, and to initiate the appropriate response. Radar and sonar operators also required high levels of skill. In general, the wartime equipment worked well, but mistakes were frequent. The most precise bombsight ever developed was not leading to accurate bombing. Friendly ships and aircraft were being misidentified and fired upon. Whales were mistaken for submarines. Although the machinery seemed to be functioning properly, the system—the interaction of the person and the machine—clearly was not.

It was this wartime need that spurred the development of engineering psychology, similar to the way the screening and selection needs of the army in World War I gave rise to mass psychological testing. Authorities recognized that human abilities and limitations would have to be taken into account while designing machines if the overall system was to operate efficiently. Psychologists, physiologists, and physicians soon joined engineers to design aircraft cockpits, submarine and tank crew stations, and components of military uniforms.

An example of this early work helped American pilots stay alive. At the time, there was no consistent or standard arrangement of displays and controls within the cockpits of different models of aircraft. A pilot used to one type of plane who was suddenly assigned to another would be confronted by a different set of displays and controls. The lever to raise the wheels in the new plane might be in the same place as the lever to operate the flaps in the old plane. Imagine trying to drive a car in which gas pedal and brake pedal are reversed. In an emergency you would probably step on what you thought was the brake pedal, but you would be stepping on the gas instead.

There was also no consistency in the operating characteristics of aircraft controls. Within the same cockpit, one control might be pushed upward to turn something on and another switched downward to turn something on. A number of separate controls with identical knobs were often placed close together so that a pilot whose attention was diverted would not be able to distinguish among the controls by touch alone. As these problems were recognized, they were corrected, but many pilots were killed because their machines had been designed poorly from the reference point of the pilot, whose job was to direct and control the aircraft's power.

Poor design has also led to other kinds of accidents. In 1979 a disastrous situation occurred at the nuclear power plant at Three Mile Island, Pennsylvania. The accident occurred during the night shift when the operators were less alert, but part of the problem involved a lack of attention to human needs. In the power plant's control room, instrument dials and controls had been placed too far apart. When operators detected a dangerous reading on one of the displays, valuable time was lost because the employees had to run to another part of the room to activate controls to correct the malfunction. To prevent a recurrence, the Nuclear Regulatory Commission ordered modification of nuclear power plant control rooms to consider the abilities of the human operators.

To deal with human factors in aircraft accidents, 66 percent of which can be traced to pilot error, the National Transportation Safety Board added engineering psychologists to its staff. Their job is to investigate pilot and crew fatigue, shift work schedules, health issues, stress, and equipment design, all of which can contribute to accidents.

Much human factors research has been conducted on passenger vehicles in an effort to make them safer. Variables studied include the brightness of automobile and motorcycle headlights; the position, color, and brightness of brake lights; and the layout of dashboard controls and displays. Since 1985, passenger cars driven in the United States must have a brake light mounted in the rear window. This requirement is a result of human factors research on 8,000 vehicles that showed that a high-mounted brake light reduced the incidence of rear-end collisions by 50 percent.

Engineering psychologists are studying ways to make license plates and traffic signs more legible and noticeable at night. They investigate the effects of alcohol on driver behavior and conduct research on driver reaction time—how drivers perceive and comprehend risky situations and make decisions about responding.

Another problem engineering psychologists are tackling is the effect on visibility of tinting or solar film on car windows. Research results show that the detection of objects, such as pedestrians or other cars, through the rear window while backing up is significantly reduced when that window is tinted. In some cases, a tinted window admits only half of the available light, a finding that has led many states to regulate the use of solar film for safe visibility. Older drivers are more affected by dark window tints than are younger drivers. One study found that drivers between the ages of 60 and 69 experienced a greater reduction in contrast sensitivity to light than did drivers between the ages of 20 and 29 (LaMotte, Ridder, Yeung, & DeLand, 2000).

Research by engineering psychologists has demonstrated that using cell phones while driving reduces reaction time, particularly among older drivers, and can lead to a higher accident risk among drivers of all ages. These and similar research findings are instigating state regulation of cell phone use.

Engineering psychologists contribute to the design of a variety of other products, including dental and surgical implements, cameras, toothbrushes, and bucket seats for cars. They have been involved in the redesign of the mailbags used by letter carriers. Why? Because more than 20 percent of letter carriers suffer from musculoskeletal problems such as low back pain from carrying mailbags slung over their shoulders. A mailbag with a waist-support strap, and a double bag that requires the use of both shoulders, have been shown to reduce muscle fatigue.

The most well-developed human factors programs in the United States and in several European and Asian nations are in the automobile, electronics, and food industries, as well as in the design of work stations for a variety of businesses. Some of the leading companies in applying human factors findings to their workplaces and products include General Motors, DaimlerChrysler, SAAB, Volvo, and IBM and other computer makers (see Hagg, 2003).

An analysis of the economic benefits to corporations of applying ergonomic research showed net gains between 1 and 12 percent over the cost of the human factors intervention. These financial gains almost always accrued in less than a year after incorporating human factors changes. One example is the introduction of the high-mounted brake light on automobiles, which cost the industry about $10 per car. The annual return on that modest initial investment has been approximately $434 million in lower car repair costs resulting from the 50 percent drop in rear-end collisions (Stanton & Baber, 2003).

Because the field of engineering psychology is a hybrid, it is not surprising that its practitioners have diverse backgrounds. The membership of the Human Factors and Ergonomics Society consists primarily of psychologists and engineers but also includes professionals from medicine, sociology, anthropology, computer sciences, and other behavioral and physical sciences. Over the past decade there has been a substantial increase in the number of masters-level psychologists undertaking careers in engineering psychology. The growth of the field remains dynamic, and its work extends to many types of organizations.

TIME-AND-MOTION STUDY

Time-and-motion study was an early attempt to redesign work tools and equipment and to reshape the way workers performed their jobs. It stemmed from the efforts of three pioneers who focused on ways to make physical labor more efficient.

The first systematic attempt to study the performance of specific job tasks began in 1898 when Frederick W. Taylor, the promoter of scientific management, undertook an investigation of the nature of shoveling at the request of a large U.S. steel manufacturer. Taylor observed the workers and found that they were using shovels of many sizes and shapes. As a result, the loads being lifted by each man ranged from 3½ pounds to 38 pounds. By experimenting with different loads, Taylor determined that the optimum shovel—the one with which workers were most efficient—held 21½ pounds. Lighter or heavier loads resulted in a decrease in total daily output. Taylor introduced shovels of different sizes for handling different materials—for example, a small one for heavy iron ore and a larger one for ashes. These changes may sound trivial, but Taylor's work saved the company more than $78,000 a year, an enormous sum at that time. With the new shovels, 140 men could accomplish the same amount of work that previously required 500 men. By offering an incentive of higher pay for greater productivity, the company allowed workers to increase their wages by 60 percent (Taylor, 1911).

Taylor's work was the first empirical demonstration of the relationship between work tools and worker efficiency. The next pioneers in the field were Frank Gilbreth, an engineer, and Lillian Gilbreth, a psychologist, who did more than anyone else to promote time-and-motion study. Whereas Taylor had been concerned primarily with tool design and incentive wage systems, the Gilbreths were interested in the mechanics of job performance. Their goal was to eliminate all unnecessary motion (Gilbreth, 1911).

It began when Frank Gilbreth at age 17 was working as an apprentice bricklayer. During his first day on the job, he noticed that the bricklayers made many unnecessary motions in doing their work. He thought he could redesign the job to make it faster and easier, and within a year he was the fastest bricklayer on the job. Once he persuaded his co-workers to try his methods, the entire crew was accomplishing far more work without becoming exhausted.

Gilbreth designed a scaffold that could be raised or lowered so that the worker would always be at a height convenient to the task. By analyzing the hand and arm movements involved in laying bricks and changing to the most efficient ones, he found that workers could lay 350 bricks an hour instead of 120. This increase in productivity was not brought about by forcing men to work faster but by reducing the number of motions needed for laying each brick from 18 to 5.

Frank and Lillian Gilbreth organized their household and their personal lives around the principles of time-and-motion economy. Every activity was scrutinized for wasted motion. For example, Frank Gilbreth always buttoned his vest from the bottom up because it took four seconds less than buttoning it from the top down. He used two brushes, one in each hand, to lather his face for shaving, a savings of 17 seconds. He tried shaving with two razors simultaneously but lost more time bandaging cuts than he had saved in shaving. The efforts to schedule the activities of the 12 Gilbreth children were recounted in a popular book and

Time-and-motion study
An early attempt to redesign work tools and to reshape the way workers performed routine, repetitive jobs.

Newsbreak   World's Greatest Woman Engineer

Lillian Moller thought she was so plain that no one would ever marry her, so she decided to have a career. This was an unpopular notion for a 22-year-old woman in the year 1900. She graduated from the University of California at Berkeley that year and was the first woman ever to be chosen as the school's commencement speaker. She stayed on at Berkeley to study for her PhD in English literature with a minor in psychology. In 1904 her plans were upset when she met a handsome, charismatic, wealthy owner of a construction company.

Frank Gilbreth was ten years older than Lillian. He lived in Boston, where Lillian and some friends had stopped on their way to Europe. When they returned, Frank was waiting at the dock with flowers. Before long, he traveled to California to meet her parents and set the date for the wedding. Frank wanted a wife, children, and all the pleasures of domesticity, but he also desired a partner for his work. At his urging, Lillian changed her major to psychology and enrolled in graduate school at Brown University. She started working alongside him at construction sites, climbing ladders and striding across steel girders high in the sky. A fearless and fast learner, Lillian was soon helping Frank with decisions that would make construction work more efficient. She encouraged Frank to give up the construction business and become a management consultant, so they could apply their ideas about work performance and efficiency to a broad range of jobs.

But the times decreed that women couldn't do such things. That was made clear to Lillian in many ways. In 1911, for example, Lillian and Frank wrote a book, *Motion Study,* but the publisher refused to list her as coauthor, claiming that a woman's name would detract from the book's credibility. The same thing happened a year later with their next book. In 1914 Lillian completed her PhD in psychology, but when she tried to publish her dissertation in book form, the publisher would not let her use her first name, insisting that hardheaded businessmen would never buy a book on the psychology of management that was written by a woman. (Consequently, the title page listed the author as L. M. Gilbreth.)

Twenty years later, with a thriving consulting business to run and 12 children to raise, Lillian Moller Gilbreth found herself a widow. She tried to carry on their work, but most of the business executives for whom she and Frank had done consulting work for many years now cut her off. They had been willing to tolerate her as a wife helping her husband but wanted nothing to do with her on her own.

If she could no longer apply time-and-motion study in the workplace, the business she and Frank had built, she decided to teach others how to do it. She organized workshops on industrial management, which attracted participants from many countries. These workshops, and the quality of the trainees she turned out, enhanced her reputation so that, eventually, business and industrial organizations began to seek her advice.

Over the years, Lillian Gilbreth became immensely successful and influential. She was awarded several honorary degrees, received appointments to presidential commissions, and won accolades from the male-dominated engineering community. One business leader called her "the world's greatest woman engineer." She and Frank earned an additional measure of fame when the movie *Cheaper by the Dozen* was made in 1950 about how they reared their 12 children according to the principles of time-and-motion study. (A remake of the movie, starring Steve Martin, was released in 2003.)

Lillian Gilbreth died in 1972, in her nineties, still working in the field of scientific management. She applied her ideas to problems of efficient work at home as well as in the factory. The next time you open your refrigerator, notice the shelves on the inside of the door. That was her idea. Does your trash can have a foot-pedal to operate the lid? That's easier to use than having to bend down to lift the lid, isn't it? That was her idea, too. Although these may seem like trivial examples to us today, Lillian Gilbreth's contributions in applying the principles of time-and-motion economy were so extensive that they touched everyday tasks not only at home, but in factories, shops, and offices, making work for everyone a little easier. Her influence and popularity remain secure, in the 21st century, through the publication of a new biography (Lancaster, 2004).

Source: R. M. Kelly & V. P. Kelly (1990). Lillian Moller Gilbreth (1878–1972). In A. N. O'Connell & N. F. Russo (Eds.), *Women in psychology: A bio-bibliographic sourcebook* (pp. 117–124). New York: Greenwood Press.

movie, *Cheaper by the Dozen*. To learn more about the life and work of Taylor, see www.netmba.com/mgmt/scientific/. For more about Frank and Lillian Gilbreth, see www.gilbrethnetwork.tripod.com.

Time-and-motion engineers (sometimes called *efficiency experts*) have applied the Gilbreths' techniques to many types of jobs, with the goal of reducing the number of motions required. The familiar operating room procedure of having nurses place each tool in the surgeon's hand is an outgrowth of time-and-motion analysis. Previously, surgeons sought out tools themselves, a practice that greatly increased operating time.

The next time you see a United Parcel Service truck stop to make a delivery, watch how the driver behaves. Every move has been dictated by time-and-motion analysis to ensure a fast delivery. Drivers carry packages only under their left arm, step out of the truck with their right foot, cover three feet per second when they walk, and hold their truck's keys with the teeth face up. Unnecessary and wasteful motions have been eliminated. These procedures allow the drivers to work faster and more efficiently without creating extra work and stress.

The most significant results of time-and-motion analysis have been with routine and repetitive work. In a typical motion study the worker's movements are recorded on video and analyzed with a view to modifying or eliminating inefficient and wasteful motions. (The same technique is applied by sports psychologists and coaches to analyze the performance of athletes.)

From years of research, psychologists have developed guidelines for efficient work. Some rules for increasing the ease, speed, and accuracy of manual jobs include the following:

1. Minimize the distance workers must reach to get tools and supplies or to operate machines.
2. Both hands should begin and end their movement at the same time. Movements should be as symmetrical as possible. The right hand should reach to the right for one item as the left hand reaches to the left for another item.
3. The hands should never be idle except during authorized rest breaks.
4. The hands should never do tasks that can be performed by other parts of the body, particularly legs and feet. A foot control can often be used, thus relieving the hands of one more operation.
5. Whenever possible, work materials should be held by a mechanical device, such as a vise, instead of being held by hand.
6. The work bench or table should be of sufficient height that the job can be performed when standing or when sitting on a high stool. Alternating positions relieves fatigue.

You might think that these guidelines for simplifying jobs would be received with enthusiasm. After all, the company reaps a greater output and employees' jobs are made easier. Although management has generally been pleased with the results of time-and-motion study, workers and labor unions have been suspicious, even hostile. They have argued that the only reason for time-and-motion study is to force employees to work faster. This would lead to lower pay and to dismissals because fewer workers would be needed to maintain production levels. These concerns do have some validity. Other worker complaints are that job simplification leads to boredom, to a lack of challenge and responsibility, and to low motivation, which is manifested in lower productivity.

Time-and-motion analysis is most applicable today for routine tasks such as assembly-line jobs. When operations, equipment, and functions are more complex and the total relationship between person and machine must be considered, a more sophisticated approach to the person-machine interaction is needed.

PERSON-MACHINE SYSTEMS

Person-machine system
A system in which human and mechanical components operate together to accomplish a task.

A **person-machine system** is one in which both components work together to accomplish a task. Neither part is of value without the other. A person pushing a lawnmower is a person-machine system. A person driving a car or playing a video game is a more complex person-machine system. At a more sophisticated level, an airliner and its crew of specialists, each responsible for a different operation, is a person-machine system. An air traffic control network includes a number of separate person-machine systems, each an integral part of the whole. If one part—mechanical or human—fails, all other parts of the system will be affected.

In all person-machine systems, the human operator receives input on the status of the machine from the displays. On the basis of this information, the

An airplane cockpit is a complex person-machine system. Displays present information on the machine's status. The flight engineer processes the information and initiates action by operating the appropriate controls.

operator regulates the equipment by using the controls to initiate some action (see Figure 13–1). Suppose you are driving a car on a highway at a constant speed. You receive input from the speedometer (a display), process this information mentally, and decide that you are driving too fast. Through the control action of easing your foot off the accelerator, you cause the computer-aided fuel injection system to reduce the flow of gasoline to the engine, which slows the speed of the car. This decrease in speed is displayed on the speedometer for your information, and so the process continues.

Drivers also receive information from the external environment, such as a sign noting a change in the speed limit or a slow car blocking your lane. You process this information and dictate a change in speed to the machine. Verification of the altered status of the machine—the new speed—is displayed on the speedometer. The principle is the same for even the most sophisticated person-machine systems. It is the total system that is the starting point for the engineering psychologist's job.

Person-machine systems vary in the extent to which the human operator is actively and continuously involved. In flying an airplane or controlling traffic at a busy airport, operators are necessary most of the time. Even when an airplane is on automatic pilot, the flight crew must be prepared to assume control in an emergency. In other person-machine systems, humans interact less extensively. Many large-scale production processes, such as those in oil refineries, are highly automated. Some products and components can be assembled entirely by

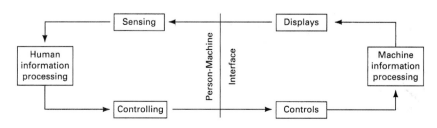

FIGURE 13–1. A person-machine system. (Adapted from "Human Factors in the Workplace" by W. C. Howell, 1991. In M. D. Dunnette and L. M. Hough (Eds.), *Handbook of Industrial and Organizational Psychology,* 2nd ed., vol. 2, p. 214. Palo Alto, CA: Consulting Psychologists Press.)

industrial robots. Although this automated equipment can operate itself, it cannot design, build, or maintain itself, or replace its own lightbulb. Humans remain important components of such automated manufacturing systems even when they are not directly or continuously operating the equipment.

Automation has complicated the task of engineering psychologists. Employees who are required to monitor automated equipment find that task to be more fatiguing and boring than the job of actually running a machine. Engineering psychologists must design monitoring equipment to keep observers alert and vigilant so that they can detect errors and malfunctions and respond immediately and appropriately.

In general, the definition and requirements of person-machine systems are the same, regardless of the degree of involvement of the worker with the machine. No one has yet developed a machine that can design, build, and maintain other machines. Humans are still vital to the system.

Allocating Functions

The initial step in the design of a person-machine system involves making decisions about the division of labor between the human operator and the machine. To do that, each step or process in the functioning of the total system must be analyzed to determine its characteristics: the speed, accuracy, and frequency with which it is performed and the stress under which it occurs. When this information is evaluated, the engineering psychologist can proceed to match the requirements of the system with the abilities of the person and of the machine. Each component—person and machine—has its advantages and its limitations.

Research by psychologists, physiologists, and physicians has provided considerable information about human strengths and weaknesses, revealing those functions for which humans are superior or inferior to machines. In general, machines are better than humans in performing the following functions:

1. Machines can detect stimuli such as radar wavelengths and ultraviolet light that are beyond human sensory capacities.
2. Machines can monitor reliably for lengthy periods as long as the stimulus in question is programmed or specified in advance for the machine.
3. Machines can make large numbers of rapid, accurate calculations.
4. Machines can store and retrieve huge amounts of information with a high level of accuracy.
5. Machines can apply greater physical force continuously and rapidly.
6. Machines can engage in repetitive activities with no performance deterioration as long as proper maintenance is applied.

Of course, machines are not perfect. They have several weaknesses and limitations.

1. Machines are not very flexible. Even the most sophisticated computer can do only what it is programmed to do. When the system requires the ability to adapt to changing circumstances, machines are at a disadvantage.
2. Machines cannot learn from errors or modify their behavior on the basis of past experience. Any change in operation must be built into the system or initiated by the human operator.

3. Machines cannot improvise. They are unable to reason or to examine un-programmed alternatives.

Some engineers believe that they should automate every possible function in a person-machine system, relegating the operator to a peripheral role. However, fully automated systems can fail, sometimes with disastrous results. Consider modern mass transit systems. In some subway lines, drivers do not control the train's speed, nor do they bring it to a stop at station platforms. Those functions are computer controlled. In a study of the Metrorail system in Miami, Florida, trains fail to stop at stations 10 percent of the time, forcing the drivers to press an emergency button to stop the train quickly, usually overshooting the station platform. Without the driver to intercede, the train proceeds automatically to the next station, delivering its passengers to the wrong place. Drivers in this system have been reduced to being little more than monitors, acting only when the machine malfunctions. They say they find it hard to remain alert when they have so little to do. The job is boring, lacking challenge and responsibility, and it rarely requires the drivers to use their skills. As the operators become more dependent on the computer-controlled equipment, they become less capable of making crucial decisions in emergencies. No matter how thoroughly they have been trained, if their job skills are rarely used, those skills will deteriorate.

A similar problem has been found in passenger aircraft. Consider the different philosophies behind the design of the European-built Airbus and the U.S.-built Boeing 777. The Airbus is largely computer controlled and limits the actions pilots are allowed to take in flying the plane. In general, Airbus pilots are unable to override the computer. In the Boeing airplane, pilots can take the controls themselves at any time to negate or override the onboard computer. Nevertheless, all large passenger aircraft today have such efficient flight computers, navigational equipment, and automatic pilots that much of the human pilot's time is spent merely monitoring the informational displays rather than actively controlling and flying the plane. As a result, pilots can easily become bored and inattentive. The Federal Aviation Administration (FAA) has officially expressed concern that pilots' basic flying skills are deteriorating because they rely so much on automation. One could say that too many functions in modern aircraft are being allocated to the machine component of the system and not enough to the human.

A study of 27 commercial airline pilots found that half of them relied more on the *feel* of the airplane's controls when determining the appropriate action to initiate when ice built up on the wings, than on a status indicator that displayed the actual extent of the ice buildup. Thus, they placed more trust in their own judgment than in the machine's display of factual information (Sarter & Schroeder, 2001).

Research on 30 pilots from a major U.S. airline found that automated systems increasingly communicate only with other machine parts of the system, making decisions and initiating actions, without interacting with the human operator. In experimental tests in flight simulators, pilots under time pressure were unable to detect situations in which flight systems were initiating inappropriate or incompatible control decisions that could have harmful consequences for the aircraft. The human part of the person-machine system was being bypassed in critical decision-making situations (Olson & Sarter, 2001).

For information on a variety of issues in engineering psychology, see www.ergonomics.ucla.edu and www.ergonomics.org/uk/ (the home page of the Ergonomics Society).

Newsbreak	# Who's Right—The Person or the Machine?

At 11:40 on the night of July 1, 2002, two aircraft were on a collision course over southern Germany. Unless one or both of them took evasive action immediately, they would collide in less time than it will take you to read this paragraph. One plane was a cargo jet with a crew of two. The other was a chartered airliner from Russia with 71 people on board, including 43 children. Both planes were equipped with computerized collision avoidance systems that had recognized the impending disaster and triggered audible and visible warnings in each cockpit with urgent instructions for the pilots.

The automated systems told the pilot of the cargo jet to descend to a lower altitude, an action he began to initiate. A similar system told the Russian pilot to climb to a higher altitude, but he hesitated, first contacting an air traffic controller to ask for additional instructions.

Two controllers were scheduled to be on duty that night, but one was taking a break while the other tried to keep track of the five aircraft in his sector. The controller also had a computerized alarm system, which at that instant could have provided him with the information that the two planes were on a collision course. But the system had been shut down for routine maintenance. There was no backup.

When the Russian pilot reported the alarm in his cockpit, the controller told him to descend, the opposite of what his warning system was telling him to do. So now, with 70 lives in his hands, he had two conflicting instructions: go up, or go down. Was he to believe the human—the air traffic controller—or was he to believe the insistent alarm from the machine? He chose to believe the human. At 11:43 the two planes smashed into each other. Everyone aboard was killed.

There is a postscript to this tragedy. Many months later, on February 26, 2004, the unfortunate air traffic controller answered a knock on the door of his house near Zurich, Switzerland. The visitor, whose wife and two children had died in the crash, stabbed the man to death.

Sources: G. Johnson, To err is human. *New York Times,* July 14, 2002; Revenge suspected as motive for killing of air controller, *Chechen Times,* February 26, 2004 (www.chechentimes.org/); Silence for slain air controller, BBC News, World Edition, March 5, 2004 (www.news.bbc.co.uk).

WORKSPACE DESIGN

The harmful effects of poor workspace design were seen in the U.S. Army's M-1 Abrams tank. The interior of a tank is the crew's workspace, and its design can influence job performance—in this case, the tank crew's fighting efficiency. The tank was designed without benefit of engineering psychology research and thus without regard for the needs and abilities of the crew. When the tank was tested, 27 of the

We don't buy just any seats. We design them.

GM begins with detailed studies of the human body. Biomedical research. The kind of comprehensive investigation of anatomy da Vinci undertook in the 1500s.

As a leader in the field of Human Factors Engineering, we design interiors scientifically to minimize the possible distractions from your driving.

It may take us two years and countless clay models to arrive at a more comfortable, durable seat for new GM cars and trucks. But we think it's worth it.

And we believe old Leonardo would have thought so, too.

We believe in taking the extra time, giving the extra effort and paying attention to every detail. That's what it takes to provide the quality that leads more people to buy GM cars and trucks than any other kind. And why GM owners are the most loyal on the road.

That's the GM commitment to excellence.

Engineering psychologists help design components for various workspaces. (Reproduced by permission of General Motors Corporation.)

29 test drivers developed such severe neck and back pains that they required medical attention. Also, the drivers were unable to see the ground in front of the tank for a distance of nine yards, making it difficult to avoid obstacles or to cross trenches.

When the engine and turret blowers were operating, more than half the tank's gunners, loaders, and drivers reported that they could not hear one another well enough to communicate because the noise of the machinery was too loud. All crew members reported visibility problems at their work stations. When drivers and tank commanders rode with an open hatch, they found that the front fenders had been so poorly designed that they did not protect the crew from rocks, dirt, and mud churned up by the tank's treads. It was obvious that the designers of the M-1 tank had given no consideration to the human factor, to the people who would have to operate the machine.

The effective design of the human operator's workspace, whether it is a bench for an electronic parts assembler, a display screen for a newspaper copywriter, or a locomotive cab for a driver, involves the following established principles from time-and-motion study and engineering psychology research:

1. All materials, tools, and supplies needed by the workers should be placed in the order in which they will be used so that the paths of the workers' movements will be continuous. Knowing that each part or tool is always in the same place saves the time and annoyance of searching for it.

2. Tools should be positioned so that they can be picked up ready for use. For example, for a job requiring the repeated use of a screwdriver, that tool can be suspended just above the work area on a coil spring. When the tool is needed, the worker can reach up without looking and pull it down ready for use.

3. All parts and tools should be within a comfortable reaching distance (approximately 28 inches). It is fatiguing for workers to change positions frequently to reach beyond the normal working area.

As an example of good workspace design, see Figure 13–2, which illustrates the work station of a radar operator or power plant monitor. Typically, the worker is seated before a panel or console of lights, dials, and switches. The job involves monitoring and controlling the operation of complex equipment. The monitoring console is designed so that operators can see and reach everything necessary for successful job performance without leaving their chair or reaching excessively beyond normal seated posture.

Another important consideration in workspace design is the size and shape of individual hand tools that must be used repeatedly. Applying engineering psychology principles can improve even basic tools such as hammers to make them easier, safer, and less tiring to use. Hand tools should be designed so that workers can use them without bending their wrists. Hands are less vulnerable to injury when the wrists can be kept straight. Engineering psychology principles applicable to the design of pliers are shown in Figure 13–3.

The proper design of hand tools affects productivity, satisfaction, and physical health. The continuous use of tools that require bending the wrist while working can lead to nerve injuries, such as carpal tunnel syndrome, caused by the repetitive motion. Carpal tunnel syndrome can be painful and debilitating. It is also prevalent among people who spend a great deal of time playing the piano, knitting, or playing video games, a finding that may influence your choice of hobbies.

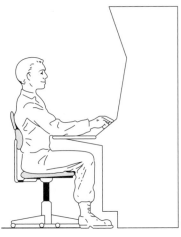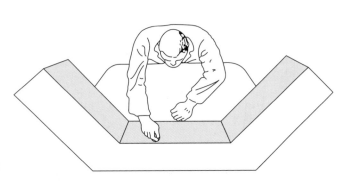

FIGURE 13–2. Monitoring console work arrangement. (From K. Kroemer, H. Kroemer, & K. Kroemer-Elbert, *Ergonomics: How to design for ease and efficiency,* 2nd ed., Upper Saddle River, NJ: Prentice Hall, 2000, p. 384.)

A study of 87 clerical employees in a municipal office building investigated the effects of redesigning the work stations to apply ergonomic principles. The human factors alterations were in four areas: seating, keyboards, computer relocations, and computer screen modifications. Some of the modifications included new chairs and chair cushions, back supports, wrist support pads, and glare guards for computer monitors. Most of the changes were simple and inexpensive yet they resulted in significant benefits to the workers in terms of decreased upper back pain and greater satisfaction with the design and efficiency of the work stations (May, Reed, & Schwoerer, 2004).

A branch of engineering psychology called **human anthropometry** is concerned with the measurement of the physical structure of the human body. Complete sets of body measurements have been compiled from a large, representative sample of the population in the performance of various activities. Specific data include height (standing and sitting), shoulder breadth, back height, chest depth, foot and hand length, knee angle, and so on (see Figure 13–4). These measurements are applied to the design of work areas to determine, for example, normal and maximum reaching distances, tool and desk height and arrangement, size and shape of seats, and viewing angles for video display terminals.

Human anthropometry A branch of engineering psychology concerned with the measurement of the physical structure of the body.

FIGURE 13–3. Application of human factors principles to the design of pliers. (From "Ergonomics," 1986, *Personnel Journal, 65*(6), p. 99.)

Avoid short tool handles that press into the palm of the hand. The palm is very soft and easily damaged.

Avoid narrow tool handles that concentrate large forces onto small areas of the hand.

Tools and jobs should be designed so that they can be performed with straight wrists. Hands are stronger and less vulnerable to injury when the wrists are kept straight.

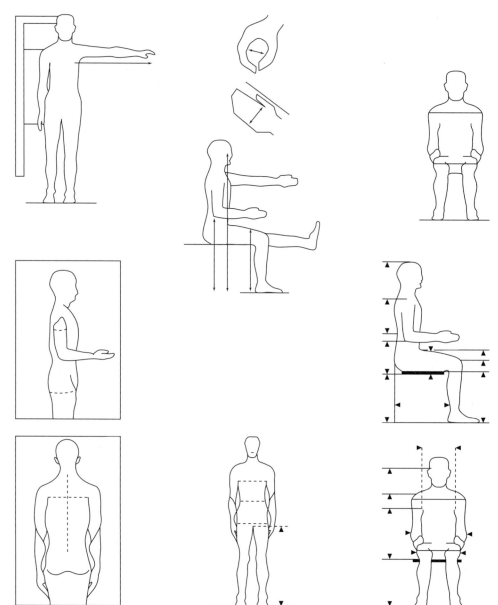

FIGURE 13–4. Typical postures used in gathering body measurements (anthropometric data). (From R. S. Bridger, Introduction to ergonomics, 2nd ed., London & New York: Taylor & Francis, 2003, p. 64.)

With the increasing globalization of the workforce, efficient design of work stations must consider that "average" body measurements and dimensions may vary with workers from different cultures. This was demonstrated in a study comparing anthropometric measurements of Chinese workers (to represent Asians) and German workers (to represent Caucasians). Chinese workers were typically found to have longer torsos and shorter legs than German workers, as well as larger heads and arms. Thus the same work stations, ergonomic chairs, tools, and uniforms would not be suitable for both groups (Shan & Bohn, 2003).

For the millions of people who work at a desk or work bench, the seats we use, if improperly designed, can cause back and neck pain and lead to fatigue, which, in turn, reduces productive efficiency. Research has been conducted on every conceivable aspect of the design of workplace seating, and guidelines are available for various kinds of jobs. For example, you may have noticed that seats are getting larger and wider—because we are! With the notable exception of seats in airplanes, the seats in stadiums, movie theaters, and subway cars have become roomier. The ferries crossing Puget Sound in Washington State used to hold 250 people in seats 18 inches wide. Because the operators had to install wider seats, each boat now carries only 230 people.

For an interesting, often humorous, look at bad human factors design of items from maps to toothbrushes, log on to www.baddesigns.com/index.shtml.

DISPLAYS: PRESENTING INFORMATION

In person-machine systems, operators receive inputs from the machine through the physical senses. For example, in driving a car you receive information on the operating status of the machine from visual displays (speedometer, temperature indicator, gas gauge) and from auditory displays (the chime alerting you to fasten your seat belt or remove the ignition key). More informally, you receive inputs tactually, such as when a balky engine causes the car to vibrate.

One of the earliest decisions to be made about the presentation of information in the design of a person-machine system is to select the most effective means of communication. Visual presentation of information, the mode most frequently used, is more appropriate in the following instances:

- The message is long, difficult, and abstract.
- The environment is too noisy for auditory messages.
- The auditory channels of communication are overloaded.
- The message consists of many different kinds of information that must be presented simultaneously.

The auditory presentation of information is more effective in the following instances:

- The information is short, simple, and straightforward.
- The message is urgent; auditory signals typically attract attention more readily than visual ones do.
- The environment is too dark or otherwise does not allow for visual communication.
- The operator's job requires moving to different locations. The ears can receive messages from all directions, whereas the eyes must be focused on the display to receive messages.

Visual Displays

A common error made in the visual presentation of information is to provide more input than the operator needs to run the system. For example, most drivers do not need a tachometer to indicate engine rpm. Although this may not be a major concern in a passenger car, in an airplane, where large amounts of vital information must be displayed, any unnecessary input adds to the display problem and is potentially confusing for the pilot. The engineering psychologist must ask:

Visual displays in an air traffic control tower present information in words, symbols, and graphics.

Is this information needed to operate the system? If the system can function without it, then that is one less item for the busy human operator to confront. If the information is vital to the operation of the equipment, what is the most effective way to display it?

Three types of visual displays commonly used in person-machine systems are quantitative, qualitative, and check reading.

Quantitative visual displays Displays that present a precise numerical value, such as speed, altitude, or temperature.

Quantitative Displays.   **Quantitative visual displays** present a precise numerical value. In situations dealing with speed, altitude, or temperature, for example, the operator must know the precise numerical value of a condition of the system. A pilot must know if the altitude is, say, 10,500 feet, as dictated by the flight plan. An approximate indication of altitude instead of an exact one could lead the plane into the path of another aircraft or into a mountain in fog.

Five displays for presenting quantitative information and their relative reading accuracy are shown in Figure 13–5. You can see that the open-window display was read with the fewest errors. The vertical display was misread more than one-third of the time. These results, from a now-classic research study, were obtained from a laboratory experiment on instrument dial shapes in which subjects were required to read displays in a brief fixed time period.

A quantitative display that is easier to read than the open-window type is the digital display, or counter, in which actual numbers are shown. The familiar digital clock or wristwatch is an example of this type of display. Digital displays are common in electronic consumer products such as DVD players and microwave ovens.

Although digital displays can be read faster and with fewer errors than any other type of display, they cannot be used in all situations. If the information being presented changes rapidly or continuously, a set of numbers may not remain in place long enough to be read and processed by the human operator. Digital displays are also unsuitable when it is important to know the direction or the rate of change—for example, whether engine temperature is rising or falling, or whether it is rising rapidly or slowly.

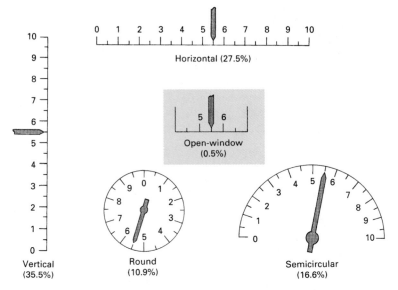

FIGURE 13–5. Percentage of errors in reading five types of quantitative display. (From "The Effect of Instrument Dial Shape on Legibility" by R. Sleight, 1948, *Journal of Applied Psychology, 32,* p. 177. Copyright 1948 by the American Psychological Association. Reprinted by permission.)

Qualitative Displays. **Qualitative visual displays** can be used when a precise numerical reading is not necessary. For example, most drivers do not need to know the precise temperature of their car's engine. All most of us want to know is whether the temperature is in the safe operating range. With many components of person-machine systems, the operator needs to know only whether the system is functioning within the proper range and whether the values are increasing or decreasing over time.

A typical qualitative display is shown in Figure 13–6. The operating ranges are often color coded with the dangerous, or hot, portion in red and the safe portion in green. Such a display permits quick, accurate verification of the system's status and reduces the amount of technical information the operator must absorb.

When several qualitative displays must be checked frequently, consistent patterning makes them easier to read accurately (see Figure 13–7). Placing the dials so that they always face the same way in the normal operating range makes it easier to scan the display and detect an abnormal reading. Unpatterned displays force the operator to read each dial separately. Patterned displays are used in aircraft cockpits, power plant control rooms, and automated manufacturing plants.

Qualitative visual displays Displays that present a range rather than a precise numerical value. They are frequently used to show whether components, such as engine temperature, are operating in the safe or unsafe range.

Check Reading Displays. **Check reading visual displays** are the simplest kind of visual display. They tell the operator whether the system is on or off, safe or unsafe, or operating normally or abnormally. For example, with the engine temperature gauge in your car, a warning light is sufficient to indicate whether you

Check reading visual displays Displays that tell the operator whether the system is on or off, safe or unsafe, or operating normally or abnormally.

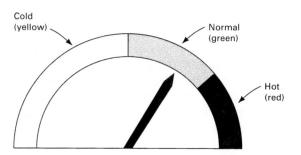

FIGURE 13–6. A qualitative visual display. (Adapted from *Human Factors in Engineering and Design* (p. 76) by E. J. McCormick, 1976, New York: McGraw-Hill.)

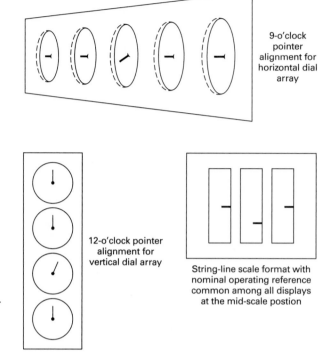

9-o'clock pointer alignment for horizontal dial array

12-o'clock pointer alignment for vertical dial array

String-line scale format with nominal operating reference common among all displays at the mid-scale postion

FIGURE 13–7. Patterned and unpatterned dial displays with pointers aligned for rapid reading. (From K. Kroemer, H. Kroemer, & K. Kroemer-Elbert, *Ergonomics: How to design for ease and efficiency,* 2nd ed., Upper Saddle River, NJ: Prentice Hall, 2000, p. 491.)

can continue to drive safely or should stop because the engine is in danger of overheating. This kind of display is sometimes referred to as "go/no go." Either the system is in condition to operate (to go) or it is not.

The most common check reading display is the warning light. When the light is not illuminated, the system is functioning satisfactorily. When the light comes on, it indicates a system malfunction serious enough to require the operator to take immediate corrective action.

Among the considerations in the design of warning lights is level of brightness. On a display panel that contains several sources of light, it is vital that a warning light be at least twice as bright as the background to get the operator's attention. Location of warning lights is also important. They should be centrally located within the operator's field of vision. Warning lights too far to one side of a console may not be noticed when the worker is paying attention to more centrally located displays and controls. Also, flashing lights attract attention more quickly than continuous warning lights.

Visual displays today include more than the familiar lights, dials, and gauges. Much information is displayed on video screens and in words, symbols, and graphics. The electronic flight information system used in aircraft and in air traffic control radar screens combines lines, numbers, and pictorial symbols to present precise information about location. Adding color to cockpit displays reduces errors and response times for aircraft crew members in reading and processing information.

Not all visual displays are high-tech. For example, the common push/pull door signs are used every day by millions of people entering and exiting stores, factories, and office buildings. Some doors need to be pushed, others pulled. To find out how best to display this basic information visually, so that users would follow directions accurately, a study was conducted using 60 subjects under laboratory conditions and 1,100 subjects in the real world. Eleven different kinds of

> ## Newsbreak   Let Jack Do It
>
> "In his 15 years on the job," wrote a reporter for the *New York Times,* "Jack has been trapped in coal mines and forced to lift and carry objects that could break his back, and once while pregnant—yes, pregnant—was stuffed into a car to see if he could fit behind the wheel and reach the pedals. Jack never complains, however, because Jack is a piece of software, a virtual reality representation of a person who can take on various forms. Jack can walk, avoid obstacles, reach, and lift. But if he cannot perform a certain task, an image of the character will signal a problem, sometimes by turning a body part a different color on a computer screen. Jack rolls with the punches so that we don't have to."
>
> By wearing virtual reality helmets, real people, such as designers of cars or aircraft cockpits or work stations, can see through Jack's eyes as he becomes a driver or pilot, a factory worker or office manager. Thus, the engineering psychologists or human factors engineers can see how something works—or fails to work—before they actually build it.
>
> For example, they might find out whether by reaching to change a radio station in your sports car, you could accidentally nudge the gear shift lever into neutral. They might find out whether the farmer driving the redesigned tractor has a clear view of the blades that are tilling the soil behind it. When the John Deere company learned that Jack couldn't see those blades from the new tractor cab, it was no big deal to change the design at that stage. But had the tractors already started rolling off the assembly line, it would have been tremendously expensive to redesign them.
>
> Good ol' Jack never fails. And never gets tired or cranky or comes in late or stays home with the flu. And he costs only $25,000. In today's market, Jack's a bargain.
>
> ---
>
> *Source:* Jack is put through the wringer so you won't be. *New York Times,* May 11, 2000.

signs were tested. The most effective signs (those quickly identified or eliciting the greatest compliance) combined a drawing of a hand with an arrow and the word push or pull displayed horizontally (see Figure 13–8). Even a simple visual display can be improved through engineering psychology research.

Auditory Displays

An **auditory display** can be more compelling than a visual display for the following reasons: (1) Our ears are always open, but our eyes are not; (2) we can receive auditory information from all directions; and (3) our visual sense is often taxed to capacity. Table 13–1 presents the major types of auditory alarms.

No matter how loud or effective an auditory alarm is, it is only as good as the human operator's response to it. We learned this from the case of the Russian airline pilot, described above, who chose not to believe what the auditory collision warning system told him to do. Ignoring alarm systems is not such unusual

Auditory displays Alarms or warning signals in person-machine systems. Auditory displays can be more compelling than visual displays.

Most effective (word plus symbol)

 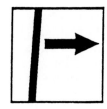

FIGURE 13–8. Most effective and least effective door pull signs. (Adapted from T. J. B. Kline & G. A. Beitel, "Assessment of push/pull door signs: A laboratory and a field study." *Human Factors,* 1994, *36,* 688.)

Least effective (symbol only)

behavior; people often fail to respond properly. For example, a long-term study of employees monitoring the daily operation of nuclear power plants in Canada found that more than 50 percent of the alarms did not provide useful or meaningful information for the human operator, so that he or she could initiate some corrective action. These so-called "nuisance alarms" served only to add clutter or confusion to a critical and demanding job (Mumaw, Roth, Vicente, & Burns, 2000). A study of highly trained registered nurse-anesthetists in 24 surgical cases found that almost half of the auditory alarms from the medical equipment were ignored. No corrective

TABLE 13–1

Characteristics of Auditory Alarms

Alarm	Intensity	Attention-Getting Ability
Foghorn	Very high	Good
Horn	High	Good
Whistle	High	Good, if intermittent
Siren	High	Very good, if pitch rises and falls
Bell	Medium	Good
Buzzer	Low to medium	Good
Human voice	Low to medium	Fair

Note: Adapted from "Auditory and Other Sensory Forms of Information Presentation" by B. H. Deatherage, 1972. *Human Engineering Guide to Equipment Design,* Washington, D.C.: U.S. Government Printing Office.

action was taken because none was needed. The surgical team had learned that the warnings were probably nuisance alarms (Seagull & Sanderson, 2001).

Sometimes, even the most carefully designed person-machine system does not work as intended because the human operator violates the conditions under which the system is supposed to function. On the night of May 17, 1987, aboard the navy frigate USS *Stark* on duty in the Persian Gulf, a radar operator was monitoring a complex system that was tracking all nearby radar signals. The system had visual and auditory warning devices to alert the operator if hostile radar was detected. The system designers believed that with both visual and auditory displays, there was no way the operator could miss a warning. If the operator was looking away from the visual display screen, the auditory signal—a rapid beeping—would surely be noticed.

Yet, when hostile radar was detected that night and the visual warning signal flashed on the screen, the operator was looking away and the auditory signal failed to sound. That operator, or an operator from an earlier shift, had disconnected the auditory alarm because he found it to be annoying. Because the ship was in enemy territory, the alarm was beeping frequently, and the sailor had decided that it was a nuisance.

With the auditory alarm disabled and the visual warning signal unseen, a jet fighter plane from Iraq fired an Exocet missile at the USS *Stark*, killing 37 American sailors. In this case the equipment portion of the person-machine system functioned satisfactorily, but the human operator did not.

Auditory signals may be used to transmit complex information. One example is the shipboard use of sonar for detecting underwater objects. A high-frequency sound is transmitted from beneath the ship through the water. When it strikes a large enough object, the signal is reflected back to the ship and reproduced as the familiar pinging sound heard in old war movies. The job of interpreting the message or information that the sound conveys can be difficult. Extensive training is required to be able to discriminate among the sound's various qualities. With sonar, if the detected object is moving away from the ship, the reflected sound is of a lower frequency than is the transmitted sound. An object moving toward the ship provides a higher frequency of returning sound.

Humans can receive and interpret a variety of information through the auditory sense. We are capable of responding to formal signaling procedures (warning horns, whistles, and buzzers) and to informal cues (the misfire of a car engine, the wail of a miswound audiotape, or the beep of the computer that lost your term paper).

CONTROLS: TAKING ACTION

In person-machine systems, once the human operators receive input through the displays and mentally process that information, they must communicate some control action to the machine. They transmit their control decisions through such devices as switches, push buttons, levers, cranks, steering wheels, mouses, trackballs, and foot pedals. Engineering psychologists analyze the nature of the task to determine whether it involves, for example, turning on a light or activating some other system component. Does the task involve a fine adjustment, such as selecting one radio frequency from the spectrum of frequencies? Does it require frequent and rapid readjustment of a control, or is a single setting sufficient? How much force must the operator exert to accomplish the job? If the control must be activated in cold temperatures, will the wearing of gloves interfere with proper operation? If the control must be activated under low lighting conditions, can it be easily identified by shape alone?

Guidelines for Controls.   For a task that requires two discrete settings of a control, such as "on" and "off," a hand or foot push button is suitable. For four or more discrete settings, a group of finger push buttons or a rotary selector switch is preferred. For continuous settings, knobs or cranks are the best choice. For selecting elements on a computer display, devices such as a mouse, light pen, or touch pad can be used. A selection of controls and the actions for which they are appropriate are shown in Figure 13–9. In addition, controls should satisfy the following two criteria:

1. *Control-body matching.* Although some controls could be activated with the head or the elbow, most of them use hands and feet. It is important that no one limb be given too many tasks to perform. The hands are capable of greater precision in operating controls, and the feet are capable of exerting greater force.

FIGURE 13–9.   Control devices and the type of information they best transmit. (From M. S. Sanders & E. J. McCormick, *Human factors in engineering and design,* 6th ed., p. 261. New York: McGraw-Hill, 1987. Copyright 1987, McGraw-Hill Book Co. Used with permission.)

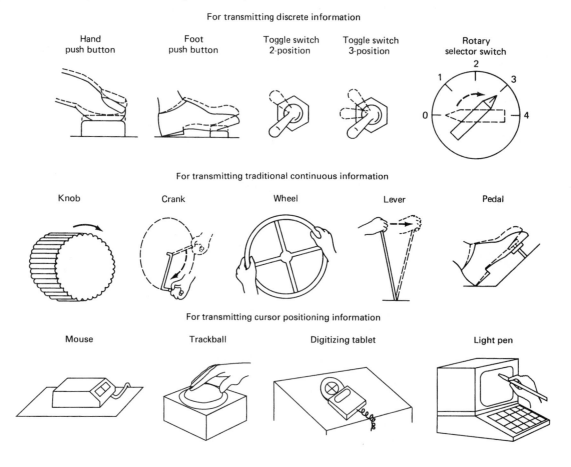

2. *Control-task compatibility.* A control action should imitate the movements it produces. For example, pulling an airplane's control column to the right pulls the plane to the right; the control movement and the machine's response are parallel. To lower aircraft flaps or landing gear, the control should move downward. Typically, we turn a control knob to the right (clockwise) to turn a machine on. Most people would have difficulty adjusting to a knob that turned to the left to activate a machine.

Combining Related Controls.   Wherever possible, it is more efficient to combine controls that perform similar or related operations. For example, simple radios have three control functions—on/off, volume, and station selection—yet there are only two controls. The on/off and volume controls, which perform related functions, are combined to reduce the number of separate actions required of the human operator and to save space on the control panel.

Identification of Controls.   Controls must be clearly marked or coded to assure their correct and rapid identification. Automobile manufacturers code instrument panels by using pictorial symbols to represent control functions (for example, a miniature wiper blade identifies the windshield wiper switch). On a crowded instrument panel, easily identifiable controls can minimize errors caused by activating the wrong control.

Shape coding means designing each knob on a console or control panel in a recognizably different shape (see Figure 13–10). This allows for rapid visual identification of the correct control and permits identification by touch in low-lighting conditions or when the eyes must focus elsewhere. Sometimes the control's shape symbolizes its function. In U.S. Air Force planes the landing flap control looks like a landing flap, and the landing gear control looks like a tire. Each control is unique in touch and appearance, and the control functions can be learned quickly. Standardizing the controls on all aircraft reduces the opportunity for pilot error.

Shape coding Designing knobs for control panels in recognizably different shapes so that they can be identified by touch alone.

Placement of Controls.   Once the kind and shape of the controls have been selected, engineering psychologists determine their placement on the control panel. They also consider the control's relationship to an informational display. A primary requisite for control location is consistency or uniformity of placement.

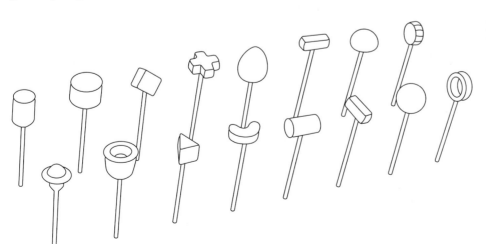

FIGURE 13–10.
Recommended handle shapes for coding. (From W. Woodson, B. Tillman, & P. Tillman, *Human factors design handbook,* 2nd ed., New York: McGraw-Hill, 1992, p. 439.)

For example, we expect the gas pedal to be located to the right of the brake pedal on automobiles, and for the Enter key to be on the right side of the keyboard. The greater the standardization of control arrangement, the easier and safer it is for people to work with different models of the same system. This sounds like common sense, but it took many years before engineering psychology research was accepted and for aircraft instrument panels to be standardized. This basic design principle is still being ignored in many consumer products.

Consider the kitchen range. Typically, there are four burners on top and four knobs on a panel to control the burners. However, there is little consistency in the relationship between control knobs and burners. A survey of 49 electric and gas ranges revealed six different knob-burner operating linkages. Although this does not create as serious a problem as lack of standardization in an airplane, it can lead to burns and other accidents. With a gas range, we receive immediate feedback when we turn a knob to activate a burner, but with an electric range, we could touch a burner, thinking it is cold, to find out it had been turned on.

In the global marketplace, where a product manufactured in one country may be sold in many others, human engineers must be aware of cultural differences that may influence the product's use, such as the linkage between displays and controls. For example, research subjects in Taiwan preferred a different burner-control link when operating a four-burner stove than subjects in the United States. They automatically reached for different knobs than the American subjects to operate the same burners. This probably reflected the Taiwanese practice of reading characters vertically and from right to left, whereas English-speaking people read horizontally and from left to right. Thus, the so-called natural approach to the use of these controls differed for people in the two cultures.

Controls that are associated with emergency functions must be placed in the normal line of sight where they can be distinguished from other controls. The operator should be able to reach emergency controls quickly. The controls should be protected with a cover or shield so that they cannot be activated accidentally.

When displays are associated functionally with controls—such as a dial that must be set by turning a knob—they should be placed as close together as possible. It is desirable to group related displays and controls according to function. For example, in an aircraft cockpit, displays and controls involving engine performance are grouped. When the order of operation is consistent, displays and controls can be grouped sequentially.

HUMAN FACTORS IN EVERYDAY LIFE

Research and application of ergonomics findings can be found in many areas of everyday life, from driving your car to using the voice menu in a telephone call. Human factors are no longer confined to tanks, airplanes, or work areas. The relatively new field of *telematics,* for example, refers to the wireless information technology you may already have in your car, such as a GPS navigation system, a satellite radio, or a built-in wireless phone. The automatic collision notification system, such as OnStar, that seems to know where your car is at all times and alerts authorities when your airbag deploys, is another example. Currently being researched are e-mail and Internet access for your car, Bluetooth support, and built-in PDAs. The obvious problem with these devices, however, is that they can distract the driver and lead to accidents. Engineering psychologists are involved with determining the nature and extent of these distractions and how best to equip the human operator to deal with them.

The use of cell phones while driving is also believed to be a major contributor to accidents, but the data are incomplete to date. Most jurisdictions do not yet require information on cell phone use in traffic accident reports. The currently accepted figure is that the chance of being involved in a car crash is 4.3 times greater when the driver is using a cell phone as when he or she is not using a cell phone.

Research on drivers in Japan showed that the primary cause of accidents was answering a call while driving. The second most frequent cause was placing a call while driving. Third was talking on the phone while driving. No significant differences were found between the use of handheld phones and hands-free phones. The nature of the distraction was found to be similar in both cases (Green, 2003).

Preliminary research on the GPS navigation system while driving in urban traffic showed that drivers were able to make visual-manual destination entries using a touch screen in an average time of 3.4 seconds. The average glance time at the screen to check on location was 1.32 seconds. The researchers of this study suggested that being able to enter destinations by voice activation rather than manual activation would simplify the driver's task and reduce the time the driver's attention would be focused on the screen (Chiang, Brooks, & Weir, 2004).

Studies conducted in automobiles on the road, as well as in a realistic laboratory driving simulator, showed that an auditory warning system that sounded when drivers were too close to the car ahead led these drivers to maintain a greater distance behind other cars and thus reduced the number of rear-end collisions by 50 percent (Ben-Yaacov, Maltz, & Shinar, 2002; Lee, McGehee, Brown, & Reyes, 2002).

Other human factors research has focused on telephone voice menu systems. A study of 114 research participants, ranging in age from 18 to over 60, found that older people had greater difficulty than younger people in identifying the menu choices they wanted. Providing a graphic aid with the recorded spoken instructions significantly improved the performance of older people in selecting the appropriate menu options (Sharit, Czaja, Nair, & Lee, 2003).

Desks and chairs for your school classroom have also been the subject of human factors research. Anthropometric measures of 180 primary school students (ages 7–12) in Greece found that the furniture was poorly designed for the use and comfort of the children. Chairs were too high and the seats and desks were too deep for the reach of most students. This situation led to uncomfortable and unnatural sitting postures, leading to slumping and pressure on the spine and back (Panagiotopoulou, Christoulas, Papanckolaou, & Mandroukas, 2004). These findings supported a similar study in Michigan in which 80 percent of the students (ages 11–14) had seats that were too high and deep and desks that were too high. Attention to the anthropometric measurements for children in these age ranges could have prevented much discomfort and harm.

Moving on to airplanes, have you noticed that passengers in first class often get leather seats while the rest of us in the rear of the plane have fabric-covered seats? Do you envy them? You shouldn't. A study conducted in Germany found that fabric upholstery was rated more comfortable because fabric breathes and leather does not. People are more likely to perspire in a leather-covered seat (Bartels, 2003).

And what about kitchen utensils, say ice cream scoops and spatulas? Ergonomics researchers have been working in that area, too. Research has shown that the physical stress of repeated scooping by employees of retail ice-cream shops can be reduced if the ice cream is kept no colder than minus 14 degrees Celsius.

Scooping is also less physically difficult if the edge of the scoop is sharpened at least once a month. In addition, the job was found to be easier when an antifreeze liquid was encapsulated within the scoop but as yet designers haven't found a way to keep the antifreeze from leaking onto the ice cream, which would not be good for business (Dempsey, McGorry, Cotnam, & Braun, 2000).

Ergonomics researchers in China found that spatulas used by restaurant cooks to turn over food while it is cooking can lead to carpal tunnel syndrome and other trauma disorders in the upper limbs. They tested spatulas with different handle lengths and various angles between the handle and the turning surface. Both factors significantly affected the twisting, or flexion, angle of the cook's wrist. The straighter the wrist could be held, the less physical strain occurred. From a human factors design viewpoint, then, the best spatula was found to be one that minimized the flexing of the wrist: 25 centimeters in length with a lift angle of 25 degrees. With a tool of those dimensions, the restaurant cooks were able to manage more food with less physical damage and pain (Wu & Hsieh, 2002).

These and similar research findings continue to be applied to transportation, furniture design, kitchen items, home workspaces, and other consumer products to make them more comfortable and efficient and to minimize discomfort from long-term use.

COMPUTERS

Millions of us use computers on the job and in everyday life. When the human engineering aspects of the design of computer terminals and computer furniture are ignored, the result is physical strain and discomfort. Concern about the effects of prolonged computer use on employee health stems from the 1970s when two employees of the *New York Times* reportedly developed cataracts, which they attributed to working at video display terminals. Many computer users have since complained of blurred vision, eyestrain, and changes in color perception. However, the National Academy of Sciences concluded that there is no scientific evidence that computers caused visual damage.

Engineering psychologists suggest that most employee complaints about visual disturbances result not from the terminals but from equipment components and from the design of the work station. Equipment factors identified as potential hazards include the color of the phosphor in the cathode ray tube, the size of the screen, the degree of flicker of the characters on the screen, and the rate at which characters are generated.

In addition, level of illumination and glare in the workplace can be sources of eyestrain. Antiglare coatings and shields can be applied to reduce the problems. The overall lighting of the work area can be reduced, and walls can be painted in darker colors. Fluorescent overhead lights can be replaced by indirect lighting. All these changes can enhance visual comfort for computer users.

There is evidence that people read more slowly from computer screens than from paper. Research is focusing on specific factors of the display and the user—such as length of time spent at the terminal—to explain this phenomenon. I-O psychologists suggest that slower reading speed may be related to the quality of the image on the screen (size, type style, clarity, and contrast with background).

Many people have a better understanding of what they read on paper than what they read on the screen. This was shown in a study of 113 college students who read and answered questions about two magazine articles. One group was presented with the material on paper; the other group read the articles on a computer. More readers of the paper version reported that the articles were interesting and persuasive than did the readers of the computer version. The readers of the paper version also showed a higher degree of comprehension of the content of the articles (Greenman, 2000).

Other complaints from computer users are fatigue and pain in wrists, hands, shoulders, neck, and back, all of which can be related to a lack of attention to human engineering concerns. For example, desks and chairs used with computer equipment are often poorly designed for jobs that involve sitting for long periods. The best chair is adjustable, enabling computer operators to adapt it to their height, weight, and posture. Periodically changing position can reduce fatigue, and this is easier to do with an adjustable chair. Desks with split and adjustable tops that hold keyboard and display screen components at different heights can also increase user comfort. Comparisons of the standard flat keyboard and the split adjustable keyboard, using experienced typists as subjects, have found no differences between the two designs in terms of their causing musculoskeletal pain. However, people who use a padded wrist rest report less pain in elbows and forearms than people who do not use a wrist rest.

A great deal of human factors research has been conducted on the design of computers and work stations. Some well-established guidelines are illustrated in Figure 13–11. For example, research findings indicate that a downward-sloping computer keyboard at an angle of 15 degrees decreases discomfort in the neck and shoulders. Locating the monitor too high or too low creates pain in the neck and lower back. Viewing angle has a significant effect on posture; an angle of approximately 17 degrees permits the best postural alignment of back, neck, and shoulders (see Psihogios, Sommerich, Mirka, & Moon, 2001; Simoneau & Marklin, 2001; Sommerich, Joines, & Psihogios, 2001).

Studies have also been conducted on the standard mouse, comparing it with other types of control devices. The mouse requires extensive movement of wrist

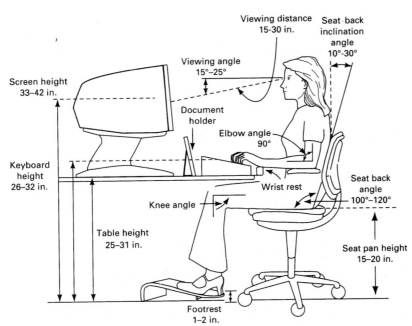

FIGURE 13–11. Guidelines for the design of computer work stations. (Adapted from M. S. Sanders & E. J. McCormick, *Human factors in engineering and design,* 6th ed., p. 358. New York: McGraw-Hill, 1987. Copyright 1987, McGraw-Hill Book Co. Used with permission.)

TABLE 13–2

Ergonomics Questionnaire on the Design of Work Stations

Employees answer YES or NO

1. Are you able to view your computer screen without tipping your head forward or backward?

2. Are you looking straight ahead at your screen?

3. Is your copyholder next to your screen and at the same height and distance from your eyes?

4. Can you easily view your work without leaning forward and hunching your shoulders and back?

5. Are the screen contrast and brightness levels set correctly for your visual comfort?

6. Is the screen free of glare, reflections, or white spots that might be caused by the surrounding work environment?

7. Can you avoid bending your neck or hunching your shoulders when you hold your telephone?

8. When you work at your desk or keyboard, is your elbow at about a 90-degree angle?

9. Are your wrists almost straight (in a neutral posture) as you work?

10. Is your work area free of sharp edges that might rub against your wrists or forearms?

11. Can you reach frequently used items (such as your mouse, files, coffee mug, or pen) without stretching?

12. Can you sit all the way back in your chair without feeling pressure against the back of your knees?

13. Does your chair provide good support for the lumbar region of your back?

14. Are your feet fully supported by the floor or by a foot rest?

15. Do you take mini-breaks during the workday to stand up, stretch, and focus your eyes on something far away?

Source: Adapted from Eastman Kodak Company (2004). *Kodak's Ergonomic Design for People at Work* (2nd ed.). New York: Wiley, p. 131.

and forearm. Research conducted in Sweden suggests that it is less comfortable to work with, and is related to lower productivity, than a virtual mouse shaped like the joystick used to play video games (Gustafsson & Hagberg, 2003). With the virtual mouse, the hand is maintained in a vertical position wrapped around the stick, with the thumb operating the click button. Thus, there is no strain on the muscles of the wrist and forearm.

The Ergonomics Group at the Eastman Kodak Company developed a questionnaire to determine the kinds of problems employees faced in their daily interaction with computers. The goal was to gather information from employees so that work stations could be redesigned to reduce fatigue, stress, and neuromuscular disorders (Eastman Kodak, 2004). So sit down in front of your computer, answer "yes" or "no" to the questions in Table 13–2, and see how you score.

Don't Take Your Laptop to Lunch

It happens every day. You've probably done it yourself. You're leaning over your computer, intent on surfing the Web or sending an e-mail, and you drop food on the keyboard. Chocolate chip cookie crumbs, pizza, cheese curls, or worse—coffee or soda—can destroy a computer. The high-tech wonders of the workplace, which have so transformed the way we live and do our jobs—these marvels of design and engineering—can be totally ruined by a diet cola. No joke! This is a serious problem as more and more people stay at their desks to eat lunch or take their laptops to the cafeteria.

All that food and drink is messing up today's sensitive electronics. At the ExecuSpace company in Chicago, a woman trashed a $1,000 digital telephone when she spilled iced tea on it. Sticky liquids with sugar are the worst. They jam keys and push buttons, clog openings, and also attract bugs. An exterminator in Chicago, whose business is obviously increasing, was quoted as saying, "We're seeing more and more cockroach, mice, and ant problems in [office] cubicles." To solve this growing problem, the Amherst-Merritt International company of Dallas, Texas, is marketing a computer condom. A simple plastic sheath, called the SafeSkin, keeps those nasty crumbs out of your keyboard.

But suppose you've already done the damage. Is it too late to save the mechanism? An official from Gateway advises, "Take the keyboard into the shower [unplugged, of course]. Give it a good going over with warm water. Let it sit upside down for two weeks. There's a slight possibility it will work again."

Source: Desk dining may be hazardous to office's health. *St. Petersburg (FL) Times,* April 18, 2000.

If your answers to all the questions were "yes," congratulations! You are working comfortably and are not experiencing computer-related physical problems. If you answered "no" to any of the questions, then something about your work area probably needs to be readjusted.

Summary

Engineering psychology is concerned with the design of tools, equipment, and workspaces to make them compatible with the abilities of employees. Psychologists consider the limitations and capacities of workers as well as the characteristics of the equipment to produce an efficient **person-machine system.** A precursor to engineering psychology was **time-and-motion study,** pioneered by Frederick Taylor and Frank and Lillian Gilbreth, which attempted to redesign tools and wage-incentive systems and to eliminate wasted motions on the job. Time-and-motion study is applied to routine jobs, whereas engineering psychology focuses on higher-level jobs involving more complex systems.

The initial step in designing a person-machine system is allocating functions between human operators and machines. Humans are superior in detecting a range of stimuli, detecting rare or low-level stimuli from a confusing background, sensing and recognizing unusual or unexpected stimuli, recalling relevant information, using past experiences in making decisions, responding quickly to diverse situations, using inductive reasoning, and showing flexibility in problem solving. Machines are superior to humans in detecting stimuli beyond human sensory powers, monitoring for long periods, calculating rapidly and accurately, storing and retrieving large amounts of data, applying physical force, and engaging in repetitive tasks with no performance deterioration.

Workspace design involves principles of motion economy as well as data from **human anthropometry** (measurements of the body's physical structure). Three types of visual informational display are quantitative, qualitative, and check reading. **Quantitative displays** provide a precise numerical value. **Qualitative displays** provide an indication of relative operating conditions. **Check reading displays** tell whether a system is operating normally or abnormally or whether it is on or off. **Auditory displays** can attract attention more readily than can visual displays because the ears receive sound from all directions.

Controls to initiate action must be compatible with the task and the worker's abilities. Controls should be combined for similar or related operations and must be easily identifiable. Control identification can be aided by pictorial symbols or by **shape coding.** Controls may have to be modified for users from different cultures. Engineering psychology research is being applied to daily life, from the impact of telematics (wireless information technology) in our automobiles to the design of classroom desks to the shape of ice cream scoops and cooking utensils.

Computers are person-machine systems that may cause problems for the human operator. Computer use can lead to a downgrading of human skills, job dissatisfaction, boredom, muscle strain, and pain, much of which can be eliminated by paying attention to human factors considerations in designing computer work stations.

Key Terms

auditory displays	qualitative visual displays
check reading visual displays	quantitative visual displays
engineering psychology	shape coding
human anthropometry	time-and-motion study
person-machine system	

Review Questions

1. Define *ergonomics* and describe its role and function in the workplace.
2. When did the field of human factors begin? How did its early efforts help save the lives of military pilots?
3. Give an example of how human factors research has reduced the chances of being involved in a car crash.
4. Who was Frederick Taylor and what did he do to improve the job of shoveling?
5. How did Frank and Lillian Gilbreth change the way jobs are performed?
6. How did the Gilbreths apply time-and-motion study to everyday life?
7. Describe several rules for increasing the ease, speed, and accuracy of manual jobs that developed from the findings of time-and-motion studies.

8. What is the relationship of displays, controls, and the human operator in a person-machine system? Give an example of a person-machine system.

9. What advantages do humans have over machines? In what ways are machines superior to humans?

10. How would you design a workspace for a person who is assembling and testing cell phones so that the job can be performed rapidly and safely?

11. What is *human anthropometry?* How is it applied to workspace design? How is it used in the field of transportation, such as subway cars?

12. Under what conditions is the visual presentation of information superior to the auditory presentation of information? Give an example that involves your automobile.

13. Describe three types of visual displays and note what kind of information is best displayed on each.

14. What are some problems with auditory alarm systems? How would you correct these problems?

15. What is the field of *telematics?* Why is it important in engineering psychology?

16. What has human factors research learned about (a) the use of cell phones while driving, (b) leather versus fabric seating, and (c) furniture for the classroom?

17. How would you design a study to determine the most efficient ice cream scoop to minimize muscle strain?

18. What factors should be considered in designing a computer work station?

19. What are the most frequent complaints from computer users?

20. Would you rather read a magazine article on your computer screen or printed on paper? Which format provides for faster reading and better understanding?

Additional Reading

Carroll, J. M. (1997). Human-computer interaction. *Annual Review of Psychology, 48,* 61–83. Reviews research and applications in the field of human-computer interaction focusing on the development of user-centered systems.

Chiles, J. R. (2001). *Inviting disaster: Lessons from the edge of technology.* New York: Harper Business. Describes dramatic incidents such as mine shaft explosions, chemical plant mishaps, sunken ships, drilling rig accidents, airplane crashes, and spacecraft disasters. Suggests that such events show a chain of human errors (mismanagement, fatigue, panic, carelessness, and insufficient training) in response to machine malfunctions.

Dekker, S. W. A. (2004). *Ten questions about human error: A new view of human factors and system safety.* Mahwah, NJ: Erlbaum. Deals with questions asked in accident investigations, policymaking, training, and research on human errors. Suggests models to deal with the complexities of these situations.

Lancaster, J. (2004). *Making time: Lillian Moller Gilbreth: A life beyond "Cheaper by the Dozen."* Boston: Northeastern University Press. A lively and detailed biography of Lillian Gilbreth, who combined marriage, motherhood, and a career in a so-called man's profession. A high-profile engineer and efficiency expert, she helped develop time-and-motion study and showed empathy toward workers. She served as an adviser on women's issues to five U.S. presidents. The daily problems she faced still resonate with working women today.

Meister, D., & Enderwick, T. P. (2002). *Human factors in system design, development, and testing.* Mahwah, NJ: Erlbaum. A comprehensive review of human factors issues from task analysis to formal experimentation.

Nelson, N. A., & Silverstein, B. A. (1998). Workplace changes associated with a reduction in musculoskeletal symptoms in office workers. *Human Factors, 40,* 337–350. Identifies workplace factors associated with hand/arm and neck/shoulder/back complaints among office workers.

O'Brien, T. G., & Charlton, S. G. (Eds.) (1996). *Handbook of human factors testing and evaluation.* Hillsdale, NJ: Erlbaum. A sourcebook on assessing the components of a person-machine system.

Shih, H. M., & Goonetilleke, R. S. (1998). Effectiveness of menu orientation in Chinese. *Human Factors, 40,* 569–576. An example of cultural differences in human factors applications. Studies reading and writing flow (for example, vertical versus horizontal) in the effectiveness of computer menus.

Part Six

Consumer Psychology

Not everyone works for an organization, but all of us are consumers of the products and services of many organizations. We buy cars, cosmetics, clothes, and cell phones. We vote for political candidates and express our opinions on issues in public opinion polls. We respond to appeals from charities and special interest groups.

We are bombarded by communications from all these organizations—messages from business, government, and other groups urging us to behave in one way or another. These thousands of advertising appeals appear on television and computer screens and billboards, and in the pages of our magazines and newspapers.

Consumer psychologists are concerned with the interactions between consumers and organizations. Advertisers spend billions of dollars to influence our choices, and many of their persuasive techniques were devised by psychologists. Consumer psychology is also important to you as an employee. If people do not buy what your company produces, then it will not be in business for long.

Chapter 14 deals with the major facets of the producer-consumer interaction—the ways of studying consumer behavior and preferences; the nature of advertising; the importance of packaging, trademarks, and product images; and the assessment of reactions to television programs.

Chapter 14

Consumer Psychology

SUMMARY
KEY TERMS
REVIEW QUESTIONS
ADDITIONAL READING

THE SCOPE OF CONSUMER PSYCHOLOGY

There is no escaping the influence of consumer psychology. Pick up a magazine, turn on the radio or TV, go online, or drive down a billboard-lined road, and almost everywhere you will be bombarded by thousands of advertising messages every day. Your phone company sends advertising flyers with your monthly bill. The supermarket prints ads on the back of your cash register receipt. Theaters showing popular films also run commercials. Public buildings post ads on the inside of the stall doors in the restrooms.

Banks run ads on their ATMs and spew out money-saving coupons with your cash. Office buildings install high-resolution color monitors in elevators to beam ads to the captive audience. Cable TV presents a running band across the bottom of the screen to show news headlines, sports scores, weather and traffic reports, and—you guessed it—ads! Supermarket checkout lines, gas pumps, the post office, doctors' offices—you'll find high-tech ads running wherever people have to wait.

Scented paper forces us to smell a product, even if we do not look at the ad for it. Aromas of perfumes, chocolates, detergents, and the leather upholstery of the Rolls-Royce automobile fill the glossy pages of our magazines. More than a billion scent strips a year are distributed, creating severe problems for people who suffer from allergies. Thanks to microchips the size of a grain of salt, it is possible to hear advertisements in print. Several years ago, a popular brand of vodka spent $1 million on a Christmastime ad that played "Jingle Bells" when readers turned the page. The company claimed that the ad produced the largest holiday season sales in its history.

It is not possible for us to pay attention to or respond adequately to all the messages directed toward consumers, nor should we, if we want to maintain our sanity. We do not consciously perceive the majority of the messages around us, but even if we remain unaware of the details of many ads, we are certainly aware that the process of advertising is ongoing, and many of us don't like it. A large-scale nationwide survey conducted in 2004 for the American Association of Advertising Agencies yielded results that did not make the ad agencies happy. Here are a few of the findings (Elliott, 2004):

1. 54 percent of those surveyed said they deliberately avoided products that overwhelmed them with advertising.
2. 60 percent said their opinions about advertising were much more negative than they were a few years ago.
3. 61 percent reported that the amount of advertising they were exposed to was "out of control."

4. 69 percent expressed interest in products and services that would help them eliminate or block ads.

5. 45 percent said that the amount of advertising and marketing detracted from the quality of everyday life.

Although it is true that advertising can annoy us, it can also inform and entertain us. Ads tell us about new products, new models of current products, product specifications and pricing, places to purchase the product, and sales. Some ads are attractive, clever, and funny. Advertising is part of daily life and a major topic of research for industrial-organizational (I-O) psychologists.

Indeed, consumer behavior has been of interest to I-O psychologists since the beginning of the field. It was the study of consumer behavior that launched I-O psychology. Industrial psychology dates from the early-twentieth-century work of Walter Dill Scott on advertising and selling. In 1921 John B. Watson, founder of the behaviorist school of psychology, began to apply his ideas about human behavior to problems in the business world. He proposed that consumer behavior could be conditioned—and, therefore, predicted and controlled—just like any other kind of behavior. He brought the experimental and survey methods to marketing and he insisted that advertisements should focus on style and image rather than substance and fact. He also pioneered the use of celebrity endorsements.

Since those early days, the field has continued to expand in scope and influence. In the late 1960s, the Association for Consumer Research was founded and the first consumer behavior textbooks were published. The Society for Consumer Psychology was founded in 1960 as Division 23 of the American Psychological Association. Besides psychology, researchers in the field of consumer behavior come from sociology, anthropology, economics, and business administration.

RESEARCH METHODS

Most consumer psychology research relies on the techniques described in Chapter 2, such as laboratory experiments and surveys, and is conducted in various settings, such as university laboratories, downtown intersections, homes, shopping centers, the offices of manufacturers and advertising agencies, and online.

Surveys and Public Opinion Polls

The premise underlying the use of surveys is simple—that is, most people can and will express their feelings, reactions, opinions, and desires when somebody asks them. This assumption holds whether we are trying to determine reactions to a new brand of peanut butter or to a presidential candidate. We have only to recall how accurately most preelection polls have predicted election results or how successfully new products have been introduced on the basis of market testing to know that the survey method often works well. However, there have also been spectacular failures to predict election results or to forecast a product's success. Table 14–1 shows advantages and disadvantages of different survey techniques.

Part of the difficulty is the complex and changeable nature of human behavior. Some people will tell a pollster on Friday that they intend to vote Republican

TABLE 14–1

Advantages and Disadvantages of Various Survey Techniques

	Mail	Telephone	Personal Interview	Online
Cost	Low	Moderate	High	Low
Speed	Slow	Immediate	Slow	Fast
Response rate	Low	Moderate	High	Self-selected
Geographic flexibility	Excellent	Good	Difficult	Excellent
Interviewer bias	N/A	Moderate	Problematic	N/A
Interviewer supervision	N/A	Easy	Difficult	N/A
Quality of response	Limited	Limited	Excellent	Excellent

Source: L. Schiffman & L. Kanuk (2004), *Consumer Behavior* (8th ed.). Upper Saddle River, NJ: Prentice Hall, p. 351.

and then will change their mind and vote Democrat on Tuesday. Respondents may tell an interviewer that they drink expensive imported beer, but a glance inside their refrigerator would reveal cans of some generic "lite" brand. They may have claimed to drink the imported brand because they thought it would make them appear sophisticated.

Searches of trash cans have revealed that on the average people drink twice the amount of beer and liquor than they report in consumer surveys. Survey respondents consistently underreport the amount of junk food they eat and over-report the amount of fresh fruit and diet soft drinks they consume. People tend to respond to surveys and polls with statements they believe will enhance their status, and on such vagaries elections are lost and manufacturers go bankrupt.

A survey of 2,448 people who had received mail-order catalogs reported that 10 percent of those who had purchased products from the company said they had *never* purchased anything from that company. In addition, 40 percent of those who had made no purchases reported that they had, indeed, bought something. Whatever the cause of such false responses—memory lapses or deliberate distortions—the results highlight the problem of inaccurate responses to survey questions (Woodside & Wilson, 2002).

Other research on survey methods found that for mail surveys, sending post-cards to potential respondents that contained a contact telephone number to establish the survey's validity significantly increased the response rate over simply mailing the survey without advance notice or contact information (McPheters & Kossoff, 2003).

We noted in Chapter 2 that it has become increasingly difficult to conduct telephone surveys. Response rates have declined significantly since the development of Caller ID systems and the federal "Do Not Call" registry. Research has shown that 43 percent of those who own answering machines or subscribe to Caller ID services screen their calls and tend not to answer those whose names they do not recognize. The tendency to screen calls is higher among ages 18–29, single persons, African-Americans, and people with young children at home. The

Much consumer psychology research relies on surveys. Shoppers may be asked about the products they are using, how often they purchase them, and why they have chosen a particular brand.

behavior is also higher in large cities and their surrounding suburbs than in smaller cities and towns (Tuckel & O'Neill, 2002).

Therefore, many market researchers are turning to online surveys, which have become a fast and less expensive way to obtain data on consumer behavior and attitudes. Web sites have been developed that offer incentives (such as the chance to win a vacation or a television set) to respond to a survey online. One survey site, www.GreenfieldOnline.com, has signed up 1.2 million respondents by advertising on various Web sites.

In 2000 only 10 percent of all market research surveys were carried out online. By 2003 that had increased to 23 percent; by 2006 the figure is estimated to reach 33 percent. The Consumer Reports organization conducted its first annual product survey in 2003, reaching four million online subscribers. The return rate was 25 percent, compared to 14 percent in previous years when questionnaires were sent by mail. The cost of the online survey was half that of the mailed surveys (Jackson, 2003).

Focus Groups

A widely used type of survey involves **focus groups,** which are small samples of consumers who meet in groups of eight to 12 to describe their reactions to a product, package, or ad, or to the ideas and issues being promoted by a political candidate. Members of focus groups are usually paid for their participation and are selected to match the profile of the average voter or consumer of a particular type of product. For example, only pet owners would be selected for a focus group to test an ad for dog food. Only mothers of infants would be chosen to evaluate a new disposable diaper. Focus groups can be structured on the basis of age, income, educational level, or any other variable relevant to the product.

Focus groups A method of surveying public opinion through the paid participation of eight to 12 group members who meet to describe their reactions to a product or advertisement or to specific issues.

Newsbreak

How to Make a Living from Focus Groups

You can make a living from focus groups—if you tell them what they want to hear! Read this article from a popular magazine and draw your own conclusion.

"I have been many men in my career as a focus-group member. For a travel study, I was a hardy adventurer who'd backpacked through Mongolia. For a deodorant group, I claimed a glandular problem that caused me to sweat profusely, no matter the conditions. . . . It all began when I woke up to my status as a card-carrying member of the advertiser-horny 18-to-34-year-old, single-white-male segment of society. As such, my opinions are valuable. Focus groups pay serious money: anywhere from $75 to $300 an hour for sitting with a bunch of other guys and commenting on everything from alcohol packaging to the elastic waistband of your tighty-whities. These 'screenings' are constructed as theoretically perfect control groups, with men off the street full of fresh, unspoiled insights. To that end, most focus companies have a rule that no one can participate in a group more than once every six months. This is complete bunk. If you know how to game the system, you can do one of these a week, sometimes even more. . . . If [recruiters] ask you whether you've done [a focus group] in the past six months, just say no. They never check. If they ask you something off-the-wall, like 'Have you purchased a treadmill in the past year?' say yes; they wouldn't ask if that weren't the answer they wanted. If they ask you what brands you purchase most often, always name big ones: Sprint, Budweiser, Marlboro. They're representing either one of those companies or a smaller one trying to figure out how to steal you away. And, most important, let the recruiters lead you. Before you answer a question you're not sure about, pause for a couple of seconds. They'll tip their hand every time.

"Once you're actually in the group, it's vital to be as invisible as possible. If you're tagged as an 'outlier' who has opinions that don't jibe with an advertiser's research, it's less likely you'll be invited back. You are not a human; you are a demographic stereotype. So act manly: Refer to any pink product packaging as 'feminine' or 'wussy,' or mention that you're always 'tossing down a few after work with my buddies.' In one group for Johnnie Walker Black, it was obvious the marketers wanted us to consider their beverage upscale, for special occasions. Recognizing this, I made up a story about learning my best friend was engaged and telling him, 'It's Johnnie Walker time!' The interviewer looked like he wanted to hug me.

"It's also important to be vague. During the focus group on travel, the interviewer asked me if there were any countries I might have moral qualms visiting. The correct answer was 'Oh, none at all.' But I blurted out, 'South Africa,' sharing some underdeveloped thoughts I had about apartheid. The interviewer's face sharpened, and he began to pepper me with questions. I had forgotten the cardinal rule: They don't want your opinion; they want you to confirm what they already think. You're whatever they want you to be, baby."

Source: W. Leitch, Group thinker. *New York,* June 21, 2004.

Focus groups need to be structured differently for different segments of the population. For example, the approach suitable for groups of adolescents must be modified for the lesser attention span of children or the perceptual and cognitive differences of the elderly. A study of focus groups in Britain, whose members ranged in age from 60 to 88, showed that the older members responded better with shorter sessions, simpler and briefer questions, better lighting, larger-print materials, and familiar surroundings (Barrett & Kirk, 2000).

The focus group sessions are observed through one-way mirrors and video-taped for later analysis. The data produced by the focus groups—the comments and responses of the participants—are more qualitative than are those obtained from questionnaires in large-scale empirical surveys. Sometimes, focus group members are not asked direct questions but are observed as they try to use a new product. In a session to evaluate a disposable razor, observers found that many men cut themselves while shaving because the package directions were not clear.

As in surveys, focus group participants may distort their answers, saying what they think others want to hear—or what they want others to hear. Consider the focus group that was discussing ads for a company that performed surgical hair replacements (Lauro, 2000). The men in the group all insisted that they were not bothered, personally, by losing their hair, yet they were all wearing hats—on a hot day in Atlanta, Georgia! Their behavior may have been more truly reflective of their attitude about hair loss than what they said to others in the group, but how could we know for sure?

Virtual focus groups conducted online function in a similar way as face-to-face groups and offer the advantages of lower cost and greater efficiency. They can sample a more diverse group of people who might lack the time and transportation to come to a central meeting place for the focus group session.

The responses of members of actual and virtual focus groups may differ. Usually, in a face-to-face meeting, one person at a time expresses an opinion. Sometimes, one individual will dominate the group. In an online meeting, all participants have the chance to speak simultaneously and thus will tend to be less influenced by the opinions of others. When dealing with sensitive topics such as health issues, the privacy and anonymity of an online session enable people to speak more candidly (Collins, 2000).

Motivation Research

We cannot uncover all human motivations by asking questions that permit people to mask or distort their true intentions and feelings. To probe these deeper, hidden motivations, some psychologists use in-depth interviews and projective techniques. The pioneer in this field of motivation research was Ernest Dichter (1907–1992), a Vienna-born and trained psychologist who lived across the street from Sigmund Freud. Dichter emigrated to the United States in 1938. Building on Freudian psychoanalysis to discover unconscious motivations for neurotic behavior, he applied the approach to consumer behavior—why some people purchase particular products or decline to purchase other products.

Dichter's first success was with packaged cake mix, a product introduced around 1940. Everything needed to bake a cake was included in the box: sugar, flour, shortening, and dried egg. Just add water, stir, pour in a pan, and bake. The product promised a revolution in cake baking—an easy, quick, no fuss, and homemade cake with that just-baked aroma that never failed. The only problem was that consumers rejected it. Why? Dichter solved the problem for the General Mills company, using psychoanalytic techniques to uncover the real reason for customer resistance. Questioning a sample of female consumers, so-called typical homemakers of the day, he found that the women felt guilty about doing little or no work to bake a cake for their family. The solution? Give the consumer something to do, to help fulfill the urge to be creative. In this case, Dichter recommended that the company omit the dried egg and let the consumer add fresh eggs to the packaged mix. As a result, sales soared, Dichter became rich and famous, and his motivation research techniques became essential tools in the understanding of consumer behavior (see Schiffman & Kanuk, 2004; Smith, 2004; Stern, 2002).

We described some of these projective techniques in Chapter 4—namely, the Rorschach Inkblot Test, the Thematic Apperception Test, and the sentence completion test. The theory behind the use of projective techniques is the same whether they are applied to employee selection or to consumer behavior. When people are presented with an ambiguous stimulus, such as an inkblot, it is assumed that they will project their needs, fears, and values onto the stimulus in the act of interpreting it. A classic example of the use of projective techniques to study consumer behavior involved the reaction of low-income Southern women to a new brand of roach killer packaged in small plastic trays. Surveys showed that consumers said they believed the plastic trays were far more effective than the old-style sprays, yet they continued to buy the sprays. To determine the reasons for this inconsistency, groups of women were asked to draw pictures of roaches and to write stories about them. The researchers reported the following about the possible motivation of the female consumers:

> The results were very informative—all the roaches in the pictures were male, "symbolizing men who the women said had abandoned them and left them feeling poor and powerless." The women were said to be expressing their built-up hostility by spraying the roaches and watching them squirm and die!
> (Foxall & Goldsmith, 1994, p. 162).

Direct questioning would not have revealed this motivation.

In theory, the projective approach offers the same advantages as projective tests for employee selection, namely, the ability to reach deeper levels of motivation and to uncover feelings and desires that cannot be assessed by objective tests and questionnaires. However, projective tests are low in reliability and validity. There have been successful uses of projective techniques to study consumer behavior, but because the advertising industry does not publicize its failures, it is difficult to determine the extent of that success.

Observations of Shopping Behavior

Consumer surveys and the kinds of techniques used in motivation research share a basic weakness. They reveal only what people say they believe or will do. These expressed intentions do not always coincide with behavior. Because of this discrepancy, some consumer psychologists prefer to observe what people do when purchasing a product or when expressing their preference by selecting one brand over another. Common sense suggests that acceptance of a new product or advertising campaign will be reflected in subsequent sales figures. For example, if sales of a toothpaste brand double in the six months following an ad campaign, then the campaign must have been successful. However, unless all other variables capable of

Newsbreak

Are You a Minivan or an SUV?

Consumer researchers tell us that different products attract different kinds of people. This seems particularly true for the kinds of automobile we drive. A survey of 5,400 owners of minivans and sport utility vehicles revealed that what you drive tells the world a lot about your personality. And maybe that's why you chose it.

The research showed that SUV owners tend to be more restless, more devoted to pleasurable pursuits, less social, and more fearful of crime than are people who purchased minivans. Minivan owners tend to be more self-confident and sociable and more comfortable with the idea of being married and having children than are SUV drivers.

Both groups said they wanted to be "in control" of their vehicle, but they don't mean the same thing by that phrase. Minivan people want to be in control in terms of safety, the ability to maneuver well in traffic, and to park easily. SUV people want to be in control in the sense of dominating everyone around them.

It is not surprising, then, that SUV drivers have been found to be more aggressive and less concerned with behaving courteously to drivers of other vehicles. A French anthropologist who is a consultant to Ford, General Motors, and DaimlerChrysler said, "Sport utilities are designed to be masculine and assertive, often with hoods that resemble those on 18-wheel trucks and vertical metal slats across the grilles to give the appearance of a jungle cat's teeth. Sport utilities are designed to appeal to Americans' deepest fears of violence and crime."

SUVs are like weapons, he concluded, "armored cars for the battlefield." Their message is "Don't mess with me."

What do you drive? Hmmmmm?

Source: K. Bradsher. Was Freud a minivan or an SUV kind of guy? *New York Times,* July 17, 2000.

influencing sales were controlled, we cannot conclude with certainty that the new advertising program was solely or even partially responsible for the boost in sales.

Suppose the company's aggressive sales staff arranged for more prominent shelf display of the toothpaste during the six-month period. That increased visibility could have contributed to higher sales, independent of the ad campaign. Or suppose the company's leading competitor was faulted in a government report for adding an allegedly harmful ingredient to its toothpaste formula. That criticism could contribute to higher sales for all other toothpaste manufacturers. Thus, sales data can reflect factors other than the one being evaluated, and without adequate control over all possible influencing variables, we cannot determine precisely what caused any increase or decrease in sales.

The most direct way to investigate purchasing behavior is to site video cameras or place human observers in stores. Researchers have watched mothers with young children as they shopped for cereals and snack foods. More than 65 percent of the time, children ask for a particular product. And more than half the time, the mothers buy the products their children demand. This kind of data is especially valuable because it indicates that children, not adults, should be the target of ads for cereals and snack foods. Had the mothers been questioned directly in a survey, however, they might have said that *they* were the ones to choose these products, not wanting to appear to be dominated by their children, or perhaps not realizing the extent of their children's influence.

Another observation of purchasing behavior resulted in a change in how a product was stocked. Supermarket observers noted that while adults purchased dog food, dog treats were more often selected by children or older persons. However, dog treats were usually stocked on the upper shelves. Hidden cameras caught children climbing on the shelves to reach the dog cookies. Elderly women were observed using boxes of foil or other long objects to knock down a favorite brand of dog biscuit. By moving the dog treats to lower, more accessible shelves, sales improved almost overnight.

Although observations of actual purchasing behavior can be useful, they are costly and time-consuming. There are other problems as well. One relates to adequate sampling of shopping behavior. Stores in different locations (such as inner city versus suburban) attract customers with different needs and income levels. As you might expect, city and suburban shoppers preferred different kinds of stores, chose different types of products, and had differing amounts of disposable income for shopping.

Various types of shoppers can be found in the same store at different times of the day or week. People who shop in the evenings and on weekends may have different buying habits from those of people who shop during the day. The research design must compensate for this problem by providing for observations at an adequate sample of locations and shopping hours, but this increases the cost of the research.

Another problem with behavioral observations of purchasing behavior is the lack of experimental control over other influencing variables; this is a weakness of all types of observational research studies. In observing supermarket shopping patterns in urban and suburban locations, for example, it is difficult to determine whether the differences found are a function of socioeconomic level, ethnic composition, shelf arrangement, or inventory. All these factors could affect the outcome of the research. Despite such limitations, however, direct observation of shopping behavior has often revealed valuable marketing information that would have been difficult to obtain any other way.

Brand Identification and Preference Research

Consumer psychologists are also interested in how well shoppers recognize, identify, or recall specific product brands. Much of this research focuses on the ability to discriminate among competing brands of a product. When all recognizable cues are removed—such as product name and distinctive packaging—can consumers truly distinguish, say, one brand of cola from another? Studies consistently demonstrate that many people cannot discriminate among brands of products such as soft drinks, cigarettes, beer, and margarine. Researchers have concluded that many consumer preferences and loyalties are based on factors other than the product's taste or other intrinsic qualities.

Testing Reactions to Advertising

A major research activity of consumer psychologists is testing the effectiveness of advertising and promotional campaigns. The most direct approach is to ask people for their reactions to an ad. Does the ad make them want to buy the product? Do they believe the ad? Which of two ads for a product do they find more interesting? It is necessary that the respondents be a representative sample of the population for whom the product is intended. Using single men or elderly women to pretest an ad for baby food is not likely to yield useful results.

Aided Recall. The most popular technique to test advertising effectiveness is **aided recall,** which is used to determine the extent to which the contents of an ad can be remembered. Once an ad has appeared in a magazine or broadcast on radio or television, a sample of consumers is questioned, usually the following day, about whether they read the magazine or heard or saw the program in which the commercial appeared. If so, they are asked to tell as much of the selling message as they can recall. The interviewer asks specific questions about the nature of the ad; this aids the recall. However, a high rate of recall for an ad's message did not necessarily lead the consumer to purchase the product.

> **Aided recall technique** A test of advertising effectiveness to determine the extent to which ad content can be recalled. The interviewer aids the recall by asking specific questions.

Recognition.   Another technique for testing the effectiveness of ads is **recognition.** People who have seen a particular television program or magazine are shown copies of the ads and are questioned about them. Do the consumers recognize the ad and remember where they saw it? Do they recall the name of the product? Had they read the message? Unfortunately, people may say that they have seen an ad or commercial even when they have not. When researchers showed people ads that had not yet appeared in the media, some respondents claimed to have seen them. A comparison of aided recall and recognition techniques showed that recognition was the more sensitive measure of memory for TV commercials.

> **Recognition technique** A technique for testing advertising effectiveness by asking people if they recognize a particular ad, where they saw it, and what they can recall about it.

Physiological Measures.   Because TV commercials are designed to elicit an emotional response in viewers, physiological measures of those emotions are an effective way to measure a commercial's usefulness. For example, a group of consumers serving as research participants could be exposed to a variety of television commercials while their physiological responses are measured by electromyography (EMG), which detects changes in the electrical activity of the muscles. When applied to certain facial muscles, it measures a person's reaction to emotional stimuli. These consumers would be questioned some time later and asked to rate each commercial or ad on the basis of how much they liked it or how much pleasure (or other emotion) it aroused in them. If the results show that facial EMG data correlate strongly and positively with the ratings of the commercials, then the ads would be considered effective.

Sales Tests.   Some psychologists argue that the only meaningful test of advertising effectiveness is whether it results in higher sales. However, we have noted the limitations of using sales data as a measure of advertising success. The **sales test technique** is designed to reduce those problems because it permits experimental control of extraneous variables. Sales tests have been found to be a highly accurate way of assessing the impact of advertising on sales.

> **Sales test technique** A way of testing the effectiveness of an advertising campaign by introducing the new advertising in selected test markets.

Newsbreak   Coupons Make a Lot of Cents

It started in 1895, more than a hundred years ago, when Asa Chandler, of Atlanta, Georgia, distributed coupons for a free glass of Coca-Cola at his soda fountain. Today, an estimated 335 billion cents-off, free-product, and rebate coupons are distributed annually, an average of more than 3,000 for every U.S. household. We cut them out of newspapers and magazines or download them from the Internet and take them to stores to redeem for our purchases of toothpaste, headache remedies, cookies, and breakfast cereal. Pharmacies give them out for discounts on prescription drugs, department stores offer them for special sales, and cemeteries have dollars-off coupons for gravesites.

Coupons can save real money. The average family that uses coupons can count on saving approximately $700 a year, a substantial hourly payback rate for the time required to clip, assemble, and organize the coupons. Hardcore coupon users, who have been known to purchase several copies of the Sunday newspaper to get additional coupons, save even more money.

Most people still obtain their coupons from the Sunday newspapers and use them primarily at the supermarket, but that situation is changing rapidly as more people search for coupons online. It is easy to print them out at home and redeem them at stores and service providers such as travel agencies. In 2003 U.S. consumers downloaded 242 million coupons, an increase of 111 percent over the previous year. Although still a small share of the coupon market, the growth of online coupon delivery may soon reach and exceed coupon clipping from newspapers and magazines.

Online coupons provide a major benefit to marketers and researchers: instant personal information about the person who is downloading the coupon. For example, one company that issues coupons online is www.SmartSource.com. Users who log on to their Web site must register, providing details about themselves, family members, pets, income, and preferred stores. In return, they get free access to up to 35 coupons a day worth approximately $14. When they use a coupon, its code number tells the company who redeemed it, where it was redeemed, and for what product. That data cannot be obtained from a coupon cut out from a newspaper supplement.

So log on and get your coupons, but you'll give away a bit of your privacy. Do you think it's a fair trade?

Sources: No more clipping. *Newsweek,* April 1, 1996. It all started with a coupon for a free Coke. *St. Petersburg (FL) Times,* January 11, 1996. More consumers are clicking for online coupons. *St. Petersburg (FL) Times,* April 21, 2003.

In a sales test, an advertising campaign is introduced in selected test markets, such as a specific neighborhood, city, or other geographical area. Other locations, chosen to be as similar as possible to the test markets, serve as controls; the new advertising is not presented in these control areas. If the test and control areas are comparable, then any change in sales within the test areas can be attributed to the advertising campaign. The control over possible influencing variables is the major advantage of sales tests. The researcher is not measuring interest in an ad or what subjects say they remember, but whether they actually buy the product on the basis of the ad.

The use of sales tests for studying advertising effectiveness also has limitations. An adequate sales test is costly. It takes time to arrange, and it requires precise accounting of the purchasing behavior of a large number of people. Another problem involves the areas selected for the control group. By not exposing people in the control markets to the new ad campaign, the company risks losing sales to its competitors.

Coupon Returns.   The effectiveness of magazine and newspaper advertising can be tested by evaluating coupon returns. When coupons are returned to the manufacturer to obtain a product sample or to enter a contest, they provide a measure of reader interest. When coupons are used to purchase a product or receive a discount (cents-off coupons), they measure actual buying behavior. However, if the inducement to return the coupon is attractive, such as when a West Coast mail-order retailer offered a free pair of sweat socks to introduce a house brand, there is the danger that people will respond even though they have no interest in the product. Many people just want to get something free. There are also people who will return virtually any coupon because they like to get mail. It is difficult to determine how many coupon returns come from habitual coupon clippers and how many come from people genuinely interested in the product.

Coupon returns may indicate the attention-getting value of an ad, but they do not provide a direct measure of the ad's impact on sales. When coupons offer a reduced price for a product, they are effective in inducing people to change brands, at least temporarily. A price reduction obtained by redeeming a coupon at the supermarket promotes greater sales than an equivalent price markdown given at the store.

In one study, more than 900 shoppers were given questionnaires as they left various stores and asked to mail them to the researchers. The results showed that those who used coupons differed from those who did not. The high coupon users considered themselves to be smart shoppers, believed in the economic benefits of using coupons, were more price sensitive and value conscious, and were willing to invest the time required to obtain coupons in order to save money. High coupon users also reported that they enjoyed the shopping experience more than did low coupon users (Garretson & Burton, 2003).

THE NATURE AND SCOPE OF ADVERTISING

Let us examine some of the techniques the sellers of goods and services use to encourage, persuade, stimulate, or manipulate you, the consumer, to buy their products. There are several different types of advertising. Although the most frequently used is the direct sell type, designed to elicit an immediate response from the consumer, other advertising is created for different purposes.

Consumer Awareness.   Another type of advertising is designed to create consumer awareness of a new product, an improved product or package, or a price change. This advertising also tries to reinforce the brand name. Because so much purchasing behavior is linked to brand names, companies spend considerable sums creating and maintaining public awareness of company and product names.

Ford Mustang LX Convertible

It's just what the doctor ordered... plenty of fresh air, fun and relaxation. The Ford Mustang LX Convertible. Power windows, power door locks, power mirrors...the easy life. Push a button and the power convertible top moves to uncover wide open spaces, while the power under the hood really lets you enjoy the open road.

The Ford Mustang LX Convertible. "Ahhh..."

Transferable 6/60 Powertrain Warranty.
Covers you and future owners, with no transfer cost, on major powertrain components for 6 years/60,000 miles. Restrictions and deductible apply. Ask to see this limited warranty at your Ford Dealer.

Quality is Job 1.
Our goal is to build the highest quality cars and trucks in the world.

Open up and say "ahhh."

Buckle up–together we can save lives.

Have you driven a Ford...lately?

This direct-sell ad promotes consumer awareness of the product and tries to establish an image of luxury and fun. (Courtesy of Ford Motor Company.)

To help awaken them to the plight of the world's rainforests, Julie Gawel's students created one of their own.

Julie, an art teacher at Killough Middle School in Houston, Texas, designed the multi-disciplinary program for her students utilizing reading, writing, science, and art. After researching the rainforest environment, the students practiced drawing its inhabitants; learning about paint, color mixing, and texture in the process. Then they transformed their classroom with wall-size murals and papier-mâché trees filled with a menagerie of plants and wildlife.

Finally, the students invited parents and local business leaders to their rainforest, where the children made presentations and passed along the lessons they learned about conservation.

For teaching her students how to be wild about art – and the world's rainforests – Julie Gawel is our newest Good Neighbor Award winner.

State Farm is pleased to contribute $5,000 in her name to Alief Independent School District.

GOOD
NEIGHBOR
AWARD
STATE FARM INSURANCE COMPANIES
Home Offices: Bloomington, Illinois
www.statefarm.com

The Good Neighbor Award was developed in cooperation with the National Art Education Association.

Institutional advertising promotes the idea that the company is a good neighbor and community benefactor. (Reproduced by permission of State Farm Insurance Companies.)

Product Image.   Some advertising tries to establish an image for a product or service. Many products cannot be distinguished from one another on the basis of ingredients or quality, so advertisers try to create differences in terms of images, symbols, or feelings. For example, an automobile must do more than provide transportation; a lipstick must provide more than color. It must, through its image, make the owners feel younger, sportier, or more attractive, or enhance their prestige and economic status. As the president of a firm that makes men's and women's fragrances said, "In the factory we make cosmetics. In the store we sell hope."

Institutional Advertising.   The goal of institutional advertising is to persuade the public that the company is a good neighbor and community benefactor. An example is the campaign conducted by an oil company to promote highway safety rather than simply to sell its brand of gasoline. Companies advertise that their products are good for the environment, that they contribute a share of their profits to charities, or that they support Little League baseball teams. Institutional advertising can build public goodwill, boost sales, help recruit employees, improve employee morale, and drive up the price of the company's stock.

Informational Advertising.   Some advertising comes under the heading of informational advertising when it enables consumers to make more intelligent purchasing decisions. The type of information provided in such an ad can include price, quality, performance data, components or contents, availability, nutritional information, warranties, and safety record. The use of informative advertising has increased from an average of 20 percent of all ads a decade ago to more than 65 percent today. Magazine ads tend to be more informative than television ads. More cable television commercials than network television commercials are of the informative type.

Advertising Placement.   The outlets for advertising—of every type—have changed over the past several years. For example, McDonald's devotes one-third of its marketing budget to television ads, but only five years ago that figure was two-thirds. Many other companies are also cutting back on the money earmarked for TV advertising, spending it instead on other media outlets in an effort to reach more targeted audiences. For McDonald's, the money they used to spend on 30-second network spots now goes to closed-circuit sports programs piped into bars with a large Hispanic customer base, to ads in *Upscale* magazine (distributed to barber shops with a Black clientele), to in-store videos at Foot Locker, to print ads in women's magazines, and to pop-ups on Web sites such as Yahoo!. What happened to television advertising? Many consumers prefer to spend time in front of their computer instead of their TV set. And even when people watch television, they are more likely to ignore the commercials or zap past them with personal video recorders such as TiVo. Table 14–2 shows the growth in our lack of interest in TV ads for various consumer products (Bianco, 2004).

Types of Advertising Appeals

The major way in which an ad campaign can persuade you to buy a product is through its appeal—that is, what it promises to do for you. Look at some magazine ads. Which human needs or motivations does the product promise to satisfy? Psychologists have identified many human needs: the innate or primary needs, such as food, water, shelter, security, and sex; and the learned or secondary needs, such as power, status, achievement, esteem, and affiliation. These secondary motivations depend on our personal experiences and thus will vary from one person to another and one culture to another.

To sell their products and services, advertisers must identify the relevant needs and direct their messages toward the appropriate segment of the population. Most ads attempt to satisfy more than one need. For example, an ad for imported beer can promise to quench thirst (a primary need) and to satisfy the desires for status

TABLE 14–2

Interest in Various Types of Television Advertising

Product	Percent of Viewers Ignoring These TV Ads	Percent of Ads Skipped by Using Personal Video Recorders
Beer	5	32
Soft drinks	22	83
Fast food	45	96
Automobiles	53	69
Credit cards	63	94
Upcoming TV programs	75	94

Source: Business Week, July 12, 2004.

and belonging (secondary needs). Ads for mouthwash and deodorant promise to help us avoid embarrassing situations and thus be more likable. If we use the right cologne, we are assured by advertisers that we will find love and thus fulfill the needs for social support and self-esteem. Driving the right car can provide power, prestige, and achievement, along with the hope of attracting a mate. Advertisers use several techniques to appeal to these diverse human needs.

Celebrity Endorsements.   A product endorsed by a celebrity entertainer or sports figure invites the audience to identify with that person's success. Celebrities are often used to sell products, although there is little published evidence of the impact of such endorsements on actual purchasing unless the celebrity is believed to be qualified to promote that product. A study of college students investigated the influence of celebrity status, attractiveness, trustworthiness, and perceived expertise on their expressed intentions to purchase particular items. Only the perceived expertise of the celebrities was positively related to buying intentions. For example, a tennis pro was considered to be a believable endorser of tennis rackets, a good-looking male movie star was an effective promoter of men's cologne, and a fashion model an appropriate spokesperson for a line of designer jeans.

Some celebrities endorse more than one product, which can cause problems for some sponsors or manufacturers. Research shows that as the number of products endorsed by a celebrity increases, ratings of the celebrity's credibility decrease significantly. In addition, attitudes toward the ads became significantly less favorable.

Positive and Negative Appeals.   Advertising appeals can be positive or negative. The message can suggest that something good will happen to you if you use the product or that something unpleasant will happen if you don't use the product. An ad for deodorant soap can show a room full of happy people who are obviously desirable because they use the featured soap, or it can show a person sitting at home alone, dateless and dejected because he or she failed to bathe with the soap. A related approach is to make the person feel guilty for not buying the product, a tactic that is particularly effective with mothers of young children.

Negative appeals are effective for certain types of products, but they do not work when the consequences are overly unpleasant. Pictures of gruesome

Some advertisers attempt to appeal to emotional needs and feelings such as affection, romance, and beauty. (Reproduced by permission of Perugina Chocolates.)

automobile accidents to promote safe driving or depictions of diseased lungs in antismoking campaigns have been shown to be ineffective. Such fear-laden appeals distract people from the message. The same holds true for guilt appeals. Research has shown that strong appeals are significantly less effective than moderate appeals in inducing feelings of guilt. A strong guilt appeal can easily generate anger toward the ad and the company that sponsored it. A frequently used approach combines both types of appeal, first showing the negative consequences of not using the product and then showing the positive consequences of using the product.

Whereas negative appeals may not be effective in advertising, shock appeals (ads that deliberately startle or offend the audience) may work. A series of three ads— one to inform, one to instill fear, and one to shock—were shown to 105 college students. The messages related to the use of condoms as a way to prevent HIV/AIDS. The shock ad showed a nude couple embracing; the message read "Don't be a f---ing idiot." The fear ad showed a driver's license with the expiration date circled; the message was "If you get the AIDS virus now, you and your license could expire at the same time." The information ad showed the acronym AIDS and the words "Acquired Immunodeficiency."

The results showed that the shock appeal produced significantly greater scores on recall, recognition, and attention paid to the message than the other types of appeals. Also, more people in the shock-ad group and the fear-ad group took AIDS-related informational materials from the items displayed on a table in the experimental treatment room (Dahl, Frankenberger, & Manchanda, 2003).

Implied Superiority.   A widely used appeal is implied superiority, in which the superiority of one product over its competitors is not stated directly but is inferred by the consumer. For example, if all headache remedies take the same amount of time to bring relief, one company may claim that no competitor provides faster relief than its product. The claim is true—no one product is faster than another— but the phrasing may lead people to conclude that this brand is superior because it sounds as if it works faster. The ad also suggests indirectly that its claim is based on scientific research.

Trademarks

A familiar trademark can facilitate advertising effectiveness because it serves as a shorthand symbol of the feelings and images associated with the product (see Figure 14–1). Key aspects of the product come to be identified with and exemplified by the trademark. Most trademarks are brand names—for example, Coca-Cola, Kleenex, and Xerox. When a trademark is well established in the marketplace, it alone, without any other advertising message, can stimulate consumers to recall the product.

A survey of brand names and trademarks asked executives to rate them on the reputation, management strength, and investment potential of their companies. A second survey asked a random sample of more than 10,000 people to rate the brand names on product quality, corporate vision, and leadership. The rankings are shown in Table 14–3, in descending order of popularity. Only three names—Coca-Cola, Walt Disney, and Johnson & Johnson—appear on both lists. Otherwise, the companies selected by the executives are different from those

FIGURE 14–1. Trademarks. (Reproduced by permission of Wal-Mart Stores, Inc.; AT&T Corporation; and Toyota Motor Sales USA, Inc.)

selected by the random sample of consumers. Thus, it is clear that the "best" brand names depend on who is being asked to pick them.

Companies spend a great deal of time and money on the development of product trademarks and brand names. Identity consultants specialize in naming

TABLE 14–3	
Rank Order of U.S. Companies by Reputation and Brand Name Recognition	
By Executives	**By Random Sample**
Coca-Cola	**Johnson & Johnson**
Microsoft	**Coca-Cola**
Walt Disney	Hewlett-Packard
Campbell Soup	Intel
Johnson & Johnson	Ben & Jerry's
General Electric	Wal-Mart
FedEx	Xerox
Procter & Gamble	Home Depot
Hershey Foods	Gateway
Harley-Davidson	**Walt Disney**

and renaming products and companies. For example, California Airlines changed its name to AirCal when focus-group interviews revealed that the new name had greater consumer impact. Allegheny Airlines changed its name to USAir (now US Airways) to make it sound more like a national than a regional carrier.

Research can also tell manufacturers how recognizable their product name is to the consuming public and what it means to the target audience. This is especially crucial for U.S. companies marketing products in other countries. Sometimes a trademark can have an unintended, or unfavorable, meaning in another language. The Chevrolet Nova, named for a star that suddenly increases in brightness and energy, became in Spanish "no va," which means "doesn't go"—not a very good name for a car. Coca-Cola changed its product name in China when the company discovered that in Chinese, Coca-Cola meant "bite the wax tadpole." Pepsi had a similar problem. "Come alive with the Pepsi generation" translated into Chinese as "Pepsi will bring your ancestors back from the dead." Remember Kentucky Fried Chicken's "finger-lickin' good"? In Chinese it became "eat your fingers off." Oops. One U.S. airline boasted in Spanish-language magazines about the leather upholstery on its seats; in translation the message meant "sit naked." The Scandinavian vacuum cleaner company, Electrolux, pulled an ad that promised, "Nothing sucks like an Electrolux," when informed by their American distributors that this was not quite the image they wanted associated with their brand.

A trademark can be so effective that it comes to stand for all brands of a product. For example, "kleenex" is now used to mean any kind of facial tissue, "xerox" any type of photocopier, and "fedex" any express mail carrier. When this occurs, the company can lose its identifiability and its exclusive share of the market.

Trademarks that have worked successfully for years may have to be altered to reflect changes in the culture of the marketplace. The image of Betty Crocker, the fictional woman trademark for many General Mills's food products, was updated in 1996 to reflect the greater racial and ethnic diversity of the American population. The new Betty Crocker is a computer-generated hybrid of 75 real American faces. Designed to represent many races, she now looks multicultural, in an attempt to depict more accurately American society.

Product Image

Often allied with a product's trademark is its image—the ideas, thoughts, and feelings associated with the product's personality. The development of a successful product image, one with which consumers will want to identify, can bring a company from obscurity to prosperity. Indeed, the image can be more important than the qualities of the product itself.

Sometimes product image is transmitted by a symbol, such as the tiny alligator on some popular knit shirts. This symbol is supposed to convey the image of the person wearing the product. A now-classic study compared consumer perceptions of a person wearing a plain knit shirt and wearing shirts with alligator, fox, and polo player logos. The person wearing the plain shirt was judged to be self-confident, tolerant, satisfied, and friendly. The same person in the fox emblem shirt was described as self-confident, enthusiastic, and a leader. In the polo player shirt he was perceived as less self-confident, tolerant, enthusiastic, satisfied, and friendly than in any of the other shirts. In the alligator shirt, the same person was described as preppy but neither a leader nor a follower. The shirt was identical in all cases; the only difference was the logo (Swartz, 1983).

The most difficult problem in developing a product image is determining the qualities that will attract potential buyers. One technique for studying product image involves group interviews with selected samples of consumers in which they are questioned about their perceptions of various products. This in-depth approach attempts to elicit positive and negative feelings about the products.

A more objective approach involves the adjective checklist, which is what was used in the study of the shirts with the logos. Consumers are given a list of descriptive adjectives and phrases and are asked to select those that characterize their feelings about the product or their conception of the person who would buy the product.

Product Packaging

Another important aspect of an advertising campaign is the product's package, the part of the product that consumers see at the critical point of sale, the moment of deciding whether to purchase. Shoppers looking for a box of crackers on a supermarket shelf who are confronted by an array of competing brands may not remember the TV commercial they saw last night or the magazine ad they read last week. At the instant of purchase, the packaging may be the deciding factor.

There is an old saying about not judging a book by its cover, but many people make various decisions on just that basis. We often evaluate people by their clothing or their car, and we make similar judgments about the products we purchase. Consumer attitudes are often shaped not by the quality of an item but by the wrapping in which it is offered.

The most famous example is an early consumer study on the taste of coffee. Two groups of people were questioned. For one group, the coffee was poured from an ordinary electric coffeemaker. For the other group, the coffee was served from an ornately engraved antique silver urn. You guessed it. The consumers rated the taste of the coffee poured from the silver urn much higher than the coffee from the electric coffeemaker, though the coffee was the same in both cases. It was the container—the package—that accounted for the difference in the way people perceived the taste.

In other research on this concept, pills of two sizes were shown to groups of patients and physicians, who were asked to rate the potency of each drug. Both groups reported that they believed that the larger pill was the more potent. In fact, the larger pill was less than half as strong as the smaller pill.

Overall, the package must reinforce the product's image or personality as established by its advertising campaign. For example, a men's hair gel should not be packaged in a pink bottle with letters in script but in a sturdy box with bold stripes and colors. The design and matching of product and package can be determined through consumer research. Consumers may be asked to free-associate to the designs of current or proposed packaging, telling researchers the positive or negative images elicited by the designs. Surveys and projective techniques can also be used to determine packaging impact and preference.

Packaging is an expensive part of the manufacturing and marketing process, accounting for more than one-third of the cost of most supermarket items. For every dollar you spend on food, drugs, cosmetics, clothing, and electronics, approximately 35 cents goes for the container, not for what is in it.

Sex in Advertisements

The use of attractive and scantily clad models of both sexes is popular in advertising, so we might assume that their effectiveness is beyond question. However, the value of sexy images in ads has been accepted on faith, with little empirical research support. Sex appeal does have a high attention-getting value. Studies using the eye camera show that most consumers reading magazines, when confronted with several ads on a page, will immediately look at the ad that contains an element of sex. But what then? In general, the information in the ad that features provocative pictures of women is read more often by women than by men. Men look at the pictures, but women read the message, which usually means that the ad is communicating with the wrong audience. Similar results have been found with ads featuring pictures of attractive men; the messages are read more often by men than by women, again attracting the wrong audience.

More discouraging is research evidence suggesting a very low rate of recall for information that accompanies sexy illustrations. One company published two versions of a magazine ad, each containing a mail-in coupon for additional information. One ad showed a bikini-clad young woman; the other ad did not. Coupon returns were significantly higher for the ad without the sexy model.

Laboratory research supports these field observations. In one study, male subjects viewed several ads; some of the ads had sexy illustrations and some did not. The subjects were then shown the same ads with the brand names deleted and were asked to identify the product or advertiser. They were questioned again 24 hours later. There was no difference in the rate of recall for the sexy and nonsexy ads. After seven days, the subjects had forgotten significantly more of the sexy ads than the nonsexy ads.

A study in which 324 male and female adults were shown a sexually explicit or a neutral television program found that those who saw the sexy program had significantly lower recall and recognition scores for nine ads that were shown during the program than did those who saw the neutral program. In another experimental condition, those who watched a violent television program reacted similarly to the sexy-program group. Neither could recall or recognize the products advertised during the program as well as could those who watched the neutral program (Bushman & Bonacci, 2002).

It appears, then, that the wrong audience reads the messages accompanying sexy ads, and although many people enjoy looking at the ads, they are not likely to remember the product. However, advertisers continue to rely on the shock value, and their promotions—especially for fragrances, underwear, and jeans—grow more daring every year.

Effectiveness of Advertising Campaigns

The most important question for the seller is whether its advertising campaign is effective in increasing the sales of its product or service. In many cases, neither the advertising agency nor the company knows the answer, because effectiveness is difficult to determine. Further, companies are reluctant to go public with their failures and are apt to exaggerate their successes.

Research on television ad campaigns consistently shows that most people dislike commercials. Television viewers watch fewer than half the commercials broadcast. They leave the room during commercial breaks, turn off the sound or switch channels with the remote control device, and erase or fast-forward through commercials on video-recorded programs. A study of 360 television viewers in Hong Kong found that fully 81 percent avoided watching commercials (Tse & Lee, 2001).

Advertising agencies recognize that most people are not sitting through or paying attention to television ads. They describe viewers as "nomads," because they wander or surf from one channel to another. Consumer psychologists have described three types of viewers:

1. *Channel nomads:* people who surf from channel to channel looking for a program of interest. In New York City, viewers change channels on the average of every 3 minutes 26 seconds.
2. *Mental nomads:* people multitasking, concerned with other activities such as preparing dinner, talking on the phone, or playing with their children. Only occasionally do they glance at the TV set.
3. *Physical nomads:* people busy in other parts of the house who watch snatches of programs and commercials when they pass through the room containing the television set.

In laboratory test situations, where people watching TV commercials were unable to tune them out, channel surf, or leave the room, subjects typically misunderstood or forgot approximately one-third of what they had seen when questioned immediately after viewing the ads. A day later, the subjects had forgotten or misunderstood three-fourths of what they had seen. The figures were higher for magazine ads. Of course not everyone can avoid all commercials all the time. A study of advertising during the Super Bowl broadcast, where a 30-second spot can cost more than $2 million, showed that movies promoted in ads during the game grossed nearly 40 percent more than movies released at the same time but not advertised during the Super Bowl. In this instance, the ads were watched by enough people to more than pay for their cost (Yelkur, Tomkovick, & Traczyk, 2004). For current ratings of your favorite television programs, go to www.ytv.yahoo.com/nielsen/ and to learn about Internet ratings, see www.nielsen-netratings.com/.

You may have noticed that when you go to a movie theater nowadays, more ads are shown on the screen before the movie you paid to see even begins. A study of 14,400 people in South Africa who viewed commercials in movie theaters and on television, and 1,291,800 additional reviewers who reported on the same ads seen only in the theater, found that the recall rate for ads in the movie theaters was higher than the recall rate for ads shown on television. This result was the same for young adults (the primary movie audience) and for older adults. The researchers suggested that perhaps we pay more attention to ads in the theaters because we have little chance of avoiding them (Ewing, DuPlessis, & Foster, 2001).

A number of other factors can influence ad recall. For example, a telephone survey of 418 adults found that they were significantly more likely to remember an ad they had liked than an ad they had disliked. Whereas 65 percent of the subjects were able to describe ads they had disliked (which in itself is a respectable level of recall), more than 90 percent were able to describe ads they had liked (Stone, Besser, & Lewis, 2000).

How we feel about commercials in general can affect how well we remember them. In one study, the attitudes of 1,914 adults toward ads were measured first. Although 45 percent of the subjects believed that advertising was informative, 77 percent believed that ads were annoying and manipulative and that many

Some advertisers recognize the buying power of women for products that are beyond the scope of the traditional homemaker role. (Reproduced by permission of Samsonite Corporation.)

products failed to live up to their claims. These results tell advertisers that even people who think ads can be useful may also hold negative attitudes toward them. When these subjects were shown a series of magazine ads and asked on the following day to recall them, people with highly favorable attitudes toward advertising recalled significantly more of the ads they had seen than did people with highly unfavorable attitudes toward advertising (Mehta, 2000).

Racial identification can be a factor in our attitudes toward advertisements. A group of 160 Black adults participated in an experiment in which some of them viewed an ad featuring a White woman holding a garment bag and some viewed an ad featuring a Black woman holding the same bag. Their reactions were shown to depend on their level of identification with Black culture. Those with a high identification regarded the ad with the Black model more favorably. Those with a low identification with Black culture showed no preference for either model (Whittler & Spira, 2002).

Much research has been conducted on the effectiveness of magazine advertising. One study dealt with the controversial but widespread practice of advertisements for prescription drugs. A Gallup survey of 1,475 women over age 18, who described themselves as frequent magazine readers, showed that prescription ads were effective, especially among women who believed they had one of the symptoms described in the ad, which the drug claimed to cure. Half of those with such a symptom claimed to read the ads, and 43 percent reported that they asked their physicians about the medication. Older respondents had a higher rate of recall for the ad content and 62 percent of those surveyed, regardless of age, believed that prescription drug advertising provided vital information (Mehta & Purvis, 2003).

Mass-market advertising is a relatively recent, but rapidly growing, phenomenon in China. Research on the effectiveness of advertising there, conducted in a telephone survey of 825 adults ages 18–64, found that people in China held more positive attitudes toward ads than adults surveyed in the United States. A majority of the respondents (69 percent) reported that they found advertising to be informative, and 56 percent said they often used ads when making purchasing decisions. Younger people exhibited the most positive attitudes; they found advertisements to be entertaining and informative. Those with greater formal education held more positive attitudes toward advertising than did those with less education (Zhou, Zhang, & Vertinsky, 2002).

Advertising on the Web

The Internet is providing a new way for advertisers to spread their messages, although the effectiveness of their banner ads is still undetermined. To date, the effort is small, but it has the potential to grow. One survey reported that 40 percent of the people who use the Internet do so primarily for shopping. Even consumers who do not actually make purchases from Internet sites find it a good source of consumer information. Popular purchases include computers, books, flowers, music, travel services, and investment products. Yet for all the success stories, particularly around the Christmas shopping season, many companies have been disappointed by the response to their Web sites. A great deal more research is needed to identify the characteristics of potential Internet shoppers and the best ways to attract them.

One survey found that 85 percent of those who considered using, or actually used, online shopping reported frustration with the level of customer service.

TABLE 14–4

Reasons for Not Shopping Online

Reasons	Percent
Shipping charges	51
Cannot see and handle items	44
Cannot return items easily	32
Concern about credit card safety	24
Cannot ask questions	23
Takes too long to load screens	16
Worry about delivery time	15
Enjoy shopping in person	10

Source: W. Wells, J. Burnett, & S. Moriarty (2003). *Advertising: Principles and Practice* (6th ed.). Upper Saddle River, NJ: Prentice-Hall, p. 489.

Another 68 percent wanted to be able to contact a salesperson by e-mail or telephone but found that 40 percent of the shopping sites did not provide that capability. Some 51 percent said they cancelled an online purchase just before completion because the Web site requested too much personal information (Wells, Burnett, & Moriarty, 2003). Another survey cited several reasons some people refuse to shop online (see Table 14–4).

One consumer researcher sought to identify the types of direct-mail print ads that were likely to draw customers to commercial Web sites. Five different ads for a company that manufactured antique reproductions were mailed to 2,000 antique dealers, interior decorators, and designers. A Web address was included. The ads that produced the greatest number of hits were those that mentioned the Web address the greatest number of times. The ad that drew the fewest responses was the one that listed the Web address only once, at the end of the ad. The ad designed to look like a Web page, with a line of Web-like graphics across the top, drew the highest response rate (Bellizzi, 2000).

Research with groups of employed adults and college students on the design of Web pages has shown that complexity has a negative influence on advertising effectiveness. The simpler the Web page design, the higher was the stated intent to purchase the product displayed. Also, simpler Web pages engendered more favorable attitudes toward the company and the ad (Bruner & Kumar, 2000; Stevenson, Bruner, & Kumar, 2000).

A study of 311 adults who reviewed four hotel Web sites found that a high level of perceived interactivity with the site, as well as features such as a virtual tour of the facilities and an online reservation system, resulted in highly positive attitudes toward the companies and the sites. Web sites lacking these features did not receive positive ratings (McMillan, Hwang, & Lee, 2003).

An online survey of the purchasing behavior of 307 Internet users ages 16–40 showed that frequent Internet users bought books, CDs and other music products, electronic goods, and entertainment and travel services more often than did respondents who were infrequent Internet users. Age was not a factor in this study of Internet shopping behavior; older respondents purchased as many items as did younger respondents. Men were more likely than women to be more active buyers, and persons with higher incomes bought more items online than did those with lower incomes (Kwak, Fox, & Zinkhan, 2002).

An international study of 299 Internet users in 12 countries in Europe and South America, as well as the United States, found that consumer trust in a Web site was a major determinant in making the decision to purchase a product online. Trustworthiness was perceived to be higher when the site featured customer-service guarantees, reviews and testimonials from prior customers, and certification from an independent source such as a respected consumer organization (Lynch, Kent, & Srinivasan, 2001).

We noted that men shop online more frequently than women. This finding was confirmed in a questionnaire study of 227 adults over age 18 who had made at least one purchase online. The women in the sample shopped online less often and reported that they found online shopping to be less emotionally satisfying and less convenient than men did. Women were less trusting and more skeptical of Web site advertising claims than men were (Rodgers & Harris, 2003).

An international market research firm, Harris Interactive (www.harrisinteractive. com), suggests, on the basis of their survey results, six types of online shoppers (see Table 14–5).

Increasing amounts of research data are being published on the effectiveness of Web site advertising. In one study, pop-up questionnaires on 13 sites advertising and selling a variety of products were completed by more than 13,000 people who had logged on. The effectiveness of banner ads was measured by the length of the visit to the site and the number of clicks made to obtain additional information. The results showed that sites for so-called high-involvement products such as luxury cars provided more effective advertising (people spent more time on the site and clicked through more levels of information) than sites for low-involvement products such as baby diapers or diary products (Dahlen, Rasch, & Rosengren, 2003). Apparently, people will spend more time tracking down information on products that are more important, attractive, and desirable to them than on products that are merely functional.

This raises the question whether people who spend more time looking at ads on a Web site, or in any other medium, remember more of the ad content than do those who spend less time with the ad. A study conducted in New Zealand suggested yes. Some 149 university students were exposed to different ads on Web sites for various lengths of time (20 to 60 seconds per page). Then they were given aided recall and recognition tests on the ads they had just seen. The longer a person was exposed to a Web page containing an ad, the more likely they were to recall and recognize the ad after the exposure (Danaher & Mullarkey, 2003).

Personal interviews with 105 residents of Seoul, Korea, who used the Internet at least one hour per week, showed that their online time was greater for high-involvement products than low-involvement products; these results are similar to those of a study described earlier. Overall, however, the researchers did not find Internet ads to be as effective as television ads for enticing new consumers to consider luxury products. TV ads were more effective for all four products studied: luxury cars, expensive watches, fast food, and shampoo. Newspapers,

TABLE 14–5

Six Types of Internet Shoppers

E-bivalent newbies
Approximately 5% of the online shopping population, this group is the newest to the Internet, is somewhat older, likes online shopping the least, and spends the least money online.

Time-sensitive materialists
Approximately 17% of online shoppers, this group is most interested in convenience and time-saving and is less likely to read product reviews, compare prices, or use coupons.

Clicks and mortar
Approximately 23% of online shoppers, this group tends to shop online but prefers to make purchases in stores, is more likely to include women homemakers, expresses concerns about privacy and security when buying online, and visits shopping malls more often than other groups.

Hooked, online, and single
Approximately 16% of online shoppers, this group is more likely to be young, single men with high incomes, has used the Internet the longest, likes to play games, download software, bank, invest, and shop online the most often.

Hunter-gatherers
Approximately 20% of online shoppers, this group is typically age 30–49 with two children and most often visits Web sites that provide analysis and comparison of products and prices.

Brand loyalists
Approximately 19% of online shoppers, this group is the most likely to connect directly to the site address of a company they know, expresses the greatest satisfaction with online shopping, and spends the most money online.

Source: Adapted from L. Schiffman & L. Kanuk (2004), *Consumer Behavior* (8th ed.). Upper Saddle River, NJ: Prentice Hall, p. 70, after www.harrisinteractive.com.

magazines, and radio were also effective in enticing people to buy new products (Yoon & Kim, 2001).

An overall measure of the effectiveness of Web site advertising is the number of people who shop online. Although online purchases account for a smaller percentage of sales than direct purchases in stores or from catalogs, the growth rate for online shopping is increasing. Table 14–6 shows the annual growth rate in sales for ten types of goods and services.

Fully half of today's online shopping occurs at work, from the office computer. About one-third is done from home. Approximately 15 percent of online shopping with U.S. companies comes from consumers in other countries, which indicates the huge potential market for international online sales of American products and services (Cappo, 2003).

Convenience and price are often cited as the major advantages of online shopping. A survey of 147 adults ages 22–44 confirmed these as the major reasons for shopping online. The respondents also indicated that they were much more likely to shop online for what are called "search goods," such as books or music,

TABLE 14–6		
Fastest-Growing Categories of Consumer Online Spending		
Category	**2002 Sales**	**Percent Change from 2001**
Furniture and appliances	$ 316,189,127	154%
Home and garden	899,882,381	101%
General services	201,415,914	80%
Sports and fitness	482,503,210	77%
Travel	14,773,387,316	71%
Event tickets	1,249,576,972	68%
Office	3,218,368,617	51%
Video games	121,492,909	47%
Computer hardware	4,662,862,978	45%
Movies and video	434,872,979	39%

where they can obtain information such as reviews, than for "experience goods," such as clothing, which shoppers prefer to feel or try on (Chiang & Dholakia, 2003).

Finally, Table 14–7 shows the relative advantages and disadvantages of advertising in the most frequently used media: direct mail, television, radio, periodicals, newspapers, and the Web. As you can see from the data, the Web has the potential for being the most effective source.

TABLE 14–7						
Advantages and Disadvantages of Advertising in Different Media						
Marketing Quality	**World Wide Web**	**Radio**	**Newspaper**	**Periodicals**	**Television**	**Direct Mail**
Large national audience	Yes	Maybe	Maybe	Maybe	Maybe	Yes
International exposure	Yes	No	No	Maybe	Maybe	No
Can be targeted to a specific audience	Yes	No	No	Maybe	No	Yes
Audience members can view ads at their convenience	Yes	No	Yes	Yes	No	Yes
Relative expense	Low	Medium	Medium	High	High	High
Instant customer interaction	Yes	No	No	No	No	No

Source: T. Kuegler (2000), *Advertising and marketing* (3rd ed.). Rocklin, CA: Prima Publishing.

CONSUMER BEHAVIOR AND MOTIVATION

Consumers can be influenced by marketplace factors other than advertising when they make their purchasing decisions. A store's atmosphere and cleanliness, the ease of parking, the length of the aisles—all these things can affect buyer behavior. For example, research on supermarket shopping behavior found that people will look down short aisles rather than walk down them. They are much more likely to walk down long aisles and to make more impulse buys as a result. In addition, the products more likely to be purchased on impulse are those displayed at the ends of the aisles and around the checkout lanes. You can readily see where manufacturers would want to shelve their products for maximum visibility.

Personal factors that affect consumer behavior include the standard biographical variables—age, sex, educational level, socioeconomic status, and ethnic origin—along with cognitive variables such as perceived time available for shopping, attitudes toward shopping, purpose of the shopping trip, and the shopper's mood and personality. For example, people who are self-conscious in public (overly concerned about the impression they make on others and what others think of them) tend to be concerned about the labels on the products they buy. Perhaps they believe that people will think more highly of them if they purchase national brands rather than store brands or generic brands of the same product.

Other factors that influence consumer behavior of interest to psychologists are brand placement, buying habits, brand loyalty, and the effect of product pricing.

Brand Placement

If you watch television or go to movies, it is impossible to avoid brand placement. When a film character drives a particular sports car or drinks a certain brand of beer, you are seeing an example of brand placement within the context of the story, rather than as a separate commercial or ad. A review of 112 hours of prime-time television programs showed an average of 30 brand placement appearances every hour (Avery & Ferraro, 2000). Advertisers like brand placement in movies, TV shows, and video games because they know the audience is not going to mute it, zap through it, leave the room, or channel surf the way they are likely to do when commercials come on. In addition, brand placement usually involves the use of the product by a popular star and thus can have the impact of a celebrity endorsement.

Studies have shown that when the lead character in a movie is shown using, driving, or drinking the product, viewer recall of that brand is increased. Viewers tend to evaluate the product more positively when a well-known actor appears to use the product. People also report that brand placement enhances their viewing experience because it makes the movie or television program seem more realistic (Yang, Roskos-Ewoldson, Roskos-Ewoldson, 2004).

In a study of 105 children ages 6–12, half were shown a brief film clip in which the Pepsi-Cola soft drink was mentioned and spilled on a table. The other group of children saw the same film clip but instead of Pepsi, unbranded food and milk were used. Then they were offered a choice between Coca-Cola and Pepsi-Cola, after which they were asked to describe the film clip. Significantly more of the children exposed to the brand placement selected Pepsi over

Newsbreak   Here's a Tip for You

Consumer psychologists try to amass as much information as possible about human behavior and motivation—where we shop, what we purchase, why we buy it, what ads we like, what ads turn us off. There's not much that escapes the scrutiny of consumer psychologists, even leaving a tip in a restaurant. To the people who serve meals and clear tables, the tips make up the bulk of their income. Therefore, the amount you decide to leave for their service is vital to them.

The money left on restaurant tables as tips totals more than $12 billion a year. Researchers have found that tipping has little to do with your opinion of the quality of the service you received and much more to do with the waiter's opinion of you! In other words, so researchers claim, we tip to please the waiter because we believe he or she is judging us. Do you buy that?

How do you decide on the size of the tip you leave at a restaurant? Do you tend to tip excessively? Do you tip only a token amount and hurry to leave before the waitperson notices? Here are several other factors that may influence the size of your tips:

- *How big was your bill?* The size of the tab you run up is the single best predictor of tip size. The larger the bill, the larger the tip.
- *How friendly was your server?* This should be the first thing a new server learns. The friendlier they are, the larger tip they receive. Waiters who smile and introduce themselves by name tend to make more money than those who do not. Also, waiters who crouch or bend down to your level while taking your order get better tips than those who remain standing. Women servers who draw smiley faces on the bill get higher tips than those who do not, but men servers who draw smiley faces get lower tips.
- *How professional was the service?* Studies show a weak relationship between customer evaluations of the quality of service and the size of the tip. Thus, friendliness may compensate for making a mistake with the order.
- *How attractive was the server?* As with many social activities, more attractive people fare better than less attractive people. In this case, they tend to receive somewhat larger tips, although the difference is not significant.
- *How many in your party?* Do you expect to leave a bigger tip when you are eating alone than when you're with a group? Tip size seems to decrease with the size of the party. Single diners leave an average of 20 percent of the bill. Two diners tip an average of 17 percent apiece. But when the group includes four or more, tip size drops to around 13 percent.
- *How often do you eat there?* Regulars at a restaurant tend to tip more than first-time customers or people who eat there only occasionally. Apparently, people feel differently about tipping when they expect to patronize the restaurant again.

- *Cash or charge?* People who charge meals leave larger tips than those who pay cash. Perhaps it doesn't seem like "real money" when you're using plastic.

A recent nationwide survey found that 30 percent of Americans do not know that it is customary to leave a 15 to 20 percent tip in a restaurant; they didn't have a clue about how much to leave for the server! A consumer behavior professor at Cornell University, who conducted the survey, was surprised by the results. He wrote that "a fair number of that 30 percent said 'I leave a buck or two.' I was shocked. I figured about 90 percent of the population would know that you leave 15 or 20 percent, and maybe there was that 10 percent of people living under a rock who didn't know." Hmm. How much do you tip?

_____

Sources: S. Daley, Hey, big spender. *Washingtonian Magazine*, May 1996, p. 194. W. Grimes, Tips: Check your insecurity at the door. *New York Times*, February 3, 1999. J. Sharkey, He parked your car. She retrieved it. Who gets a tip? *New York Times*, April 25, 2004.

Coke. This was true even for children who said they did not recall seeing Pepsi in the movie segment. Fewer younger children than older children were able to recall the brand they had seen, but there was no age difference in their choice of Pepsi over Coke. In this case, the brand placement was effective (Auty & Lewis, 2004).

Buying Habits and Brand Loyalty

Many of the stores in which we shop and the products we select are chosen on the basis of habit. Once we find a product we like, it is simpler to continue to buy it than to find a new one. To demonstrate the strength of shopping habits, one supermarket rearranged its display of canned soups. The soups had been grouped by brand name but were changed to alphabetical order by type of soup, thus intermixing all the different brands. Although signs were posted to explain the new arrangement, more than 60 percent of the customers were fooled. Habit led them to the space on the shelf where they had previously gotten the desired soups. When questioned, customers said that the soups had been stocked in their usual order. They were amazed to find the wrong cans in their shopping cart. When consumers shop in new stores, where habit does not automatically lead them to the shelf locations of their preferred products, they tend to buy many more different brands than in the past.

The design of an ad campaign to change persistent buying habits presents a challenge. Studies show that consumer loyalty to major brands can remain unchanged up to eight years. Sixteen brands that were top sellers in their product category in 1923 retained their primacy 60 years later: these included Campbell soup, Lipton tea, Kodak cameras, and Wrigley chewing gum. These findings reinforce the importance to advertisers of establishing brand preferences in childhood. Once committed, consumers tend to remain loyal to a particular brand for many years and to pass that loyalty on to their children.

It is sometimes difficult for researchers to distinguish between buying habits and brand loyalty. Both can be defined in terms of repeat purchase behavior, with the result that the consumer is relatively impervious to ads for competing brands. Some companies, notably airlines, hotels, and car rental agencies, have developed effective brand loyalty programs by offering a rising scale of rewards for repeat business. For example, airline frequent-flier plans offer rewards such as free flights, first-class upgrades, VIP check-in lines, early boarding, and sky-lounge memberships. These programs have been shown to be highly successful in inducing customer loyalty. Many people will make longer or more circuitous flight arrangements on their chosen airline just to accumulate additional miles.

A survey of 643 adults showed that the promise of a low to moderate reward for buying a product, in an effort to establish brand loyalty, was more cost-effective than the offer of a higher reward in return for an intention to purchase. This finding contradicted the results of a survey of 300 brand managers who believed that offering high rewards would be more cost-effective for their company in establishing brand loyalty (Wansink, 2003).

Product Pricing

The price of a product can be an important influence on buying behavior, independent of advertising and product quality. Consumers frequently use price as an index of quality on the assumption that the more an object costs, the better it must be. Some manufacturers capitalize on this belief and charge a higher price than their competitors do for a product of equal quality. Identical products, differing only in price, are often judged solely by their cost, with the more expensive product rated higher in quality.

Some consumers, however, do not consider price when shopping for certain items. Observations of supermarket shoppers reveal that most do not pay attention to price information when shopping for staples such as breakfast cereal,

Supermarket shoppers may judge certain products to be superior solely on the basis of price.

coffee, and soft drinks, and they cannot accurately report current prices. Because of different package weights and sizes, shoppers are often unable to make the calculations necessary to determine which of several brands is the best buy. When supermarkets provide unit pricing information, such as cost per serving or cost per item, some shoppers use this information in making purchasing decisions.

A popular technique to gain sales for a new product or package is to charge a low price as an introductory offer. The idea is that once shoppers purchase the product, they will continue to do so out of habit, even when the price is raised to the level of competing products. Research does not support this notion. Sales are usually high during the introductory price period but drop when the price is raised. In stores that do not lower the price during the introductory period, sales typically remain stable. Rebates are a more effective way of offering a price reduction as an inducement to purchase. A price decrease in the form of a rebate usually produces higher sales than an equal point-of-sale price reduction.

Advertising to Ethnic Groups

Research has identified important differences in consumer values, attitudes, and shopping behavior among people of different ethnic groups. Studies of Whites, Blacks, Hispanic-Americans, and Asian-Americans have documented preferences for various products. In many large cities, Blacks and Hispanics account for the majority of the residents, forming sizable markets with considerable purchasing power. Consumer Web sites for ethnic groups include www.nationalbcc.org, the National Black Chamber of Commerce, which offers discounts from major corporations and other benefits; www.blackplanet.com, which offers college databases and financial tools; www.starmedia.com, which offers Spanish-language shopping and travel services; and www.zonafinanciera.com, which provides banking, insurance, auto, and real estate services.

In 2002 Hispanics became the largest minority group in the United States; their population is expected to increase by 30 percent by 2010. The non-Hispanic White population is expected to increase only 6 percent during that time, and the Black population by less than 12 percent. The U.S. Census Bureau estimates that Hispanics will account for nearly one-third of the U.S. population by 2050.

Corporations such as Kraft, General Foods, and Pepsi-Cola have created special organizational units to develop advertising targeted to appeal to Hispanics. Studies show that as a group, Hispanics have positive attitudes toward advertising and rely on it, more than do other minority groups, to provide information about consumer products and services (Torres & Gelb, 2002). Recognizing this characteristic, Procter & Gamble spent $90 million in the year 2003 on advertising designed for Hispanic media outlets for a dozen products including toothpaste and laundry detergent. The company established a 65-member bilingual team to identify the needs and desires of Hispanic consumers. One result of this market research is the finding that Hispanic consumers like to be able to smell certain household products, such as toiletries and detergents. This has led the company to add new scents for this market (Grow, 2004). Market researchers have identified other characteristics of Hispanic shoppers (see Table 14–8).

TABLE 14–8

Characteristics of Hispanic-American Shoppers

- Prefer well-known or familiar brands
- Buy brands perceived to be prestigious
- Are fashion conscious
- Prefer to shop at smaller, more personal stores
- Buy brands advertised by their own ethnic group stores
- Tend not to be impulsive buyers
- Tend to clip and use cents-off coupons
- Prefer to purchase the products and brands their parents bought
- Prefer fresh or freshly prepared food items rather than frozen foods

Source: Adapted from L. Schiffman & L. Kanuk (2004), *Consumer behavior* (8th ed.). Upper Saddle River, NJ: Prentice Hall, p. 441.

Spanish-language television programs shown on the Telemundo network (owned by NBC) and the Univision network have been highly successful in reaching the greater Hispanic audience. Univision is the fifth most frequently watched network in the United States. Advertisers have learned that even Hispanics who are fluent in English prefer to watch Spanish-language programming, making them an ideal audience for advertisers. Spanish-language magazines such as *Latina, Urban Latino,* and *Glamour en Español* are popular outlets for advertising. General Motors spends more than $7 million annually for ads in such magazines. Kmart began a Spanish-language entertainment and lifestyle magazine, *La Vida,* with a circulation in excess of one million in ten key markets including Los Angeles and San Diego, California.

A major source of advertising to the Hispanic market is the telecommunications industry. As a group, Hispanic consumers spend more of their monthly household budget on cell phones and long-distance phone service, driven by the strong need to keep in touch with family members residing in other countries (Noguchi, 2004).

Blacks constitute nearly 13 percent of the U.S. population, making them also a desirable market with rapidly increasing purchasing power. During the decade of the 1990s, the buying power of Black consumers grew 73 percent, as more and more Blacks earned middle-class and upper-class incomes. Black consumers, more than any other group, demonstrate a high level of brand loyalty. Once a brand is selected, they are highly unlikely to switch to a competing grand.

Black households tend to spend a larger share of their income on food, clothing, entertainment, and health care than other groups. They also prefer to make more separate trips to grocery stores in the course of a week than do other groups. In general, Black consumers are more willing to pay more for what they consider to be products of higher quality. This includes a preference for high-fashion items and name-brand products that serve as a visible indicator of success. Blacks, in general, look to the media, movies, TV programs, and advertisements for cues as to which items of clothing, jewelry, and other products will define success in the mainstream culture (Schiffman & Kanuk, 2004).

Surveys of Black and Hispanic consumers show that both groups are attracted to upscale images and attributes of products and the stores in which they shop. For Blacks, unlike Hispanics, family and friends are an important reference point and source of information in making purchasing decisions. This indicates the value of word-of-mouth advertising and of showing images of friends and family using a particular product in the ads (Kim & Kang, 2001).

Surveys indicate a general level of distrust of advertising in the Black community. Because many people appear to believe that ads are designed for a White audience, Black adult consumers have greater trust in Black-centered media outlets as sources of information about consumer products. Consequently, major companies are spending millions of dollars designing ads to appeal to the Black community for Black-oriented print media, and radio and television programs. As with the Hispanic market, advertisers have learned that, contrary to the popular saying, one size does *not* fit all. An ad that may be highly successful with White consumers may fail to reach other groups.

The Asian-American community in the United States is approximately 4 percent of the population but is the fastest-growing segment. Asians have a reputation for being industrious, disciplined, and hard working, eager to achieve a middle-class lifestyle. Thus, they constitute another desirable market for advertisers. They tend to be better educated than the general population and to be more computer literate. About 60 percent of this group earns more than $60,000 a year; approximately half have professional positions in the workforce.

Asians tend to value high quality, to buy established and well-known brand names, and to remain loyal customers. They are a particularly diverse community of some 15 different ethnic groups with different buying and spending habits. Thus they can be expected to respond differently to advertising appeals. For example, almost 80 percent of the Vietnamese living in the United States were not born in this country; fewer than one-third of the Japanese community in the United States were not born here. Most Vietnamese prefer to use their native language and are highly committed to maintaining their cultural traditions. They do not like to make purchases on credit, because owing money in their culture brings disapproval. In contrast, Korean and Chinese people who have spent more years in the United States are highly agreeable to the use of credit as being the "American way" of being a good consumer in the marketplace (Schiffmann & Kanuk, 2004).

Advertising to Children and Adolescents

The 4-to-12 age group contains 35 million children with control over approximately $15 billion in disposable income. Fast-growing spending categories for these young consumers are shoes, clothing, breakfast cereals, candy, soda, and other snack foods. One explanation psychologists have advanced for the children's high degree of purchasing power is parental guilt. Consumer psychologists suggest that in single-parent families, in families with both parents employed outside the home, and in families in which parents have postponed childbearing until their thirties, the children have been indulged with more money to spend and more influence over family purchasing decisions.

Marketing to children uses techniques such as placing products on lower supermarket shelves, airing cartoon commercials on children's TV programs, and distributing in schools pencils, magazines, and book covers featuring a product's name or logo, but the primary way of reaching children in the marketplace is through electronic media.

Many teenage shoppers are responsible for household grocery purchases.

Children are exposed to an average of 40,000 television commercials annually. In the United States, children between the ages of two and 18 spend nearly 40 hours per week with some form of electronic media including television, computers, videos, movies, video games, cell phones, and radio. The average American child apparently spends more time staring at a screen than doing anything else (Levin & Linn, 2004).

Teenagers spend an estimated $30 billion a year on clothing, cosmetics, and other personal items such as videotapes, audiotapes, and CDs. They have also assumed responsibility for much household spending. Many adolescents compile the household grocery list, make decisions about specific brands, and do the family shopping. More than 60 percent of teenage girls and 40 percent of teenage boys are believed to do routine grocery shopping.

A study of nearly 200 teenagers found that half reported spending up to three hours a day watching television and one-third spent the same amount of time listening to the radio (LaFerle, Edwards, & Lee, 2000). Teenagers are also increasing their use of the Internet, spending more hours surfing the Web at home and at school. So much advertising is directed at adolescents about the importance of having the popular brand of shoes, jeans, cell phones, or cars that it has changed they way they view themselves and their interactions with peers and adults. One child psychologist noted that "By the time children reach their teens, a developmental stage when they're naturally insecure and searching for a personal identity, they've been taught that material possessions are what matter" (Kersting, 2004, p. 61). They define themselves, all too often, by the images they see in movies and on TV.

A survey of 329 college students ages 18–24 asked how informative they found the ads in different media. Television ads were ranked high in value for information, as were newspaper and magazine ads. Considering all media outlets, women in this sample found advertising to be more informative than men did (Wolburg & Pokyrwczynski, 2001).

Newsbreak Does Advertising Exploit Children?

The answer is yes. In 2004 the American Psychological Association reported that ads directed at children under age eight should be restricted because young children tend to assume that what they see and hear is truthful and unbiased. And even advertisers admit that their marketing exploits children. The head of one ad agency said, "Advertising at its best is making people feel that without their product, you're a loser. Kids are very sensitive to that. If you tell them to buy something, they are resistant. But if you tell them they'll be a dork if they don't, you've got their attention. You open up emotional vulnerabilities, and it's easy to do that with kids."

Advertisers refer to a product's "nag factor"—how much they can get kids to nag their parents before they give in and purchase the product. One clinical psychologist reported that parents experience considerable emotional turmoil over how they should respond to such nagging. They feel guilty about surrendering and buying their children the junk food or violent video games the kids want, because the parents believe these things are bad for their children. And the parents feel guilty if they don't agree, thinking that maybe their decision will lead to a child's depression or anxiety or lowered self-esteem if he or she doesn't get the right shoes or backpack.

Advertisers also like to develop materialistic attitudes as early as possible, which, critics say, can lead children to grow up defining their self-worth in terms of their possessions instead of their personal qualities.

Now, how about that manipulation and deception, which critics charge is done on a massive scale? Psychologists agree that it happens, even though some of them help advertisers develop effective techniques to persuade children to buy products. As one psychologist put it, "The fake promise of popularity, success, and attractiveness that marketers routinely make for their products are such common lies that we have become inured to their dishonesty. Yet we know that when adults chronically deceive and manipulate a child it erodes the youngster's ability to trust others and to feel secure in the world."

Do children learn from a young age that advertising is not like real life and that they shouldn't take it seriously? Is this part of growing up, learning who and what to trust? And even if no psychologists were involved, wouldn't advertisers be doing the same thing? Here's the bottom line, according to the advertising industry: If companies did not use advertising ploys to sell products, they'd go out of business and would have to fire hundreds of thousands of employees, most of whom have children. Do you agree?

Sources: R. A. Clay, Advertising to children: Is it ethical? *Monitor on Psychology,* August 2000, 52–53; A. D. Kanner & T. Kasser (2000). Stuffing our kids: Should psychologists help advertisers manipulate children? *The Industrial-Organizational Psychologist, 38*(1), 185–187. Ads that target kids are unfair, studies say. *St. Petersburg (FL) Times,* February 24, 2004.

Advertising to Older Persons

Changing demographic trends have produced another important market for advertisers: working people over the age of 50. This consumer segment, growing in numbers and affluence, will, by the year 2020, constitute more than one-third of the population. The over-50 group now includes the first of the baby boomers, a market of 76 million consumers with a large disposable income that they are used to spending freely. People over 50 have half the discretionary income in the United States, and people over 65 have twice that of people between 25 and 34, in their prime earning years.

The over-50 age group represents a multibillion-dollar market for goods and services. Advertisers have responded to this trend by revising their image of older people in ads and by eliminating stereotypes about the older consumer. Ads featuring attractive older models now promote cosmetics, hair care products, luxury travel, automobiles, clothing, jewelry, health clubs, and investments.

Retired people over age 65 constitute a large market for clothing, home furnishings, travel, entertainment, and health care products and services. They tend to read more newspapers and magazines, and their television preferences include news and sports programs. Thus, they rely on mass media advertising and also use the Internet for shopping. There are more Internet users over age 50 than under age 20. The over-50 group tends to shop online for books, stocks, and computer equipment more frequently than the under-50 group. More than 90 percent of people over age 65 who have access to computers shop online. Older consumers are highly critical of ads suggesting that young people are the only ones who have any fun.

Advertising to the Gay Community

An increasingly vocal and visible consumer group, gay persons are better educated and more affluent than the general population. A survey of 20,000 homosexuals that was conducted by a Chicago opinion polling firm found that approximately 60 percent of gay men and women were college graduates, compared to about 20 percent of the U.S. population as a whole. As a large potential market of people with high discretionary incomes, they are increasingly coming to the attention of advertisers.

Interviews with 44 gay men in Canada found that they preferred making consumer purchases only from companies that were perceived as "gay positive." These were companies that advertised in gay media, supported gay and lesbian employee groups, and offered same-sex domestic-partnership benefits. These companies also supported the gay community at large—for example, by making corporate contributions to AIDS charities. In addition, the survey showed that these gay consumers actively boycotted companies perceived as being homophobic or practicing discrimination in hiring (Kates, 2000).

Another survey of 372 homosexuals in the United States confirmed their status as a better-educated and more affluent segment of the population, but these upscale characteristics applied more often to men than to women. The questionnaire responses indicated that these gay consumers preferred to read the *Wall Street Journal, Business Week, Fortune, Money, The New Yorker, Sports Illustrated,* and *National Geographic;* they were less likely to read *TV Guide* or *Readers' Digest.*

Television preferences included network news programs, CNN, "Late Night with David Letterman," and "60 Minutes." They rarely watched game shows, soap operas, or talk shows. This information tells companies where to target their ads. However, the survey also reported that the participants in this research claimed to have little use for advertising in making their purchasing decisions. They tended not to believe advertising in general and described most of it as condescending to homosexuals (Burnett, 2000). Note that the Web sites www.gay.com and www.planetout.com offer chat rooms, personal ads, shopping information, HIV information, investment opportunities, news, and links to gay-owned businesses.

Let us conclude by noting that manufacturers and advertisers respond to changing markets with new products and marketing techniques. Consumers should be aware of the varied nature of advertising—sometimes valuable and informative and sometimes manipulative and deceptive. As a consumer, you should remember one of history's oldest lessons: *caveat emptor.* Let the buyer—whether of ideas, political philosophies, values, theories, research findings, and even psychology textbooks—beware.

Summary

Consumer psychology studies consumer behavior through surveys, **focus groups,** motivation research, behavioral observations, and brand identification and preference research. Testing for advertising effectiveness is done through direct questioning, **aided recall** and **recognition,** physiological measures, **sales tests,** and coupon returns. Advertising types include direct sell, product image, consumer awareness, and institutional. Advertising appeals can be positive, negative, or mixed, or they may include celebrity endorsements. Many ads involve claims of implied superiority, which consumers tend to believe.

Trademarks can be effective advertising aids, as can the product image. Packaging can also be influential at the point of purchase. Sexy images are commonly used in ads; they attract people to the ads but do not seem to influence how much of the advertising message is recalled. Most people dislike TV commercials, avoid watching them, and fail to remember three-fourths of the ads they see. Internet advertising has increased; simpler Web page design is effective in getting people to purchase the advertised products, although some consumer resistance to online shopping still exists, typically related to shipping charges, credit card safety, and the inability to actually touch or see the product. Men shop more frequently online than women do. Trust in a Web site is also a factor in online shopping. People who spend more time looking at an online ad are more likely to recall the message and recognize the product.

Brand placement (having a product used by a character in a movie or TV program, for example) is effective in influencing consumer opinion about the product. Brand loyalty can render buyers immune to advertising for competing products. Product price is often used as an indication of quality.

Hispanic, Black, and Asian ethnic groups in the United States have become targeted audiences for advertising campaigns designed to appeal to their specific cultural needs and values; these can be seen most often in magazine ads and television commercials. Other groups likely to receive targeted ads include children, adolescents, elderly persons, and gay persons.

Key Terms

aided recall technique
focus groups

recognition technique
sales test technique

Review Questions

1. What did John B. Watson contribute to the study of consumer behavior?
2. Describe some of the results of the nationwide survey by the American Association of Advertising Agencies on popular opinions toward advertising.
3. What are the advantages of online consumer surveys over surveys conducted by telephone or in person?
4. Describe how focus groups are conducted. Discuss advantages and disadvantages of focus groups compared to surveys.
5. How did the study by Ernest Dichter on packaged cake mixes influence consumer research?
6. If you had the job of conducting research on the behavior of consumers shopping for cookies at supermarkets in your city, how would you design the project? What problems would you have to resolve in conducting this research?
7. Describe techniques used by consumer psychologists to test reactions to advertising.
8. How effective is the use of coupons in determining effectiveness of newspaper and magazine ads? What are the advantages of obtaining coupons online compared to cutting coupons out of the newspaper?
9. Which appeals are more effective in advertising: positive or negative appeals? Shock or fear appeals? Give an example of each type.
10. Describe the impact on consumer behavior of product packaging, product pricing, and the use of sex in advertisements.
11. What factors help us remember an ad we have seen? How effective are ads for prescription medications?
12. What are the advantages and disadvantages of advertising on the Web?
13. How do people who like online shopping differ from those who do not like online shopping?
14. What kinds of products are people more likely to purchase online? What are they least likely to buy online?
15. What is brand placement? How effective is brand placement when targeted at adults? At children?
16. How would you devise an ad campaign for upscale furniture if your target was the Hispanic consumer? The Black consumer? The Asian-American consumer? What media would you use for your ads?
17. Describe the major differences between the consumer behavior of Hispanics and of Blacks.
18. What characteristics define the Asian-American population in the United States?
19. Do you think it is ethical to advertise to children under the age of eight? Why or why not?
20. How do gay people appear to differ from nongay people in their consumer behavior?

Kasser, T., & Kanner, A. D. (Eds.) (2004). *Psychology and consumer culture: The struggle for a good life in a materialistic world.* Washington, D.C.: American Psychological Association. An in-depth psychological analysis of consumerism and its effects on people's lives and on society as a whole. Relates consumer behavior to ethnicity, childhood development, gender roles, work stress, and psychopathology.

Lewis, D., & Bridger, D. (2000). *The soul of the new consumer: Authenticity—What we buy and why in the new economy.* London: Nicholas Brealey. Market researchers present findings from consumer surveys on shopping experiences and television commercials. They describe the modern consumer as individualistic and well informed.

Longinotti-Buitoni, G. L. (1999). *Selling dreams: How to make any product irresistible.* New York: Simon & Schuster. The CEO of Ferrari North America describes his research on the emotional link between a product's image and its function. He applies his ideas to cars, hotels, magazines, beauty products, wines, clothing, and electronics.

Reichert, T., & Lambiase, J. (Eds.) (2003). *Sex in advertising: Perspectives on the erotic appeal.* Mahwah, NJ: Erlbaum. Attempts to answer questions about sex in advertising: What is it? Doses it work? Why is it so popular? How does it affect different consumer groups? How is it used by new media? What are its effects on society?

Simonson, I., Carmon, Z., Dhar, R., Drolet, A., & Nowlis, S. M. (2001). Consumer research. *Annual Review of Psychology, 52,* 249–275. Reviews theories of consumer behavior, social and cognitive influences, and research methods (including online behaviors, field experiments, and laboratory research).

Tourangeau, R., Rips, J. L., & Rasinski, K. (2000). *The psychology of survey response.* New York: Cambridge University Press. Summarizes and reviews research on the psychological mechanisms of the survey response. Shows how minor variations in the wording of survey questions can affect employee comprehension, judgment, and response.

Twitchell, J. B. (2001). *20 ads that shook the world: The century's most groundbreaking advertising and how it changed us all.* New York: Crown. A look back at classic ad campaigns for Coca-Cola, Volkswagen, Listerine, Nike, and Lydia E. Pinkham's Vegetable Compound, showing how a market can be created for a product we never knew we needed.

Underhill, P. (1999). *Why we buy: The science of shopping.* New York: Simon & Schuster. An urban geographer presents his findings based on 20 years of observations of shoppers in supermarkets, bookshops, and department stores.

Williams, J. D., Lee, W.-N., & Haugtvedt, C. P. (Eds.) (2004). *Diversity in advertising: Broadening the scope of research directions.* Mahwah, NJ: Erlbaum. Reviews research on diversity in advertising covering prejudice and discrimination, gender bias, language, group differences in information processing, social context, celebrity endorsements, ethnic identity and targeted marketing, culturally embedded ads, religious symbolism, and social values.

References

Alcohol and drug abuse in America today. (2004). Washington, D.C.: U.S. Department of Labor.

Allen, T., Eby, L., Poteet, M., Lentz, E., & Lima, L. (2004). Career benefits associated with mentoring for proteges: A meta-analysis. *Journal of Applied Psychology, 89*, 127–136.

Antonioni, D. (1994). The effects of feedback accountability on upward appraisal ratings. *Personnel Psychology, 47*, 349–356.

Antonioni, D., & Park, H. (2001). The effects of personality similarity on peer ratings of contextual work behavior. *Personnel Psychology, 54*, 331–360.

Aquino, K., Tripp, T., & Bies, R. (2001). How employees respond to personal offense: The effects of blame attribution, victim status, and offender status on revenge and reconciliation in the workplace. *Journal of Applied Psychology, 86*, 52–59.

Arthur, M. (2003). Share price reactions to work-family initiatives: An institutional perspective. *Academy of Management Journal, 46*, 497–505.

Arthur, W., Bennett, W., Edens, P., & Bell, S. (2003). Effectiveness of training in organizations: A meta-analysis of design and evaluation features. *Journal of Applied Psychology, 88*, 234–245.

Arthur, W., Day, E., McNelly, T., & Edens, P. (2003). A meta-analysis of the criterion-related validity of assessment center dimensions. *Personnel Psychology, 56*, 125–154.

As, S. (2001). *The measurement of accident proneness*. Groningen, Netherlands: Groningen University.

Atkins, P., & Wood, R. (2002). Self-versus others' ratings as predictors of assessment center ratings: Validation evidence for 360-degree feedback programs. *Personnel Psychology, 55*, 871–904.

Atkinson, J. W., & Feather, N. T. (1996). *A theory of achievement motivation*. New York: Wiley.

Atwater, L., Waldman, D. A., Atwater, D., & Cartier, P. (2000). An upward feedback field experiment. *Personnel Psychology, 53*, 275–295.

Auty, S., & Lewis, C. (2004). The "delicious paradox": Preconscious processing of product placements by children. In L. Schrum (Ed.), *The psychology of entertainment media: Blurring the lines between entertainment and persuasion*. Mahwah, NJ: Erlbaum.

Avery, D. (2003). Reactions to diversity in recruitment advertising: Are differences Black and White? *Journal of Applied Psychology, 88*, 672–679.

Avery, R., & Ferraro, R. (2000). Verisimilitude or advertising? Brand appearance on prime-time television. *Journal of Consumer Affairs, 34*, 217–244.

Bailey, D. (2004). Number of psychology PhDs declining. *Monitor on Psychology, 35*(2), 18–19.

Bandura, A., & Locke, E. (2003). Negative self-efficacy and goal effects revisited. *Journal of Applied Psychology, 88*, 87–99.

Bargh, J., & McKenna, K. (2004). The Internet and social life. *Annual Review of Psychology, 55,* 573–590.

Barling, J., Kelloway, E., & Iverson, R. (2003). High-quality work, job satisfaction, and occupational injuries. *Journal of Applied Psychology, 88,* 276–283.

Barling, J., Loughlin, C., & Kelloway, E. (2002). Development and test of a model linking safety-specific transformational leadership and occupational safety. *Journal of Applied Psychology, 87,* 488–496.

Barling, J., Zacharatos, A., & Hepburn, C. G. (1999). Parents' job insecurity affects children's academic performance through cognitive difficulties. *Journal of Applied Psychology, 84,* 437–444.

Barrett, J., & Kirk, S. (2000). Running focus groups with elderly and disabled elderly participants. *Applied Ergonomics, 31,* 621–629.

Barrick, M., Stewart, G., & Piotrowski, M. (2002). Personality and job performance: Test of the mediating effects of motivation among sales representatives. *Journal of Applied Psychology, 87,* 43–51.

Barron, K., & Harackiewicz, J. (2001). Achievement goals and optimal motivation: Testing multiple goal models. *Journal of Personality and Social Psychology, 80,* 706–722.

Baruch-Feldman, C., Brondolo, E., Ben-Dayan, D., & Schwartz, J. (2002). Sources of social support and burnout, job satisfaction, and productivity. *Journal of Occupational Health Psychology, 7,* 84–93.

Bass, B., Avolio, B., Jung, D., & Berson, Y. (2003). Predicting unit performance by assessing transformational and transactional leadership. *Journal of Applied Psychology, 88,* 207–218.

Beal, D., Cohen, R., Burke, M., & McLendon, C. (2003). Cohesion and performance in groups: A meta-analytic clarification of construct relations. *Journal of Applied Psychology, 88,* 989–1004.

Bellizzi, J. A. (2000). Drawing prospects to E-commerce Websites. *Journal of Advertising Research, 40,* 43–53.

Bennett, J., & Lehman, W. (2001). Workplace substance abuse prevention and help seeking: Comparing team-oriented and informational training. *Journal of Occupational Health Psychology, 6,* 243–254.

Bennett, R. J., & Robinson, S. L. (2000). Development of a measure of workplace deviance. *Journal of Applied Psychology, 85,* 349–360.

Ben-Yaacov, A., Maltz, M., & Shinar, D. (2002). Effects of an in-vehicle collision avoidance warning system on short- and long-term driving performance. *Human Factors, 44,* 335–342.

Bergman, M., Langhout, R., Palmieri, P., Cortina, L., & Fitzgerald, L. (2002). The (un)reasonableness of reporting: Antecedents and consequences of reporting sexual harassment. *Journal of Applied Psychology, 87,* 230–242.

Birnbaum, M. (2004). Human research on data collection via the Internet. *Annual Review of Psychology, 55,* 803–832.

Bishop, G. D., Enkelmann, H., Tong, E., Why, Y., Diong, S., Ang, J., & Kaader, M. (2003). Job demands, decisional control, and cardiovascular responses. *Journal of Occupational Health Psychology, 8,* 146–156.

Bishop, J. W., & Scott, K. D. (2000). An examination of organizational and team commitment in a self-directed team environment. *Journal of Applied Psychology, 85,* 439–450.

Bobko, P., Roth, P. L., & Potosky, D. (1999). Derivation and implications of a meta-analytic matrix incorporating cognitive ability, alternative predictors, and job performance. *Personnel Psychology, 52,* 561–589.

Bolino, M., & Turnley, W. (2003). Going the extra mile: Cultivating and managing employee citizenship behavior. *Academy of Management Executive, 17*(3), 60–71.

Bond, F., & Bunce, D. (2001). Job control mediates change in work reorganization intervention for stress reduction. *Journal of Occupational Health Psychology, 6,* 290–302.

Bond, F., & Bunce, D. (2003). The role of acceptance and job control in mental health, job satisfaction, and work performance. *Journal of Applied Psychology, 88,* 1057–1067.

Bono, J., & Judge, T. (2003). Self-concordance at work: Toward understanding the motivational effects of transformational leaders. *Academy of Management Review, 46,* 554–571.

Booth-Kewley, S., & Friedman, H. S. (1987). Psychological predictors of heart disease. *Psychological Bulletin, 101,* 343–362.

Boudreau, J., Boswell, W., Judge, T., & Bretz, R., Jr. (2001). Personality and cognitive ability as predictors of job search among employed managers. *Personnel Psychology, 54,* 25–50.

Brett, J., & Stroh, L. (2003). Working 61 plus hours a week: Why do managers do it? *Journal of Applied Psychology, 88,* 67–78.

Bridger, R. S. (2003). *Introduction to ergonomics* (2nd ed.). London: Taylor & Francis.

Brief, A., & Weiss, H. (2002). Organizational behavior: Affect in the workplace. *Annual Review of Psychology, 53,* 2979–307.

Broad, W., & Wade, N. (1982). *Betrayers of the truth.* New York: Simon & Schuster.

Brooks, M., Grauer, E., Thornbury, E., & Highhouse, S. (2003). Value differences between scientists and practitioners: A survey of SIOP members. *The Industrial-Organizational Psychologist, 40*(4), 17–23.

Brown, K. (2001). Using computers to deliver training: Which employees learn and why? *Personnel Psychology, 54,* 271–296.

Brown, M., Sturman, M., & Simmering, M. (2003). Compensation policy and organizational performance: The efficiency, operational, and financial implications of pay levels and pay structure. *Academy of Management Journal, 46,* 752–762.

Bruner, G. C., II, & Kumar, A. (2000). Web commercials and advertising hierarchy-of-effects. *Journal of Advertising Research, 40,* 35–42.

Burnett, J. J. (2000). Gays: Feelings about advertising and media used. *Journal of Advertising Research, 40,* 75–84.

Bushman, B., & Bonacci, A. (2002). Violence and sex impair memory for television ads. *Journal of Applied Psychology, 87,* 557–564.

Button, S. (2001). Organizational efforts to affirm sexual diversity: A cross-level examination. *Journal of Applied Psychology, 86,* 17–28.

Bycio, P., Hackett, R. D., & Allen, J. S. (1995). Further assessments of Bass's (1985) conceptualization of transactional and transformational leadership. *Journal of Applied Psychology, 80,* 468–478.

Cable, D., & Parsons, C. (2001). Socialization tactics and person-organization fit. *Personnel Psychology, 54,* 1–23.

Caligiuri, P. M. (2000). The Big Five personality characteristics as predictors of expatriates' desire to terminate the assignment and supervisor-rated performance. *Personnel Psychology, 53,* 67–88.

Callister, R. R., Kramer, M. W., & Turban, D. B. (1999). Feedback seeking following career transitions. *Academy of Management Journal, 42,* 429–438.

Campion, M., & Berger, C. (1990). Conceptual integration and empirical test of job design and compensation relationships. *Personnel Psychology, 43,* 525–554.

Campion, M., Outtz, J., Zedeck, S., Schmidt, F., Kehoe, J., Murphy, K., & Guion, R. (2001). The controversy over score banding in personnel selection: Answers to ten key questions. *Personnel Psychology, 54,* 149–185.

Cappo, J., (2003). *The future of advertising: New media, new clients, new consumers in the post-television age.* New York: McGraw-Hill.

Cartwright, S. (2000). Taking the pulse of executive health in the U.K. *Academy of Management Executive, 14*(2), 16–23.

Cascio, W. F. (1998). The virtual workplace. *The Industrial-Organizational Psychologist, 35*(4), 32–36.

Cavanaugh, M. A., Boswell, W. R., Roehling, M. V., & Boudreau, J. W. (2000). An empirical examination of self-reported work stress among U.S. managers. *Journal of Applied Psychology, 85,* 65–74.

Chandler, A. D., Jr. (1988). Origins of the organization chart. *Harvard Business Review, 66*(2), 156–157.

Chattopadhyay, P., & George, E. (2001). Examining the effects of work externalization through the lens of social identity theory. *Journal of Applied Psychology, 86,* 781–788.

Chen, G., & Klimoski, R. (2003). The impact of expectations on newcomer performance in teams as mediated by work characteristics, social exchanges, and empowerment. *Academy of Management Journal, 46,* 591–607.

Chiang, D., Brooks, A., & Weir, D. (2004). On the highway measures of driver glance behavior with an example automobile navigation system. *Applied Ergonomics, 35*(3), 215–223.

Chiang, K., & Dholakia, R. (2003). Factors driving consumer intention to shop online: An empirical investigation. *Journal of Consumer Psychology, 13,* 177–183.

Church, A. (2001). Is there a method to our madness? The impact of data collection methodology on organizational survey results. *Personnel Psychology, 54,* 937–969.

Clay, R. A. (2000). Advertising to children. *Monitor on Psychology, 31*(8), 52–53.

Clevenger, J., Pereira, G., Weichmann, D., Schmitt, N., & Harvey, V. (2001). Incremental validity of situational judgment tests. *Journal of Applied Psychology, 86,* 410–417.

Colella, A., Paetzold, R., & Belliveau, M. (2004). Factors affecting co-workers' procedural justice inferences of the workplace accommodations of employees with disabilities. *Personnel Psychology, 57,* 1–23.

Collins, C., & Stevens, C. (2002). The relationship between early recruitment-related activities and the application decisions of new labor-market entrants: A brand equity approach to recruitment. *Journal of Applied Psychology, 87,* 1121–1133.

Cortina, L., Magley, V., Williams, J., & Langhout, R. (2001). Incivility in the workplace: Incidence and impact. *Journal of Occupational Health Psychology, 6,* 64–80.

Coy, P. (2004, March 22). The future of work: Flexible, creative, and good with people? You should do fine in tomorrow's job market. *Business Week,* 50–52.

Cropanzano, R., & Greenberg, J. (1997). Progress in organizational justice: Tunnneling through the maze. In C. Cooper & I. Robertson (Eds.), *International review of industrial and organizational psychology.* New York: Wiley.

Cropanzano, R., Rupp, D., & Byrne, Z. (2003). The relationship of emotional exhaustion to work attitudes, job performance, and organizational citizenship behaviors. *Journal of Applied Psychology, 88,* 160–169.

Crosby, F., Iver, A., Clayton, S., & Downing, R. (2003). Affirmative action: Psychological data and the policy debates. *American Psychologist, 58,* 93–115.

Crowley, B., Hayslip, B., Jr., & Hobdy, J. (2003). Psychological hardiness and adjustment to life events in adulthood. *Journal of Adult Development, 10,* 237–248.

Dahl, D., Frankenberger, K., & Manchanda, R. (2003). Does it pay to shock? Reactions to shocking and nonshocking advertising content among university students. *Journal of Advertising Research, 43,* 268–280.

Dahlen, M., Rasch, A., & Rosengren, S. (2003). Love at first site? A study of Website advertising effectiveness. *Journal of Advertising Research, 43,* 25–34.

Danaher, P., & Mullarkey, G. (2003). Factors affecting online advertising recall: A study of students. *Journal of Advertising Research, 43,* 252–264.

Davidson, O. B., & Eden, D. (2000). Remedial self-fulfilling prophecy. *Journal of Applied Psychology, 85,* 386–398.

Davis, B. L., & Mount, M. K. (1984). Design and use of a performance appraisal feedback system. *Personnel Administrator, 29*(3), 91–97.

Davis-Blake, A., Broschak, J., & George, E. (2003). Happy together? How using nonstandard workers affects exit, voice, and loyalty among standard employees. *Academy of Management Journal, 46,* 475–485.

Day, D., Schleicher, D., Unckless, A., & Hiller, N. (2002). Self-monitoring personality at work: A meta-analytic investigation of construct validity. *Journal of Applied Psychology, 87,* 390–401.

Dayan, K., Kasten, R., & Fox, S. (2002). Entry-level police candidate assessment center: An efficient tool or a hammer to kill a fly? *Personnel Psychology, 55,* 827–849.

DeAngelis, T. (2000). Is Internet addiction real? *Monitor on Psychology, 31*(4), 24–26.

deCroon, E., Sluiter, J., Blonk, R., Broersen, J., & Frings-Dresen, M. (2004). Stressful work, psychological job strain, and turnover: A two-year prospective cohort study of truck drivers. *Journal of Applied Psychology, 89,* 442–454.

Deatherage, B. H. (1972). *Human engineering guide to equipment design.* Washington, D.C.: U.S. Government Printing Office.

DeFrank, R. S., Konopaske, R., & Ivancevich, J. M. (2000). Executive travel stress. *Academy of Management Executive, 14*(2), 58–71.

de Jong, G. M., & Emmelkamp, P. M. G. (2000). Implementing stress management training. *Journal of Occupational Health Psychology, 5,* 309–320.

Dembowski, J. M., & Callans, M. C. (2000, April). Comparing computer and paper forms of the Wonderlic Personnel Test. Paper presented at the meeting of the Society for Industrial and Organizational Psychology, New Orleans, LA.

Demerouti, E., Bakker, A., Nachreiner, F., & Schaufeli, W. (2001). The job demands–resources model of burnout. *Journal of Applied Psychology, 86,* 499–512.

DeNisi, A. S., & Kluger, A. N. (2000). Feedback effectiveness. *Academy of Management Executive, 14*(1), 129–139.

Dietz, J., Robinson, S., Folger, R., Baron, R., & Schulz, M. (2003). The impact of community violence and an organization's procedural justice climate on workplace aggression. *Academy of Management Journal, 46,* 317–326.

Dineen, B., Ash, S., & Noe, R. (2002). A Web of applicant attraction: Person-organization fit in the context of Web-based recruitment. *Journal of Applied Psychology, 87,* 723–734.

Dirks, K., & Ferrin, D. (2002). Trust in leadership: Meta-analytic findings and implications for research and practice. *Journal of Applied Psychology, 87,* 611–628.

Donovan, M. A., Drasgow, F., & Probst, T. M. (2000). Does computerizing paper-and-pencil job attitude scales make a difference? *Journal of Applied Psychology, 85,* 305–313.

Donovan, J. J., & Radosevich, D. J. (1999). A meta-analytic review of the distribution of practice effect. *Journal of Applied Psychology, 84,* 795–805.

Dormann, C., & Zapf, D. (2004). Customer-related social stressors and burnout. *Journal of Occupational Health Psychology, 9,* 61–82.

Douglas, S., & Martinko, M. (2001). Exploring the role of individual differences in the prediction of workplace aggression. *Journal of Applied Psychology, 86,* 547–559.

Druskat, V., & Wheeler, J. (2003). Managing from the boundary: The effective leadership of self-managing work teams. *Academy of Management Journal, 46,* 435–457.

Eagly, A., Johannesen-Schmidt, M., & Van Engen, M. (2003). Transformational, transactional, and laissez-faire leadership styles: A meta-analysis comparing men and women. *Psychological Bulletin, 129,* 569–591.

Eisenberger, R., Armeli, S., Rexwinkel, B., Lynch, P., & Rhoades, L. (2001). Reciprocation of perceived organizational support. *Journal of Applied Psychology, 86,* 42–51.

Eisenberger, R., Stingchamber, F., Vandenberghe, C., Socharski, I., & Rhoades, L. (2002). Perceived supervisor support: Contributions to perceived organizational support and employee retention. *Journal of Applied Psychology, 87,* 565–573.

Eklund, J. A. E. (1995). Relationships between ergonomics and quality in assembly work. *Applied Ergonomics, 26*(1), 15–20.

Ellin, A. (2004, February 29). When it comes to salary, many women don't push. *New York Times.*

Elliott, S. (2004, April 14). Advertising: A survey of consumer attitudes reveals the depth of the challenge that the agencies face. *New York Times.*

Ellis, A., West, B., Ryan, A., & DeShon, R. (2002). The use of impression management tactics in structured interviews: A function of question type? *Journal of Applied Psychology, 87,* 1200–1208.

Ely, R. J. (1995). The power in demography. *Academy of Management Journal, 38,* 589–634.

Epitropaki, O., & Martin, R. (2004). Implicit leadership theories in applied settings: Factor structure, generalizability, and stability over time. *Journal of Applied Psychology, 89,* 293–310.

Ettner, S., & Grzywacz, J. (2001). Workers' perceptions of how jobs affect health: A social ecological perspective. *Journal of Occupational Health Psychology, 6*(2), 101–113.

Evans, D. (2003). A comparison of other-directed stigmatization produced by legal and illegal forms of affirmative action. *Journal of Applied Psychology, 88,* 121–130.

Evans, G. W., & Johnson, D. (2000). Stress and open-office noise. *Journal of Applied Psychology, 85,* 779–783.

Evans O., & Steptoe, A. (2001). Social support at work, heart rate and control: A self-monitoring study. *Journal of Occupational Health Psychology, 6*(4), 361–370.

Everton, W., Mastrangelo, P., & Jolton, J. (2003). Surfin' USA: Using your work computer for personal reasons. *The Industrial-Organizational Psychologist, 40*(4), 90–93.

Ewing, M., DuPlessis, E., & Foster, C. (2001). Cinema advertising reconsidered. *Journal of Advertising Research, 4*(1), 78.

Facteau, J., & Craig, C. (2001). Are performance appraisal ratings from different rating sources comparable? *Journal of Applied Psychology, 86*, 215–227.

Farmer, S., Tierney, P., & Kung-McIntyre, K. (2003). Employee creativity in Taiwan: An application of role identity theory. *Academy of Management Journal, 46*, 618–630.

Feinstein, A. (2002). A hazardous profession: War, journalists, and psychopathology. *American Journal of Psychiatry, 159*, 1570–1579.

Feldman, D., & Klass, B. (2002). Internet job hunting: A field study of applicant experiences with online recruiting. *Human Resource Management, 41*, 175–192.

Ferdman, B. (2003). Accounts of inclusion (and exclusion). *The Industrial-Organizational Psychologist, 40*(4), 81–86.

Fiedler, F. E. (1978). The contingency model and the dynamics of the leadership process. In L. Berkowitz (Ed.), *Advances in experimental social psychology.* New York: Academic Press.

Fiedler, F. E. (2002). The curious role of cognitive resources in leadership. In R. Riggio, S. Murphy, & F. Pirozzolo (Eds.), *Multiple intelligences and leadership* (pp. 91–104). Mahwah, NJ: Erlbaum.

Fitness, J. (2000). Anger in the workplace: An emotion script approach to anger episodes between workers and their superiors, co-workers, and subordinates. *Journal of Organizational Behavior, 21*, 147–162.

Florey, A. T., & Harrison, D. A. (2000). Responses to informal accommodation requests from employees with disabilities. *Academy of Management Journal, 43*, 224–233.

Forth, J., & Millward, N. (2004). High-involvement management and pay in Britain. *Industrial Relations, 43*, 98–119.

Foxall, G. R., & Goldsmith, R. E. (1994). *Consumer psychology for marketing.* London: Routledge.

Frame, J. H., & Beaty, J. C., Jr. (2000, April). An investigation of high-technology survey methods at Hewlett-Packard. Paper presented at the meeting of the Society for Industrial and Organizational Psychology, New Orleans, LA.

French, H. (2003, July 25). Japan's neglected resource: Female workers. *New York Times.*

Frese, M., Beimel, S., & Schoenborn, S. (2003). Action training for charismatic leadership: Two evaluations of studies of a commercial training module on inspirational communication of a vision. *Personnel Psychology, 56*, 671–697.

Friedman, M., & Rosenman, R. H. (1974). *Type A behavior and your heart.* New York: Knopf.

Frone, M. (1998). Predictors of work injuries among employed adolescents. *Journal of Applied Psychology, 83*, 565–576.

Frone, M. (2003). Predictors of overall and on-the-job substance abuse among young workers. *Journal of Occupational Health Psychology, 8*, 39–54.

Fugate, M., Kinicki, A., & Scheck, C. (2002). Coping with an organizational merger over four stages. *Personnel Psychology, 55,* 905–928.

Fuller, J., Stanton, J., Fisher, G., Spitzmueller, C., Russell, S., & Smith, C. (2003). A lengthy look at the daily grind: Time series analysis of events, mood, stress, and satisfaction. *Journal of Applied Psychology, 88,* 1019–1033.

Fulmer, I., Gerhart, B., & Scott, K. (2003). Are the 100 best better: An empirical investigation of the relationship between being "a great place to work" and firm performance. *Personnel Psychology, 56,* 965–993.

Galaif, E., Newcomb, M., & Carmona, J. (2001). Prospective relationships between drug problems and work adjustment in a community sample of adults. *Journal of Applied Psychology, 86,* 337–350.

Ganzach, Y. (1998). Intelligence and job satisfaction. *Academy of Management Journal, 41,* 526–539.

Ganzach, Y., Pazy, A., Ohayun, Y., & Brainin, E. (2002). Social exchange and organizational commitment: Decision-making training for job choice as an alternative to the realistic job preview. *Personnel Psychology, 55,* 613–637.

Garretson, J., & Burton, S. (2003). Highly coupon and sale prone consumers: Benefits beyond price and savings. *Journal of Advertising Research, 43*(2), 162–173.

George, J., & Zhou, J. (2001). When openness to experience and conscientiousness are related to creative behavior: An interactional approach. *Journal of Applied Psychology, 86,* 513–524.

Glomb, B., & Liao, H. (2003). Interpersonal aggression in work groups: Social influence, reciprocal, and individual effects. *Academy of Management Journal, 46,* 486–496.

Gilbreth, F. B. (1911). *Motion study.* Princeton, NJ: Van Nostrand.

Goldman, B. (2001). Toward an understanding of employment discrimination claiming: An integration of organizational justice and social information processing theories. *Personnel Psychology, 54,* 361–386.

Goldstein, H., Yusko, K., & Nicolopoulos, V. (2001). Exploring Black-White subgroup differences of managerial competencies. *Personnel Psychology, 54,* 783–807.

Gomez, C., & Rosen, B. (2001). The leader-member exchange as a link between managerial trust and employee empowerment. *Group and Organization Management, 26,* 53–69.

Gomez-Mejia, L., Larraza-Kintana, M., & Makri, M. (2003). The determinants of executive compensation in family controlled public corporations. *Academy of Management Journal, 46,* 226–237.

Gosling, S., Vazire, S., Srivastava, S., & John, O. (2004). Should we trust Web-based studies? A comparative analysis of six preconceptions. *American Psychologist, 59,* 93–104.

Gowan, M. A., Riordan, C. M., & Gatewood, R. D. (1999). Test of a model of coping with involuntary job loss following a company closing. *Journal of Applied Psychology, 81,* 75–86.

Graen, G., & Schliemann, W. (1978). Leader-member agreement. *Journal of Applied Psychology, 63,* 206–212.

Green, P. (2003). Motor vehicle driver interfaces. In J. Jacko & A. Sears (Eds.), *The human-computer interaction handbook* (pp. 844–860). Mahwah, NJ: Erlbaum.

Greguras, G., Robie, C., Schleicher, D., & Goff, M. (2003). A field study of the effects of rating purpose on the quality of multisource ratings. *Personnel Psychology, 56,* 1–21.

Griffith, K., & Hebl, M. (2002). The disclosure dilemma for gay men and lesbians: "Coming out" at work. *Journal of Applied Psychology, 87,* 1191–1199.

Grow, B. (2004, March 15). Is America ready? *Business Week.*

Gustafsson, E., Delive, L., Edlund, M., & Hagberg, M. (2003). The use of information technology among young adults: Experience, attitudes, and health beliefs. *Applied Ergonomics, 34,* 565–570.

Gustafsson, E., & Hagberg, M. (2003). Computer mouse use in two different hand positions: Exposure, comfort, exertion and productivity. *Applied Ergonomics, 34,* 107–113.

Haaland, S., & Christiansen, N. (2002). Implications of trait-activation theory for evaluating the construct validity of assessment-center ratings. *Personnel Psychology, 55,* 137–163.

Hackman, J. R., & Oldham, G. R. (1976). Motivation through the design of work. *Organizational Behavior and Human Performance, 16,* 250–279.

Hackman, J. R., & Oldham, G. R. (1980). *Work redesign.* Reading, MA: Addison-Wesley.

Hagg, G. (2003). Corporate initiatives in ergonomics: An introduction. *Applied Ergonomics, 34,* 3–15.

Haight, F. (2001). *Accident proneness: The history of an idea.* Irvine, CA: University of California Institute of Transportation Studies.

Hardy, G., Woods, D., & Wall, T. (2003). The impact of psychological distress on absence from work. *Journal of Applied Psychology, 88,* 306–314.

Harned, M., Ormerod, A., Palmieri, P., Collinsworth, L., & Reed, M. (2002). Sexual assault and other types of sexual harassment by workplace personnel: A comparison of antecedents and consequences. *Journal of Occupational Health Psychology, 7,* 174–188.

Harris, M. (2003). Speeding down the information highway: Internet recruitment and testing. *The Industrial-Organizational Psychologist, 41*(2), 103–106.

Hart, P. M. (1999). Predicting employee life satisfaction. *Journal of Applied Psychology, 84,* 564–584.

Harter, J., Schmidt, F., & Hayes, T. (2002). Business-unit-level relationship between employee satisfaction, employee engagement, and business outcomes: A meta-analysis. *Journal of Applied Psychology, 87,* 268–279.

Harvey, S., Kelloway, E., & Duncan-Leiper, L. (2003). Trust in management as a buffer of the relationships between overload and strain. *Journal of Occupational Health Psychology, 8*(4), 306–315.

Hausknecht, J., Trevor, C., & Farr, J. (2002). Retaking ability tests in a selection setting: Implications for practice effects, training performance, and turnover. *Journal of Applied Psychology, 87,* 243–254.

Hechanova-Alampay, R., & Beehr, T. (2001). Empowerment, span of control, and safety performance in work teams after workforce reduction. *Journal of Occupational Health Psychology, 6*(4), 275–282.

Heil, G., Bennis, W., & Stephens, D. (2000). *Douglas McGregor, revisited: Managing the human side of the enterprise.* New York: Wiley.

Hepworth, W., & Towler, A. (2004). The effects of individual differences and charismatic leadership on workplace aggression. *Journal of Occupational Health Psychology, 9*(2), 176–185.

Herbert, B. (2003, December 29). The white-collar blues. *New York Times.*

Herold, D., Davis, W., Fedor, D., & Parsons, C. (2002). Dispositional influences on transfer of learning in multistage training programs. *Personnel Psychology, 55,* 851–869.

Herscovitch, L., & Meyer, J. (2002). Commitment to organizational change: Extension of a three-component model. *Journal of Applied Psychology, 87,* 474–487.

Herzberg, F. (1966). *Work and the nature of man.* Cleveland: World.

Herzberg, F. (1974). Motivator-hygiene profiles. *Organizational Dynamics, 3*(2), 18–29.

Hofmann, D., Morgeson, F., & Gerras, S. (2003). Climate as a moderator of the relationship between leader-member exchange and content specific citizenship: Safety climate as an exemplar. *Journal of Applied Psychology, 88,* 170–178.

Hogan, R., Curphy, G. J., & Hogan, J. (1994). What we know about leadership. *American Psychologist, 49,* 493–504.

Hollingworth, H. L. (1929). *Vocational psychology and character analysis.* New York: Appleton.

Holton, B., Lee, T., & Tidd, S. (2002). The relationship between work status congruence and work-related attitudes and behaviors. *Journal of Applied Psychology, 87,* 903–915.

Hosodo, M., Stone-Romero, E., & Coats, G. (2003). The effects of physical attractiveness on job-related outcomes: A meta-analysis of experimental studies. *Personnel Psychology, 56,* 431–462.

Hough, L. M., & Oswald, F. L. (2000). Personnel selection. *Annual Review of Psychology, 51,* 631–664.

House, R. J. (1971). A path-goal theory of leader effectiveness. *Administrative Science Quarterly, 16,* 321–338.

House, R. J., & Mitchell, T. (1974). Path-goal theory of leadership. *Journal of Contemporary Business, 3,* 81–97.

Hovorka-Mead, A., Ross, W., Jr., Whipple, T., & Renchin, M. (2002). Watching the detectives: Seasonal student employee reactions to electronic monitoring with and without advance notification. *Personnel Psychology, 55,* 329–362.

Howell, J. M., & Hall-Merenda, K. E. (1999). The ties that bind. *Journal of Applied Psychology, 84,* 680–694.

Hsueh, Y. (2002). The Hawthorne experiments and the introduction of Jean Piaget in American industrial psychology, 1929–1932. *History of Psychology, 5,* 163–189.

Huffcutt, A., Conway, J., Roth, P., & Stone, N. (2001). Identification and meta-analytic assessment of psychological constructs measured in employment interviews. *Journal of Applied Psychology, 86,* 897–913.

Huffcutt, A., Weekley, J., Wiesner, W., DeGroot, T., & Jones, C. (2001). Comparison of situational and behavior description interview questions for higher-level positions. *Personnel Psychology, 54,* 619–644.

Huseman, R. C., Hatfield, J. D., & Miles, E. W. (1987). A new perspective on equity theory. *Academy of Management Review, 12,* 222–234.

Ilies, R., Hauserman, N., Schwochau, S., & Stibal, J. (2003). Reported incidence rates of work-related sexual harassment in the United States: Using meta-analysis to explain reported role disparities. *Personnel Psychology, 56,* 609–631.

Ilies, R., & Judge, T. (2003). On the heritability of job satisfaction: The mediating role of personality. *Journal of Applied Psychology, 88,* 750–759.

Iverson, R., & Deery, S. (2001). Understanding the "personological" basis of employee withdrawal: The influence of affective disposition on employee tardiness, early departure, and absenteeism. *Journal of Applied Psychology, 86,* 856–866.

Jackson, N. (2003, August 3). Opinions to spare? Click here. *New York Times.*

Jacobs, D. (2004). Douglas McGregor: The human side of enterprise in peril [book review]. *Academy of Management Review, 29,* 293–296.

Jamal, M., & Baba, V. (2003). Type A behavior, components and outcomes: A study of Canadian employees. *International Journal of Stress Management, 10,* 39–50.

James, E., Brief, A., Dietz, J., & Cohen, R. (2001). Prejudice matters: Understanding the reactions of Whites to affirmative-action programs targeted to benefit Blacks. *Journal of Applied Psychology, 86,* 1120–1128.

Jansen, P., & Stoop, B. (2001). The dynamics of assessment-center validity: Results of a nine-year study. *Journal of Applied Psychology, 86,* 741–753.

Janssen, O., & Van Yperen, N. (2004). Employees' goal orientations, the quality of leader-member exchange, and the outcomes of job performance and job satisfaction. *Academy of Management Journal, 47,* 368–384.

Jawahar, I. (2001). Attitudes, self-monitoring, and appraisal behaviors. *Journal of Applied Psychology, 86,* 875–883.

Jeanneret, P., & Strong, M. (2003). Linking O*NET job analysis information to job requirement predictors: An O*NET application. *Personnel Psychology, 56,* 465–492.

Jett, Q., & George, J. (2003). Work interrupted: A closer look at the role of interruptions in organizational life. *Academy of Management Review, 28,* 494–507.

Jex, S., Bliese, P., Buzzell, S., & Primeau, J. (2001). The impact of self-efficacy on stressor–strain relations: Coping style as an explanatory mechanism. *Journal of Applied Psychology, 86,* 401–409.

Jockin, V., Arvey, R., & McGue, M. (2001). Perceived victimization moderates self-reports of workplace aggression and conflict. *Journal of Applied Psychology, 86,* 1262–1269.

Johnson, J. W., & Ferstl, K. L. (1999). The effects of interrater and self-other agreement on performance improvement following upward feedback. *Personnel Psychology, 52,* 271–303.

Judge, T., & Bono, J. (2000). Five-factor model of personality and transformational leadership. *Journal of Applied Psychology, 85,* 751–765.

Judge, T., & Bono, J. (2001). Relationship of core self-evaluations traits—self-esteem, generalized self-efficacy, locus of control, and emotional stability—with job satisfaction and job performance: A meta-analysis. *Journal of Applied Psychology, 86,* 80–92.

Judge, T., Bono, J., Ilies, R., & Gerhardt, M. (2002). Personality and leadership: A qualitative and quantitative review. *Journal of Applied Psychology, 87,* 765–780.

Judge, T., Bono, J., & Locke, E. (2000). Personality and job satisfaction. *Journal of Applied Psychology, 85,* 237–249.

Judge, T., & Cable, D. (2004). The effect of physical height on workplace success and income: Preliminary test of a theoretical model. *Journal of Applied Psychology, 89,* 428–441.

Judge, T., Colbert, A., & Ilies, R. (2004). Intelligence and leadership: A quantitative review and test of theoretical propositions. *Journal of Applied Psychology, 89,* 542–552.

Judge, T., Heller, D., & Mount, M. (2002). Five-factor model of personality and job satisfaction: A meta-analysis. *Journal of Applied Psychology, 87,* 530–541.

Judge, T., & Ilies, R. (2002). Relationship of personality to performance motivation: A meta-analytic review. *Journal of Applied Psychology, 87,* 797–807.

Judge, T., Piccolo, R., & Ilies, R. (2004). The forgotten ones? The validity of consideration and initiating structure in leadership research. *Journal of Applied Psychology, 89,* 36–51.

Judge, T., Thoresen, C., Bono, J., & Patton, G. (2001). The job satisfaction–job performance relationship: A qualitative and quantitative review. *Psychological Bulletin, 127,* 376–407.

Judge, T., Thoresen, C., Pucik, V., & Welbourne, T. M. (1999). Managerial coping with organizational change. *Journal of Applied Psychology, 84,* 107–122.

Kacmar, K., Witt, L., Ziunuska, S., & Gully, S. (2003). The interactive effect of leader-member exchange and communications frequency on performance ratings. *Journal of Applied Psychology, 88,* 764–772.

Kalimo, R., Taris, T., & Schaufeli, W. (2003). The effects of past and anticipated future downsizing on survivor well-being: An equity perspective. *Journal of Occupational Health Psychology, 8*(2), 91–109.

Kammeyer-Mueller, J., & Wanberg, C. (2003). Unwrapping the organizational entry process: Disentangling multiple antecedents and their pathways to adjustment. *Journal of Applied Psychology, 88,* 779–794.

Kanner, A. D., & Kasser, T. (2000). Stuffing our kids. *The Industrial-Organizational Psychologist, 38*(1), 185–187.

Kark, R., Shamir, B., & Chen, G. (2003). The two faces of transformational leadership: Empowerment and dependency. *Journal of Applied Psychology, 88,* 246–255.

Kates, S. M. (2000). Out of the closet and out on the street! *Psychology and Marketing, 17,* 493–513.

Katkowski, D., & Medsker, G. (2001). SIOP income and employment: Income and employment of SIOP members in 2000. *The Industrial-Organizational Psychologist, 391,* 21–36.

Kelly, R. M., & Kelly, V. P. (1990). Lillian Moller Gilbreth (1878–1972). In A. N. O'Connell & N. F. Russo (Eds.), *Women in psychology* (pp. 117–124). New York: Greenwood.

Kerr, N., & Tindale, R. (2004). Group performance and decision making. *Annual Review of Psychology, 55,* 623–655.

Kersting, K. (2004a). How do you test on the Web? Responsibly. *Monitor on Psychology, 35*(3), 26–27.

Kersting, K. (2004b). Driving teen egos and buying through branding. *Monitor on Psychology, 35*(6), 60–61.

Kim, Y., & Kang, J. (2001). The effects of ethnicity and product on purchase decision making. *Journal of Advertising Research, 41*(2), 39.

Kinicki, A., McKee-Ryan, F., Schriesheim, C., & Carson, K. (2002). Assessing the construct validity of the Job Descriptive Index: A review and meta-analysis. *Journal of Applied Psychology, 87,* 14–32.

Klein, H. J., & Kim, J. S. (1998). A field study of the influence of situational constraints, leader-member exchange, and goal commitment on performance. *Academy of Management Journal, 41,* 88–95.

Klein, H. J., Wesson, M. J., Hollenbeck, J. R., & Alge, B. J. (1999). Goal commitment and the goal-setting process. *Journal of Applied Psychology, 84,* 885–896.

Klein, K., Conn, A., & Sorra, J. (2001). Implementing computerized technology: An organizational analysis. *Journal of Applied Psychology, 86,* 811–824.

Kluger, J. (2004, April 5). Just too loud. *Time.*

Kobasa, S. C. (1979). Stressful life events, personality, and health. *Journal of Personality and Social Psychology, 37,* 1–11.

Kobasa, S. C. (1982). The hardy personality. In G. Sanders & J. Suls (Eds.), *Social psychology of health and illness* (pp. 3–32). Hillsdale, NJ: Erlbaum.

Kodak's ergonomic design for people at work (2nd ed.). (2004). New York: Wiley.

Kolmstetter, E. (2003). I-O's making an impact: TSA transportation security screener skill standards, selection system, and hiring process. *The Industrial-Organizational Psychologist, 40*(4), 39–46.

Korsgaard, M., Brodt, S., & Whitener, E. (2002). Trust in the face of conflict: The role of managerial trustworthy behavior and organizational context. *Journal of Applied Psychology, 87,* 312–319.

Korsgaard, M., Sapienza, H., & Schweiger, D. (2002). Beaten before begun: The role of procedural justice in planning change. *Journal of Management, 28,* 497–516.

Koys, D. (2001). The effects of employee satisfaction, organizational citizenship behavior, and turnover on organizational effectiveness: A unit-level longitudinal study. *Personnel Psychology, 54,* 101–114.

Kraut, R., Olson, J., Banaji, M., Bruckman, A., Cohen, J., & Couper, M. (2004). Psychological research online: Report of the Board of Scientific Affairs' Advisory Group on the Conduct of Research on the Internet. *American Psychologist, 59,* 105–117.

Kravitz, D. (2003). More women in the workplace: Is there a payoff in firm performance? *Academy of Management Executive, 17*(3), 148–149.

Kravitz, D., & Klineberg, S. L. (2000). Reactions to two versions of affirmative action among Whites, Blacks, and Hispanics. *Journal of Applied Psychology, 85,* 597–611.

Kroemer, K., Kroemer, H., & Kroemer-Elbert, K. (2000). *Ergonomics: How to design for ease and efficiency* (2nd ed.). Upper Saddle River, NJ: Prentice Hall.

Kuegler, T. (2000). *Advertising and marketing* (3rd ed.). Rocklin, CA: Prima Publishing.

Kuncel, N., Hezlett, S., & Ones, D. (2004). Academic performance, career potential, creativity, and job performance: Can one construct predict them all? *Journal of Personality and Social Psychology, 86,* 148–161.

Kwak, H., Fox, R., & Zinkhan, G. (2002). What products can be successfully promoted and sold via the Internet? *Journal of Advertising Research, 42*(1), 23–39.

LaFerle, C., Edwards, S. M., & Lee, W.-N. (2000). Teens' use of traditional media and the Internet. *Journal of Advertising Research, 40*(3), 55–65.

Lam, S., Yik, M., & Schaubroeck, J. (2002). Responses to formal performance appraisal feedback: The role of negative affectivity. *Journal of Applied Psychology, 87,* 192–201.

LaMotte, J., Ridder, W., Yeung, K., & DeLand, P. (2000). Effect of aftermarket automobile window tinting films on driver vision. *Human Factors, 42,* 327–336.

Lancaster, J. (2004). *Making time: Lillian Moller Gilbreth: A life beyond "Cheaper by the dozen."* Boston: Northeastern University Press.

Landrum, R., & Harrold, R. (2003). What employers want from psychology graduates. *Teaching of Psychology, 30*(2), 131–133.

Lawler, E. E., III. (1986). *High-involvement management*. San Francisco: Jossey-Bass.

LeBlanc, M., & Kelloway, E. (2002). Predictors and outcomes of workplace violence and aggression. *Journal of Applied Psychology, 87*, 444–453.

Lee, J., McGehee, D., Brown, T., & Reyes, M. (2002). Collision warning timing, driver distraction, and driver response to imminent rear-end collisions in a high-fidelity driving simulator. *Human Factors, 44*, 314–334.

Lee, K., & Allen, N. (2002). Organizational citizenship behavior and workplace deviance: The role of affect and cognitions. *Journal of Applied Psychology, 87*, 131–142.

Lefkowitz, J. (1970). Effect of training on the productivity and tenure of sewing machine operators. *Journal of Applied Psychology, 54*, 81–86.

Legree, P., Heffner, T., Psotka, J., Medsker, G., & Martin, D. (2003). Traffic crash involvement: Experiential driving knowledge and stressful contextual antecedents. *Journal of Applied Psychology, 88*, 15–26.

Levin, D., & Linn, S. (2004). The commercialization of childhood: Understanding the problem and finding solutions. In T. Kasser & A. Kanner (Eds.), *Psychology and consumer culture: The struggle for a good life in a materialistic world* (pp. 213–232). Washington, D.C.: American Psychological Association.

Lewis, K. (2000). When leaders display emotion: How followers respond to negative emotional expression of male and female leaders. *Journal of Organizational Behavior, 21*, 221–234.

Liao, H., Arvey, R., Butler, R., & Nutting, S. (2001). Correlates of work injury frequency and duration among firefighters. *Journal of Occupational Health Psychology, 6*(3), 229–242.

Liden, R. C., Wayne, S. J., & Sparrowe, R. T. (2000). An examination of the mediating role of psychological empowerment on the relations between the job, interpersonal relationships, and work outcomes. *Journal of Applied Psychology, 85*, 407–416.

Lievens, F., Harris, M., Van Keer, E., & Bisqueret, C. (2003). Predicting cross-cultural training performance: The validity of personality, cognitive ability, and dimensions measured by an assessment center and a behavior description interview. *Journal of Applied Psychology, 88*, 476–489.

Lim, V. (2003). Managing HIV at the workplace: An empirical study of HIV and HR managers in Singapore. *Journal of Occupational Health Psychology, 8*(4), 235–246.

Locke, E. A. (1968). Toward a theory of task motivation and incentives. *Organizational Behavior and Human Performance, 3*, 157–189.

Locke, E. A., & Latham, G. P. (1990). *A theory of goal setting and task performance*. Upper Saddle River, NJ: Prentice Hall.

Locke, E. A., & Latham, G. P. (2002). Building a practically useful theory of goal setting and task motivation: A 35-year odyssey. *American Psychologist, 57*, 705–717.

Locke, E. A., & Latham, G. P. (2004). What should we do about motivation theory? Six recommendations for the 21st century. *Academy of Management Review, 29*, 388–403.

Lord, R., Brown, D., & Freiburg, S. (1999). Understanding the dynamics of leadership: The role of follower self-concepts in the leader-follower relationship. *Organizational Behavior and Human Decision Processes, 78*, 167–203.

Lord, R., & Maher, K. (1993). *Leadership and information processing: Linking perceptions and performance*. London: Routledge.

Lundberg, U., & Lindfors, P. (2002). Psychophysiological reactions to telework in female and male white-collar workers. *Journal of Occupational Health Psychology, 7*(4), 354–364.

Lynch, P., Kent, R., & Srinivasan, S. (2001). The global Internet shopper: Evidence from shopping tasks in 12 countries. *Journal of Advertising Research, 41*(3), 15–31.

Lyness, K., & Thompson, D. (2000). Climbing the corporate ladder. *Journal of Applied Psychology, 85,* 86–101.

Maier, G., & Brunstein, J. (2001). The role of personal work goals in newcomers' job satisfaction and organizational commitment: A longitudinal analysis. *Journal of Applied Psychology, 86,* 1034–1042.

Mainiero, L., & Gibson, D. (2003). Managing employee trauma: Dealing with the emotional fallout from September 11th. *Academy of Management Executive, 17*(3), 130–143.

Major, V., Klein, K., & Ehrart, M. (2002). Work time, work interference with family, and psychological distress. *Journal of Applied Psychology, 87,* 427–436.

Margulies, A. (2004). 2004 SIOP tour: Hamburger University. *The Industrial-Organizational Psychologist, 41*(3), 168–169.

Markham, S., Scott, K., & McKee, G. (2002). Recognizing good attendance: A longitudinal, quasi-experimental field study. *Personnel Psychology, 55,* 639–660.

Martell, R., & Desmet, A. (2001). A diagnostic-ratio approach to measuring beliefs about the leadership abilities of male and female managers. *Journal of Applied Psychology, 86,* 1223–1231.

Martin, D., Brooks, R., Ortiz, D., & Veniegas, R. (2003). Perceived employment barriers and their relation to workforce-entry intent among people with HIV/AIDS. *Journal of Occupational Health Psychology, 8*(3), 181–194.

Maslach, C., & Jackson, S. E. (1986). *Maslach Burnout Inventory manual* (2nd ed.). Palo Alto, CA: Consulting Psychologists Press.

Maslach, C., Schaufeli, W., & Leiter, M. (2001). Job burnout. *Annual Review of Psychology, 52,* 397–422.

Maslow, A. (1970). *Motivation and personality* (2nd ed.). New York: Harper & Row.

Maslyn, J., & Uhl-Bien, M. (2001). Leader-member exchange and its dimensions: Effects of self-effort and others' effort on relationship quality. *Journal of Applied Psychology, 86,* 697–708.

Maurer, T., Solamon, J., Andrews, K., & Troxtel, D. (2001). Interviewee coaching, preparation strategies, and response strategies in relation to performance in situational employment interviews. *Journal of Applied Psychology, 86,* 709–717.

Maurer, T., Weiss, E., & Barbeite, F. (2003). A model of involvement in work-related learning and development activity: The effects of individual, situational, motivational, and age variables. *Journal of Applied Psychology, 88,* 707–724.

May, D., Reed, K., & Schwoerer, C. (2004). Ergonomic office design and aging: A quasi-experimental field study of employee reactions to an ergonomics intervention program. *Journal of Occupational Health Psychology, 9*(2), 123–135.

Mayer, R. C., & Davis, J. H. (1999). The effect of the performance appraisal system on trust for management. *Journal of Applied Psychology, 84,* 123–136.

McClelland, D. C. (1961). *The achieving society.* New York: Free Press.

McClelland, D. C. (1975). *Power.* New York: Irvington.

McClelland, D. C., Atkinson, J. W., Clark, R. A., & Lowell, E. L. (1953). *The achievement motive.* New York: Appleton-Century-Crofts.

McDaniel, M., Morgeson, F., Finnegan, E., Campion, M., & Braverman, E. (2001). Use of situational judgment tests to predict job performance: A clarification of the literature. *Journal of Applied Psychology, 86,* 730–740.

McElroy, J., Morrow, P., & Rude, S. (2001). Turnover and organizational performance: A comparative analysis of the effects of voluntary, involuntary, and reduction-in-force turnover. *Journal of Applied Psychology, 86,* 1294–1299.

McFadden, K. (2002). DWI convictions linked to a higher risk of alcohol-related aircraft accidents. *Human Factors, 44,* 522–529.

McFarlin, S. K., Fals-Stewart, W., Major, D. A., & Justice, E. M. (2000, April). Alcohol use and workplace aggression. Paper presented at the meeting of the Society for Industrial and Organizational Psychology, New Orleans, LA.

McGregor, D. (1960). *The human side of enterprise.* New York: McGraw-Hill.

McKinney, A., Mecham, K., D'Angelo, N., & Connerly, M. (2003). Recruiters' use of CPA in initial screening decisions. *Personnel Psychology, 56,* 823–845.

McLean, L., Tingley, M., Scott, R., & Rickards, J. (2001). Computer terminal work and the benefit of microbreaks. *Applied Ergonomics, 32,* 225–237.

McMillan, S., Hwang, J., & Lee, G. (2003). Effects of structural and perceptual factors on attitudes toward the Web site. *Journal of Advertising Research, 43*(14), 400–410.

McNatt, D. B. (2000). Ancient Pygmalion joins contemporary management. *Journal of Applied Psychology, 85,* 314–322.

McPheters, R., & Kossoff, J. (2003). Effects of differential enhancements on mail response rates. *Journal of Advertising Research, 43*(1), 14–16.

Mehta, A. (2000). Advertising attitudes and advertising effectiveness. *Journal of Advertising Research, 40*(3), 67–72.

Mehta, A., & Purvis, S. (2003). Consumer response to print prescription drug advertising. *Journal of Advertising Research, 43*(2), 194–206.

Melamed, S., Fried, Y., & Froom, P. (2001). The interactive effect of chronic exposure to noise and job complexity on changes in blood pressure and job satisfaction: A longitudinal study of industrial employees. *Journal of Occupational Health Psychology, 6*(3), 182–195.

Meyer, J. P., & Allen, N. J. (1991). A three-component conceptualization of organizational commitment. *Human Resource Management Review, 1,* 61–98.

Morrison, E. (2002). Newcomers' relationships: The role of social network ties during socialization. *Academy of Management Journal, 45,* 1149–1160.

Morrison, E. W., & Phelps, C. C. (1999). Taking charge at work. *Academy of Management Journal, 42,* 403–419.

Muchinsky, P. (2004). When the psychometrics of test development meet organizational realities: A conceptual framework for organizational change, examples, and recommendations. *Personnel Psychology, 57,* 175–209.

Mumaw, R., Roth, E., Vicente, K., & Burns, C. (2000). There is more to monitoring a nuclear power plant than meets the eye. *Human Factors, 42,* 36–55.

Munson, L. J., Hulin, C., & Drasgow, F. (2000). Longitudinal analysis of dispositional influences and sexual harassment. *Personnel Psychology, 53,* 21–46.

Münsterberg, H. (1913). *The psychology of industrial efficiency.* Boston: Houghton Mifflin.

Naglieri, J., Drasgow, F., Schmit, M., Handler, L., Prifitera, A., Margolis, A., & Velasquez, R. (2004). Psychological testing on the Internet: New problems, old issues. *American Psychologist, 59,* 150–162.

Nelson, D. L., & Burke, R. J. (2000). Women executives. *Academy of Management Executive, 14*(2), 107–121.

Neubert, M., & Cady, S. (2001). Program commitment: A multi-study longitudinal field investigation of its impact and antecedents. *Personnel Psychology, 54,* 421–448.

Neuman, G. A., & Wright, J. (1999). Team effectiveness. *Journal of Applied Psychology, 84,* 376–389.

Noguchi, Y. (2004, June 6). Hola! Stay in touch? Telecom companies are eager to help Hispanic families do just that. *Washington Post.*

Offermann, L., & Malamut, A. (2002). When leaders harass: The impact of target perceptions of organizational leadership and climate on harassment reporting and outcomes. *Journal of Applied Psychology, 87,* 885–893.

Olson, G., & Olson, J. (2003). Human-computer interaction: Psychological aspects of the human use of computing. *Annual Review of Psychology, 54,* 491–516.

Olson, W., & Sarter, N. (2001). Management by consent in human-machine systems: When and why it breaks down. *Human Factors, 43,* 255–266.

O'Neil, B., & Mone, M. (1998). Investigating equity sensitivity as a moderator of relations between self-efficacy and workplace attitudes. *Journal of Applied Psychology, 83,* 805–816.

Panagiotopoulou, G., Christoulas, K., Papanckolaou, A., & Mandroukas, K. (2004). Classroom furniture dimensions and anthropometric measures in primary school. *Applied Ergonomics, 35*(2), 121–128.

Parasuraman, S., & Purohit, Y. S. (2000). Distress and boredom among orchestra musicians. *Journal of Occupational Health Psychology, 5,* 74–83.

Parker, S. (1998). Enhancing role-breadth self-efficacy. *Journal of Applied Psychology, 83,* 835–852.

Parker, S., Axtell, C., & Turner, M. (2001). Designing a safer workplace: Importance of job autonomy, communications quality, and supportive supervisors. *Journal of Occupational Health Psychology, 6*(3), 211–228.

Parker, S., & Griffin, M. (2002). What is so bad about a little name-calling? Negative consequences of gender harassment for overperformance demands and distress. *Journal of Occupational Health Psychology, 7*(3), 195–210.

Parker, S., Griffin, M., Sprigg, C., & Wall, T. (2002). Effect of temporary contracts on perceived work characteristics and job strain: A longitudinal study. *Personnel Psychology, 55,* 689–719.

Parkes, K. (2003). Shiftwork and environment as interactive predictors of work perceptions. *Journal of Occupational Health Psychology, 8*(4), 266–281.

Paronto, M., Truxillo, D., Bauer, T., & Leo, M. (2002). Drug testing, drug treatment, and marijuana use: A fairness perspective. *Journal of Applied Psychology, 87,* 1159–1166.

Payne, N., Jones, F., & Harris, P. (2002). The impact of working life on health behavior: The effect of job strain on the cognitive predictors of exercise. *Journal of Occupational Health Psychology, 79*(4), 342–353.

Peterson, N., Mumford, M., Borman, W., Jeanneret, P., Fleishman, E., Levin, K., Campion, M., Mayfield, M., Morgeson, F., Pearlman, K., Gowing, M., Lancaster, A., Silver, M., & Due, D. (2001). Understanding work using the occupational information network O*NET: Implications for practice and research. *Personnel Psychology, 54,* 451–492.

Peterson, R., Smith, D., Martorana, P., & Owens, P. (2003). The impact of chief executive officer personality on top management team dynamics: One mechanism by which leadership affects organizational performance. *Journal of Applied Psychology, 88,* 795–807.

Ployhart, R., Weekley, J., Holtz, B., & Kemp, C. (2003). Web-based and paper-and-pencil testing of applicants in a proctored setting: Are personality, biodata, and situational judgment tests comparable? *Personnel Psychology, 56,* 733–752.

Posig, M., & Kickul, J. (2003). Extending our understanding of burnout: Test of an integrated model in nonservice occupations. *Journal of Occupational Health Psychology, 8*(1), 3–19.

Posthuma, R., Morgeson, F., & Campion, M. (2002). Beyond employment interview validity: A comprehensive narrative review of recent research and trends over time. *Personnel Psychology, 55,* 1–81.

Potter, P., Smith, B., Strobel, K., & Zautra, A. (2002). Interpersonal workplace stressors and well-being: A multi-wave study of employees with and without arthritis. *Journal of Applied Psychology, 87,* 789–796.

Powell, G., & Butterfield, D. (2002). Exploring the influence of decision-makers' race and gender on actual promotion to top management. *Personnel Psychology, 55,* 397–428.

Price, R., Choi, J., & Vinokur, A. (2002). Links in the chain of adversity following job loss: How financial strain and loss of personal control lead to depression, impaired functioning, and poor health. *Journal of Occupational Health Psychology, 9*(4), 302–312.

Probst, T. (2000). Wedded to the job. *Journal of Occupational Health Psychology, 5,* 63–73.

Probst, T. (2004). Safety and insecurity: Exploring the moderating effect of organizational safety climate. *Journal of Occupational Health Psychology, 9*(1), 3–10.

Probst, T., & Brubaker, T. (2001). The effects of job insecurity on employee safety outcomes: Cross-sectional and longitudinal explorations. *Journal of Occupational Health Psychology, 6*(2), 139–159.

Psihogios, J., Sommerich, C., Mirka, G., & Moon, S. (2001). A field evaluation of monitor placement effects in VDT users. *Applied Ergonomics, 32,* 313–325.

Ragins, B., & Cornwell, J. (2001). Pink triangles: Antecedents and consequences of perceived workplace discrimination against gay and lesbian employees. *Journal of Applied Psychology, 86,* 1244–1261.

Ragins, B., & Cotton, J. L. (1999). Mentor functions and outcomes. *Journal of Applied Psychology, 84,* 529–550.

Reilly, R. R., Smither, J. W., & Vasilopoulos, N. L. (1996). A longitudinal study of upward feedback. *Personnel Psychology, 49,* 599–612.

Rhoades, L., & Eisenberger, R. (2002). Perceived organizational support: A review of the literature. *Journal of Applied Psychology, 87,* 698–714.

Rhoades, L., Eisenberger, R., & Armeli, S. (2001). Affective commitment to the organization: The contributions of perceived organizational support. *Journal of Applied Psychology, 86,* 825–836.

Richtel, M. (2000, July 6). The lure of data: Is it addictive? *New York Times.*

Roberts, B., Caspi, A., & Moffitt, T. (2003). Work experiences and personality development in young adulthood. *Journal of Personality and Social Psychology, 84,* 582–593.

Rodgers, S., & Harris, M. (2003). Gender and e-commerce: An exploratory study. *Journal of Advertising Research, 43*(3), 322–330.

Roethlisberger, F. J., & Dickson, W. J. (1939). *Management and the worker.* Cambridge, MA: Harvard University Press.

Rogelberg, S. G., Luong, A., Sederburg, M. E., & Cristol, D. S. (2000). Employee attitude surveys. *Journal of Applied Psychology, 85,* 284–293.

Rosenthal, R., & Jacobson, L. (1968). *Pygmalion in the classroom.* New York: Holt.

Rospenda, K. (2002). Workplace harassment, services utilization, and drinking outcomes. *Journal of Occupational Health Psychology, 7*(2), 141–155.

Roth, P., Bevier, C., Bobko, P., Switzer, F., & Tyler, P. (2001). Ethnic group differences in cognitive ability in employment and educational settings: A meta-analysis. *Personnel Psychology, 54,* 297–330.

Rothbard, N., & Edwards, J. (2003). Investment in work and family roles: A test of identity and utilitarian motives. *Personnel Psychology, 56,* 699–736.

Rotundo, M., Nguyen, D., & Sackett, P. (2001). A meta-analytic review of gender differences in perception of sexual harassment. *Journal of Applied Psychology, 86,* 914–922.

Rotundo, M., & Sackett, P. (1999). Effect of rater race on conclusions regarding differential prediction in cognitive ability tests. *Journal of Applied Psychology, 84,* 815–822.

Ryan, A., West, B., & Carr, J. (2003). Effects of the terrorist attacks of September 11, 2001, on employee attitudes. *Journal of Applied Psychology, 89,* 647–659.

Rynes, S., Brown, K., & Colbert, A. (2002). Seven common misconceptions about human resource practices: Research findings versus practitioner beliefs. *Academy of Management Executive, 16*(3), 92–102.

Sacco, J., Scheu, C., Ryan, A., & Schmitt, N. (2003). An investigation of race and sex similarity effects in interviews: A multilevel approach to relational demography. *Journal of Applied Psychology, 88,* 852–865.

Saks, A. (2002). So what is a good transfer of training estimate? *The Industrial-Organizational Psychologist, 39*(3), 29–30.

Saks, A., & Ashforth, B. (2002). Is job search related to employment quality? *Journal of Applied Psychology, 87,* 646–654.

Salas, E., & Cannon-Bowers, J. (2001). The science of training: A decade of progress. *Annual Review of Psychology, 52,* 471–499.

Salgado, J., Anderson, N., Moscoso, S., Bertua, C., & Fruyt, F. (2003). International validity generalization of general mental ability and cognitive abilities: A European community meta-analysis. *Personnel Psychology, 56,* 573–605.

Salgado, J., Anderson, N., Moscoso, S., Bertua, C., Fruyt, F., & Rolland, J. (2003). A meta-analytic study of general mental ability validity for different occupations in the European community. *Journal of Applied Psychology, 88,* 1068–1081.

Sanders, M. S., & McCormick, E. J. (1987). *Human factors in engineering and design* (6th ed.). New York: McGraw-Hill.

Sarchione, C. D., Cuttler, M. J., Muchinsky, P. M., & Nelson-Gray, R. O. (1998). Prediction of dysfunctional job behavior among law enforcement officers. *Journal of Applied Psychology, 83,* 904–912.

Sarter, N., & Schroeder, B. (2001). Supporting decision making and action selection under time pressure and uncertainty: The case of in-flight icing. *Human Factors, 43,* 573–583.

Savicki, V. (2002). *Burnout across 13 cultures: Stress and coping in child and youth care workers.* Westport, CT: Praeger/Greenwood.

Schat, A., & Kelloway, E. (2003). Reducing the adverse consequences of workplace aggression and violence: The buffering effects of organizational support. *Journal of Occupational Health Psychology, 8*(2), 110–122.

Schaubroeck, J., Jones, J., & Xie, J. (2001). Individual differences in utilizing control to cope with job demands: Effects on susceptibility to infectious disease. *Journal of Applied Psychology, 86,* 265–278.

Schaubroeck, J., & Lam, S. (2002). How similarity to peers and supervisor influences organizational advancement in different cultures. *Academy of Management Journal, 45,* 1120–1136.

Schaubroeck, J., Lam, S., & Xie, J. (2000). Collective efficacy versus self-efficacy in coping responses to stressors and control. *Journal of Applied Psychology, 85,* 512–525.

Schiffman, L., & Kanuk, L. (2004). *Consumer behavior* (8th ed.). Upper Saddle River, NJ: Prentice Hall.

Schmidt, F. L., & Hunter, J. E. (1998). The validity and utility of selection methods in personnel psychology. *Psychological Bulletin, 124,* 262–274.

Schmidt, F. L., & Hunter, J. E. (2004). General mental ability in the world of work: Occupational attainment and job performance. *Journal of Personality and Social Psychology, 86,* 162–173.

Schminke, M., Ambrose, M. L., & Cropanzano, R. S. (2000). The effect of organizational structure on perceptions of procedural fairness. *Journal of Applied Psychology, 85,* 294–304.

Schmitt, N., & Kunce, C. (2002). The effects of required elaboration of answers to biodata questions. *Personnel Psychology, 55,* 569–587.

Schmitz, N., Neumann, W., & Oppermann, R. (2000). Stress, burnout, and locus of control in German nurses. *International Journal of Nursing Studies, 37*(2), 95–99.

Schneider, K. T., Hitlan, R. T., & Radhakrishnan, P. (2000). An examination of the nature and correlates of ethnic harassment experiences in multiple contexts. *Journal of Applied Psychology, 81,* 3–12.

Scholz, U., Dona, B., Sud, S., & Schwarzer, R. (2002). Is general self-efficacy a universal construct? Psychometric findings from 25 countries. *European Journal of Psychological Assessment, 18*(3), 242–251.

Schriesheim, C. A., Neider, L. L., & Scandura, T. A. (1998). Delegation and leader-member exchange. *Academy of Management Journal, 41,* 298–318.

Schweitzer, M. E., & Kerr, J. L. (2000). Bargaining under the influence. *Academy of Management Executive, 14*(2), 47–57.

Scott, W. D. (1903). *The theory and practice of advertising.* Boston: Small.

Seagull, J., & Sanderson, P. (2001). Anaesthesia alarms in context: An observational study. *Human Factors, 43,* 66–78.

Seashore, S. E., & Bowers D. G. (1970). Durability of organizational change. *American Psychologist, 25,* 227–233.

Segerstrom, S., & Miller, G. (2004). Psychological stress and the human immune system: A meta-analytic study of 30 years of inquiry. *Psychological Bulletin, 130,* 601–630.

Seibert, S., Crant, J., & Kraimer, M. (1999). Proactive personality and career success. *Journal of Applied Psychology, 84,* 416–427.

Seibert, S., Kraimer, M., & Crant, J. (2001). What do proactive people do? A longitudinal model linking proactive personality and career success. *Personnel Psychology, 54,* 845–874.

Seifert, C., Yukl, G., & McDonald, R. (2003). Effects of multisource feedback and a feedback facilitator on the influence behavior of managers toward subordinates. *Journal of Applied Psychology, 88,* 561–569.

Shah, P. P. (2000). Network destruction. *Academy of Management Journal, 43,* 101–112.

Shalley, C. E., Gilson, L. L., & Blum, T. C. (2000). Matching creativity requirements and the work environment. *Academy of Management Journal, 43,* 215–223.

Shan, G., & Bohn, C. (2003). Anthropometrical data and coefficients of regression related to gender and race. *Applied Ergonomics, 34,* 327–337.

Sharit, J., Czaja, S., Nair, S., & Lee, C. (2003). Effects of age, speech rate, and environmental support in using telephone voice menu systems. *Human Factors, 45,* 234–251.

Shaw, J., Duffy, M., Mitra, A., Lockhart, D., & Bowler, M. (2003). Reactions to merit pay increases: A longitudinal test of a signal sensitivity perspective. *Journal of Applied Psychology, 88,* 538–544.

Sherony, K., & Green, S. (2002). Co-worker exchange: Relationships between co-workers, leader-member exchange, and work attitudes. *Journal of Applied Psychology, 87,* 542–548.

Shin, S., & Zhou, J. (2003). Transformational leadership, conservation, and creativity: Evidence from Korea. *Academy of Management Journal, 46,* 703–714.

Shore, L., Cleveland, J., & Goldberg, C. (2003). Work attitudes and decisions as a function of manager age and employee age. *Journal of Applied Psychology, 88,* 529–537.

Simoneau, G., & Marklin, R. (2001). Effect of computer keyboard shape and height on wrist extension angle. *Human Factors, 43,* 287–298.

Simons, T., & Roberson, Q. (2003). Why managers should care about fairness: The effects of aggregate justice perceptions on organizational outcomes. *Journal of Applied Psychology, 88,* 432–443.

Simonson, I., Carmon, Z., Dhar, R., Drolet, A., & Nowlis, S. (2001). Consumer research. *Annual Review of Psychology, 52,* 249–275.

Smith, D. (2004, April 14). When flour power invaded the kitchen. *New York Times.*

Smith, D., & Ellingson, J. (2002). Substance versus style: A new look at social desirability in motivating contexts. *Journal of Applied Psychology, 87,* 211–219.

Smith, D., Hanges, P., & Dickson, M. (2001). Personnel selection and the 5-factor model: Reexamining the effects of applicant's form of reference. *Journal of Applied Psychology, 86,* 304–315.

Smither, J., London, M., Flautt, R., Vargas, Y., & Kucine, I. (2003). Can working with an executive coach improve multisource feedback ratings over time? A quasi-experimental study. *Personnel Psychology, 56,* 23–44.

Smither, J., & Walker, A. (2004). Are the characteristics of narrative comments related to improvement in multirater feedback ratings over time? *Journal of Applied Psychology, 89,* 575–581.

Smith-Jentsch, K. H., Jentsch, F. G., Payne, S. C., & Salas, E. (1996). Can pre-training experiences explain individual differences in learning? *Journal of Applied Psychology, 81,* 110–116.

Smith-Jentsch, K. H., Salas, E., & Brannick, M. (2001). To transfer or not to transfer? Investigating the combined effects of trainee characteristics, team leader support, and team climate. *Journal of Applied Psychology, 86,* 279–292.

Snape, E., & Redman, T. (2003). An evaluation of a 3-component model of occupational commitment: Dimensionality and consequences among United Kingdom human resource management specialists. *Journal of Applied Psychology, 88,* 152–159.

Sommerich, C., Joines, S., & Psihogios, J. (2001). Effects of computer monitor viewing angle and related factors on strain, performance, and preference outcomes. *Human Factors, 43,* 39–55.

Sonnentag, S. (2003). Recovery, work engagement, and proactive behavior: A new look at the interface between nonwork and work. *Journal of Applied Psychology, 88,* 518–528.

Spector, P. E., Chen, P. Y., & O'Connell, B. J. (2000). A longitudinal study of relations between job stressors and job strains while controlling for prior negative affectivity and strains. *Journal of Applied Psychology, 85,* 211–218.

Spector, P. E., et al. (2004). A cross-national comparative survey of work-family stressors, working hours, and well-being: China and Latin America versus the Anglo world. *Personnel Psychology, 57,* 119–142.

Stajkovic, A. D., & Luthans, F. (1998). Self-efficacy and work-related performance. *Psychological Bulletin, 124,* 240–261.

Stajkovic, A. D., & Luthans, F. (2003). Behavioral management and task performance in organizations: Conceptual background, meta-analysis, and test of alternative models. *Personnel Psychology, 56,* 155–194.

Stanton, E. (2002, December 29). If a resume lies, truth can loom large. *New York Times.*

Stanton, N., & Baber, C. (2003). On the cost-effectiveness of ergonomics. *Applied Ergonomics, 34,* 407–411.

Stark, S., Chernyshenko, O., Chan, K., Lee, W., & Drasgow, F. (2001). Effects of the testing situation on item responding. *Journal of Applied Psychology, 86,* 943–953.

Steers, R., Mowday, R., & Shapiro, D. (2004). The future of work motivation theory. *Academy of Management Review, 29,* 379–387.

Stern, B. (2002). The importance of being Ernest: A tribute to [Ernest] Dichter. *Journal of Advertising Research, 42,* 19–23.

Sternberg, R. (2003). WICS: A model of leadership in organizations. *Academy of Management Learning and Education, 2,* 386–401.

Stevenson, J. S., Bruner, G. C., II, & Kumar, A. (2000). Web page background and viewer attitudes. *Journal of Advertising Research, 40,* 29–34.

Stone, G., Besser, D., & Lewis, L. E. (2000). Recall, liking, and creativity in TV commercials. *Journal of Advertising Research, 40,* 7–18.

Sutton, R. I., & Rafaeli, A. (1998). Untangling the relationship between displayed emotions and organizational sales. *Academy of Management Journal, 31,* 461–487.

Sverke, M., Hellgren, J., & Naswall, K. (2002). No security: A meta-analysis and review of job insecurity and its consequences. *Journal of Occupational Health Psychology, 7(3),* 242–264.

Swartz, T. A. (1983). Brand symbols and message differentiation. *Journal of Advertising Research, 23,* 59–64.

Tan, H., & Aryee, S. (2002). Antecedents and outcomes of union loyalty: A constructive replication and an extension. *Journal of Applied Psychology, 87,* 715–722.

Taylor, F. W. (1911). *Scientific management.* New York: Harper.

Taylor, S. E., Klein, L. C., Lewis, B. P., Gruenewald, T. L., Gurung, R. A. R., & Updegraff, J. A. (2000). Biobehavioral responses to stress in females. *Psychological Review, 107,* 411–429.

Tenopyr, M. L. (1992). Reflections of a pioneering woman in industrial psychology. *Professional Psychology, 23,* 172–175.

Tepper, B., Duffy, M., & Shaw, J. (2001). Personality moderators of the relationship between abusive supervision and subordinates' resistance. *Journal of Applied Psychology, 86,* 974–983.

Thompson, L., Surface, E., Martin, D., & Sanders, M. (2003). From paper to pixels: Moving personnel surveys to the Web. *Personnel Psychology, 56,* 197–227.

Tierney, P., & Farmer, S. (2002). Creative self-efficacy: Its potential antecedents and relationship to creative performance. *Academy of Management Journal, 45,* 1137–1148.

Tierney, P., Farmer, S., & Graen, G. B. (1999). An examination of leadership and employee creativity. *Personnel Psychology, 52,* 591–620.

Toegel, G., & Conger, J. (2003). 360-degree assessment: Time for reinvention. *Academy of Management Learning and Education, 2,* 297–311.

Torres, I., & Gelb, B. (2002). Hispanic-targeted advertising. *Journal of Advertising Research, 42*(6), 69–76.

Tourangeau, R. (2004). Survey research and societal change. *Annual Review of Psychology, 55,* 775–801.

Trimmel, M., Meixner-Pendleton, M., & Haring, S. (2003). Stress response caused by system response time when searching for information on the Internet. *Human Factors, 45,* 615–621.

Tse, A., & Lee, R. (2001). Zapping behavior during commercial breaks. *Journal of Advertising Research, 42*(3), 3–28.

Tuckel, P., & O'Neill, H. (2002). The vanishing respondent in telephone surveys. *Journal of Advertising Research, 42*(5), 26–51.

Van der Ploeg, E., Dorresteijn, S., & Kleber, R. (2003). Critical incidents and chronic stressors at work: Their impact on forensic doctors. *Journal of Occupational Health Psychology, 8*(2), 157–166.

Van der Zee, K., Bakker, A., & Bakker, P. (2002). Why are structured interviews so rarely used in personnel selection? *Journal of Applied Psychology, 87,* 176–184.

Van Dierendonck, D., Schaufeli, W., & Buunk, B. (2001). Burnout and inequity among human service professionals: A longitudinal study. *Journal of Occupational Health Psychology, 6*(1), 43–52.

Van Vianen, A. E. M. (2000). Person-organization fit. *Personnel Psychology, 53,* 113–149.

Van Yperen, N., & Hagedoorn, M. (2003). Do high job demands increase intrinsic motivation or fatigue or both? The role of job control and job social support. *Academy of Management Journal, 46,* 339–348.

Van Yperen, N., & Janssen, O. (2002). Fatigued and dissatisfied or fatigued but satisfied? Goal orientations and responses to high job demands. *Academy of Management Journal, 45,* 1161–1171.

Vecchio, R., & Bullis, R. (2001). Moderators of the influence of supervisor-subordinate similarity on subordinate outcomes. *Journal of Applied Psychology, 86,* 884–896.

Venkatesh, V., & Johnson, P. (2002). Telecommuting technology implementations: A within- and between-subjects longitudinal study. *Personnel Psychology, 55,* 661–685.

Vera, D., & Crossan, M. (2004). Strategic leadership and organizational leaving. *Academy of Management Review, 29,* 222–240.

Viswesvaran, C., Schmidt, F., & Ones, D. (2003). The moderating influence of job performance dimensions on convergence of supervisory and peer ratings of job performance: Unconfounding construct-level convergence and rating difficulty. *Journal of Applied Psychology, 87,* 345–354.

Waclawski, J., Church, A., & Berr, S. (2002). The 2002 SIOP member survey results. *The Industrial-Organizational Psychologist, 40*(1), 16–27.

Wagner, S., Parker, C., & Christiansen, N. (2003). Employees that think and act like owners: Effects of ownership beliefs and behaviors on organizational effectiveness. *Personnel Psychology, 56,* 847–871.

Waldman, D., & Korbar, T. (2004). Student assessment center performance in the prediction of early career success. *Academy of Management Learning and Education, 3*(2), 151–167.

Walker, A. G., & Smither, J. W. (1999). A five-year study of upward feedback. *Personnel Psychology, 52,* 393–423.

Wallace, J., & Vodanovich, S. (2003). Workplace safety performance: Conscientiousness, cognitive failure, and their interaction. *Journal of Occupational Health Psychology, 8*(4), 316–327.

Walsh, M. (2002, November 19). Number of women in upper ranks rises a bit. *New York Times.*

Walz, S., & Niehoff, B. (2000). Organizational citizenship behaviors; Their relationship to organizational effectiveness. *Journal of Hospitality and Tourism Research, 24*(3), 301–319.

Wanberg, C. R., & Banas, J. T. (2000). Predictors and outcomes of openness to changes in a reorganizing workplace. *Journal of Applied Psychology, 85,* 132–142.

Wanberg, C. R., & Kammeyer-Mueller, J. D. (2000). Predictors and outcomes of proactivity in the socialization process. *Journal of Applied Psychology, 85,* 373–385.

Wansink, B. (2003). Developing a cost-effective brand loyalty program. *Journal of Advertising Research, 43*(3), 301–310.

Wayne, S., Shore, L., Bommer, W., & Tetrick, L. (2002). The role of fair treatment and rewards in perceptions of organizational support and leader-member exchange. *Journal of Applied Psychology, 87,* 590–598.

Weber, M. (1947). *The theory of social and economic organization.* New York: Oxford University Press.

Wells, M., & Perrine, R. (2001). Critters in the cube farm: Perceived psychological and organizational effects of pets in the workplace. *Journal of Occupational Health Psychology, 6*(1), 81–87.

Wells, W., Burnett, J., & Moriarty, S. (2003). *Advertising: Principles and practice* (6th ed.). Upper Saddle River, NJ: Prentice Hall.

Whittler, T., & Spira, J. (2002). Model's race: A peripheral cue in advertising messages? *Journal of Consumer Psychology, 12*(4), 291–301.

Wilk, S., & Cappelli, P. (2003). Understanding the determinants of employer use of selection methods. *Personnel Psychology, 56,* 103–124.

Witt, L., Burke, L., Barrick, M., & Mount, M. (2002). The interactive effects of conscientiousness and agreeableness on job performance. *Journal of Applied Psychology, 87,* 164–169.

Witt, L., & Ferris, G. (2003). Social skill as moderator of the conscientiousness-performance relationship: Convergent results across four studies. *Journal of Applied Psychology, 88,* 809–820.

Wogalter, M., Conzola, V., & Smith-Jackson, T. (2002). Research-based guidelines for warning design and evaluation. *Applied Ergonomics, 33,* 219–230.

Wolburg, J., & Pokyrwczynski, J. (2001). A psychographic analysis of Generation Y college students. *Journal of Advertising Research, 41*(5), 33–53.

Woodside, A., & Wilson, E. (2002). Respondent inaccuracy. *Journal of Advertising Research, 42*(5), 7–20.

Woodson, W., Tillman, B., & Tillman, P. (1992). *Human factors design handbook* (2nd ed.). New York: McGraw-Hill.

Wright, T., & Bonett, D. (2002). The moderating effects of employee tenure on the relation between organizational commitment and job performance: A meta-analysis. *Journal of Applied Psychology, 87,* 1183–1190.

Yang, M., Roskos-Ewoldson, B., & Roskos-Ewoldson, D. (2004). Mental models for brand placement. In L. Shrum (Ed.), *The psychology of entertainment media: Blurring the lines between entertainment and persuasion* (pp. 79–98). Mahwah, NJ: Erlbaum.

Yang, N., Chen, C. C., Choi, J., & Zou, Y. (2000). Sources of work-family conflict. *Academy of Management Journal, 43,* 113–123.

Yelkur, R., Tomkovick, C., & Traczyk, P. (2004). Super Bowl advertising effectiveness: Hollywood finds the games golden. *Journal of Advertising Research, 44*(3), 143–159.

Yoon, S., & Kim, J. (2001). Is the Internet more effective than traditional media? Factors affecting the choice of media. *Journal of Advertising Research, 41*(6), 53–61.

Yrle, A., Hartman, S., & Galle, W. (2002). An investigation of relationships between communication style and leader-member exchange. *Journal of Communications Management, 6*(3), 257–268.

Yukl, G., & Taber, T. (1983). The effective use of managerial power. *Personnel, 60*(2), 37–44.

Zellars, K., & Perrewe, P. (2001). Affective personality and the content of emotional social support: Coping in organizations. *Journal of Applied Psychology, 86,* 459–467.

Zellars, K., Tepper, B., & Duffy, M. (2002). Abusive supervision and subordinates' organizational citizenship behavior. *Journal of Applied Psychology, 87,* 1068–1076.

Zhou, D., Zhang, W., & Vertinsky, I. (2002). Advertising trends in urban China. *Journal of Advertising Research, 42*(3), 73–82.

Zohar, D. (2002). Modifying supervisory practices to improve subunit safety: A leadership-based intervention model. *Journal of Applied Psychology, 87,* 156–163.

Glossary

Accident proneness   The idea that some people have personality traits that predispose them to have accidents, and that most accidents are caused by or involve these same few people. This theory is not supported by research.

Achievement motivation   The theory of motivation that emphasizes the need to accomplish something, to do a good job, and to be the best.

Adverse impact   When a group of job applicants or employees is treated markedly worse than the majority group in staffing decisions.

Aided recall technique   A test of advertising effectiveness to determine the extent to which ad content can be recalled. The interviewer aids the recall by asking specific questions.

Apprenticeship   A training method for skilled crafts and trades involving classroom instruction and on-the-job experience.

Aptitude tests   Psychological tests to measure specific abilities, such as mechanical or clerical skills.

Assessment centers   A method of selection and training that involves a simulated job situation in which candidates deal with actual job problems.

Attribution   A source of error in performance appraisal in which raters attribute or assign positive or negative explanations to an employee's behavior.

Auditory displays   Alarms or warning signals in person-machine systems. Auditory displays can be more compelling than visual displays.

Authoritarian leadership   A leadership style in which a leader makes all decisions and tells followers what to do.

Average rating error   A source of error in performance appraisal in which a rater is unwilling to assign very good or very poor ratings. Consequently, most ratings fall in the middle of the rating scale.

Banding   A controversial practice of grouping test scores for minority job applicants to equalize hiring rates.

Behavior modeling   A management training technique in which trainees attempt to imitate the job behaviors of successful supervisors.

Behavior modification   A training program of positive reinforcement to reward employees for displaying desirable job behaviors.

Behavioral observation scales (BOS)   A performance appraisal technique in which appraisers rate the frequency of critical employee behaviors.

Behaviorally anchored rating scales (BARS)   A performance appraisal technique in which appraisers rate critical employee behaviors.

Biofeedback   A stress-reduction technique that involves electronic monitoring of physiological processes, such that people can learn to control muscle tension, blood pressure, and brain waves.

Biographical inventory   An employee selection technique covering an applicant's past behavior, attitudes, preferences, and values.

Bureaucracy   A formal, orderly, and rational approach to organizing business enterprises.

Burnout   A condition of job stress that results from overwork.

Business games   A training method that simulates a complex organizational situation to encourage the development of problem-solving and decision-making skills.

Carpal tunnel syndrome   A repetitive motion disorder that may involve numbness; tingling; or pain in fingers, hands, and forearms.

Case studies   A method of executive training in which trainees analyze a business problem and offer solutions.

Change agents   Organization development facilitators who work with business groups to implement change and develop group confidence and effectiveness.

Charismatic leadership   A leadership style characterized by a self-promoting personality, a high energy level, and a willingness to take risks. Charismatic leaders stimulate their followers to think independently.

Check reading visual displays   Displays that tell the operator whether the system is on or off, safe or unsafe, or operating normally or abnormally.

Computer-assisted instruction (CAI)   A computer-based training method in which trainees learn material at their own pace and receive immediate feedback on their progress.

Computerized adaptive tests   A means of administering psychological tests in which an applicant's response to an item determines the level of difficulty of succeeding items.

Concurrent validity   A way to establish criterion-related validity that involves administering a test to employees on the job and correlating their scores with job performance data.

Consideration leadership functions   Leadership behaviors that involve awareness of and sensitivity to the feelings of subordinates.

Constant bias   A source of error in performance appraisal based on the different standards used by raters.

Construct validity   A type of validity that attempts to determine the psychological characteristics measured by a test.

Content validity   A type of validity that assesses test items to ensure that they adequately sample the skills the test is designed to measure.

Contingency theory   A leadership theory in which a leader's effectiveness is determined by the interaction between the leader's personal characteristics and the characteristics of the leadership situation.

Control group   In an experiment, this is the group of research participants that is not exposed to the independent variable.

Correlation   The relationship between two variables. The strength and direction of the relationship is expressed by the correlation coefficient.

Criterion-related validity   A type of validity concerned with the relationship between test scores and subsequent job performance.

Critical-incidents technique   A means of identifying specific activities or behaviors that lead to desirable or undesirable consequences on the job.

Democratic leadership   A leadership style in which a leader and followers discuss problems and make decisions jointly.

Dependent variable   In an experiment, this is the resulting behavior of the subjects, which depends on the manipulation of the independent variable.

Descriptive statistics Ways of describing or representing research data in a concise, meaningful manner.

Diversity training Training programs to make employees aware of their personal prejudices and to teach them to be more sensitive to the concerns and views of others.

Employee assistance programs (EAPs) Counseling and rehabilitative services for various employee problems, notably alcohol and drug abuse.

Engineering psychology The design of machines and equipment for human use, and the determination of the appropriate human behaviors for the efficient operation of the machines. The field is also called human factors, human engineering, and ergonomics.

Environmental psychology The study of the effect of workplace design on behavior and attitudes.

Equity theory The theory of motivation that states that our motivation on the job is influenced by our perception of how fairly we are treated.

Equivalent-forms method A way to determine test reliability that involves administering similar forms of a new test to the same group of subjects and correlating the two sets of scores.

Executive coaching A management training technique involving personal sessions with a coach to improve a particular aspect of job performance.

Experimental group In an experiment, this is the group of research participants exposed to the independent variable.

Experimental method The scientific way to determine the effect or influence of a variable on the subjects' performance or behavior.

Face validity A subjective impression of how well test items seem to be related to the requirements of a job.

Fixed-alternative questions Survey questions to which respondents limit their answers to the choices or alternatives presented. They are similar to multiple-choice questions on college exams.

Flextime A system of flexible working hours combining core mandatory work periods with elective work periods at the beginning and end of the workday.

Focus groups A method of surveying public opinion through the paid participation of eight to 12 group members who meet to describe their reactions to a product or advertisement or to specific issues.

Forced-choice technique A performance appraisal technique in which raters are presented with groups of descriptive statements and are asked to select the phrase in each group that is most descriptive or least descriptive of the worker being evaluated.

Forced-distribution technique A performance appraisal technique in which supervisors rate employees according to a prescribed distribution of ratings, similar to grading on a curve.

Frequency distribution A graphic representation of raw data that shows the number of times each score occurs.

Goal-setting theory The theory of motivation based on the idea that our primary motivation on the job is defined in terms of our desire to achieve a particular goal.

Group cohesiveness   The focus, closeness, and commonality of interests of a small work group.

Group tests   Psychological tests designed to be administered to a large number of people at the same time.

Halo effect   The tendency to judge all aspects of a person's behavior or character on the basis of a single attribute.

Hardiness   A personality variable that may explain individual differences in vulnerability to stress. So-called hardy persons believe they can control the events in their lives and thus may be more resistant to stress.

Hawthorne studies   A long-term research program at the Hawthorne, Illinois, Western Electric Company plant. It documented the influence of a variety of managerial and organizational factors on employee behavior.

Human anthropometry   A branch of engineering psychology concerned with the measurement of the physical structure of the body.

Implicit leadership theory   A leadership theory that describes a good leader in terms of one's past experiences with different types of leaders.

Impression management   Acting deliberately to make a good impression, to present oneself in the most favorable way.

Inadequate information error   A source of error in performance appraisal in which supervisors rate their subordinates even though they may not know enough about them to do so fairly and accurately.

In-basket technique   An assessment-center exercise that requires job applicants to process memos, letters, and directives found in a typical manager's in-basket.

Independent variable   In an experiment, this is the stimulus variable that is manipulated to determine its effect on the subjects' behavior.

Individual tests   Psychological tests designed to be administered to one person at a time.

Inferential statistics   Methods for analyzing research data that express relationships in terms of probabilities.

Initiating structure leadership functions   Leadership behaviors concerned with organizing, defining, and directing the work activities of subordinates.

Interest tests   Psychological tests to assess a person's interests and preferences. These tests are used primarily for career counseling.

Interpersonal affect   Our feelings or emotions toward another person. In performance appraisal, the emotional tone of the relationship between manager and employee, whether positive or negative, can influence the assigned ratings.

I-O psychology   The application of the methods, facts, and principles of the science of psychology to people at work.

Job analysis   The study of a job to describe in specific terms the nature of the component tasks performed by the workers.

Job congruence   The match between our abilities and the requirements of our jobs.

Job engagement   The true enjoyment of work, characterizing people who score high in energy, involvement, and efficacy.

Job enrichment   An effort to expand the scope of a job to give employees a greater role in planning, performing, and evaluating their work.

Job rotation   A management training technique that assigns trainees to various jobs and departments over a period of a few years.

Job satisfaction   Our positive and negative feelings and attitudes about our jobs.

Job simplification   The reduction of manufacturing jobs to the simplest components that can be mastered by unskilled or semiskilled workers.

Job-characteristics theory   The theory of motivation that states that specific job characteristics lead to psychological conditions that can increase motivation, performance, and satisfaction in employees who have a high growth need.

Leaderless group discussion   An assessment-center exercise in which job applicants meet to discuss an actual business problem under the pressure of time. Usually, a leader emerges from the group to guide the discussion.

Leader-member exchange   A leadership theory that focuses on how the leader-follower relationship affects the leadership process.

Locus of control   One's belief about the source of one's rewards. People with an internal locus of control believe that job performance, pay, and promotion are under their control and dependent on their own behavior. People with an external locus of control believe such events depend on outside forces such as luck.

Management by objectives (MBO)   A performance appraisal technique that involves a mutual agreement between employee and manager on goals to be achieved in a given period.

Mass psychogenic illness   A stress-related disorder manifested in a variety of physical symptoms that spread rapidly among a group of workers; popularly called assembly-line hysteria.

Matched group design   A method for ensuring similarity between experimental and control groups that matches subjects in both groups on characteristics, such as age, job experience, and intelligence, that could affect the dependent variable.

Mean   The arithmetic average; a way of describing the central tendency of a distribution of data.

Median   The score at the midpoint of a statistical distribution; half the scores fall below the median and half above.

Merit pay   A wage system in which pay is based on level of performance.

Merit rating   Objective rating methods designed to provide an objective evaluation of work performance.

Meta-analysis   The large-scale reanalysis of the results of previous research studies.

Mode   The most frequently obtained score in a distribution of data.

Most-recent-performance error   A source of error in performance appraisal in which a rater tends to evaluate a worker's most recent job behavior rather than behavior throughout the period since the last appraisal.

Motivator-hygiene (two-factor) theory   The theory of motivation that explains work motivation and job satisfaction in terms of job tasks and workplace features.

Naturalistic observation   The scientific observation of behavior in its natural setting, without any experimental manipulation of the independent variable.

Needs assessment   An analysis of corporate and individual goals undertaken before designing a training program.

Needs hierarchy theory   The theory of motivation that encompasses physiological, safety, belonging, esteem, and self-actualization needs.

Negative affectivity   A personality dimension characterized by a generalized life and job dissatisfaction and by a focus on negative aspects of life events.

Nominal working hours   The prescribed number of hours employees are supposed to spend on the job; not all of these hours are actually spent performing job tasks.

Normal distribution   A bell-shaped distribution of data in which most scores fall near the center and few fall at the extreme low and high ends.

Objective tests   Tests for which the scoring process is free of personal judgment or bias.

Occupational health psychology   The field of study dealing with the health effects of job stress and other aspects of employee well-being.

On-the-job training   Training that takes place directly on the job for which the person has been hired.

Open-end questions   Survey questions to which respondents state their views in their own words. They are similar to essay questions on college exams.

Organizational culture   The organization's pattern of beliefs, expectations, and values as manifested in company and industry practices.

Organizational development (OD)   The study and implementation of planned organizational changes.

Organization-based self-esteem   A personality dimension relating to our assessment of our adequacy and worth with regard to our place in the employing organization.

Paired-comparison technique   A performance appraisal technique that compares the performance of each worker with that of every other worker in the group.

Path-goal theory   A leadership theory that focuses on the kinds of behaviors leaders should exercise to allow their subordinates to achieve personal and organizational goals.

Peer rating   A performance appraisal technique in which managers or executives at the same level assess one another's abilities and job behaviors.

Performance appraisal   The periodic, formal evaluation of employee performance for the purpose of making career decisions.

Personality tests   Psychological tests that assess personal traits and feelings.

Person-machine system   A system in which human and mechanical components operate together to accomplish a task.

Person-organization fit   The congruence between an employee's values and the organization's values.

Power tests   Tests that have no time limit. Applicants are allowed as much time as they need to complete the test.

Predictive validity   An approach to establishing criterion-related validity in which a new test is administered to all job applicants, and all applicants are hired, regardless of test scores. Later, when a measure of job performance can be obtained, test scores are correlated with job performance to see how well the test predicted job success.

Proactivity   A tendency to take action to try to influence or change one's environment.

Probability   The idea that the differences between the means of experimental and control groups could have occurred by chance.

Probability sampling   A method for constructing a representative sample of a population for surveys or polls. Each person in the population has a known probability or chance of being included in the sample.

Projective techniques   A personality assessment technique in which test-takers project their feelings onto an ambiguous stimulus such as an inkblot.

Prosocial behavior   Behaviors directed toward supervisors, co-workers, and clients that are helpful to an organization.

Protective exclusion   The practice of barring certain groups of employees, such as women of childbearing age, from potentially hazardous jobs because of fear of lawsuits.

Pygmalion effect   A self-fulfilling prophecy in which managers' expectations about the level of their employees' job performance can influence that performance.

Qualitative visual displays   Displays that present a range rather than a precise numerical value. They are frequently used to show whether components, such as engine temperature, are operating in the safe or unsafe range.

Quality-of-work-life (QWL) programs   Organizational programs based on active employee participation in decision and policy making.

Quantitative visual displays   Displays that present a precise numerical value, such as speed, altitude, or temperature.

Quota sampling   A method for constructing a representative sample of a population for surveys or polls. Because the sample must reflect the proportions of the larger population, quotas are established for various categories such as age, gender, and ethnic origin.

Race norming   A controversial practice, now outlawed, of boosting test scores for minority job applicants to equalize hiring rates.

Random group design   A method for ensuring similarity between experimental and control groups that assigns subjects at random to each condition.

Ranking technique   A performance appraisal technique in which supervisors list the workers in their group in order from highest to lowest or best to worst.

Rating scales   A performance appraisal technique in which supervisors indicate how or to what degree a worker possesses each relevant job characteristic.

Rational validity   The type of validity that relates to the nature, properties, and content of a test, independent of its relationship to job performance measures.

Realistic job previews   A recruitment technique that acquaints prospective employees with positive and negative aspects of a job.

Recognition technique   A technique for testing advertising effectiveness by asking people if they recognize a particular ad, where they saw it, and what they can recall about it.

Relaxation training   A stress-reduction technique that concentrates on relaxing one part of the body after another.

Reliability   The consistency or stability of a response on a psychological test.

Reverse discrimination   The phenomenon that may occur when recruiting, hiring, promoting, and making other human resources decisions in favor of members of a minority group result in discrimination against members of the majority group.

Role ambiguity   A situation that arises when job responsibilities are unstructured or poorly defined.

Role conflict   A situation that arises when there is a disparity between job demands and the employee's personal standards.

Role playing   A management training technique in which trainees play the role of a supervisor, acting out various behaviors in situations with subordinates.

Sales test technique   A way of testing the effectiveness of an advertising campaign by introducing the new advertising in selected test markets.

Scientific management   A management philosophy concerned with increasing productivity that regarded workers as extensions of the machines they operated.

Scientific method   A controlled, objective, and systematic approach to research.

Selection ratio   The relationship between the number of people to be hired (the number of jobs) and the number available to be hired (the potential labor supply).

Self-managing work groups   Employee groups that allow the members of a work team to manage, control, and monitor all facets of their work, from recruiting, hiring, and training new employees to deciding when to take rest breaks.

Self-ratings   A performance appraisal technique in which managers assess their own abilities and job performance.

Self-report personality inventories   Personality assessment tests that include questions dealing with situations, symptoms, and feelings. Test-takers are asked to indicate how well each item describes themselves or how much they agree with each item.

Shape coding   Designing knobs for control panels in recognizably different shapes so that they can be identified by touch alone.

Situational interviews   Interviews that focus not on personal characteristics or work experience but on the behaviors needed for successful job performance.

Situational testing   An early term for the assessment-center technique for employee selection and performance appraisal. Employees are placed in a simulated job setting so that their behavior under stress can be observed and evaluated.

Skewed distribution   An asymmetrical distribution of data with most scores at either the high or the low end.

Social loafing   The idea that people do not work as hard in a group as they do when working alone.

Socialization   The adjustment process by which new employees learn their role in the organizational hierarchy, their company's values, and the behaviors considered acceptable by their work group.

Speed tests   Tests that have a fixed time limit, at which point everyone taking the test must stop.

Split-halves method   A way to determine test reliability that involves administering a new test to a group of subjects, dividing in half the total number of items, and correlating the two sets of scores.

Standard deviation   A measure of the variability of a distribution, the standard deviation is a precise distance along the distribution's baseline.

Standardization   The consistency or uniformity of the conditions and procedures for administering a psychological test.

Standardization sample   The group of subjects used to establish test norms. The scores of the standardization sample serve as the point of comparison for determining the relative standing of the persons being tested.

Statistical significance   The level of confidence we can have in the results of an experiment. Significance is based on the calculation of probability values.

Stress Physiological and psychological responses to excessive and usually unpleasant stimulation and to threatening events in the environment.

Structured interviews Interviews that use a predetermined list of questions that are asked of every person applying for a particular job.

Subjective tests Tests that contain items such as essay questions. The scoring process can be influenced by the personal characteristics and attitudes of the scorer.

Survey research method Interviews, behavioral observations, and questionnaires designed to sample what people say about their feelings or opinions, or how they say they will behave in a given situation.

Test norms The distribution of test scores of a large group of people similar in nature to the job applicants being tested.

Test-retest method A way to determine test reliability that involves administering a new test twice to the same group of subjects and correlating the two sets of scores.

Theory X/Theory Y The Theory X approach to management assumes that people are lazy and dislike work and therefore must be led and directed. Theory Y assumes that people find satisfaction in their work and function best under a leader who allows them to participate in working toward both personal and organizational goals.

Time-and-motion study An early attempt to redesign work tools and to reshape the way workers performed routine, repetitive jobs.

Total quality management (TQM) Participative management programs characterized by increased employee involvement and responsibility.

Transactional leadership A leadership style that focuses on the social interactions between leaders and followers, based on followers' perceptions of and expectations about the leader's abilities.

Transformational leadership A leadership style in which leaders are not constrained by their followers' perceptions but are free to act to change or transform their followers' views.

Type A/Type B personalities Personality patterns related to one's ability to tolerate stress; Type A persons have been associated with heart disease, anger, hostility, time urgency, and depression; Type B persons may work as hard as Type As but show fewer stress effects.

Unstructured interviews Interviews in which the format and questions asked are left to the discretion of the interviewer.

Valence-instrumentality-expectancy (VIE) theory The theory of motivation that states that people make choices that are based on their perceived expectations that certain rewards will follow if they behave in a particular way.

Validity The determination of whether a psychological test or other selection device measures what it is intended to measure.

Validity generalization The idea that tests valid in one situation may also be valid in another situation.

Vestibule training Training that takes place in a simulated workspace.

Wage-incentive system The primary pay system for production workers, in which the more units produced, the higher the wage.

Work analysis   The study of certain tasks and skills that workers can transfer from one job to another.

Work overload   Too much work to perform in the time available or work that is too difficult for the employee to perform.

Work underload   Work that is too simple or insufficiently challenging for one's abilities.

Workaholism   So-called addiction to work because of anxiety and insecurity or because of a genuine liking for the job.

Credits

Name Index

Subject Index

The coming hardenability test